DAVID HALBERSTAM'S LONG [AWAITED FOLLOW-?]
UP TO HIS #1 NATIONAL BESTSELLER *THE BEST AND THE BRIGHTEST*

WAR IN A TIME OF PEACE

"Riveting, merciless . . . indispensable to anyone interested in that confused period between the Cold War and the Terrorist War about to begin."

—John Lehman, *The Wall Street Journal*

"[David Halberstam] has produced a book that most journalists would give their right arm to have written, a tour de force of reportorial narration very much of the *Best and the Brightest* genre."

—Richard Bernstein, *The New York Times*

"A sprawling tapestry of exquisite bottom-up reporting and powerful vignettes. . . . Now that foreign affairs have come home to the United States in the most crushing of ways, are the American people ready to read an account of foreign policy and its makers by one of the most astute writers in the trade? If they want to learn from the past decade, they should. If they want to think seriously about the future, they must."

—Jane Perlez, *The New York Times Book Review*

"A finely crafted and enjoyable account of the shared culture and personal chemistry of America's political and military power-brokers."

—*The Economist*

"The best war reporter of his generation, Halberstam has become one of the great synthesizers of modern American history."

—Mark Bowden, *The Washington Post Book World*

"I sat down with this galley, forcing myself to open it, because I thought I already knew everything about this all-too-recent history. Seven hours later I was closing the pages, having absolutely devoured the book as if it was the most lurid, engaging, and unbelievable work of fiction."

—Liz Smith, *New York Post*

"A brilliant study of how the fault line between Washington and the military, magnified by Vietnam, has determined recent foreign policy."

— Joan Didion, *New York* magazine

"Well-written and lucid, his narrative reveals a military that continues to be ill-coordinated to meet—and sometimes opposed to—the political ends of its civilian overseers, who in turn often seem terminally confused about the rest of the world. Excellent, as is Halberstam's custom, and instructive for those seeking to understand geopolitical realities."

— *Kirkus Reviews* (starred)

"Events and personalities clash in this extraordinary sequel to Halberstam's classic examination of America's road to Vietnam. . . . This is vintage Halberstam, combining sharp portraits of the political players—Bush, Clinton, Powell, Madeleine Albright, and so many others—with nuanced reportage of the events they shape and are shaped by."

— *Publishers Weekly* (starred)

"A work that adds to the legendary status of David Halberstam as an author and historian. As he did in *The Best and the Brightest,* the number one national bestseller about the Vietnam War, the Pulitzer Prize–winning Halberstam probes the bureaucracy to reveal the interplay between the White House, the Pentagon, the State Department, and Congress. His perceptive portraits of powerful U.S. and foreign government officials and military officers offer clues to explain not only what they did, but why they did it. Halberstam's last eleven books have attained *New York Times* bestseller status. *War in a Time of Peace* might well make it an even dozen."

— Alan Prince, *BookPage*

"Grade *War in a Time of Peace* as a big, important and fascinating book—big in its scope, important in its subject, fascinating in its tale-telling. Halberstam writes with great insight about the tension between military people and the civilians to whom they report."

— Harry Levins, *St. Louis Post-Dispatch*

WAR IN A TIME OF PEACE

BUSH, CLINTON, AND THE GENERALS

DAVID HALBERSTAM

A TOUCHSTONE BOOK
PUBLISHED BY SIMON & SCHUSTER
NEW YORK   LONDON   TORONTO   SYDNEY   SINGAPORE

TOUCHSTONE
Rockefeller Center
1230 Avenue of the Americas
New York, NY 10020

The Epilogue is adapted from an article that was originally published in *Vanity Fair*.

First Touchstone Edition 2002

For information regarding special discounts for bulk purchases,
please contact Simon & Schuster Special Sales at 1-800-456-6798
or business@simonandschuster.com

DESIGNED BY ERICH HOBBING

Manufactured in the United States of America

3   5   7   9   10   8   6   4

The Library of Congress has cataloged the Scribner edition as follows:
Halberstam, David.
War in a time of peace : Bush, Clinton, and the generals / David Halberstam.
p. cm.
Includes bibliographical references (p.).
1. United States—Foreign relations—1989– . 2. United States—Politics and
government—1989– . 3. Bush, George, 1924– . 4. Clinton, Bill, 1946– .
5. United States—Military policy. 6. Intervention (International law).
7. Vietnamese Conflict, 1961–1975—Influence. I. Title.

E881.H34 2001
327.73—dc21   2001038416

ISBN-13: 978-0-7432-0212-1
ISBN-10:   0-7432-0212-0
ISBN-13: 978-0-7432-2323-2 (Pbk)
ISBN-10:   0-7432-2323-3 (Pbk)

For Russell and Mimi Baker

CHAPTER ONE

For a brief, glorious, almost Olympian moment it appeared that the presidency itself could serve as the campaign. Rarely had an American president seemed so sure of reelection. In the summer and fall of 1991, George Bush appeared to be politically invincible. His personal approval ratings in the aftermath of the Persian Gulf War had reached 90 percent, unheard of for any sitting president, and even more remarkable for someone like Bush, a competent political insider whose charisma and capacity to inspire had in the past escaped most of his fellow citizens. Of his essential decency and competence there had been little doubt, and the skill with which he had presided over the end of the Cold War had impressed not merely the inner club that monitored foreign policy decision-making, but much of the country as well. With exceptional sensitivity, he had juggled and balanced his own political needs with the greater political needs of his newest partner in this joint endeavor, Mikhail Gorbachev. For Bush was quite aware that Gorbachev's political equation was much more fragile than his own, and he had been careful to be the more generous member of this unlikely two-man team that was negotiating the end of almost forty-five years of terrifying bipolar tensions.

One moment had seemed to symbolize the supreme confidence of the Bush people during this remarkable chain of events. It came in mid-August of 1991, when some Russian right-wingers mounted a coup against Gorbachev and Bush held firm, trying at first to support Gorbachev and, unable to reach him, then using his influence to help the embattled Boris Yeltsin. The coup had failed. A few days later, Gorbachev, restored to power in part because of the leverage of Washington, had resigned from the Communist Party. To the Bush people that attempted coup had been a reminder that with the Cold War officially ended or not, the Berlin Wall up or down, the world was still a dangerous place, which meant that the country would surely need and want an experienced leader, preferably a Republican, at the helm. Aboard *Air Force One* at that time, flying with his father from Washington back to the Bush family's vacation home in Maine, was George W. Bush, the president's son. He was just coming of age as a political operative in his own right, and he was euphoric about the meaning of these latest events. "Do you think the American people are going to turn to a Democrat *now?*" he asked.[1]

Bush himself believed he was invulnerable. He had presided over the end of the Cold War with considerable distinction. He had handled the delicate job of dealing with the complicated international events that had led to the end of European communism, thereby freeing the satellite nations of Eastern Europe, and perhaps most remarkably of all, gaining, with Russian approval, a unified Germany that was a member of NATO. But typically he had held back on participating in any kind of celebration to mark those stunning events.

When the Berlin Wall had come down, many in the right wing, and a number of people around Bush himself, wanted some kind of ceremony, for this was a historic moment and they believed it deserved a commemoration not unlike those that had attended V-E and V-J Days in World War II, the victories in Europe over Germany, and in the Pacific over Japan. The destruction of the wall represented not merely the West's triumph in a long, difficult struggle against a formidable adversary, but equally important, a triumph in their minds of good over evil, proof that we had been right *and they had been wrong,* and that our system was politically, economically, ethically, and spiritually superior to theirs. At the very least there should be, they believed, one momentous speech to recount the history of the Cold War and celebrate the victory of the forces of light over darkness.

But Bush was uncomfortable with the idea of a celebration, aware that he had little flare for the dramatic. "I'm not going to dance on the wall," he told his aides. Even as the wall was coming down, Marlin Fitzwater, his press officer, had invited a small group of reporters into the Oval Office to talk with the president, but they found his answers cautious, curiously without emotion, almost joyless. Bush was sparring with them. Why wasn't he more excited? a reporter asked. I'm not an emotional kind of guy, he answered. "Maybe," he said later by way of explaining his self-restraint, "I should have given them one of these," and he leapt in the air in a parody of a then popular Toyota commercial portraying a happy car owner jumping and clicking his heels together.[2] On *Saturday Night Live,* comic Dana Carvey, who often parodied Bush, showed him watching scenes of Berliners celebrating the destruction of the wall but refusing to join in. "Wouldn't be prudent," he said. Then Carvey-as-Bush pointed at himself: "Place in history? *Se-cure!*"

So, much to the disappointment of many on the right, Bush was anxious to minimize the event as a symbolic occasion. It was against his nature. Taking personal credit for any kind of larger success, not all of which was his, conflicted with the way he had been brought up. He believed—an attitude that was surely old-fashioned and quite optimistic in an age of ever more carefully orchestrated political spin, when the sizzle was more important than the steak—that if you did the right things in the right way, people would know about it. You should never call attention to yourself or, worse, advertise your accomplishments. Besides, Bush put a primacy on personal relationships, and by then he had begun to forge one with Mikhail Gorbachev and was obviously unwilling to do anything that would make things more difficult for his new ally. The more Bush celebrated, the more vulnerable Gorbachev and the other more democratically inclined figures in the Soviet Union were likely to be. Celebrating was like gloating and Bush would not gloat. (A few months later, getting close to an election campaign, Bush was more emboldened, and when he delivered his January 1992 State of the Union speech, with an election year just beginning, he did give the United States credit for winning the Cold War. Gorbachev, by then ousted from power, was not amused and said that the end of the Cold War was "our common victory. We should give credit to all politicians who participated in that victory.")

It was probably just as well that Bush did not try to grab too much credit for the collapse of communism, for what had transpired was a triumphal victory for an idea rather than for any one man or political faction. The Soviet Union had turned out to be, however involuntarily, the perfect advertisement for the free society, suggesting in the end that harsh, authoritarian controls and systems did not merely limit political, intellectual, and spiritual freedom, but economic freedom and military development as well. They limited not just the freedom of the individual, something that many rulers in many parts of the world would gladly accommodate, but in the end limited the sum strength and might of the state, which was a very different thing. Therefore, what the proponents of an open society had long argued, that freedom was indivisible, and that the freedom to speak openly and candidly about political matters was in the long run inseparable from the freedom to invent some new high-technology device, or to run a brilliant new company, was true. The rights of man included not merely the right to compose and send an angry letter to a newspaper complaining about the government, they included as well as the right to choose where he went to work, and his right to garner, if he so chose and worked hard enough and with enough originality, far greater material rewards than his neighbors. The Soviet system was a devastating argument for what the lack of choice did, and what happened when a society was run top to bottom, instead of bottom to top. When George Bush had taken office, the Soviet system had begun to collapse of its own weight. Clearly by the eighties, communist rule, as critics had long suggested, had undermined the nation itself, weakening it, particularly in a high-tech age when there was such an immediate and direct connection between the vitality of the domestic economy and a nation's military capacity, and when the gap between American weaponry and that of the Soviets had begun to widen at an ever greater rate.

Symbols had never been Bush's strength, and those who were dissatisfied with his innate caution liked to imagine what Ronald Reagan—who was always so brilliant with symbols and had a God-given sense of when and how to use them—might have done had he still been president when the wall fell.

Possibly he would have ventured to Berlin for some wonderful kind of ceremony that the entire nation, perhaps the entire free world, could have shared. But Reagan was then and Bush was now, and unlike his predecessor (and his successor), Bush tended to downplay ceremonial moments. Many in the right wing who had often found him to be of too little ideological faith were again let down. Once more he had proven himself unworthy, placing success in a delicate and as yet unfinished geopolitical process above the temptation to savor what might have been a glorious historic moment.

Bush's belief that process always took precedence over image confirmed his reputation, essentially well-deserved, as a cautious insider rather than a public figure who knew how to rise to historic occasions and use symbols to bring the nation together. In a way it was Bush at both his best and worst. At his worst, he failed to take a memorable event and outline what it meant in larger terms of the long, hard struggle of a free society against a totalitarian state, and perhaps at the very least to showcase those remarkable people in Eastern Europe whose faith in a better, more democratic way during the long, dark hours of communist suppression was finally being rewarded. But it was also Bush at his best, because he was unwilling to exploit a vulnerable colleague—Gorbachev—and his distress and humiliation for political profit. Bush, after all, was first and foremost a team player, and unlikely though it might have seemed just a few years earlier, Gorbachev was now his teammate.

Whether or not he celebrated the end of the Cold War, it appeared to be just one more significant boost to his presidency. And it came at virtually the same time that American military forces, as the dominating part of the United Nations coalition, had defeated the Iraqi army in a devastating four-day land war, a rout preceded by five weeks of lethal, high-precision, high-technology air dominance. The stunning success of the American units in the Persian Gulf War, the cool efficiency of their weapons and the almost immediate collapse of the Iraqi forces, had been savored by most Americans as more than a victory over an Arab nation about which they knew little and which had invaded a small, autocratic, oil-producing duchy about which they knew even less. Rather, it had ended a period of frustration and self-doubt that had tormented many Americans for some twenty years as a result of any number of factors: the deep embarrassment of the Vietnam War, the humiliation suffered during the Iranian hostage crisis, and the uneasiness about a core economy that was in disrepair and was falling behind the new muscle of a confident, powerful Japan, known now in American business circles as Japan Inc.

The Gulf War showed that the American military had recovered from the malaise of the Vietnam debacle and was once again the envy of the rest of the world, with the morale and skill level of the fighting men themselves matching the wonders of the weapons they now had at their disposal. The lessons of the Gulf War were obvious, transcending simple military capacity and extending in some larger psychological sense to a broader national view of our abilities. We were back, and American forces could not be pushed around again. Perhaps we had slipped a bit in the production of cars, but American goods, in this case its modern weapons, were still the best in the world. The nation became, once again, strong, resilient, and optimistic.

The troops who fought in the Gulf War were honored as the troops who had fought in Vietnam were not. Colin Powell and Norman Schwarzkopf, the presiding generals of the war, were celebrated as William Westmoreland had never been. Shades of World War II: Powell was the new Eisenhower, the thoughtful, careful, tough but benign overall planner; and Schwarzkopf was the new Patton, the crusty, cigar-chomping, hell-for-leather combat commander. There was a joyous victory parade in Washington, and then they were honored again at a tumultuous ticker-tape parade in New York. Powell's security people had suggested that he wear a flak vest, but he felt he was heavy enough without one, and he was driven along the parade route in an open 1959 Buick convertible without protection. Both Schwarzkopf and Powell were from the New York area, Schwarzkopf the son of the head of the New Jersey State Police, and Powell the son of parents who had both worked in the garment district. Powell's memory of occasions like this was of newsreel clips of parades for Lindbergh, Eisenhower, and MacArthur. Now riding through a blizzard of ticker tape raining down on himself and Schwarzkopf, he was delighted; all this fuss, he thought, for two local boys who had made good.[3]

Nineteen ninety-one had been an excellent year for George Bush. It had ended with the ultimate Christmas present for an American president when Gorbachev had called to wish him well personally, and to inform him that the Soviet Union had ceased to exist. Gorbachev, the last leader of the USSR, was resigning and turning over power to Boris Yeltsin, the new leader of Russia. Earlier in the day, Gorbachev had told Ted Koppel of *Nightline* that he was something of a modern-day Russian pioneer because he was participating in the peaceful transfer of power, acting in accordance with a formula that was democratic, something relatively new in Moscow. Then, in a warm, rather affectionate conversation with Bush, he said he was turning over what he called the little suitcase, the bag that contained the authorization codes to activate the Soviet nuclear arsenal, to the president of the Russian Republic. Even so, he could not bear to mention Yeltsin, his sworn enemy, by name.[4] The deed was done and Gorbachev was gone. (As Raisa Gorbachev had shrewdly observed after returning from an immensely successful trip to the United States in June 1990, "The thing about innovations is that sooner or later they turn around and destroy the innovators."[5])

Some of that special call announcing the end of the Soviet Union was even watched on television. Gorbachev, the product of the most secretive society in the world, was now a media-savvy man who had learned to play to international as well as domestic opinion. Bush would later discover that Gorbachev had allowed Koppel and *Nightline* to televise his end of their two-person phone call. It was the climax of a year that most American presidents only dream of. It seemed like the rarest of times, when almost all the news was good and Bush was the primary beneficiary. His presidency was an immense success and his reelection appeared to be a sure thing.

But there were already signs that a powerful new undertow was at work in American politics, and Bush and the people around him were, for a variety of reasons, most of them generational, slow to recognize it. But the signs of significant political and social change were there nonetheless. They reflected a certain lack of gratitude on the part of all kinds of ordinary people for the successes of the last three years, and a growing anger—indeed perhaps rage—about the state of the American economy. There was also a concurrent belief that George Bush was certainly capable of being an effective world leader, but domestic problems and issues, in this case, principally, the economy, did not matter as much to him as foreign affairs. A number of different pollsters were picking up on this undertow of discontent, among them Stan Greenberg, a former Yale professor who was polling for the young would-be Democratic presidential candidate Bill Clinton, and Fred Steeper, who had impeccable Republican connections and was polling for the Republican National Committee. Steeper was working out of the office of Bob Teeter, a leading Republican public opinion expert, who was one of George Bush's closest friends and political allies and would be among the men directing his campaign for reelection. Normally Steeper would have been polling for Bush directly, but due to a temporary breakdown in polling in 1991 because of factional differences in the White House, he had ended up working for the RNC.

By the early nineties, polling had become an ever more exact and important instrument of American politics, though some old-timers from an earlier political era were made uneasy by it. They especially distrusted those politicians who used it on all occasions for all purposes and appeared to have no inner value system or beliefs that could withstand the alleged truths produced by polling. But used properly, polls could reveal some things. Used properly, they could serve as a good DEW-line alert system for forces that might soon represent important shifts of public opinion. At the very least they could reveal the primacy of issues, and this would turn out to be one of those occasions. Fred Steeper thought he had been detecting signs of a growing economic malaise for quite a while and a resulting public disenchantment with Bush's attempts to deal with the economy. The huge budget deficits produced by Reagan's tax policies had led to a bitterly debated decision in 1990 on the part of George Bush to go for a tax increase. Campaigning for election in 1988, he had vowed not to raise taxes—"Read my lips. No new taxes," he had said during the campaign. By breaking that promise he had angered many in his own party. The bright and angry young Republican conservatives in the House, led by Newt Gingrich, had broken with him on that issue, and he had got the tax increase through Congress largely with support from the Democrats. But it would become a not-insignificant wound.

By the summer and fall of 1991, the polls had begun to show a potential vulnerability for Bush. His personal ratings still remained high, but there was a growing public restlessness about the direction of the economy and therefore of the country. The economy was turning into a slow-burning but eventually inflammatory issue for the incumbent. Several regions in the nation were suffering from a recession, and by the end of 1991, the entire country would be declared in a recession. One type of economy, a blue-collar industrial one, was coming to an end, and the new high-tech, digital one that would soon replace much of it had not yet arrived with sufficient impact to compensate for its predecessor's decline. The Japanese were producing heavy-industrial goods of a higher quality than we were, and America's industrial heartland was being called the Rust Belt. The budget deficit was growing larger every year, as was the trade imbalance with Japan. Ordinary people who did not usually monitor such economic trends felt squeezed and believed they were working harder and harder just to stand still. It was one of those moments in American life, despite the continuing growth of the postwar economy, when economics and politics converged because normally abstract economic numbers were becoming deeply personal.

Steeper had discovered in late 1990 and early 1991 that there were increasingly serious political problems stemming from what was a stagnant economy. The irony of the Gulf War was that it had momentarily changed the lead topic on the national agenda from a growing concern about the economy to pride in our newly manifested military might. That, of course, was of immediate political benefit for Bush, resulting in the quantum increase in his personal popularity. Yet his vulnerability on economic issues was there. Right before the Gulf War, despite the success of the administration in ending the Cold War, the responses to the most elemental question a pollster can ask—"Is the administration on the right track or the wrong track?"—had been disturbing. Steeper's polls showed that roughly two out of three Americans thought the country was headed down the wrong track. Clearly there had not been much domestic political bounce to the amazing events that marked the end of the Cold War. But then came the triumph of the Gulf War. A mere two days into the fighting, a poll had shown a complete reversal of that most important index: two out of three Americans now thought we were headed in the right direction.

The Gulf War, however, had only temporarily obscured deep dissatisfaction in the country, particularly about the economy. That was new problem number one. Problem number two was that despite the warm and enthusiastic welcome accorded the returning troops, the Gulf War itself had surprisingly little traction. Yes, the country had sat transfixed for those few days, watching the television coverage released by the Department of Defense—video clips of high-technology bombs landing precisely on their intended targets. And yes, everything had gone not only as well as it was supposed to, but unlike most events in warfare, even better than expected. The entire country had fallen in love with the troops and their amazingly swift victory. If not everyone loves a sword, then almost everyone on the winning side loves a swift sword. But in truth, it was a war without real resonance. The actual land combat had lasted just four days, and it had been conducted by an elite professional army, thereby touching relatively few American homes. For much of the country it was a kind of virtual war, something few people were engaged in or had sacrificed for. Thus, like many things celebrated in the modern media, it was distant and oddly nonparticipatory; when it was over, it was over, leaving remarkably little trace. People had tied yellow ribbons to their mailboxes or gateposts as a sign of their support for those fighting, but it was very different, indeed, from the time during World War II when small flags with stars were displayed in windows to signify that a member of the family was in service, probably overseas and in harm's way.

The different pollsters tracking George Bush in the period after the Gulf War, from March until well into the fall of 1991, found a steady decline in the president's approval ratings, a decline, depending on the pollster, of some twenty or twenty-five percentage points. That was bad enough, but it was relatively easy to justify—after all, his ratings at the moment of victory in the desert had been almost unconscionably high. What went up that high certainly had to come down. Much more alarming was that people were again becoming mutinous over the economy, even as the aura of good feeling about the Gulf War was beginning to vanish.

The White House, for a variety of reasons, tended to cut itself off from that ominous trend. Steeper's polls and those of other pollsters showed that much of the country, perhaps as many as 80 percent of those polled, thought the country was in a recession. But the president's economic advisers—Michael Boskin, who was the head of the Council of Economic Advisers, effectively Bush's own personal economist; Dick Darman, his budget director; and Nick Brady, his secretary of the treasury—all told him that the recession was over. Some of his political people were furious with that stance; they thought the economists were dead wrong and were underestimating a potentially destructive political issue in order to justify their past advice. Nonetheless, Bush, in the fall of 1991, went public and declared that the recession was over. That was a critical mistake; it put him in direct conflict with the way a vast majority of Americans felt on an issue that was growing ever more serious in the public mind.

This was the predicament of the Bush White House at the end of 1991. It had been Bush's best year in office, yet a powerful political current was beginning to work against him. Furthermore, he was being given little credit for his considerable skill in negotiating the end of the Cold War. In fact, the end of the Cold War was now possibly also working against him, as the release from Cold War tensions accelerated the change in the primacy of issues, from foreign affairs, where the Republicans in general and Bush in particular had been the beneficiaries, to domestic affairs, at a time when the economy was soft and the chief beneficiaries on economic issues were the Democrats.

Among the first to spot this change was Fred Steeper. In December 1991, at exactly the time when the Soviet Union was breaking up and a once-feared adversary was losing its strength, he was holding a series of focus groups with ordinary citizens, trying to figure out how they felt about the issues that would face the Republican Party in the upcoming election year. The results were deadly. Not only was the primary issue the economy, not only did most ordinary people feel the country was mired deep in a recession, in contrast to what the president and his economic advisers were saying, but they were furious with Bush, who, they believed, was not that interested in them and their problems. Even more devastating, there were signs that it was already too late for him to right himself on this issue.

Because of these findings Steeper wrote a memo for his boss, Bob Teeter, suggesting the possibility of what he termed the Churchill Factor or the Churchill Parallel. At the end of July 1945, just after Germany had surrendered, a tired England had not even waited for the war to end in the Pacific before voting out Winston Churchill, its gallant and beloved wartime leader, whose bulldog determination had symbolized England's strength and faith during Europe's darkest hour, and replacing him with the obviously less charismatic Labor Party leader, Clement Attlee. (He is a modest man and has much to be modest about, Churchill once said of Attlee.) The British had believed that Churchill's primary passion was defense and foreign policy, not domestic affairs, and they wanted someone who they thought would pay more attention to their postwar needs.

The same thing might now happen to George Bush, Steeper warned, and it was imperative that the president not bank too heavily on his foreign policy successes in the campaign ahead. The economy was hurting a wide range of people and becoming preeminent in their minds. Bob Teeter warned Bush of much the same thing. But the president was more confident, loath to move against his top people—his economists—and still content to believe their rosier economic forecasts. Thus, a critical election year would begin with Americans bothered by the state of the economy and yearning for benefits from the end of the Cold War, and with George Bush under assault from a Democratic challenger for paying too much attention to foreign policy and too little to domestic policy. All of this would take place as the Balkan state of Yugoslavia began to unravel with horrendous human consequences.

CHAPTER TWO

The campaign for the young Democratic presidential hopeful began in the fall of 1991 because, as much as anything else, he had nothing to lose. In the late summer and fall of 1991, the glow from the Persian Gulf War still existed, manifesting itself in George Bush's unprecedented popularity. But it also had a formidable effect on the better-known potential candidates on the opposition Democratic side—for it helped suppress their desire to run against Bush. Thus for William Jefferson Clinton, the governor of Arkansas, if a presidential race was not exactly a lark, then there was little reason not to try. Clinton was aware that if he entered the race, he would be going against a relatively thin field. He was young enough so that if he did not win, he could chalk it up as a wonderful apprenticeship during which he had learned the landscape while surely at the same time impressing the national media and influential politicians with his abilities. At the very least, a good showing, and the chance to exhibit his political skills on a national platform could catapult him into leading mention as a vice-presidential nominee.

Others might have had doubts about Clinton's talents and whether they measured up to a presidential campaign, but Clinton himself, at age forty-five, had none. He was bright and gifted, a natural politician, and he was absolutely sure of his abilities. Each increment of his career had taught him that he was as talented, or perhaps even more talented, than his peers, even though many of them might be better known because they came from bigger states with larger, more powerful constituencies, were far better financed, and, of course, had greater access to the media. He had been measuring his potential adversaries carefully over the years, and again and again had decided that his political skills and talent were superior to theirs, and he was aware as well that when he had met with the media giants who judged political horseflesh, he had always made a dazzling impression. Perhaps because he was the governor of a poor, small Southern state, their expectations were relatively low, and they came away with a favorable opinion of a young man who was so well-read, so knowledgeable and articulate about such a vast variety of issues, and whose attractive young wife seemed equally bright and knowledgeable. Clinton's ability to charm big-time power brokers, whether in the media or in the party apparatus, might not yet be known nationally but it was hardly a secret to one person—Bill Clinton.

In general, Clinton himself and the men and women around him were rather optimistic about the possibility of a race—or at the very least a testing of the waters. That idea had been on the table with the governor, his wife, and their closest allies for more than four years. In the months preceding the 1988 campaign, he had seriously thought about it but had pulled back because of whispers about relationships with women other than his wife. But the idea had never been put aside. In 1990, Clinton had faced a difficult reelection campaign, but he and his advisers had in time fashioned a successful strategy and he had again won handily. The governorship safely secured, he; his wife, Hillary; his campaign adviser Frank Greer; Stan Greenberg, the pollster; and a few close friends had immediately started thinking about a 1992 presidential run, all of them quietly believing that Clinton was the most talented *centrist* Democrat around. Their meetings had started as early as December 1990, and they had grown more serious in the early months of 1991. But then came the Gulf War, Bush's popularity shot through the roof, and even Clinton, with so little to lose, entertained doubts about taking on the race.

"Have you ever heard of the American people throwing out a president who conducted a successful war?" he asked Greer. No, Greer answered, he had not, but this was a very different, much more volatile age. Because of the force of modern media, the old rules no longer applied. Political tides changed more quickly and less predictably, Greer suggested. "But I didn't even serve in the army and I was against the Vietnam War," Clinton said. "I didn't serve either and I was against it, too," said Greer, who had helped run one of the antiwar moratoriums. Then Greer added, "And most of the country didn't serve either." Eventually, Clinton decided to enter the race.

Clinton's chief political rival appeared to be Mario Cuomo, the governor of New York, he of the eloquent phrases and a big bloc of votes, a darling of those traditional Eastern liberals still longing for the cadences of the New Deal. Clinton appreciated the New York governor's verbal skills, but he never thought of Cuomo as more talented than he was, nor in any way better at governance—who really knew how good Cuomo was at governance? he would say to friends. Cuomo might look like a marvelous candidate, but Clinton had a shrewd, intuitive sense of the self-doubts and limitations that might keep Cuomo from ever making a presidential run. Was it, Clinton had wondered, a great hidden fear of rejection, a man so proud that he could not bear risking this, the ultimate rejection? Besides, if the Cuomo candidacy *did* pan out and he got the nomination, what better fit for a New York Catholic of Italian origins than a bright, attractive, young Protestant governor from the South? But when Cuomo took himself out of the race, Clinton did not see anyone on the horizon whom he thought invincible, and that included George Bush. He might be the sitting president, but he did not, Clinton confided to close friends, strike him as having exceptional political gifts.

As he entered the primaries, Clinton was aware that he had little knowledge about foreign policy, and if he was going to get up to speed on it, he needed a foreign policy connection. So he hooked up in the fall of 1991 with a talented young man who was one of the few surviving Democratic gurus in the world of foreign policy, Tony Lake. The original link to Lake had come through a man named Samuel (Sandy) Berger, who had been an antiwar activist while in college, had worked in the 1968 campaigns of both Gene McCarthy and Bobby Kennedy, and had first met Clinton in the failed George McGovern campaign in 1972. Berger had thereafter worked for Lake in the Carter administration when Lake was the director of Policy Planning in the State Department under Cyrus Vance.

In 1991, Berger had a full-time job as a Washington trade lawyer, while Lake was at something of an impasse in his life. He was still relatively young by the standards of the foreign policy establishment, barely in his fifties, talented, extremely well-credentialed, and still a favorite of Vance's. By the fall of 1991, he was teaching courses about contemporary foreign policy at several colleges in western Massachusetts, while at the same time working on a book, which did not seem to be going well. It was a book, as Lake described it, about the Democrats and foreign policy and "why we always screw up." Berger made the connection between Clinton and Lake—suggesting to Lake that at the very least any time spent with this talented young Democratic politician might help him with his book.

Lake and Clinton first got together in Boston in the fall of 1991. Clinton, just beginning to test the political waters, was there to give a speech. Lake drove over from his farm in western Massachusetts for the meeting, and he was vetted first by George Stephanopoulos, Clinton's bright, young, all-purpose aide, and Hillary Clinton. Only then, after passing muster, did he meet the candidate himself. Like almost everyone else who met Clinton for the first time, Lake was immensely impressed by his remarkable intelligence and the exceptional level of concentration he seemed to bring even to peripheral meetings. One of Clinton's great strengths, it was to help him greatly during the forthcoming campaign. Though as governor of Arkansas he was technically still a small-timer, the politicians and media people usually sensed upon meeting him that he was a big-time player, as good as anyone they had ever seen.

The first time Clinton and Lake met, they spoke primarily about domestic matters, and Clinton was intrigued by Lake's stories of how badly his neighbors in rural Massachusetts were faring economically. What struck Lake first about the governor was his intellect, and then his empathy, a word that would often be used to describe Clinton. The two men seemed to get on well, and Lake's curriculum vitae—his dissent from American policies in Vietnam after serving as a young and eager foreign service officer there early in the war, culminating in his resignation from Henry Kissinger's staff during the Cambodian incursion—was something that would pass the litmus test of both Clintons, who had been active in the antiwar movement. Lake was soon invited to come to Little Rock to consult with the candidate. En route on the plane, he sat next to an Arkansas woman who was deeply disenchanted with her governor and was quick to let Lake know why. When he later mentioned it to Clinton, he was impressed by Clinton's immediate reaction—"Did you get her name?" It was retail politics at its most elemental, Lake decided.

Lake was not unhappy about being pulled back into politics. He was having trouble with his book, there was something of a vacuum in his life, and he was uneasy with the general drift of the country as voiced by some of his students who, in this new post–Cold War era, were arguing with him that foreign policy had lost not merely its primacy, but virtually all of its importance. This argument, which was bad enough coming from students, would be even worse when Lake heard it either from members of the Congress and the executive branch of the government. Besides, Lake liked the sheer talent of the candidate. You never had to repeat yourself with him. Foreign policy might not be his natural field, but he was nothing if not a quick study. Clinton, Lake decided early on, had an extraordinary intellect—one that was not always linear, though it certainly had a linear baseline. Clinton was well-read, but much of his intelligence, or certainly the most interesting part, was intuitive. His instincts on issues and people, Lake thought, were simply uncommon, and he had clearly learned long ago to trust them.

Somewhat against his will, for he had a rather Hamlet-like ambivalence, Lake discovered that he was being drawn into a Democratic presidential campaign. One of the pluses was that in the beginning it did not really seem like a full-time commitment. Clinton appeared to be a long shot, a talented young candidate, surrounded by bright young people, up against great odds. Besides, Lake was underemployed at the moment and he quite liked Clinton. Why not join him?

Helping to prepare a foreign policy speech, Lake was impressed by one additional aspect of working with Clinton. When he had prepared speeches for other candidates, it had always been about the bottom line—what was the sum position of the speech? With Clinton it was somewhat different; he went through the speech far more carefully than other pols, and Lake was intrigued by what he would say at the end of each paragraph: yes, I believe that, or, yes, I agree with that, instead of saying something to the effect that the audience would agree with it.

The first foreign policy speech, given at Georgetown, went well, and Lake was asked to stay on, which he did, working with Sandy Berger. The early days in New Hampshire were not, of course, easy, and foreign policy was hardly of the essence. "Those of us doing foreign policy were always aware that we were a wholly owned subsidiary of the campaign," Lake later noted, "that is, we were very much apart from the center. The center was the economy, and we were aware that the campaign would be driven by one phrase: 'It's the economy, stupid.'" But Lake also knew that if foreign policy was no longer the defining issue in American politics, that if Clinton's domestic political advisers were right about the importance of the economy and of domestic issues, they might be underestimating another critical element in any presidential campaign; the American people were, when they voted for a president, measuring him as a man who would become commander in chief.

That was a critical test, Lake believed, and one that Michael Dukakis had failed miserably four years earlier. The photo taken of him in a tank during the 1988 campaign wearing both a tanker's helmet and a big grin had been a candidate killer; the Republicans had seized on it, running and rerunning it endlessly as a television commercial. New world order or no, candidate Clinton would do well to be aware that some old-fashioned tests were still out there. No one knew what crises lay ahead, and somehow in the mysterious process that took place inside the voting booth, there would be a moment when voters considered how the candidate might behave during an international crisis. Clinton had to pass that test. If he failed it, then no matter how well the other issues worked for him, he would lose.

Foreign policy was not a strength, either of the candidate himself or of his party, and was hardly at the center of his campaign. But Clinton would, it was decided early on, handle foreign policy by protecting himself on it without making it a major issue. If he got the nomination, which began to appear ever more likely after the New Hampshire primary, he did not want to be associated with Jimmy Carter or Michael Dukakis, both of whom seemed—though the former had once been elected, and Clinton had once coveted a place on the ticket with the latter—ghosts from Democratic disasters past. The Clinton people were aware of their candidate's—and their party's—vulnerability in foreign policy, but even in the wake of the Gulf War they believed Bush had his own vulnerabilities.

Clinton and his advisers like Lake decided from the start to neutralize Bush on foreign policy if their man got the nomination. "We would try and clinch him the way a boxer tries to clinch another boxer in the ring when he thinks the other boxer is stronger," said George Stephanopoulos, a veteran of the Dukakis campaign. Added Lake, "We were also going to keep jabbing him, on the theory that if we were jabbing him, he would have a harder time hitting back at us." Or as James Carville, Clinton's top political strategist, so delicately explained the zeitgeist of the Clinton campaign, "It's hard for some-body to hit you when you've got your fist in his face."

The Clinton people studied the Bush record and saw—and this was par-ticularly important to Lake—that he was most vulnerable on Bosnia, part of the old Yugoslavia, where the world was watching the beginning of what would become a human catastrophe. They would hit Bush hard on Bosnia and on China, where there were also human rights violations. That would be tailor-made, they believed, to put Bush on the defensive and show that they were tougher than the Democrats who had run in recent years. Their words on Bosnia would also show that Democrats need not be wimps. It might help win back Reagan Democrats who took issues like these seriously. They would also make the case for the importance of the domestic economy in terms of foreign policy: for America to be a leader and the most powerful voice in world affairs, its economy had to be made stronger.

CHAPTER THREE

Yugoslavia had started as the smallest of crises, a blip on the radar at a historic time when so much else that was taking place was so positive. The end of the Cold War inaugurated a period of almost unparalleled optimism, particularly in central Europe and most especially among the countries that had involuntarily been part of the Soviet Union's empire for so long: Poland, Hungary, and Czechoslovakia. Finally, in countries where democracy had been suppressed for almost forty-five years, ordinary people were passionate about long-awaited democratic reforms and a chance at embryonic capitalism, which might provide a better material life, not only for their children in the future, but perhaps even for themselves in the present.

The one exception to the generally hopeful picture in the old communist world was Yugoslavia, where it was not so much democracy that had been suppressed—the Yugoslavs had enjoyed considerably more personal and economic freedom than the people of any other Eastern European country—but nationalism. The price of surface unity in Yugoslavia had been the forceful restraint of the great ethnic differences among the various components of this unlikely country, one that had been stapled together after the end of World War I, and where Serb Orthodox Catholic, Croatian and Slovenian Roman Catholic, and Bosnian and Kosovar Muslim lived in uneasy accord, an accord ensured by the authoritarian regime. In Yugoslavia as the Cold War ended, many non-Serb Yugoslavs were growing particularly nervous about Serb nationalism emanating from Belgrade. On a map of Europe that was otherwise full of bright promise, of people gaining greater freedom, Yugoslavia was the one country that cast a dark shadow.

By early 1990, it was increasingly clear that Yugoslavia would probably not hold together as a unified country. The forces of freedom that had come with the collapse of the communist empire and the destruction of the Berlin Wall had an additional and somewhat different meaning in many parts of Yugoslavia. In both Slovenia and Croatia, for example, it meant not merely freedom from Moscow and from communism, but freedom from rule by Belgrade. Both the Slovenians and the Croatians were anxious to leave the Yugoslav federation and become independent nations. At the same time, a virulent Serb nationalism seemed on the rise, and any move toward independence by any of the country's former components might be used as an excuse for the Serbs to move against them. The most likely targets were Bosnia, perhaps parts of Croatia, and a part of the country that had almost unique historical significance for the Serbs— Kosovo.

In late February 1990 with Yugoslavia moving steadily toward what appeared to be a breaking point, Larry Eagleburger, then deputy secretary of state in the Bush administration and one of the most experienced American foreign service officers of the last twenty-five years, visited his old stomping grounds in Belgrade. He had spent eight years in Yugoslavia as a foreign service officer. He had been only thirty-two years old when he began his first tour of duty in 1962; and shortly after he had arrived, there had been a catastrophic earthquake in Skopje, the capital of Macedonia, which was a part of the federation. Eagleburger had taken over and directed the immensely successful relief activities, including the construction of an army field hospital in the city, thereby earning from the Yugoslavs the nickname Lawrence of Macedonia. His second tour had come in the late seventies, when Jimmy Carter was president and Eagleburger was named ambassador to Belgrade. He had been welcomed back as something of a national hero.

Now in 1990 he was returning again, this time as a senior administration official to deal with the internal tensions that had been escalating in Yugoslavia since the collapse of the Berlin Wall, and to try to reconcile, as one friend said, the irreconcilable. In part because he knew the terrain well, Eagleburger was, his close friends thought, quite reluctant to make this trip. He was unhappy about coming back to a place he knew and had once loved, and averse to dealing with explosive forces he wanted no part of as the nation seemed to be careening toward some kind of violent end. For he sensed that the kind of military commitment it might take to stop the violence on the part of the Western world, most notably the United States of America, was almost surely lacking.

But the pressure on him to give it one last try had been mounting for weeks, most of it from people in the American embassy in Belgrade. There it was believed that if any outsider had the authority and the leverage to make these people see what Westerners believed was a rational solution to their problems, it was their old friend Larry Eagleburger. He had been visiting some of the emerging democracies in Eastern Europe at the time, and arrangements were made for him to visit Belgrade as well. Privately he was quite ambivalent about the trip. There were several reasons, one of which was a commitment he had made to the Senate during his confirmation hearings several months earlier not to get involved in Yugoslav affairs. He had, during a relatively brief period out of government, served with Kissinger Associates, a high-powered, supremely well-connected lobbying and consulting firm, where he had made some minor representations for Yugoslav companies, including the maker of the ill-fated Yugo. The net value of his services was small, but there had been the possibility of a conflict of interest. Some of the attacks upon him were viewed by his friends as driven not so much by a genuine belief in that possibility, but by the fact that Jesse Helms, a powerful force on the Senate Foreign Relations Committee, though like Eagleburger a Republican, was far to the right of Eagleburger and regarded him as Henry Kissinger's man, a representative of the old moderate bipartisan foreign policy establishment, which, of course, he was. But a more important reason for his reluctance, some of his colleagues believed, was a prescient sense that things were not going to end well in Yugoslavia. He had just enough knowledge of the forces at work in both countries, Yugoslavia and the United States, to know that there was no conceivable happy ending to this story. Yugoslavia was heading into a downward spiral where the leverage of the United States was likely to be minimal. Besides, he already knew something that all the bright, idealistic, younger officers underneath him who were pushing for greater activism did not know, that the deal was done. The Bush administration had already made its decisions. So it did not matter which options appeared to be open, for in reality they were already closed.

Because James Baker, the secretary of state, was preoccupied with higher-priority issues, such as the evolution of the new Russia, the creation of a single, unified Germany, and events in the Middle East, once Eagleburger was drawn back into Yugoslavia, the issue was likely to remain in his permanent custody. That was not something he sought—an endlessly draining loser that offered few positive options. Some friends felt he had a sixth sense of the future. Yugoslavia would continue to unravel.

As he had suspected, it did not turn out to be a pleasant visit. Eagleburger met with almost every player in this mounting psychodrama. All the more powerful forces suddenly at play, unlike those in Poland, Hungary, and Czechoslovakia, were heading in what the United States and others in the West would deem a negative direction. He had warned the Slovenes and Croats not to break away from the federation, but he sensed that his words had little weight. They were going to do what suited them and seek long-awaited independence. Then he had engaged in a long, hard session with Slobodan Milosevic, the shrewd, aggressive, jingoistic leader of the Serbs. Eagleburger was well aware that Milosevic had been deliberately fanning the rising ethnic tensions and exploiting them for more than three years as a means of enhancing his own power. Once the two men had been close, or relatively close for an American ambassador and a young, rising apparatchik in a communist country, and some in the embassy had thought of Milosevic, if not exactly as a protégé of Eagleburger's, as one of his favorites. Milosevic was, it seemed, a bright young man on the rise who in Eagleburger's eyes represented the new breed of Yugoslav leader, someone who could and would help navigate his country toward the more blessed shores of capitalism. As the head of one of Belgrade's banks, Milosevic, in comparison with those who had gone before him, appeared to Eagleburger to be remarkably free of dogma. That would certainly turn out to be true—opportunism rather than dogma was at the heart of his every move.

There were, however, a number of Slobodan Milosevics. There was Milosevic One, the original, dutiful Communist Party believer. The man Eagleburger had liked and had tried to take under his wing was Milosevic Two, the young banker flirting with capitalism. To the Americans stationed in Belgrade, tired of the old communist leaders with their closed minds and ideological mantras, Milosevic Two had seemed like the kind of man who was the hope for the future, a new kind of leader, a modern technocrat, more pragmatic, better educated, less bound by all the old communist orthodoxies. Or as one American said, "Our kind of guy, not one of the old brain-dead Tito hacks, but instead a guy you could go to a nightclub drinking with and he would order Scotch instead of slivovitz." In the view of Eagleburger, the new generation of ascending leaders like Milosevic was simply smarter, quicker, and more open than the generation preceding them, which, Americans believed, had learned nothing since its leadership had come down from the mountains with Tito in 1945. The new technocrats had less to unlearn than their seniors, and Milosevic, quick, surprisingly facile, able to understand what Westerners wanted and the benefits of dealing with them, was clearly a rising star.

Then in more recent years as the communist world around him had begun to implode, Milosevic had changed again and started his ruthless exploitation of the latent and ever-potent Serb nationalism, playing in particular on Serbian fears of the Kosovo Albanians. That was Milosevic Three, the supernationalist Milosevic, a new and truly dangerous figure. No wonder that Eagleburger had not been eager to meet with his latest incarnation. The real Milosevic, it now appeared, represented a breed as old as time itself, a complete cynic who believed in nothing save his own rise to power, used situational ethics in all critical moments, and therefore was the principal author of the tragic chapter about to unfold in the history of Yugoslavia. While many other bright, new democratic leaders were coming to the fore in much of the former communist world, men and women who had paid a high price for their beliefs in the past and were now looking to the future, Milosevic intended to sustain the past by exploiting the ethnic hatreds that had existed in his country just under the surface for centuries.

The Milosevic and the Eagleburger who were about to meet in 1990 were very different from the two men who had met just two years earlier in the summer of 1988, when Milosevic Two was just beginning to morph into Milosevic Three. Few Westerners had yet detected the change. Eagleburger had come back to Belgrade for a brief visit, and Jack Scanlan, then the American ambassador and something of an Eagleburger protégé—he had been deputy chief of mission under Eagleburger when the latter was ambassador—took his former boss to see the Serb leader. Their meeting was one of genuine warmth and affection, two old friends exceptionally glad to see each other and discovering that they wanted the same things and were still in tune. But just a year later, it became clear that Milosevic Three had replaced Milosevic Two and was playing the most important role in tearing the fabric of Yugoslavia apart. By then, his tour of duty in Belgrade over, Scanlan was back in Washington, and he dropped by Eagleburger's office to see his sponsor, who was deputy secretary of state. "Your friend Milosevic is beginning to cause a lot of trouble over there," Eagleburger said. "But, Larry," Scanlan answered, "I met him at your dinner table."[1]

Now, in February 1990, summoned back to Belgrade, Eagleburger was not thrilled about meeting his former protégé. "I thought he was a liberal; he talked so convincingly about westernizing Yugoslavia's economy," Eagleburger told another of his protégés, Warren Zimmermann, the American ambassador who had replaced Scanlan. "I just must have been wrong." Zimmermann did not think Eagleburger had been wrong, just that Milosevic was a more flexible apparatchik than most, with a chameleon-like ability to adjust to different circumstances, and a remarkable lack of commitment to ideology, which had served him well in the rapidly changing political arena in which he had come to power.[2] Eagleburger's meeting with Milosevic was particularly heated. Milosevic insisted that he was being accused unfairly for everything that was going wrong in Yugoslavia. Why did the West always blame the Serbs? he asked. Look what has been done to us by our enemies over the years. It was a typical Milosevic performance, one that all too many Westerners would come to recognize in the following months and years. Of the things being done to the Serbs by others in the country, Milosevic was infinitely well-informed; of the many things being done to others by the Serbs, he always knew absolutely nothing but would be glad, if given the right information, to check them out.

There was no common ground. Eagleburger and Milosevic, once relatively good friends, could, like their respective countries, find no acceptable accord. The United States had sent its best player to play its best card, and it had not worked. There was no reward for stored-up goodwill or favors done in the past, nor was there any reward for appeals to Milosevic about the economic and political benefits of a more humane Yugoslavia, one that avoided human rights violations. The only thing that would catch Milosevic's attention, Eagleburger suspected, was a cold-blooded threat backed by genuine military force.

On the second night of Eagleburger's visit, Warren Zimmermann did something that, for an American in Belgrade, was groundbreaking. He invited about fifteen members of opposition groups representing the different ethnic factions throughout the country to a meeting at his residence. Invisible men became, for the first time, visible, people who had never been to the American ambassador's residence came, and many who had never spoken before spoke freely that night. Some voices were for the dismemberment of the country, some for making it more of a true confederation, some for holding on if possible to the best of what existed. Eagleburger went around the room asking people what they thought was going to happen next. If years later the evening could be remembered for the warning signals of what was soon to come, it was also, in its pluralism, a reminder of what might have been. Louis Sell, the embassy's political counselor, was intrigued by the diversity of it, but later the thing he recalled most clearly was the voice of the Slovenians.

When Eagleburger asked if anyone in the room favored the end of Yugoslavia as a unified country, Peter Jambrek from Slovenia was the only one to answer in the affirmative. He also said that his party, the noncommunist DEMOS, was likely to win the upcoming election in Slovenia, and that it would quickly move toward independence, both of which predictions would prove true. Then at the very end of the evening, Jambrek turned the tables and quietly asked Eagleburger a question: If we leave Yugoslavia, what will the United States do? At first Eagleburger was a bit taken aback; it was hardly a question he was eager to respond to. Finally, he answered that the United States hoped Slovenia would not leave the federation, but in the end we would not do anything to force the Slovenian government's policies. Jambrek thanked Eagleburger for his answer.

It had not at first seemed like the highlight of the meeting, but almost ten years later, what Louis Sell, by then retired from the foreign service, recalled most vividly were Jambrek's question and Eagleburger's answer. The Slovenians, Sell remembered, unlike some of the others, had been polite and had not made a lot of noise, but they had got what they wanted, effectively a green light. The deed was done. Word of what Eagleburger had said spread like a brush fire throughout Slovenia, where it was viewed as the final step in the move to independence, for the Slovenians were already aware that the Germans, culturally, socially, religiously, and historically their allies, favored their independence. Nor was it likely to be a solitary act. Slovenian independence would trigger Croatian independence, which would, it was believed by many, inevitably trigger Serbian military moves against Croatia as well as against an extremely naked and vulnerable part of the federation, Bosnia. Thus the stage was being set for tragedy.

To Eagleburger the trip to Yugoslavia was immensely disheartening. When he returned to Washington, he was much chastened. "You guys told me it was bad and getting worse," he told his aides. "Well, I want you to know that it's much worse than anyone thought. It's going to be much bloodier than we thought." But it had been a small dark moment, a rare exception to the general mood in that region, where, because of the end of communism, almost all the news was good. The events in the Soviet Union and in Germany, not to mention Warsaw, Prague, and Budapest, were much more positive and were all viewed as far more important. Strikingly, in a book written by Michael Beschloss, the diplomatic historian, and Strobe Talbott, then the *Time* magazine Washington bureau chief, an excellent, almost minute-by-minute chronicle of critical events from 1989 to 1991 in Washington, Moscow, and Germany, there is only the most fleeting mention of Yugoslavia, and not a single mention of Slobodan Milosevic.

The Eagleburger trip to Yugoslavia marked, without anyone realizing it, the end of one era and the beginning of another. We had sent as able a man as the State Department had produced in the postwar era, and one relatively predictable question had revealed a complete lack of a policy for the future in that area. Perhaps there was a generational divide. Men like Eagleburger and many others in the administration he served had done extremely well in confronting previous crises and tensions, where for more than forty years those who wore the black hats were always clearly labeled—they were communists. But now these experts seemed to have trouble adjusting to a new kind of crisis, where the men wearing black hats in Europe were no longer controlled or driven by Moscow. They were just men in black hats capable of doing a great deal of harm. In this new era, evil was simply evil, albeit localized. It no longer bore a recognizable brand name that would cause Washington to spring to readiness, and where there would be large domestic American political constituencies pledged to counteraction. The talents and the experiences of the last forty years had left many senior national security people somewhat slow to spot a very different kind of crisis and ill-prepared to respond.

CHAPTER FOUR

The official unraveling of what had once been Yugoslavia began in late 1990, and every single participant in the drama, from all the different sides, seemed to be playing an assigned role. In Slovenia, Peter Jambrek's DEMOS party, as he had predicted to Larry Eagleburger, won the election and a referendum in favor of independence in December 1990, and he announced plans to secede from Yugoslavia in late June 1991. The Croats immediately declared that they would follow the Slovenians.

So it began. The willingness of Slovenia and Croatia to leave the federation became, of course, the rationale for Milosevic to move against them—a brief little ten-day military flurry at the border against the Slovenians soon followed. The Serbs got a bloody nose, but that was of little consequence to Milosevic. Slovenia did not interest him greatly; there were not many Serbs there. Most assuredly it was not sacred ground. But the Serbs did covet a vast part of eastern and central Croatia called the Krajina, an area that resembled a snake about to coil and strike. Like much of the land in Yugoslavia, it was disputed terrain with a considerable number of longtime Serb residents, and Milosevic wanted it to be part of his Greater Serbia, which would also give him a chance to wrap his arms and his land around a region of the old Yugoslavia called Bosnia.

Skirmishes between Serb forces and local Croatian military units began to break out in the summer of 1991, and Serbs who had long lived in Croatia began to flee as the tensions rose and news of fighting in other towns spread. That became an even more powerful excuse for the Serbs to use the Yugoslav National Army (JNA) to attack that part of Croatia. The Serbs had from the very beginning been the dominant military force in the country. In the last few years, Milosevic had virtually turned the JNA, the third or fourth largest in Europe, depending on how you counted reservists, into a de facto Serbian army, moving out officers of other nationalities and promoting not just Serbs, but Serb officers who were in accord with his political ambitions.

The Croatians were poorly prepared for this opening phase of what would be a prolonged civil war (it would last episodically for four years), and the early Serb victories came quite easily. By the fall of 1991 the Serbs had two Croatian cities under siege, Vukovar in eastern Croatia, and Dubrovnik, the beautiful city on the Adriatic, much admired not only by the Yugoslav people, but by the many Europeans who had gone there on vacation because Yugoslavia, an attractive land with attractive people and an attractive soft currency, was a much cheaper package tour than, say, Italy. It was the brutal siege of Dubrovnik, the destruction of a city of historic reknown, that first brought the growing violence in Yugoslavia to the attention of the West.

As these early events unfolded, and as two parts of what had been a once-favored nation fought with each other, Washington essentially stood on the sidelines. The Bush administration was slow to act in Yugoslavia for two prime reasons. The first and more obvious was the ghosts of Vietnam, the immense resistance of the Pentagon to direct military involvement, the great fear of being sucked into a Balkan quagmire. As Larry Eagleburger, who was as important as any other high-level official in the decision-making—or the non-decision-making—of that time, later said, "When I thought of what might happen if we intervened, what I always feared was Vietnam—the tar baby. Something that started out small but kept growing."[1] But that was hardly the only reason, especially among the top civilian officials. George Bush, James Baker, the secretary of state, and to some degree Brent Scowcroft, the national security adviser, among others, had their own reasons for not wanting to get militarily involved on behalf of a breakaway part of a once sovereign nation. Not only were they exhausted from the complicated job of putting together the Gulf War alliance and overseeing the end of the communist empire in Eastern Europe, but the importance of dealing with Russia was constantly on their minds.

Thus a fascinating critical issue, which overshadowed the violence in Yugoslavia, came from a third country—not what was good for the people of Yugoslavia, but what was good for Mikhail Gorbachev and American-Soviet relations. Gorbachev was attempting to navigate his way through the difficult—indeed treacherous—period that came with the collapse of a once great empire. The stakes in his success as far as American policy makers were concerned were immense. That he wanted to keep Russia communist did not bother Washington at first, because the Russia that was evolving was essentially a defanged one. If Gorbachev was successful, it would mean nothing less than the end of a rival superpower and an entire forty-year era of terrifying nuclear tensions.

That consideration, therefore, dwarfed all other foreign policy issues. Washington would watch, with its fingers crossed, as Gorbachev tried to morph the Soviet Union into a new and somewhat more democratic incarnation, and above all a smaller, less adversarial one. It was the trickiest job imaginable, attempting to modernize and, indeed, even democratize an awesome, bulky, incompetent communist state that had never really worked—other than in its military and secret police operations. But the question for the Bush administration from the start had been, how far could Gorbachev go?

What, in the opinion of his potentially powerful domestic enemies in Moscow, constituted Russian soil, and what parts of the old Soviet empire could be let go without paying too high a political price? What would Moscow do, for example, about Ukraine, a part of the Soviet Union and perhaps even of Russia that nonetheless thought of itself as historically independent? It was, Gorbachev was learning, a lot easier to build an empire than to hold one together. In addition, the pace of change tended inevitably to accelerate toward warp speed as different parts of the empire, their own independence long suppressed, looked around, saw changes elsewhere, and began to sense weakness in Moscow and demand their own freedom.

At a time when the first sure signs of the Yugoslav breakup became clear, and when American influence there might have been at its greatest, we were wedded to Gorbachev. The Soviet Union, and then eventually Russia, as far as Bush and the men around him were concerned, was like a baby in an oxygen tent, entering its new life tentatively and awkwardly. As that process took place, Yugoslavia was very much a peripheral issue in Washington. Already there were signs of the immense benefits to be derived from the change in Russian-American relations. Russia had been an invaluable ally in the Gulf War, with Gorbachev greatly angering his own military people, who were closely wedded to Saddam Hussein (Milosevic and much of the JNA were also pro-Saddam, and indeed the JNA flagrantly violated the United Nations arms embargo on Iraq). Moreover, with Gorbachev and Eduard Shevardnadze's uneasy acceptance, Germany was on its way not merely to unification, but unification within NATO, a geopolitical coup unimaginable a few years earlier.

Thus, in the eyes of the top Bush people, Gorbachev's political problems greatly outranked whatever signals were coming from Yugoslavia. Gorbachev feared the accelerating potential for breakaway provinces in his empire and the rage it would stir up among his more jingoistic enemies on the domestic right and in the military. That, too, had repercussions in our dealings with Yugoslavia. For America could not appear to back a breakaway province in Yugoslavia without setting a dangerous precedent for a Soviet Union and Russia that might also splinter apart. If the United States tolerated the birth of Croatia and Slovenia and recognized them, then we might have to recognize Ukraine as a newly incarnated nation and God only knew how many other parts of what had been the Soviet Union now yearning for their independence. They would surely point to our acquiescence—or sponsorship—of new nations in the Balkans. That might trigger uprisings against our new and suddenly most important friend. Therefore, at a time when our leverage was at a maximum in the Balkans, we tended to disregard reports that not only suggested the inevitability of a Balkan breakup, but perhaps its desirability if it was done under mandated international supervision. Our policy was not just, as some critics later decided, Serbo-centric, driven by a traditional diplomatic preference for Serbs rather than Croatians, Slovenians, or Muslims, and a belief that the real Yugoslavia was Serbian. It was, at that moment, Gorba-centric.

Then there were the military complexities that worked against any kind of involvement. By the fall of 1991, Croatia and Serbia were at war, with the Serbs the primary aggressors. That had been obvious during the prolonged shelling of Dubrovnik and Vukovar. The Serbs had attacked Dubrovnik with land-based artillery and with the guns aboard some of their naval vessels. They were, given the nature of the conflict, far better armed than the Croats but extremely naked to any enemy with first-rate technology, such as American or NATO forces. American retaliation, either by jet fighters and bombers or by ships from the Sixth Fleet, would have been a piece of cake. They could have taken out the Serb batteries in a few minutes and sunk any number of Yugoslav ships. The air and sea belonged, if we so wanted it, to NATO and the Americans.

To some civilians in State, ahead of the existing curve in sensing how murderous the intentions in Belgrade were and how much more murderous they might become unless we checked them soon, the equation was immensely tempting. They thought that Serb forces were historically overrated. After all, relatively weak Slovenian forces, made up primarily of a few well-armed policemen, had bashed the Serbs when Milosevic had made his early move on Slovenia. In Croatia the Serb victories had come only when they used vastly superior firepower against underarmed local militia; when contested by real opposition, they had performed with only the most marginal success.

Yet there was little in the way of a constituency, either in or outside the government, for taking military action against the Serbs. The State Department tended to be split, along hierarchical lines. At the lower and middle levels, younger people, less steeped in Cold War orthodoxies and reacting to the events on the ground, were pushing for some kind of action. At the upper levels, people were reacting to policy, to the political signals coming *down* from the administration and men like Eagleburger. Those signals were simple enough to read: minimize what was happening in Yugoslavia. More important things were on the menu, a presidential election was coming up, and the administration was in no way anxious to be drawn into military action in the Balkans. The Balkans, the administration line went, constituted a problem that the European nations were going to handle.

The American military was also wary of any commitment to Yugoslavia. General Colin Powell, the head of the Joint Chiefs of Staff, and other senior people in the military saw Yugoslavia as a potential nightmare. They were confident of the initial success of any early American military moves. But since war tends to be a disorderly business that rarely follows a predictable schedule, they worried what would happen next. A quick American sea and air strike might prove effective against the guns shelling Dubrovnik, Powell and others in the

Pentagon believed, but it would not leave the Serbs without the capacity to strike elsewhere, particularly at remote targets deep in the interior that would be a logistical horror for the West. A direct confrontation with the Serb-dominated Yugoslav National Army would be no problem. The American army, fresh from its stunning triumph in the Gulf War against the Iraqi army, was at a high point in its morale and confidence. The new high-technology weaponry had been an exceptional success in that war, and the military leadership—from the top right down to the NCO level—had demonstrated that the army had recovered from the troubled days of the Vietnam era. The people who were most enthusiastic about military intervention in Yugoslavia wanted to use American airpower against the Serbs to dissuade them from their aggressive path. But what bothered the American military planners was the what-if factor, a factor much neglected by the Vietnam planners.

What-if in this case meant what would happen if the Serbs suffered heavy initial casualties from our high-tech weaponry, but instead of folding their hand and bowing to pressure, acted like the proud warrior nation they were long reputed to be, broke their forces down into smaller guerrilla-like units, and used the harsh terrain to their advantage and continued to attack their neighbors? What if we then sent in ground troops and the Serbs assaulted the long, extremely vulnerable American lines of supply and communication? What if there were American casualties, perhaps not many, but enough to get the war on television: first the images of American soldiers where they had just been killed (or captured), and then images from some American small town of their funerals, accompanied by an interview with a grieving and angry parent who said he did not know why his son had been sent to die in so foreign a place?

What sometimes seemed easy on paper, the use of awesome American technology against smaller, poorly armed forces, was not so easy in reality when the smaller, poorer forces had the option of appearing and disappearing as they saw fit. Colin Powell had learned that in two painful tours of Vietnam, which was the defining experience of his life and where he had dealt on the ground with the ferocious military forces the civilians and his military superiors had so casually underestimated. That was a war that had taken place before the coming of CNN, the all-day news network that would immediately highlight— to be followed by the other networks—any American deaths and create ever greater doubt about American purpose. What some people in State saw as pieces of cake were never pieces of cake to Powell and the men around him, all of whom had gone through the same haunting experience in Vietnam. They had a visceral sense that the technology of modern communications had more than kept up with the technology of modern armaments and had made the sustaining of war and the taking of casualties in distant places far harder for civilian politicians in ways that they discovered only too late. A number of ratios had changed in modern warfare, especially in wars in distant lands. Not the least of these changes was the coming of instantaneous communications, which gave politicians something they did not always comprehend at first, a ticking clock, transforming a military equation into a more political one in which a critical factor would be our innate national impatience that might, eventually, undercut the military. Powell and others in the Pentagon believed that if we got entangled with the Serbs in some way, it might become like Vietnam, a distant, peripheral war for our people and politicians, but an all-encompassing blood war of survival for the Serb people and politicians. Powell did not see us being either more passionate or more patient about any conflict in Serbia than the Serbs were.

Years later some of the young men who had served at the median level in State during the Bush years, as well as some of the civilians who were part of the top level in the Clinton administration, would judge Powell and the military quite critically in this period, claiming that he had been wrong and had overestimated the potential for Serb resistance. But in truth, in 1991 and 1992 and even 1993, when these decisions were being made, no one knew if he was wrong or not. An equally large truth was that the civilian teams under Bush and Clinton never gave Powell the most important requisite of all for a green light: the belief that acting militarily in Yugoslavia was a high priority for American national security and that it was worth the price of implementation if the consequences, as often happened in cases of military intervention, turned out to be more severe than imagined. Under Bush, and again under Clinton, when the top civilians asked what it might cost to intervene militarily, Powell would show his lack of enthusiasm by giving them a high estimate, and they would quickly back off. The figure never went under two hundred thousand troops.

Nothing reflected the difficulty of a potential American military move more than did dealing with two of the cities that had first begun to penetrate Western consciousness, Dubrovnik and Vukovar. Dubrovnik, where the Serb assault had started in October 1991, was a tempting target and would have been easy for the West to defend. A beautiful city, the jewel of the Adriatic, it was under siege from Serb gun positions that would not have been hard to nail. But well beyond Dubrovnik, far removed from Western journalistic eyes, a much uglier assault was taking place upon Vukovar, a mining city in eastern Croatia some 180 tortuous miles inland, a place that was about as logistically difficult to reach as any officer back in the Pentagon could imagine. The siege of Vukovar, which was significantly harsher and crueler than that of Dubrovnik, had begun in mid-September. In terms of Serb atrocities, Vukovar was to be far worse than Dubrovnik and would stand as one of the early examples of what became known as ethnic cleansing.

Outwardly it was a small, quiet city on the Danube whose classic baroque architecture might, in a more peaceful time, have fascinated the few Western tourists who were hardy enough to make their way that deep into Yugoslavia. It appeared to be of little strategic importance to anyone in the world, and yet it was a good deal closer to Belgrade than Zagreb, the capital of Croatia, a geographical fact that placed it in jeopardy. Milosevic had a large army at his disposal, and Franjo Tudjman of Croatia did not, and so the Serbs pounded the city with artillery. Why they brutalized it so badly no one was ever quite sure, though some, knowledgeable about Milosevic, thought it was because the different ethnic groups had lived there together in rather easy accord, not unlike Sarajevo in Bosnia, a place where the old Yugoslavia had worked surprisingly well, and where the local Serbs had not rallied with adequate enthusiasm to his nationalistic ambitions. Punish Vukovar, Milosevic did. The siege of the city was one of the ugliest battles of the early days of the Balkan war, a battle that was not really a battle, since only one side had weapons. The Serbs surrounded it with heavy artillery pieces and simply hammered away for several months. By the time the siege was over in mid-November, Vukovar looked like one of those cities in eastern Germany that had had the misfortune to be in the way of the advancing Red Army during the final days of World War II. Its fine old buildings had been reduced to rubble. Like a growing number of towns in Croatia and many, many more to come in Bosnia, Vukovar had been the site of a massacre. When the Serb soldiers entered the city, they swept into the local hospital and executed all the people they found there, civilian as well as military patients. When Vukovar surrendered, the Serbs invited all the foreign journalists, long barred from the area, to lunch, roasted some pigs for them, then handed out—the ultimate insult—postcards of the old Vukovar.[2]

If one thing had changed at the highest levels of the Washington power structure, Larry Eagleburger noted years later, it was how both the State Department and the Pentagon differed some two decades after Vietnam. In the old days, Eagleburger believed, the Pentagon had tended to be gung ho about military involvement and brought a can-do attitude to all its endeavors, while State tended to be cautious. Vietnam had changed that—the army had gone in there and paid a high price both in blood and in its psyche. Now the roles were reversed. State had a number of activists among its younger officials, many of whom had come along after the Vietnam experience, and at the Pentagon most of the senior people were extremely cautious. There the memory of Vietnam was a little longer, because almost all of the top army people, unlike those at State, had served directly in that war and the experience had been a bitter one in almost all instances. The Pentagon had an all too personal understanding of what happens, first, when the architects of an interventionist policy underestimate the other side, and second, when so many of those in the political process who were its architects soon orphan their own handiwork and go on to other jobs, leaving the military to deal with a war that no one could get right.

The American military, therefore, remained dubious about military intervention in the Balkans, and that, in turn, meant that the Serbs became increasingly audacious. It was the start of what would become a well-known Milosevic (and Milosevic-proxy) dynamic: a quick military probe to see if there was any Western resistance, and if none, then an even more brazen assault.

Colin Powell and most of the top people in the Pentagon were not only unalterably opposed to any seemingly quick and easy flexing of American military might, a flash of airpower or sea power in places where it was convenient, they were also nervous about assuming any simple humanitarian role that might be poorly thought out, too open-ended, and might somehow draw the country into an unwanted combat commitment: Serbs attacking a small group of American troops ferrying refugees or supplies to and from a city under siege, the Americans suffering casualties, some Americans firing back, the Serbs reinforcing, the conflict escalating on its own, with what the Pentagon assumed would be unsympathetic coverage generated by television journalists both on location and back home. An interventionist policy might look easy, but the best-case scenario, as often happened in military matters, might turn into a worst-case scenario. If that happened, Powell and others like him believed, the army would be left holding the bag, while many of the other people in the bureaucracy would deftly distance themselves from the policy, something that had happened when Vietnam turned into a disaster.

To the military, therefore, the two cities that had come to the fore early on were always entwined: Dubrovnik would be easy to handle, the logistics made to order for the West, but Vukovar would be a military nightmare. As the Serb assault on the two Croatian positions began, the American commander in Europe, General Jack Galvin, an army four-star, was on the phone with Powell every day. Could you protect Dubrovnik? was Powell's first question. Easily, Galvin would say. Silencing the Serb batteries would be a relatively simple task. Could you protect Vukovar easily? Not very easily—the price would go up. Then there was the question: Could you protect Dubrovnik, the easy one, and walk the hard one, Vukovar? That was a very different question. Galvin, stationed in Brussels and distant from the Washington-insider rumor machinery, sensed that some civilians were pushing hard for an attack on the Serbs at Dubrovnik—just set up seaborne counterbatteries to hit the Serbs, or use air force muscle or run ships in from the Sixth Fleet to clear out the Yugoslav navy.

But the proponents of action, Galvin felt, never took into account the steps left open to the Serbs in the more distant reaches of the country. Like Powell, he believed, as he would later say, that you could not just put your toe in. Galvin was a highly decorated veteran of Vietnam, thoughtful, judicious, much admired by almost everyone who dealt with him, a man both tempered and strengthened by Vietnam, and he agreed that if you put in your toe at Dubrovnik, the foot would inevitably follow, and if the foot was in, the rest of the body might also be pulled in. If we went in, who was with us? How far would our allies go? Where was the Congress and where would the media be?

In Galvin's mind, doing Dubrovnik demanded doing Vukovar as well. But if that happened, the Serbs might readily take the initiative in other distant places. They would have at least as many options as we did. Galvin had a clear understanding of the ambivalence in Washington about intervention in Yugoslavia because Powell, who read Washington better than any other senior military figure in years, would pass the word on to Brussels. It was, thought Galvin, absolutely fascinating to get a sense of the byplay. What made Powell so good, in Galvin's opinion, was that he had a feel for what was real in Washington and what existed only on the surface. There was a pseudopolicy driven by today's headlines and film clips, and the spin that an extremely agile spokesman could put on the administration's view of these events, as opposed to long-term policy goals that emanated from deep within the administration and the bureaucracy—Washington's own unspoken but important truths. Powell knew when the rhetoric was all posture and when it represented something real. He knew when a proposed policy was a kind of trial balloon, even an unconscious use of a trial balloon, something inflated in the uncomfortable vacuum of an absent policy, and when, in contrast, it reflected well-considered policy agreed upon by most of the decision-making apparatus. Powell seemed to symbolize a Pentagon that was adamant against any interventions. Only one member of the Joint Chiefs dissented from him, General Merrill (Tony) McPeak, the air force chief of staff, but his dissent was marginalized because Powell was so dominating a figure at the JCS resulting from his unique post-Vietnam personal stature, enhanced as it was by the Gulf War victory, his remarkable skill in dealing with all facets of the Washington political world as well as the media, and because his bitter feelings about the careless civilian decision-making in Vietnam were shared by almost all the other members of the JCS. McPeak alone thought we could use air power effectively, if not decisively, to limit what the Serbs were doing in Bosnia.

McPeak had been a last-minute addition to the JCS on the eve of the Gulf War, when the then incumbent, General Mike Dugan, had held what was considered to be an intemperate press conference in Riyadh that offended both the civilians and the brass back in the Pentagon in multiple ways, most notably his statement that the American people would support this war until the body bags began to come home. Dick Cheney had fired Dugan, and Powell had chosen McPeak as his successor. In comparison with his peers on the JCS, McPeak was very much a Bosnian activist. America was a great power, standing well above all the other military powers in the world, he believed, and if you were a great power, then on occasion you had to use your power. Certain crises—and to his mind the brutality in Bosnia had turned that crisis into a small-scale Holocaust—demanded action. If America did not act with its unique military domi-

nance in a place like that, then what other country would, and on what occasion? he wondered. McPeak did not necessarily believe that airpower alone
could do it, but he thought the skilled use of contemporary airpower might play
an important role and put the price of Balkan imperialism up much higher for
the Serbs. We could easily take out their artillery positions and headquarters in
Bosnia, disrupt their lines of communication, take out a number of bridges and
thereby limit their ease of entry into the country, and hit their weapons and
ammunition storage sites. At the very least, we could even out the battlefield for
the opposing indigenous forces and quite likely compel peace negotiations.

McPeak also believed that the air force had come into its own during the
Gulf War, and that for the first time in its history, it was a force unto itself with
its own munitions capability, no longer dependent upon munitions designed
by other services. In World War I, he liked to muse, it had been so bad that the
early bombing runs were made by pilots dropping previously *unexploded,* dud
artillery shells over the side of their planes in order not to waste any good
ammunition. That pretty well summed up the service's past, he thought.
McPeak realized that all his peers on the JCS—as well as members of the
Joint Staff who were going over to the Hill to testify—were saying that airpower used alone was a bad idea, that traditional pre–Desert Storm doctrine
still held. But he disagreed. He thought that confining the use of military force
only to those situations where America's strategic interests were directly
threatened was far too limiting for a great power, almost handcuffing the top
civilians and the military if carried to its logical extreme. It also excused us
from taking any responsibility in what seemed to him to be the most likely
kind of crisis now facing America—the implosion of countries in the
post–Cold War era. A great power, he believed, had to be prepared to act in
more ambiguous circumstances.

McPeak was very admiring of Powell, who was a neighbor and personal
friend and had appointed him to his chair. He thought Powell was, in his own
words, the most effective public servant he had ever dealt with in or out of uniform. But there was one difference between McPeak and many of the senior
army officers he knew. McPeak believed that he and others in the air force had
been less damaged by Vietnam than the army. Certainly, he and his peers who
had flown there (he had flown more than one hundred sorties over Laos and
North Vietnam) had been frustrated by what they felt were appalling rules of
engagement, and they had often taken fire from places along the Ho Chi Minh
Trail that were outside the zone of returnable fire. But the burden of combat for
the air force had been carried by an elite officer corps. There had been no wide-
spread smoking of dope or fragging of officers as he believed there had been
in the army. Morale had never deteriorated within his service. They had lost
men and overcome bitter frustrations, but somehow it had not gone as deep or
as corrosively into the bloodstream of the air force as it had into the army, he

thought. Many of the army people, he felt, had returned from the war deeply hurt, almost emotionally wounded, as if there were an element of personal humiliation in what had happened that greatly affected the army's view of succeeding crises. If the president wanted to do something in a place like Bosnia where war crimes were taking place, McPeak had come to believe, then he had a right to try. But among the army people, particularly those involved in Vietnam, he sensed a need to talk him out of it.

McPeak made his dissent within the Pentagon starting in 1992. Both his bosses in the Bush years, Cheney and Powell, were against using airpower, and in the early Clinton years, Powell remained McPeak's boss. He did not go public with his doubts. It was not in his mind an issue where you threw yourself down on your sword. No one criticized him for his opinions. The general view of his dissent was that of senior army people, who thought he was speaking for the air force, and the air force had always overestimated its military muscle, in World War II, Korea, and Vietnam; and because McPeak was an air force man, he had an institutional justification for pushing airpower. He, in turn, thought privately that the other Joint Chiefs had an institutional bias *against* using airpower as the sole or at least the primary weapon. When McPeak made the arguments on behalf of what airpower had done in the Gulf War, discussing the amazing accuracy of the bombing runs—an accuracy that two years later was even more precise—they had all argued back that because Iraq was a desert, the targets had been easy; they virtually stuck out, asking to be hit. He could not persuade them that the weaponry would in most circumstances be just as accurate in the Balkans.

When the issue came up of whether we could do anything in Bosnia, McPeak said simply, yes, we could do something. We could use airpower and make things difficult for the Serbs, make them pay a high price for their incursions into Croatia and Bosnia. But his colleagues argued that airpower would not be decisive because the terrain was so difficult and the weather would be so much worse. They also argued that some risk would be attached. Planes might be lost, and CNN or some other network would seize on any fatalities. To that there was no counterargument. McPeak's dissent was never angry or especially heated, but he made no progress and picked up no other votes. Though he never went public, it became known that he was making the airpower-alone argument, and he was on occasion described in the media as the mad bomber. He understood the equation was stacked against him. "I was on the short end of a lot of five-to-one votes," he said later. Powell, he decided, simply had no intention of intervening in Bosnia. Powell did not like the lay of the land in either Yugoslavia or Washington. McPeak thought Powell's own description of himself as a reluctant warrior was a healthy one; warriors at that level should be reluctant. But McPeak also felt that the world had changed and that sooner or later the military would have to figure out how to use the forces they were being paid so much for—a ticket of $275 billion a year in the budget—in smaller wars, and that the current doctrine was simply too rigid.

Powell apparently believed that an air campaign in the Balkans might turn out to be unending and we would get bogged down. Again McPeak did not agree. He thought we could be effective with airpower at a relatively low cost and in a relatively short time. In this continuing debate, the weapons were new but the arguments were old. The other services distrusted the confidence of the air force men about what they could do. Powell, like many army men who had fought in Vietnam, was particularly distrustful. Or as he said after one meeting in which a civilian had extolled airpower as a dominating instrument for stopping Slobodan Milosevic, "When I hear someone tell me what airpower can do, I head for the bunker." At this time no one was giving Powell a sense of anything approaching a consensus in Washington for serious military action against Yugoslavia. One reason he had always put the number of troops needed to do the job so high—over two hundred thousand—was not necessarily that he felt it would take many. It was a test for the civilians: How much do you really want this, how high a price are you willing to pay? Are you willing to cover worst-case-scenario possibilities? It was as if he were asking how much do you love me, and the troop figure were a symbol of how much love the civilians really had to provide.

No one in the Bush administration at a high level was eager for any kind of commitment like that. Yet one of the many ironies of what was taking place in the Balkans was that the Bush administration, unlike the Clinton administration, which succeeded it, was in no way short of people seemingly knowledgeable about Yugoslavia. Both Brent Scowcroft, the national security adviser, and Larry Eagleburger had served there, Eagleburger for eight years, Scowcroft as a military attaché for one tour. They were to some degree well-informed and knew a good deal about the nation that had once existed, if not of the polyglot society that was now erupting into armed conflict. In fact, Eagleburger noted years later, one of the principal criticisms leveled at both of them by those younger and more proactive was that they knew too much about Yugoslavia and were therefore too fearful of what the Serbs might do if we responded militarily. Perhaps, Eagleburger added, there was some truth in that criticism.[3]

Both Eagleburger and Scowcroft had some limited sense of the violence that might take place, one ethnic faction against another. They were aware of the dangers inherent in any military commitment there, and of the harsh quality of the terrain. They knew the hatreds that would drive the violence, Serb against Muslim, Croat against Serb, Muslim against both, were historic and had existed for hundreds and hundreds of years. "A very tough, nasty neighborhood," Scowcroft would say in private. Eagleburger, in particular, found himself deeply ambivalent about events in Yugoslavia. He hated not just the dissolution of a country he had loved, but also the ferocity on the part of those who had once been his friends. He had assumed that there would be some level of violence, as Serb struck against Croat and vice versa, and as one or the other moved against the Bosnians. But he had expected a more traditional kind of violence, the kind that took place on the battlefield, and where eventually some sort of settlement could be reached because the respective parties had exhausted themselves militarily. He was aware that the two people above him, George Bush and James Baker, for a variety of reasons, wanted to make no additional military commitment, not immediately after the Gulf War, and that the Pentagon might be the most skittish and conservative of all. It was his job, however, to defend the administration's inaction, and he was fond of quoting Bismarck on the Balkans, that they were not worth the life of a single Pomeranian grenadier; and Eagleburger would sometimes add that nothing could be done until the various parties to this historical hatred had killed each other off in sufficient numbers.

Scowcroft, who met with Bush every day and often several times a day—there had probably never been a national security adviser so close to a president and so tuned in to him—thought the breakup of Yugoslavia posed a dreadful dilemma for the president. Scowcroft was at once wary of the terrain and wary of being pulled into the middle of so ancient a struggle, but he also had a sense that something terrible was happening. Torn in two directions, he found himself pondering the use of force more seriously in the summer of 1992 as the worst atrocities in Bosnia became known. Though he was originally an air force man, he was quite dubious that airpower alone could end the violence. If we intervened with airpower and it didn't work, what then? What would the next step be? Without answers to those questions Scowcroft found his own voice muted.

In the last year of the Bush presidency, a time of ever crueler events in Yugoslavia, of ever more barbarous Serbian acts inflicted upon its former partners in Croatia and particularly upon Bosnian Muslims, Scowcroft had to bring the latest news from the Balkans to the president and discuss it with him. It was important, Scowcroft believed, to remember the context of that moment. The Americans had just finished up the largely successful Gulf War, but it had been an exhausting, complicated political process, putting together and then holding together the alliance and the immense force necessary, steering the package through the Senate, getting and keeping the Pentagon on board, and making sure that the Israelis, in their anger over Scud missiles, did not go off on their own and break up the fragility of the new alliance. Scowcroft knew it had been an immensely draining experience for Bush. He also knew that no president wanted to go to war—on any sizable scale—twice in one term.

When Scowcroft briefed the president, he always felt Bush's sense of distance on this issue. The president would seem puzzled about the complexity of the Balkans, asking again and again which side was which, who were the Bosnians, who were the Bosnian Serbs, who were the Bosnian Muslims, who were the Kosovars, and who were the Croats and the Slovenians. To Bush it was obviously an odd country, one where the forces that divided people were so much more powerful than the ones that united them. It clearly confused him, all these disparate places, strange names, and different ethnic groups who were supposed to be one country but clearly were not—Bosnian Serbs, Bosnian Muslims, Albanians, Macedonians, Montenegrans.

There was a ritual to their briefings. Bush would be reading the foreign intelligence reports on Yugoslavia, look up, and ask Scowcroft, "Now, tell me again what this is all about." Then Scowcroft would go through the details of the conflict, describing the different parties involved, why they hated each other, how deep these hatreds were, who was a threat to whom, and who had inflicted the latest outrage on which group. The more Scowcroft talked, the more the shadow of perplexity seemed to come over Bush's face. It was clear, Scowcroft thought, watching the president struggle with the complicated ethnic rivalries that were driving the conflict, that if Bush himself could barely understand the differences and the issues, how could ordinary Americans understand them? How then could Bush justify sending their sons and daughters to a place so far away, with towns whose names were so difficult to pronounce, for a cause that was so perplexing even to him? By contrast, the challenge in the Gulf War had seemed infinitely simpler. One country had invaded another. A border had been crossed. The balance of power in the Middle East might change if the Iraqis had access to Kuwaiti oil and could thereby continue to arm themselves at ever more excessive levels, thereby intimidating their neighbors. America's technological weaponry was likely to be effective in the desert. All of that had been easy for Bush to understand, and thus, he believed, for the American people to understand as well. Not so Yugoslavia.

So at the very top, the most important person of all did not want to buy in. In the case of Kuwait, the intervention had been driven from the start by the president. The Pentagon had not been eager for a military operation there, nor had Jim Baker. Both in Panama and in the Gulf, tough and flinty as he might seem to outsiders dealing with him in different high-level meetings, Baker did not like to choose force. It was Bush who was outraged by what the Iraqis had done and brought the bureaucracy along with him. But Yugoslavia did not fit into his existing geopolitical mind-set of where America could and should use its power. It sounded like the most complicated kind of civil war imaginable, much of it within the recognized boundaries of an existing nation-state, with no easy mission or exit strategy, and with unusually high possibilities of things going wrong according to the people he respected the most, his military men. Bush's resistance to intervention was immediate and constant.

That attitude—how difficult a call it might be—permeated even those who tilted slightly toward intervention. To respond and limit Serb aggression, Scowcroft once told Zimmermann (who would eventually make an appeal for the use of force), you had to be ready to send in ground troops. No one was anxious to do that, certainly not in an election year, and certainly not in the numbers the Pentagon was talking about.[4] That figure varied—sometimes it was two hundred thousand and sometimes it was even more—but the numbers were always big. There was, in addition, much talk about the difficulty of the terrain, and how the Yugoslav partisans had tied down so many German troops during World War II. At one point David Owen, the former British foreign secretary, appointed to be one of the peace seekers in the region in 1992, and hearing how many German divisions had been tied down by the partisans—was it only twenty-five divisions or as many as thirty-six?—did a check and found out that it was only six, still not insignificant, a figure of around one hundred thousand men.[5]

Every time they looked at Yugoslavia, experience had taught the military planners that they could not think in terms of airpower alone. Only illusionists (and top air force generals), they believed, thought that could solve the dilemma. Most of these men, going back to Korea where airpower was more valuable tactically than strategically, and particularly in Vietnam, where its shortcomings had been all too apparent, had come of age aware of its limitations. That was especially true of the Pentagon's leading generals, like Powell, all of whom had served one or two terms in Vietnam and were skeptics about airpower as a cure-all. If it proved ineffective, then we might need to deploy ground forces, and then we would begin to be gradually sucked into a full-scale war. Just like Vietnam.

The most telling line on what American policy would be in Yugoslavia had been delivered by Jim Baker after an unsuccessful trip to Yugoslavia in late June 1991, in a desperate attempt to keep the country from breaking up. It was hardly his kind of mission, for those who had studied Baker carefully over the years had learned that he did not lightly seize on issues that had the almost sure look of losers. He was not fond of difficult, dangerous places, filled with bitterly aggrieved people who presented political and human questions that, if not exactly insoluble, were as close to that as you could get. Questions like that tended to be handed off to deputies, in this case Eagleburger, whose terrain it ought to have been anyway by dint of his two tours of duty there and the alleged affection the people had for him.

Baker's trip to the Balkans was one of the most unrewarding of his professional career, worse, he later said, than dealing with the leaders of the competing forces in the Middle East, who, he had decided long ago, left a great deal to be desired as listeners. He had patiently pointed out all the many reasons why the varying Yugoslav leaders should follow the advice of the United States and the Europeans and not inflict a suicidal war on each other, and he noted the obvious economic consequences if they went ahead. It would be a disaster for a region already desperately poor. Baker also noted that he held the proxies of all the European nations. That mattered not at all. It was as if he were speaking to the deaf. No one, least of all Milosevic, paid any attention to him. Baker left Yugoslavia angry and frustrated, feeling, his close aides believed, that these Balkan leaders had no earthly sense of what was good for them. Why waste rational words on irrational people? Why waste your breath? What happened there, he seemed to think, was what they deserved, and we should wash our hands of the whole thing.

After that, the administration's policy in the Balkans, as articulated by Baker in terms that ordinary Americans would readily understand, was "We don't have a dog in that fight." It was a good phrase, but there was a danger, critics of the administration believed, that it summed up the Bush-Baker view of the entire new turbulent post–Cold War world, a place that was so messy, with so few choices that were positive rather than negative, that it was better, all in all, simply to ignore them.

CHAPTER FIVE

The irony of the Gulf War victory was that quite possibly the wrong branch of service and the wrong military leaders had been celebrated at its conclusion. American ground troops led by their armored units had humiliated an allegedly mighty but now bedraggled Iraqi army, and the final and most permanent images of that war were of pitiful Iraqi prisoners stretched out as far as the eye could see. The sight was so pathetic to much of the world that the war's architects decided to terminate it more quickly than they might normally have, fearing the negative consequences such scenes might have when they were shown in the Arab world. The final impression of the war was that it had been a singular victory for ground troops, and the two heroes who emerged had both been army men, Norman Schwarzkopf and Colin Powell. Some analysts, however, believed that the victory belonged more to the air force and the advent of its new precision-guidance munitions and highly sophisticated delivery systems.

If one man was responsible for this most original aspect of the Gulf War, these analysts believed, it was a brilliant but little-known air force strategist, Colonel John Warden, called affectionately by some of his junior officers (but not to his face) Mad John. If one of the newsmagazines had wanted to run on its cover the photograph of the man who had played the most critical role in achieving victory, it might well have chosen Warden instead of Powell or Schwarzkopf. Moreover, they believed that although what had taken place in the Gulf War was merely a beginning, it marked a decisive change in the nature of America's air strategy that now allowed the nation to maximize its use of these supremely sophisticated new weapons. Precision-guided weapons, in their embryonic stage in Vietnam, had come of age in this war, and America was obviously far and away the leader in their production and use. Thus America had been catapulted into a potential position of unmatched military power—short of nuclear weapons—that had never before existed in the post–World War II era, and the consequences of this unprecedented power might be far-reaching in both political and military terms.

A large coterie of senior military officers had watched the unique progress of the high-technology air campaign in the first five weeks and were convinced that the war was effectively over before ground forces joined the battle, the Iraqi army already battered to the point of disintegration by the unprecedented use of airpower. But the forty-three-day air campaign had lacked faces and humanity, while the ground war had given the American people what they wanted: faces and a final visual—and very palpable—victory. As a result, a truly revolutionary moment in modern warfare might have been significantly underestimated, not just by the public at large, but by many civilians who were in charge of national security, and quite possibly by some senior military men.

At the time of the Gulf War, Warden was the head of a top-secret air force group working inside the Pentagon known as Checkmate. He was considered by some military experts to be an important figure, emblematic not just in the air force but across the board among a younger generation of officers eager to adjust military thinking, planning, and structure to the uses of the new weaponry. The principal opponents of Warden's radical ideas turned out to be not, as one might expect, army men or even civilians, but senior officers in his own branch of service, especially the three- and four-star officers who dominated much of air force strategy and theology and came from the Tactical Air Command (TAC). They had a much more conventional view of the order of battle and believed that airpower was there to support the army on the ground and to interdict enemy forces. They despised Warden and his ideas, a hostility that never lessened.

In preparation for Desert Storm, Schwarzkopf had immediately requested an air plan, and from the moment Warden took on the assignment, he had a number of powerful enemies in the Washington area and particularly in TAC, where he was known as a maverick who was assaulting the orthodoxy of his own profession. The TAC people were influential within the air force, constituting, one officer said, a powerful mafia all its own. Normally the request from Schwarzkopf would have gone to Lieutenant General Jimmie Adams, air force deputy chief of staff for plans and operations, another old-fashioned TAC strategist. But Adams was away on leave and the request was funneled to Warden. The difference in their respective philosophies could not have been greater. Adams and the other senior TAC officers wanted to use the new weaponry in the traditional manner, supporting American ground forces and interdicting enemy armies in the field. They viewed Warden as both too radical and too theoretical. Warden, in turn, saw them as men from another century who did not understand the possibilities that the new generation of weapons offered strategists.

An iconoclastic officer who had graduated from the Air Force Academy in 1965, Warden had flown fighter planes and aerial reconnaissance missions in Vietnam and had left there immensely frustrated by what he believed was the misuse of airpower. When he thought of Vietnam, what he remembered were the castrating rules of engagement. Enemy trucks parked along borders of the Ho Chi Minh trail, their lights still on, were targets that he and his colleagues were not allowed to hit until they started down the trail, by then with lights off. He recalled with some bitterness his farewell dinner in Thailand, when he had gotten up and said he never wanted to be part of anything like that again. He thought it was immoral—not the war itself, fighting the North Vietnamese, but the way we had fought it, with so many restraints. His fellow airmen gathered at the party were all in agreement and cheered him enthusiastically, although an army special forces captain, misunderstanding what he had said about the immorality of the war, later challenged him to a fistfight outside the restaurant.

By the mideighties, when he was in midcareer, Warden was considered brilliant, truly innovative, and equally difficult, a man who did not know how to stay within the chain of command. He burned so brightly with his own ideas, was so sure that he was right *on every issue,* that he rarely listened to those who dissented from him. Another of his nicknames among his peers was "Right Turn" Warden because if he had a compelling idea and a superior rejected it, he simply took a right turn and went to the next higher level. Failing there, he would take yet another right turn and go to the next higher level, infuriating in the process a long line of his superiors. Predictably, the system hated him, although isolated, young iconoclastic officers working inside the system and often frustrated by it thought he was one of the most original thinkers in the service. But even an admirer once noted that Warden had no sense of proportion. Convinced of his rightness in all matters, he would argue as hard on some small, peripheral issue as on a matter of global strategy and refuse to back down. He had commanded a wing very briefly in the eighties in Germany, but it had not gone well. His subordinates had chafed over his edicts that women on the base had to wear dresses instead of pants at the PX and the various clubs, and over parking privileges. His tour as a wing commander was cut short.

To the TAC people the air force was for pilots, and pilots *flew,* and if you did not fly, if you wrote or planned, you were not really an air force man. You were somehow outside the culture, not really one of them. Their disdain for Warden was palpable, but somehow he managed to survive inside the system, always able to find one important sponsor who would harbor him on the lee side of the bureaucratic storms where the traditionalists could not get at him. At the start of the Gulf War, that role was played by General Mike Dugan, the air force chief of staff, himself soon to be fired by Dick Cheney for what were considered to be outrageous statements made on the eve of the war. Warden had been preparing for a war like this long before Iraqi soldiers crossed into Kuwait. In the seventies and especially the eighties, as the technology of modern munitions had become increasingly sophisticated, he had worked on a strategy that would give the United States (and the air force), both leaders in this new high-technology game, the maximum effect from such innovative weapons and technologies. The problem with most senior military strategists, air force or otherwise, Warden believed, was that when given what were virtually brand-new weapons with brand-new capabilities, they tended to use them with the old strategies, thus to no small degree neutralizing their full potential.

That was more true than ever with the coming of Stealth fighters and precision-guided bombs. Most senior TAC officers had been trained to think of airpower as a formidable weapon of attrition in case we fought the Soviets in a land war in Europe. In that eventuality, we would arm our Stealth fighters with these amazingly accurate weapons and use them to interdict Soviet troops and matériel on their way across Eastern Europe. Warden could barely contain his contempt for that strategy as a misuse of energies.

Instead he eventually came up with his own strategy, based on the modern state's unusual vulnerability to these new weapons. The more modern the state, the greater its dependence upon electrical power, communications systems, sources of petroleum, and transportation systems, then the more it was endangered by this kind of warfare. With the accuracy of modern airpower it was possible to paralyze the modern state by taking out its central nervous system, as if quickly and swiftly injecting it with a temporary poison that stilled its capacity to function both militarily and otherwise as a state. Moreover, it could be done with limited risk on the part of American forces, it caused limited collateral damage given the amount of munitions dropped, and it even caused comparatively limited physical damage, or at the least, the physical damage could be fairly accurately controlled. With this strategy you could harm the people who had started the war, not the poor grunts whose misfortune it was to be soldiering out in the field.

Warden understood that because of the immense success and dynamism of the American domestic economy and the great strides in computer and satellite technology, the United States was far ahead of the rest of the world in its techno-military progress and that these advances accrued primarily to the air force, perhaps a little to the navy with the cruise missiles, and very little to the army. By the late eighties, these advances had been taking place for some twenty years, incrementally increasing the degree of accuracy until what existed was nothing less than a quantum change. We could now, he believed, use airpower as no nation had ever been able to do in even the recent past, and we even had a remarkable new delivery system for these precision-guided bombs, the F-117 Stealth fighter (actually more a small bomber than a fighter), which was largely immune to radar detection.

Warden saw the enemy as a bull's-eye on a target, with five concentric rings around it, and inside each ring something of high value to the targeters: the power grid, the military communications system, the fuel supplies, the normal communications system, which was ancillary but almost as important as the military communications system, and the transportation systems, both military and civilian. You could, he believed, paralyze an enemy and bring him to the table without destroying his people. When he finally presented his plan first to General Schwarzkopf and then to General Powell, it was notable for the primacy of its assault upon the Iraqi political and military communications systems, and its almost complete indifference to the Iraqi army in the field, which he, unlike the two army generals, saw as being of little consequence once the Iraqi central nervous system was numbed. Adjustments were eventually made at Schwarzkopf's and Powell's requests to pay more attention to attacking Iraqi field forces.

In the past, most notably in the air assault upon Germany in World War II, bombing had been *serial* instead of *parallel*. Because the bombing techniques were so primitive and the accuracy so limited, it would take a week of sustained effort for the Eighth Air Force to inflict relatively severe damage on a target, often only partially crippling it. Then the bombers would go on to the next target, while the Germans would have a chance to repair the latest damage. That in Warden's definition was a serial campaign. But the new technology allowed the planners to go after as many different targets as they wanted on the first day or two and take them out with remarkable precision. The new weaponry had reversed the traditional equation of airpower. In World War II, it had been a question of how many planes were needed to take out one target; now it was a question of how many targets *one* plane with precision-guided weapons could take out. Warden had studied the air campaign against Germany, and in all of 1943 when the Allies were going after German targets, they had hit only fifty of them. But now if you had fifty or sixty key targets, you could hit them all with devastating accuracy in the first few hours of the war. Thus you had a parallel rather than serial campaign.

When Schwarzkopf's request for an air campaign came through to Warden in August 1990, it was the assignment he had always wanted. The pressure for immediate results was on, and in just two days he put together a master plan for using airpower based on his ideas and strategies. The TAC people were sure to be against it, but one of Warden's superiors shrewdly delayed a briefing Warden was supposed to give them until *after* Warden had briefed Schwarzkopf, so that it would be a fait accompli. Not everyone was happy with it, and at one high-level briefing a senior air force officer said that it was all wrong. The way to do it was to drop one big bomb relatively near Baghdad to demonstrate to Saddam what we could do, and if that did not bring him to the table, then drop the bombs closer and closer to him.

To Warden that was bizarre, a kind of gradualism reminiscent of Vietnam. Still bitter over the misuse of airpower in Vietnam and the incremental use of airpower in Rolling Thunder, he had deliberately entitled his campaign Instant Thunder. "This is not your Rolling Thunder. This is real war," he told the junior officers in his own shop, "and one of the things we want to emphasize right from the start is that this is not Vietnam! This is doing it right! This is using airpower!"[1]

Of all the top people in the chain of command who responded to Warden's early briefings, the most enthusiastic was Schwarzkopf himself, who wanted desperately to limit American and allied casualties in the war and understood immediately the possibilities that Warden was offering him. At first Schwarzkopf had been suspicious of Warden, thinking he was, in Schwarzkopf's words, a new-age Curtis LeMay clone who believed airpower was the answer to everything. But Schwarzkopf was delighted with the flexibility and originality of Warden's plan, quite pleased that it had been put together so quickly.[2] The American commander would eventually disagree on some points with Warden; he, like Colin Powell, wanted more emphasis on bombing the Iraqi army in the field. But he listened carefully to Warden's presentation and his belief that we had the capability to knock out the Iraqi airpower and air-defense systems in just six days. "This is exactly what I needed," Schwarzkopf said. Warden was, of course, thrilled to have so powerful a sponsor, and from of all places the *army*, and he was not shy about trying to hold on to him. As he was finishing his briefing, he went over to Schwarzkopf and told him, "General, if you do this, you'll be the first person since Douglas MacArthur landed at Inchon to have so complete a victory." One of the senior air force officers who had escorted Warden to the Schwarzkopf briefing, Major General Robert Alexander, was appalled by Warden's blatant flattery—fearing that it might jeopardize the entire plan. Schwarzkopf did not say anything, but he seemed to beam and expanded a bit.[3]

Colin Powell was also impressed by the plan, as was Dick Cheney. By then Warden had learned that no small part of his problem was making people who had little knowledge of the specifics understand the dramatic change in weaponry that had taken place in the last ten years or so. So he and his people pointed out that during World War II, an average B-17 bomb during a bombing run missed its target by some 2,300 feet. Therefore, if you wanted a 90 percent probability of having hit a particular target, you had to drop some nine thousand bombs. That required a bombing run of one thousand bombers and placed ten thousand men at risk. By contrast, with the new weaponry one plane flown by one man with one bomb could have the same level of probability. That was an improvement in effectiveness of approximately ten-thousand-fold. At the end of the briefing, Cheney sat back and said, "Now for the first time I understand why you people are so confident about this whole thing."

This was the moment when the new age in air force tactics was colliding with the old one. For Warden, dealing with men like Schwarzkopf, Powell, and Cheney turned out to be easier than dealing with his own superiors. The biggest roadblock was Lieutenant General Charles Horner, the man who would command all the American airpower in the theater. Horner was a TAC man through and through, a traditionalist closely linked to both General Robert Russ, the four-star TAC commander based at Langley, and Jimmie Adams. Schwarzkopf told Horner that Warden and his team were coming to brief Horner, and Schwarzkopf knew that his top air commander was furious at the idea of a campaign created by junior subordinates in Washington. "Sir, the last thing we want is a repeat of Vietnam where Washington picked the targets! This is the job of your air commander," Horner angrily told Schwarzkopf over the phone.[4] To Horner, a strategy that emanated from Washington brought back painful memories of Vietnam, as well as a sense of the possible diminution of his own role as commander.

The meeting in Riyadh was nothing less than brutal. Warden had expected that it would be a difficult session as he would finally have to deal with the formidable TAC opposition he had deftly bypassed back in Washington. But he was stunned nonetheless, as he later told friends, by the degree of personal venom he encountered. Knowing he might have a tough sell, he had brought some goodies he had been told were hard to get in Saudi Arabia—Chap Stick and sunscreen. He tried to give them to Horner as a peace offering at the beginning of their briefing, but Horner asked, "What is this shit?" and swept the goodies across the table. It was not an auspicious start for a colonel trying to brief a three-star on a brand-new strategy. The rest of their meeting did not go much better. One witness remembered that from time to time Horner turned his chair away from Warden so that he was talking to Horner's back. Whatever Warden said, Horner challenged. Unlike Warden, he did not have much confidence in either the new strategy or the new F-117 Stealth fighters. He was also worried that Warden's plan, aimed in the beginning at virtually everything in the Iraqi military component save its vast army already in the field, some of it sitting very close by on the Saudi borders, would leave Horner open to a major assault from Iraqi tanks. He was hardly eager to listen to some bright young theoretician dispatched from Washington—even one who already had Schwarzkopf's approval.

It was, indeed, a collision between the old air force and the new air force. Horner was, some of Warden's people thought, openly contemptuous of him, and at one point Horner asked one of his aides, as if had been talking to a madman, "I'm being very, very patient, aren't I?" The aide said he was. "I'm being very, very tolerant, aren't I?" The aide again agreed. "I'm being really nice not to make the kind of response that you would expect me to make, aren't I?" he then asked. Again the aide agreed.[5] Finally, near the end of the meeting, Horner turned to some of his people and said, "And you didn't think I could hold my temper, did you?"[6] He thought Warden's plan much too theoretical.

That meeting marked the end of an era in the use of airpower: one strategy replaced by an entirely new one. Horner had pounded Warden mercilessly. Then, the meeting virtually over, he pointed at Warden's top four aides and asked them, one by one, if they would join Horner's staff, which they did. It was over, he had humiliated Warden, taken his staff and his strategy—Horner had no choice about that; it was what his boss, Schwarzkopf, wanted—and sent Warden back to Washington alone. In an odd way, Warden thought, even severing him from the plan and returning him to Washington, painful though it was, had an upside. He could now work the corridors of Washington, explaining the plan to influential doubters. The TAC resentment of Warden, despite the fact that the essence of his strategy had been adopted by the air force, remained intense. Even Lieutenant General Mike Short, who eventually commanded the air component in Kosovo and used some of Warden's tactics, spoke disparagingly of him. (Warden never made general, but was assigned to teach at the air force's elite war college in Montgomery, Alabama, where he dealt with the institution's brightest young officers and, ironically, became more influential than ever.)

Part of Warden's air campaign was based on the ability to use the Stealth fighter, the F-117 Nighthawk, as a lead instrument of battle. The Stealth fighter, which could elude enemy radar, was just coming into its own. Two squadrons would fly in the Gulf War and were instrumental in taking out the most heavily defended targets, thus opening corridors for more traditional fighters and bombers. But they were hardly at the core of Warden's plan. The key was the accuracy of the weapons they carried, which allowed them to do parallel rather than serial bombing. It would have been essentially the same strategy without the Stealth fighters, Warden later noted, though the casualties would almost surely have been a good deal higher. The military success that Warden had promised Schwarzkopf was in fact close to the one he received. For six weeks, the American forces, using land-based aircraft, naval aircraft, and missiles, systematically pounded the Iraqi military and its parallel civilian instruments of power, paralyzing them and making them virtually useless. Iraqi airpower was suppressed, communications interrupted. Iraqi tanks, waiting in the field for the coming battle, provided marvelous target practice for the air force, and the phrase *tank plinking* was born.

Stationed in the desert, where the daytime heat was extraordinary, the tanks, like everything else, became very hot. In the evening, however, the sand cooled much faster than the tanks, and so American F-111s, each armed with six five-hundred-pound, laser-guided bombs and a thermal guidance system, could pick them out virtually at will because of the infrared signal they gave off. Some fifteen hundred tanks were readily destroyed that way. After the war an Iraqi tank commander told his American captors that war had become a kind of hell for the Iraqi tankers. During their war with Iran, he said, the tanks had been where they took refuge at night, but against the Americans they had been terrified to be in them at night for fear they would be killed.

What happened in Iraq was a precursor to the future. During the Gulf War, only about a third of the bombs were precision instruments, whereas *two-thirds* of the targets were hit by them. That meant precision munitions were giving the commanders a level of accuracy and efficiency never before known, and an advantage almost unprecedented in warfare. It was as if the airpower available during World War II had been enjoyed exclusively by one of the major combatants in World War I. In terms of what might soon be accomplished because of rapidly developing new technologies, it was just a beginning. The bombs were likely to become ever more precise and the ability to avoid enemy radar through Stealth flights even greater.

To show that we had only scratched the surface, when the Gulf War was over, Warden put a bright young man on his staff, Lieutenant Colonel Robert Owen, in charge of an unusual assignment. He was to take the level of accuracy now available to American fighters and project it onto the aerial needs of the World War II campaign against Germany, as if we had had the technological ability then that we had now. It had been a three-year campaign requiring as many as six thousand aircraft to shut down German military production. It was crude, not necessarily accurate, and caused innumerable casualties, both among the bomber crews and civilians. One thousand planes might be needed to hit a target. The circle of error—that is, the circle into which you could realistically expect to put 50 percent of your bombs—was comparatively large, some twenty miles for the night bombing in the beginning, closing to about one thousand meters near the end. Collateral damage was immense. By the Gulf War that figure had dramatically changed; the circle of error was closer to six feet or even smaller. Owen estimated that two squadrons of F-117s (a total of forty-eight Stealth fighters, not even the B-2 Stealth bombers soon to come) would have shut down the production of Germany in approximately six weeks.

Thus had the strategy been matched up with the weaponry. But the conversion would be both slow and difficult, in part because both civilians and military men (especially senior army men) felt that the air force had often boasted before about what airpower alone could do, without any real proof. Most people in the ruling elite in both civilian and military circles had attitudes shaped by previous wars and were slow to adjust to new possibilities.

What was exceptional and would be of importance if the United States ever went to war in the Balkans was that the air campaign in Iraq was just the start. The air force and navy were rapidly switching over most of their planes to precision-guided platforms, and the munitions themselves, laser-guided and photo-image-driven, were becoming more accurate all the time. The military was gaining the ability to pick out a building and not merely hit it, but also determine which floor and which side of the building to hit. It was a fascinating part of the technological revolution. As the technology of modern communications was making it more difficult for a democracy to go to war and risk casualties, the modern technology of armaments was offering for the first time the possibility of a new kind of war, waged at a distance with superior precision, demanding fewer risks and inflicting less permanent physical damage on the enemy—a campaign, said the foreign policy analyst Les Gelb, "of immaculate destruction." Virtual war, it would soon be called.

The technology was at hand, but knowledge of it and confidence about using it had yet to permeate the military-civilian thinking. Also uncertain were attitudes about whether this kind of military success could create parallel political value. But its temptations were obvious in terms of American domestic politics. For future administrations, anxious to exert American force overseas, but wishing to minimize risk, unsure of public and congressional support, and distrusting of an intrusive media, it might seem like manna.

CHAPTER SIX

Some of the Bush foreign policy people would later acknowledge their impotence in face of the mounting tragedy in Yugoslavia. That they had stumbled was obvious in retrospect to all of them. Larry Eagleburger, the number two man in the State Department for much of that period, and the number one man in the final few months of the Bush administration and among the most influential men in that administration, knew that he had fallen short. It was, he said, the issue about which he had most come to doubt himself after he left government. Every day when I look at myself in the mirror when I shave, he added, I question myself on what happened there. Should we have done more, should I have expressed my doubts harder with the president? Yes, he had warned about what might happen, but he had never gone to Bush and said, "Mr. President, you've got to do something on this one." Late in the game, he had suggested some kind of action, he remembered, but he had never really *pushed* for military intervention, always aware of the cost of that kind of commitment. The figure of two hundred thousand ground troops had frightened him off, as it had the others.

Some younger people at State, and some critics of the administration, thought it a rare moment lost to history. Not only was American power at its absolute maximum, but probably more could have been done for less in the Balkans. Ironically, the Bush people comprised, arguably, one of the most experienced foreign policy teams to come to power in the postwar era. Many of them, including the president himself, had spent a great deal of time in high-level national security positions. Foreign policy, rather than domestic affairs, was the administration's area of expertise, interest, and passion. Even more ironically, they tended to be men much more committed to America's role in the world, more truly internationalist, than the congressional leadership of their own party, the leadership of the Democratic Party, the news executives of the three main television channels, and the country as a whole.

If a generational divide was taking place in the country toward foreign policy and the overall importance of internationalism, they were all on the traditionalist side, one that greatly valued foreign policy and thought it was at the very heart of governance. The young men and women coming of age in their own party and the Democratic Party, in the Congress and in the media, did not have the history of commitment, the experiences that made internationalism seem so necessary. They had never suffered the consequences of isolationism, and they were receiving very different signals from their even younger constituents. Different political polls were already beginning to show a mutinous feeling in the country because of the president's preoccupation with foreign policy, and the young challenger emerging from the Democratic primary season was preparing to use Bush's obsession with foreign policy as a weapon against him. We need, Bill Clinton was saying at every stop in his campaign as a kind of mantra, a president who cares about the Middle West as well as the Middle East. That meant, of course, that Bush was ignoring America's domestic problems, particularly the economy.

So as the 1992 election year dawned, not only was the president himself reluctant to use force in a conflict that seemed so complicated and bewildering to him, but a de facto pincer movement was also working against intervention, formed by his national security people in one phalanx and his political people in the other. His three top national security advisers, all of whom were supposed to know a good deal about issues like this, and two of whom were experts on this country, men he trusted and admired—Larry Eagleburger, Brent Scowcroft, and Colin Powell—were apprehensive about military intervention in Yugoslavia. And his political advisers, men like Bob Teeter and Jim Baker (who, in the growing anxiety about how poorly the reelection campaign was going, would soon switch from being a national security man to a top political adviser), were warning him that he was too involved in foreign policy and needed to show, in as dramatic a way as possible, greater concern for domestic issues.

No one watching the way the Bush team had handled the end of the Cold War questioned the level of its talent. Some of the top people, like the president himself, had served in the Nixon, Ford, and Reagan administrations. They were by and large the most careful of men, internationalists, anticommunists, but not ideologues or moralists. Typically, they had watched the Gorbachev revolution skeptically at first—much of the U.S. government, most notably the CIA, had been slow to pick up on it—but when they had finally accepted that it was real, they had dealt with it deftly. Most of them had roots in the moderate, internationalist wing of the Republican Party, rather than in the competing Reagan wing, which often seemed more concerned about the morality of foreign policy. The Bush people tended to see the Cold War as an ongoing conflict between two superpowers; the Reagan people had seen it as a clash between good and evil.

Before the end of the Cold War, the pragmatic Bush people had generally been détenters, seeking small slices of mutual accord with the Soviets and a reduction in nuclear tensions. By contrast many of the Reagan people had cared not just about national security but rather which side was right and which side was wrong. Not by chance had Reagan himself called the Soviet empire "evil"; that was a word unlikely to come from Bush's mouth. To the Reagan people, *détente* was a dirty word. They had never accepted the idea of coexistence with Moscow and looked on their Bush cousins as compromisers without true beliefs. Of the high-level Bush people, only Dick Cheney, the secretary of defense, was considered, by the standards then employed in calibrating ideology in Washington, a true conservative.

The top civilians in the Bush administration were cautious in general, befitting men who had grown up and come to power during a prolonged period of relentless Cold War tensions, tensions made ever more dangerous by the mutual availability of nuclear weapons. They had come of age when you inherited a difficult, divided world, and if all went well during your tour of office, you handed off to your successor a difficult, divided world. The principal military men were cautious, too, but in a different way, befitting men who had experienced the full bitterness of the Vietnam War. Thus for all of the men around Bush, the geopolitical tensions in their lifetimes had been constant, the victories essentially incremental. Keeping things from getting worse was, in itself, a victory. These men were all survivors; yet when their predecessors and in some cases their colleagues in office had some fifteen years earlier begun to advocate the policy aimed at reduction of conflicts with the Soviet Union known as détente, a vast wing of their own party had rejected that concept and had gradually, under Ronald Reagan, become the majority wing.

Some Bush people, like Scowcroft and Eagleburger, were associated in various ways with the most dominant figure of American foreign policy in the late sixties and seventies, Henry Kissinger, and on occasion they would even tease each other during high-level meetings about whether they had received their orders from Park Avenue yet. That was a mocking reference to the fact that not only did Kissinger, who had a consulting firm in New York on Park Avenue, like to feel he was still influential, but to emphasize that in the minds of their more conservative critics they were always going to be seen as pawns of Kissinger—the master of realpolitik—waiting for secret word about how to carry out his orders.

In their years under Reagan and even to some degree Bush, it had been important not to look as if they were too close to Kissinger, who had become something of a bête noire to many of the new Sun Belt conservatives. Kissinger's policies of détente, to many centrist Americans among the most laudable of his achievements during his tenure, had openly and angrily been repudiated during the 1976 election year, principally at the GOP convention, which gave its nomination to Jerry Ford but its heart to Ronald Reagan. The convention had nearly been torn asunder by a debate over ideology and foreign policy. Oddly enough, though an internal fight, it was quite possibly the fiercest battle over foreign policy of the previous twenty-five years. The repudiation of détente at the 1976 convention—the rejection by a ruling party of its own foreign policy—remained something of a shadow over those actually charged with foreign policy under Bush. They always had to be aware that they were significantly more internationalist than the rest of the party, which took a much harder line on the Soviet Union. It was also a reminder that they were becoming, if not an anachronism, then something of a minority, their domestic hold on power ever more fragile, and the Republican Party as it existed in Congress, and in future primary runs and conventions, not necessarily behind them. On some issues—like the collapse of the Soviet Union—it would be relatively easy to keep everyone in line, but in other, more subtle international crises, particularly those that might demand the use of the American military in a multinational force, it would not be easy to gain support.

The Bush people were by and large an anomaly, practical men and women of an earlier era in what had been a stronger, more muscular centrist wing of the party. That wing had come on harder times in the sixties and seventies, even as these men rose higher and higher in the national security hierarchy. Bush himself had served Reagan, a more obviously ideological figure, with singular loyalty over eight years, never allowing even a glimmer of dissent to come out of his office about anything the Reagan people did with which he might disagree. Yet Bush, finally running on his own after those eight years, got the most tepid of endorsements imaginable from Reagan. The true Reagan enthusiasts did not really trust Bush in 1988, when he made his first presidential run on the Republican ticket, because they had never trusted him. He was not one of them, and no matter how hard he tried, he never would be. They might one day accept his son, who spoke like a real Texan, but the jury was always out on the father. It was hardly Bush's fault. He had more than paid his dues. A kind of old-fashioned loyalty was at the center of his personal codes. He played the game by old-fashioned rules, never leaking anything that might cast him in a better light at the expense of those he served. Those were his values and they reflected the way Bush had been raised.

No one could have served Reagan more faithfully, but Bush was what he was and he could never pass certain tests, if not from his boss, then from the president's considerably more judgmental wife, Nancy, and other people who loved and admired Reagan so much they were probably truer Reaganites than the ever supple Reagan himself. Indeed the very word that defined the centrists' search for a less troubled, less divided world—détente—was a red flag to the more ideological people in the party. Détente meant you accepted the right of the communists to occupy a large part of the world, which was not to be tolerated.

Fortunately for the Bush people, once they took office in 1989, the leadership of the newly ascending political right seemed to be far more interested in domestic issues—abortion, crime, and gun control, for example—than the things Bush cared about, foreign policy issues, and they tended to allow the people in the executive branch considerable freedom to deal with foreign policy within certain proscribed limits. After all, the Cold War was winding down and becoming less of a concern. That evil had been defeated, and now other forms of evil had to be taken on, this time in domestic guise. But the limits of the party's political support for an essentially centrist president were always there, right in the background, as was an implied lack of congressional support if the president went too far. This meant that by the time Bush took office there were two wings of the Republican Party, a somewhat more internationalist and centrist one in the executive branch, and a far more conservative and isolationist one in the Congress and in the party machinery that controlled future nominations.

This division within the party structure had begun in the midsixties when there had already been an immense shift of power and affluence from the Eastern and Middle Atlantic states to the Sun Belt, a shift that would dramatically change national politics. Moreover, the 1965 Voting Rights Act had been passed, after brutal beatings inflicted upon blacks trying to register to vote in Alabama and Mississippi. It would be hard to think of a precedent for a piece of liberal domestic legislation—designed to empower those most powerless in our society—that had so profound an effect on the nation's political alignment. It caused the backlash of all backlashes. Lyndon Johnson had pushed it through, and it was quite possibly his single greatest legislative triumph. But even at the time it was a bittersweet victory for Johnson, something he was doing because it was so obviously right, even though it would have dire consequences for his own political party.

On the night the act was passed, Bill Moyers visited Johnson in his bedroom expecting to find the president exhilarated by his victory. Instead he found him quite depressed. What was wrong? Moyers asked. "I think we've just handed the South over to the Republican Party for the rest of our lives," Johnson answered sadly and prophetically.[1] That he was right was immediately evident within the boundaries of the old Confederacy when thousands and thousands of Democrats became Republicans virtually overnight. With that, the Democrats lost their last great bastion, the Solid South, to the Republicans, and liberal Southern Democrats were very much in jeopardy. If passage of the act devastated the Democrats, it had an even more profound effect on the Republican Party. It meant that Sun Belt Republicans were on the rise both in the nation and in the party, and they were a very different breed from the Eastern establishment Republicans, who had long held power within the party. This new breed was narrower of view, particularly on foreign policy, warier of foreign involvements, especially with international organizations like the United Nations, more connected to the agenda of and dependent on the support of the fundamentalist right, and significantly more conservative in general. They regarded America's interaction with the rest of the world with greater suspicion. Nothing could be more reflective of the rise of Sun Belt Republicanism than one of the men the party sent to the Senate Foreign Relations Committee. In the old days George Aiken of Vermont and Chuck Percy of Illinois had served on that committee. Now it was Jesse Helms of North Carolina, whose suspicions of all foreign nations seemed to be a constant, unless, of course, they showed themselves willing to import American cigarettes.

Bush and those around him were viewed with a guarded tolerance by the conservative Republicans who were coming to dominate the party. Still, even critics and opponents admired their foreign policy professionalism. They were well credentialed, worked harmoniously with each other, and perhaps most fortunate of all, operated in the area that the president cared most about. By contrast, from the very start, Bush's domestic political team was considered highly inadequate, and it was operating in an area that barely interested the president and which he instinctively neglected—the kind of neglect that inevitably led to a series of costly miscalculations.

The foreign policy people were probably the last of a kind of public official, almost all of whom had grown up in the post–World War II and the Cold War era, bright young men who had gone into public service, anxious to deal with foreign policy rather than domestic issues because that was where the action was and where the fate of the world might be decided. Issues of foreign policy always took primacy in their minds. They assumed that when they got to the highest levels in government, they would have the full attention of the president himself—which at that time was still true. There was the president, who had served in World War II, surely the last World War II president the nation would elect. There was Brent Scowcroft, born in 1925, who had gone to West Point hoping to be a fighter pilot in the days when there was no Air Force Academy. He had been injured in a crash landing, which had ended his flying career, and he then went on to become first an academic within the military and eventually one of its reigning policy experts. Also on board were James Baker, who had served in the marines at the tail end of the Korean War, Colin Powell, who had served two difficult tours in Vietnam, and Larry Eagleburger, who had served in the army in the early fifties and then had a career operating at the highest level of the State Department under several different presidents. By the time these men entered the White House in 1988, most of them had worked with each other for a decade or more. But their service would mark the end of an era. For running in the election against Bush would be a young man born in 1946, after the end of World War II, who in some cases was the age of their own children.

They understood that in some ways Bush's term in office was accidental. If Jim Baker had not convinced him to withdraw early enough in the 1980 primaries in favor of Reagan, more damage would have been done at a personal level between the two men. Bush would not have made the ticket as the vice-presidential nominee and got as his just reward eight years later what the commentator Mark Shields called Reagan's third term.

Unlike previous groups of foreign policy advisers, the Bush administration had an unusually high quotient of men who had considerable domestic political experience. Jim Baker was widely admired as one of the most skillful operators not just in national politics but within the bureaucracy over several decades, a man so gifted at the highest levels of policy that when Reagan had been elected in 1980, Stu Spencer, one of his most senior advisers from California and among the architects of his political rise, had gone to Nancy Reagan and urged her to make sure that Baker, even though he was a Ford man and had run two successive campaigns against Ronald Reagan, be made chief of staff instead of Ed Meese, the ultimate Reagan loyalist. Baker got the job, which helped ensure that the Reagan White House worked with great efficiency, and it left the ideologues in the party free to blame Baker and others like him for the sin of preventing Reagan from being Reagan, even of course when the exact opposite was true and Reagan *was* being Reagan.

By the time Baker emerged as secretary of state in Bush's administration, he was widely admired for his skills in running Reagan's first term and in minimizing any potential damage caused by some of the president's somewhat limited attention span. Baker as chief of staff had been considered something of a nonpareil, able to anticipate Reagan's needs and act on his behalf, even without consulting him. Baker had made sure that the president's seemingly casual, laissez-faire attitude toward events did not encourage those around him to try to move into a vacuum. Baker was always aware of the political equations of all decisions—most memorably, when he had decided that Paul Volcker, as head of the Federal Reserve, was not bringing interest rates down quickly enough and had squeezed him out of his job. Baker was brilliant at reading the needs, desires, and priorities of his boss, thereby allowing Reagan to be Reagan.

Because Baker was so cold and tough and efficient, the general belief was that the Reagan White House got into serious trouble only after Baker, wanting a portfolio of his own, had switched jobs with Donald Regan and went over to Treasury. Indeed, there had been a brief moment when Baker seemed destined to go to the NSC chair instead of Treasury, a change shot down by some of the old-time Reagan people. Michael Deaver, who would have been chief of staff if that had taken place, wrote later that if it had happened, "There would have been no arms sold to Iran, no Swiss bank accounts, or secret funds diverted to the Contras, no foreign policy seemingly created by Rube Goldberg."[2]

As secretary of state, Baker brought both his skills and extensive political connections to the job. He was extremely knowledgeable about American politics, having served at the highest level in several state and national campaigns, going back to the failed Bush Senate race of 1970. He had also been the top vote counter in the 1976 Ford conquest of Reagan. His close personal relationship with the president was not the least of his many assets. He was conservative in the old sense of being a traditionalist, but a pragmatic conservative, someone who liked to get things done. If one of the true disappointments of Baker's life was that he was never able to translate his skill in working the upper bureaucracy and handling the Washington press corps into a national political constituency for his own presidential candidacy, he was nonetheless an immensely successful figure for a dozen years in the domestic and foreign policy decision-making of two Republican administrations. Young, ambitious Republicans, coming to Washington during the Reagan years, looking for interesting jobs and meeting both Vice President Bush and his close friend Jim Baker, usually went away thinking Baker was the brighter and more charismatic of the two, the man who would surely go farther. Because a good many other people also thought that Baker was more talented politically and most certainly more verbally gifted than Bush, the relationship between the two men was not without its own complexities, even when Bush was president and Baker secretary of state. Baker, unlike the candidate and the president he served, was a masterful manipulator of the press, articulate, shrewd, always knowing not just where things stood in terms of reality, but able to spin them for the occasionally quite different reality they wanted reflected in the media. That was something Bush was almost completely incapable of doing. Baker always managed to come out looking good in the media, whereas Bush was perceived as being, in a generous phrase, media-challenged. As a result, Bush was as skeptical of the media as they were skeptical of him, and he often managed to appear maladroit.

Baker was *very* tough and not a man to tangle with. If you wanted something from James Baker, his probable answer would be, what's in it for me? Your leverage with him was usually based on what you could do for him and his candidate; Jewish groups, for example, believed that he had once said of them, "Fuck the Jews. They never voted for us [the Republicans]." Whether he had said it or not was difficult to prove, but it certainly sounded like quintessential Baker: your leverage with him equaled the weight of your votes. He was also *very* territorial, within the accepted boundaries of the administration he served, and something of a control freak; he was not likely to let Defense dominate State in high-level meetings.

When Larry Eagleburger was first proposed as the number two man in the State Department, Baker had not been enthusiastic. He had finally accepted him with a good deal of reluctance because not only had Eagleburger been a Kissinger man, his long and distinguished career had given him a value system of his own and a considerable sense of independence. Eagleburger was known to have been loyal to everyone for whom he had worked from Nick Katzenbach to Henry Kissinger, but he also spoke his mind. Baker finally accepted him as his deputy but never as a member of his inner team. That meant Eagleburger was at the top, but always something of an outsider. On many an occasion when Eagleburger wanted to push an idea to the president, he did so through his old friend Scowcroft, who had the NSC chair, and with whom he could speak a kind of shorthand based on their long years of friendship and service together.

If Baker had no great philosophical vision of foreign policy, he was as professional as you could get, and he negotiated with considerable ability. He was exceptionally talented at letting others at any table know in all kinds of subtle and not so subtle ways that he represented the might and majesty of the United States of America, a big and powerful country whose displeasure you did not lightly want to incur. If he was participating in the Middle East peace process, no one was likely to do it better, but he also wanted to waste no energy and had little time for the traditional amenities of diplomatic statecraft. No, he did not want to go to some ceremonial dinner with the host foreign minister after a long, hard day of negotiating. The Israelis and Egyptians just had to accept him for what he was, someone who worked hard, negotiated tough, and declined traditional diplomatic pleasures, which were rarely pleasures anyway. One might discount him as a player once, but never twice.

Brent Scowcroft at the NSC was a different sort of man—with fewer edges and fewer enemies. He was exceptionally modest, almost consciously so, much admired across a broad political spectrum, low-key, and good at what he did, though often overshadowed by men with a greater hunger for power and fame like Kissinger and Baker. Because of that it was easy to underestimate him. He never seemed to want anything for himself, more power or a grander title. In time that became not just a strength but a source of power. Only when the Bush years were over and other members of the administration were assessing what had been accomplished did they realize how much intelligence, judgment, and decency he had brought to his job. Scowcroft was, thought the people who had worked closely with him, quite possibly the ablest national security adviser of recent times. Though extremely well-informed and knowledgeable, he was exceptionally skilled at making sure that ideas with which he disagreed went forward to the president, something that had never been a Kissingerian specialty. He seemed, at the end of the Bush administration, to be almost physically joined to the president, and when Bush wrote a memoir, he not surprisingly did it jointly with Scowcroft, each of them writing alternate sections, as if acknowledging Scowcroft's unusually influential role in foreign policy. The book said something about both men and their respective qualities of modesty. One could not imagine a comparable literary collaboration, for example, after their years in government were over, of Richard Nixon and Henry Kissinger.

Bush was not the first president whom Scowcroft had served that faithfully. He had been a favorite of Jerry Ford's as well. Scowcroft had, thought Jim Cannon, a Rockefeller man who had served in the Ford White House and had watched him carefully, the rare gift of being able to bring to two different presidents unwanted news that other men might not have been able to deliver without giving significant offense. The perfect example of this had come in the 1976 campaign when Ford made a horrendous mistake and claimed that Poland was not behind the Iron Curtain. It was a clinker of the worst kind—a possible election-loser that even a high school student should have gotten right—and an immediate retraction was called for. But Ford was so adamant—in no small part because he had screwed up on such a grand scale—that none of his staff dared to talk to him about it. Finally Dick Cheney, who was then Ford's chief of staff, knowing that if anyone could turn the candidate around, it was the beloved Scowcroft, went to him and beseeched him to try to reach the candidate and get the retraction. But Ford was still mad—mad at the world, but mostly mad at himself—and he turned even Scowcroft down. "I said what I said, I know what I said, I know what I meant, and I'm not going to change it," he told Scowcroft.

Dick Cheney, the third major civilian player in the Bush administration, had become secretary of defense almost as a fluke, when the Senate, bothered by reports of John Tower's womanizing and drinking, had rejected him for the job. There was something brisk, almost brusque, about Cheney as a senior government official. It was as if—either for reasons of time or of professional objectivity—he wanted to keep his distance from his top people at all times. He was judged by those who worked with him as not particularly likable but adept at making a bureaucracy work. He appeared to care almost nothing about elemental popularity. He did not schmooze, he did not socialize, and memorably when, in January 1993, the Bush people began to close out their offices, Colin Powell, who had worked intimately with Cheney for three years as chairman of the Joint Chiefs, went by his office to say good-bye, he found that the secretary had packed and left hours earlier. Yet Cheney was a considerable talent scout and had reached down to pick Powell when he was a brand-new four-star general to be chairman even though fourteen more senior four-stars were ahead of him.

Cheney was an egalitarian man with little time for pomp and circumstance. Norman Schwarzkopf had, without knowing it, almost lost the chance to command the United Nations troops in the Persian Gulf War not just because he had a reputation for being extremely volatile—a screamer—but because Cheney had once flown to Saudi Arabia with Schwarzkopf and had not liked his behavior. The crowded flight had a long line to the rest rooms, and

Cheney had not been pleased to see a major standing in line, finally get to the toilets, and then call out to Schwarzkopf to take his place. Nor had Cheney been pleased to see another officer on his hands and knees ironing the general's uniform. Cheney did not approve of that kind of use of hierarchical perks.[3]

Cheney was significantly more conservative than the others in the inner group, his personal politics by the time he took the job closer to those of the Reagan wing of the party than the Ford-Bush wing. But he had originally come out of the centrist Ford wing, and in the early days of their administration the Reagan people remained leery of him. At one point they were looking for a secretary of the interior, and Cheney, by then a Wyoming congressman, was on the short list. But Paul Laxalt, the conservative senator who was one of Reagan's closest friends, was in charge of the screening and thought Cheney too much of a Ford man.

Cheney was not given to small talk. He was good at working efficiently inside a killer bureaucracy like the Pentagon. But he was hardly dashing as a candidate for elective office, and something of a Washington hostess's nightmare, notorious for making a minimal social effort. He was the son of a soil conservation agent in Lincoln, Nebraska, who had moved to Casper, Wyoming, when Cheney was a boy. He had won a scholarship to Yale, dropped out after a year, and took a variety of blue-collar jobs before going back to school in Wyoming. Showing talent as a political writer, he won a fellowship that landed him on the staff of the governor of Wisconsin, where he served while also working toward a graduate degree at the University of Wisconsin. In 1968 he won another fellowship, which brought him to the staff of William Steiger, a Wisconsin Republican.

In 1969, a year later, when the Nixon administration was just taking office, Cheney was singled out by Don Rumsfeld, a great Republican talent scout in those days who was heading the Office of Economic Opportunity. In 1974 when Ford replaced Nixon as president, Rumsfeld came over as the de facto chief of staff, bringing Cheney to the White House with him. His rise there had been meteoric. In the Ford years Rumsfeld instituted a policy under which everyone in the White House had to have a deputy who could speak for him in his absence. The policy was designed to cut back on the waste of White House time, and Cheney became Rumsfeld's deputy and alter ego. Ford quickly came to like and trust Cheney. Rumsfeld, a man with limitless ambitions of his own, had his eye on a cabinet post—he tried for Treasury and Bill Simon beat back that thrust—but he soon ended up with Defense, and Cheney, at the age of thirty-four, became chief of staff of the White House.

When Jimmy Carter was elected in 1976, Cheney went back to Wyoming to run for Congress, won, and quickly emerged as one of the more talented of the young conservative Republicans. Because of his previous experience in Washington, he did not act like a new boy at the old school and was soon catapulted into a leadership role. Yet there was always a certain question within Republican circles about Cheney, who had come to prominence first as a skilled functionary in a moderate White House (Ford) under the right hand of a moderate chief of staff (Rumsfeld) and later served a moderate president (Bush), but who on his own voted somewhat even to the right of the new Gingrich Republicans. Wyoming was a conservative state anyway, but Cheney as a congressman stood out as being far right.

In the summer of 2000 when George W. Bush picked his father's onetime defense secretary for his vice-presidential candidate, those old House votes, on abortion, gun control, and keeping Nelson Mandela in prison (it was a procedural vote, Cheney explained, which must surely have been of great comfort to Mandela), became something of a burden for the ticket. The one thing about Cheney that the Democrats had quickly learned was that for all his bland exterior, he played very, very tough inside politics. He had been the leader in the movement that had ousted Jim Wright from his job as Speaker because of some violations over the House honorarium rule. Wright did not lightly forgive or forget and when a reporter later caught up with him back in Texas after he had left Washington to ask what happened, Wright answered, "What happened was that that goddamn son of a bitch Dick Cheney—he's mean as a snake. No wonder he's had three heart attacks."[4]

When George H. W. Bush was elected president in 1988, a number of his close assistants had pushed Cheney for a top job, but Bush was hesitant. Cheney had been a protégé of Rumsfeld's, and Rumsfeld and Bush, ambitious young men working the same political sector, both with presidential ambitions, had always been suspicious of each other, and Rumsfeld had often spoken with open contempt of Bush. To Bush the word *Cheney* meant Rumsfeld. But at the beginning of his presidency, when John Tower's nomination failed, Cheney, still a Wyoming congressman, was Bush's fallback choice, largely regarded as a good one. Cheney moved over to the Pentagon and made it clear that he was going to *run* it. Anyone who crossed him on an issue of policy might pay dearly for it.

CHAPTER SEVEN

Because George Bush had come of age during World War II and had served in that war, his attitudes toward the world and America's involvement in it were shaped by that experience, by the isolationism that had preceded the war and allowed darker forces on two continents to move against their weaker neighbors, and by the need for collective security in the years following, as two new superpowers faced off in an atomic age. To many in the generation coming home after World War II, a generation that knew firsthand the tragedy of the war itself and the death of so many close friends, old-fashioned isolationism was no longer acceptable. And it was even less acceptable as the buffers that had formed the premise of American isolation in the past, our two great oceans, were turned into ponds by modern weaponry, intercontinental rockets with nuclear warheads, atomic submarines and other instruments of war into which high technology was blended for the purpose of mass destruction.

That particular background, his service in World War II in the navy even before he attended college and his instinct to resist overt aggression, had been of singular importance in Bush's decision to mount a full-scale military mission some sixty-five hundred miles away to oust Saddam Hussein from Kuwait. During that crisis, Bush had been the most hawkish member of his own administration, surprising a number of his closest advisers and the senior people in the Pentagon alike with his singular sense of purpose. To him what the Iraqi army had done was a replay of World War II, naked aggression of the strong against the weak, and that was intolerable. Besides, it potentially changed the balance of power in the oil world, and his roots were in the oil business. The decision not merely to block the Iraqis at the Saudi border, which everyone in the administration agreed with, but to turn back the seemingly huge and powerful Iraqi army from Kuwaiti soil was very much George Bush's decision.

Among those less hawkish than he were the Joint Chiefs, who were not in any way quick to come up with plans to dislodge Saddam Hussein from Kuwait. Colin Powell, extremely cautious about any use of American troops, favored instead drawing a line around Saudi Arabia that the Iraqis would dare not cross. Still smarting from the Vietnam experience when the Joint Chiefs, in his words, had been docile in allowing the civilians to go to war without spelling out clear objectives, he had pushed his superiors to state quite precisely what it was they wanted to do and what price they were willing to pay. At a certain point his caution became something of an irritant. Finally Cheney went to him and said, "Colin, you're chairman of the Joint Chiefs. You're not secretary of state. You're not the national security adviser anymore. And you're not secretary of defense. So stick to military matters."[1]

Bush was sixty-four years old when he took office, which meant that virtually all of his adult life had been spent in the shadow of the Cold War. It had not only shaped him, but like most internationalist Americans of his generation, it dovetailed with his personal view of the world. He had never doubted America's role in securing the Western alliance and drawing a line against the constant Soviet pressures in central Europe. Others in his generation had been affected by the Vietnam War and had slowly migrated from hawk to dove. But Bush's views on the subject remained quite hawkish. If he harbored any doubts about the nature of the American commitment in Vietnam and why it had failed, they remained a secret to most serious students of that subject. On the day that Lyndon Johnson, his presidency ravaged by the war, had left Washington to return to Texas in January 1969, one of the relatively small number of politicians who came out to see him was the young Republican congressman George Bush. The other Republicans of his generation tended to look down on Bush, during his rise through the ranks of his party, as the legatee of a class, not necessarily gifted, but hardworking and willing to take on jobs that others might scorn. His class, it was believed, might once have entitled him to a seat in the inner circle, but now left him, fingers holding on to the windowsill, eager to take whatever was handed him.

Over the years Bush had filled a number of relatively senior foreign policy posts: head of the CIA, ambassador to the United Nations, U.S. envoy to China. As vice president he had been actively involved in foreign policy, far more so than most men who had held that office. He did not merely attend the regular early-morning briefings from the top CIA people assigned to update him on events of the last twenty-four hours, he lovingly and enthusiastically read the cables themselves—a sure sign that he was a foreign policy junkie. In that, too, he was generational—someone who believed that the true instruments of power resided in foreign policy. That, however, would change at an accelerating rate during his presidency, for the disappearance of an adversarial superpower immediately devalued foreign policy issues. But to Bush, and to everyone whose political viewpoint he respected, foreign policy remained at the core of his job. You ran for the presidency because you wanted to play a part in determining the direction of the world.

Bush was aware of his own strengths and weaknesses, that he was better at one-on-one relationships than he was at dealing with abstract issues. His personal courtesies were already legendary when he entered office. Running for the presidency, the core of his support had been the thousands of people he had met over the years who had stayed on as personal friends—many of them fellow Yale alumni—and to whom he had written countless bread-and-butter notes. When asked once what the basis of his presidential candidacy would be, he had answered, "I've got a big family and *lots* of friends." Or as the writer Richard Ben Cramer noted in his book on the 1988 election, Bush "was trying to become President by making friends, one by one, if need be."[2] The Bush Christmas card list was endless, thousands and thousands of cards, hand-addressed, a process that probably started the day after the holiday season ended. His politics were primarily personal, rather than driven by the impulse of ideas. He also represented the politics of a kind of old-fashioned attitude of class: We come from certain backgrounds, we went to certain schools, we survived certain common historic experiences, we believe in the nobility of service when service is required, we look at the world in much the same way, we agree on what is good and what is bad. Moreover, we don't know many people who have done their homework and don't agree with us on everything that really matters.

Bush as a presidential candidate was an imperfect and often uncomfortable hybrid of old, traditional Eastern Republican liberalism and the new Sun Belt conservatism. He had started life as a scion of the Eastern establishment, son of Prescott Bush, a good liberal Republican senator, an unusually well-credentialed man who had created his own considerable shadow: St. George's School, superb athlete at Yale in three sports, captain in the artillery during World War I, early vice president of Brown Brothers, Harriman, the symbolic center of establishment finance in its day, member of the Yale Corporation, Connecticut head of the United Negro College Fund. Young George was quite properly raised as an upper-class son of Greenwich, Andover (chosen for him because it was considered more democratic than some of the East's more snobbish prep schools), Yale (Skull and Bones, captain of the baseball team), and marriage to a handsome young woman who came from exactly the same class. After college he had moved to Texas to make his fortune in the oil fields, living first in West Texas and eventually moving to Houston. Yet even though he would eventually win a congressional seat from that state, he was never entirely accepted as a Texan. The imprint of the East was always on him: the force of his family upbringing, and those perfect, old-fashioned manners, which so impressed any number of his more senior sponsors within the Republican Party. Texans are supposed to be at least partially raw and unfinished, and there was nothing raw and unfinished about George Bush.

Many of his old-line WASP qualities were increasingly out-of-date in America by the sixties, but no place more so than in Texas with its almost self-conscious contemporary informality. Bush's good manners were by Texas standards stiffness, and he could never pass as a real Texan. All hat and no cattle, John Connally had once said of him. He was also a Republican caught in the party's momentous transition both ideologically and geographically. He could no longer be an old-fashioned New England moderate because that wing of the party was dying all around him, but he could never be a Sun Belt conservative either, for his past was hard to escape. In 1980 in the New Hampshire primary, Bob Dole, trying to make sure that Bush did not change his stripes, kept referring to him as "the Rockefeller candidate." It would take another generation, and the rise of his son George W. as governor, before a Bush could be accepted as a true Texan.

Even so, Bush continually moved to the right on certain domestic issues, adapting gradually from the political codes and social attitudes of the class and culture into which he had been born to the class and culture that now surrounded him. It is not always easy to reinvent yourself, and for Bush, it was harder than most. He did not adjust to the changed political culture of Texas with complete success and was often more than a little uncomfortable and awkward with his new right-wing allies in both speeches made and positions taken. Sometimes Bush seemed to be caught between duty and ambition as well as between his past and his future. When his presidential ambitions had flowered, he had moved away from his roots, in the period just before the 1980 campaign resigning from both the Trilateral Commission and the Council on Foreign Relations—in a perfect Bush mode, for manners were always important—with, it was said by officials at both places, a small personal note requesting that his resignation not be made public.

Bush had been added to the Reagan ticket—and thus cleared for the big time—only at the last minute. The idea of a Reagan-Ford ticket (with Henry Kissinger in charge of foreign policy and Alan Greenspan in charge of economic policy) had thrilled and excited much of the media, but failed to entice Reagan himself, and at the last moment he had chosen Bush at the suggestion of his pollster, Richard Wirthlin, who had in the convention's final moments said that Bush helped as much as anyone else. The conservatives, the true-blue Reagan people, were not happy. They had always regarded Bush with great skepticism. He was in every way different from them. Was there an Eastern elite entitlement there? some of them wondered. Bush had called Reagan's fiscal policies voodoo economics during the primaries, a phrase that might as easily have come from a liberal economic critic like John Kenneth Galbraith. But after taking office as Reagan's vice president, no one could have been more loyal than Bush; the good soldier, Bush accepted all vice-presidential obligations, no matter how odious or menial, without complaint. Even when he disagreed with a policy, his people were under orders never to show any daylight between what they felt and what the president was doing. There were to be no leaks. Still, total loyalist or not, the Reagan true believers always knew that he was not one of them and never would be. They did not have to give him a test to know that if they did, he would in some way fail it. They were, of course, right. He was not a true believer, and the changeover from the Reagan administration to the Bush administration in terms of the national security team was not insignificant. Given the centrist nature of American foreign policy over most of the postwar era, it was almost greater than the changeover from most Republican to most Democratic administrations, or vice versa. James Baker, for example, taking over at State, was delighted to get rid of some of the more conservative Reagan appointees. "Remember, this is *not* a friendly takeover," he said as he cleaned house.[3]

Bush knew that he could not compete with Reagan in many ways, that their skills were completely different. But his interest in process, the long years in grade working his way carefully and cautiously up in the world of national security, and his interest in foreign policy, would serve him well in office. The irony was that the president and his most senior people had come to power in a period that was the exact opposite of what they had trained for. They had spent all those years preparing for the worst, the approach of doomsday, and readying themselves for a dangerous increase in tensions and aggressiveness on the part of the sworn adversary in Moscow. Instead, the sworn enemy had become, if not yet an ally and a candidate for membership in NATO, momentarily a friend. In those turbulent, unpredictable days, dangerous because this was the last gasp of a dark empire, and old adversaries are often most dangerous in their dying moments, Bush and his team seemed to have perfect pitch. They knew how far to go at each moment, how much to push for change, when to back off and let events take their own course, and when to nudge them forward. At one point as the Soviet empire was breaking up, James Baker told his closest aides that the only question left was whether it would be, in his words, "a crash or a soft landing." Largely thanks to the skills of the different members of the Bush administration, it was a soft landing.

The post–Cold War era was another thing. There was no training for that at all, and what to act upon and what to let go by was much harder to measure, because few of the new trouble spots represented, in the truest sense, direct threats to the national security of the United States. The all-purpose directive that had defined American policy for forty years—all eyes on Moscow, with quick glimpses toward Beijing, Western democracies good, communist countries and satellites bad—had suddenly been pulled from the table. In the Cold War not only had international politics been relatively simple, if ever dangerous, but domestic political attitudes toward foreign policy had been equally uncomplicated. Any president who took a hard line against the communists was almost automatically guaranteed the support of most Americans, but challenges posed by the communists, which made for easy calls when they existed in the center of Europe, were quite different when they surfaced in the third world, as with the postcolonial struggle in Vietnam, where the threat of communism was blended with potent nationalism.

The dominant question in American presidential campaigns had in those days been who was best prepared to stand up to the Soviet dictator of the moment. Both parties assaulted the other on this issue, although the competition inevitably favored the Republicans, for they were, by their roots, the party of business, of true capitalism, and therefore virtually by birthright more fiercely anticommunist. The simplistic way in which they often viewed the world translated into an advantage in domestic politics, for they saw no gradations out there, and they left no doubts about what our foreign policy should be. By contrast, the Democrats might possibly have been tainted in the past by their more liberal origins and views and could even on occasion be accused of fellow-traveling. So the Cold War had favored the Republicans, and some of the leaders of the communist world seemed to understand that they had a freer hand in negotiating with Republicans than with Democrats because the Republicans were less likely to be on the defensive. "I like rightists," Chairman Mao told Nixon at their first meeting, ". . . I am completely happy when these people of the right come to power."[4]

Then, almost overnight, that era had not only ended with the collapse of communism, but the world became infinitely more complex. Long-repressed indigenous forces were released everywhere, and they were dangerous in their own right even if they did not fit the old-fashioned, tried-and-true test as a global Soviet threat. It was as if true north had been erased from the compasses of the men and women who had worked all their lives in national security. The domestic political reaction to the new forces at play in the world would also change; that which had once been a whole would now become very fragmented. The foreign policy crises faced by Washington would in part evolve from the newly gained freedom of certain midsize powers to cause mischief, countries whose ability to act on their own had until recently been limited by their powerful benefactors. It is doubtful that Iraq, for example, a Soviet client state that had benefited immeasurably from knowing how to play the angles of the American-Soviet competition, but also a nation held in check because of its sponsor's caution, would have felt free to move against Kuwait during the height of the Cold War.

Other crises would stem from the implosion of poor, embryonic African countries stocked to the gills with B- and C-level modern weaponry, countries that were barely countries at all, and in which most civic institutions of government, save the army and the secret police, had effectively atrophied. The rise of nationalism, indeed tribalism, in several parts of the world and ethnic anger over arbitrary boundaries would cause the outbreak of bitter, unusually cruel fratricidal violence and, in time, masses of refugees flowing across international borders. These were "teacup wars," as the writer and defense expert Les Gelb called them. The issues they presented evoked not so much any immediate question of American national security as a question of American goodness and generosity of spirit and a long-term view that the less killing there was, the safer the globe was for everyone. If military commitments were made, they tended to be seen by the Pentagon as values-driven commitments, not national security commitments.

No one knew the right answers to the questions presented by these crises, if indeed there were right answers. Sometimes it seemed as if all the answers were wrong. Rarely was the security of the United States in any direct or even indirect way threatened, and on such crises the Bush people—other than for the Gulf War, which was to the president a mirror example of Germany's naked aggression in World War II or North Korea's in June 1950—moved slowly and uncertainly. They could talk the talk about foreign policy in the New World Order, as the president called it. But they, like the bright young men about to challenge them in the 1992 presidential election and then to replace them in office, were not yet sure where the walk would lead them.

There were also new, vexing political problems for Bush and any potential successor. As the Soviet threat to the United States receded, so, too, did the political support for any kind of foreign policy issue that was not immediate in its import. A generation was coming of age in the Congress who cared less about foreign affairs, elected by a generation of voters who cared less, and reported on by a media that paid less attention. Thus at a time when low-risk, largely humanitarian involvement in different parts of the world might have been possible, the necessary domestic support for it was on the wane. The country, to be blunt, was more powerful and more influential than ever before, but it was looking inward. It was the most schizophrenic of nations, a monopoly superpower that did not want to be an imperial power, and whose soul, except in financial and economic matters, seemed to be more and more isolationist.

CHAPTER EIGHT

I n retrospect, it was not a surprise that the first great test of the post–Cold War era would take place in Yugoslavia, a country that embodied so many of the conflicts and contradictions of Europe in the twentieth century, which, as the century neared its end, remained almost completely unresolved. Yugoslavia was an uneasy composite of smaller, tribal factions rather than one true nation; it had survived as a nation for the last forty years largely because of its unusual geopolitical location and the unique talents of its leader, Josip Broz, or Tito as he was popularly known. Tito had ruthlessly suppressed various competing forces, most particularly the potentially powerful nationalism of the different component groups, and formed if not a whole out of the many parts, then the veneer of a whole.

Yugoslavia had been cobbled together in the period after World War I, an unlikely composite of smaller nations and tribes that were part of the detritus of the end not merely of the most murderous war imaginable, but the final collapse of two great empires, the Ottoman and the Hapsburg. Most of the terrain included in Yugoslavia was on the outer reaches of those two empires, where their magnetic fields were just strong enough to cause problems for those who lived there, and where there had been a constant ebb and flow of ruling groups. The original name for the country reflected the unlikely quality of national consensus; it was to be called the Kingdom of Serbs, Croats, and Slovenes. In time that was changed to Yugoslavia, which essentially meant the "country of southern Slavs." The historical tribal grievances ran deep, and for a variety of economic, cultural, and educational reasons, the forces that worked to divide the nation remained more powerful than those that united it. During the worst of the Cold War, when it had been ruled by the communists under the semi-iron hand of Tito, the quip had been that it had six republics, five nations, four languages, three religions, two alphabets, and one political party.[1]

Still there was considerable admiration—a surface admiration, to be sure— on the part of visiting foreigners, like the Americans, for the people of the country, in no small part because we disliked their enemies and therefore concentrated on their better rather than their lesser qualities. During World War II the enemies of Yugoslavia—Serb Yugoslavia—had been the Germans, so the French, British, and Americans had liked that; during the Cold War, Yugoslavia had carved out a position of partial independence from Moscow, and we had all liked that as well. The people of Yugoslavia were "at once brawny, animated—a tough brusque lusty folk," John Gunther, one of the ablest American journalists of his generation, once wrote, reflecting how Yugoslavs were viewed and admired in the West for the way they had fought the Germans in World War II and stood up to the Russians during the Cold War, although, of course, some of the Yugoslavs, most notably the Croatians, had for their own historic reasons behaved quite murderously on the side of the Germans.[2]

Worse, the internecine hatreds that existed there were a curious blend of the old and new. Their history was not easily escaped, based on what the different ethnic groups had done to each other for over six hundred years, medieval grievances that remained remarkably fresh and bitter as they emerged into more modern incarnations. As the journalist Ed Vulliamy noted, after covering endless battles among Serbs and Croats and Serbs and Muslims, and listening to the commanding officers on both sides explain what they had done and why they had done it, "The answer to an artillery attack yesterday will begin in the year 925, invariably illustrated with maps [of that year]."[3]

The country rested in an unusually backward part of Europe, a good deal of it mountainous and therefore poor farming land, much of it outside the pull of the more positive economic and social forces of the industrial revolution, which had helped bring steady growth to the rest of Europe, particularly in the years after World War II. Others had modernized; Yugoslavia had remained poor. Not by accident had it been a source of cheap labor for the booming West German economy, for a grim factory job that did not greatly appeal to a young German male with a number of vocational choices was a handsome, middle-class opportunity to a Yugoslav. Many of the powerful political leaders in the region had instinctively fought modernity unless they could manipulate it for their own narrow uses. In Yugoslavia the past not only lingered, but looked to all too many people like the future. In June 1989, Congressman Stephen Solarz of New York, a member of the House Foreign Affairs Committee, had visited Yugoslavia, just before the country's breakup, accompanied by a bright young foreign service officer named Chris Hill. "So what do you think about it?" Hill asked Solarz as his tour ended. Solarz answered, "It's a nineteenth-century museum piece."

Not only had the political system been frozen for so long, but the religious order was as well. Many of the major churches in the West—that is, Western Europe and North America—in the years after World War II had taken a more enlightened and tolerant view of competing religions and thereby the different faces of ethnicity that went with them. That was notably true in the Roman Catholic Church under the papal encyclical of Pope John XXIII in 1963. But that was not true of the Balkans. The religious leaders there were unusually anxious to hold on to the old ways, even when the old ways seemed to outsiders to be as burdened by historical prejudices as they were ennobled by belief. It was like a part of the world where in an age of ever-greater light, the shades on the windows remained drawn. Time did not bring greater tolerance. In Bosnia, as David Owen, the former British foreign minister who made a gallant effort to bring some form of peace to the region, once noted, "Time does not move on, it deteriorates."[4]

Many of the illusions about Yugoslavia had been created during the Tito years; he had been both wartime partisan leader and the leader of postwar Yugoslavia. Unlike other nations of Eastern Europe, which were liberated by the Red Army, Yugoslavia was effectively liberated by its own people and therefore had its own mythic patriot as chief of state. Unlike most of the dictators installed elsewhere by the Russians largely because of the Red Army's conquest (and often deliberately selected by Stalin because of their lack of local popularity and therefore their dependence on him), Tito started with true legitimacy. Because of Yugoslavia's unique geopolitical position (it did not have the Red Army stationed either inside it nor surrounding it nor to the west of it), its physical and cultural connections to the West as well as the East, and its harsh territory, potentially as great a threat to the Russians as it had been to the Germans, Tito had been able to follow a policy somewhat independent of Moscow.

From 1948 when he led his nation out of the communist bloc (or was expelled from it, depending on who was telling the story) to the time of his death, Tito was more than a mere head of state; he ruled the nation like a cunning and deft and occasionally brutal paterfamilias, hero of World War II, and evader of the Soviet shadow. Unfortunately, it was a one-man show, and his legitimacy was personal, not lightly passed on to the representatives of another generation. There was no heir apparent—he seemed not to want one. Like many a dictator before him, he apparently did not believe in the concept of succession. He had loomed far above the political landscape when he first took over, and regrettably, he loomed even further above it when he died. A great oak tree in whose great shadow no other tree could grow, one countryman called him.[5] "Even before his death the system didn't function," Slobodan Milosevic, one of his successors, once noted, "Tito functioned."[6]

Tito was half-Slovene, half-Croat, and the political dilemma he faced was not so much, as it was in other countries in Eastern Europe, in suppressing democratic impulses on the part of his people. Rather it was in suppressing the powerful tendencies toward *nationalism*—always there, always right under the surface—among the different and always restless ethnic groups that made up the whole. This he did ruthlessly, sending some nationalists into exile, others to prison. Anyone who proselytized on behalf of Serb separatism or hegemony during the Tito years was, in one of those wonderfully clumsy communist phrases of that era, guilty of "reactionary nationalism."[7] Tito was as good at defeating the actuarial tables as he was in suppressing the forces that might threaten his vision of the country. But when he died, at eighty-eight in May 1980, it was the end of an era, of a kind of one-man, one-nation rule. He left behind a country in which none of the burning issues of nationalism had ever been dealt with. Was Yugoslavia actually a country or not? Should it remain unified? "We all cried [at the time of his death]," said Mahmut Bakalli, a leader among the ethnic Albanians in the nation, "but we did not know that we were also burying Yugoslavia."[8]

If the death of Tito was the first great step in the breakdown of Yugoslavia, the second was the fall of the Berlin Wall. It changed dramatically the greater East-West geopolitical equation in which Yugoslavia had been so valuable a prize—a showpiece—being sought after by the two giant superpowers. It was like having been the prettiest girl at the dance whom everyone had always courted but now for whatever reason—the coming of other more beautiful girls from the neighboring town—no one wanted to date anymore. What happened then was a fascinating exhibit for those who argued that, in the postwar years, America's foreign policy had come to represent not so much true internationalism as a thin veneer of internationalism that covered policies that were first, foremost, and finally almost completely anticommunist. As long as there was a Soviet threat, we were ready to be engaged in Yugoslavia, perhaps even—worst-case scenario—willing to go to war if need be on behalf of the freedom-loving Yugoslavs. But remove the Soviet threat, and our commitment to the people of Yugoslavia would drop alarmingly. The immediate post–Cold War attitude toward Yugoslavia certainly reflected the conundrum of an American policy from a previous era that had more or less evaporated and been replaced by nothing else. A country that we had thought of as a place to be weaned away from the Soviets, and into which we had poured a great deal of foreign aid and shipped a great deal of high-quality military hardware, had been almost completely devalued in American eyes; and that had happened even as the dangers of fratricidal fighting became far more grave.

In early 1989, Warren Zimmermann, newly minted as the first American ambassador to post–Cold War Yugoslavia, had dropped by to see his friend and superior Larry Eagleburger, then the number two man in the State Department, to discuss his marching orders. Zimmermann, like the young Eagleburger just a few years earlier, was considered one of the department's rising stars. This would be his second posting to Belgrade, and like Eagleburger, he had loved his earlier tour. A certain excitement had come with being right on the border of the Soviet empire, of dealing daily with these rough-hewn, audacious people, who were, the embassy hoped, always searching for greater increments of personal freedom. Zimmermann and Eagleburger were both aware of the potential for violence in Yugoslavia, yet the country was declining in terms of American foreign policy interest. The Congress was not only significantly more isolationist than the executive branch, but dramatically more isolationist than fifteen or twenty years earlier. Given the growing budget deficit at home, ever less foreign aid was being handed out. And the degree of altruism in American foreign policy, greater in the period right after World War II when we had become aware of the cost of neglect and of acting too late in distant places before the war, was also in sharp decline.

Zimmermann and Eagleburger's meeting reflected that. The prospects for helping Yugoslavia financially on any large scale were already bleak, they agreed. We were still interested in the country, Zimmermann should tell its leaders, just as we had always been. Yugoslavia was important, of course, but, well, it was not *very* important. It was lagging behind other former satellite states that were now breaking with the past and creating new democratic orders. Nor did we need it as a buffer against the Soviet Union, which itself was in great disrepair, on its way to becoming a nonempire and then a noncommunist Russia. Poland and Hungary were to be cited by Zimmermann as examples of the countries that we now preferred, the prettier new girls just come to the dance. Yugoslavia's transgressions in human rights, something we had looked away from in the past, were of particular concern. They were especially odious in Kosovo, where Serbian violations of the rights of the Kosovo Albanians had been accelerating, and which had been a principal instrument for the rise of Slobodan Milosevic, to whom, among others, Zimmermann would presumably be making this pitch. The message was clear. In terms of significant American aid, Yugoslavia was on its own, ironically just when it might need help more than ever before. The coda to the message was equally clear. We were judging Yugoslavia not on the old scale—brave little Yugoslavia standing apart from Moscow—but on a new and far more demanding scale: how it treated its own people and how quickly it emulated the way we thought a struggling former central European country should behave.

The new and now more favored states of Eastern Europe—Poland, Hungary, and Czechoslovakia—would, in fact, make an easier transition from the old order to the new than Yugoslavia. Though there would probably be a split in Czechoslovakia between the Czech and Slovak Republics, it seemed likely, because of the indigenous democratic leadership, to be a cordial one. Both Poland and Hungary were unitary states, with little in the way of tribal or ethnic problems to tear them apart or hinder their future democratic development. Moreover, all three of these countries had formidable nascent democratic movements with readily identifiable leadership—the identification having been made by the former communist rulers themselves, who had placed the most passionate democrats of a generation in jail. Equally important in countries like Poland, Hungary, and Czechoslovakia, unlike in Yugoslavia, the old leadership was completely discredited; it had been imposed by Moscow, courtesy of the Red Army, and then the secret police, whereas in the Serb part of Yugoslavia, the leadership had a certain legitimacy. It had produced indigenously, first Tito and his partisans, and now the children of Tito and his partisans. The existing leadership in Belgrade was not discredited and hated as the regimes in Warsaw, Budapest, and Prague had been hated and discredited. In terms of national coherence, Poland, Hungary, and Czechoslovakia offered everything that Yugoslavia lacked. They looked like the easier ones; Yugoslavia, because of its internal ethnic divisions, the hard one. Thus, we decided to put our prime effort into those countries and to cut back our interest in Yugoslavia.

Yugoslavia had by chance come on hard times economically at that moment, which made it unusually ripe for appeals to age-old hatreds. There was runaway inflation, the virulence of which in any country tended to be political and social dynamite. The Yugoslav prime minister, Ante Markovic, a decent democratic man whom the United States had chosen as its horse, soon pleaded with Zimmermann for financial aid in this extremely difficult time; in a highly inflated economy, he badly needed debt relief. He asked for $4 billion. In the old days that might not have been too great a sum—who knew what the Soviet Union might match it with? But now with Washington feeling a need to help the countries of Eastern Europe and weary of carrying a heavy international financial burden, that suddenly looked like a lot of money, especially for a country that seemed to offer us no benefits in return.

Zimmermann was polite with Markovic and said he would check back with his superiors. But he already knew the answer: Poland and Hungary were coming our way even faster, and they did not, as Zimmermann noted, have the additional baggage of bitter ethnic nationalism. They were obviously better bets. That these very qualities that made Yugoslavia so fragile might also make it a more important prospect for serious aid—the potential threats to itself, to the well-being of southern Europe, and to world peace of mind—was not yet an operative observation. So America was no longer quite as interested or committed, just as Yugoslavia's darker forces were being stirred.

The man stirring them was a self-declared new nationalist who had spent most of his career as a dutiful beneficiary of the Communist Party, an apparatchik's apparatchik, Slobodan Milosevic. Milosevic was, as Robert Kaplan has pointed out, an odd legatee of a flawed ancien régime looking now to play an entirely different hand of cards in an era that renounced the old totalitarianism, "the only European Communist leader who managed to save himself and his party from collapse [and] did so by making a direct appeal to racial hatred."[9] He was one of those men coughed up by history in its more cataclysmic moments. If nationalism rather than communism was the new game, Milosevic was ready to play it. His ethics were truly situational—he responded to what was around him with innate quickness and skill, but with no larger vision. He was, no one dealing with him would doubt, quicker and more astute than the other politicians with whom he competed, be they Serb or non-Serb. It was a mistake to underestimate him, and a number of his Balkan peers and people in Washington underestimated him for a long time.

Leave the Communist Party he might, but he had hardly changed his stripes. True, the portrait of Tito came down from behind his desk. True, he purged himself of that unique, heavy-handed, semi-intelligible, deliberately obfuscating language that all communist leaders had seemed to favor. True, in time, his position of power more secure, he would seem to defy Yugoslav history by speaking negatively of Tito and how the great man had liked to rape young Serbian girls. But little else changed, and certainly not the modus operandi: the way of going after power and holding it, the dependence on secret police and state-controlled media, and the skillful use of the army led by people chosen for their personal loyalty. Milosevic was a born infighter, trained in a system that placed great emphasis on how to work your way up in a closed, one-party operation, mimicking those above you when it suited you, and squeezing those beneath you. "Milosevic knows only servants and enemies," his former information minister Aleksander Tijanic once said of him, in what was an almost perfect description of a successful Communist Party apparatchik. "Partners and allies do not exist for him."[10]

By the late eighties the most powerful political force in Yugoslavia was Serb nationalism, a belief among many influential as well as ordinary Serbs that somehow the complicated form of the Yugoslav government, the sharing of power with other groups, particularly the Muslims in Kosovo, went against their historic right to have their own country. They also believed that the Kosovo Albanians had been granted too much autonomy in the later Tito years and were exploiting it at the expense of the security of local Serbs. Some of these beliefs were, given the tortured history of Kosovo, quite legitimate, but Milosevic's manipulation of them was singularly political. He would seek not to address raw grievances in Kosovo and make life more bearable for the Kosovo Serbs, but instead to exploit it ruthlessly as a ticket to hold power everywhere else in the country.

Nationalism was a powerful force throughout Yugoslavia, but nowhere was it more powerful than in Kosovo, where the ethnic Albanians, who were also Muslims, comprised the majority and the Serbs the minority by a ratio of roughly ten to one, and where the two great empires, the Hapsburg and the Ottoman, had been entwined in a long, sad, bitter, and violent history. In Kosovo, six hundred years earlier, the Serbs had fought the most famous battle in their history, and this land, though primarily settled now by Albanian Muslims who were the legatees of the victors in that battle, remained their most sacred territory. The hatreds went so deep, so much was still unresolved, that it often seemed as if the original struggle for this land had taken place not six hundred years earlier, but on the day before.

In April 1987, two years before the fall of the Berlin Wall, but already a time when Eastern Europe was changing at a rapid pace, Milosevic, substituting by chance for Serbian president Ivan Stambolic, went to meet with the local leadership in Kosovo. A huge crowd of Serbs from all over the region gathered outside the government center where Milosevic was talking with Albanian officials. As they pushed forward closer and closer to the building, local ethnic Albanian police—Kosovars as they would be known—tried to hold them off. Some Serbs were beaten. Milosevic came to the balcony and surveyed the huge crowd in front of him. "No one should dare to beat you," he shouted. That in time became a rallying cry for Serb nationalism. Suddenly the enormous crowd, until then quite mutinous, changed its mood and started chanting, "Slobo! Slobo!"[11] At that moment, he became a Serb hero; it was the making of an increasingly successful demagogue in a part of the world where few politicians had ever heard genuine roars of approval from the populace.

From then on Milosevic moved ruthlessly and single-mindedly to exploit the anti-Albanian hatred of the Serbs. He used it as an instrument to take out his longtime sponsor and friend Stambolic, who was still wedded to the old Titoist idea of a pluralist Yugoslavia. Milosevic repeatedly scorned the advice of the American ambassador, Jack Scanlan, about trying to limit the rising ethnic tensions. Perhaps most important of all, he gained control over the state-dominated media and used it to maximize any incident that might inflame Serb feelings. That was something new in an East European country, where in political terms television had been used primarily to broadcast boring party conferences. Now in September 1987 when an Albanian draftee unraveled mentally and went on a killing spree, Milosevic said, "This is God-sent,"[12] and ordered the media to exploit the incident.

In the view of Nebojsa Popov, an old Titoist hand, Milosevic used television the way he was sure Hitler would have used it had there been television in his day. The intense exploitation of nationalism through the use of television, Popov added, had turned his own country into "a real Orwellian dictatorship of the proletariat."[13] It was something new and very ugly—the use of the power of state-controlled media to escalate the darkest fears and hatreds of the people. "You Americans would become nationalists and racists too if your media were totally in the hands of the Ku Klux Klan," noted Milo Vasic, one of the country's most independent journalists, talking of that period.[14]

The country was turning ugly. What had been for many Westerners a joyous place where the negative energy had largely been focused on Moscow and the Russians had changed; now it was aimed at fellow Yugoslavs, albeit those of different ethnic groups. High-level Belgrade dinner parties quickly degenerated into angry, bitter denunciations of one group by another. Westerners (and Yugoslavs, too) who had been away for a few years were stunned by the viciousness in the Belgrade media—the relentless promotion of negative propaganda about all non-Serbs, the manipulation of traditional Serb paranoia, the ugliness with which non-Serb politicians and their ambitions were treated, and the inevitable result of it all: the surfacing among old and trusted friends of a new element of ethnic hatred.

The tensions between the Serbs and the Kosovars, orchestrated and escalated now by Milosevic, continued to mount. Two years after his surprise role as a defender of the Serbs, on June 28, 1989, Milosevic, by now the Serb president, returned to Kosovo for a dramatic repeat performance. This time it was on the most important of Serb national days, one that commemorated the time and the place, six hundred years earlier, when the Turks had defeated the Serbs on a battlefield known as the Field of Blackbirds. Not many nations transform the date of their greatest defeat, one that inaugurated five hundred years of foreign domination, into a sacred day, but that day, June 28, 1389, had deep emotional significance for all Serbs. Tsar Lazar, the most noble of Serb heroes, offered a choice by the Turks between surrendering or fighting to his death, chose to fight to his death.

On this, the six-hundredth anniversary, more than a million Serbs, sensing the beginning of a new age, turned out for Milosevic, and this time he was ready to hit all the right buttons. "Six centuries [later] we are engaged in battles and quarrels. They are not armed battles, but this cannot be excluded either."[15] The huge crowd loved it and chanted back its own battle cry: "Tsar Lazar, you were unfortunate not to have Slobo on your side."[16] It was a clear warning to the rest of the nation, and to the world, about which way Milosevic intended to go.

In January 1990, the Yugoslav League of Communists—until then the only party in the nation—dissolved itself. By doing so it became the first Communist Party in all of Eastern Europe to disappear, although, of course, it did not in any real way disappear. Milosevic and his supporters were now, in the technical sense, no longer communists. But it was at best merely the most marginal change of nomenclature, for all the other aspects with which the communists had exercised power in Eastern Europe—the control and manipulation of media, the dependence upon the secret police, the fear of genuine democratic procedures, the instinct to suppress dissident groups—remained much the same. Milosevic's vision was the creation of a Serb state, and his eye, thought some Westerners, was on Bosnia and Kosovo, and perhaps part of Croatia, too.

The larger question now posed for the Western powers as Yugoslavia was poised on the brink of dissolution was what their response would be if war broke out. Here one additional factor was at work, the belief among the different European powers that with the end of the Cold War this was their own special moment in history; whatever happened in Yugoslavia would be on their terrain, and therefore, they could handle it. The Europeans, eager to show the force and muscle of a newly united continent, were anxious to play a decisive role on this issue. Later it would be clear that they had greatly overestimated their influence, but there was no doubt about their enthusiasm for the task at first. "The age of Europe has dawned," said Jacques Poos of Luxembourg, the chairman of the European Union, in a statement that would be much repeated and mocked in the ensuing months and years.[17]

CHAPTER NINE

In 1991 and 1992 as Yugoslavia was beginning to rise in importance as a topic of conversation, there was great optimism on the Continent about what the European nations would now be able to do to control their own destiny. For the Cold War was over and they no longer needed, as they had for some forty-six years, the security umbrella offered by the Americans. The European Union was about to come to an end, to be replaced by the far stronger European Community. To many that signaled more than the arrival of Europe as an economic unit; it would be a political and military entity as well, one with great potential for the future of the region's collective security. The divisions that had haunted the Continent for so long and created so many mass graves would be a thing of the past. All the energy that had been used so destructively could now be used in common cause to strengthen each other economically, socially, and, if need be, militarily. It was a heady vision. If that was true, and the Europeans seemed to think it was, then Yugoslavia could be a test case, a European issue, one handled on the Continent by people who were believed to know both the players and the territory. The great, muscular giant across the Atlantic, ever protective but equally clumsy and, often, it was believed (particularly by the French), appallingly insensitive to local nuance, the United States, need not be summoned.

Stationed in Brussels at that time, one of the more interested spectators was a senior American army officer named John Shalikashvili, an army four-star, a man who because of his unique boyhood was all too familiar with the ashes of postwar Europe. "We forget this now," he said a few years later, "but everywhere you went in Europe in 1991 and 1992 there was this enormous optimism about what the new Europe could do, and this idealistic belief in the possibilities for the new positive forces about to be unleashed. The Europeans would handle this one, they were saying, and the Americans, who had just finished the Gulf War and were playing out their role as the overseer in the end of the Soviet empire, were only too glad to accommodate them."

The sequence of events at this time was quite important for all parties concerned. The Berlin Wall had come down in November 1989, setting loose powerful forces that had not merely changed the map of Europe, but given it a great psychic lift about the future. Then the Gulf War had taken place, and it had been primarily an American show. The Western forces had quickly and easily triumphed, but it had not been an entirely positive experience for some of the European participants. In fact, for some it had been downright depressing. The Americans had called most of the important shots, and the role of the NATO allies had been, though they did not like to admit it publicly, somewhat marginalized. In the end, the Gulf War had brought home to many of the European nations a sense once again of their impotence on any larger security issue. They were frustrated by one more reminder of the limits of their power outside their continent when the stakes were high and the big boys—that is, the Americans and whomever their adversary was—came to play. But they were also excited about what was taking place on the Continent now that the Russian satellite regimes were falling, and Warsaw, Prague, Budapest, and East Berlin were free to be *European* again. If the Russians were departing, would not the Americans be far behind? Would they ever again need the Americans that badly?

Probably not, and that led to the heightened awareness of what the Europeans could do for themselves. Perhaps they did not have the muscle or the reach for the big-time stuff, a huge multinational force aimed at an outlaw nation in some distant part of the world, but now the consensus was that they could come together, on their own continent, and be a dominating force. Europe would be theirs once again. They would be, as they had not been since before World War II when they were all bitter rivals, their own guardians. They would deal with the growing crisis in the Balkans, an idea with which the Americans eagerly agreed. The American attitude was oddly passive, something that we would later regret. We signed on in advance to a policy we did not shape, in effect telling the Europeans to let us know what their policy was and we would accept it as ours. We did not try to formulate a course of action that would be palatable to everyone involved, and which would cover the darker possibilities of a breakup in Yugoslavia. What ensued therefore was quite tragic: diplomatic hopes not backed up by military muscle.

The policy was not done through NATO, or at least in conjunction with NATO, which would have brought to any agreement—or even a vision of Europe—considerable American military strength. At the time, Will Taft, technically William H. Taft IV, descendant of a long line of Republican luminaries, was the American ambassador to NATO, and he felt that NATO should be involved in any peacekeeping process in the Balkans. He understood Washington's reluctance to take on any additional military responsibilities, but he also felt that we had played too small a role in what was subsequently decided on. We had effectively given the Europeans carte blanche to write the terms themselves, rather than trying to help shape them as a quiet partner and to come up with something with more muscle. But Washington was adamant about not getting involved. It was exhausted and overloaded by other events.

If the Europeans wanted to handle this one, let them have it, and we would sign on to their decision.

Later, looking back on the events of 1991 and 1992, Dick Holbrooke, who would become a principal Clinton negotiator in the area, thought that had been the fateful error—not including NATO as the determining organization from the start, and not having the United States, in some active way, as a military guarantor of whatever decisions were made about the Balkans. The Americans, he believed, had just played a critical part in helping to create and strengthen the new post–Cold War Europe, most notably with the unification of a Germany that had remained in NATO. But now on virtually the first important question about the future of the Continent, we had decided to stand aside, to abdicate our responsibilities. Instead the critical decisions were made on the Continent by a new group, still in its infancy, which knew neither its strengths nor, far more important, its weaknesses. John Shalikashvili largely agreed. "What took place at that moment was what I would call a holiday from leadership," he said years later, referring to the attitude of both sides—on the Continent and in America—as the crisis in Yugoslavia grew. "The Europeans were not yet up to it, and the Americans were for a variety of reasons taking time off."[1]

Moreover, not everyone in Europe was on the same page. A significant difference of opinion existed about which way Yugoslavia should go, a difference of vision that was never resolved. The British and the French were pro-Serb and pro-Belgrade, with a desire to sustain, in lieu of any other attractive possibilities, the existing Yugoslav union, which was, of course, Serb-dominated. But others had a very different view of what should happen. The Germans, who were now emerging as an important force, united for the first time since 1945, sympathized with the Croats and the Slovenes, *their* old allies from World War II, and favored their independence. As that question was being discussed, the most important figure to emerge among the major European powers was Hans Dietrich Genscher, the German foreign minister. He was a powerful influence, not just more senior than the other foreign ministers, but "a man who seemed," in the words of Will Taft, "to have been foreign minister back when some of the rest of them had been born." Genscher, a formidable personality, was not a man to disagree with when he really wanted something.

The Germans were formidable players in those critical days and were determined to push for Croatian and Slovenian independence—something that most assuredly did not displease the Serb nationalists, waiting in the wings. Thereafter, having helped set these catastrophic forces in play, the Germans essentially departed the game. So be it. Cyrus Vance, the former American secretary of state, already operating in one of the many peace-seeking missions in the Balkans, had warned that independence would trigger a chain of events that would make war in Bosnia inevitable. Washington, led by Larry

Eagleburger, argued vigorously with Genscher, trying to slow down the process. But the Germans had moved ahead and accelerated the timetable, yet were restrained by their own constitution from using their military in what was to come.

Why they pushed so hard at that moment was a question that puzzled their colleagues both then and later. Part of the answer was the same history that tied the French and the British to the Serbs, for the Slovenes and the Croats had been Germany's allies twice in the great wars of the past. Another part, as Helmut Kohl, the German head of state, told the French leaders, was pressure from the large number of Croatian workers who lived in Germany and had become a strong indigenous political force. A third part was the excitement and idealism of the new Europe, something the Germans themselves had just become the beneficiary of, the belief that this chance for greater national independence and personal freedom should be shared by all. Germany itself was now being reconstituted and becoming whole, and arbitrary borders inflicted on it by conquering foreigners were being erased. Therefore, went the reasoning, why should not the same thing happen for these smaller friendly nations—historically and militarily their proxies—who had shared cultural values? To the Germans, Croatia and Slovenia were seen as legitimate countries that had a right to long-awaited independence.

The truth was, of course, that most of the Europeans, like the Americans, were quite ill-prepared for the events to come. They did not really know Yugoslavia. They knew the *illusion* that Tito had created, and like the Americans they had quite eagerly accepted it. As Tony Judt, the distinguished European historian, pointed out, the Tito model was unusually popular across a broad political spectrum in both Europe and America. The left liked it because Yugoslavia was as close to a success as the communist world had been able to produce in Europe, and it seemed to put a relatively humane face on European communism. If it was not exactly an economic success, it was not an obvious total failure like the rest of Eastern Europe and the Soviet system. And the political right always had a certain sympathy for Yugoslavia because Tito had broken with Moscow and negotiated a path of substantial independence.[2]

As events in Yugoslavia speeded up, two truths about the European Community's attitude toward those events and the people involved would be revealed. First, the Europeans were greatly overestimating their military muscle and their ability to handle a crisis that was going to be brutal and therefore primarily military. They had been cutting back on their defense budgets as a percentage of their GNP ever since the Korean War, always content to let the United States carry the burden financially. They had been getting a cut-rate defense ride for a long time, did not realize it, and had an inflated sense of their accomplishments and abilities. As Tony Judt said, "They did not know their political-military thinking 101—that your political policy must have genuine defense underpinnings. As events in Yugoslavia deteriorated, as the crisis mounted, the Europeans had the troops and in some cases, like the British and the French, the willingness to put them in harm's way. But they lacked the means to deliver them, the helicopters and the air cover and the other instruments of support."[3]

The second truth would soon have echoes in American policy. As the Europeans became more and more aware of their lack of power in this most difficult, complicated, and treacherous area, the two most important countries, Britain and France, were at the very least Serbo-centric, and in the case of the French, particularly under François Mitterrand, Serbo-philiac. These loyalties had spanned most of the century and were the result of the French and British fear of the rise of a modern, ever more aggressive Germany. Once sworn enemies, England and France now looked fondly on each other and also wanted Russia and its Slavic friends as allies as a counterweight to the German threat.

In the two great wars of this century, the Serbs had been on the same side as the French and British. During World War I, Serbia, overrun by England's enemies—the Germans, Austro-Hungarians, and Bulgarians—had been known in Britain almost generically as "gallant Little Serbia."[4] Then in the spring of 1941, at one of the darkest moments in the war, Winston Churchill had broadcast to the Yugoslavs, "Serbs, we know you. You were our allies in the last war, and your arms are covered with glory. Croats and Slovenes, we know your military history. For centuries you were the bulwark of Christianity. Your fame as warriors spread far and wide on the Continent . . ."[5] His appeal had greater resonance with the Serbs than with the Croats; in World War II, as in its predecessor, the Croats had aligned themselves with the Germans. If anything, the Serbs' relationship with France was even closer than with the British. The French had earlier in the century trained the Serb army and, through special purchasing incentives, essentially supplied it with French military equipment. To understand where the most important European powers stood in relation to the Balkans in 1992, it was only necessary to see where they had been in 1914 and 1940.

Technically, Washington also greatly preferred to keep Yugoslavia unified, albeit for slightly different reasons. To be sure, we had been allies with the Serbs in both wars, and there was a natural affinity there; most of our senior diplomats favored, almost without realizing it, Serb over Croat and Belgrade over Zagreb. They had spent much more time in Belgrade than Zagreb (more often than not, a few years in Belgrade and a few days in Zagreb), their closest friends were much more likely to be Serbs than Croats, and they tended to see any impulse toward Croatian independence or separatism as an irritant, which was much the same way the Serbs saw it. A good Croat, in the eyes of most Western embassies, was someone who backed the concept of a greater Yugoslavia. Anyone else was a troublemaker.

For many Westerners, the Croat cause, as the breakup of the country neared, was harmed by the Croatian leader, Franjo Tudjman, who was a truly loathsome figure capable of spouting some of the worst ethnic garbage since World War II. So Washington had a Serbo-centrist sympathy as well. That Croatia (and Slovenia) saw themselves as unitary countries with well-defined histories, cultures, and religions, all of which made them different from and therefore separate from Belgrade, was greatly underestimated in Washington as it was elsewhere.

One additional factor applied to Bosnia, a largely unspoken one, built into the subconscious rather than the overt attitudes of the European nations. The Bosnians were Muslims, and if a new Bosnian state emerged, the kind envisioned by Alija Izetbegovic, the leader of the Bosnian Muslims, some degree of past pluralism of the area notwithstanding, it could be Islamic. It might not be a fundamentalist one, and many of his constituents were what would be viewed in the Arab world as lapsed or assimilated Muslims, Europeanized men and women who drank alcohol and ate pork, but there was nonetheless an uneasiness about a Muslim state in southern Europe.

The other European nations might not see this as the Serbs did, just one more battle with the hated Turks in a war that had been going on for six hundred years, but any degree of freedom for the Bosnian Muslims seemed somehow alien. Alija Izetbegovic, after all, took his religion seriously, prayed five times a day, and seemed to have a mystical quality in his public pronouncements. Who knew how secular a leader he would turn out to be if Bosnia gained independence? Therefore in the grading system that the other Europeans used to determine their policy—a grading system based on a belief that first and foremost nothing good ever happened in the Balkans, that you had to be wary of all the different groups, that it was a dark, violent swamp where you could only be pulled down—the Serbs were favored, the Croats had their kinship with the Germans, and the Bosnian Muslims were essentially without sponsors.

Thus as the Americans and others in the West watched the heightening storm clouds gather over Yugoslavia, they saw no real upside. Slobodan Milosevic was obviously the most dangerous figure in the country. But Franjo Tudjman of Croatia was an equally ugly nationalist. Among the factors that limited empathy for him in the West was his steadfast sympathy for what seemed like a neo-Nazi ideology, his enthusiasm for what he called Aryan values, and his insistence that much of the history of the Holocaust was a hoax. "Thank God my wife is a not Jew or a Serb," he had said during one memorable campaign speech in 1990.[6]

To Alija Izetbegovic of Bosnia, Tudjman was a Croatian Hitler and Milosevic a Serbian Stalin.[7] "One of the reasons that it was hard to have a good policy there is how terrible all sides were," said John Deutch, a high-ranking Defense Department official who later headed the CIA for a time. "To whom would you give a Thomas Jefferson Award? Not Milosevic certainly. And not Tudjman, equally certainly. Izetbegovic? Not a great candidate himself. The question of which one of them left to their own devices would kill the most people belonging to the other group is a good question. Probably Izetbegovic would kill the fewest, but perhaps only because he lacked the means. It took a long time for arms to get to the Bosnian Muslims."

With Yugoslavia moving to the brink of dissolution and the potential for great violence, and with Europe wanting somehow to prevent it, but not really ready for the task, the role of the United States in 1990–92 would turn out to be crucial. Would Yugoslavia fragment into different countries? And would the dissolution be a peaceful one? Those were the questions that had defied easy answers when Larry Eagleburger had reluctantly made his way to Belgrade in February 1990, met with the various opposition leaders, argued bitterly with his onetime friend Milosevic, and somehow signaled to the Slovenians and the Croats that the United States would not stand in the way of their independence.

CHAPTER TEN

Events, George Ball wrote in one of his dove papers on Vietnam just before the fateful commitment of American combat troops, quoting from Emerson, are in the saddle and ride mankind. So it was in the Balkans in 1990, as events began to move swiftly to a head. Slobodan Milosevic was driven by an irresistible impulse for the creation of a Greater Serbia. The cover story, and the cover story was always important, would be the necessity of holding together the old Yugoslavia. In the coming months Milosevic would make the JNA, already a Serb-dominated force, an essentially Serbian army and upgrade Serb control of other critical institutions. His state-controlled media would escalate its reporting on atrocities inflicted by other ethnic groups on Serbs. There was a historical precedent: Hitler had done exactly this before invading Poland a little more than fifty years earlier.

In December 1990, the Croats, increasingly the principal targets of Belgrade's nationalistic propaganda, sensing the likelihood of coming violence and aware of Belgrade's superiority of men and arms, contacted Mike Einek, the American consul general in Zagreb, to ask for what they called "technical assistance in police improvements." That translated into a request for arms shipments. Warren Zimmermann recommended that Washington turn it down because it would be, among other things, one more way for the Croats to suppress the Serb minority in Croatia. The request was quickly denied; Washington felt little connection with the Croats, and most American officials actively disliked Tudjman. It was, in effect, part of a larger embargo that would penalize Milosevic's enemies. He had all the arms he needed because of the rich stocks of the JNA, while his adversaries would start out with a considerable shortfall.

In 1991 and 1992, he and his forces began to inflict, particularly on the Muslims of Bosnia, the worst ethnic crimes in Europe since the rise of Hitler. As he made his various military moves and his forces shelled essentially defenseless cities, the West issued warnings, which he shrewdly understood to be essentially toothless. What he was listening for was a sign or sound that force might be used against him, and what he heard, despite all the bluster from a series of European and American officials over the next four years, was that it would not. Diplomacy without force would not work with someone like Milosevic.

One of the ironies of the tragedy that unfolded in Yugoslavia was that there had been no lack of American diplomatic, military, and intelligence talent dispatched to the region over the previous forty years. Because of Yugoslavia's critical position in the Cold War, it had been an unusually good listening post. Through skillful use of occasionally dissident JNA officers, American military and intelligence experts could learn a good deal about the Warsaw Pact military, and we had regularly sent our best people there. Not by chance had the young Larry Eagleburger and the young Brent Scowcroft first gone and made their mark in Belgrade. The reporting from Yugoslavia, a high-priority station, was often very good. In the fall of 1990, for example, the CIA did a full-scale analysis that was largely accurate. It predicted that in one year Yugoslavia would no longer function and in two years it would begin to dissolve. It saw the dangers of armed conflict between the different ethnic groups throughout the country. Neither the United States nor the European nations could do anything to stop the breakup, the agency reported.

But as with many of the views we had held during the Cold War, there was considerable illusion in the way we saw Yugoslavia. We had, one old Yugoslavian hand said later, seen only what we wanted to see, as happens in cases like this, and we had not seen what we did not want to see. The American view of the country at the end of the Cold War was romanticized. We significantly underestimated the rage on the part of the Croats and the Slovenes to be free of the shadow of Belgrade, and the fear on the part of the Muslims generated by the Serbs. The Croats and the Slovenes tended to be seen by the American embassy and in high circles in Washington as pesky constituencies who were acting a little big for their britches and ought to know what was good for them, which was a unified Yugoslavia.

The Serbs and the Croats, in particular, nursed a deep-seated hatred for each other. Their history was gnarled and mutually ugly, a legacy of the great cruelty of a distant, brutal past. In many areas the wounds were not ancient but fresh, still open, remembrances of World War II, where under the guise of fighting either alongside the Allies or the Axis, the Serbs and Croats had waged a de facto civil war. Terrible Croat crimes had been committed against Serbs in World War II, and equally terrible Serb crimes against Croats. Lord Owen, assigned to be a peacemaker in 1992, checking into the violent recent past while trying to create a passable modern peace, estimated that of the 1.7 million Yugoslavs killed during the war, more than half had died at the hands of fellow countrymen, a most enlightening statistic.[1] To this day Serbs and Croats argue over exactly how many people—Serbs, Jews, Gypsies, Muslims, but mostly Serbs—were killed by the Croat Ustashe (fascist police) at a death camp called Jasenovac, a name that in Yugoslavia has the same resonance as Auschwitz has for the world's Jewry. Was it perhaps one million, or merely, as some believed, around one hundred thousand to half a million? The Ustashe who ran Jasenovac were not nearly as meticulous in keeping records as their German counterparts.

The Croats had their grievances as well. For them the most resonant name, the one that inspired the greatest hatred for the injustices inflicted upon them, was Bleiburg, that of a town just across the border in Austria. As the war was winding down and the Red Army was driving eastward, Croatian soldiers who had served alongside the Germans fled west to escape the Russians. A large number, perhaps fifty thousand or perhaps one hundred thousand—the numbers were always vague, subject to exaggeration by the Croats or to stonewalling by the Serbs—gathered at Bleiburg and surrendered to British Allied authorities. The British, in turn, handed them over to the Yugoslav partisans under Tito, and almost all of them were subsequently murdered. Bleiburg is a name that has little importance in the West, but in Croatia it has great significance. It stands as Katyn Wood does for Poles, where the cream of the Polish officer corps, desperately trying to escape from the advancing Germans in order to fight another day, were rounded up by officers of the Red Army and, on Stalin's orders, executed on the spot, thousands of men buried in mass graves. Bleiburg was a part of recent history of which the West was largely unaware, but it meant a great deal to the Croats, who perceived the executioners to be essentially communist and Serbian. "We Croats don't drink wine, rather we drink the blood of Serbs from Knin" went a slogan that began to appear all over Croatia as the Yugoslav federation broke up.[2]

Yet if the Serbs and the Croats loathed each other, they quite possibly felt an even greater hatred for the Muslims in Bosnia. On March 25, 1991, as the Serbs were escalating their propaganda and their preparations for war, Milosevic and Tudjman met secretly at one of Tito's favorite hunting lodges. There they tried to make a mutually advantageous deal to carve up Bosnia, the multiethnic, exceptionally vulnerable state that lay between them. Tudjman, not nearly as shrewd or cunning as Milosevic, and not as well armed either, seemed to be lulled by the meeting. Eventually as the Croats belatedly started to arm themselves, smuggling some forty thousand Kalashnikovs in from Hungary and Austria, the Serbs were aware of it and filmed it instead of stopping it. They used the film clip on Belgrade television to heighten anti-Croat feelings among the general Serb population about what the nation's enemies were about to do.[3]

Tudjman, playing a fast game with a tough operator, came to the table with far fewer chips. He apparently did not realize that. Milosevic was way ahead of him and led Tudjman to believe that the Serbs would not attack Croatia; Bosnia was the only object of their aggression. Their meeting was brief, amicable, and a number of their deputies followed it up with a series of meetings designed to draw maps from which Bosnia essentially disappeared. Lord Carrington, brought in by the Europeans to negotiate some kind of settlement, was appalled by the consequences of the meeting, the carving up of a sister state, the Serb areas going to Serbia, the Croat areas to Croatia, "and they weren't worried too much, either of them, about what was going to happen to the Muslims."[4] Slowly and steadily the country was moving to the brink of civil war.

It would all begin as a border skirmish between Serbs and Croats over disputed territory, provocations planned in Belgrade, for which Zagreb was woefully ill-prepared. The symbolic incident that was later remembered as the sign that Yugoslavia was disintegrating took place on May 1, 1991, in the eastern Croatian village of Borovo Selo. The occasion was May Day, still a major workers' holiday in a part of the world where the governments had for so long been communist. Four Croatian policeman from the city of Osijek, the third-largest city in Croatia, hearing that Borovo Selo had been left unguarded, drove over there that night. Local Serb villagers had hoisted the old Yugoslav flag with the communist star on a number of buildings. That, the policemen decided, was an act of rebellion, and they intended to replace them with red-and-white checkerboard Croatian flags. But the Serbs, who were still guarding the town, fired on the policemen and wounded two, capturing the two and holding them prisoner.

The two policemen who escaped returned to Osijek, where they told their story to colleagues. Soon a busload of Croatian policemen set out from Osijek to rescue the two captured men. But the local Serbs were more than ready. The village was now on red alert. All the intersections were guarded by heavily armed men. On the rooftops covering them with unobstructed fields of fire were more armed men. What happened that morning was nothing less than a massacre. Twelve Croatian policemen were killed and about twenty more were wounded. It caused, in the words of Laura Silber and Allan Little, "a sea change in Croatian public opinion." Where there had been wariness, now there was open Serbo-phobia. Zagreb television reported that the dead had been tortured and mutilated. Even worse, Serbian authorities seemed to boast about what they had done.

No one was more appalled by the ugliness than an American reporter named Roy Gutman, who was in Yugoslavia at the time and who was just starting to write what was to be a series of unusually prophetic dispatches for *Newsday,* the New York suburban daily. Because this was his second tour in Yugoslavia, Gutman was already undergoing what he later called a mandatory reeducation, taking apart the old construct of Yugoslavia—what was good and what was bad about it, and how valid it was as a nation—and creating a new one, piece by piece. He had to unlearn everything he had once believed in, the romantic Western view of this unusual, complicated country where the people who had seemed so admirable, brave, and generous could become so difficult, headstrong, and intolerant—indeed even savage.

If there was a turning point in Gutman's reappraisal, it came in May 1991 when he visited Borovo Selo. He had heard about it first from a small news service the Tudjman people were operating in Zagreb. Not only had there been a massacre, it was said, but the bodies had been mutilated, a reference that added an additional degree of horror to the story. Gutman immediately went to Borovo Selo, but by the time he arrived, things were already being tidied up. Serb paramilitary forces were running the town and no one was eager to talk about what had happened. But Gutman was struck from the beginning by the brutality of the massacre, that it had been so carefully orchestrated—a small provocation that had been turned into a deliberate, murderous, big-time ambush. For Gutman, the incident did not stem from a local ethnic antagonism that had simmered for a long time before finally erupting into violence. Rather it had been arranged and triggered by forces in Belgrade and bore the unofficial stamp of Belgrade's approval—its new direction and purpose. Serb officialdom, unconcerned about such raw ethnic divisions, seemed to be gloating about the incident.

For Gutman it was more like an execution than a mere ambush, and the architect was a notorious figure named Vojislav Seselj, an ultranationalist Serb who had once been jailed by Tito for his ethnic views and was known, even in the harsh world of the Balkans, for his personal cruelty. At one point, before the two of them eventually broke, Slobodan Milosevic liked to say that Seselj was his favorite policeman. It was obvious to Gutman that Seselj had been in Borovo Selo, and that the massacre was his handiwork. Seselj personified the worst of the violent new nationalism now being orchestrated by Belgrade— the belief that it was not enough to vote against those who were ethnically different; it was better to kill them. What Seselj represented, the advent of well-organized, well-armed Serb paramilitary units, which assaulted ill-prepared Croatian (and in time Muslim) officials in small towns, was to be a critical ingredient in the kind of ethnic cleansing soon to come. Nor was Seselj alone. There were others, most notably a man known as Arkan, Zeljko Raznatovic, with his infamous Tigers, who on occasion made Seselj look like something of an amateur. (As happens with men like Seselj and Arkan, their feelings for each other were not always benign and collegial. Seselj once turned to Arkan during a debate on state television and told him, "I bet you've put a black sock on your face more than on your foot.")

To Gutman, what had happened at Borovo Selo was appalling, but what made it worse was how blatant it was. He was quite sure that the mutilation— the policeman's eyes had been gouged out—had taken place, but by the time he was ready to do the story, the Croats were putting a lid on that part, fearful that news of this kind would enrage their own people and lead to even more violent incidents. That was precisely what the Serbs wanted—localized Croatian assaults upon Serb neighbors in small villages and towns, which would become the justification for bringing in the JNA. But the role of Seselj unnerved Gutman. He had already heard a good deal about this man who operated like an outlaw, but an outlaw armed with the imprimatur of the sitting government who liked to go around boasting of the violent end he had in store for non-Serb Yugoslavs.

Gutman decided to do a story on Seselj himself, went looking for him in Belgrade, but found to his surprise that he was not there because he was running for the parliament. He finally caught up with him in northern Serbia in a town called Vojvodina. To Gutman, Seselj was quite open about what had happened at Borovo Selo. Yes, he had been there and had been in charge. Moreover, if elected, he promised to assault many other villages. Borovo Selo would be but a beginning. The men under his command, Seselj said, were his own Chetniks, *Chetnik* being a hateful word to non-Serb Yugoslavs, recalling memories of soldiers of the old Orthodox Serb empire, monarchists who marched—and killed—under the banner of the Orthodox Church and could do what they wanted to any non-Serbs; men who saw the non-Serb world as one vast free-fire zone. Then Seselj spoke quite candidly about how he planned to break up the existing Yugoslavia—he even had a map. A city located on the Slavonian-Hungarian border might go to the Hungarians. Split on the Adriatic Coast might go to the Italians. Most of the rest of the country would be Serbian. To Gutman, this brief discourse was both chilling and hypnotic, a war criminal speaking openly about his deeds past and his hopes for deeds future. At the end of the interview, expecting they might talk again, Gutman gave Seselj his card. ("You did *what!*" his wife, Betsy, later said. "You gave him your card with *our* address on it!")

Gutman's interview with Seselj left him with no doubt about Serb intentions. He filed his story on Seselj but felt that what he had written was somehow hopelessly inadequate. The calm, understated nature of professional journalism had not been equal to the sheer horror of the deed and the threat. Something sinister was beginning to happen, with no restraints to limit the brutality. The kind of paramilitary units Seselj employed represented the dregs of society, and their behavior startled even old-line, traditionalist JNA officers. "They were the types who would kill a man of ninety for a lamb," said General Slavko Lisica, who commanded JNA soldiers on the Dalmatian coast. "My men in the front lines come to me and say, 'The paramilitaries rob, they rape, they steal. Why are we fighting and what are we fighting for?' "[5]

Gutman was an experienced reporter who, when he arrived the second time in Yugoslavia, flattered himself that he knew the region well because of an earlier, happy tour there. He had grown up in West Hartford, Connecticut, gone to Haverford College and the London School of Economics, and worked for a time for the United Press before joining Reuters in Europe. As a Reuters correspondent he had been stationed in Belgrade from 1973 to 1975, and like many Western reporters he loved the country—"the golden age of Tito," he later called it. The Serbo-centrism that tempered the vision of many Western diplomats was something he knew well because he had unconsciously indulged in it himself. The Yugoslavia he knew back then had basked in the glow of being more independent than the other Eastern European countries. Its citizens had more personal freedom than the Poles or the Hungarians. The economy seemed to be developing at a much faster rate with more material benefits than those in other communist countries—more meat, better clothes, possibilities of travel in the West, even the chance to own a car. The people he met were attractive, independent, feisty, and talented. Moreover, the different ethnic groups seemed to get on reasonably well with each other, and there was little sense of the tragedy to come.

Like many an American who went to Belgrade in those years, Gutman had found the entire ambience seductive. But by the time he returned in 1989, everything was beginning to change. He was then in midcareer, based in Bonn for *Newsday*, the affluent suburban Long Island paper that was then making an effort to create a Manhattan constituency. He had been away from Yugoslavia for some fifteen years, and he now saw many signs that it was becoming a very different country. Serb officials felt free to make inflammatory statements about other nationalities. Political extremism was the new virus; ultranationalism on the part of one group soon bred it in another. Milosevic had not only come to power, he appeared determined to crush fledgling democratic forces in the country, most particularly university students who were calling for more, rather than less, freedom.

As far as Gutman could tell, the symbol of how quickly the country was changing from the old to the new reality was the growing division between Western journalists and diplomats. The journalists were lined up on one side in their view of how bad things were, and a great many of the diplomats were on the other, still holding on to their traditional view of the country. Gutman had some sympathy for the diplomats. Journalists, he decided, were luckier than diplomats because they were always out working the story, involuntarily on the cutting edge, meeting people from all walks of life, and the more they worked the story, the more evidence they found that what they had once believed in no longer existed. Gutman doubted that any high-level diplomat had ever had an enlightening interview with Seselj. Journalists could also change directions much more easily; they were tied to events rather than to policies.

Gutman's early stories were, in terms of the human tragedy he was soon to report, rather prosaic. "Yugoslavs Need West's Intervention" was the headline on an early one that ran in *Newsday* on November 21, 1991, and it suggested that the United States was the one country that might stop Serb aggression. The story quoted an expert on the Balkans at a London think tank who said that American policy needed a degree of brinkmanship there, and if the United States was willing to make a show of force, the Serbs would quickly back off. It also recounted a series of gestures of appeasement made by the European nations as Serb aggression had mounted. A month later, on December 22, 1991, Gutman followed up with a story of considerable significance, forecasting that the decision by European nations to recognize Croatian independence would trigger an explosion of catastrophic proportions in Bosnia, and implying as well that this was precisely what the Serbs wanted. He quoted the Bosnian foreign minister as saying, "There could be two hundred thousand to three hundred thousand people slaughtered within a few months." The likely epicenter for the slaughter, he reported, was Banja Luka, a city in northern Bosnia. Gutman would with great sadness discover in the months to come just how prophetic he had been.

CHAPTER ELEVEN

B y the summer of 1992, George Bush and a great many of his fellow countrymen were beginning to learn how skillful a politician Bill Clinton was. He had decided to make the race for the presidency and had become an immediate beneficiary of both the end of the Cold War and, ironically enough, the quick American victory in the Gulf War. The former was a boon because it had dramatically changed the American political agenda, and the latter because it had suppressed the ambitions of better-known Democratic politicians. No one who ever knew Clinton thought that his political career was bedeviled by bad luck—some of the good luck he made himself, and some of it was simply the most fortunate of political inheritances. That was demonstrably true in 1992. But his talent was also surpassing. "The best horse I've ever seen," said his first campaign manager, James Carville, and by that he meant that Clinton was born to run, and the higher the office for which he ran, the better he did.

If Clinton's political career, some believed, had been confined only to running rather than to governance, he would have been a sure bet for Mount Rushmore. One could somehow imagine him not governing, but it was almost impossible to think of him not running. Even late in his presidency, when his wife was running for the Senate and his vice president, Al Gore, was finally running on his own to succeed him, Clinton, knowing that what he said could detract from their races and their sense of independence, could not discipline his irresistible impulse to campaign and seemed determined to run their races for them, always ready, should someone amend the Constitution in time, to run for a third term himself.

Clinton was arguably one of the two most gifted American politicians of the latter third of the twentieth century, sharing that title with Ronald Reagan, whose almost magical political gifts allowed his fellow countrymen to excuse his limitations and failings and see only his strengths—that is, see him as he wanted to be seen. But Reagan had arrived at a time when conservativism was on the rise, when the demographics of America were changing dramatically, and when political power and economic affluence were shifting from the East and Middle Atlantic states to the Sun Belt, a region whose values he shared and came to represent. He was the perfect candidate for a postindustrial, increasingly suburban America, where millions of people, while technically living better than ever, were cut off from their immediate pasts and roots and were restlessly searching for reassuring images of a safer and simpler time. Reagan did not merely reflect these changing political values, he helped drive them as well. He brought the forces he represented from the political fringe, where they had been early in the sixties, when he'd first come on the national stage, to the very center of American life. Moreover, he did that so effortlessly that he never seemed to be a politician.

Bill Clinton, on the other hand, was the candidate of a declining, seriously fragmented Democratic Party and had started his political career as a young, ostensibly liberal Southern governor with the weakest of constituencies. Given the frailty of his base, the diminishing muscle of his political party, and his lack of personal wealth, he was destined for a political life of constant compromise as well as rhetoric that was always a bit grander than his deeds. In rhetoric, he was instinctively slightly liberal, deftly to the left of the center, with a few symbolic conservative acts to balance it all off. In deeds, he was instinctively centrist, as gifted a straddler of complicated issues as the political system had coughed up in years.

Politics was a deadly serious business for Clinton. It was not just his avocation, it was his very being. The only jobs he had ever held for any length of time were political. There had been a brief tour after his Rhodes scholarship when he had served with marginal enthusiasm as an instructor at the University of Arkansas law school. But even there he had devoted himself less to the work of his students than to surveying the political terrain. "Am still doing dull law school," he had written in 1971 to his friend Willie Morris, also a Rhodes Scholar, who was then editing *Harper's,* "laying the foundation for who knows what, but it will be done with a good spirit and a wry grin." For politics was all Clinton knew and all he did. For most of their adult lives, he and his wife lived in government-owned housing, first in Little Rock and then in Washington. He had come on the scene as a political wunderkind so early and had such staying power that, by 1992, when he was still in his midforties, Sam Nunn, the Georgia senator, could refer to him as a rising star in the Democratic Party in three different decades. There was one other critical thing about him. Given the constancy of the odds against him throughout his entire career, he understood that nothing could be wasted and there was no downtime. Everything he did was political, and everything he did was likely to be politically driven. He was *always* campaigning. He never stopped. His life, at the age of fifty-four, had been one long, uninterrupted political campaign. He was not merely a brilliant survivor, he was more truly a survivalist, someone for whom survival was the sole purpose of his being.

Clinton seemed to defy all the forces of late-twentieth-century American politics. At a time when high-level politics had become something of a millionaires' club, he was a man without any wealth of his own. He and Mrs. Clinton did not even own a home until they finally bought a handsome house in New York's Westchester County, a requisite for her campaign for the Senate, a home that was to be financed at first with help from one of his principal fundraisers. He came from a small, poor state with marginal political leverage, and he was a product of a divided, inchoate Democratic Party. Yet, his political instincts were almost pure. No one could read a crowd and sense what the people in it felt and wanted better than he. Reagan had only to be Reagan, warm and sunny and confident, and the crowd would move to him; Clinton had a weaker base and so had to make adjustments to every crowd.

Clinton was also addicted to polls, and his administration would set a new high in its sensitivity to them. At one point, polling was even done on where the president and first lady should spend a summer vacation, with Wyoming the winner. The country, it appeared, would love to see photos of him in rough outdoor clothes and checked Western shirts, top button unbuttoned. But in truth, his own antennae were so good, his feel for the country and its mood so true, that he needed the polls, perhaps, only as confirmation of what he already knew. He was especially good out in the field, touching voters, seeing them and responding to them and making them respond to him. He had an essential humanity that always came to the surface, on occasion both evangelical and intellectual at the same time. In contrast, when he went into a room filled with a group of academics and policy professionals—the governance-is-serious-business-but-never-fun crowd—he immediately became drier and more didactic, his mood matching theirs. Because of that, there was no telling with Clinton when he was going to be at his best, when he would reach back and come up with something simply dazzling. Once in an open meeting during the 1992 New Hampshire primary, a voter asked a question about what Bush had awkwardly called the vision thing. Clinton, tired and worn-out that night, nonetheless immediately jumped on the question and exploited it brilliantly. "I hope you never raise a child without the vision thing," he said. "Life would be bleak and empty without the vision thing."

Clinton's instinct for the changing moods of people was extraordinary. As president he could, it seemed, get up in the morning, take a walk around the White House, and by the time he got back inside for coffee, having in effect conducted his own poll, would know the national mood. "He sees himself," said one top member of his administration who worked closely with him over the years, "as the doctor and the country as the patient, a patient who on occasion has been sick, and Clinton feels he knows the patient's mood and temperature to the most infinitesimal degree at all times. And he believes he knows what should be prescribed at all times—and what should not be prescribed." Oddly enough that quote from a close Clinton associate dovetailed with something Brent Scowcroft, Bush's national security adviser, once said of Clinton and his preoccupation with the pulse of the American people: "The president has to do more than take the pulse of the people, which Clinton does with great skill. He has to lead as well."

One of the most important things about Bill Clinton was his capacity— indeed his need—to win people over. Those who had tracked him for a long time, going back to his boyhood in Arkansas, believed that it was a product of the disorderly home in which he had grown up. Favored in intelligence, but not favored in social position and wealth, he had needed to impress and win over all those around him, teachers, bandleaders, peers, to show that he was as good as everyone else. It was almost a compulsion, this need to win over doubters. He was, thought a number of journalists who had covered him over the years, a lot more interested in reporters who seemed just outside his reach than those who coveted his favors. As Bob Reich, one of his oldest friends and for a time his secretary of labor, once noted, if you're in his cabinet and you called him often, he would downgrade you. But if you didn't call him for a time, he'd get nervous and he'd call you.[1]

It sometimes seemed as if his political skills were too great. In his desire to please various audiences, he occasionally tended toward rhetoric that exceeded his capacity to deliver; he did not merely charm people, he overcharmed them. Many of those listening to him decided that he was the one politician who agreed with all of their ideas, the man they had been looking for all their life. But he often disappointed the very same people who had once believed so completely in him. Those who defended him against criticism like this noted that whatever his failings were, given the political climate in the country at the end of the century, he was as good a deal as they were likely to get. That was probably true, but it did not ease their disappointment.

The Democratic Party, as Clinton rose to power, was very much a minority in national terms, the forces that had propelled it to prolonged hegemony back in the thirties through the fifties long since dissipated. Of its own it did not have a real center; it had a center only when someone as talented as Clinton, with his unerring sense of where the center ought to be and how to balance all the conflicting forces, became the party's leader. It was increasingly short of a broad purpose as well, overtaken by profound historical and technological changes and engaged in bitter fratricidal struggles. Labor, once a dominating force nationally, was in serious decline because of the critical changeover from a blue-collar to a white-collar economy, the outmigration of blue-collar jobs to countries overseas, and the coming of a modern high-technology workplace. All in all, labor was more powerful within the party than it was within the nation.

One of the forces that faced Clinton and any Democratic politician in the latter part of the twentieth century was the sheer affluence of America and the unparalleled long-term postwar success of its economy. America, especially *white* America, judged on any comparative international scale, was a very rich and thus a very conservative country. That made it much harder on any party even marginally rooted on the left. The liberalism that had been created in the thirty-year period of the New Deal and Fair Deal, when millions of Americans had been crushed economically by forces outside their control and were grateful for the programmatic aid sponsored by the federal government, had waned greatly in so long a period of seemingly limitless prosperity. What Americans regarded as a brief recession looked like a time of prosperity to most foreigners. Starting in the fifties and sixties, throughout the country, for it was hardly a regional phenomenon, the children of white New Dealers had gradually become more affluent, had moved to the suburbs, and had become more conservative on both cultural and economic issues. In time they spoke of themselves as independents and often voted Republican.

Nor did this change extend only to those Americans who were fortunate enough to go to college and thereby managed to jump upward a grade in class. It included blue-collar Americans as well, workers who had once voted solidly Democratic but who now began to split off from the party. Their alliance with urban blacks, never an easy marriage, had begun to break down in the mid and late sixties. Back in the thirties, forties, and fifties, when both groups were outsiders trying to work their way up the American ladder, they had a shared wariness of the ruling business elite and were allies in an edgy relationship that was probably better on paper than in reality. But by the seventies, blue-collar whites enjoyed enough success to feel they had made it, and the gap between their aspirations and those of many blacks had widened. Blue-collar whites were especially resentful of any new governmental attempts to adjust the existing societal balance in favor of blacks, such as court-ordered busing or affirmative action. The big-city political machines, which had once been able to guarantee the Democrats not only urban control in a number of big industrial states, but the ability to carry those states in national elections, had become pale shadows of their former selves. White flight from the cities had escalated, creating new conservative patches in the suburbs.

On foreign policy issues the Democratic Party was still badly bedeviled by Vietnam. Two Democratic presidents, Kennedy and Johnson, had been the principal architects of the ill-advised escalation, and yet most of the antiwar protest had come from the liberal-left faction of the party, along with some moderate centrist Republicans. That was the perfect description of a family in serious conflict with itself. The Republican Party had largely taken a bye on the issue. In 1968, a seminal year in American life, the tensions over Vietnam had not only pitted two great forces in the Democratic Party against each other, the more conservative hawks and the more liberal doves, but cops representing the last great city political machine, that of Richard Daley, had assaulted the young peace protesters (just as the leaders of the protest had hoped) at a disastrous convention in Chicago. This was the convention where the sitting president was originally supposed to be renominated. Now his vice president stood in as his proxy, his own top political people bitterly divided from those of the president over how many degrees of separation he was allowed at a decisive moment like this. Ordinary citizens, watching on television in their homes, could take away only one lesson from the ugliness of Chicago: that the Democrats had lost control of the convention *and* the country. Vietnam had put the party at war with itself. It was, said the liberal columnist Mark Shields, as if an unusually violent football game were being played. One team was led by Lyndon Johnson and the people who favored the war, and the other was a team led by Bobby Kennedy, Gene McCarthy, George McGovern, and assorted other Democrats. In the stands were thousands and thousands of cheering fans having the time of their lives—all of them Republicans.[2]

Those divisions within the party had never entirely healed. The peace that had evolved between the two main factions over the years was not so much a peace as a thinly concealed truce; and, in fact, they soon found other issues with which to challenge each other. For a brief time there had been a faint glimmer of hope that the party might evolve into a Kennedy party, for the Kennedys were seen as both tough enough to handle the old political forces, yet sensitive enough to deal with the new forces now at play, and with the ability to hold a fragile, largely outdated coalition together. But Robert Kennedy was assassinated before the 1968 convention, and thirteen months later, Ted Kennedy drove off a bridge on Chappaquiddick with a young female staff member who drowned in the accident. With that, the increasingly frail dream of a Kennedy party died.

The tensions, particularly in foreign policy, remained. Vietnam evolved into other divisions, once again between hawk and dove, over a broad range of foreign policy and defense issues. Some foreign policy people, uneasy with what they considered the dovish direction of the party, began an outmigration to the GOP in the seventies and eighties. The old-fashioned ability to forge a sort of compromise and come together on something of a centrist policy no longer seemed to exist in the new television age, which tended to create one-issue constituencies. It also created greater egos among the leaders of each one-issue group, with less and less capacity to compromise.

Many old-line Democrats left their party in the eighties to become Reagan Democrats. Jeane Kirkpatrick, a former Democrat, spoke for these dissidents at the Republican convention in 1984. There, her voice ringing with pure contempt, she talked of "the San Francisco Democrats," as if it were a party of the spoiled, the effeminate, and the anti-American. That was the convention that had nominated Walter Mondale and, in her opinion, had lost touch with the mainstream of America. Ronald Reagan beat the candidate of the San Francisco Democrats by the largest landslide in American presidential elections, in what would be one of the low points in the history of the modern Democratic Party (Mondale had carried only his home state of Minnesota). The post–New Deal political, social, and economic realignment of America was, on the occasion of Reagan's second inaugural, complete. By 1992, the Democrats had held power for only four years of the last twenty-four.

In the 1992 campaign Bill Clinton negotiated his way through the terrible detritus of his partially crippled party with singular dexterity. It was as if he, raised as he had been in a dysfunctional home with an alcoholic stepfather, had long ago mastered the ability to defuse tensions in a warring and dysfunctional family—which most assuredly the Democrats were. He knew at every moment how bold or how cautious to be, how big a step to take and when to stand still. He knew how to tempt the more liberal wings with winning rhetoric when he chose, and how to straddle divisive issues when necessary. He knew how to charm, to beguile, to cajole. He was unusually good at the implication of his support if not at support itself. He knew how, and this was no small talent, to disappoint those who supported him when need be. He knew as well how to play his last best card, the idea that if the Democrats did not go along with him, they would surely get something far worse from the other side of the aisle.

Clinton was a leader of the New Democrats, a faction of the party that did not want to be tagged as too liberal, which was trying to move toward the national political center. Unlike most Democrats, he had supported the Gulf War. He was more willing than most liberals who had gone before him to speak out on issues like crime, which up until then had been in the sole custody of the Republicans, as if somehow Democrats were pro-crime. He was considered passionate on the issue of race, and yet as governor of Arkansas he had accepted the death penalty, one of the great hot-button issues of American life. He had appalled many hard-core liberals when, as governor and by then running for the presidency in 1992, he refused to stay the execution of a retarded murderer, a man named Rickey Ray Rector, who was so mentally deficient that, when offered his final meal, he asked the warden to save the dessert, pecan pie, so he could eat it when he returned from what was for him just a brief walk. It was the kind of decision the young Clinton and his wife, newly arrived in Arkansas, might once have opposed; it was obviously a terrible thing to do, but failing to do it would open him up to all kinds of charges and recriminations on an issue where it appeared that rational debate had long ago ended.

Clinton was always aware that making the necessary accommodations to the needs of the more conservative voters of Arkansas might damage him nationally. He once told his good friend Tom Kean, a popular, attractive fellow governor, a liberal Republican, and like him a centrist, that both of them could win a national election, but that their problem would be getting their respective nominations. Kean, he postulated, was too liberal to get his party's nomination, and he, Clinton, was too conservative to win the Democratic nomination.

He projected not merely intelligence and youth but an elemental humanity; he did not seem plastic or colorless, but rather, more than any other quality, engaged. That was clear from the start of his campaign, his innate empathy for ordinary people, his ability to identify with them, listen to their problems, and sympathize with them. The byword of his candidacy and his presidency was the phrase "I feel your pain." Some eight years later, his tour as president over, a cartoon in *The New Yorker* showed a couple, presumably watching the inaugural on television, and one asking the other if this meant, the guard having changed, they now had to feel their own pain. Over the years an increasingly skeptical press corps would come to think of Clinton as the national empathizer, believing that he did empathy better than he did solutions to social problems. But he was too good at it for all of it to be faked, and much of it was surely genuine.

Watching him wade into all kinds of different crowds, seeing how good he was at what might be called the empathy thing, Ed Rollins, the former Reagan political consultant, had an epiphany about how dramatically American culture had changed in the twelve years since Reagan's first election. Driven by various technological, social, and economic forces, that change was now being seen in American politics. Reagan, Rollins believed, had been the final political reflection of the popular culture of his time, derived primarily from the movies of the John Wayne, Jimmy Stewart, and Gary Cooper days when the American self-image called for one lonely man to stand up and do the right thing, whether it was popular or not. That self-image during the worst of the Cold War was comforting; it might not be true, but as they used to say in the West, when there was any difference between the truth and the legend, print the legend. Clinton, by contrast, was the political extension of a new popular culture, the age of empathy television, symbolized by Oprah Winfrey, the need to feel better about yourself in a difficult, emotionally volatile world where the greatest daily threat was posed not so much by the nuclear warheads of a foreign power, or by severe economic hardship, but by the inner demons produced by an unhappy childhood. Indeed Clinton himself was good at telling different audiences that when he was young, he was overweight and unhappy and had not been popular. It was, Rollins said, the *Oprah* show as presidential politics,[3] and a reflection that the country no longer felt threatened by exterior enemies.

During the second Bush-Clinton-Perot debate, a young black woman asked the three candidates how they had been affected by the soft economy. The different reactions of the three men were fascinating and uncommonly revealing. Perot spoke of how he was giving up his private life to run, a sacrifice that few listening thought of as a sacrifice. Bush completely stumbled, obviously greatly puzzled by the question itself. "I'm not sure I get it," he said. Clinton, of course, nailed it. He walked toward the woman and spoke of his personal experiences as governor of a small state in a bad time, and of the people whose lives had been hurt by the weak economy. He all but embraced the woman; her pain had become his pain. It was a truly memorable moment, indicative of a profound generational change in American politics. James Carville was sure that it was the moment when Bush lost the election.

Good politicians are always audacious, and in his audacity, Clinton picked the perfect year for his presidential run. For 1992 was a watershed largely because of the end of the Cold War. No one realized it at first, but as the campaign unfolded, first in the primaries and then in the general election, it became evident that one era of America politics was over, and another, in the most incipient way, was beginning. By 1992, Gorbachev, the last Soviet first secretary, had not only been defanged, his attempt to bring reform to the dying empire a failure, but he had fallen from power, replaced by the first postwar *Russian* president.

The post–Cold War world was not, of course, something that was born in 1989 with the fall of the Berlin War; it had been coming incrementally over some twenty-seven years, probably ever since the high-water mark of tensions that had been reached during the Cuban missile crisis in October 1962. The two superpowers had still regarded each other with great hostility. But for some time in the minds of ordinary citizens, the sheer terror generated by the other side had gradually abated. People had come to accept living in a bipolar nuclear world, in which there were now slow, systematic, albeit occasionally grudging attempts at arms reduction. By the late eighties, the nuclear threat was simply not as raw as it had once been. The Cold War, driven in its later stages by institutions uniquely powerful in Washington, had probably remained a far more important part of the fabric of life in the capitol than it had nationally, particularly among younger people.

The generation that had fought in World War II was older now. The first representative of that generation who had served at the combat level—Eisenhower had been a commander—to take the presidency, Jack Kennedy, a man who on his election had appeared almost too young to be president, would have been seventy-five in 1992. Now members of that generation were increasingly a minority in political terms, and perhaps a minority in terms of their values as well. Formed by a pretelevision, popular culture, shaped by the Great Depression, World War II, and a general lack of affluence, their values were those of sacrifice, obligation, and personal modesty, which often seemed outmoded in contemporary America. Military service was no longer compulsory. Political candidates were not required to be war heroes; they did not even have to have been in uniform.

The definition of patriotism had probably changed with finality on the day the first atomic bomb was dropped on Hiroshima, and in the period thereafter as the United States began to acquire a vast first-strike capacity—SAC,

ICBMs, nuclear subs. Patriotism in its purest sense, which had served the nation so well in the days after Pearl Harbor, was the impulse, both proud and immediate, to defend your country against enemy aggression. It was not necessarily the impulse to go thousands of miles away for obscure political causes in countries where no border had been crossed by an invading army, and where the conflicting forces were not only indigenous but likely to be both poor and raggedy, to fight on behalf of people who did not pose a threat to the United States. Patriotism in an age of distant, political wars was a more complicated concept. Did an ordinary person have to be as patriotic in the present as in the past if his nation had an immense nuclear arsenal and a professional all-volunteer army?

The Vietnam War had divided the country, frustrated the country, and scarred the country, but it never really threatened the country. There was never a danger of North Vietnamese or Vietcong forces landing south of San Francisco and sweeping down in a great arc to capture Los Angeles (although a great many people on the far right might not have been too unhappy if they had). In fact, as the tensions of the Cold War began to move away from central Europe to distant places in the third world where the proxies of both superpowers were aligned against each other, the cause of patriotism became even less immediate. A young American was more likely to be fighting to save an odious local oligarchy and thus prop up a rather debatable domino than to protect his hometown in Iowa.

One of the nation's less attractive and not very secret secrets was gradually being unveiled in this political season: that the educated, the talented, and the privileged had by and large not served in Vietnam. Some like Clinton had not served because they opposed the war but others who appeared to favor it had not deigned to go for other reasons. Newt Gingrich, a rising star in the House, might now be a hawk, but had not chosen to serve in Vietnam, accepting instead a number of educational deferments. Trent Lott, a soaring luminary of the Southern wing of the Republican Party, already on his way to becoming Senate majority leader, a man who had an ideological affinity for the war and was almost the perfect age to go, had been able to come up with deferments for family reasons. Bush's sitting vice president, Dan Quayle, with powerful connections in Indiana—the head of the Indiana National Guard was a top-level newspaper editor who worked for his family—found a safe place in the Indiana Guard and yet managed without any inner conflict to hold a hawkish view of the war, a rare combination of both love and abstinence. In fact, it was barely noticed that Dick Cheney, the sitting secretary of defense, had not served in Vietnam though he also had been the perfect age to go and had rather casually told the *Washington Post*'s George Wilson, when asked about it, "I had other priorities in the sixties than military service."[4]

Indeed, that profound generational difference in terms of the attitudes toward their defining wars existed in the home of President George Bush himself. The elder Bush could not wait to sign up as a naval aviator in World War II. His oldest son, George W., like many privileged and well-connected young men, had, by contrast, found a haven in an Air National Guard unit, a place that was in at least the partial lee of the storm in the midsixties. Vietnam was simply a very different war in a different time, creating very different attitudes among the young men who were destined to become part of the leadership class. Those who had wrestled with the moral complexity of whether to serve were by 1992 no longer kids. They were, like Bill Clinton, well into their forties, and they had surveyed a large body of evidence that the war had been a monumental mistake. They were now an important part of the voting body politic—the demographic center, according to the actuarial tables. That meant there was a generation—or even two—of Americans even younger than candidate Clinton, to whom the debate about Vietnam had as much meaning and immediacy as a debate about how badly the British generals had wasted their troops during World War I, sending them again and again into mass assaults against German machine guns.

This profound generational change and therefore the change in issues showed up in the primaries. In New Hampshire, the Democratic candidate who was the early favorite and whose curriculum vitae looked good on paper, Bob Kerrey, former governor of Nebraska, now senator, never found his stride. Before New Hampshire, Kerrey was thought to be a nineties reincarnation of John Kennedy. He was bright and interesting and very attractive, ironic and quirky, never predictable and extremely popular with the Washington press corps. He was, it appeared, a genuine war hero, a navy SEAL who had won the Congressional Medal of Honor for his service in Vietnam, where he had lost a leg. He had won election as governor of a conservative state that did not normally elect Democrats, he had been a successful businessman, and he was a bachelor who dated an attractive movie star, Debra Winger. Or as his rival Bill Clinton had said about him somewhat enviously in one of the conversations with his girlfriend Gennifer Flowers, which she had taped, Kerrey had "all the Gary Hart/Hollywood money, and because he's single, looks like a movie star, won the Medal of Honor, and since he's single, nobody cares if he's screwing around."[5]

Kerrey was presumed to be the perfect Democratic candidate because he could reclaim the issue of patriotism, which had rested for so long with the Republicans. If he were nominated, the Republicans, as they had for a number of elections, would no longer have sole title to the flag. But Kerrey was a disaster in New Hampshire. He had undertaken the run largely because a number of more senior political figures in Washington, who seemed to know much more about this than he did, had looked at his qualifications and told him he ought to do it and would do well. He had no idea that, as one of his top aides said, "By running for the presidency in the modern era, he was leaving politics and entering the circus." Kerrey might have been an ideal candidate, but he lacked the requisite passion (or madness), the all-or-nothing glandular need to make a run for the White House. In New Hampshire, he was appalled by how little he liked campaigning for the presidency and what an extraordinary intrusion it was into his personal life, how little it seemed to be about substantive issues and how much it was about everything he detested in contemporary politics—the theater rather than the essence of governance. Day by day he grew increasingly puzzled about why he was there. Early in the campaign, his visit to a senior citizens' center in Concord had gone poorly. Afterward he returned to his van, obviously tired and somewhat discouraged. Even as someone shoved a microphone and a camera in his face, Kerrey turned to the reporters covering him and asked, "What the hell am I doing here?"

"You mean being in Concord, Senator?" one reporter responded.

"No, running for president—remind me of that."[6]

What the media (and certainly many of his party's leaders who were tired of the Democrats being portrayed as not loving the flag sufficiently) wanted from Bob Kerrey was to take his biography—his Vietnam War record, his heroism as a SEAL, and his Congressional Medal of Honor—and contrast it with Bill Clinton's biography. Obviously that matchup had a good deal more drama than a comparison of their respective health programs. But that was precisely what Kerrey did not want. He did not want to run for the presidency as a war hero, and if he had his misgivings about how Clinton had played the draft, he did not want it to be the defining issue of a presidential campaign. It was as if, for him, Vietnam was not only in the past, but it was then and this was now. Most important of all, it was personally painful, perhaps even sacred and not to be exploited. What he had done—the sacrifice, the loss, the comradeship, the loyalty, the pain, the darkness, and, not insignificantly, the love—was between him and those who had served with him, and it was not to be devalued by bartering it for political advantage. For there had been an earlier operation, one before he lost his leg, which still haunted Kerrey and his fellow SEALs. In February 1969 they had conducted a nighttime raid in an area that was completely controlled by the Vietcong and probably had been for three generations. There had been a firefight, and women and children had been killed, as Kerrey and others on his team remembered it. One member recalled it differently and claimed that the SEALs had rounded up the women and children and executed them. The rest of Kerrey's team recalled the events as he did, as something terrible and cruel that had happened in the darkness and fog of war. But it had always operated—the grimness of his own memory—as a caution when he spoke about the war, especially in political campaigns. Too many ghosts were already there.

There were the rare times when he was with his old buddies from the SEALs and they would sing the bitter antiwar Australian song "And the Band Played Waltzing Matilda." But those were private, not public moments, and they were most assuredly not to be manipulated for public consumption. He had gone to Vietnam, he had paid a high price, both physically and emotionally, and that was all the public needed to know; if it hungered for more, then something was very wrong with the system. Most of his staff pushed him hard to go after Clinton on the draft, especially after Kerrey had faltered in New Hampshire and all the candidates headed to the South for the next round of primaries, but Kerrey was determined that it would not be a defining issue.

Clinton, the all-time natural, took one look at Kerrey in action and knew that he had him, that somehow Kerrey's heart was not in it. That a man whose strength was precisely Clinton's weakness would not use it as an electoral weapon in New Hampshire was an early sign to Clinton that the political winds had changed and Vietnam as an overt issue might be less and less important. The press corps covering Clinton had in general accepted him at face value on his draft record and his lack of service; many members of it were roughly the same age, and they apparently liked him or at least saw him as the ablest candidate in the race, which was the same as liking him. In addition, their own relationship with Vietnam in most cases was just as distant as the candidate's. (On Valentine's Day, Billy Shore, Kerrey's chief of staff, irritated by what he thought was media softness on Clinton, wrote a brief valentine poem to the media: "Roses are red / Violets are blue / Clinton dodged the draft / And so did most of you.")

But not just the media turned away from Vietnam, thought Stan Greenberg, Clinton's pollster; it was the country itself. Greenberg was aware of the danger to Clinton from the draft issue and had carefully polled about it throughout the New Hampshire primary, meticulously scrutinizing opinions. From the start he had been relieved to see the degree to which the war was not an issue, even among focus groups with Vietnam veterans. It had little traction in most of the demographic samplings he was taking. Only a tiny number of baby boomers had actually served in the military, let alone gone to Vietnam, and among those younger than the boomers, the postboomers, the number was infinitesimal. Almost none of the people in these two groups wanted the issue of Vietnam reopened.

New Hampshire, nonetheless, turned into a brutal test for Clinton. Early on he did well, the ablest campaigner in an essentially weak field. In mid-January he was leading Paul Tsongas, who was from neighboring Massachusetts, by twelve points in a *Boston Globe* poll. Then the Gennifer Flowers story—an alleged affair with a young woman who had been an Arkansas state employee—broke in the tabloid *Star.* Clinton at first dismissed it, saying the report had been printed in a newspaper "that says Martians walk on earth and cows have human heads." But the story, added to a broad general awareness of Clinton's philandering—there had always, even among those who admired him, been talk that he had what was euphemistically called a zipper problem—did not go away. Moreover, he ended up making a specific denial of it ("the affair did not happen"), a departure from an earlier decision not to discuss the somewhat tainted aspect of his private life.

With that he began to slip in the polls, and at virtually the same time his draft record became an issue. It began with a detailed story in the *Wall Street Journal,* which went over what was by then relatively familiar ground. But the *Journal* story had a new twist. Colonel Eugene Holmes, the ROTC officer at the University of Arkansas who had enrolled Clinton in the Arkansas unit, was now saying that Clinton had manipulated the draft so that he did not serve. That was a major change. In the past Colonel Holmes had defended Clinton's record on the draft. The Clinton people thought of him as their first line of defense in this extremely touchy area, and they had often sent inquisitive reporters off to talk to the then quite friendly Colonel Holmes. Now Holmes had switched sides. That was bad news.

A few days later, things took a turn for the worse when Clinton's letter to Colonel Holmes, written some twenty-three years earlier, became public for the first time. Someone had handed a copy of it to Mark Halperin, a producer, and Jim Wooten, a correspondent for ABC. Holmes had befriended Clinton during the tumultuous period when he was at Oxford and was wrestling with his conscience about what would be the right thing to do about Vietnam. Holmes had enrolled him in the Arkansas ROTC unit while Clinton was still at Oxford. The original exchange between the two men had taken place at a moment when the question of receiving his draft notice was in no way theoretical. The timing of the draft notice now being released was also important. Clinton had received a place in the ROTC *after* receiving his draft notice, which meant entry in the unit was technically illegal, though for a time he denied this. At first, in the midst of the campaign, Clinton claimed he could not remember whether he had already received his draft notice when he started working the ROTC gambit, but later he came around and admitted that he had.

The presumption made when he first entered the ROTC under the guidance of Colonel Holmes was that he would finish his second year at Oxford, return home to Fayetteville, and enter law school and the ROTC at the same time. It appeared quite clear that, as often happened with National Guard units, which were *never* immune from local politics, the skids had been greased. For if Clinton was not exactly to the manner born, he was by the time he arrived at Oxford to the manner handsomely apprenticed and connected. Already quite active politically, he had powerful Arkansas benefactors on Senator J. William Fulbright's staff who were sponsoring him. Since appointments to National Guard units, particularly in the South, were always part of the political fabric, his connection to Colonel Holmes appeared to have been aided by influential friends in Fulbright's office, where Clinton had worked part-time.

So be it. Clinton was not the first bright, well-connected young man to find a home in the National Guard. But then the game had changed. In 1969, while Clinton was still at Oxford, the papers admitting him to the National Guard already being processed, President Nixon, in an attempt to defuse the antiwar movement and separate its leadership from the mainstream of American college kids, changed the rules governing the draft. When that happened, Clinton's game plan changed, too. On December 1, 1969, with the newly introduced lottery finally in place and in use for the first time since World War II, Clinton found himself with a number that was both literally and figuratively bulletproof—his birthday was the 311th day picked. Just two days after getting so magical a number, he had written Colonel Holmes, the man he had so artfully stroked to get into the ROTC unit, this time withdrawing from the slot Holmes had saved for him.

The letter was prototypically Clinton, reflecting both the best and the worst of him, charming, passionate, manipulative, wildly honest and deeply disingenuous, full of personal flattery for Holmes, and yet containing a serious critique of the war and what it was doing to a young, high-minded, almost pathologically ambitious twenty-three-year-old. In some ways parts of the letter spoke for a generation. Its tone of personal anguish was unmistakable. But at its core was Clinton's request to withdraw from the agreed-upon ROTC slot because, he now claimed, his original decision to join was unacceptable to him on moral grounds and he had no true interest in the ROTC. Liberated by the lottery from any fear of the draft, he was now resigning a safe ROTC slot he had almost surely received illicitly. The letter and the dazzling series of moves Clinton had put on poor, unsuspecting Colonel Holmes offered a fascinating insight into the man the country would get to know better and better in ensuing years. No one else was quite as smart as he was, he believed, and therefore he could manipulate people and somehow manage to get away with it.

In the end Clinton went into neither the army nor the ROTC. Clinton, David Maraniss later wrote, had "played the draft like a chess player." His draft record had surfaced on occasion in the past but had never been damaging in part because Colonel Holmes had defended him. Now, twenty-three years later, when he was embroiled in a difficult primary race in New Hampshire, with his entire political future at stake and already shaken by the Gennifer Flowers accusations, his letter withdrawing from the ROTC slot, so full of contradictions, had found its way into the public domain. The timing could not have been worse. Clinton's approval rating in the polls, which had once been as high as thirty-seven, was slipping badly and was now under twenty. Paul Tsongas was comfortably in the lead. Jim Wooten of ABC was absolutely sure the ROTC gambit had been preceded by a draft notice, though he could not prove it. But he had not put the story on the air immediately, seeking first to authenticate it and then get the governor's reaction. Wooten went to the tiny airport in Keene, New Hampshire, where the Clintons were to arrive shortly after spending several days in Little Rock, and handed his copy of the letter to Clinton, his wife, and his top political aides, James Carville, Paul Begala, and George Stephanopoulos. Clinton saw the letter and looked ashen, Wooten remembered. The five immediately excused themselves and held a high-level strategy meeting in the ladies' room of the airport.

At this point Carville's role was critical. He was both talented and combative, a student of the modern high-technology eye-for-an-eye, or better still one-eye-of-ours-for-two-of-theirs, school of politics. This campaign, he had vowed earlier, would not be a repeat of the murderous Bush-Dukakis campaign; the Clinton people would fire back and they would fire back immediately. Carville was also the least conventional of the Clinton political people. He always trusted his own reactions and experiences, and they were very different from those of most mainstream liberal Democratic advisers. His roots were among the very people with whom the Democrats had done so poorly in recent years, good-old-boy, flag-loving, blue-collar (and often redneck) Southern patriots, who had become Reagan Democrats. Reading Clinton's letter he was struck by its humanity, its anguish, and the degree to which it spoke, in its passion, confusion, and, above all, doubt, for the young men Carville knew of his generation—not the least of all himself.

For the Carvilles of Baton Rouge, Louisiana, were old-fashioned patriots. James Carville's grandmother had been a five-star mother during World War II, four sons and a son-in-law serving in the armed forces at the same time. James had been born in 1944 at Fort Benning, Georgia, where his father was stationed during that war. Upon graduation from Louisiana State in June 1966, he did what young men of his background always did. He went into the service as a marine lieutenant, eager to get to Vietnam. All his friends had gone, but to his consternation he served stateside. That bothered him greatly for a time, that he had missed the big show and was perhaps not as much a man as his pals, who might someday hold his lack of combat experience against him. But instead, as they began to return home, he learned something surprising. They thought he was the lucky one. They had by and large hated the war and congratulated him on his good fortune, which until then he had thought of as his shame. His failure to serve had in no way separated him from the defining experience of his generation, he discovered; for a number of his close friends it had been a negative experience and he had been spared it. Carville believed a serious political lesson was to be drawn from that. Now as he read his candidate's letter, the doubts he saw reflected the feelings of his friends, those who had gone and those who had not gone, as well as his own. They were generational doubts. In fact, Carville wished he could have written that letter himself when he was twenty-three years old. He believed that it was a classic example of something that people in the media and Washington often got wrong, the importance of the role of doubt in how ordinary people felt about complicated issues.

So as he huddled with the candidate in this impromptu Keene airport strategy session, Carville spoke forcefully and with a sure sense of how many of the young men of his generation would react to the letter. Wooten, waiting outside, could hear him, emotional and emphatic in the best of circumstances, shouting at the candidate inside the ladies' room in language that was distinctly Carvillian: "Goddamnit, Governor, this letter is your mother-fucking friend! This can work for you! You've got to distribute it!" The conference was brief and Clinton emerged, the color back in his face, and said, yes, the letter was his, and then he began a period of waffling with Wooten and others about whether his draft notice had preceded his signing on for the ROTC unit. Wooten, some ten years older than Clinton, born of a generation where things like this mattered greatly and candidates always emphasized their service in the nation's wars, was sure that it was a big-time story and an extremely damaging one, potentially the end of the bright career of an otherwise gifted young politician. In their brief meeting, Clinton assured Wooten that he had not yet received his draft notice when he applied for the ROTC. It was, of course, a lie. "Governor, why don't I believe you on this?" Wooten asked. "Because no one wants to believe me," Clinton answered, then added, "Jim, one of the reasons that both Hillary and I love you is because you've always been so fair with us." Wooten thought the story might be a campaign killer, and he was extremely careful in checking it out; he wanted no details to be wrong.

His exceptional fairness cost him a scoop. *Nightline,* another wing of ABC News, got a copy of the letter and beat him on the story. Two days later, Clinton appeared on *Nightline* with Ted Koppel to talk about the letter; the strategy was now clear: he was going to brazen it out. Koppel, the most talented live interviewer on television, was at his best, but Clinton was simply brilliant—he was following the Carville line. They had worked out ground rules with Koppel; Koppel, not Clinton, would read the letter on a split screen, with Clinton looking on sagely. It worked. Clinton managed to stiff-arm Koppel and held turf; he had made the issue the war, rather than his reaction to it. He had, in the process, sacrificed his truthfulness to one of the best and most respected reporters in America, and though he won a short-range victory, his lies to Wooten became a cornerstone of why so many other journalists never completely trusted him again. But he had dodged a bullet and survived for another day.

At almost the same time, Carville was busy taking out full-page ads in various New England newspapers, reprinting the letter in its entirety, and within a day or two Wooten realized that he had been wrong about the importance of the letter and the draft. Clinton and the people around him, Wooten decided, had sensed something about the country and its changes before he had. It was like a wake-up call. If there were contradictions in Clinton's record on Vietnam, they were not that different from the contradictions throughout the country. Clinton, Wooten realized, represented both the strengths and weaknesses of postwar, baby-boomer America, an era in which success came largely without sacrifice. Clinton represented more than a mere ideological gap with the existing administration. Rather, what Wooten was covering and watching was more like a generational changing of the guard. The generation he knew best, and the rigidity of whose values he had often been at tension point with, those Americans of a distinctly more Calvinist era, who had been through both the Depression and World War II, and whose lives had been marked both by sacrifice and lower expectations, were no longer the force they had once been. Replacing them was something very different, a younger, infinitely more successful generation of Americans, surely better educated, whose talent produced not merely higher levels of accomplishment but equally high expectations. Wooten, then in his midfifties, felt himself at tension point with them, too; it was as if success had all come too easily for them, and worse, they had too little respect for the past. They believed their uncommon good fortune was entirely the product of their own hard work and they owed little to those who had gone before them. Like many Americans, Wooten could feel the new political and cultural lines cut through him; he might be politically more sympathetic to the ideas of Clinton and the younger generation, but culturally more sympathetic to those being replaced. The country, Wooten decided, was different now; it wanted to forgive a politician like Clinton because it wanted to forgive itself.

The draft issue turned out to be one that New Hampshire did not seem to care passionately about. Clinton began to close on Paul Tsongas. People liked the way he fought back. Though Tsongas went on to carry the state—as a kind of cross-the-state-line favorite son—Clinton was the real winner, because Tsongas was unlikely to travel well elsewhere. Clinton had hung in the wind for a moment and then come back to do exceptionally well. Whatever else was unknown about him as the primary season advanced, one critical bit of information was now available to the general public and to working politicians and journalists: Bill Clinton could take a hit and keep coming. In that he resembled no one so much as the man whom many of his devotees considered his polar opposite, Richard Nixon. Other men might have pulled out of the race immediately, deciding that whatever office they were seeking was not worth the continuing public dissection. Instead, Clinton seemed to reach back and find new sources of strength.

Whatever the accusations against Clinton, particularly the Gennifer Flowers stories, if the public did not like him, it liked his critics even less, and his real accusers, among the ever more predatory press corps that pursued him on the issue. As a result he was beginning to be perceived by the general public as under assault first and foremost by the media. The press, of course, is never popular, even when it is doing its best work—covering a dangerous foreign assignment or the civil rights movement—because it often brings unpalatable but necessary news to ordinary people.

But this was, given the changing nature of the media, the increased power of television, and the almost compulsive appetite for tabloidlike scandal brought on by the coming of cable television, a very different press corps, chasing a very different kind of story. Moreover, the longer the story went on and the larger the posse of pursuing media people grew, the less popular and the less innocent the press corps became in the public mind. Its members, gathered together outside an airport gate or in front of a high school where the candidate was to speak and, shouting the most brazen of questions, looked like sharks disguised as humanoids, hounding Clinton on an issue that seemed to many Americans private rather than public information.

To some of the more senior people in network television, who had grown up in an age when things like this were not considered legitimate stories, the fierce impulse for tabloid-style reporting was unwanted. They might finally accept that these stories were already in the public domain and therefore legitimate to cover, but the frenzy with which they were pursued, the disproportionate emphasis on them rather than on other stories that might reveal true *political* character, was troublesome. Yet they went ahead anyway; they might as well do it, they finally decided, because everyone else was doing it. "The crack cocaine of American journalism," Carville, never short of sound bites himself, once shrewdly called the Gennifer Flowers story and other similar stories that came after it. "You could," he said, "see the need in their faces, even the top print people. They would be sitting there telling you, 'I don't want to do this' [to write about Ms. Flowers], but then you'd look in their faces and see the hunger, the desperation to do it, and the fact that they were loving it."

These stories, thought Carville, himself a shrewd student of the new media game, connected now to career; they got reporters onto the myriad new cable talk shows, and that, in turn, with a bit of luck might lead to lectureships and books. But what the public understood in some visceral way, he added, was that the candidates were not necessarily the ones lowering the quality of discourse in a campaign. It was the media themselves, draped more often than not in their own false piety. The justification for the press covering other important stories—the people's right to know—was not in the minds of many people a powerful rationale in a case like this. About some aspects of a candidate's personal life (as of some aspects of their own personal life) they were not so sure that the public had a right to know. People looked at the media examining the candidate and rightfully wondered what it would be like if the media stars themselves, instead of the candidate, were being scrutinized, and how much hunger there would be for news of their private lives.

The scenes from New Hampshire of the governor surrounded by a horde of television reporters, all of them bearing in on him and shouting at him about his personal life—*"Governor, did you sleep with Gennifer Flowers? Governor, did you do it?"*—were ugly. At Ms. Flowers's own press conference at the Waldorf-Astoria in New York, carried live on CNN, another crowd of reporters shouted questions at a young woman who seemed way in over her head (Had Clinton worn a condom? someone asked). Yet accusations of infidelity did not damage Clinton that much in the long run. There was simply too much of it in the media; it violated in the most basic way what many Americans felt was a sense of fair play. Moreover, it was being done by highly paid media people who themselves were influential in society, but whose own personal lives, on occasion equally messy, were permitted to remain private. The Clinton pollsters, appalled at first by the nature of these accusations and worried that they might be a potentially fatal wound, were impressed by what they found in their focus groups: that people quickly came to dislike what the media people were doing to the candidate. Instead, they liked the way that the candidate, a big man, seemed to lean into the media physically during these impromptu encounters— not backing down a bit.

What happened to Clinton when he took the worst of the hits aimed at him was fascinating. He became more committed, more centered, those around him decided. This was Clinton at his best, more focused on his purpose than ever. That was when he showed his true strengths and went from the genial, ever-agreeable young Arkansas governor who was so eager to please everyone to the man who gradually came into focus in the White House, a tough, shrewd, immensely skillful politician capable of making hard decisions, willing, if need be, to jettison almost anything and anyone, no matter how old the friendship, in behalf of his own interests. Empathetic he might seem in his normal public mode, but cold and tough he could be if his political future was at stake. When his back was to the wall, he became the total politician engaged in the one thing he excelled at more than anything else—survival.

CHAPTER TWELVE

The Serb attacks on the parts of Croatia that Milosevic orchestrated and the early successes were simply the first round in what was to become a brutal fratricidal war. Milosevic had never coveted Croatia that much; certainly it was nice to have the Krajina, but what he really wanted was a large slice of Bosnia and perhaps, eventually, the capacity to dominate Kosovo, place it under Serb, not Yugoslav, hegemony, and eventually resettle it with Serbs. But Bosnia at first had a higher priority. With Croatia and Slovenia having left the federation, the Bosnians now wanted their turn. In late February 1992, as the federation broke down, a referendum was held in Bosnia about whether to seek independence. The resident Serbs, who represented about 30 percent of the population, boycotted the election, but roughly 99 percent of those who voted wanted to become a new nation.

A few weeks later, on April 6, the European Community recognized Bosnia as an independent nation. The Serbs celebrated the occasion by shelling Sarajevo, the beautiful multiethnic city that was the capital of Bosnia. Eleven people were killed in the first day's fighting. A day later, on April 7, 1992, the United States also recognized Bosnia. Thus Bosnia as a crisis point, a nation that would undergo some of the worst genocidal crimes seen in Europe since World War II and would therefore challenge the West's view of its morality, came into existence. What was happening there would only slowly penetrate the American political consciousness. At the time it all began, George Bush was still feeling some glow from his past successes. Even the Republican Party's own pollsters, with their increasingly negative reports, had not yet shaken the existing White House optimism. In the other party, Bill Clinton was just beginning to pull away from his competitors in the Democratic primaries. Sarajevo, surrounded by Serb forces and under a relentless heavy-weapons attack, seemed a world apart.

To many in the West, Sarajevo was the showplace of the country, a symbol of the Yugoslavia that might have been. In this sophisticated urban venue, the educational level was higher than in the rest of the country, pluralism seemed to work, and ethnic tensions were largely dormant. More than a quarter of the marriages in Bosnia were ethnically mixed. Of the Bosnian population, 44 percent was Muslim, 31 percent Serb, and 17 percent Croatian. It had in the past been something of an advertisement for the pluralism of the larger nation, and Sarajevo had been greatly admired by foreigners during the 1984 Winter Olympics. Rarely had the citizens of an Olympic city so favorably impressed visitors from other countries. Sarajevo represented, as Edward Vulliamy noted, the exact opposite of the Milosevic and Tudjman vision of a nation, theirs, of course, conceived in racial separatism and ethnic hatred.

If the Croatians had been ill-prepared for the Serb onslaught against them, then the Bosnians were in even worse shape. The Croats had a long coastline through which it would be relatively easy to smuggle in arms, and they had a great many protector nations in Europe, particularly the Germans and the Austrians. Bosnia was landlocked and, as an essentially Muslim nation in Europe, relatively devoid of friends in the immediate region. The Bosnian leadership had behaved curiously without guile, seeking independence without making any military preparations for it. Both Serbs and Croats were hostile to Bosnian independence, and both had a deep-seated hatred for the Bosnians far greater than the feelings of Serb about Croat and vice versa, even though both were then fighting each other. When a reporter asked the deputy president, Ejup Ganic, what Bosnia's preparations were for defending itself, he answered, "We are just talking, talking, talking. When you are face-to-face with a wolf, the only option is to work with it, until it becomes a pet."[1] The Serbs, needless to say, did not make good pets.

If the Bosnians had not been ready for the assault upon their territorial integrity, the Serbs were more than ready. In early 1992, with the fighting over on the Croatian front and the entire Krajina under Serb control, the Yugoslav National Army began to move its forces, particularly its armored and artillery units, from Croatia to Bosnia. As part of the charade being played out, Milosevic had created a Bosnian Serb army, with Serb officers serving elsewhere in the JNA quickly transferred to it. It was in all ways a de facto part of the JNA, and at the beginning of hostilities, the so-called Bosnian Serbs had a well-equipped armed force of ninety thousand men at their disposal, in addition to a number of exceptionally violent paramilitary units ready to undertake what would be unspeakable and systematic human cruelties.

When the Serbs surrounded Sarajevo with their artillery, it was like shooting fish in a barrel. The first full day of heavy, lethal bombardment aimed at Sarajevo was April 21, 1992. It became in the weeks and months that followed a civilized European city under siege, where people tried to live normal lives while constantly dodging Serb artillery fire. Slowly and quite systematically, the Serbs squeezed out every aspect of life in what began to seem like a doomed city. It was a stunning sight: an army inflicting so much damage on a much-loved city largely without defenses. For every round fired by the badly underarmed Bosnians in their own defense, Edward Vulliamy noted, 180 were fired into the city by the Serbs. By the end of June of 1992, the Bosnian government reported that seventy-two hundred people were known dead and some thirty thousand more were missing.[2]

Food and water disappeared, people slept in their cellars for protection. There were so many dead that the local cemeteries soon ran out of space and many bodies were buried in gardens. The hospital was at least as much a morgue as a medical center, and international doctors working there soon had to warn the local doctors to start burning the remains of the dead. The problem of sewage grew more desperate all the time. The Serbs soon cut the gas lines. As the mordant local joke went, "What is the difference between Sarajevo and Auschwitz?" The answer: "In Auschwitz at least they had gas." Two Serb attacks in particular were memorable. During one of them, on May 27, 1992, artillerymen hit a large number of Bosnians waiting in a breadline in the city center. Twenty people were killed and an estimated 160 were wounded. A month later the Serbs hit another line, this time of people waiting to take money out of one of the city's banks. Twenty-one people were killed and 135 wounded.

The world watched Sarajevo with great fascination and in horror. Yet in some ways the Serbs were not unhappy to have attention fastened on Sarajevo, where they had the city completely bottled up and could squeeze the population or ease the pressure when the West and the United Nations complained particularly loudly. But the real campaign was taking place elsewhere in small villages in Bosnia where, largely unscrutinized by Western journalists, a well-organized campaign of ethnic cleansing was under way. The Serb irregulars were driving the Bosnians out of their villages, taking their property, and transporting the men to camps from which they were often never seen again. While the West focused on the siege of Sarajevo, Bosnia was disappearing off the map.

Long after the campaign was over, one of its architects, Mikola Koljevic, an intellectual leader of the Bosnian Serbs, told Ed Vulliamy that Sarajevo had been nothing but theater designed to take the West's eyes off the real campaign, which was the disappearance of Muslims, particularly Muslim men, from countless villages. He chided Vulliamy and all other Westerners for their innocence about what was happening: "It amazes me that you all took so long to get the point. Poor Sarajevo! That was all you could think about. The crossroads of Europe! None of you had ever been on holiday in Trnopoljie [a small town brutally cleansed]." Then Vulliamy remembered that Koljevic began to laugh, pleased that they had so deftly snookered the press corps and the world.

Some American witnesses were just beginning to sense that Sarajevo, for all its horrors, was the equivalent of what in football is called the draw play, a fake to draw attention away from the real purpose of the play. In the summer of 1992, even as the presidential campaign was just beginning to gear up, one of the aspiring candidates for the Democratic Party's foreign policy team, Richard Holbrooke, made a trip to Yugoslavia and, in time, to Bosnia. He became the first member of the putative Democratic national security team to have a personal stake in the terrible crisis unfolding there. Holbrooke went at the suggestion of Winston Lord, an old friend who earlier had struggled with the country's Asian policies. Lord was now the vice chairman of the International Rescue Committee, and he had suggested that Holbrooke go on a fact-finding mission for the IRC, which was one of the most influential of the various refugee organizations. A few weeks later, Holbrooke left for Yugoslavia in the company of Bob deVecchi, the IRC's president, and Sheppie Abramowitz, a forceful and effective person who had been drawn into refugee work when her husband was the American ambassador to Thailand and a flood of Vietnamese and Cambodian refugees had found their way to what was effectively her neighborhood.

During the trip deVecchi took Holbrooke from Zagreb to Banja Luka in Bosnia. It had been an eerie day. The IRC team had arrived to the accompaniment of constant Serb machine-gun fire, and their driver politely asked Holbrooke to stop videotaping local scenes in order to make them less of a target for the Serb militia. That night they had drinks at the local hotel bar and overheard a Serb woman say in the most casual way that Muslims made good lampshades. They spent the night at the hotel, and the next morning they were intrigued by an odd sight. Outside a very ordinary building near their hotel, deVecchi noticed a long line of people standing with their suitcases.

These people, many of whom were obviously tired and dejected, and some of whom were actually crying, were waiting their allotted turn. In time, they entered the building for a few minutes, then came out and got on a bus. DeVecchi made sure that Holbrooke witnessed the scene. They checked out what was happening and found they were watching nothing less than what was now being called ethnic cleansing. Muslims who had lived in this town all their life were going into Serb headquarters and signing away their property in exchange for what was alleged to be a guarantee of safe passage to Croatia. The building even had a name: Office for Population Resettlement and Property Exchange. The property the Muslims signed away would be given to Serbs, either Serbs who lived there or were imported from other parts of the country into the region specifically for Serbianization. It was all strictly legal.

Holbrooke learned that this procedure had been expedited by Serb irregulars who had already worked the town, killing some Muslims, abducting others, threatening the lives of those remaining if they did not sign over their property and leave. Some of the Bosnian Muslims were stoic about it. Others were less so. All were leaving the land where their families had lived for centuries to undergo a passage, unwanted, without real guarantees of safety, to another country where they might not be welcome. DeVecchi, watching Holbrooke, thought he was overwhelmed by the spectacle. It would be hard not to be. On his return to America, Holbrooke had not only written op-ed pieces about the mounting crisis but he had called his old friend Strobe Talbott, then a senior *Time* foreign affairs writer and a close friend of the Democratic candidate Bill Clinton, to tell him that Bosnia was on its way to becoming a horrendous tragedy. It might be "George Bush and Larry Eagleburger's revenge if Clinton wins," Holbrooke said.[3]

Not since Vietnam, Holbrooke later wrote, had he seen a problem so difficult or compelling. His first op-ed piece on Bosnia for *Newsweek* was unusually prophetic. "By its inadequate reaction so far, the United States and, to an even greater extent, the European Community may be undermining not only the dreams of a post–Cold War 'common European House' but also laying the seeds for another era of tragedy." He urged the end to an arms embargo that punished the Bosnians but not the Serbs and wrote that every day the killing went on, the chances of preventing a long-term tragedy decreased. What would the West be doing now, he asked, if the religious convictions of the combatants were reversed and a Muslim force was trying to destroy 2 million beleaguered Christians and Jews? In addition to his op-ed piece, Holbrooke began to push the idea of a proactive policy with friends of his who were close to candidate Bill Clinton.

In fact, the rest of the world was not sitting by idly. It tried to stop the hostilities, but from the start it moved weakly and inadequately. Under United Nations security resolutions, it first sent troops to monitor the Croat-Serb ceasefire, and then in 1992, as the violence moved to Bosnia, it dispatched even more troops as a humanitarian peacekeeping force to stop the fighting and suffering there. What it did was probably well intentioned but surely inadequate, and it represented a tragic underestimation of the violence in the hearts of the aggressors.

For, given the sheer brutality of what was taking place in Bosnia, given the countless areas now under assault, and given the weak mandate of the UN troops, known as UNPROFOR, United Nations Protection Force, the United Nations ended up being more in the fig-leaf business than the security business. It was supposed, as one diplomat said, to keep the peace where there was no peace and where one side, exceptionally well-armed, had no intention of keeping the peace. It was supposed to be impartial in a conflict between violent aggressors and obvious victims. Its soldiers, some of whom behaved with considerable dignity and courage, and many of whom did not, were almost always outnumbered and underarmed, and they never knew whether they should return fire. If they did, they might move from being impartial peacekeepers to armed participants, and not only would the mighty Serbs turn on them, but their superiors at UN headquarters in New York would be furious. Again and again, they were damned if they did and damned if they didn't. In all, UNPROFOR turned out to be a horror, representing not so much the weakness of the United Nations, though the UN command had little to be proud of in the Balkans, but the weaknesses and indecisiveness of the member nations. The Europeans who had thought they could deal with the problem were now overwhelmed by the sheer fury and cruelty of the Serb assault, while the Americans still resisted military intervention.

Poor Bosnia. On the geopolitical Richter scale, the inevitable conflicts and internal battles of the Balkans had not at first seemed to be sufficient cause for the use of American troops and the risk of American lives. Only when the genocidal actions became so obvious, and the issue changed from geopolitical to moral *and* geopolitical, did the attention of America become engaged. "My favorite quote is from Hegel," said a distinguished professor of international relations at Princeton, Dick Ullman, who later served as a consultant to the State Department in Policy Planning and wrote about these events, "and it is, 'Minerva's owl flies at dusk.' That is, the most important signs that will warn you of important issues still to come happen too late—by the time we know enough to act, it's often likely to be very late."[4]

The Serb assault against Bosnia had been very deliberately planned and organized. In no way was it random. Milosevic and the Serbs were well prepared for the assault. In June 1991, six months before Yugoslavia disintegrated, Milosevic had lunched with the ambassadors from the European Community and had warned them that if the country broke up, he would carve out a new Serbia. Slovenia meant nothing to him, he said, and it could go, and perhaps Macedonia, too. But the Serb-populated regions of Croatia, Bosnia, and Montenegro would become part of this new country, "a fatherland of all Serbs," as he had put it.

Regrettably, the UNPROFOR troops played right into Milosevic's hands, involuntarily helping legitimize (at least momentarily) his territorial gains. They were like manna from heaven for him, giving him extra protection against his greatest vulnerability, the possibility that the West, choosing a low-cost use of maximum force, would strike out against him with NATO airpower. Instead they had become potential hostages, completely exposed, whom Milosevic could easily take prisoner as he kept moving toward his goal of a Greater Serbia. They were always there, ready to be plucked in case the Americans threatened the use of airpower, a gift chip made of platinum for him. The alliance against him had a fatal flaw. The European nations, however inadequately, had placed troops on the ground, while the Americans, with far greater technological weaponry at their disposal, were unwilling to send any ground troops. The West's policy was thus bastardized from the start, a signal of the tensions between the Americans and the Europeans, and the uncertainty of the Americans about playing a full internationalist role now that the easy enemy of communism had disappeared off the map. The question that events in Bosnia raised again and again was how internationalist America really was. It was a monopoly superpower, but was it truly internationalist? That was not an easy question to answer.

No one had a better sense of how to play the divisions between his enemies than Milosevic. Brilliant, visionary, and farsighted he might not be, but he had an unerring ability to spot the weaknesses of his enemies. He knew how to probe for their frailties and how to exploit any vulnerability he discovered. He knew how to disassociate himself from many of his odious deeds. Ugly genocidal incidents? Violations of agreed-upon safe areas? That was the Bosnian Serbs, he would say, and he had little control over them; they were a separate nation. So a cruel and prolonged charade began in which the Serbs initiated assaults upon the Muslims, and the West reacted always a little too late and always a little too weakly.

It became, for a time, a wonderful war for the Serbs. The people they were fighting were always underarmed. The UNPROFOR forces had proved to be an almost perfect instrument for the Serbs, too weak to resist them, but a valuable asset because they offered an inviting opportunity for hostages, thus negating the dreaded potential of U.S. (or NATO) airpower. The UN command was notoriously weak, and because of all the divisions among the great powers, there were simply too many voices and too many internal political differences to stop the Serbs. The early months of Serb aggression took place largely without resistance.

There was an animal shrewdness to all the Serb moves. They were able to push just hard enough to get what they wanted without pushing too hard and thereby enraging the more powerful NATO nations. When a momentary crisis of conscience occurred in the West, they would sense it and pull back, waiting for the right moment to push again. Even their military tactics had that same animal cunning. They would encircle a town, bring up their artillery, and pound away, exhausting and terrifying the Muslims inside the besieged spot. Then they would make a probe, a little tentative for fear that the UNPROFOR forces might actually retaliate this time or someone might call in a NATO air strike. If there was no Western response, then more emboldened than ever, with more swagger than ever, they would attack again. In the beginning it was a wonderful war.

CHAPTER THIRTEEN

The United States was going to sit this one out and let the Europeans handle it. Nothing highlighted that policy quite so clearly as an incident that took place in the late spring of 1992 at the time when Sarajevo was being systematically shelled. Richard Johnson, the State Department desk officer for Yugoslavia, was probably at the exact fulcrum in the department between the dissenters at the lower level and the upper-level figures who wanted to sustain the status quo. Johnson heard that the people in the national security world— years later he was not sure whether it was the NSA or the CIA—who did the satellite imagery not only had uncommonly good photos of what the Serbs were doing at Sarajevo, they also had excellent—and precise—photos of the Serb gun positions there. This kind of satellite technology was a uniquely American marvel; we did it better than anyone else in the world, and it had proven exceptionally valuable during the Gulf War.

The connection had been made through INR, the bureau of Intelligence and Research, which was State's own mini-CIA. A briefing by the imagery experts was set up in the State Department building. Invitations were sent out up to the deputy assistant secretary level. On the scheduled day, Johnson gathered himself together and went to the briefing. He was the only person from State who attended; that of itself was revealing, as if there were a need *not* to know. The briefing lasted roughly an hour and a half. The satellite photos were devastating; they showed about ninety-five Serb artillery and antiaircraft emplacements. One of the things that struck both the briefer and Johnson was how brazen the Serbs were. The guns were neither camouflaged nor given even the slightest physical protection—no bunkers protecting them, no sandbag walls built up. The briefer, having been through the Gulf War, was quite surprised by how exposed the Serb gun positions were.

Johnson asked the briefer if the guns would be difficult to take out and he answered not at all. Based on what had happened in the Gulf War, he said, it would be simple; it would take at best a day or a day and a half for American airplanes to destroy them. The briefing over, Johnson wrote a one-page memo to Tom Niles, the assistant secretary for European and Canadian affairs, describing what he had learned and how easy it would be to obliterate the guns of Sarajevo. He did not hear back on it. Instead his immediate boss, Mike

Habib, who had been out of town when the briefing took place, rapped Johnson's knuckles for having sent the memo, scolding him for trespassing outside the proper boundaries of State and venturing into territory that belonged to the military.

Milosevic, not surprisingly, quickly became aware of what the West was *not* going to do. It had not come to the rescue of Vukovar and Dubrovnik, so it was unlikely to come to the aid of Bosnia either. In 1993, David Owen, his peacekeeping mission in tatters, was accused at a meeting in New York of acting as an appeaser, as Neville Chamberlain, representing the Western powers, had appeased Hitler at Munich before World War II. Angered by the accusation, Owen had answered coldly, referring to what had happened in late 1991 in Vukovar, which had been subjected to a brutal siege and had fallen to the Serbs a month before Christmas, "Munich was last year."[1]

If for a variety of political reasons the official American government sources were unwilling to report the truth of the genocide in Bosnia, the role of the press inevitably became far more important, and as in Vietnam, when the government was in denial about military failures, reporters in the field in Bosnia linked up with more junior members of the bureaucracy. What senior Western diplomats were learning from their intelligence sources and from representatives of nongovernmental organizations (NGOs), they were quite content to keep secret because of the enormous disparity between the horrors that were being committed and the impotence of their response. But at the same time, a handful of Western journalists began to pursue the story actively. Roy Gutman, the *Newsday* reporter who was by then relatively well advanced in his personal reeducation about the Serbs, virtually stumbled onto what were the worst atrocities in Europe since those of the Third Reich. The timing was intriguing; Gutman's first major piece on the cruelties inflicted on the Bosnian Muslims by the Serbs ran on July 3, 1992, just as the United States was gearing up full-time for an election campaign. Gutman was beginning to uncover evidence of genocidal crimes at precisely the moment when the incumbent Bush administration, already criticized for being more concerned with foreign policy than domestic issues, was preoccupied by an increasingly difficult reelection drive.

Almost from the start, Gutman's reporting had been well ahead of the curve. In early July, one of his stories on the deportation of Muslims from Bosnia to Hungary bore a particularly prophetic headline: "Ethnic Cleansing: Yugoslavs Try to Deport 1,800 Muslims to Hungary." That was just the beginning. Within a few days he got an emotional phone call from one of the Muslim leaders he had met earlier in Banja Luka: "Please try to come here. There is a lot of killing. They are shipping Muslim people through Banja Luka in cattle cars. Last night there were twenty-five train wagons for cattle crowded with women, old people, and children. They were so frightened. In the name of humanity please come." With that Gutman managed to get to Banja Luka, where he heard reports of concentration camps set up by the Serbs for Muslims in northern Bosnia, the worst of them at a place called Omarska, which was an open iron-mine pit north of Banja Luka. The stories he heard were terrible, and there was good reason to take them seriously; he could vouch for a number of the people he was talking to. "All the grass has been eaten by the people," one source told him. "Every day in Omarska between twelve and sixteen people die. . . . Two-thirds of them are living under open skies. It is like an open pit. When it rains, many of them are up to their knees in mud."

Gutman could not get to Omarska—the Serbs said they could not guarantee his safety—but a Serb official offered him another trip to a prisoner-of-war camp in a place called Manjaca. Gutman and his photographer and interpreter went there, and again the images—this time of emaciated men with shaved heads—were hauntingly similar to those from Nazi Germany. On August 2, *Newsday* published Gutman's story on Omarska under the headline "There Is No Food, There Is No Air." It was the most damning account yet of the new culture of genocide. "The corpses pile up. There is no food. There is no air to breathe. No medical care. Even the grass around the pit has been completely clawed away," he quoted one relief agency official as saying. Two days later, Gutman filed another story about the mass deportations of Muslims in railroad cars. "There was no food, no water, and no fresh air. There was no toilet, just holes in the floor, piled high with excrement." A number of people, children and old people, had died on the trains, he quoted an eyewitness as saying. The eyewitness spoke of seeing the people packed in the train like cattle, their hands visible through the tiny ventilation holes. "It was like the Jews being deported to Auschwitz," said a Muslim official who had witnessed it. The headline over his story said it all: "Like Auschwitz." Under it was the subhead "Serbs Pack Muslims into Freight Cars." The Muslim men who were at Omarska and other camps weren't idly chosen, since little about this campaign was idly done. They were the elite of these Muslim towns, the political leaders, the police officials, the doctors, the businessmen, and the teachers. Many of them would never be seen again.

Now there were witnesses in the West to the catastrophe, and the lingering sense of indecision in Washington and in European capitals eventually created a complicated new political constituency in America. This constituency was different from those that had preceded it in recent foreign policy debates, no longer divided by traditional ideological bias, but instead driven by a memory that connected these events to the atrocities of the Nazis and therefore demanded that other nations ask themselves what their larger purpose was. What was happening in Bosnia began to crystallize, however slowly, into a new foreign policy issue, one that, if it failed to meet the standard national-security definition for American involvement, obviously met a more complicated new moral test involving a great nation's self-definition, and one that recalled memories of a previous failure on the part of Western leaders to act in time to stop genocide.

It was interesting, Gutman thought years later, that with all the diplomatic services of the developed nations involved, with all their intelligence services on the case, and with all the NGOs with roots in the West able to report on the tragedy in Bosnia, it took reporters working in the field to break the story. This was the age of satellite spy cameras, he liked to point out, and there were at least one hundred Serb concentration camps in Bosnia. So the claim that there were no photos of what was happening readily available to Western intelligence agencies was laughable. A rich, powerful nation could easily have this kind of information at its fingertips. If Washington officials did not want to know about it, it was for a good reason: to know about it and not to act was a profound embarrassment. Therefore, for as long as possible, that is, for much of 1992, it was better not to know.

Gutman understood from the beginning that this was going to be a tough sell for most American newspapers. In the past, the easy button to push for a foreign correspondent had always been the Cold War: good anticommunists struggling with bad communists. Or if on occasion fewer moral distinctions existed between the two forces as they contested each other in the third world, then at least editors and readers could be reassured that the contest was a part of the larger East-West confrontation and give it decent play. For there was no doubt that any kind of confrontation with the communists (or at least the leftists) was the mother's milk of foreign reporting over more than forty years, with an unspoken assumption that the communists were the forces of darkness. It was not that the Balkans story lacked evil. Quite the reverse. Evil obviously abounded. But it was evil without a larger context and without the dramatic framework that most top bureaucrats in Washington, people on the Hill, and senior news executives at home had been trained to recognize. The form of evil Gutman was writing about did not fit the preconception of evil that existed in the minds of many of the people he was writing for—a definition created by over forty years of the Cold War.

The lack of television coverage also made it more difficult for print reporters to get the story of Bosnia to American homes. In an earlier time, print had defined news stories, thereby setting the agenda, and network television had broadcast them to the mass audience. But that had ended in the late seventies, probably with the Iran hostage story. Now not only was foreign news in decline—the Vietnam War had disillusioned many people about the nature of foreign involvements—but the country simply felt less threatened; and the networks were emphasizing domestic stories, which were presumed to be more important to viewers than foreign news. Equally important, the networks, feeling their ascending power and influence compared with print, were beginning to operate on norms of their own. The gravitas of a story that normally defined elite print coverage meant less and less to the new generation of executive producers. Pictures—images—meant more and more. Replicating the *New York Times* or the *Washington Post* with a televised version of their front-page stories was now considered boring. Going for high-voltage action shots was more exciting, even if the action shots often meant little.

Other than a flash of interest in the siege of Sarajevo, television did not cover events in Bosnia with any great intensity. This absence of network coverage meant that the government did not have to respond to the isolated or episodic stories carried primarily by elite, middle-class newspapers. Though gaining some momentum, until the story became a television story, it was not in the American mainstream and the administration would not have to respond.

An American press corps was, however, beginning to come together in Yugoslavia: Blaine Harden of the *Washington Post* and John Burns of the *New York Times,* whose coverage, Gutman believed, was critically important because he represented the paper with the most powerful constituency in the country and the world. Burns, a distinguished reporter who had already covered a number of tough assignments, brought with him a considerable reputation as well as a Pulitzer prize, and his stories could not lightly be written off as the emotional outbursts of a young cub reporter who did not know how the real world worked.

Because of Gutman's coverage, the story of Bosnia was beginning to wend its way upward into the middle levels of the Washington bureaucracy. John Fox, a young man who was working at State for Policy Planning, thought that Gutman's early stories on genocide were a turning point. To his mind, Gutman was a highly respected reporter in Washington and *Newsday* was a highly respected paper. In addition, Gutman's bureau chief, Saul Friedman, was one of a group of diplomatic correspondents who often traveled with James Baker, and he was an old friend of both Baker and his press aide, Margaret Tutwiler. That added a sense of legitimacy because Friedman was vouching for Gutman and making sure that his stories got to the top State Department people immediately. But Gutman's stories—confirmation of what so many people were sure was happening—had the greatest impact at a lower level in the department. There the stories were photocopied and circulated throughout the department. It was, thought Fox, what the old samizdat days must have been like in the Soviet Union. Gutman's reports were exactly what Fox wanted, for he was trying to make as strong a case as possible for some form of American military intervention, often working with other people who were equally frustrated at comparable levels elsewhere in the bureaucracy. Moreover, Fox thought the NGOs were not to be underestimated. They were out there on the spot, most of them were humanitarian rather than ideological by nature—and this was a humanitarian not an ideological conflict—and some of them had excellent intelligence about what was going on. Fox was sure that their reports, particularly reports of Serb atrocities inflicted on Bosnian Muslims brought back by the International Red Cross, had reached the highest level of the U.S. government. Why, then, didn't the government act on them?

It was a struggle in the summer of 1992 to get the top people in the government even to admit that genocide was taking place in Bosnia. Fox was constantly working the bureaucracy, talking to like-minded people in other agencies and with friends in the NGOs, in an attempt to document the atrocities. "I was," he said years later, "like a fact-checker at *The New Yorker* trying to confirm certain things, working with people who felt the same way I did throughout the government. There was a network of us, working for different agencies both in and out of government, sharing information and keeping each other tuned. And we had a lot of information very much like that which Gutman came up with about the camps and the atrocities. The camps, we had discovered, were not even the worst of it. The worst of it was, village by village, the systematic execution of all village leaders by the Serbs." That was why Gutman's story of August 2, 1992, about the horrors of Omarska was so important. "We knew it was going to be a big day and a lot was going to be in play," Fox remembered, "because here was a major reporter for a major newspaper reporting concentration camps in very considerable detail."

For weeks the State Department press guidelines had stated that rumors of Serb atrocities in Bosnia could not be confirmed. But that day the answer in the press guideline to any questions about Gutman's report in *Newsday* was a startling reversal. *Yes,* it stated, *we can confirm this, there are concentration camps in this part of the world.* The admission was important because if these camps existed, then the United States had to have a policy in response to them. When Fox saw the press guideline that day, he was stunned. He called around asking what had happened and found that the editor of the guidelines, a man who was famously anti-interventionist and whose role was critical in controlling what went into the guidelines, was on vacation. "It was a great opportunity, with the cat away, for the mice to play," Fox said.

Larry Eagleburger, the person at State in charge of the policy to minimize the atrocity story, was very unhappy with the changed position. The next day, a preliminary version of the press guideline had a complete turnaround. The department's press officers, when asked about the story, were to say, no, they could not confirm it after all. Fox got wind of it and decided to challenge this latest attempt to sustain what he believed was a cover-up. His superiors had told him that the reversal had come from people at the top, which meant Eagleburger, and that the denial was being driven from the top down. If Fox wanted to change it, he would have to engage them.

So in a series of E-mails, Fox challenged what the department was trying to do. The U.S. government had plenty of information to confirm these atrocities. A denial, he said, could not stand up. We know it's true and yet we're saying that we don't know what we, in fact, do know. Then he added one single killer of a sentence: we did this once before, and we must never do it again. By that he meant the United States—due in no small part to the negligence and indifference of the State Department—had turned away from Germany's annihilation of the Jews during World War II and it must never happen again. Never again, he believed, meant exactly that: never again. Talking with the people in Eagleburger's office, he also played his best card. He let them know that he had access to a great deal of material that confirmed Gutman's story.

In the end, Fox got his superiors in Policy Planning to change the latest directive and confirm Gutman's story. It might, he thought, seem like a small victory to people on the outside, but in a place like the State Department, a victory of any kind, even if it was on paper, was an immense one in the slow and difficult process of changing a policy that had been frozen for so long. Fox was amused to learn that Tom Niles, the assistant secretary for Europe, had gone to the Hill that day, where he tried to defend the hear-no-evil, see-no-evil policy. He was challenged by Tom Lantos, a Democratic congressman who had been born in Hungary and was already one of the most outspoken members of Congress in decrying the Serb atrocities. Lantos had reliable sources of his own and scoffed at Niles's story.

By chance, there was soon more graphic evidence of the death camps. A British television team had managed to work its way to Omarska and got some film clips. As one of the journalists on the team, Ed Vulliamy, later wrote of what he saw, "Nothing could have prepared us for what we see when we come through the back gates of what was the Omarska iron mine and ore processing works. . . . [The prisoners] run in single file across the courtyard and into the canteen. Above them in an observation post is the watchful eye, hidden behind reflective sunglasses, of a beefy guard who follows their weary canter with the barrel of his heavy machine gun. There are thirty of them running; their heads newly shaven, their clothes baggy over their skeletal bodies. Some are barely able to move. . . . They line up in obedient and submissive silence and collect their ration: a meager, watery portion of beans augmented with bread crumbs and a stale roll. The men are at various stages of human decay and affliction; the bones of their elbows and wrists protrude like pieces of jagged stone from the pencil-thin stalks to which their arms have been reduced. Their skin is putrefied, the complexions of their faces debased, degraded, and utterly subservient, and yet they fix their huge hollow eyes on us with looks like the blades of knives. There is nothing quite like the sight of the prisoner desperate to talk and to convey some terrible truth that is so near yet so far, but who dares not."[2]

One of the most intriguing things about that period, thought Richard Johnson, the Yugoslav desk officer, was the dance of nomenclature. Starting in the Bush years, but extending well into the Clinton years, an attempt was made to avoid or at least modify the G-word; that is, genocide. To admit outright that what the Serbs were doing was, in fact, genocidal was a critical decision because the need to act would be that much greater. The most inventive kind of descriptions were demanded, the use of words and phrases the like of which had not been seen around the department in years, perhaps since the early days of Vietnam when, in the face of continued terrible news about the war, the government had steadfastly announced that it was cautiously optimistic.

Johnson noted that even when State Department spokesmen gradually began to edge toward saying how terrible it was in Bosnia, there were still gradations that allowed the press officers to stop short of calling it genocide. Certain acts, they said, could be described as "tantamount to genocide." Or they had "bordered on genocide." Or a particular act was genocidal, as if the sum of everything the Serbs were doing was not and there was a difference between an act of genocide and genocide itself.[3]

The pivotal figure at State at this point was Eagleburger, and he was not in an enviable position. He had been the deputy secretary of state, and the deputy traditionally gets the assignments the secretary does not want. Dealing with the Balkans most clearly was a job that James Baker did not fancy; it was messy, with no plausible rational outcome. That meant Eagleburger had faced a resistant secretary, a resistant president who obviously did not want to engage there, and a very resistant Pentagon. By August of 1992, however, he had been promoted—a rare honor accorded a professional foreign service officer—and had been named acting secretary of state. A most unhappy Baker, in the growing recognition of the crisis in Bush's drive for reelection, had been dragooned out of State and brought back to the White House to run the political campaign. Shortly thereafter Eagleburger was named secretary of state, a special moment somewhat diminished because the foreign country he knew best and perhaps loved best was breaking down into genocidal conflict.

Eagleburger was aware of the doubts and reservations of the rest of the administration, particularly of the two men directly above him, Baker and Bush. He shared many of those doubts himself. He was not sure that there was a right course of action, certainly there was no easy one, and he feared like others in the administration that America could be dragged into something difficult and costly. But he was gradually beginning to feel that the status quo could no longer stand. What was happening in Bosnia was far worse than anything he had ever imagined.

Eagleburger's change of opinion was driven by events and by the bright, passionate people under him. He was, in effect, a somewhat compromised man, unhappy with what would occur if they followed the current policy, but no more happy with any alternative to it. Like his close friend Brent Scowcroft, Eagleburger believed that we could not depend solely on airpower. He could envision the Serbs breaking down their regular military forces into small guerrilla units. That alone could bedevil America's high-technology military, which depended upon quick results in distant places while, of course, taking few casualties. "What I always worried about in those days," he later said, "was the shadow of Vietnam. I had a very strong sense of how tough the Serbs could be from my time there, how stubborn and how resilient they were."

But the cruelty being inflicted by the Serbs on the Bosnians was another thing. When Yugoslavia began to break apart in 1991, he had assumed there would be violence—"a terrible, bloody mess," in his words. He had always been aware of the potential for ethnic conflict in Kosovo because of the historical blood hatreds, and he regarded that as a special place where the United States had to make clear to Milosevic that it would not tolerate any brutality inflicted by the minority Serbs on the Albanian majority. In the rest of Yugoslavia, however, Eagleburger had envisioned a very different level of violence than that which was now taking place. There would be some bitter struggles between the Serbs and the Croats, but they would be waged within a traditional military context. Eventually the map would probably be redrawn, the Serbs would come away with a slice of Croatia or the Croats would have a slice of Serbia, and either might grab a slice of Bosnia. Then having expended so much energy in a number of battles, they would find themselves, however involuntarily, exhausted, and an uneasy, probably unwanted, and certainly uncomfortable equilibrium would take hold. The map of the Balkans would once again be redrawn, and those who had gained more than they had started out with would be happy, and those who had lost a little would be unhappy. The fighting would end of itself when the different sides simply ran out of energy.

What Eagleburger had not expected was the genocide, the relentless cruelty inflicted by the Serbs on civilians. He had seen photos of the emaciated Muslim men looking like the Jews either on their way to the Nazi camps or already there. He had read the stories in the newspapers, and one particular cover of *Time* magazine in August 1992 (with the cover line, appropriately enough, "Must It Go On?") showing Bosnian men looking through the fence of a concentration camp had told him he had been wrong and had underestimated the catastrophic nature of what was taking place.

That summer the pressure mounted within the lower and middle levels of the State Department to do something about the Balkans, and most of it centered around reaching Larry Eagleburger. Below him in the department almost everyone wanted a more aggressive policy toward Yugoslavia. Above him almost no one did. Though he was from the foreign service and not a political appointee, he was a moderate to liberal Republican and a committed, old-fashioned internationalist. By the time he had risen to become the number two man in the department, he had survived in the bureaucracy under different presidents, from Johnson through Bush, and had managed to operate at a very high level.

His father, a doctor first in Milwaukee and then Stevens Point, Wisconsin, had been "somewhat to the right of Genghis Khan," Eagleburger remembered. But growing up in Republican student politics in the years after World War II, the son had emerged as a committed member of the internationalist Vandenberg wing of the party. At the age of eighteen, Eagleburger had been a supporter of Earl Warren in the 1948 presidential primaries, and as a college student he was the relatively rare Wisconsin Republican who had fought the state's own senator, its best known, if not most admired, politician, Joe McCarthy.

Eagleburger was immensely popular with high-level people across a wide political spectrum. He had served as a special assistant to Dean Acheson when Acheson was running errands for Lyndon Johnson, worked on European affairs on the NSC staff under Walt Rostow, and then slipped away from Rostow and the NSC to become Nick Katzenbach's special assistant when Katzenbach was undersecretary and was beginning to question the Johnson policies in Vietnam. Eagleburger had served with distinction through to the Reagan years, working under George Shultz at State, and was believed by others in that administration to have played a critical role in some of Shultz's successes, particularly during his long, hard struggles with Cap Weinberger at Defense. Eagleburger was bright, with a practical rather than an abstract intelligence, and his greatest strength was his shrewd reading of the people around him. He had natural political skills and was virtually without peer in knowing how to work within the bureaucracy and actually make things happen. He had made his most important political connection in late 1968, linking up with Henry Kissinger while Kissinger was working for Nixon during the transition period just before becoming Nixon's NSC assistant. Kissinger, about to trade academe for government, understood immediately how good Eagleburger was, how well he operated in a complicated bureaucracy. In that area, Kissinger was then something of a virgin.

During the following year Eagleburger devoted himself, among other things, to protecting Kissinger's flank, which was virtually a full-time job because of the animus felt toward Kissinger by the right. Typically, he tried to buffer a badly wounded Kissinger through the famed 1976 Republican convention in Kansas City, where not only his policies of détente but the entire concept of bipartisan internationalism came under assault. The noisy, heated convention in the end gave, however reluctantly, its nomination to Jerry Ford, but the most memorable speech was by Ronald Reagan, who did not mention Ford's name. Kissinger, something of an embarrassment at the convocation of this party that was changing so radically, was smuggled into Kansas City and kept there, in the words of the columnist Jules Witcover, "under virtual house

138 / DAVID HALBERSTAM

arrest." Aware of his boss's hurt feelings, Eagleburger had called the Republican organizers and asked if they could put on some kind of demonstration to make Kissinger feel welcome when he arrived. That was easy enough to do, and when Kissinger finally got to his Kansas City hotel, a nice crowd of clean-cut, freshly scrubbed young Republicans were cheering and waving placards in his honor—*Kansas City Welcomes Secretary of State Henry Kissinger!* The ever-mordant Kissinger took one look at the crowd, turned to Eagleburger, and said, "You organized this, didn't you?"

Eagleburger was not by instinct an idea man; rather he was one of those rare people whose native human talents suited him exceptionally well for being in government. He was straightforward, surprisingly candid with everyone, and played by rules of old-fashioned loyalty. But he was not viewed as a foreign policy visionary or conceptualizer. The relationship with Kissinger was ideal, some people believed. Kissinger was the conceptualizer and Eagleburger knew how to work the bureaucracy, and, of course, to clean up after Henry.

Eagleburger had left government in the mideighties. Partly burned-out and somewhat out of step with the Reagan people, he had gone to work for Kissinger Associates, where his clients included Yugoslavia. He made considerable money in those years, certainly a good deal more than foreign service officers usually make, though not as much as some well-credentialed Americans were about to make as America's role in what was now a global economy became preeminent, the line between government official and former government official blurred, and the financial rewards became infinitely greater. (A few years later when the world of the Internet was just being born and Eagleburger had retired again, he was besieged with offers to join boards. Some he accepted, some he turned down. One offer was from a new company in California, and as far as he could tell it was one board too many, demanding too many cross-country flights on which he would not be able to smoke his omnipresent cigarettes. So he suggested that the head of the company take his old sidekick Brent Scowcroft instead, and Scowcroft, a mild and unassuming man of no wealth and considerable personal modesty, went on the board of the company, which was called Qualcomm, and the value of his stock was at one point some $75 million.)

After working with Kissinger Associates, Eagleburger came back to the State Department to serve as Baker's deputy secretary. Once again he proved of value because of the trust he had created. Typically, in the midst of the Gulf War after the Israelis had been hit by a series of Iraqi Scud missiles and were threatening to jump the tracks and respond on their own, thereby shattering the delicate bond that held the Arab nations in the otherwise predominantly Western alliance, it was Eagleburger who was sent to plead with them not to retaliate. The Israelis obviously trusted him as they trusted no one else at that level in the administration, especially not Baker.

Eagleburger was particularly good at a kind of pseudocandor, admitting a weakness in his own position before anyone could point it out, as if to show how straight he was. He was the rare high-ranking foreign service officer who was so politically savvy that he could as easily have been Speaker of the House had he followed a slightly different career track. In a world where successful men and women in the foreign service, as in most parallel professions, appeared to be ever sleeker physically and colder of demeanor, Eagleburger was somehow old-fashioned and endearing. There he was, short, appallingly overweight, far too many pounds distributed on a body whose contours seemed to defy the State Department prototype, his health always terrible, suffering from severe asthma, yet still chain-smoking, alternating cigarettes with his antiasthma inhaler.

He was, his staff thought, oddly fatalistic about the Balkans at that time. He knew the old Yugoslavia, knew the hatreds suppressed and thought them dangerous. He was always decrying the world of the Balkans in private. "They're all liars out there," he would say again and again. Aides feared he would one day say it in public, and in time at a press conference in Europe, he did, but it passed without a diplomatic ripple. With a few close confidants, he would talk cautiously about the political dilemma they faced. Nothing was going to happen at the level above him because it was an election year, and because the president he served was already under severe attack for being too interested in foreign policy. At the very least, his aides thought, he was telling Bush and the other top people how bad things were in Bosnia. Bill Montgomery, his deputy, thought Eagleburger was immensely frustrated. Montgomery had quietly been urging Eagleburger to take a more proactive position. The two had argued heatedly over what was happening in the Balkans and the American failure to act. Years later when Montgomery eventually became ambassador to Croatia, in his office in Zagreb was a signed photo from Eagleburger dedicated to "my nag, conscience, scold and friend."

Montgomery was aware, as few of the people pushing for greater action on Yugoslavia were, that the Bush administration was focused on the fledgling and very uncertain Russia. As far as Bush, Baker, and Scowcroft were concerned, the threat of secession of former parts of greater Russia was uppermost in their minds, much more important than Yugoslavia. That was one of the obstacles Eagleburger ran into whenever he suggested a more aggressive policy at the White House. The other was the military. At the urging of the people underneath Eagleburger, he might make their arguments to his peers, but when he returned to the department and repeated what they had said, the opinions they had the most trouble countering were those of Colin Powell. What would happen if any early military move did not work? What happens, Eagleburger would ask, his questions echoing Powell's, if a plane is shot down and they parade prisoners through the streets of Belgrade? What's your advice now, guys?

For a brief period in the summer of 1992, Jim Hooper and Richard Johnson worked on a special committee headed by Warren Zimmermann, the former ambassador to Belgrade, who had become Eagleburger's point man on the Balkans. Both Hooper and Johnson were activists and had been placed on the committee by Montgomery, a covert activist who wanted them to move Zimmermann forward a bit. But they soon felt stalemated on the Zimmermann committee and asked for a meeting with Eagleburger. It took place in mid-September, when the presidential campaign was in full swing and Bush was running badly. They had been granted fifteen minutes, and Eagleburger gave them thirty. Hooper and Johnson were very blunt. American policy in the Balkans was a complete failure. Milosevic had a strategy and we did not. We were reacting to military aggression with empty words. Eagleburger was low-key at the meeting—in no way hostile. That, Hooper suspected, was because he and Johnson were playing by the rules, not resigning loudly and publicly, but working within the system. At one point Eagleburger turned to them and said, "I want to thank you for telling me that my policy is full of shit." "I see you've been paying attention to us," Johnson replied. At the end of the meeting they asked for the right to do a critique of the policy and Eagleburger agreed. Some ten days later, they handed in a tough twenty-five-page dissent. After that they heard nothing. Finally they put their paper in the dissent channel, which guaranteed that it would at least be part of the historical record.

Some two months later, Hooper and Johnson went back to see Eagleburger. It was, they remembered, Veterans Day, November 11. The election was over. Bush had lost and Clinton would be the next president. This time Eagleburger was surprisingly candid with them. He had read their paper, he said, read it carefully. But he had not wanted to talk too much about it before because of the election. Nothing, he said, was going to happen until it was over. But if they wanted him to make any changes, now was the time, because he was going to bring the matter up with Cheney and Powell. He and the two dissidents went back and forth, with Eagleburger essentially making the military's case. They tell me, he said, they do deserts, not mountains. "Before Kuwait they didn't do deserts," Hooper replied. What about the allies, how do we handle them? Eagleburger wanted to know. You don't ask them, you tell them what American policy is going to be, Johnson and Hooper answered.

Then a strange thing happened. Eagleburger critiqued the policy himself and his critique was even harsher than theirs. "I knew something like this was going to happen," he said. "I knew it was going to be violent. I just didn't know it would be this bad." With that the meeting was over. But at one point, because he thought this was not leading anywhere and because he felt there was a moral imperative to act, Johnson said something to the effect that history was going to judge them all. "Don't use that stuff on me—I'm not going to be judged," Eagleburger said. Later when told by a reporter that Eagleburger had remarked long after leaving government that each day he looked in the mirror and wondered whether he should have done more, Johnson said, "Good—I'm glad to hear that." The problem, Bill Montgomery thought years later, was that even when you pumped Eagleburger up, he would go to the White House virtually without allies. In the past when they had got him to make the case for intervention, he had been forced to go against Bush, Powell and the uniformed military, Cheney, and Baker. In addition, Montgomery believed, Eagleburger was a divided soul, fighting an undertow within himself, his own heart at least partially on the side of the people he was ostensibly arguing with.

What dissent there was in the Pentagon came from the civilian side, and its leader was the undersecretary of defense under Cheney, Paul Wolfowitz, who represented the new complexity of political currents at work in Washington. He was a Scoop Jackson Democrat who, disenchanted with his party's foreign policy, had gradually turned into a Reagan Republican, which meant that he was something of a social liberal and a combination of hard-liner and ideological purist in foreign policy. Like many of the proactive people at State, Wolfowitz thought that American participation in an arms embargo toward Bosnia was absolutely appalling. It was morally unacceptable to permit the aggressor the luxury of arms but to deny those under attack the ability to defend themselves. He agreed with both Powell and Cheney on the need to keep American ground troops out of a potential Balkans quagmire, but disagreed on the practical effect of the arms embargo. He was certain that it would almost surely guarantee that the United States would be drawn into the conflict rather than preventing it. It made the Bosnians more vulnerable than they already were and encouraged the Serbs to think no one would stand in their way.

If the indigenous forces in Bosnia were not able to defend themselves, then the international community would eventually have to do it, Wolfowitz believed. In his mind the Europeans lacked the muscle, the force, and the will to handle so difficult a situation. There was already considerable evidence of their limitations, evidence that they were unconsciously playing into Serbian hands. He was sure that matters would continue to disintegrate, and as they did, the burden would eventually fall on the United States. Therefore, American self-interest demanded that we allow the Bosnians access to weapons.

Wolfowitz met with Colin Powell, who heard him out and made sure that one of his top people was in the room. Powell was immune to most of the pleas coming from the interventionists. He thought that no one in Washington was willing to pay the price that a commitment like this might demand. To him the interventionists were talking a policy based on hope rather than reality, a hope that things could be affected with a minimum, casualty-free application of airpower. But what Wolfowitz told him was intriguing. It was based on a hard look at the forces at play, not a humanitarian call to arms on the part of those who might not be there if and when things went sour. The hearing he received from Powell was, Wolfowitz thought, as serious as you could get in the top level of the bureaucracy. Powell obviously listened attentively and quite possibly agreed with him. "And what about your friends in the State Department," Powell asked at the end of their meeting, "what do they think about this?" They were, Wolfowitz admitted, against arming the Bosnians. "Come back to me," Powell told Wolfowitz, "when they're on board."

Powell, Wolfowitz knew, was already unhappy with the policy he had been handed, which had come through State, for American forces to be part of a humanitarian aid mission, carrying food and medical supplies into troubled areas. That put his troops, as far as he was concerned, right in the middle of an ugly war, one without rules. He had his own suspicions about humanitarian missions anyway because of the ease with which they could be expanded or escalated if something went wrong, if a plane was shot down or troops were taken prisoner. If he was going to switch policies for one that, in fact, might make more sense, he wanted everyone on the same page. But no one was close to that. Any chance at lifting the arms embargo and letting the Bosnians handle the Serbs on their own ended there.

CHAPTER FOURTEEN

George Bush ran a terrible campaign for reelection. In the beginning the White House was arrogant because of the immense success in overseeing the end of the Cold War and the comparable success of the Gulf War. One of the most grievous mistakes that a number of the Bush people, most particularly the president himself, made was to underestimate Bill Clinton, to compare the two candidates, as it were, by weighing their respective curriculum vitae: where they came from, what jobs they had held, and how they had handled the issue of patriotism. That was fatal. Political campaigns are all too intense and unpredictable, and candidates, as many a front-runner had learned over the years, most notably Jerry Ford running against Jimmy Carter, are rarely the sum of their résumés.

The people around Bush also forgot that their man had never been a particularly good or charismatic candidate. If the growing importance of television was tilting the presidential race from the tortoise to the hare, then Bush would surely lose that race, the sum of his years in governance far more impressive than his sound bites. He was an attractive man up close, someone of considerable personal grace and warmth. His good manners were a constant, but he was often oddly awkward, and in projecting his better qualities in public forums, his civility tended to come off as stiffness. His occasional struggles with the English language made it seem as if it were a somewhat alien instrument.

Bush was very much aware of his limitations. Words were not his strength. His voice was hardly mellifluous. The simplest of presidential responses were often blurted out. Experts on learning disabilities often sensed that they had found a longtime sufferer. Emotions were always to be buttoned up, not, as with many more naturally skillful politicians, to be used deftly in the right way at the right time for political effect. In addition, speaking publicly of his accomplishments might imply that he was promoting himself, and he had been raised in a culture of ego austerity, alien as that was to presidential politics. When Peggy Noonan, the ablest conservative speechwriter of a generation, who had written several of Ronald Reagan's best speeches, tried to make a lateral move to Bush, she found it hard going, not just because of the difference in their politics, but because of the candidate's modesty and reluctance to use the first-person singular.

Once, in 1988, engaged in a bitter do-or-die struggle with Bob Dole for the Republican nomination, Bush had summoned Ms. Noonan to write a speech for him—she who had supplied so many poetic phrases for Ronald Reagan. She made a draft but Bush did not like it. What was wrong? she asked. "Oh," he answered, "the me-me-me stuff."[1] Noonan learned quickly and became adept at writing pronounless speeches, because he would kill any sentence that had the word *I* in it. So instead of "I moved to Texas and soon we joined the Republican Party," she wrote, "Moved to Texas, joined the Republican Party . . ."[2] Bush absolutely shrank from the very idea of being eloquent. Not only was he unable on his own to find a graceful sentence or a phrase that would lift his words to match the occasion, but he remained on red alert lest those around him try to slip in something tending to upgrade either him or the moment. "That's not me," he would say, spotting a dangerously eloquent phrase, and out it would come. He was always on the watch for what he called "the poetry stuff," and for moving phrases that were, in his opinion, "Noonanesque."[3]

Vice presidents who are not charismatic often spend much of their time, even when they are out on their own, fighting the shadow of the more charismatic figure who has gotten them so close to the presidency. So it had been for Lyndon Johnson, ever fighting the shadow of Jack Kennedy. So it would one day be for Al Gore following Bill Clinton. So it was in 1992, when the person Bush was always running against, other than Bill Clinton or Ross Perot, was Ronald Reagan. Even as president he somehow remained in Reagan's shadow. The Reagan connection had turned out to be a two-edged sword. It had helped Bush get the 1988 nomination, but it also hung over him as a measurement he could never quite live up to in the minds of many Americans who hungered not merely for Reagan's policies, but for the comfortable feeling provided by the man himself. That was what the faithful longed for, the conservative faithful, and the Reagan Democrats as well, and that was where Bush was forever doomed to fall short.

Bush was determined to be true to himself in public no matter how bland that made the occasion; he would never be out of his own context. His lack of eloquence was surely a political weakness. But unlike Johnson, Bush was smart enough to know that the single worst thing he could do was compete with Reagan at being Reaganesque. The more he did that, the more he would surely fail. The contrast between the private and public Reagan and the private and public Bush, the difference between reality and image, was fascinating. When Bush graduated from Andover in the spring of 1942, graduation day had been his eighteenth birthday and he had signed up for the service. He had been the youngest naval pilot in World War II, had won the Air Medal and the Distinguished Flying Cross, and was by traditional American standards not an inconsiderable hero. Reagan, who was the right age to serve, had taken something of a bye during that conflict; his main contribution had been making propaganda films for the military. His war record was, in modern terminology, a virtual one, though he did not always seem to remember that. But it was Reagan, with that marvelous natural confidence, the lack of doubt in his voice, even the audacious macho walk born of many a cowboy film, who was considered a hero (and who even implied in speeches that he had, in fact, served in combat in World War II). It was Bush whose manliness appeared to be in doubt. In 1980, when he was first running for the presidency, *Newsweek,* a magazine where most of the editors had never heard a shot fired in anger, ran a devastating cover story about him saying that he was fighting the Wimp Factor.

Reagan had been a hard act to follow politically. Symbols had been the mother's milk of his longtime profession, and he understood not merely their importance but the timing implicit in their use. More than anyone around him, he had a sense of when to use them with perfect pitch politically. After all, no one has a highly successful career in Hollywood without understanding not merely the importance of symbols but how to make them work. He was an American everyman; he knew exactly what the American people felt and needed at different times because it was more often than not the way he felt, and the most natural thing in the world for him was to excel at being the person they wanted him to be. That particular quality separated the more cerebral analysts and critics of American politics from the American voters on the subject of Reagan. The former, watching him in action, aware of his acting background, often privately disagreeing with much of what he believed, saw him as plastic and inauthentic, a man of Hollywood; the voters, by contrast, sensing that what he said was what he felt, that he had come by these feelings naturally, and more, that what he felt was the way *they* felt about so many of the same things, saw him as being absolutely authentic.

Reagan knew a very few things, but his strength was that he was completely faithful to those few things and strongly believed in them: the government was too big, it shouldn't tinker in the affairs of ordinary people if at all possible, and if let alone, America was a great regenerative society. To many people who were more sophisticated politically, he was an easy man to discount because of the simplicity of his beliefs, his unshakable faith in them, and his carelessness with what seemed to be facts. He could get all his facts wrong, yet in the minds of the people voting still be completely right. Underestimating him was both easy and fatal—the graveyard of American politics was littered with the headstones of those men who had made the deadly mistake of underestimating Ronald Reagan.

The things that political writers and pundits valued most, complexity and subtlety of thought, accuracy in factoids and anecdotes, meant little to Reagan, and America's political analysts saw him as a lightweight, instead of what he was, someone unique, an American original whose sense of the country's hopes, fears, and expectations was remarkably true. What he had about the country was faith. Like Dwight Eisenhower, he understood how much to know and how much not to know on all occasions; he was sure that ordinary people would trust him on major issues, and in fact they did. The rhetoric was in no way a sham. He believed absolutely in what he said about the greatness of America, and his remarkable career was proof of those verities and of that rhetoric: America worked and indeed worked magically. Why not therefore be confident? That inner core of confidence helped him greatly once in office. He never went around fighting himself. The small things, the personal insecurities and inadequacies that were so dramatically magnified in most men once they became president, the doubts that could explode into full-fledged paranoia and had made the presidency so difficult for men like Johnson and Nixon, never bothered him. The importance of his personal confidence was not to be ignored. Who else, upon election as president, would hire Jim Baker as his chief of staff, a man who had run two campaigns against him?

Moreover, his natural ebullience helped him in one additional way as he began to seek the presidency. The seventies had been a dark time nationally, a time not so much of American weakness as of *perceived* weakness. First, there had been the humiliating departure from Vietnam, then the catastrophic events in Iran, amplified again and again on national television—Day 323, America Held Hostage, Walter Cronkite would say—and the soaring energy prices and a belief that the American industrial manufacturing core was losing ground to the Japanese. In that period, Reagan, ever self-assured—no American politician had a jauntier walk—was the welcome antidote. He was perfectly cast for the moment, and it was not by surprise that the emotional (as opposed to the geopolitical) issue that burned so intensely with him, the Panama Canal, burned with the electorate as well. He believed in America, and America, of course, believed in him. Whatever else, with the Cold War still on, no one was going to push America around, not while Ronald Reagan was president—not, as he liked to say, on his watch.

Now Reagan was gone, leaving behind a deeply divided Republican Party. That made it a much harder equation for Bush, who could never match Reagan in natural appeal. Nor, unlike Reagan, could he so easily fuse the two adversarial wings of his party, the new right, driven by the fundamentalists, and the old traditionalists, who were often made uncomfortable by their Sun Belt colleagues. Bush simply lacked the political and human skills to pull it off. He was too much the product of his own background. If he tried to do Texasy things, he always looked a little stiff and sounded a little tinny, as when he spoke of a situation in which, if things went wrong, he would be in deep doodoo.

Bush had existed in an odd compromise with the far right of his own party for the past four years. The right had been hard on him, ever suspicious that his heart was not where it ought to be. George Will had once called him a lapdog, and it did not get much worse than that. At heart, and almost everyone knew it, despite his protestations to the contrary, Bush was a centrist in a party whose center was very much under assault. What worked somewhat to his advantage was that the issues of primacy, for him, foreign policy ones, were less and less vital to the new forces in his party. For the right wing of the party was, as the threat of the Soviet Union receded, far more interested in domestic political and cultural issues—what were now known as family values, most particularly abortion—and its power was centered in the electoral primaries and the Congress. The overriding interest of the more moderate centrist wing was foreign policy, and its power and influence were manifest in the executive branch in Washington and often in different governorships.

The most tangible evidence of the split had come during the tax battles of 1990, when Bush had broken his pledge and approved a tax increase because of the rising deficit. Newt Gingrich and his pals sat that one out in the Congress. The damage to Bush politically was dual: not only was he wounded by breaking a pledge, but having done the right thing for the good of the nation's economy, he remained fearful of much of his own party on the issue. He would back off from talking about it during the campaign—thereby taking no credit for having done what was self-evidently the right thing. Because his own party was so emotionally locked into tax-bashing, doing something reasonably courageous had become something shameful.

In matters of foreign policy the two wings of the party were more than a little uncomfortable with each other. The people running the executive branch still had roots in the old Dewey-Vandenberg-Eisenhower internationalism, but the people ascending in both houses of the Congress, many of them from the Sun Belt, were very different. They might be anticommunist, but they were more jingoist than internationalist, less traveled, in many instances, than their predecessors, and an ever-stronger current of isolationism ran through their thinking. They were especially apprehensive about any kind of multilateral foreign policy commitment. Describing them in one of his columns, the *New York Times'* Tom Friedman, the paper's gifted foreign policy analyst, had referred to them "as a hard core of Republicans in Congress whose motto on foreign policy could be summed up as 'Stupid and proud of it' or 'Dumb as we wanna be.' This is the crowd that favors everything from nonpayment of UN dues to further cuts in foreign aid, to outright isolationism."

The Bush people saw the congressional leadership very much the same way. When they spoke about the right-wingers in private, they did so with raised eyebrows and a deft negative shake of the head. The word *yahoos* was often used. These were people, they would say, whom you needed in the party to get the requisite 51 percent and to hold on to committee chairs, but in all other ways they seemed alien, their thinking far more adversarial than that of old colleagues from the other party who had for so long comprised the great centrist bipartisan internationalism of the postwar years.

In the past, domestic politics had not greatly interested Bush. He had spoken during the 1988 campaign about being the education president, but that had been the most casually uttered of promises, and the thought of reeducating millions of young Americans had not much burdened him thereafter. Once in office Bush and the team around him had thrown any number of bones—a Supreme Court appointment here, a few district judgeships there—to the right wing. But Bush's relationship with this powerful, aggressive force in his own party, at the end of eight years as vice president and the four years of his presidency, represented at best a loveless, passionless marriage.

The 1992 Bush campaign was troubled from the start. Almost everything that could go wrong went wrong. The president appeared sluggish, slow to pay much attention to mounting distress signals and make the moves necessary to streamline his team. Some of Bush's closest friends thought afterward that his health had been a problem—medication for a thyroid illness that the doctors had never quite got right—and the candidate who was usually the most upbeat and focused of men, indeed almost hyperactive, often seemed listless and behind the beat. The White House, in early 1992, was poorly run. John Sununu had departed, chased out by an undertow of minor scandal and the hostility of a great many centrist Bush traditionalists, who thought him not only too ideological but too arrogant. Sam Skinner, who had replaced him, was hardly up to running either the White House or a presidential campaign.

Many Bush advisers, aware of how damaging the polls had become, were pushing hard for some kind of domestic program, some new booster shot of energy. But the Bush political people were divided. The hard-liners were so taken with Clinton's negatives, particularly his lack of service in Vietnam, that they believed that no matter what the numbers said, he was beatable. Another, more moderate wing was worried by the polls and the degree to which they showed that people blamed Bush for the economy and felt he was indifferent to their problems. This latter group was increasingly aware that the reelection campaign promised to be hard, that Clinton, the certain Democratic nominee, might prove to be a formidable candidate. "We face," Fred Steeper wrote in the spring of 1992, "a twenty-month recession, a 78 percent 'wrong track' number, and a Southern Conservative Democrat. In my mind this is our worst political nightmare."[4]

By August, as things went from bad to worse, a most unhappy and reluctant James Baker was pressured into leaving the State Department and coming back to his old job in the White House to run the campaign. He brought with him a few top people, and he was absolutely appalled by the state of the campaign. He later told close friends that it had been lost as early as May. No one was ready for a big-time campaign. Baker had returned to an empty cupboard. Only one speechwriter was on hand. No one had been hired to do the television commercials. They were behind in every department, and this time they were up against some tough professionals.

Baker, the people around him thought, seemed to be in virtual shock—or as close to shock as someone that tough-minded ever got. His heart was obviously not in this race; he had not wanted the job and thought the campaign was a disaster. Despite the closeness of their friendship, an undercurrent of competition had always existed between Bush and Baker. Bush got the top job and Baker did the heavy lifting for him, and yet Baker had always impressed the opinion makers in Washington more than Bush. Perhaps coming back to the White House was one test of loyalty too many. Baker had been at the pinnacle of his career as secretary of state, a job he loved, and now he was back at the White House in a mere political job, once more playing the role of Tonto to Bush's Lone Ranger.

Ensconced in a familiar but unwanted role, Baker seemed almost melancholic to old friends and, for a man who usually took complete command of what he did, somewhat disengaged. His energy level was not good, and if after his defeat George Bush was disappointed, Barbara Bush, who reflected the family's feelings about loyalty more openly and was generally less forgiving than her husband, was furious at Baker. Eight years later when George W. Bush was preparing to run, and many of the older Bush people came together as an informal group of consultants, notable for his absence from that group was James Baker. He was essentially removed from the inner circle until the moment right after the election, when, summoned once again from his place on the Bush bench, he was miraculously resurrected and became the point man for George W. Bush in the legal wrangles over the Florida vote—even a distinguished former secretary of state, it was implied, says we won. He carried out this particular role with such partisan enthusiasm and passion that he began to lose the admiration of some who had thought him an uncommonly talented secretary of state.

Things that had once looked so rosy had begun to look bleak in the winter and spring of the campaign. Bush continued to slip in the polls. Pat Buchanan had run against him in New Hampshire, the worst possible state for Bush, and had exploited the weak economy as well as nativist feelings to wound him. As summer arrived, the campaign obviously needed a boost, and some of the people around Bush believed that the ideal way to do that was to get rid of the weight of an inconsequential vice president and add someone of greater gravitas whom the center of the electorate would take more seriously. It would also show that this was a newer, more professional Bush team. That meant, in blunt English, dropping Dan Quayle from the ticket. The Dump Quayle movement had begun as far back as the fall of 1991 and included some of Bush's top peo-ple. The chief coconspirators were Baker, then still secretary of state, and Bob Teeter, Bush's pollster and an old personal friend with roots in moderate to lib-eral Republican politics, who was slated to run the 1992 campaign. Neither man liked Quayle, neither valued him greatly as a man or a politician, and both regarded Bush's original selection as more or less inexplicable. Moreover, they now thought they had a new ally, Bush himself, who believed that Quayle had been too open in his flirtation with the religious right, a violation of the crucial Bush code of loyalty. Bush and the people closest to him held that the funda-mentalists should be kept just happy enough to prevent them from being mutinous, but in no way encouraged or allowed across the moat. "Do you think all this right-wing stuff that Dan is doing these days is helping us?" Bush asked Teeter one day. No, Teeter answered. "I don't think so either," Bush said, and he suggested that perhaps Teeter should talk to Quayle about it—though obviously the person to do that was the president himself.

If Quayle was to go, it was decided, the best signal that this was a dramat-ically new team would be his replacement by Colin Powell. But if Powell was to be approached, it would have to be done in a way that was completely deni-able. Deniability was important if people were proffering vice-presidential bids to Republican hopefuls when there already was a Republican vice president. So one day very much on his own, Stu Spencer, the California consultant who had played an instrumental role in the creation of Ronald Reagan's political career, dropped by the Pentagon to talk with his friend Powell. Bush was not in on this, of course, and Spencer was just making a social call. Everything was discussed in a hypothetical way—a hypothetical place for a hypothetical general on a hypothetical ticket. In turn the general made clear that he, who existed in a real and not hypothetical world, liked being a real general in a real army, and that for a variety of reasons he was not interested in being a politi-cian. He had no desire to go on a Republican ticket, and some of the people who thought they wanted him might not like all of his social positions. But if the president badly wanted the general to be on his ticket, and the president himself asked, the general, good soldier that he was, would, of course, accept. But the general would prefer not to be asked.

There were other possibilities—Baker himself and Dick Cheney; there was enough post–Desert Storm aura still attached to Cheney to make him an attractive candidate. Two weeks before the convention, the Dump Quayle peo-ple were sure they were going to nail Quayle, for Bush was paying more and more attention to polls showing who would and would not help the ticket as a Quayle replacement. The plotters were certain they had Bush's support, and the one problem, since Bush did not like confrontation, was who would tell Quayle. But then Bill Kristol, who was Quayle's political man and infinitely more nimble at the political game than his boss, set a marvelous trap for Bush.

With about two weeks to go, Quayle went to the White House for breakfast and asked the president if he was happy with him. Bush hesitated for just a moment, failed to bite the bullet, and said, yes, he was. Kristol immediately gave the media the Quayle version of events, and a story went out that day in effect reaffirming Quayle's place on the ticket. Bush was furious with the leaked story but did nothing. Quayle stayed on the ticket in no small part because it was now so much harder to dump him. With that the last chance to strengthen the ticket by adding Powell or Baker and perhaps to change the outcome of the election was lost.

The convention was a disaster. Rarely had a sitting president allowed his enemies to dominate what under most circumstances was a democratic form of coronation. It should have been Bush's show and a celebration of his not inconsiderable achievements in foreign policy. But it was not. Instead, the convention showcased angry right-wingers whose principal concern was not a safer post–Cold War America with exceptional new possibilities for the grander uses of the nation's extraordinary energies. Rather it was primarily concerned with whether American women had the right to choose an abortion, not necessarily a subject about which Bush had strong convictions.

The Bush and Buchanan people had had prolonged negotiations over how much exposure Buchanan would get as the price for his support of the president. The White House had clearly given away too much: not merely prime time but on the first night of the convention, the primest of prime time. Worse, when Buchanan had sent in his speech for clearance, the White House people had chiefly been concerned about the degree of enthusiasm for Bush. Because of that they failed to catch the harsh, unnerving rhetoric—the call for a religious and cultural war, exactly the wrong message for most moderate Americans, who were notoriously uneasy with any display of zealotry, especially religious zealotry.

All too many speakers at that convention did not sound like people who had been in power for the last twelve years. They sounded like people angry at the people who had been in power, particularly for the last four. The convention was hungry for red meat, and it came right off the bones of George H. W. Bush. In the end both the burden and the fault were Bush's, and it cut to what was wrong with his campaign and perhaps what had always been missing from his political career. It was not that Buchanan (rather predictably) gave one of the ugliest speeches in the history of modern national conventions. It was that Bush, the party's nominee, failed to answer it himself because he was intimidated by the delegates at his own convention. Reagan could handle these people; he could not.

There was an additional problem, the entrance into the race of a third-party candidate named Ross Perot, a billionaire who seemed to bear far greater personal animus toward Bush than toward Clinton. Perot systematically and

effectively attacked Bush on the economy, relieving Clinton of that responsibility and allowing him to run on a higher plane. Perot's was the kind of campaign that the opposing vice-presidential candidate usually runs, and it
allowed both Clinton and Gore to take the high road while Perot served as
their hit man.

The Perot candidacy was, if not a fatal wound, one not to be underestimated. But the deepest wounds were self-inflicted. There were simply too
many people in the White House, including the president himself, who were
so personally offended by all the baggage that the young Democratic candidate carried, particularly what they considered to be draft dodging, that the
idea that the America they knew would reward Clinton for a life, in their view,
so poorly led was inconceivable. In some ways they were right. Just a few
years earlier, the Clinton challenge might have been laughable. But the world
had changed and the America now voting was no longer the America they
knew.

The Clinton people were sure that Bush and the people around him were
living in the past, unable to adjust to new circumstances. The transition from
Cold War politics to post–Cold War politics, something that Reagan might
have made with uncommon ease, was too difficult an adjustment for the less
nimble Bush. In fact, Stan Greenberg thought Clinton was now not only
closer than Bush to the demographic center of the country, he was closer to the
cultural and political center as well. The draft issue was a dangerous one for
Bush, Greenberg believed. The young men of the country had not been subject to the draft for a generation and they wanted that issue closed.

If Bush criticized Clinton on this one, he was also criticizing millions of
young American males. As soon as the Republican convention was over,
Greenberg did a memo for Clinton and his top people disguised as a memo
that Bob Teeter might write for George Bush—a kind of know-your-enemy-
and-see-yourself-as-they-see-you document. The subject, based on Greenberg's own polling, was how to attack Clinton most effectively, thereby to
prepare him as best they could for the coming assault. The fake Teeter memo
said that if Bush ran on the economy, he would lose. The ideal way to run
against Clinton, Greenberg suggested, was first to attack his political record,
thereby diminishing his place on the larger national landscape, and to portray
him as an untested, small-time operator from a poor, unimportant state who
aspired to too big a job. Only then should they deal with his draft record. That
done, they could go after his character and try to exploit the issue of trust. If
they reversed the order of the assault, Greenberg discovered from his polls, it
was likely to fail because the American people did not want that kind of attack
at the very outset of a campaign. They wanted to measure the candidate on his
fitness for the job.

To the delight of the Clinton team, the Bush people went after his character and the draft issue from the start. That begot a great sigh of relief from the Clinton camp. The Bush people had fallen into a trap they had set for themselves. Later in the campaign, when Bush finally did begin to talk about domestic issues, he did not introduce them properly, Greenberg believed, failing to segue from his foreign policy successes to his ability now to use the same energies and talents on the domestic front. Only near the end of the campaign, when it was far too late, did the Bush people go after Clinton's political record with ads that made Arkansas look like it was right out of the dust bowl of the thirties. Ironically, Clinton, who had not been that bothered by the assault on his personal life and his draft evasion, went ballistic with the attacks on his record and was sure they would hurt him. They did not. In all ways, Greenberg thought the Bush campaign never went to its strengths and never adjusted to the new political realities. What had worked so handsomely for Bush just four years earlier against Michael Dukakis no longer worked in this very different era against the shrewder, wilier Clinton and his team, particularly James Carville, ever combat ready. Carville was like a liberal-Democratic version of Lee Atwater, the young Republican adviser who had specialized in a scorched-earth policy toward political opponents.

Carville had come to prominence in an off-year Senate election in Pennsylvania in 1991 for the seat of the late Jack Heinz. The race was not without parallels to the 1992 presidential race. Dick Thornburgh, a popular former governor, a member of the Bush cabinet, and a somewhat patrician politician like Bush, had been willing to resign from the cabinet to make the race. Against him was the relatively unknown Harris Wofford, a former head of the Peace Corps and a college president. At one point Thornburgh led by forty-seven points in the polls. Carville's way to celebrate the end of the Cold War and cast attention on the soft Pennsylvania economy was his simple phrase "It's time to take care of our own," which was the forerunner of his later "It's the economy, stupid." Wofford had gone on to win, but the big winner was Carville with his combative style.

Perhaps the biggest surprise of the 1992 campaign was the lack of bounce Bush got from the Gulf War. The ground war had been prosecuted with brilliance and had lasted only a few days, the casualties minimal. It had been watched on television by an entire nation. The coming of the twenty-four-hour news channels and the ability to watch Pentagon film of American bombs and rockets hitting Iraqi targets had made it seem like a great national video game. It had been prosecuted by a professional army—a very professional army, it would turn out. The country had been thrilled, and afterward both Colin Powell and Norman Schwarzkopf, the most different of men, had emerged as national heroes. There had been marvelous celebratory parades in Washington and New York, which much of the nation had watched. Then very quickly it was all gone.

Perhaps it was the very nature of the war. Its brevity and the fact that the soldiers fighting it were from an elite professional army meant that few American homes actually shared in the danger, diminishing its impact. On the eve of war, David Maraniss of the *Washington Post* had gone down to Vanderbilt University in Nashville, where he interviewed seven young men, each either twenty or twenty-one, about the same age as the young men ready to fight in the Gulf. In this Southern citadel of traditional patriotism, five of the seven supported the war, but none was willing to fight in it. "This might sound selfish, but I think it would be a shame to put America's best young minds on the front line," said one young man.[5] Maraniss's piece was unusually telling; it was as if war had turned into a spectator sport, with most American homes immunized from the reality of it all. Perhaps the television coverage itself made it seem more like an entertainment event and helped turn many Americans into viewers rather than patriots. For most citizens, whatever the pleasure in seeing this awesome display of American might, the Gulf War was like watching a movie rather than a genuine participatory experience. When it was over, it was over quickly. The boost that Bush got from it was quick and impressive, but not long-lasting. It was not a deeply shared national experience. A new political coda seemed to be at work here: ask little of a nation and instead ask sacrifice from only a few people, and in the end the nation will care little.

Defeat was hard for George Bush, who believed up until the final days of the campaign, despite the polls, that he was going to win. He was sure that on Election Day the country would experience a blinding moment of reality and vote for him. The America he knew would not turn on him and vote for a man who had refused to serve his country, a man he sometimes in private and in public referred to as Elvis, a man who had played the saxophone on a goofy television talk show and was comfortable appearing on a channel called MTV, which surely had greater appeal to Bush's grandchildren than to the president himself. In the closing moments of the campaign, Bob Teeter, the pollster, and Marlin Fitzwater, the press secretary, went to Bush and tried to cushion the news of the inevitable. But Bush still refused to believe them and was sure that his faith in the wisdom of the American people would be validated.

In the final days of the Bush administration, Larry Eagleburger made one last try on Bosnia. In a sign of how far his own views had evolved, he had become the most proactive member of the administration. In early December he got permission to talk to our European allies about endorsing a new policy of "lift and strike"; that is, lifting the arms embargo on the Bosnians and using American airpower to deter Serb aggression. He did not have high hopes. He knew the European concerns about the vulnerability of their troops on the ground, but he thought it was worth the attempt. Nothing else was working and the atrocities were getting worse.

The election was over, so an element of restraint had now passed. At State, Eagleburger had been getting hit with the issue every day, and his trip was taken as much as anything else out of frustration. But it indicated the gradual change within the U.S. government that someone who had been perceived as an obstacle to an escalated American response was now going to his old European friends and asking them to up the ante. His trip changed neither hearts nor minds. The Europeans were in as deep as they wanted to be, pleas of an old friend or not. It was one more sign, as the Bush administration left office, of the failure of its policy toward Bosnia.

Eagleburger and Scowcroft recommended and got one other thing in the final days of the administration. The day before Christmas the president issued a warning—it became known as the Christmas warning—to Milosevic and the Serbs to leave Kosovo alone. Eagleburger drew it up. "In the event of conflict in Kosovo caused by Serbian action, the United States will be pre-pared to employ military force against Serbians in Kosovo and in Serbia proper." Because of their time in Yugoslavia both Eagleburger and Scowcroft knew that Kosovo remained the true flashpoint. Milosevic was delighted to extract as much as he could from Bosnia, but his political star had risen with his exploitation of ethnic tensions in Kosovo.

One final revealing discussion about the role of Europe and the United States in the Balkans also came in the last days of the Bush administration. In late December 1992, a group of central European foreign ministers, all part of what was called the Visegrad group, came to Washington to meet with both James Baker and George Bush. The Visegrad group, named after a small town in Hungary, was composed of the leaders of the countries in Europe that had recently been communist and were now coming together to improve their rela-tions with each other and show that they could be part of a new, more demo-cratic Europe, perhaps even members of NATO. Many of these men had known each other since the days when they had been suppressed by commu-nist regimes, and thus they had an innate collegiality. The group traveling to Washington included Polish, Czech, and Hungarian officials. The Austrians were at that moment quite oriented toward a new, democratic Europe, and the Austrian ambassador to the United States, Friedrich Hoess, was shepherding them through Washington and had arranged for a meeting with Baker and then with the president.

Two things were important about the meeting. The first was the immense stature of George Bush at that moment. To these men he was nothing less than the liberator of Europe, the man who had presided over the policies of the most powerful nation in the world when the cruel yoke of Soviet totalitarian-ism had been lifted from their shoulders. Never mind that their own heroism and the heroism of their people—the innate instinct of ordinary people to resist brutal totalitarian control—were more critical to the outcome than any action of the Americans. But they had nonetheless a great admiration for the policies of the American leaders who had helped stay the course over some forty-five years, and for Bush, in particular, for being the sitting president when it had all ended. Bush had visited their countries and capitals as a hero, the president of a nation whose troops had come to their distant countries for noble ideals during World War II, and whose leadership had stayed true to those ideals during the Cold War.

The second important thing was that these men were all passionate about what was happening in Yugoslavia. They knew the area well, it was in some cases right on their borders, and they knew Milosevic, or, perhaps more accurately, his type. They knew the Milosevics of the world because most of them had spent the last thirty years with the feet of Milosevic-like figures planted firmly on their necks. To them, the idea of Milosevic rising under the aegis of a system that they had fought for a lifetime, then switching over as the battle was won and declaring himself on the side of the new forces, was the height of cynicism. Most important, they knew the antidemocratic nature of what was going on, and they had a strong sense of what the larger cost might be to the people in Yugoslavia and to the general well-being of a more democratic Europe.

They made a passionate pitch to Bush and took turns speaking. For the sake of your legacy, for the sake of peace and decency in our region, we ask you to intervene. Only the United States can end the tragedy before it grows even worse. Bush heard them out but did not really respond. His term was coming to an end and he was not about to undertake a new military endeavor. The delegation was devastated. Leaving Bush's office, the Slovenian foreign minister, Dimitri Rupel, shook his head, turned to his colleagues, and said, "We hear a lot about the new Europe, but the truth is that the political will of the free world begins and ends in the Oval Office."

CHAPTER FIFTEEN

Foreign policy had remained a relatively minor issue in the Democratic primaries. Even before the 1992 campaign, it was obviously not a burning concern among the different Democratic Party constituencies. Rather, it was something that most of the party's principal candidates had distanced themselves from. In 1988 when the early signs of profound upheaval in Eastern Europe were already in evidence, the party's primary campaigns were even then noticeable for the lack of energy and substance on the subject. Of the younger Democratic candidates ascending in the eighties, only Gary Hart had a genuine passion for foreign policy and defense issues. He had sensed even before the Berlin Wall came down that the end of the Cold War would have profound consequences for both superpowers. Gorbachev had kept him at a distance at first but, increasingly intrigued by Hart's evident seriousness on issues, began to warm to him. Then Hart self-destructed, an early victim of the media's preoccupation with the personal lives of candidates, and the possibility of a meaningful debate about foreign policy died. (Gorbachev later tipped his hat to Hart, when the latter was out of presidential politics and practicing as a lawyer in Denver, by throwing an immense telecommunications contract to one of his Denver clients.)

That disengagement on foreign policy was largely still true in 1992. Gradually as Clinton escaped New Hampshire in surprisingly good shape, it became clear that he would be the Democratic nominee. In New York, where the Clinton team had all gathered for the convention, Tony Lake and Sandy Berger were standing around in Lake's hotel room, and Berger, who was about to go to Madison Square Garden for the nomination, glanced at Lake and saw a look of considerable sadness on his face.

"What's the matter?"

"I think it's going to work," Lake said. "I think he's going to get elected, and I'm going to have to make a choice about going back into government." Would he go back? he wondered. He was momentarily ambivalent about it. He knew how destructive working at that level in the government was to a marriage. It had damaged his once before and would eventually help destroy it. But he also knew he would say yes.

Clinton and his running mate, Al Gore, had capitalized in 1992 on the harsh rhetoric of the Republican convention by going out on their famed bus tour, and it had captured the imagination of the country, these two young men with their attractive young wives who apparently represented a new and dynamic post–Cold War America finally getting back to the business of America being America and not so involved in distant places. Clearly the country wanted some kind of reward for having soldiered through the hard years of the Cold War, an economic and psychological, if you will, peace dividend. To emphasize that point, there was Clinton, out on the hustings, attacking Bush again and again for paying too much attention to the rest of the world and not enough to his own country.

Having Al Gore on the ticket was a plus from the start, a serious political figure picked for what was, in volatile modern times, an increasingly important job. Whatever else about Gore—to some he appeared too straight, too stiff—no one ever doubted his ability and the degree of his preparation. If Clinton was serious about politics, Gore was just as serious about government. One could not imagine a teacher calling on Gore and young Al not having all his homework done. He tended to give long answers to short questions; and his problem on any essay exam would be never having enough time to make all the points he wanted.

In an earlier America, a ticket like this would never have been nominated. Tickets were supposed to be balanced, older men with younger, North with South or East with West, preferably New York with California, someone to the right of center with someone to the left of center, most certainly not Arkansas with Tennessee with both men of the same generation. But this was a new age and Gore's strengths had outweighed the demographic-geographic construct. Unlike most of the other talented young Democratic senators, he had not been standoffish or snobbish when he was interviewed by Warren Christopher during the preliminary search for vice-presidential candidates. When he subsequently met with Clinton, their session had gone very well.

Though no clear delineation of responsibilities emerged between Gore and Clinton, from the start they were reasonably comfortable with each other, with Gore having considerably more experience in foreign policy, in which Clinton was a neophyte. Gore had served on the Senate Armed Services Committee and was more hawkish than most members of his party. He had run as a hard-liner on the Middle East in his ill-conceived and abortive 1988 race, and he had voted for the Gulf War authorization. He was also very concerned about the Balkans. He was a sharp critic of American policy there, which he considered impotent, and was eager to lift the arms embargo. Almost from the beginning he had urged Clinton to take a stand against Slobodan Milosevic and to speak out on the Balkans.

During the campaign, Gore was far ahead of Clinton not merely in his knowledge of foreign policy, but in his *confidence* about his knowledge of foreign policy. At first Clinton tended to defer to his running mate on the matter, as if Gore were the professor and he the student. When Gore had pushed for a tougher line on the Balkans, Clinton seemed responsive. One memorable conference call early in the campaign included the Clinton foreign policy team: Tony Lake, Sandy Berger and Nancy Soderberg, Leon Fuerth, who was Gore's foreign policy staffer, as well as Gore, Clinton, and George Stephanopoulos. Gore strongly advocated arming the Bosnians, there seemed to be an agreement, and they appeared ready to go ahead with that policy, the candidate not merely on board, but surprisingly eager to take a harder line. *Yes, that's what we should be doing,* he said with a new vigor and confidence in his voice as if relieved from the indecision that had burdened his own attitude toward the region. But then they gradually decided that the new policy was, if not exactly precipitous, a little too specific. It put the Clinton people too far out on a limb and might make them vulnerable to criticism not just from Bush, but from the Europeans and the Pentagon, and so they backed down and made it a bit more general. Instead of presenting a clear-cut policy of their own, they would continue to nick away at the Bush people for their failings.

The race for the Democratic nomination was the hard part. After the nomination, Clinton could sense things beginning to turn in his direction. His feel for the way the campaign was going was eerie. His antennae were so good that he could tell from the reaction of the crowds that his issues were the ones that had resonance, that what he stood for was what the country wanted—the economy, stupid. He knew that, despite all the empirical arguments against him and in favor of Bush, all the conventional wisdom that said Bush should win, the issues were his. In Washington, taking a brief break from the campaign early in September, Clinton had turned to Stephanopoulos and said, "You think we're going to win, don't you?" "Yes, I do," Stephanopoulos answered. "I do, too," Clinton said, and Stephanopoulos was impressed. For Clinton to say something like that was new; he was usually much more cautious in talking about which way it was all going.[1] After that, Stephanopoulos noted, Clinton began to change. Because he sensed that his wildest dream was close to becoming a reality, he tempered his rhetoric, aware that he might actually become president and have to act on his words. Indeed, he might be a prisoner of them, and therefore it wasn't the wisest thing in the world to exaggerate.

The generational change taking place in American politics was also taking place in the larger culture as well, particularly in the media and national network television. Network television, always so sensitive to public opinion, much more so than elite print, picked up on changes in popular attitudes with astonishing rapidity, lest its ratings spiral downward with millions of dollars lost. Even as the American people were deciding in 1992 that domestic rather than foreign policy issues were paramount, the same thing had been happening in less dramatic form for more than a decade in network news, which was a remarkably faithful thermometer of the national psyche.

Nothing reflected the changes in American attitudes toward foreign policy more clearly than the way the three main television networks—ABC, CBS, and NBC—had gradually been moving away from serious foreign coverage in the eighties. They might, it was said with only a certain amount of exaggeration, be the only places where polling was as addictive as it was soon to become in the Clinton White House. In that decade the networks had largely turned away from the generation of distinguished correspondents who had built their reputations the old way, by covering the most difficult and important foreign stories, to a new, more telegenic kind of correspondent, both male and female, who worked for what were now called magazine shows and covered stories that were in general more tabloid or fluffier and were indicative of America's preoccupation with itself. It was a major professional shift. Some fifty years earlier, the networks—then in the radio, not the television, business—had made their reputations as a critical part of the fabric that bound the nation together with shared concerns by their foreign coverage during World War II. They had at that historic juncture helped the nation bridge the two oceans, a first step in America's coming of age as a world power.

That tradition, born of need and circumstance, had continued into the television age, and foreign correspondents had been the stars of the networks. The first generation of high-ranking, high-visibility television journalists had made their bones as foreign correspondents. Some of them, like Ed Murrow and Eric Sevareid, Walter Cronkite and Charles Collingwood, had begun as radio broadcasters and then in midcareer had been reincarnated as the leading figures of television news. That remained the case through the Vietnam War, which had been, in the writer Michael Arlen's apt phrase, not merely the first television war, but the first living room war.

By the eighties all of that was changing. Foreign correspondents began to encounter an increasingly difficult time getting on air. Many once-cherished foreign assignments lay open because bright young men and women were no longer eager to go to dangerous but interesting places where events were not sufficiently exciting to make the twenty-two-minute news shows. By the midnineties, places like Moscow, which offered great stories and where young print reporters from the *Times* and the *Washington Post* could still make their reputations, went unoccupied for extended periods because back home the young television reporters who wanted to be stars—to make your name in print, it was enough to be a good reporter; in television you had to be a *star*—knew they would end up with a tough, messy, difficult assignment that would only rarely make the evening news.

In effect, the networks had become essentially isolationist, or neo-isolationist, both reflecting and at the same time increasing the nation's self-absorption. America was only interested in itself. The rest of the world had become far more distant, less important, indeed more *foreign,* than it had been a decade earlier. Foreign news aired on the network news shows only when the connection to American concerns was unusually direct, or when the footage was so good and violent—lots of carnage—that it made for exceptional television. Or as the saying about many television news shows went, if it bleeds, it leads. Where once the daily news budget for the networks had closely paralleled that for the front pages of the great national newspapers such as the *New York Times* and the *Washington Post,* there was now a marked divergence. The national newspapers still carried a variety of foreign stories on their front pages, while the networks rarely reported on the same events unless they could air great footage. (Though one of the principal results of World War II was a powerful postwar generational commitment to internationalism, by the end of the century, Tom Brokaw, a network anchorman who had never been based overseas, was writing a series of encomiums to the World War II generation while presiding over the essential dissolution of its foreign correspondents.)

The impulses that the television news shows executives were responding to were exactly the same ones that Bill Clinton had responded to as he set off on his presidential campaign. It was a different America, one with a narrower focus. As the worst of the confrontations with the Soviets slipped into the past, the American people no longer felt threatened or scared. The interest in foreign news had been high in the years right after World War II, when the coming of nuclear warheads, attached as they were to intercontinental missiles, had shrunk the Atlantic and Pacific oceans, and it had ended when America felt safe from the rest of the world. Probably the most surprising aspect of the fall of the Berlin Wall and the end of the Cold War was the effect it had on the American media executives; they seemed released from being serious not just about foreign news, but in domestic reporting as well.

The entire economic structure of the networks had also changed. The proprietorial generation of Paley, Sarnoff, and Goldenson was gone; the new owners were giant corporations run by the new managerial class. To members of that class the only thing that mattered was increasing the value of the stock; foreign reporting was perceived as expensive and bad for ratings, which was bad for the stock. The new managerial class cared little about the iconic stature of Ed Murrow and Walter Cronkite. In addition, cable television had profoundly affected the networks. By the mideighties, cable had begun to come into its own, and the large audience that the three networks had always shared so comfortably—no one ever lost—began to fragment under the competition from cable.

The world of cable, with its desperate need for even the smallest rating point, brought a different value system, one more like tabloid newspapers, emphasizing sex and scandal and celebrity and violence and, with luck, perhaps all four at the same time as memorably with the O. J. Simpson murder trial. Their share of the audience in decline, the networks began to emulate not those who had gone before them in the world of serious journalism, but those who were now challenging them from the land of cable. Their magazine shows—which often gathered surprisingly good ratings and were inexpensive to produce—became increasingly tabloid. In the old days, the way to earn a position as a prominent and above all successful journalist who got a lot of airtime was to take on the most serious stories of the day—civil rights, Vietnam, Watergate. The new track was different. The big money was in magazine shows, and young reporters wanted to get on them because the seven-figure salaries were made there. What emerged in the world of the networks in the eighties and nineties was not great reporters, but television *personalities*. "Ours has become," John Chancellor, the former NBC anchor and one of the most distinguished men of broadcasting, said shortly before his death, "a world I no longer recognize and a world I do not very much like."[2]

Nothing indicated the changes taking place in the world of network news more vividly than the career of Garrick Utley, one of the most gifted foreign correspondents of two eras. Covering international news was literally in his blood. His father, Clifton Utley, who had headed the Chicago Council on Foreign Relations, was an early radio correspondent for an NBC-owned station. In fact, Clifton Utley had hired the young John Chancellor back in the forties. When Garrick Utley came along in 1963, just out of Carleton College in Minnesota, he was hired as an office boy by Chancellor in Brussels about a month before the network went from a fifteen-minute to a thirty-minute news show. Chancellor, one of the most admired men in the profession, gave Utley simple instructions on how to write and report for television: keep your sentences short and your voice low.

That was the beginning of a truly distinguished thirty-five-year career for Utley, during which he covered every major story all over the world, and where his very appearance on the screen signaled that a story of considerable substance was being reported. But that, as he liked to say, was yesterday, and this was today, and Utley understood by the early eighties that the profession he belonged to and loved was changing. Great, irreversible economic pressures were gathering against it, and the people charged with defending the traditional values were either weaker in their positions or not necessarily on the same side as he was. The open conflicts generated by the Cold War had essentially died down, undercutting the profession. Journalists love conflict; they might be fascinated by the ideas that drive the conflict, but on television the collision itself (because it produces great images) is what matters, and as the tensions of the Cold War abated, so did the pictures and the fears that it had generated. As there was less immediate threat, there was less story.

By 1982 Utley was chief foreign correspondent for NBC, heir to a great if somewhat brief tradition, based in New York and traveling the world without budgetary restrictions, still able to do longer pieces on serious foreign policy issues. But he soon began to realize that what he did and what he represented were coming to an end. NBC was bought by General Electric, the managerial class took hold, and that was immediately felt in the newsroom. Foreign bureaus—the exact same thing was to happen soon at CBS and in time at ABC—were considered unduly expensive. The idea of a talented, highly paid reporter waiting around until a story came his or her way was not something modern corporate financial officers liked. Bureaus at all three networks began to close and foreign correspondents were told to find other work.

In 1993, after thirty years with NBC, aware that the people he worked for cared little or nothing about the things that mattered most to him, knowing that it was pointless to be chief foreign correspondent for a network that did not believe in foreign reporting, Utley left NBC and went to work for ABC, which had under the leadership of Roone Arledge emerged for a time as the most serious of the three networks, until Disney merged with Capitol Cities. Utley's tour with ABC would be brief, three years, just long enough to witness, with the arrival of the Disney people, the same change in values that had already taken place at NBC.

In 1993, Utley was in London when the Balkans began to blow up, sharing his stories of woe with another ABC foreign correspondent, Jim Laurie. They had both discovered that it was increasingly difficult to get stories on the air—unless there was combat footage—and now even with that, the market was shrinking. Bosnia, they decided, was an important story, but it was also a nightmare, harder and harder to get access to, and more and more dangerous. In New York there was little enthusiasm for the story, which was becoming a tough sell to the news desks because no one thought it really connected to America. The stories they were able to file, Laurie and Utley agreed, were becoming shorter and shorter because of New York's essential lack of interest. That meant the context of their stories, which was at the core of good reporting, was being cut out, and they had less and less significance for ordinary Americans because they were devoid of the mandatory explanations. It was a kind of journalistic self-fulfilling prophecy. New York did not think the stories had much meaning and thereupon created a format that presented them with little meaning.

Laurie had a feeling that a vicious cycle was at work. The people who ran *World News Tonight* were, in ways they did not entirely understand, keying in on what first the Bush and then the Clinton administrations thought was important on the theory that what the president and his people thought was important was, in fact, important. But in this case, the relationship was intriguing. As the Clinton administration evolved, the president, for political reasons, did not want to deal with Bosnia and was deliberately downplaying it, while the failure of the network news shows to run Bosnian reports aggressively allowed him to keep minimizing the story. It was, Laurie thought, the blind leading the blind—a kind of journalistic Catch-22.

In 1992, Laurie reported one story from Belgrade that became a fifty-second spot, the first time that had ever happened. At one time his stories had been longer, two or two and a half minutes, but that was in another age, and he and Utley commiserated about that. They and many of the other American television correspondents who were covering Bosnia knew the difficulties of the story. This nasty assignment, filled with constant dangers, did not seem to excite New York. For the first time in his career, Laurie began to question his own news judgment. Here were Serb soldiers on a rampage in Bosnia, leaving terrible carnage in their wake, and yet New York did not seem to care.

Laurie and Utley were a little luckier than most, they decided, because Peter Jennings, alone among the three network anchors, had made his reputation as a foreign correspondent and still had a passion for foreign news. But after a time, a malaise overtook Laurie. He had covered many of the most dangerous stories for ABC over two decades, but the risk in Bosnia—where journalists wore helmets, flak jackets, and sometimes traveled around in armored cars—was not necessarily worth taking if nobody cared. He found himself shying away from the story, leaving it to the stringers, young men and women who were not American nationals and were willing to take appalling risks to get on the air and perhaps make their reputations. Both Utley and Laurie thought some kind of test was being failed not merely by their network, but in some way by their country. Here was America, at the zenith of its power and influence, paying so little attention to the world around it.

Rarely had there been such a sharp division between those who worked in the field (until they were almost all gone) and their superiors in New York, the anchors and the executive producers of the news shows. The roots of these senior figures were in journalism, and they had risen through the ranks when people like Ed Murrow, Walter Cronkite, and John Chancellor were giants— no one threw Murrow's name around more than Dan Rather of CBS. But the process now had a dynamic of its own, and the senior network anchors had become, like it or not, a central part of it. There were fewer and fewer real reporters, less and less real reporting, and most certainly fewer foreign correspondents. And more stars. That was the system. The anchors themselves, like the stars of the frothier magazine shows, were stars, too, and drew the salaries of stars, about $7 million or $8 million each. They did the best they could against a current running ever faster against them, but they had been made accessories to a process they did not believe in.

An issue of *New York* that gave out the salaries of the anchors also noted what the *New York Times* paid Joseph Lelyveld, its talented executive editor—some $500,000. No one who knew anything about journalism thought for a moment that any of the anchors was fourteen times the journalist Lelyveld was. But it would not have occurred to the owners of the *Times* to pay their editor at the expense of their foot soldiers or to close down foreign bureaus in order to afford gargantuan salaries. Salaries at the *Times* were representative of journalism the way it used to be; those at the networks were representative of journalism as it had transmogrified itself in an age of entertainment and self-absorption.

The one television correspondent who was making a considerable professional reputation in the Balkans was a talented young woman named Christiane Amanpour, who worked for the fledgling cable network CNN and who had the good fortune, in a profession where cosmetics were so important, to be as attractive as she was talented. She was absolutely fearless, and almost from the start staked the story out as her own. For CNN to cover it while other networks stood aside was not surprising. Its franchise was international, and this story, if it did not yet excite Americans, did have significant international implications. It was important in the Balkans and throughout the rest of Europe, it was important in Russia because of the Slavic interest in anything that happened to the Serbs, and it was important in the Muslim world because of the fate of the Muslims in Bosnia and Kosovo.

Amanpour had arrived in the Balkans in June 1991, knowing little about the region, but getting there in time to cover the breakaway of Slovenia and Croatia from Yugoslavia and the Serbian assault upon the Muslims of Bosnia that followed. "I did not," she noted, "know a Croat from a Serb when I first arrived." Child of an upper-middle-class Iranian family uprooted when the Shah fell in 1979, she grew up in England and was educated in the United States at the University of Rhode Island. Determined to be a war correspondent, she was one of the early CNN employees and had covered the Gulf War. That was a big CNN story, but one in which the technology was so dominant and the actual time of armed combat so brief that few correspondents in the field had distinguished themselves.

In Bosnia that would be different. Amanpour was thirty-four when she got there, lucky, she decided, to be a part of the changing of the guard from the generation of journalists who had come of age during the Vietnam War and had covered some of the smaller conflicts in the intervening years, most notably in Central America, and who were now in their late fifties and early sixties. She remembered believing that this was her generation's Vietnam, a war that was not only a serious ongoing military struggle, but one with a huge moral component. Amanpour brought an unusual intensity to her work. Perhaps because her own family had been devastated by events outside their control, she had exceptional sensitivity to the plight of ordinary people caught in the pull of cruel historical forces. But what was happening in Bosnia was different from anything she had seen in the Gulf War. There, armies had fought other armies. Here the Serb army was attacking civilians. She was amazed by the brazen cruelty of what she witnessed, beginning with the siege of Dubrovnik.

When that was over and Milosevic started to move on Bosnia, Amanpour had no trouble convincing her superiors that she should stay on top of the story. Some European television networks were taking it seriously, but she was surprised by the lack of interest among the other American networks. Their correspondents covered the story episodically, staying for three or four days, complaining bitterly about their inability to get anything on the air, then going back to their bases in London or Paris. It was primarily the print journalists, Amanpour believed, who brought Bosnia to the world's attention, not the diplomats from the great nations who were supposed to watch out for barbarisms like this, not the UN people who were there to keep the peace, not even the representatives of the NGOs who were trying to deal with the tragic situation. It was Blaine Harden of the *Washington Post,* Roy Gutman of *Newsday,* and John Burns of the *Times* who were keeping a record of the terrible atrocities. Amanpour became their peer, the one reporter on American television every day. She thought from the start that she was witnessing a moral catastrophe, one that brought back memories of Hitler's Germany. Perhaps the scale was not the same, but the cruelty of the genocidal impulse was, and thousands and thousands of people were being killed and raped or forced to flee only because of their ethnicity while the West was simply standing by.

Amanpour was appalled, and her emotions not only drove her reporting and made her work ever harder, they were also obvious in her voice. She did not even attempt impartiality or journalism's beloved artificial balance, the equating of forces that were not equal. She did not believe that being a good reporter in a time of genocide meant neutrality, or that she should distort what she saw and learned in order to appear to be more fair. Fairness had nothing to do with what was happening. Hers was a powerful voice, even though it was confined to the smallest of the networks, one which had on average perhaps only a million viewers a day. But her work spoke volumes about the other networks and what they were not doing. Nor did it please the Clinton administration, newly arrived in power and reluctant to get involved in Bosnia.

CHAPTER SIXTEEN

B ill Clinton was the first true post–World War II, post–Cold War president. George Bush had served some three and a half years in office from the fall of the Berlin Wall to Clinton's inaugural, but he was very much a man of the old order. Clinton represented a different political generation, driven by vastly different issues. The defining personal experience for Clinton was most assuredly racial change in the South. That seemed to be the issue to which more than any other he brought genuine commitment and passion and was what probably had motivated him to be a politician in the first place. Foreign policy remained distant to him. Yes, he had been a Rhodes Scholar, and certainly one of the assumptions of the people who gave out those cherished fellowships was that it was supposed to be a life-changing experience. Part of its purpose was to introduce talented young Americans (and others) to the rest of the world, especially England and the Continent. But once at Oxford, Clinton had performed academically in the most desultory manner imaginable. The brand name of the Rhodes Scholar was what he had wanted—and a two-year travel-o-rama.

He had not sought an Oxford degree. It would not in any way be a great career asset; he was not going to be an academic. He knew exactly where he was headed. He was going back home to law school and then run for office. He had gone to Oxford, Rolodex at the ready, eager to meet and check out the competition—the other brightest and most ambitious young men of his generation—and to decide whether a country boy from Hope, Arkansas, could take them on. If he could, all the better; he would sign them up for his future campaigns. He seemed to some of his peers to have arrived at Oxford already campaigning for national office, taking down names and addresses of anyone who might help him and, of course, trying to meet as many attractive young women as possible. He had not greatly interested himself in the study of postwar Europe, the effect of the Cold War on both sides of the Iron Curtain, nor the validity of NATO. If any foreign policy issue weighed on him in those days—and most other young men of his generation—it was Vietnam.

Clinton was interested in domestic politics by instinct. That was his strength and his natural inclination. His defeat of Bush had only served to confirm the accuracy of his political instincts. Foreign policy issues subtracted from the limited power he had, which was to be used for domestic programs anyway. Foreign policy was to be minimized and, if at all possible, kept on the back burner. Besides, he was almost excessively confident himself as a quick study, someone who could make shrewd and highly effective political calls on *any* subject, even when he came in at the last moment. The one thing Clinton did not want was an activist secretary of state who would undertake new and potentially unpredictable initiatives. He also wanted a status quo national security team in what was most demonstrably no longer a status quo world.

His months on the campaign trail had convinced him that he was politically ahead of a new curve. Nothing indicated that so clearly as a meeting he had held with a group of leading Democrats—all House committee chairmen—during the transition period. He had gone around the room asking each chairman about the problems in his area until he finally got to Lee Hamilton, the veteran Indiana congressman who headed the House Foreign Affairs Committee. Hamilton talked about a number of issues: post-Soviet Russia, the complex problems of dealing with China—there was never, he said, going to be a policy that would satisfy everyone on China. Suddenly Clinton interrupted him, "Lee, I just went through the whole campaign and no one talked about foreign policy at all, except for a few members of the press."

That set Hamilton back slightly, but then he responded, "You know, every president's tenure is marked by foreign policy issues, whether they want it or not. It just happens that way. No American president can avoid it because he's the leader of the free world. They think they can, but they can't." Then Hamilton mentioned Johnson and Vietnam, Carter and the hostages in Iran, Reagan and the Iran-contra scandal, and Bush and the Gulf War. It did not change Clinton, of course; he knew that his stand on domestic issues had elected him. Years later, Hamilton, who had by then left office, reflected on that meeting and thought that Clinton had been right. But he had also been very wrong.

The team assembling around Clinton during the transition was representative of, among other weaknesses within the Democratic Party, the lack of depth in foreign policy. The Democrats, after all, had been out of power for twelve years, and in power for only four of the last twenty-four years. They had not developed much in the way of bench strength. Nor were they a party with an easy consensus on political issues. There was still a considerable division between the old Kennedy-McCarthy-McGovern Democrats and the Hubert Humphrey–Scoop Jackson Democrats, some of whom had come back to the fold during the 1992 campaign and some of whom were still sitting on the fence. Old issues that had divided different wings of the party because of Vietnam had never entirely been resolved. In the one term in which the Democrats had managed to hold power during the prolonged Republican dominance—the Carter years—the split between the two Democratic factions had proved nearly fatal.

The Carter administration was instructive. Carter had named as his national security adviser Zbigniew Brzezinski, and as his secretary of state Cyrus Vance. The twain never met. Brzezinski, of Polish origin, was not merely a hard-liner in general, but was considered more Russophobic than the top people in State, who had been in many cases personally affected by Vietnam. He tended to believe that the smaller conflicts throughout the world were, in fact, areas where the Soviet Union was contesting the United States, whereas some of the Carter people believed that indigenous nationalist forces, arguing out age-old political and ethnic divisions, were at the core of the contention. In addition, they thought the stakes were not that high because these countries were only marginally developed, and therefore no matter which side won, it would not make much difference in realpolitik. Those arguments had their roots in the Vietnam experience; many of the early and most outspoken doves believed the decisive issue at stake there had been nationalism, and that any American commitment was doomed because we were bound to come in on the wrong side of history, reinforcing in the minds of the Vietnamese the French colonial experience. Under Carter the two warring wings of the party had come to Washington, each had held one of the two top foreign policy positions, and they had kept right on warring. That the last Democratic president had permitted a bitter internal struggle to go on so long and so openly, and that a Democratic president had allowed his national security adviser to cut his secretary of state out on critical issues, were sure signs of the party's lack of leadership in foreign policy.

The Clinton transition period did not begin well. Almost from the start there were major conflicts between the domestic political people like Stephanopoulos and Carville—the men who thought they had elected Bill Clinton—and Mickey Kantor, who was also a good friend of the president-elect's and was supposed to be an unofficial chief of staff and, at least in his own mind, in charge of the transition. The question seemed to be about whose victory this was. The degree of squabbling in the early days of the transition—how poisonous it was and how far apart were the people who should have been on the same side—quite startled the president-elect. For a time it appeared likely to force him to make an unwanted and perhaps fateful choice between close and trusted aides even before he was in office. In desperation, he called Warren Christopher and asked for his help. Christopher, who was supposed to be a relatively minor figure during the transition, flew immediately to Little Rock, thinking he might stay for a day or two. Instead he stayed on for more than a month and became, along with Vernon Jordan, the leading figure in the transition.

Christopher was sixty-seven years old, twenty-one years older than the president-elect, old enough to be his father. He was, in fact, virtually the exact same age that William Jefferson Blythe, the president's birth father, would have been had he not been killed in an auto accident as a young man. That was not unimportant because close aides would describe Christopher's early relationship to Clinton as almost paternal. Christopher was at the time the most senior figure in the Democratic Party foreign policy establishment, but not too old to serve in the new administration. Though he had been a Vance man, he had never been contaminated by the bitter divisions of the Carter years. He was the acceptable man. Not many people were excited by him or his view of the world (which by and large they didn't know since he never went around discussing whatever it was). He elicited few strong feelings—either among people who favored him or who were opposed to him. Almost everyone who knew him had some esteem for him. Ed Muskie, briefly secretary of state under Carter, was too old, and Zbig Brzezinski, national security adviser under Carter, was perhaps the perfect age, three years younger than Christopher. But Brzezinski had been a leader in the internal battles with the somewhat more dovish wing of the Democratic Party during the Carter years and was virtually persona non grata to many of the young men now returning to power who had been on the Vance side of the old factional divide.

Christopher represented the neutral center of the party. He did not know Clinton well, but he was a good friend of Mickey Kantor's, through mutual service in Los Angeles Democratic politics. Kantor had originally brought him into the Clinton campaign. Christopher had been of distinct service to Clinton on two previous political occasions. The first was during the New Hampshire primary at the height of the Gennifer Flowers crisis, a time when most of the senior figures of the Democratic Party were still extremely leery of the Arkansas governor, keeping more than the requisite distance from him. Christopher had come to Clinton's aid in one of his darkest hours, the night after he had been badly pounded at a meeting in Seattle. At a fund-raiser for Clinton in Los Angeles, Christopher, a leading figure in local Democratic circles, not only spoke, which was valuable of itself, but he, nominally the most emotionally buttoned up of men, gave a surprisingly impassioned speech. Clinton was touched that this lion of the Los Angeles Democratic establishment had come to his aid during a moment of travail, and he spoke of it often afterward to friends.

At the fund-raiser Christopher had praised Clinton's amazing resilience and his ability to keep coming despite taking hit after hit. "And he doesn't whine about the hits," Christopher added. ("Christopher found out soon enough he was wrong about that particular part of it," one of his close friends later noted. "Clinton can take a lot of hits but he always whines—it's a very important part of his makeup.")

On the second occasion, Christopher was placed in charge of the vice-presidential search, and done carefully and discreetly, it was widely regarded as the single most successful part of the entire campaign. Nothing had leaked out, and they not only got the man they wanted, but no one else's feelings were hurt. At the time they announced the choice of Al Gore, it should be remembered, Clinton was running poorly against both Bush and Perot, but the campaign took off almost immediately and the bus tour of the two young Democratic nominees was considered an exceptional plus. Christopher had twice proved himself effective, low-key, and undemanding. He was what every politician dreams of finding at a time like that—a thorough professional with lots of connections who knows the terrain and has complete control of his ego.

Working with Christopher on the foreign policy transition team was Vernon Jordan, who had been brought in somewhat earlier as a kind of tiebreaker when the Stephanopoulos-Kantor tensions had heightened. Jordan and Christopher constituted a most unlikely pair. Jordan was young, black, earthy, exuberant, the strikingly handsome son of an Atlanta country-club waiter, a man who exulted in the pleasures and perks that his newfound success had brought him. If anyone personified the victories of the civil rights movement in the thirty-eight years since *Brown* v. *Board of Education,* it was Jordan, an immensely winning man, who appeared to be on the threshold of a brand-new role for any descendant of slavery in America. For the first time in the country's history, the principal friend and fixer of a president-to-be of the United States was black, an unofficial position to be sure, but a most desirable one, and one always reserved for white political power brokers in the past. Jordan would become a ubiquitous figure in the Clinton years, perhaps the one person the president trusted on high-level appointments and on a wide range of other subjects.

Where Jordan was exuberant and energetic, Christopher was the most reserved and disciplined of men, tightly wound and completely driven, going through life as if displaying any emotion was the last thing you ever did. It was hard to imagine him with his jacket off or his tie loosened. The two men, naturally, got on perfectly from the start. Neither wanted the same thing. Jordan had long ago spent more than his share of time in public service doing pro bono work. For more than twenty years he had headed various civil rights organizations such as the United Negro College Fund and the Urban League. He had received something like fifty honorary degrees. That was the first part of his career. In the second, having already done his share of good, he wanted to do well, and instead of collecting honorary degrees, he collected memberships on America's corporate boards. As an influential lawyer-lobbyist in Washington, he had no interest in working for the president, a relationship, he knew, that would inevitably diminish him, especially with this president, whom it was possible to serve loyally, skillfully, and yet somehow manage to fail. Jordan was shrewd enough to know that he could remain a close friend only if he did not work for Clinton.

Jordan was perfectly positioned. The city, the nation, and the world knew how close he was to Clinton, the president-elect's chosen golf partner, the man he liked around him for locker room talk. What better advertising was there for both him and his law firm than that? Who else could sit in a Washington law office and be as great a rainmaker? On the first day they got together, Jordan, dropping by the hotel to pick up Christopher, drove a red Allante Cadillac convertible, a sporty car made in Italy. He had heard that Christopher—it seemed out of character to most people who knew him—loved hot cars. "We had a two-man dinner and we got on well from the start. By the end of the evening," Jordan liked to say, "we were going steady."

Warren Christopher was an old-fashioned man of another generation, his expectations always tempered by his having survived a difficult childhood in the Dakotas during the Depression. He was a ferociously ambitious man, a good deal of whose energy went into concealing how ambitious he really was. He wanted more than anything else to be secretary of state of the United States. One of his greatest disappointments had come in 1980 after Cyrus Vance resigned as secretary of state and Jimmy Carter chose, instead of Christopher, who had served both Vance and Carter so loyally for so long, Ed Muskie as the secretary. Christopher, engaged in backbreaking private negotiations to free the American hostages in Iran, was devastated by the news and thought seriously of resigning. Because he was so disciplined, he was loath to say how badly he felt at the time. Instead, in Christopher-speak, it came out simply as "that was a low point in my career."

When Christopher joined the transition team, he immediately took himself out of the running for the secretary of state's job. Still, as the search for that secretary progressed, two things became clear. First, no other candidate loomed large on the landscape. "There was," Jordan would later say, "a huge gap in age between those who had done it in the past and those who were not yet ready but wanted to." The lack of Democratic bench strength, they quickly discovered, was quite stunning. The damage done by Vietnam had effectively wounded some in the ascending generation. Some of the men coming of age, in their late fifties to early sixties, were in general too close to the now contaminated policy makers of that era, and the next generation was, as Jordan suggested, still too young. Any possible candidate of Clinton's own age would have to come from the Senate, and the most obvious Democratic senators of that generation, their reputations already assured before Clinton ever announced, had tended to look down on him as an upstart, a man whose credentials fell far short of their own.

Sam Nunn, the Georgia senator, was a possibility. The senior level of the Washington Democratic establishment was promoting him enthusiastically, but the traditional liberals in the party were dubious. His innate cultural conservatism tended to work against him, and there was something of an ideological gap between him and the president-elect. They might both be what were called New Democrats, but on a number of social-cultural issues Clinton's national constituencies were different from Nunn's Georgia ones, and their personal relationship was, at best, uncomfortable. Nunn could surely have Defense, but not State. Bill Bradley might have been another possibility, but he had alienated the Clinton people during the vice-presidential screening process. Christopher had met with him as he had met with Gore and others. But Bradley had made it abundantly clear that the only job he wanted was the presidency. The word the Clinton people used to describe him was *haughty.* Nor was he perceived as having helped greatly during the campaign itself.

The second thing that became apparent was that Warren Christopher badly wanted the job. In a polite, genteel, and unemotional way, he hungered for it. He might be a minimalist in words and in emotions, but he made clear in any number of little ways that he coveted the job. He also made clear that he thought he was the right man for it, but the initiative would have to come from someone else. Later during the transition, Jordan, by then extremely gifted at interpreting what Christopher said and did not say, understood how desperately his colleague—and now good friend—wanted the job. He got Christopher alone and said they needed to talk. He then told Christopher that he was going to see Clinton that day and turn down once and for all the job of attorney general, for which he was being recommended. But he wanted to raise Christopher's name for secretary of state. It was speak now or forever hold your ambition. "Do you want the fucking job?" Jordan asked. Yes, Christopher answered, but it would be a conflict of interest because as head of the transition team he had taken himself out of the running for any key job. Jordan told him that was not exactly a conflict of interest and went to the governor's mansion that night to talk to Clinton.

There Jordan told Clinton that under no circumstance would he take the job of attorney general, but he knew that Christopher badly wanted to be secretary of state. "He wants it, he deserves it, but he won't raise it, so I'm raising it for him," Jordan said. Clinton asked if Jordan thought Christopher was the right man and Jordan said yes. So they talked a bit more, Clinton seemed agreeable, and Jordan asked if he could tell Christopher that the deed was done. Clinton said yes. The next morning Jordan telephoned Christopher at his hotel and said, "Good morning, Mr. Secretary." (A few months later, on his first trip to the Middle East, Christopher met in Damascus with Hafiz al-Assad, the president of Syria. "How did you get to be secretary of state?" Assad asked him. "When I sat there watching CNN one day, I saw you take yourself out of the running. So how did you get the job?")

Not everyone who knew Christopher well and regarded his abilities highly thought it an inspired appointment. They agreed that he was honorable and decent, intelligent, uncommonly careful and meticulous. Above all, he was a workhorse of the first order. He had great control of his ego, which meant that he would neither be a leaker nor a glory seeker, someone likely to trumpet his own achievements at the expense of the White House. When things went well in foreign policy, the light would shine on the White House; when they went badly, Christopher was the kind of man—and there fewer of those left in the aspirant pool—who would shine the light on himself.

But something important was missing. No one really knew whether he had ideas or a vision of his own on foreign policy. It was partly why he had so few enemies, but it was also why many people who knew and rather liked him had a fair amount of doubt about his selection. He remained, thought some of the doubters, exactly what he had been under Vance, the perfect deputy, a man whose own personality and thoughts were always in the shadows. But while his abilities were considerable, his critics thought, they fell short, particularly for a job that had become extremely important now that the Cold War was over and a new, thoughtful, and wise vision of how to deal with a more turbulent world was mandatory. Christopher, they thought, was too much the functionary, a capable and highly competent bureaucrat, but probably a limited one, a man lacking originality and beliefs of his own. More than anyone else in the administration other than the president, the secretary of state at this moment in time needed the vision thing.

Some people with knowledge of the Democratic Party talent bank suggested that Christopher might be perfect for attorney general, and years later the consensus was that if he had been attorney general, it might have improved the administration in two key slots. State might have been stronger from the start under someone with a more focused sense of direction, and the administration would not have stumbled as badly as it did when its first two candidates for Justice withdrew because of nanny problems. Christopher, it was believed, would have run a clean Justice Department with just the right measure of deference to the politics of the president. But that was not to be. With Vernon Jordan passing on the job at Justice, the Clinton administration was soon publicly committed to choosing a woman to be the nation's top lawyer.

Oddly, the warnings that Clinton received about Christopher probably helped validate him for the job. Not a forceful, independent figure with strong ideas of his own about the world? The last thing Bill Clinton wanted at State was a man who might, even on some relatively minor issue, if not wander off the reservation, at least create internal tension by the force and drive of his personality and his desire to act when the president might not want to act. When people told Clinton that Christopher was immensely hardworking, but not necessarily imaginative, and finally quite lawyerlike, a man likely to be a functionary rather than a leader, that, too, was precisely what the president wanted—a deputy to run State and cause no problems. What did Clinton like most about Christopher? a top administration aide was once asked. "That he did not give off any heat" came the answer. He was smart, thorough, and he knew not only his own limitations, but the limitations of what the new president wanted in the job. One of the reasons he had always been so successful was because he read the needs of his clients with singular accuracy.

So Christopher would be the secretary of state. He would never cause the administration problems the way an activist like Dick Holbrooke might. Christopher, said one colleague, would always make the safe call. But that meant, the colleague added, that he would end up not being safe, because everything he did would be premised on conventional choices and this was a world where decisions could no longer be conventional. Christopher was better at looking back on issues and tidying up other people's messes than he was at looking ahead and anticipating where a difficult crisis might arise. He was one of those men who had moved deftly through a bureaucracy, rarely standing out, rarely creating waves, knowing when to take cover, yet always moving ahead until, to the surprise of many people who had denigrated his skills and his talents, they ended up being the boss. Many of his colleagues would later remember him for the absence of actions rather than actions. "Dean Rusk without the charisma" went the phrase used in Democratic circles among those not impressed by the choice. His selection was believed to symbolize how little Clinton was really interested in foreign policy.

One of the first things that Christopher had to do was dilute his connection to Carter. He might have been one of Carter's personal favorites, and the previous Democratic president had given him the Medal of Freedom at the end of his one term, but there were limits to loyalty, and a new Southern governor was entering the presidency, and he was hardly anxious to be linked to his predecessor. The distance between Washington and Plains, Georgia, was to be maximized. Carter, to Clinton, was a symbol of Democratic incompetence past, and Clinton would be the symbol of Democratic success in the present. The problem was that Carter was ready, willing, and able to get back in government as a special representative of the president of the United States. In flooded the calls from him announcing his availability, indeed his eagerness, to take on assignments. Yet such was the wariness on the part of Clinton and his political people about the possibility of the Carter shadow falling on them that, during the transition, when Carter, full of ideas about foreign policy, called to talk to the president-elect—not an unimportant call, the last Democratic president telephoning his younger successor, both of them Southerners—Clinton pointedly did not take his calls. He passed them on to Christopher, his foreign policy transition man, who had come to prominence in the Carter years. Christopher, in turn, tried to pass the job of handling Carter on to *his* deputy, Peter Tarnoff. It would have been hard to make a cleaner break from the recent past; Jimmy Carter watched the new team arrive in Washington, deeply wounded by its treatment of him.

CHAPTER SEVENTEEN

Christopher was appointed secretary of state partly because, of the various candidates, he had the fewest enemies. Of Dick Holbrooke, at best an outside possibility for the job during the 1992 transition, it could be said that he was the most talented candidate, but also the man with the most enemies. The antithesis of Christopher, Holbrooke had been an assistant secretary for East Asia in the Carter administration as a very young man, and now as the Clinton people prepared to enter office, he was fifty-one, perhaps a bit young, especially since the president himself was so young. But age was less a problem than personality. Holbrooke was high-talent, high-risk, and believed by almost all in the selection process to be high-maintenance. When the people picking the new team considered him, they thought first of his energy and intelligence, which were almost off the charts, and then, in the same instant, of his ego, which was also presumed to be off the charts. Keeping him tuned in as a team player and out of tribal and territorial struggles with colleagues would be a problem. He tended, some people in the new administration thought, to be too media-obsessed, taking credit for things that worked out and shying away from things that did not.

If named secretary of state, however, Holbrooke would first and foremost be a player. Not everyone who admired his abilities completely liked him. He could be bright and winning, but he was so forceful, so driven, not merely by sheer ambition but his belief in the rightness of the policies he advocated, that he often had little sense of the impact of his deeds on other people. There was no way in the world that he would be a minimalist secretary of state. Quite the reverse. He would be a full-fledged activist, pushing everyone around him on any number of issues, and if he got the job, given his considerable energy, intellect, and knowledge of how to work the bureaucracy, the State Department would not be a quiet or acquiescent place.

Issues that the new administration might want to keep relatively dormant might come hurtling to the fore under Holbrooke. That was not a recommendation as far as Clinton was concerned. Clinton himself was a formidable, quite dominating figure, and he would soon learn in the White House how to intimidate aides who brought him news he did not want to hear. But it would be hard to do that with Holbrooke. He was simply more of a force of nature. Holbrooke was also aware of his reputation for being too aggressive. Washington, he once said with some degree of melancholy, rewards people who are not passionate, who know how to play the game, and who do not make mistakes.[1] With Holbrooke you got strengths, you got talent, and you got headaches—but at the very least it was guaranteed that you would not be bored.

He was already engaged on the issue of Bosnia, which would in time dominate all Clinton foreign policy decisions. Holbrooke had been one of the early first-tier foreign policy people to visit there and write about it. That was in the summer of 1992, when things were beginning to deteriorate. Now as he was being considered for a high-level administration position, it had gotten worse. Thus if Holbrooke were to be offered a job in this administration, he would be the rare high-level player who had seen the Bosnian horror at first-hand and had been moved by it. Nor was he likely, once in office, to let an issue like that slip away. Given the other priorities of the president, that might have worked against Holbrooke.

But he had another downside as well. He tended to roll over someone when it suited him, and he had crossed many powerful people in Washington, without always knowing that he had done so. Few were neutral about him. His admirers, who tended to be confident people, thought he was immensely gifted and well worth the considerable trouble he was bound to cause. His detractors, who were many, were extremely vocal in their opposition to him for that same reason. Among those whose enthusiasm was quite limited was Warren Christopher, who had clashed with Holbrooke over human rights issues in the Carter years and saw him as exceptionally hard to contain. Holbrooke was in all emotional ways almost the exact opposite of the cautious, careful Christopher, who kept much to himself yet would play an important role in choosing the national security team. He could take one look at Holbrooke and know that on something that truly mattered to him he would be like a hammer, driving the issue all the time, whether the people above him wanted it driven or not. His respect for the ideas of others did not always match the respect he had for his own ideas, unless, of course, they were the ideas and opinions of the president himself.

Thus, as the new team came together, Holbrooke, once considered a viable, albeit outside, candidate for secretary of state, began to slip in the ratings system and fall toward the second tier. That was painful. He had been a wunderkind in the Carter years, and though he was tempestuous, demanding, and often difficult, no one had doubted the totality of his bureaucratic skill. He was respected for the talented people he had picked for his team during the Carter years—a number of gifted subordinates were named as ambassadors by Holbrooke—his willingness to fight for ideas, and his tendency on many issues to be ahead of everyone else in seeing their dangers and consequences. His ambition had always been limitless; he still wanted to be secretary of state. But he had sat out the last twelve years and was now no longer a wunderkind. He was a man in his early fifties whose star, once so bright, might be in descent, even though the Democrats were back in power.

He would not get State, he would not become deputy secretary or an undersecretary, and he would not get the UN—that was marked for Madeleine Albright. Both Clintons liked the idea of a woman there. Japan was a possibility, a job in which Holbrooke was quite interested. Because of the complexity and importance of the American-Japanese relationship and the immense trade imbalance, the post was considered something of a plum. He was, after all, an expert on Asia, and Tokyo was the biggest ticket in the region, though how much of an impact an ambassador would have there was always problematical. Fritz Mondale, the former vice president, appeared ticketed for Moscow. But then Joan Mondale, who was interested in the arts, decided that the art scene in Japan was more interesting than in Moscow, a dubious judgment, and Mondale took Tokyo.

For a time it appeared that Holbrooke might not get any job at all and he was falling without a parachute. Christopher did not want him at any high-level job at State. Nor did Tony Lake, soon to be the national security adviser and once one of his closest friends, want him to have a major appointment. But Holbrooke had one influential advocate, Strobe Talbott, who had been close to Clinton for almost twenty-five years, since the time they were roommates at Oxford. Talbott was a huge Holbrooke fan; he knew the downside but he thought this administration desperately needed his talent and energy. In one of the rare occasions when he used his personal connection with Clinton, Talbott pleaded that they find a place for Holbrooke. It was, he told the president, simply wrong to have someone of his ability off the team. Talbott was aided in this instance by Sandy Berger, who was also high on the NSC team, marked to be Lake's deputy. Holbrooke, mutual friends thought, might drive Berger nuts, but Berger knew his value, and he, too, made the case for Holbrooke with Clinton.

Germany was open, and Germany it would be. Holbrooke got it as a kind of consolation prize. He was deeply disappointed at first. He did not see the upside of it, and for a time he thought of turning it down. But friends helped convince him to do otherwise, reminding him that it would not necessarily be the last position he would get and that his talents would inevitably bring him to the fore. So he reversed himself and decided to take it. But a considerable bitterness lingered from the transition period. Holbrooke was convinced that he had been shot down by old friends, in particular Tony Lake, who had blocked him. It was true that Lake had been largely negative about a number of high-level positions for Holbrooke. It slipped out that when Holbrooke's name had come up during one of the transition meetings, Lake had referred to him as high-maintenance. Even Holbrooke's most fervent admirers would agree with the description—high-maintenance, surely, but high-value as well, they believed.

Lake, however, whatever doubts he had about Holbrooke, had not tried to block him as ambassador to Germany. His slippage in the pecking order in the world of foreign policy was especially painful for Holbrooke, friends thought, because Lake ended up with one of the two prized jobs, national security adviser. Their friendship had always had an unstated competitive quality, and now Lake seemed to be the clear winner and had, in Holbrooke's eyes, worked against his place in the administration. As a result, a simmering tension now existed between the two old friends, turning them into genuine enemies.

Holbrooke and Lake were the oldest of professional colleagues. But despite parallels in their careers, they had very different interests and ambitions and modus operandi. That showed clearly in the way they had spent their years after leaving Washington when Reagan replaced Carter. Lake headed to the relative seclusion of a dairy farm in western Massachusetts and taught political science, almost as quietly as he could. Holbrooke was pulled to the excitement and energy of the literary-journalistic-political world of New York City, where he worked successfully for a major financial house and was often seen with the well-known television figure Diane Sawyer.

By the summer of 1992, Holbrooke was passionate not just about Bosnia but about his own career. He had not, however, forged an especially close connection to Clinton as the candidate neared the nomination. Holbrooke had been a foreign policy adviser to Al Gore four years earlier when Gore had made his abortive presidential race, and Holbrooke was obviously anxious to get closer to this new Democratic star. There had been one meeting early in the primary campaign between Holbrooke and Clinton, and, Clinton's advisers believed, it had not gone particularly well, in part because Clinton was already overloaded in terms of meeting new people and was more interested in impressing the people he met than in being impressed by them. Clinton, it was thought, had sensed how bright Holbrooke was, but was a little guarded about him as well, perhaps aware of his reputation for being talented but extremely ego-driven.

It was obvious to Holbrooke's friends that summer that he was obviously not getting much traction with the Clinton team. Though careful not to say anything critical about Lake, who was the chief foreign policy adviser and ostensibly one of his oldest friends, Holbrooke was frustrated and, for someone normally so outspoken and exuberant, oddly muffled when the subject of the campaign came up. He was certainly not about to let others in the tight, gossipy world of national security know that things were not as they had once been with Lake. It would be a sign of weakness for him, but not for Lake, since he now had the inside track with Clinton. But Holbrooke was, as one friend said, "suffering quietly—which was unusual. It was not very much in character for Dick to do anything quietly, especially suffer." Whatever else, Lake was clearly not encouraging Holbrooke's attentions. What those operating in the Clinton foreign policy shop needed during the campaign, they believed, was not more foreign policy expertise, but more political leverage with the candidate and time, after the election, to impress upon him how vital foreign policy was. Otherwise, it could eventually overwhelm you.

The story of both Lake and Holbrooke, perhaps the two most talented young foreign policy figures in the Democratic Party at that moment, was instructive for a number of reasons. It told a good deal about the party itself, and the damage Vietnam had done to the talent base in the world of national security. It would be hard to imagine a more complicated relationship than the one between Holbrooke and Lake. They had arrived at the foreign service training school in Washington together in 1962, where they were among a group of bright young men and women—though it was almost all men in those days—who immediately started to hang out together. Those were glorious days, the last carefree hours of a boyhood now about to end with assignment to Vietnam and a still-small war just over the horizon. After classes they went out drinking together and played a fierce game of softball on the weekends. The first tip-off, one classmate said, that the admirable, well-bred, always polite Tony Lake was every bit as ambitious as the much more raw and unfinished Dick Holbrooke was that when they played softball, Lake was the only one who showed up wearing spikes. On brutally hot evenings, along with another contemporary, Vlad Lehovich, they played a game called fan ball, which demanded quick reflexes. You threw a tennis ball into a ceiling fan and then had to scramble to retrieve it because the fan drove it off in wildly different directions.

A year later, the two men arrived in Vietnam at virtually the same time. If you were bright and young and talented, then Vietnam in 1963 was a perfect place to exhibit your abilities. There, because they were obvious comers, both Lake and Holbrooke held a series of influential jobs, serving in time as aides to ambassadors Henry Cabot Lodge and Maxwell Taylor and, eventually, when they got back to Washington, Nick Katzenbach, the undersecretary of state. In those early days, it was Lake who got the prized special assignments first and who would do exceptionally well in the job—he was, after all, smart and disciplined and always, in both little and big things, ahead of the curve—and then, as he was leaving, point to Holbrooke as his logical successor. From the start, their career ladders differed. Older men, in search of the right kind of protégé, often came looking for Lake, who was born to a certain class, whereas Holbrooke, who was decidedly not born to that class, had to search for his mentors, his ambition always a bit more obvious in the process.

The two men had been uncommonly close at that time, brought together by their intelligence and their shared twenty-four-hour-a-day passion for this difficult war they found themselves in the middle of. It was Tony Lake who had signed Dick and Liddy Holbrooke's wedding certificate in Saigon, and Anthony Holbrooke, who as a young man working for a nongovernmental organization would urge his father to go to Bosnia, was named, in part, after Tony Lake. Holbrooke, in turn, was the godfather to one of Tony Lake's children. Both men were among the most intriguing figures produced in the national security world by the Vietnam War. They had wrestled with it as a moral and political issue during the war years and long after it was over. It still cast a considerable shadow over not only American foreign policy decisions, but over the domestic political arena as well, where a man's wartime decisions, often reluctantly made and absolutely right at the time, might later be seen through a very different domestic political prism. In addition, the war had affected the psyche of the two men themselves, because Vietnam in some way or another changed everyone who went there.

When Holbrooke was a young man, his ambition seemed more naked because he, the son of an immigrant Jewish family, had started at a lower level than the WASPier Lake, and because he wore his hunger for success so openly. One could not be with him for even the briefest period without knowing how badly he wanted to succeed, not merely to hold higher office one day, but to be a star as well. He was always brash. As a young foreign service officer stationed in the Mekong Delta, he had openly argued one day with General William Westmoreland.

"How old are you?" Westmoreland, somewhat exasperated, had finally asked.

"Twenty-four," Holbrooke answered.

"What makes you think you know so much?"

"I don't know," Holbrooke replied, "but I've been here two years and I've spent all of the time in the field."

Then and later, Holbrooke's ambition was matched only by his intelligence, and the awesome quality of both, plus his raw charm, made him likable sometimes in spite of himself.

But some who knew both men well thought that Lake in his quiet, poised, far more controlled way (he had, after all, been captain of the Harvard squash team, which was a perennial powerhouse in the semiclosed world of racquet sports) was covertly every bit as ambitious as Holbrooke, and every bit as demanding of himself. In Vietnam, they had gone through the full range of experiences—optimism, apprehension, disappointment, disillusionment, and finally considerable alienation—and it was, for both of them as they reached their fifties, the defining experience of their life. They had witnessed not just the tragedy of Vietnam but also what it had done to the political careers of some of the civilians who were its principal advocates, and to the party then in power, the Democrats, a party that would in time claim their political allegiance.

Much later in the Clinton years, watching the intensity of the byplay among the two of them and of Peter Tarnoff, a third colleague who was also one of the boys of Vietnam, Tom Donilon and Mike McCurry, both high-ranking State Department officials, used to wonder what had been in the water in Saigon back in those days that had made them so driven. If both Lake and Holbrooke were bright and hungry, of the two men Lake seemed to be marked for stardom more clearly and earlier on than Holbrooke, sure, it appeared, to be first in his class in achieving every level of success; whereas Holbrooke, slightly younger and somewhat devoid of the social graces that Lake exuded, seemed destined to be, at best, second in his class. It was said of Lake that when U. Alexis Johnson, then the number two man in the State Department, had looked at Lake's first personnel report, he had been a bit irritated. "No foreign service officer that young," he allegedly said, "is that good."

Lake's ascent in the foreign service was dramatic, and it came in part, at first, because of family connections and, in time, because of his own considerable energies and skill. While working in the consular office in Saigon when he first arrived, he dealt with a Vietnamese general named Ngyen Phu Duc. Near the end of World War II, responding to an American leaflet that promised medals and money for the return of American pilots, the general had helped one to safety, but had in the interim received neither medal nor money. He eventually came to the consular office, where he met with Lake and asked for his money and his medal. There was no doubt of the legitimacy of his request, but the air force, some eighteen years after this promise had been made, refused to honor it. The paperwork was simply too complicated, and the people who had made the promise so long ago were all gone. The money could not be arranged, but the old general still wanted the medal and it was clear he deserved one. So Lake, on his own, went to a metalworker in Cholon, the Chinese section of Saigon, had a fancy silver medal with a great deal of ribbon created and carefully inscribed as the "Anthony Lake Consular Medal Awarded for Distinguished Service to the United States of America." When Henry Cabot Lodge, who was the ambassador at the time, heard of it, he greatly approved of that kind of initiative. He knew Lake's mother back home, had already checked Lake out, and now made him his personal assistant. When Maxwell Taylor replaced Lodge, Lake was transferred to him before eventually becoming the consul in Hue.

There were high-powered jobs available for Tony Lake on his return to Washington. Yet in his own emotional ambivalence, he always longed to do something else, to escape Vietnam perhaps and distance himself from the eye of the storm. A post in a faraway African embassy, which would allow him to move around the country at ease and learn about another world while making some kind of humanitarian contribution, appeared preferable to him. Instead he was being offered jobs at the feet of the mighty in Washington, in the midst of the heightening Vietnam tensions, jobs that he did not seek because more and more he disagreed with the mighty. On his return from Vietnam, he worked for Leonard Unger, who was Bill Bundy's deputy. Bundy was the assistant secretary of state for Far Eastern Affairs and Unger was running the Vietnam Working Group. It was not the easiest of assignments. Lake was dovish, surrounded in his professional life by hawks and in his personal life by doves. At one meeting, he spoke quite pessimistically about the war and was quickly upbraided in an angry letter by a navy captain who mocked him for thinking he knew more about Vietnam than Lyndon Johnson. You sound just like Bill Fulbright, the captain added. A few days later, Lake went to dinner with his very dovish wife and his equally dovish father. They both brutally assaulted the Vietnam policy. But Lake, ever the professional, tried gamely to defend it. Finally his father turned to him and said, with considerable scorn, "God, Tony, you sound just like Dean Rusk."

He had been spared further time in the Vietnam Working Group when he was pulled away by Nick Katzenbach, the undersecretary of state, who was struggling to find a more rational, more dovish policy, though he, too, was surrounded by hawks above him in most of the key jobs. Once again Lake found himself a staff assistant. Katzenbach was a good boss and, in Lake's mind, pointed in the right direction, but the war weighed on Lake ever more heavily and he found his own views diverging from official policy at an alarming rate. He finally went to Katzenbach and said he thought it was time for him to leave the foreign service. Lake was obviously both exhausted and frustrated, Katzenbach believed, sure he was no longer doing anyone any good. Lake was also sure that his dissent on so important a policy was inevitably going to damage his career—that sooner or later a senior officer would use an efficiency report as a means of punishment for Lake's lack of enthusiasm. Katzenbach thought Lake was probably right and suggested an alternative move: take a leave of absence for a year and go to Princeton. Lake did that, spending two years there and getting his master's degree in international relations. The person who replaced him as Katzenbach's assistant, at Lake's suggestion, was Dick Holbrooke. Soon after, Holbrooke would follow him to Princeton.

By the time Lake finished his two years at Princeton, Richard Nixon had been elected president and Henry Kissinger wanted Lake on his staff. Lake had dealt with Kissinger when he was a consultant for the Democrats in the terminal days of the Johnson years. Lake again thought longingly of a small, quiet post in Africa, but accepted Kissinger's offer. Kissinger had checked him out with Bill Bundy, who was one of the previous administration's leading hawks, and Bundy had given Lake a good report card. Lake, Bundy told Kissinger, had

had serious doubts about the Vietnam policy but was always a good soldier. Kissinger had also asked Katzenbach for the names of the ablest people in the department, and Katzenbach had shortlisted, among others, Tony Lake, Dick Holbrooke, and Larry Eagleburger. "I felt badly that I might be giving away too much of State's talent, so I sent the same list to Bill Rogers, but knowing Rogers, I doubt he even read it," Katzenbach said later.

Lake talked at length with Kissinger and was convinced that even though he was in a difficult position with a volatile president, he wanted to end the war. That more than anything else was what Tony Lake wanted, too. He was certain they had all been arguing on the margin for too long about the right way and the wrong way to do it, and about finding the right, clean-cut young Vietnamese colonel who could rally and lead our forces to victory. The truth was that it could not be done because history was by now against us. The Kissinger experience meant that Lake had spent the first seven years of what was supposed to be a brilliant career totally engaged in the most exhausting, heartbreaking issue of that political era, often fighting the direction of the policy, where answers, other than the eventual acceptance of some form of defeat for America, had always proved elusive. Vietnam was a graveyard of good intentions and false hopes and artificially distilled optimism. Moreover, other than for a handful of journalists who went there, it was likely to destroy rather than enhance careers. Years later when a friend asked Lake whether working on Bosnian policy under the difficult restraints imposed by a passive presidency was the worst thing he had ever been through in government, Lake laughed and said no way. Vietnam was the worst, dealing with a terrible war that went on endlessly without possible resolution while 100 to 150 American kids were being killed each week. It was so bad, he added, not just because the original policy was so flawed, but because it was so hard to set it right.

During most of the time he served Kissinger, Lake worked on downsizing the American commitment in Vietnam, though under the unlikely Nixonian banner of peace with honor, as if the ARVN, the Army of the Republic of Vietnam, which had already been defeated in 1964 by the Vietcong, would now, despite the withdrawal of half a million Americans troops and a major cutback in American airpower, be able to win the war. Though peace with honor struck Lake as a dubious possibility, the idea of disengagement was a good one. Though he was not always in sync with the White House, he was working toward a goal they probably all shared—somehow getting out—and that made losing any number of arguments along the way bearable. It was a worthy course, if not a perfect one. But then in April 1970, Nixon and Kissinger okayed the invasion of what was called the Parrot's Beak in Cambodia. Kissinger sold it to his staff at first as if it were going to be carried out primarily by South Vietnamese troops, supported by American artillery, though in fact it was to be a full-scale American mission.

Kissinger summoned what he called his bleeding hearts, those dovish young men on his staff who, he was sure, were certain to oppose the invasion, and asked them what they thought. Predictably they were against it. It would not work, they said. There was no North Vietnamese command post to be captured—which turned out to be true—and it would simply extend the war to Cambodia, a small nation that up until then had managed to stay out of the war. That also turned out to be true, with horrendous—genocidal—consequences for everyone involved. When Lake outlined his reservations, Kissinger remarked that he had known what Lake was going to say before he even said it. With that Lake resigned. Not only did he oppose the invasion, but what Kissinger had said was doubly troubling. If Lake was so predictable, he decided, he had lost the most important thing of all in a bureaucracy, true effectiveness. That meant he was nothing but window dressing for the outside world, as if his tenure there would show to Kissinger's increasingly critical colleagues, both in academe and in the peace movement, that he was still listening to their proxies. Lake was one of three Kissinger staff members who quit. "Your view represents the cowardice of the Eastern establishment," Kissinger told one of the three, a man named Bill Watts, who thereupon jumped out of his seat and tried to take a swing at his boss. But by then Kissinger had wisely retreated behind his desk.[2]

Both Lake and Holbrooke had ended up in Democratic politics in the seventies, and when Jimmy Carter took over, they were at the top of the list of the young men coming of age in the foreign policy apparatus, tempered by the Vietnam experience, but not emotionally burned out by it. Lake was still first in his class; he got a coveted position as head of Policy Planning at the State Department, a hallowed job for a State Department intellectual once held by George Kennan himself, the most cerebral man in the Washington of his day. Holbrooke, still something of a boy wonder, thirty-six that year, still brasher than Lake, was not far behind. He got the job at State as assistant secretary for Far Eastern affairs. It was a plum, but he remained second in his class. He had, some of his close friends thought, hungered for something even grander, perhaps the national security adviser job, but he knew he was too young for it and Zbig Brzezinski was likely to get the nod.

Among those who had helped propel Holbrooke upward at the start of the Carter years was Averell Harriman, the grand old man of Democratic Party foreign policy, whom Holbrooke had gotten to know quite well during the Paris peace talks. Holbrooke was clearly a young man on the rise, always looking for sponsors, and the Harriman connection had helped him greatly. By then well into his eighties and finally realizing that he would not become secretary of state himself, Harriman had begun to counsel and push a new group of acolytes, Holbrooke among them. In the Carter years, Holbrooke was on Cyrus Vance's team at State in the fierce struggles with Brzezinski at NSC.

Given Vance's passivity and his instinct to avoid confrontation, it was the more aggressive Holbrooke who often took Zbig's hits on China policy. Holbrooke fought to keep the State Department's hold over China policy when Brzezinski, playing the China card to trump the Russian card, tried to preempt it.

There was a new dimension of realpolitik to the Holbrooke who completed his tour under Carter. He had fought hard and successfully to limit the human rights activists in State from examining too closely the regime of Ferdinand Marcos in the Philippines. Holbrooke was, he once told a colleague, particularly proud of marginalizing the role of Pat Derian, the assistant secretary of state for human rights and humanitarian affairs, a newly established branch of the department, in the Philippines during his tour. Their battles over policy—human rights versus primal realpolitik—were serious ones and reflected the growing divisions in the Democratic Party after Vietnam. One reason for continuing to support Marcos, in Holbrooke's view, was that in the years after the defeat in Vietnam, the Philippines offered the United States an important naval and air base in the region. Another reason was old-fashioned domestic politics. If Marcos fell from power during a Democratic administration and was replaced by a Marxist regime, Holbrooke was aware of the political consequences, not just for the party but for himself. A few years later when Washington finally realized that the corrupt, incompetent Marcos regime had become more of a burden than an asset and was helping a growing communist insurgency, it moved against Marcos, ironically during the Reagan years, though Reagan had once been a huge Marcos fan. Holbrooke, by then working in the world of finance in New York, told Johnny Apple of the *New York Times*, "Thank goodness it happened on a Republican watch. . . . If a Democrat had tried to do this, it would have split the country."[3]

During the Carter years at State, the differences between Lake and Holbrooke still seemed quite distinctive. Lake was quieter, more reflective, more openly anguished by the terrible Vietnam experience, and more in conflict with himself. On the surface at least, he appeared to be a man of ideas, not of action. He was at heart Wilsonian rather than Kissingerian. Holbrooke, on the other hand, was an activist first and foremost. He was for realpolitik, but not quite of the Kissingerian variety. His was a tempered, liberal realpolitik that took into consideration the importance of America's moral position in the world, but also factored in the realities of the underdeveloped world and the vagaries of American domestic politics. Vietnam had probably toughened him. You made your decisions as best you could and then got on with it. His ambition would probably not let him have it any other way. Vietnam might have been a mistake, but he had studied a mistake in action and learned from some of the top people in the department how to profit from a mistake as well as how to minimize the effect of a mistake on his career. He also learned how to be a skilled and fierce bureaucratic infighter. No one was more territorial. If you were working for him, things might be fine; but if you were challenging him for turf, you were effectively at war with him, no matter the legitimacy of your viewpoint. If Vietnam had made Lake more ambivalent about the uses of American power, it had made Holbrooke tougher and more combative. Any anguish associated with him was likely to be the anguish he caused potential bureaucratic competitors.

Holbrooke was, said one old friend in both admiration and exhaustion, the kind of person who could go in a revolving door behind you and come out ahead of you. His father, who was born in Russia and came to America as a teenager, was a doctor, and Holbrooke had grown up in Scarsdale, one of New York's more affluent suburbs. He was the sports editor of his high school paper, *The Maroon,* whose editor in chief and his best friend was young David Rusk, the son of a then Ford Foundation executive Dean Rusk. Holbrooke always dreamed of being a foreign correspondent—trench-coat-clad, surrounded by attractive but slightly mysterious women. When he went to college at Brown, he spent much of his time on the college newspaper. In his sophomore year, the paper's editor, in what he presumed would be a major journalistic coup, assigned Holbrooke, who allegedly spoke French and knew a good deal about Paris, to cover the 1960 Paris summit. There, the Western leaders led by Dwight Eisenhower were to meet with Nikita Khrushchev during what appeared to be something of a relaxation in East-West tensions.

Though the conference blew up at the start because the Russians shot down a U-2 spy plane, Holbrooke forged a connection with the *New York Times* reporters working in Paris. He made $10 a day as a de facto copyboy, and his principal job was saving seven seats each day for the seven all-star *Times* reporters covering the conference. He later served as a news clerk for the paper in New York, and when he graduated from Brown in 1962, his one dream was to work for the *Times*. He wrote James Reston in Washington asking for a job, but Reston only hired young men who had five or six years in the field, and he answered that there were no vacancies. Though he desperately wanted to be a foreign correspondent, Holbrooke tried no other newspaper, and since his friend David Rusk's father, Dean Rusk, had always spoken of the uncommon value of a career in the foreign service, he took the foreign service exam. He passed and entered a class where a number of bright young men were gearing up for exciting new careers, among them Tony Lake.

Because he was ambitious, eager to serve and both do good and do well, Holbrooke, like Lake, chose Vietnam, where in 1962 things were just heating up. Both went to Vietnamese language school. But Lake, because he was married, went to Vietnam as a traditional foreign service officer to work in the embassy, while Holbrooke, because he was single, was trained for a new program, part of AID, where he would work in the field in the rural pacification program. He was making $5,500 a year, plus another $1,375 for hazardous duty. He arrived in Saigon with a letter in his pocket from Clifton Daniel, the managing editor of the *Times*, introducing him with considerable enthusiasm to the resident *Times* reporter.[4] Holbrooke from the start was connected to journalists. To his credit, though, he also had the Rusk connection but never mentioned it to his peers.

Given the nature of the institution he had joined, where social graces were then supposed to be important, Holbrooke was an unlikely candidate for a successful career in the foreign service. He had a better understanding of the political world around him than he had about himself and his effect on people. No one would accuse him of being *raffiné*. "He's not entirely housebroken," Pamela Harriman, another of his sponsors, and by then Averell's widow and the American ambassador to Paris, said of him in the midnineties. Holbrooke would always remain both endearing and off-putting, raw and unfinished, as likely to be disliked as admired, and often for the exact same qualities. Nick Katzenbach, who had been one of his early sponsors when Holbrooke returned to Washington from Vietnam, remembered with both admiration and amusement how Holbrooke had worked endlessly to get himself on the American team that went to Paris for the 1968 Paris peace talks, wheeling and dealing simultaneously with both Katzenbach and Averell Harriman, the leader of the team, to make certain he made the traveling squad. "He was absolutely sure," Katzenbach said, "that it would be a historic time, that he could learn a lot, be of value to others because of his knowledge of the war, and that he could meet some people who would one day be of value."

Holbrooke's was a triumph of talent, energy, ambition, and hubris over more peripheral social graces, the absence of which in another age might have worked against him. What was a weakness became his strength: his occasional insensitivity to others in the singular pursuit of his goals. He did not seem as reflective as Lake, perhaps because the fire of his ambition burned so brightly, but there was no doubt about the first-rate quality of his intellect. He was as smart as any foreign service officer of his generation. He remembered everything that was ever said to him (or at least everything he wanted to remember), going back if need be thirty-five years. He also remembered everything that he had read—and he read voraciously. He was an amateur diplomatic historian, the editor for a time of the quarterly magazine *Foreign Policy*, and later the coauthor of Clark Clifford's memoirs. "The best memo I ever wrote on Vietnam," Katzenbach said years later, "was one telling President Johnson that we could not win, that it was the problem of the tortoise and the hare—that the tortoise of progress was well behind the hare of public opinion and it was going to stay that way. It was written by Dick Holbrooke." (Years later, by then the hero of the Dayton negotiations to end the war in Bosnia and ambassador to the United Nations, Holbrooke gave a speech to a group that included Katzenbach, whom he generously called "the best boss I ever had." "Thanks, Dick," Katzenbach told him later. "I'll be sure to tell Bill Clinton what you said.")

Above all, Holbrooke was a total political animal. That would later—the friendship and relationship did not blossom at first—draw him closer to Bill Clinton. They would make the same reads about people and, without a word necessarily being said, the importance of events in foreign countries to Clinton's political future. Holbrooke understood the political implications of all foreign policy situations—even the politics of some distant, unimportant African nation, tribe against tribe. Holbrooke, said a friend, would know which tribe had the greater moral cause, but he would also know which tribe had the oil. As a world-class political junky, a connoisseur of political events both foreign and American, his skills greatly exceeded those of most foreign service officers. He not only had an acute feel for the politics in the countries to which he was assigned, but equally important, and unlike so many colleagues who understood the politics of foreign nations but not of their own, his political skills extended to the United States.

Vietnam had taught Holbrooke a lesson that he never forgot, that foreign policy was almost always an extension of domestic politics, reflecting the moods, the changes, even the tremors, of American life. No one was better at projecting the connection between foreign policy and domestic politics. Had he left the foreign service and decided to write a column, he might have been one of the best foreign policy commentators of a generation.

As the Clinton foreign policy team assembled during the transition, it soon become clear that Holbrooke was very much on the outside trying to get in and somewhat frustrated by his lack of access. He had been working on Wall Street as an investment banker, where he had done extremely well. The secret to his success, his colleagues at Lehman Brothers thought, was how politically adept he was. He immediately understood the interior political hierarchy of the house, who had talent and, more important, who had power. He liked the financial game; it might not be as meaningful as top-level foreign policy, where the stakes were in his mind real, but it was a high-stakes game nevertheless, even if the money did not interest him greatly. About that he remained oddly innocent. When he was asked by a friend what he would do with all his money— now that he could sometimes make more in a day than he had once made in a year—he seemed puzzled for a moment, then answered that for the first time in his life he could buy all the books he wanted. "And every time I play tennis," he quickly added, "I can use a new can of balls." If he was disappointed by the job he got in the Clinton administration, he was smart enough to keep it to himself, aware that there would be another day.

By contrast, Lake, his onetime friend, was starting at the top, as national security adviser. Sandy Berger would be his assistant, though he could easily have had the job himself. Berger had been there first and had enough pull with the president to be the senior man in the office, but to his credit Berger suggested that Lake take the post. Berger not only understood how others in the foreign policy establishment perceived him—as a relatively minor Washington trade lawyer with strong Democratic Party connections—but he also felt that Lake was better prepared for the job because he had worked in the White House and at the NSC before, albeit under Kissinger. Berger's decision had a certain nobility—not many ambitious Washington lawyers would do that—and in the long run it helped cement his relationship with the president.

For Lake it meant he was still first in his class, the first member of his generation to get one of the top-of-the-line appointments. He had passed a crucial test during the campaign as an architect of the policy that helped neutralize Bush's greater national security experience. Lake's interest in foreign policy also paralleled that of the new president and his quite influential wife, who thought of it in humanitarian and moral terms rather than in old-fashioned strategic geopolitical ones. Not only were both Clintons the products of the anti–Vietnam War movement, but this shared humanitarian viewpoint seemed far more legitimate now that the Cold War was over and a new kind of issue, often driven by refugee problems, was about to surface.

For a brief time during the transition, Clinton apparently toyed with the idea of appointing Colin Powell, then approaching the final months of his second term as head of the Joint Chiefs, to one of the top national security jobs. Whether it would have been State or Defense, no one was ever quite sure. But aides were assigned to check out the constitutionality of such an appointment. Could a man move from being in the uniformed military and heading the Joint Chiefs directly to a high-level cabinet post? The answer was no; there were rules about that. So nothing came of it at the time, and no approach, not even a tentative one, was made to Powell. The Clinton people wanted, once in office, to honor him and yet neutralize his influence. Thus, eventually, when it was time for Powell to retire, they discussed whether they should give him, as a farewell tip of the hat, another star. They checked it out and found that the last general to get a fifth star was Omar Bradley forty-three years earlier. Powell, they decided, was not Bradley. Besides, as George Stephanopoulos noted, if they gave him one more star, it might help him one day politically.[5] These were the first glimmers of Clinton's fascination with—and wariness of—Powell as both a potential figure in his cabinet and, equally important, as a potential opposition candidate in a future election. Later as Clinton underwent an unusually stormy first year with a series of defeats in foreign policy, he often wondered aloud if he should have pushed harder for Powell. Two years into what was an increasingly troubled presidency, Clinton would try the Powell gambit with far greater energy.

The secretary of defense would be Les Aspin, the longtime Democratic congressman from Wisconsin. Aspin, who had begun his career as a McNamara Whiz Kid in the Pentagon, had as a young man gone back to Wisconsin to run for office and had been a leading Democratic Party defense expert for some three decades. He had had two ambitions as a young man, becoming head of the House Armed Services Committee and, in time, secretary of defense. Now he had achieved both goals, but he would be notably more successful at the former than the latter. He was a bright, gregarious, immensely likable figure, but the appointment was in many ways to be a disaster, unacceptable for the country and the administration, and literally and figuratively heartbreaking for Aspin. He was in person the least disciplined of men, and he was now being sent to ride herd over the most contentious and divisive of institutions.

Perhaps even more puzzling to others, and to himself, was the person chosen to head the CIA—the director of central intelligence, or DCI, in Washington terms—James Woolsey. His was a last-minute selection. At first the Clinton people had intended to put Dave McCurdy, the Oklahoma congressman, there. But McCurdy, a runner-up for secretary of defense, did not want the job. Then it appeared likely to go to Tom Pickering, a career foreign service officer, at the time ambassador to India and a man of exceptional abilities and experience—former ambassador to Jordan, Israel, El Salvador, and former U.S. representative to the United Nations. He was widely regarded in high Washington circles as the professional's professional. Within the State Department it was said that he had been dispatched from the UN to India because he had performed with such skill in New York during the Gulf War and had attracted such media attention that James Baker decided he was ready for a more distant and far less visible post. Pickering had had a flawless career, admired by almost everyone who had worked for him as the absolute best in the profession, which meant he was very good indeed.

Aware that he was about to be tapped for a high-level job on the Clinton team, Pickering had made the requisite pilgrimage to Little Rock for his one-on-one meeting with the president-elect. Things went well and the deal seemed to be sealed. He had even been told by Christopher that the job was his. But at the last minute, a number of the more conservative Democrats on the Hill, as well as Admiral Bill Crowe, the former head of the Joint Chiefs whose endorsement of Clinton had been so important during the campaign, urged Clinton to broaden his team politically and suggested he name a neoconservative. Pickering, it was said, was on his way back to New Delhi when he was paged at the Frankfurt airport and told that what he thought was a deal was no longer a deal. He eventually got Moscow, which was an important post, although the first choice for Russia had been Walter Mondale.

Woolsey's appointment did not turn out to be a happy one, either for Woolsey or for the administration. Though he was given a job of considerable potential influence, it was soon decided, in the unofficial way that these things were decided, that he was somehow not quite the right person for the administration, and his tour would be frustrating. He had served at a relatively low level in the Carter administration but was thought of as a Reagan Democrat. In late December 1992, Christopher called Woolsey and asked him to fly to Little Rock to talk to the president-elect. Woolsey had arrived thinking that the Clinton team would run its short list of would-be CIA directors by him and he would advise them which candidate was likely to be the most efficient and work best with conservative Democrats. Perhaps there might even be some kind of job offer. He knew Clinton only in the most marginal way. As a candidate Clinton had appeared before an informal group of which Woolsey was a member, men who had worked under Harold Brown in the Carter Defense Department, and he had rather liked the Arkansas governor at their one meeting.

Clinton, appearing before the group and aware of his limitations in the field of defense, where these men were said to have considerable expertise, knew that he was the new boy in a demanding classroom. In addition, New Democrat or not, a potential ideological gulf was between them, and he had shrewdly devoted the entire evening to asking questions, a vintage Clinton performance, playing to his strength as a quick study. The group liked that: no one expected a young Southern politician to flash back names, numbers, and price tags on weapons systems, but he seemed open and in no way dogmatic.

When Woolsey arrived in Little Rock in the early evening of December 21, he was told that Clinton would see him about 11:30 P.M. that night. Sometime after midnight, the two men finally got together. Clinton talked casually to Woolsey, but it was hard to ascertain his exact purpose. A few rather vague references were made to the CIA job, but Woolsey's sense of the state of the world was barely discussed. The next day Woolsey was asked to stop by the Rose Law Firm to talk to Wes Hubbell about any potential conflicts of interest, a visit not without its subsequent irony. Woolsey was beginning to suspect that a job offer would be made, and in time Christopher confirmed it. Woolsey was to proceed to a press conference for the announcement that he, Berger, Lake, Aspin, and Madeleine Albright would all be joining the administration.

Before the press conference began, Stephanopoulos and Dee Dee Myers, two of Clinton's top people who handled the media, held a quick game-planning session about what questions might be asked and what answers should be given.

"What do we say if someone suggests that this is just a bunch of Carter administration retreads?" Myers asked.

"Well, I served in the Bush administration," Woolsey said, mentioning a relatively minor job he had held dealing with the reduction of conventional forces in Europe.

"Admiral Woolsey, I didn't know you served in the Bush administration," Ms. Myers said.

"I'm afraid I'm not an admiral, Ms. Myers. I never rose above the rank of captain in the army."

"In that case I better take the word *admiral* out of the press release," Myers answered.

A few minutes later the press conference began and Clinton said that to some people out there this might look like a bunch of Carter administration retreads, but Jim Woolsey had served in the Bush administration. Clearly the Democrats lacked depth in their personnel and the old divisions in the party still existed.

But the key change among the main figures in national security was the president himself. For Bush, foreign policy had been his raison d'être. For Clinton, it was an inconvenience, something that might pull him away from his primary job at hand—domestic issues, above all the economy. Newly elected and newly installed, he demonstrated that priority from the very beginning. He had little interest in meeting foreign leaders. When he received congratulatory phone messages from them, it was Warren Christopher's job to return the calls. Democratic pols offering their congratulations had their calls answered quickly; foreign heads of state had to wait. Thus were priorities established. It was not necessarily a good way to start. Some world leaders, who had found Bush accessible, began to see Clinton as the embodiment of something they disliked greatly about America, the smug, remote superpower whose attitude on most things was don't call us, we'll call you, and by the way, we'll make all the important decisions. But that attitude was very much in tune with the mood of the country. Clinton and the country were, after all, rarely out of sync. Characteristically, when Clinton gave a major speech, say a State of the Union address, and came to the part devoted to foreign policy, his voice changed, his confidence dropped, and he spoke in a stilted and rather perfunctory manner. It was as if it had been written for someone else and he had been handed it at the last minute, something he had to get through. Only when he spoke about domestic affairs did emotion and confidence and even empathy return to his voice.

To the people in the national security world, his lack of interest in their field was dispiriting. Les Gelb, who had served in the Johnson Defense Department and the Carter State Department and had in midcareer become a foreign affairs columnist for the *New York Times,* had spotted this earlier than most. He had listened to candidate Clinton's acceptance speech at the Democratic convention and had written a prescient column entitled "A Mere 141 Words," which was the number of words about foreign policy in an otherwise long and detailed 4,200-word speech. From then on Sandy Berger was detailed by Clinton to count the number of words about foreign policy in his speeches. Though the word count on occasion went up slightly, it hardly concealed the president's essential lack of interest in the subject.

But the problem with concentrating on domestic America politics to the exclusion of the world late in this century, thought Robert Kagan, a talented, conservative foreign policy commentator and writer, was that "if you are the president of the United States, you do not find trouble, trouble finds you."[6] Or as Dick Holbrooke said, talking of the president's desire to pursue a domestic rather than an international agenda, "What Clinton did not yet understand was that foreign policy never lets an American president go." Already in Iraq, an ongoing battle, if not of strength then most certainly of wills, was taking place with Saddam Hussein. If that was not enough, three other trouble spots in the world were finding the president: Bosnia, Haiti, and Somalia, the first two of which Clinton had pledged himself to take care of during the campaign. They were not geopolitical crises, though Bosnia was on the borderline, but each represented a humanitarian crisis that would be a challenge in an area where the Clinton administration had pledged to be different from its predecessors.

CHAPTER EIGHTEEN

The difference between the easy rhetoric of a campaign and the harsh realities of the outside world hit the Clinton administration even before it took office. Haiti brought it home. One of the countries Clinton had singled out when he criticized Bush's foreign policy, Haiti was like an open sore, a nation that produced a constant flood of refugees who sailed off to the United States in a sad little armada of homemade boats under the most desperate circumstances. The Bush administration had been stopping them on the high seas and sending them back. That, Clinton as a candidate had said, was criminal, and he and his administration were not going to tolerate it. Probably in no other country in the world except perhaps Bosnia had his election been as welcome as in Haiti. Thousands and thousands of Haitians, many of them with family members already in the United States, were delighted by what they saw as a new, open-armed welcome from a friendlier administration.

But even as Clinton prepared to take office, he was given intelligence reports and photos that showed thousands of Haitians were tearing the roofs off their houses and trying to turn them into boats in order to sail to America. Very quickly, the president-elect decided it was time to back away from the campaign rhetoric. A new deal for Haiti would have to wait. For a lot of people with high hopes for the new administration it was a signature moment. Mort Abramowitz, a distinguished former foreign service officer who had been ambassador to both Turkey and Thailand and with his wife, Sheppie, had been active in humanitarian relief, heard the news that the president-elect had reversed his policy and was going to stop the boats. Clinton was not even in office, Abramowitz thought, and he had already gone back on his word. An administration that had broken its promises even before it took office was not off to an auspicious start.

But Haiti was to be a relatively minor issue compared with Bosnia. That was the stickler. There, every move produced a countermove. There, the good guys were not very good, the bad guys were very bad; moreover, the good guys could easily become the bad guys, and the bad guys the good guys. The uncertainty about what to do in Bosnia frustrated not just the Clinton administration, but the Congress and the military as well. Even relatively simple actions, the kinds of things Clinton had talked about during the campaign, such as lifting the arms embargo and using American airpower, could not be taken because of the opposition of our European allies who had troops on the ground. Perhaps Bosnia was important, but now in office Clinton quickly discovered a number of other issues—all of them connected to more pressing domestic concerns. Those priorities would shape much of his first term.

There was, in fact, no easy policy, no easy consensus, about what could or should be done in Bosnia. If the president had been passionate about it, if Bosnia had been at the top of his agenda, he could have forced a policy through the top of the bureaucracy and delivered it as a virtual ultimatum to the allies. During the campaign Clinton had spoken of a changed policy, and from time to time he gave the impression that he wanted to lift the arms embargo. But once in office he froze, set back by the intense hostility of the Europeans to any change as well as the cautiousness of his own military. After that, his interest in Bosnia became more distant, at best episodic. Secretary of State Christopher clearly had reservations about the use of force and was trying to read and reflect what the president wanted. National Security Adviser Tony Lake was proactive but prudent, feeling his way cautiously and also waiting to take his signal from the president. But Lake had told Clinton of the preeminence of the Balkans at the outset. Nothing else could be done in foreign policy until Bosnia was dealt with, he said, and the administration, in terms of foreign policy, would be judged first and foremost on Bosnia. It was said not as warning but as fact from a national security adviser who understood the limits of his leverage and knew that for a variety of political and economic reasons he had less muscle than his predecessors.

Apart from Lake, the person who strongly believed that the United States would have to do something in Bosnia was the vice president. Gore was something of a hawk, and if he did not actually force a change in policy, he kept Bosnia on the agenda. He had decided even as a senator that Yugoslavia, as it had once existed, was gone and could not be reconstituted. He thought that American efforts should go into recognizing the independence of the new states breaking away from the old and minimizing any bloodshed. From the moment he joined the ticket, Gore had made Bosnia a campaign issue. Now in office he continued to push for a tougher line against the Serbs. But he was caught in the classic limitations of being vice president. He always deferred to the president, but he worked to keep the issue alive at various meetings. Though much of his advice was private, rendered when no one else was around—he would not embarrass Clinton—his activism was indisputable. Still, he was extremely careful not to stake out a position that was different from the president's, aware that in a place as rumor-driven as Washington it would be damaging. There was an additional problem of dealing with Clinton on an issue like this where the equities were so balanced. You would make your case to the president, and he would seem to agree and even to have said yes, Gore told close aides. And then Clinton would talk to other people and what had appeared to be his assent would soften, and he would be effectively on the other side. Getting him to agree to a policy was one thing—holding him to that agreement was another, very different one.

Madeleine Albright was a champion of the use of force, but her influence was also limited. Indeed at first she was considered something of a showpiece by her peers, a very public manifestation of changes in domestic politics. Appointing a woman to the UN was a form of recognition comparable to the ethnic calculations made in an earlier era in putting Americans of Italian, Polish, or Jewish ancestry in relatively minor cabinet posts. Whether the limits imposed on Albright came from the innate sexism of the men around Clinton or whether, as some of them liked to say off the record, they did not think she was up to their level intellectually, they acted as if she had been inflicted on them by an unannounced but nonetheless very real government affirmative action committee. In the early weeks Lake, who seemed barely able to contain his irritation, was the hardest on her. He tended to look away when she was talking, as if he were terribly bored, on occasion drumming his fingers impatiently on the desk. In time, though it was not as satisfactory as being present at high-level meetings, Albright would participate electronically from her New York office, in part, she told friends, because of the hostile environment in Washington.

The situation on the ground in Bosnia had deteriorated significantly when Clinton came into power in January 1993. Slowly dawning on Western consciences was that the Serbs in Bosnia were committing the worst crimes in Europe since the era of the Nazis. There might have been comparable crimes in the Soviet Union under Stalin, but they had been committed far beyond the view and the range of the West in the most inaccessible parts of the country. In Yugoslavia, because of the work of the journalists covering the story, the West, like it or not, was becoming a witness.

On the table at the time the Clinton people took office was what was called the Vance-Owen plan for Bosnia, which was probably the best that could be produced given the vulnerabilities of the various players, the de facto military acquisitions of the Serbs, and the lack of enthusiasm in the West for displacing them from the territories they had taken by force. The plan had been negotiated by two senior diplomats, David Owen, the former British foreign secretary, and Cy Vance, the former U.S. secretary of state. (The possibilities of a real peace in the Balkans were so slim that when Owen had accepted the assignment, *Private Eye,* the British satirical magazine, ran a cover showing him and Prime Minister John Major, nominally a political opponent, with words coming out of their mouths in bubbles, Major saying, "I'm afraid it's a lost cause," and Owen answering, "Then I'm your man.") The Vance-Owen plan was hardly perfect, but its imperfections matched the imperfections of Bosnia—and Yugoslavia—as countries. It called in effect for the cantonization of Bosnia. There would be ten cantons, three with a Serb majority, two with a Croat majority, three with a Muslim majority, and one mixed Croat-Muslim, with Sarajevo as a separate canton. The Bush people had quietly given their approval to the plan. Larry Eagleburger told both Vance and Owen in the final frustrating days of the Bush administration that they would not formally endorse it, but they would not attack it either. It was likely to end the bloodshed and was the best possible solution for nations unwilling to take stronger measures. If Vance-Owen worked, fine.

The Clinton people were not so accommodating. They were uncomfortable with a settlement that seemed to legitimize Serbian gains made at gunpoint. To do so would not jibe with their campaign rhetoric. They did not want to look as if they were appeasing Milosevic and the Bosnian Serbs. Vance and his aides met with the Clinton team, and despite surface assurances that the new administration would back the settlement, Vance and Owen began to suspect a growing resistance to the agreement. Were they too much the appeasers? Was their settlement too much of an accommodation with genocide? That was what the Clinton people seemed to be asking. Vance and Owen heard from journalist friends in Washington that the Clinton people were bad-mouthing the agreement in private, saying it was soft, as if it were the work of *Carter* people like Vance, and they, the realistic new breed, were tougher. Richard Boucher, who was acting as Warren Christopher's press spokesman, was asked by State Department reporters about the Vance-Owen plan, and he expressed doubts that it could realistically be achieved. A reporter at the press briefing went one step further, having picked up the back-channel Clinton position. Did the administration believe that Vance-Owen ratified ethnic cleansing? he asked. Boucher declined to answer. That, Owen wrote later, was like "rub[bing] salt in the wound."[1]

So the Vance-Owen plan, undercut in Washington, soon faded from view, and the killing continued. Vance, finding it one of the most bitter moments in his professional career, was livid, particularly angry at his former deputy Warren Christopher. It ended what was already a complicated personal and professional relationship. Christopher had been Vance's deputy when Vance was secretary of state in 1980. At the height of the Iranian hostage crisis, Carter, Brzezinski, and people in the Pentagon planned the bizarre helicopter rescue attempt, a mission unlikely to succeed given the cantankerous nature of helicopters even in the best of circumstances. At the time, an exhausted Vance was in Florida on vacation, very much out of the loop. Carter brought Christopher into the plan and told him not to tell Vance.

Vance returned to Washington to find the operation ready to be launched. He was appalled by the idea of the mission and the fact that the secretary of state had been cut out of the action. He immediately wrote a letter of resignation. Whether or not the rescue mission succeeded, the procedural violation was unacceptable. His letter was the rarest of State Department documents, a resignation on principle.

Vance had, nonetheless, recommended Christopher as his successor; the job went to Ed Muskie. Again, in 1992, when the Clinton people came to him to ask who should get the job, Vance recommended Christopher. But this, the torpedoing of his peace plan by his former deputy, was the final blow. If they had a better plan, it would have been one thing, he said; if they were willing to use American power, that was another. But he and Owen had drawn up this plan precisely because the Europeans and the Americans were unwilling to make a serious commitment in the Balkans. Yes, it was an imperfect plan, but it was the only one possible without military intervention. That the two men who played a key role in shooting it down were his protégés, Christopher and Lake, was particularly painful to Vance. (Some Carter loyalists thereupon decided that Christopher was an uncommonly able lawyer but a man who could serve only one client at a time, being completely and unwaveringly loyal first to Carter, and later to Clinton, but never able to be loyal to both.)

So the Clinton people, taking over, found themselves trapped in a self-defeating, hopelessly incomplete policy put in play by the Europeans and the Bush administration, and by their own reluctance to use force. The tangle apparently offered no way out. A primary impulse, again and again, was to use NATO airpower, but every time it was suggested, the idea was blocked by the Europeans, who said they would be delighted to go along with it, but only if we put troops on the ground along with theirs. Years later Tony Lake would talk about the frustrations of that time. The Clinton people had been so confident of their talents and so disrespectful of their predecessors (as all new administrations are—because they believe their own rhetoric) that they were sure, when they took a fresh look at Yugoslavia, they would be able to come up with a new policy to replace the failed one they had so roundly criticized in the campaign. But everywhere they turned, Lake would later note, there was some kind of blockage. "We kept looking for something—reading and rereading everything there was about the area—and it just wasn't there," he said. "So we would go back and try again, looking for some as yet undiscovered opening, for something new that we could do, and it wasn't there." With frustration mounting, the administration was inclined to blame others, the allies, and, of course, the fates.

Even before the new administration took office, Dick Holbrooke, who had visited Bosnia in the summer of 1992 and witnessed the ethnic cleansing and was committed to a dramatically changed course, warned his colleagues of the long-range dangers for American policy if we were not willing to use military power to back up our threats. At the start of the administration, he sent a memo, calling for a more aggressive policy in the Balkans designed to stop Serb aggression, to both Lake and Christopher. It began: "Bosnia will be the key test of American policy in Europe. We must therefore succeed in whatever we attempt. The Administration cannot afford to begin with either an international disaster or a quagmire."[2] Holbrooke did not hear back from either man, and when he called Lake a few weeks later, the national security adviser said that the memo had been useful, but there were certain problems with the decisive kind of action that Holbrooke wanted. That was about as far as it went.

Holbrooke was not yet ticketed for Germany and had volunteered for some kind of role in the Balkans as a special representative of the president. But that was precisely what his superiors did not want. They sensed that with his drive, intensity, and singularity of purpose—that is, his instinct, as they saw it, to freelance—it would be hard to keep him in line with the more cautious approach the administration was about to take. The job of special negotiator eventually went to Reggie Batholomew.

A few weeks later, Holbrooke, still waiting to hear what job he would get, dropped by the White House to have lunch with Lake and recommended immediate action in Bosnia. Lake countered by saying that they were working on the problem and he was sure they were beginning to make a difference. A clear division now existed between the two former friends, who both thought of themselves as proactive on Bosnia. Holbrooke was still the activist, free, because he had not yet taken a job, to talk about Bosnia in idealistic terms, while Lake was the high-powered official saddled with dealing with the problem in an administration where its priority was relatively low. Holbrooke reminded Lake of the activist rhetoric of the campaign, which Lake had authored, a reminder not necessarily guaranteed to strengthen an already fragile relationship. "The meeting," Holbrooke later wrote with considerable understatement, "ended coolly and inconclusively."[3]

The younger men and women in the State Department who had been pushing for greater activism in Bosnia were quite hopeful when the Clinton administration first took over. Christopher's early words had stirred them. "A dark period of terror and brutality," he had called it in February 1993 in his first public words on the subject. "Our conscience revolts at the idea of passively accepting such brutality." But then the Clinton people began to back off at the top, and memos that demanded action were being stopped by Christopher's deputies lest they hand him a piece of paper he would have to reject. Soon a sense of disappointment enveloped those who thought a new administrator meant a new policy.

When the Clinton people first took office, February, March, and even April were given over to a review on Bosnia. But events in Bosnia were not quiescent; they did not wait for policy reviews. If most of the Serb assault had gone according to schedule, a number of Muslim enclaves in eastern Bosnia had managed to hold out and were enduring a special kind of hell raining down on them from heavy Serb weapons. The most notable of those was a town called Srebrenica, where the Serbs had encircled the Bosnian Muslims and where there were continuing reports of a mounting human disaster which, it was believed, might become even worse. Srebrenica, as much as any one town, acted as a kind of goad, mocking this new president, who had promised to represent a more humane America, not just domestically but in foreign policy as well.

In early 1993, much of whatever of the world's attention was on events in the Balkans was focused on Sarajevo. Though the quality of suffering in a time of genocide is hard to measure, people who knew and cared about what was happening there believed that the suffering in the eastern Bosnian enclaves was far greater than in Sarajevo. With no Western scrutiny that far east, fewer convoys, less food, and less in the way of medical supplies could reach the people there. Sarajevo, terrible though conditions were, was more closely monitored in the West, and the Serbs had periodically been forced to make some accommodations to world opinion. That was significantly less true of Srebrenica, an example of the real horror of Bosnia.

Srebrenica, a small former mining town, was unusually defenseless in the face of the Serb attacks, located as it was near the Drina River, perhaps only three or four miles from the Serbian border. Because the spring of 1992 had seen such cruel and bitter ethnic cleansing, various NGOs estimated that, by early 1993, as many as two hundred thousand Muslims had been driven from their land. As village after village in eastern Bosnia fell, a large number of them found their way to Srebrenica, which was soon to be placed under siege itself. By the time of Clinton's inauguration, Srebrenica was already swarming with thousands of Muslim refugees and was being subjected to constant Serb artillery bombardment. Its story, already tragic, was only going to become worse in the next two years. When the Serb assault on Bosnia had begun a year earlier in March 1992, Srebrenica had proved a critical target for the Serbs, and their anger toward its defenders had grown in ever greater increments. Though the first part of the Serb offensive had generally gone according to schedule—after a six-week campaign they held something like 60 percent of Bosnian territory—Srebrenica continued to frustrate them.

There the local military leadership had proved unusually strong and able. When the Serbs surrounded the town and demanded that the Muslim men surrender their weapons, the local defenders knew all too well what had happened to the men in other towns. So they resisted. Serb forces, primarily paramilitaries led by Arkan's Tigers, entered Srebrenica and began to loot and murder the elderly Muslim men they found in their way. Then two days later, Muslim soldiers counterattacked. One of their leaders was Nasir Oric, then twenty-five, a former policeman and bodyguard to Milosevic, who was as rough and tough as any Serb paramilitary leader. His irregular band, significantly underarmed but very determined, drove the Tigers from the town on April 20, 1992. Because of his success in that assault, Oric immediately became the leader of all the local resistance. Srebrenica now remained a Muslim enclave, an inedible bone in the Serb craw.

Oric became the ablest and most violent of the Muslim field officers. Under his command the Muslims, though desperately underarmed, launched a series of attacks on neighboring Serb-controlled villages, always searching for weapons and ammunition. His raids were every bit as brutal as the Serb raids on the Muslims. If his men hit a village controlled by Serbs, they massacred them. His counterattacks had taken place two weeks before Bill Clinton's inauguration. With Oric in Srebrenica and using it as a base camp from which to attack the surrounding area, Srebrenica became a marked town. The Serbs assaulted the smaller Muslim villages, cleansing them, and more and more Muslim refugees fled to Srebrenica, which had no room for them. The town was already badly overcrowded, and most of the new arrivals had to sleep in the open air. The Serbs moved heavy artillery and armored vehicles into their positions and shelled the town at will. Nor would they let any UN convoys enter.

In the spring of 1993, Simon Mardell, a World Health Organization doctor, managed to sneak into the town—an extremely dangerous fifteen-mile walk during which he hoped he would not trigger any land mines. Mardell then contacted his superiors by radio and warned that the people of Srebrenica were in desperate condition and life there was inhumane. Thousands were living in the streets with no cover. There was no food or medicine. He estimated that twenty to thirty people a day were dying from cold and starvation, and that some eighteen thousand women and children should be evacuated immediately.[4] After hearing from Mardell, General Philippe Morillon, a French officer serving in the UN force who was already aware of the catastrophic conditions in Srebrenica, audaciously forced his way into the encircled town on March 11, 1993. He did not intend to stay long. He wanted to see how bad it was, talk with the local leadership about what he could do, then leave. Certainly conditions were even worse than he had expected. But he was a prize for the Muslim leaders back in Sarajevo, and they cabled Oric not to let him leave town. Women and children started throwing themselves on his car. The Serb shelling stopped while he was in town, and the Muslims believed that as long as they kept him hostage, they would be safe. Morillon's was one of the grandest gestures ever performed by someone in the UN force. "You are now under the protection of the United Nations forces . . . I will never abandon you," he had boldly but somewhat inaccurately announced. In fact, his superiors back in New York were absolutely appalled by what he had done and the greater dangers he might impose on other UN troops stationed throughout Bosnia. He had begun, in their opinion, to be partisan and take sides.

Having made his bold promise, Morillon then tried to slip out early the next morning, but was caught by the Muslims. From then on he was busy negotiating between the Serbs and the Muslims, trying to turn Srebrenica into a demilitarized zone. He finally convinced the Serbs to let some relief convoys in. When the first few trucks arrived, a terrible riot erupted as women and children rushed to get aboard the now empty trucks and leave Srebrenica for neighboring Tuzla. The crush aboard the handful of trucks was brutal, and during the night, six women and children died of asphyxiation and exposure. A few days later another convoy made it in. Some 750 people, chosen because they were in particularly desperate condition, were supposed to be evacuated, but another riot ensued and as many as 2,400 women and children crowded onto the nineteen trucks. Young women pulled older women off and took their place. Some women threw their children aboard if they could not make it themselves.[5]

General Morillon kept negotiating with the Serbs, but always from a position of weakness, and every agreement he made collapsed. He had no real leverage. The Serbs knew that his superiors in New York were already unhappy with him for being so aggressive. Opposing him was General Ratko Mladic, who wanted nothing less than the surrender of Srebrenica. Clearly, the fig leaf of UN integrity in Bosnia, such as it was, was shrinking quickly, and the pummeling of the town continued.

Just as clearly, the American response was neutered as well. The Clinton administration was still without a real policy. Finally it was decided to drop food and medical supplies on the Muslim enclaves. The food was the kind used by soldiers in the field, MRE, that is, meals ready to eat. Fittingly enough—it seemed almost to be a symbol of the early Clinton policy—the Serb lines had changed during the night, and on the first drop most of the meals went to Serb soldiers.

In mid-April, a Serb artillery attack on Srebrenica killed fifty-six people, many of them children playing soccer. Larry Hollingsworth, a British official working with the UN, normally known for his quiet, dispassionate view of events, told reporters that day, in words he chose quite deliberately, "My first thought was for the commander who gave the order to attack. I hope he burns in the hottest corner of hell. My second thought was for the soldiers who loaded the breeches and fired the guns. I hope their sleep is forever punctured by the screams of the children and the cries of their mothers. My third thought was for Doctor of Medicine Karadzic [and other Bosnian Serb officials]. And I wonder, will they condemn this atrocity? Or will they betray their education and condone it? And I thought of the many Serbs I know around this country, and I wondered, do they want the history of the Serb nation to include this chapter in which their army drove innocent people from village to village until finally they are cornered in Srebrenica, a place from which there is no escape, and where their fate is to be transported out like cattle, or slaughtered like sheep?"[6]

When the Serbs demanded the surrender of Srebrenica, the UN Security Council quickly met and designated it and five other Bosnian towns as safe areas, which it said it would protect, even though as everyone knew, it lacked the means to protect anything. So the tragedy played on. More and more refugees poured in, conditions became more desperate, and the UN was pledged to protect the people there, a pledge it could not honor. Act One in Srebrenica was coming to an end and Act Two would take place two years later.

Srebrenica, unlike Sarajevo, was beyond the scrutiny of most journalists. Sometimes Muslims in Srebrenica would radio their colleagues in Sarajevo, who could contact Western journalists and give reports. One amazing breakthrough came in April 1993, when British journalist Tony Birtley, a freelancer working for ABC, did the most daring thing imaginable. He smuggled himself aboard a Bosnian army helicopter, slipped into Srebrenica under the Serb guns, and filed a series of stories from there by radio, which alerted the world to the disaster taking place. For his pains Birtley was immediately expelled from all Serb territory.

Sometimes in the early months of the new administration, there would be a swirl of presidential irritation. Clinton would seem momentarily energized by Bosnia, angry at the lack of a policy, furious that because of the arms embargo, we were not even able to let decent people defend themselves. That went against the American grain, he believed. Hell, he said at one meeting, if Americans were fighting against brutal oppressors, and the most powerful countries in the world kept them from getting arms, he'd have been damned pissed off. Much of his anger, in the opinion of those listening to him, was aimed at the Europeans who were blocking the easiest response: lift and strike. It did not lead to policy changes, however. Clinton would explode momentarily, curse both the fates and the allies, and then, aware of the military price, the potential for political damage, and the drain it would be on his domestic agenda, he would back off.

For Bosnia was just one of many early frustrations; the Clinton administration had not begun auspiciously. He had had trouble with the military and the Congress almost from the start. During the campaign, Clinton had promised the nation that he would end discrimination against gays in the military. He had made the promise to an important new, still-developing constituency on the political landscape: gay Americans (and, he hoped, their families and friends). But the promise was easier to make than to keep and could backfire once he was in office. It reflected the greater volatility of the American political scene, which was increasingly composed of one-issue pressure groups that sometimes worked for Clinton and the Democrats. Whenever he dealt with the equally explosive issue of abortion, one that had the support of upper-middle-class women, many of them nominally Republican (for middle-class women constituted a great new swing vote in America), he picked up in the polls. But if he spoke out on the subject of gays in the military—not gay rights in the abstract, which was not necessarily that damaging, but gays quite specifically in the military—the equation quickly changed. For this issue pitted a nascent political force against a powerful, well-connected institution, where the question of personal lifestyle represented something unusually complicated, affecting strong, deeply ingrained personal feelings.

It was an issue that could easily blow up in Clinton's face and it was bound to cause him trouble on the Hill, where conservatives in Congress could team up with conservatives in the military. Clinton's problem was not just the senior military; it included some senior members of his own party, notably Senator Sam Nunn, who was greatly respected by other centrist Democrats and had been a leading candidate for a cabinet position. Nunn was the ranking Democratic Party authority on defense policy and effectively on the other side.

Colin Powell had tried to warn Clinton and his secretary of defense designate, Les Aspin, about the gay issue. It was exceptionally explosive, Powell believed, and he said as much to Clinton in their first meeting during the transition. Powell himself was very conservative on this issue, and friends remember him becoming quite irate when the argument was made that integrating gays into the military was a step not unlike integrating blacks some forty-five years earlier. It was by no means the same, he said quite vehemently. Powell was also speaking for many of his colleagues who were decidedly unenthusiastic about the idea. Opposition on the part of the Joint Chiefs and within the entire military cadre would be very, very strong, he said, because it touched on issues of human sexuality, opening up questions far more divisive than those raised by racial integration. Powell advocated a "don't ask, don't tell policy," which would not satisfy everyone—indeed, it would probably not satisfy anyone on either side—but it would almost surely work. The military, he believed, with its inherent codes of justice and fairness, would do the rest. Put the gay issue on the back burner, he had urged.

Powell had suggested that when Clinton officially announced his nomination for secretary of defense, he announce as well that the secretary designate was going to look into the issue and come back with a recommendation in six months. At the least it would buy Clinton some time and some cover. "Don't make the gay issue the first horse out of the gate with the armed forces," Powell added. He thought Clinton agreed with him. He was wrong.[7] Clinton dove right into it, got his nose bloodied, backed off, and placed himself even more on the defensive against the powerful military faction already opposed to him.

Later the top Clinton NSC people were puzzled about why the president had gone ahead on the issue despite the obvious dangers. It was bound to cause him all kinds of trouble with the military. It was, they discovered, a decision made entirely by Clinton and his political advisers. There had been no input from his NSC people. The political people wanted a campaign promise validated and saw gays in the military solely as a broad national political issue, not one that might set off a difficult struggle with the top of the bureaucracy. That it would make the Clinton team even more vulnerable to its critics and weaken him in his overall relationship with the military, an area where he was already on thin ice, was never fed into the equation.

Gays in the military was a major stumble, but it was merely the first of several political trip wires the new administration hit. Almost everything possible that could go wrong went wrong in those first few months. Inevitably, the Clinton dilemma in governance was affected by the volatility of American politics and the fragmented Democratic Party constituencies. It said something as well about the difference between the talent required to run for the presidency and the talent required to govern. In the most elemental sense, the Clinton people were not up to speed. The president himself, despite his immense ability, had operated in a much smaller arena where his skill level was unchallengeable. In Arkansas he had known more about the issues and the people confronting the issues than anyone else; he needed little advice, save his own and perhaps that of his wife. By and large, his own political reads were faster and more acute than those of many would-be advisers. But now as president he was running on a much faster track in areas where he did not know many of the players personally, and where many of the issues remained alien and moved at warp speed.

Thirty-two years before Bill Clinton assumed the presidency, John Kennedy had swept into office, promising to represent a new generation. The Clinton people, including the president and first lady, also promised, as the Kennedys had before them, generational change and more modern leadership in the new post–Cold War era. They represented in their own minds, as well as in the minds of the American public, a generation less burdened by the tensions that had divided the world for so long. They thought of themselves as more in touch with the country than those who had gone before. In the campaign they had challenged the conventional wisdom—most notably on Clinton's Vietnam history—and had won. Not surprisingly, they looked down on traditionalist Washington and did not want too many people with old-boy ties on board.

Reagan and his colleagues on the far right had run against Washington as a city that burdened the American people with too much government and too many rules. Clinton and his wife regarded Washington differently, with a somewhat liberal-populist outlook, as a city with too many well-entrenched, wealthy fixers who represented archaic or negative interests, a city that needed a cleansing. Theirs had been a most unlikely insurgency, and it was not by surprise that, when they finally won, they brought with them to the White House an arrogance about the correctness of their views, the incorrectness of those opposed to them, and their sense that they were closer to the heartbeat of the country than their critics. Sometimes they were right and sometimes they were not. But the difference between the theory and the practice of being president was immense. Some fourteen months after Clinton took office, David Owen, his peace plan effectively scuttled, met the president at the ceremony in Washington creating the Croat-Bosnian Federation and recalled for him the time back in July 1992 when they had both favored the use of airpower in the Balkans. His was a pointed comment. "It's a lot harder in government," Clinton remarked.[8]

In the beginning no one could keep Clinton on schedule. He was always behind. He seemed determined at each meeting to show how much he knew about every issue. His talent was matched only by his lack of discipline. Meetings went on interminably, largely because the president was always talking. Mack McLarty, as old a friend as Clinton had, was uniformly regarded by those who knew him as a decent man, but in no way up to the killing job as White House chief of staff, whose most important requisite was the ability to tell people they could not see the president. Day after day the administration fell behind its own projected schedule as more things went wrong. If the first stumble had been on gays in the military, then the next was on the choice for a highly visible woman in the cabinet. An unofficial deal with the various women's groups that had been so influential in Clinton's election was that one of the major cabinet jobs would go to a woman. That major breakthrough would probably occur at the Justice Department; women were more advanced on the career track in the law than they were in a number of parallel professions. But the first nominee for attorney general, Zoe Baird, a young woman with an excellent résumé, was shot down over a brand-new issue. She had, along with her husband, not only employed illegal immigrants, but had also not paid social security taxes on them until the last minute. Baird, sure nonetheless of her qualifications and unaware of how handsome a target she presented to the president's enemies, went before the Senate Judiciary Committee, where she misread the courtesy of its members for their support. As the controversy mounted, she was reluctant to withdraw her name. The administration finally had to shove her offstage. The next potential Clinton nominee, Kimba Wood, had something of a similar problem. She and her husband, Michael Kramer, a writer, had employed an illegal alien as a baby-sitter, back when that was not actually against the law, and they had paid her social security taxes. But it was all too messy and the smell of blood was now in the air. Wood wanted no part of a bitter confirmation process, and she quickly withdrew her name.

So Clinton's political foundation was proving shaky from the start. Image was driving politics, and the political sands shifted more quickly than ever before. In the pretelevision era, when the country was less affluent, politics had been driven primarily by economic impulse, and the various politically active groups were much more broadly based and therefore reflected a certain old-fashioned solidity. Their responses to a new set of political circumstances had been largely predictable, and pollsters were rarely needed to determine changing equations day by day. By the nineties that was no longer true. Other issues, primarily social-cultural, were becoming every bit as important as the economy, and they were often keyed to events on the evening news.

The fragility all this posed to a modern politician was palpable, and never more evident than in the first months of the Clinton administration. Fickle constituencies create fickle politicians; fickle politicians, in turn, make their constituencies distrustful and perhaps more fickle. Clinton would soon start complaining about the ephemeral moods of the electorate. Political energy created by a quick flash of an image on the evening news could readily be changed by an entirely different image on a subsequent news program. The electorate, like the nation, had become more mercurial. Loyalties had less adhesion, particularly the kind of loyalties that connected Clinton to these new constituencies. He had been the beneficiary of this during the campaign—the quick collapse of Bush's post–Gulf War popularity—now he was paying for it as president.

The cycle seemed to build on itself. Because of modern technology, the two most important developments in American politics were the use of polling and television advertising, both of them joined together in zeroing in on and then manipulating what the voting public thought at a given moment. But did the voting public really feel that way, how deep were those feelings, and did the public always want to be catered to so instantaneously? If the public seemed to want its politicians to bend, a month or two later it might be skeptical of any politician who was so readily bent. Politicians had to be nimble and more poll-driven, and because they were nimble, they seemed less grounded. It was a dynamic that at the core created little in the way of traction between politician and voter and held a great potential for cynicism and mutual distrust.

It was the realization of the volatility of the issues and the almost whimsical nature of the electorate which made the Clinton administration so uniquely dependent upon media advisers, consultants, and pollsters. Other administrations had been image-driven—that was the nature of the television age—but no other administration had ever been as poll-driven. It was an admission of its vulnerability, the weakness (and the lack of roots) of its various constituencies, and a de facto recognition that the structure of American politics had irrevocably changed. The Clinton administration believed that the electorate was now a reflection of the media and of constantly shifting political winds, driven by the latest incidents portrayed on network television. In time the electorate, and certainly the media, believed that the administration was altogether too tuned in to these whims, and that the president would do nothing and go nowhere without pollsters at his side.

It was known politically as the CNN factor, in reference to the all-news television network that both captured and reflected the immediacy of the changing pulse of American politics. CNN could, with the presentation of a single unflattering image, begin a major news cycle as other news outlets would soon follow, and overnight a policy that had seemed effective would begin to look like a disaster. Clinton, so aware of all the new forces in American political life, was, not surprisingly, extremely sensitive to even the slightest flicker of change reported on CNN or the networks.

In the early days of his administration, Clinton sometimes raged about the narrowness of choices that had been forced on him. One thing that bothered him, and where he seemed to have a legitimate case, was that he, unlike other presidents, had never been given either a honeymoon or a grace period at the start of his presidency. The partisanship had been virulent from the very beginning. Part of it was due to negative television advertising, which had elevated hostile sound bites to an art form. Part of it came from the power of talk radio, which had become a powerful new national political force. If the traditional media—elite print and national networks, generally politically centrist—had always been seen by those on the right as too liberal, talk radio was undoubtedly something quite different ideologically. It was right-wing, *populist* right-wing, and it was angry.

It represented a new kind of disenchanted American, more often than not white male, and middle to lower-middle class, who thought he (or on occasion she) was disenfranchised by both the current culture, which flouted what the right wing called family values, and the current economy, which favored those who had a certain kind of education (including women) over those who did not (often blue-collar and some middle-class whites). It hated much of the agenda of the urban and suburban middle and upper-middle class; it was often rural and small town and nativist. It was also antifeminist, antigay, antiliberal, and as such vehemently anti-Clinton. Its constituents had not always been to Vietnam, although they sometimes sounded as if they had, often referring to it as Nam. Many were a little young for that war, and some who had been of age had not deigned to go (because it was so badly run, they would later explain). Talk radio spoke to people who believed they were the forgotten men and women of America, white people who were God-fearing, tax-paying citizens still trying to hold on to the simple, small-town values of the past, values passed on by their fathers (and mothers).

Clinton, at a time when the culture was changing and the economic and political power of women was dramatically surging, became the perfect target for the progenitors of talk radio, most notably Rush Limbaugh, who clearly thought of himself as a repository of all the best of American patriotic virtues (but had not, of course, quite managed to make it to Vietnam because, he said, of a bad knee, which came from playing football). His popularity seemed to

increase with Clinton's ascent to the White House. The constancy and ferocity with which both Clintons were attacked on talk radio, and the intensely
personal quality of the attacks, was something relatively new in American politics. If Limbaugh stood at the head of the class in national popularity, almost
every single major broadcast market had local talk jocks who, when they read
the daily paper or watched the nightly news, reacted angrily, aware that their
anger had immediate resonance with their listeners.

Why it was all becoming so ugly was difficult to determine. Part of it was
modern politics, driven by attack commercials, in which traditional party-
driven restraints had disappeared, and which was simply meaner of spirit than
it had been fifteen or twenty years earlier. Part of it was the changing nature of
the issues. As the nation became more involved with cultural and social concerns, American politics became edgier and more personal, as if these were not
abstract arguments about better pay for blue-collar workers or about foreign
policy, but disagreements within a family, which, in fact, they often were.
Finally, part of it was the nature of Clinton himself. Because he was a white,
Southern liberal, and because the rising tide of cultural opposition more
often than not came from white, Southern conservatives, people whose backgrounds were much like his, they expected him to be on their side in the battles they fought; if he opposed them, he was a sellout, nothing less than a traitor.
To them he was known from the start as Slick Willie. He might pretend to be
a centrist Democrat, but for them the proof that he was covertly allied with the
radical wing of the party was his marriage to Hillary *Rodham* Clinton of
Wellesley College and Yale Law School. She, in their view, was the exemplar
of all that was wrong in American politics.

When Clinton took office, the political atmosphere was harsher than anyone had expected, and it affected both the president and the first lady, who
under pressure began to cut themselves off from much of what was around
them and think of themselves as victims. There was a certain form to the
dynamic: It started, some White House people believed, with Mrs. Clinton,
who was being subjected to an unusually brutal welcome to Washington, and
who was considered by her critics, given the issues that bothered people the
most—abortion, feminism, and gay rights—to be a polarizing influence.
Some of the people who dealt with the president daily in that period thought
there was a dynamic at work, and part of their job was to jolly him out of certain moods. The president was always prone to a kind of light self-pity,
which was made worse in a regular byplay with his wife, who was suffering
many frustrations of her own, both political and, as it would turn out, personal as well. The president and the first lady, it was said, often began the day
having breakfast together, and she would pick up a story or a column in the
Times or the *Washington Post* and go at him about the injustice of it all—how
unfairly the press was treating him (read *them*). She was pushing the presi-

dent's buttons about things that went with the territory and that he would do well to ignore.

To some of the more senior staff, anxious to shake him out of a bad mood so early in the day, this represented a waste of time and energy. All administrations had to accept as a given that they were going to be critiqued in unsympathetic, unknowing, or hostile newspaper reports, particularly in the short haul. For a presidency like Clinton's, already so attuned to every drop or rise in the national political temperature or the polls, to pay too much attention to the daily responses to presidential actions was catastrophic. One of the first laws of politics was never to get in a fight with people who bought ink by the barrel.

The early firefights and defeats of his administration—the backfire and retreat on gays in the military, the reversals on both Zoe Baird and Kimba Wood—only served to underscore how thin Clinton's margin of victory was, how fragile his support was in general, and how explosive American politics could be now that cultural and domestic issues were taking center stage. It raised the question of what the true center of American politics was, and how close the Clinton administration was to it. He obviously wanted to be the heralder of the new forces in American politics and to gain as many benefits from them as he could, without being precipitous about it or paying too high a political price. But those forces were still somewhat unformed. To use them to advantage required not so much a devoted, steadfast politician of undying commitment, willing to stay the course whatever the cost, but a wondrous politician, part juggler, part tap dancer.

Clinton was most certainly that. He had been elected with only 43 percent of the vote. He was the perfect example of a leader who got to the White House before his army was fully massed. The early defeats and stumbles and his tendency to back down had not enhanced his presidency. He had, in fact, given off a most unfortunate political odor: the impression that not only were he and his administration not quite up to the job, but perhaps worse, that under pressure and opposition, he might quickly fold.

CHAPTER NINETEEN

The political equation Clinton faced, to be sure, was extremely difficult. Filled with hopes and plans to be the first president to concentrate on domestic issues in more than thirty years, he encountered a particularly daunting problem as he began to tackle the reality of office: the budget deficit. In his mind and those of his economic advisers, it was the last great gift of Ronald Reagan, and to a lesser degree George Bush, to the new Democratic administration, perhaps even one of the reasons for Clinton's election. Some thought Reagan's increased defense spending, which accounted for no small amount of the deficit, had also been among the straws that had broken the back of the Soviet empire and set in motion the series of events that had helped elect Clinton.

Other politicians and economists, many of them quite conservative, had always believed that Reagan's supply-side economics—cutting the level of personal income taxes and thereby stimulating domestic consumption—was too theoretical a philosophy and not likely to succeed. Even George Bush in 1980 had referred to it as voodoo economics before joining the Reagan ticket and becoming, however involuntarily and uncomfortably, one of its advocates. Regrettably, it had worked better in theory than in practice. Though Republicans had in the past criticized the Democrats for their deficit financing, it was under Reagan that the deficits grew ever larger, becoming near the end of his presidency a living, organic part of the budget itself. When Reagan was elected in 1980, the deficit stood at $59 billion, a relatively modest figure when compared with the nation's GNP. By the time Clinton was elected, the budget deficit was expected to be $300 billion, and the national debt, $914 billion when Reagan had entered office, had reached $4 trillion. It might have been morning in America as far as Reagan was concerned, but the bill for the party the night after had yet to be paid.

By the middle of the Bush term, the economy was proving predictably sluggish. Far too much of the nation's resources were committed to servicing debt. No small part of Ross Perot's success in his own curious and erratic campaign had come from his charts, simple, indeed almost primitive ones—as if done for schoolchildren—but effective. They showed that Americans were living well, but passing the check on to those who would come after them. Lee

Iacocca, then something of a national hero for leading Chrysler's industrial resurgence, had hit home when he had said almost casually on television one night that Americans were using their children's credit cards. Much of Wall Street, though nominally Republican, agreed and, by 1992, was unhappy with the mounting deficits. Influential people there—the kind of men and women that other Wall Street big hitters turned to in time of crisis—thought any new administration had to show greater discipline and reduce the deficit. That would be true of any administration, but particularly a Democratic one, because Wall Street, though often the beneficiary when the Democrats were in power, nonetheless tended to regard them with innate ideological suspicion.

The taming of the deficit, it should be noted, had to be done not only in a country with a growing antitax sentiment, but where the Reagan years had embedded the resistance to taxes deep into the culture of one political party, the Republicans, and made the Democrats loath to take any action that might be viewed as increasing them. No issue lent itself more readily to the skills of modern political consultants and their advertising colleagues than a brief, simplistic sound bite showing an angry but ordinary wage earner, huddled together with his family, lamenting that candidate X or Y had raised his taxes.

Four years earlier, as they were about to take office, the Bush people had been aware of the same problem that the Clinton people now faced. But in his attempt to continue to hold on to the Reagan mantle (and survive the perils of conservative New Hampshire), Bush had made that famous promise not to raise taxes and would later find himself imprisoned by it. When Bush was elected and waiting to take office, Leon Panetta, then still a congressman and eventually, four years later, a critical figure in putting together the Clinton budget, went to the vice-presidential mansion, where Bush was still residing, to talk about economic policy. He did it at the request of his Republican congressional colleague Sonny Montgomery, and Panetta explained as bluntly as he could to Bush and his economic advisers that they had to get hold of the deficit. Otherwise it would profoundly and negatively affect his entire presidency. It would be, Panetta said, like a giant cancer eating away at everything else they intended to do.

Panetta came away from the meeting with a sense that Bush knew he was caught in something difficult, a prisoner of his New Hampshire promise, but he and the people around him intended to bring some form of economic reality to what was a mounting crisis. They seemed to be telling Panetta that it was a timing thing—a matter of figuring out when they could safely break the no new taxes pledge. Dick Darman, who was the Bush administration point man on the budget, took Panetta aside and said, "We hear what you're saying. I think he'll do what is right. But we have to find the right time to do it."

Clinton had campaigned as something of a liberal-populist, with one foot always in the center. His principal economic adviser was Bob Reich, who had been one of Clinton's closest friends since they'd first met as Rhodes Scholars on the boat going over to Oxford. Reich was a liberal economist in the New Deal/Fair Deal tradition. He believed that government had an obligation to tinker with the economy to help make society more equitable for the havenots. He was the chief architect of Clinton's early domestic policy programs, and many of Clinton's ideas had their roots in Reich's book *The Wealth of Nations*. Putting People First, or PPF, the Clinton economic program was called, and its founding father was Reich. PPF was relatively modest; it was aimed at the have-nots in society who were traditionally Democratic and it called for an investment of about $50 billion for job retraining, school infrastructures, preschool education, and mass transit. It was supposed to be a stimulus package for a stagnant economy, a tip of the hat to old Democratic constituencies, and was a greatly scaled-down contemporary version of Lyndon Johnson's Great Society. The investments, given the overall size of the federal budget, were hardly huge. But by the time Clinton was elected the nation's financial leadership and general population were more concerned about deficit reduction than new social programs. The tide was clearly going the other way. "Deficit, deficit, deficit, deficit, deficit," a frustrated Reich would later write of the first few weeks of the Clinton team's economic discussions. "We have to cut it. By how much? That's all we talk about in the Roosevelt Room."[1]

A month before they took office, the Clinton team had learned from Dick Darman that the budget news was going from bad to worse. Instead of an annual projected deficit of $300 billion, it was likely to be much higher, $350 billion. So from the start the Clinton people did not crunch numbers, the numbers crunched them. The need to take on the deficit weighed heavily on every aspect of the Clinton administration, particularly in the early days when its members were setting their priorities and political goals. It dominated not just economic policy, but social, political, and defense policy as well. All the economic factors that had worked for Clinton as a candidate now worked against him as a president. The national economy was soft, unemployment was high, and the deficit was on the rise. Therefore, economic policy was at the very center of the administration's purpose as it had not been in a long time, particularly for a liberal Democratic administration. This, not foreign policy, was where the president's primary energy would go, and this, not foreign policy, was where he believed policy would bring the most critically needed change. This issue was tied most directly to the national electoratel; it was why he had beaten George Bush.

If Clinton and his top NSC advisers saw little of each other, the many meetings among his economic and political people seemed endless and often chaotic, hour after hour of talk like a college bull session. Other members of the administration, including the top NSC people, seeing how much time the president was spending with his economic people, spoke wistfully about how they wished that he cared as much about their subject matter as he did about the economy. Clinton had arrived in office surprisingly budget conscious and budget careful for a moderately liberal Democrat. Being a former governor, not a former senator, made a big difference, as he had governed a small, unusually poor state with a balanced-budget requirement. So he came to the White House, in this area at least, prepared to be disciplined on budget issues. He was therefore different from many liberal congressional Democrats, for whom the instinct to spend was the most basic part of their political creed, and who were not nearly as much in the line of fire if people resented increased taxes.

It also became clear to Clinton, as he listened to the options spelled out for him by his top economic people, that Wall Street, which represented the distilled capitalist view of the American economy, believed that the government was at something of a fail-safe point regarding the rising budget deficit. That Wall Street now expected a liberal Democrat, for whom few of its senior (or junior) people had voted, to do for it what a conservative Republican, Reagan, and a centrist-conservative like Bush had not done was one of the special ironies of the moment, and it was not lost on an often irritable new president.

Clinton was prepared to bring some financial discipline to his economic policies, but he was also furious about the tight constraints placed on him by the deficit struggle and that the numbers for the coming year were significantly worse than the Republicans had promised they were going to be. He would have to spend a lot of time doing things that economically and politically he did not want to do, instead of the things he wanted to do. He raged at this, and his rage was far greater at Reagan than at Bush. Bush, he realized, had been made especially vulnerable in his run for reelection because of the sluggish economy and the damage done to him on the subject by Ross Perot. So Clinton complained often and angrily about Reagan. He was so revered by the country, everyone loved him and thought him a great hero, and here he had left the economy in a complete mess. Everyone loves him, Clinton would say in one of his milder moods, and everyone's dumping on me, and he's left behind all this shit for me to shovel. Reagan, he said, has the status of a saint and he damn near ruined the economy.

The Clinton administration, forced to concentrate on the economic equation in front of it, would charter the least likely course of all for a liberal Democratic president: deficit reduction. In the past, conservative Republicans, complaining about free-spending Democrats, had favored deficit reduction. Thus during the transition period, the initial power structure of the first term of the Clinton administration was defined. The foreign policy people were generally untested, and they were operating in an area where the president felt uncomfortable. He was sure the country was looking homeward after the Cold

War. That elevated the status of his economic advisers and diminished that of his national security ones. To the degree that anyone on his upper-level team was involved in foreign policy, and this was an enormous change in postwar American life, it was in foreign *trade,* in fighting to open markets in Japan and elsewhere in Asia. American political and military hegemony post–Cold War was now a given; by contrast, American economic hegemony seemed in jeopardy. Thus the dramatic shift in this administration as foreign policy moved from the traditional political-military sphere to a new primacy of trade.

In addition, Clinton was extremely impressed by the economic people who were joining his team. Bob Rubin's day as a major player would come later, and by the tail end of the second Clinton administration, he would be regarded as one of—if not *the*—bright shining stars of the Clinton years. That was especially true on Wall Street, which was reluctant to give any Democratic president credit and which later assumed that the rise of the Dow some 6,000 to 7,000 points in such a brief time was surely due to Rubin. Though surrounded by perfidious liberals of dubious character, he had prevailed, overruling what was presumed to be, given the prejudices of the venue, their constant bad advice.

But in the beginning, the most influential figure in the first Clinton administration was, without question, Lloyd Bentsen. Bentsen's relationship with the young president was, observers thought, the most intriguing in the entire administration, for Bentsen's hold over Clinton was almost magical. Clinton was in awe of his treasury secretary, deferential at all times, their interaction, thought one bystander, almost worthy of a novel. Not unlike Christopher with Clinton, it was a father and son relationship, with one significant difference: it was as if Bentsen, wealthy, admired, an immensely successful man who could make other powerful men seem to cower, was the father that Clinton would have chosen. He was twenty-five years older than the president, and like Christopher, roughly the age Clinton's father would have been had he lived. But it went further than that. Bentsen was accomplished in all ways and in many fields. Clinton, monodimensional, running even when he was not running, was successful in politics alone.

Bentsen was not merely older than the new president, he had all the experience, all the graces, and, no small thing, all the wealth that Clinton knew he lacked. Their personal stories were completely different, and Bentsen's biography greatly overshadowed that of the younger man he now served. He was a genuine war hero, a B-24 bomber pilot in World War II, flying with the Fifteenth Air Force in Italy, not only a squadron leader but apparently the youngest bomber pilot in the European theater. He had grown up overnight in a unit where the casualties were brutal. But he had made it back whole, and even though he was shot down twice, he never lost a crewman. Before he returned home, he had flown the requisite thirty-five missions.

He was twenty-three when he flew most of those missions. He held, in an administration where war records were either minimal or nonexistent, the Distinguished Flying Cross and the Air Medal with three oak leaf clusters. After the war he had gone back to what is called the Valley, the Rio Grande Valley in the southernmost part of Texas, where his father was a local power, a leading landholder and businessman who had the good fortune to find oil on his land. In that area, land, oil, and money all blended into power. Bentsen ran for Congress in 1948, his war record a critical part of his campaign, won easily, and became at twenty-seven the youngest member of the House. He was a protégé first of both Sam Rayburn and Lyndon Johnson, the two great powers of Texas politics on the Hill, and then later, as the divide in Texas politics between the liberal and conservative factions grew bigger, of John Connally back in Austin.

Rayburn was grooming him for a House leadership role, but Bentsen was restless, and after three terms, somewhat against his father's wishes—his father had hoped he would stay in Congress and one day run for the presidency—he quit to go back to Texas to earn some money. He succeeded handsomely at that, making a great deal of it in the insurance, real estate, and oil businesses. After more than a decade out of politics, he thought of challenging Ralph Yarborough, the liberal Democratic senator from Texas. Normally Yarborough was anathema to Johnson, but by 1964 Johnson had assumed the presidency, was switching constituencies and becoming more liberal himself. He discouraged the race, even though his close ally John Connally, then governor, and a good deal more conservative than he was, badly wanted Bentsen to make it.

Six years later, with Johnson out of office, Bentsen went after Yarborough and beat him in a bitter and ugly race for the nomination, then he beat George Bush in the general election. He was elected four times to the Senate and quickly became a major figure there. He was one of the big boys in the Senate, part of the inner group that controlled policy on important economic issues. Dealing with tax matters, he was the epitome of the old Teddy Roosevelt slogan: speak softly but carry a big stick. He was very much a throwback to the old power barons of the Senate, a man who understood the place, how it operated, how to get things done, and who developed a reputation as someone you crossed at your peril. He was known, and it was considered an advantage at his level, to have a mean streak, and to go out of the way to pay back those who underestimated him.

Bentsen also had a certain toughness, almost iciness. He had been close to John Connally, the leading power broker in Texas politics, for more than three decades, but in the late eighties and early nineties, when Connally ran into various financial and political problems, Bentsen, his own ambitions on the rise, deftly separated himself from Connally. With that, their long friendship was over and they never spoke again. It was, thought men who knew them both well, a good example of how steely Bentsen could be.

In 1988, his presidential ambitions hopeless in the then Democratic Party, Bentsen had accepted the vice-presidential nomination and had run a race in which his abilities were palpable and had left many Democrats feeling, ideological considerations aside, that the ticket might have done better if he had been at the top and Michael Dukakis at the bottom. On one famous evening he debated Dan Quayle on national television and, in just a single sentence, with a terrible finality, put a ceiling on Quayle's political career.

Despite the brief run for the presidential nomination and the vice-presidential campaign, Bentsen was not that well-known as a public figure when he joined the Clinton team. His roots were more in the past, in a time when the prime movers in the Congress exercised their power as quietly as possible, believing that the less that was known about what they did and who they were, the better, and the less they debated publicly and the more they did behind closed doors, the better. Since Bentsen held such an influential position on the Senate Finance Committee, he did not need to become a household face. Those who needed to know how powerful he was knew; those few who should have known but did not would learn soon enough. The sources of his power were in stark contrast to those of many people now arriving in a Washington that had been created by television, where power was much more fragmented, and where it was believed that the more visible you were, the more your face was known across the nation, the more powerful you were.

Bentsen's unique position among the Clinton principals in December 1992 was the result of what feminists would call a guy thing, what happens when men are among men and they watch to see who emerges as the leader, the toughest, strongest, smartest, in the pack. Bentsen had done things that other men of his generation—and most assuredly men from the next generation or two, those who had missed the big war and Vietnam as well—wished that they had done. He wore his alpha status, his elevated place in the pecking order of powerful males and would-be powerful males, lightly, with a natural ease. His innate authority in a room of other politicians was the product of the way he had lived his life and nothing less than the sum of his career. His life and career were complete. Others in the cabinet might vie to please the president; Bentsen did not have to. In fact, it worked the other way around. The president sought to please the secretary of the treasury (asked by a reporter whether he could have voted for the Clinton health care bill if he were still in the Senate, Bentsen had icily answered, "I'm not in the Senate.")

Bentsen had not particularly wanted—or needed—the job. Most of the Texas Democrats he knew urged him not to take the Treasury portfolio for fear that whoever succeeded him would surely be a Republican. But he took the job because he was a little bored with the Senate. He had after all those years been there, done that. Bentsen was older than anyone else in any Clinton meeting he attended, four years older even than Christopher, the senior figure from the world of the NSC. On the Richter scale by which talent was judged and admired in Washington, he was significantly more accomplished than the new secretary of state, who was considered the ultimate lawyer, which was not necessarily a compliment. The admiration of his peers as a man rather than as a mere politician came easily to Bentsen as it had never come to men like Nixon or Clinton, who had to hold positions of power to gain respect.

Bentsen had a natural grace and an ease with his peers. In contrast, Clinton's relationships with peers were always somewhat limited, primarily to those who were like him, political junkies, and courted his friendship because they liked being around power. Bentsen's magnetic pull worked in a room whether he had a title or not. Clinton had to be a successful politician to be important. He was never one of the boys when he was young, while Bentsen had been the boy that other boys wanted for their friend. As a man, he hunted and fished with skill all over the world. Clinton played only one sport, golf. But even there he was famed for being granted mulligans, extra shots that were never counted against his score. Golf, therefore, was an extension of his political position, not sport as an end in itself. Ambitious men were anxious to play golf with Clinton not because he was a gifted golfer but because he held power.

Bentsen's influence over Clinton was immense. He became the dominant figure in the administration on the subject they were all struggling with and to which the president was devoting most of his time. Bentsen was a deficit hawk and had been for some time. In a memorable moment during the 1988 campaign, he had described Reaganomics: "It's easy to create the illusion of prosperity. All you have to do is write hot checks for two hundred billion dollars a year. And that's what the Reagan-Bush administration has done. That's how they doubled our national debt in seven years." Now Bentsen was in a position to do something about that debt. His two leading colleagues were also deficit hawks and exceptionally impressive men. Bob Rubin had come from Goldman Sachs and was believed to be worth more than $100 million, back when that was still big money. Leon Panetta came from the Congress and was much admired for his fairness and honesty, and for his knowledge of the Hill and the way Washington worked. All three men were pushing hard for major deficit reduction. Of all these powerful people, Bentsen seemed to stand apart, the man whom, in critical meetings, Clinton always wanted to win over. During those endless discussions about the budget deficit, Bentsen would say little. He was irritated by the length and the lack of discipline of these meetings. But toward the end Clinton would turn to him and ask, "Lloyd, what do you think?" Bentsen would answer with a sentence or two—and that was what they would do.

As the Clinton team struggled with the ugly new numbers, it became clear that the dominant figures were deficit hawks, who all came up with comparable images: a cancer eating away at the government, or a runaway train that would destroy everything else in this administration. By 1996, if they did not do something to stop it, they and the Bush people estimated, the figure would be well above $350 billion, perhaps getting closer to $400 billion a year. By the end of the century, according to reliable economic projections, it might be as high as $500 billion. If so, other industrial nations, perhaps less burdened by debt, might become leaner, tougher, and more competitive economically.

In domestic political terms, the budget deficit was a singular weapon that the Republicans on the Hill could use against any Democratic social programs that might add to the debt. Thus Clinton's domestic agenda was stymied. Nothing, most of the president's economic people agreed, could be achieved until the deficit was checked and some kind of turnaround begun. Not only would that be valuable as an end in itself, but it would signal Wall Street that this administration was serious, fiscally responsible, and could be trusted.

The people arguing for this course of action—Bentsen, Rubin, Panetta, and Bentsen's deputy Roger Altman, who was also a top-level Wall Street figure and an old friend of Clinton's from college—said that instead of the stimulus package that the Clinton team had originally planned in PPF, they should go for deficit reduction. With some luck, the effect of deficit reduction—quite possibly lower interest rates, less money spent on mortgages and servicing credit card debt, and therefore more money in circulation—might end up being the equivalent of a tax cut.

One other man was a key player in all this without seeming to be one: Alan Greenspan, chairman of the Federal Reserve Board. He was signaling to Bentsen and the other senior people that if the Democrats went after deficit reduction in a serious way, he would more than likely bring interest rates down. Greenspan had implied this himself in a long meeting with Clinton in Little Rock during the transition, where he spoke of all the benefits—both central and peripheral—that would result from a major assault upon the deficit. Among many other things, Greenspan said, long-term interest rates, then unusually high, would drop, and that of itself would spur domestic spending and juice up the economy. Because the bond market would look less attractive, he added, money would be shifted into the stock market, and the Dow would rise accordingly. Deficit reduction, he said, was a form of economic stimulus.

Clinton, listening to his own top people, sensed that they agreed with Greenspan. Nonetheless, it was an unusually risky political course for him. He might do all the things that Greenspan and others wanted about cutting the deficit. But perhaps interest rates might not come down sufficiently and perfidious Wall Street might not respond enthusiastically, or perhaps the results would come in so slowly that they would be of no help at all when he needed them most—in four years. He would be turning the single most important decision about the political future of his administration over to the whims of an alien and probably hostile place over which he had no control, Wall Street, and about which a long line of Democratic politicians had learned to be suspicious. If his administration followed the deficit reduction course, it would be pulled away from the side of its traditional constituents to the side of its traditional adversaries.

After Clinton finally decided to go after deficit reduction, Bentsen, who got on well with Greenspan, represented the president in further talks with him. Greenspan was delighted by the likelihood that this administration was tacking in the direction he had suggested. No promises were made, of course, for he would not and could not promise anything. It was not a quid pro quo kind of thing, but it was what he had hoped for, and he thought that not only would virtue be its own reward, but that lower long-term interest rates would probably be a second reward.

Bob Reich, whose populist-liberal views were being devalued in this process, thought it a form of extortion. Greenspan was not necessarily at any of the many meetings where long hours were spent discussing the politics of deficit reduction. But he was very much there in spirit, with both Bentsen and Rubin talking about how negatively Wall Street would react if this administration did not take on the deficit. To Reich and others, it was as if Greenspan were actually in the room. It struck Reich as unfair that Wall Street was able to exact the kind of leverage against a liberal Democratic president that it had never deigned to exercise with two conservative Republicans who normally represented its wishes. Why hadn't Wall Street spoken more vigorously about deficit reduction six or seven or eight years ago? he wondered.

Reich was slowly being moved aside as a central player to a more peripheral role. It was a difficult time for him, falling in stature and assigned to work on economic policies that might have come from a moderate Republican administration. He was one of Clinton's oldest friends, an early admirer of his rare talent, drive, and ambition. He represented the liberal or populist side of the candidate, and Reich's views on economic policy had been important during the campaign. He had hoped for a job as the head of the Council of Economic Advisers.

But in the changed atmosphere of the grim pressure facing Clinton's economic advisers, Reich was considered a little too radical. The price on his reinvestment and stimulus package had been put at around $50 billion, at exactly the same time the Clinton people were discussing how to cut as much as they could from the budget. Reich wanted to reach out to the vulnerable in the country as directly and immediately as possible; the others hoped to make the economy more sound and thus improve the lives of people on the lower rungs of society. Reich would become secretary of labor, his job, it sometimes seemed, to placate a large number of increasingly disgruntled labor leaders. His was not destined to be a particularly happy governmental tenure.

With the decision to emphasize deficit reduction, the progressive call to arms of PPF was effectively finished. In the eyes of many supporters, Clinton had switched sides, but it did not seem to bother him very much. His views about economic policy, his longtime friends thought, did not run particularly deep. All things being equal, Clinton probably tilted to a modestly liberal, slightly populist view of domestic action, but it was hardly a passion, and his attitude about this, as about with many other things, was tactical; he would almost always go with the prevailing winds. There was not, one of his friends thought watching Clinton swing to the deficit reduction side, a strategic bone in his body. Everything was about survival.

The liberals who wanted an emphasis on social action had lost—and were furious. Newspaper accounts of the president's economic plans made Clinton sound like Calvin Coolidge, Reich wrote the president in a memo. The same disappointment was felt by some of Clinton's political advisers like Carville, Paul Begala, and Stephanopoulos, who favored domestic programs, for example, of the kind the candidate had campaigned on. To Carville the key question was who this president was. Was he the person they had believed in when the campaign first began, someone who had such natural empathy for the problems of ordinary Americans and talked to his colleagues as a fellow liberal? Or was he someone they thought they knew but didn't? At one point Carville, a born populist, scribbled a note on a small piece of paper: "Where is the hallowed ground? Where does he stand? What does he stand for?"[2]

But it was done. The fiscal conservatives and traditionalists within the administration had defined its economic and thus its political policy. Given the fierce new budget restraints, they had also without realizing it helped set limits on foreign policy as well, particularly the use of the military in a crisis where American involvement might be deemed optional. Obviously the cost of any good-sized armed intervention, a war that demanded the use of a large force over time, would throw the budget calculations completely off. In the mid-sixties, at the high point of postwar American economic hegemony, Lyndon Johnson could take the country to war by lying to his own budget people, most particularly the Council of Economic Advisers, telling them that it was going to be a small war when he had already agreed to give the military more than four hundred thousand men. Those days were long gone; the contemporary budget restraints were far more draconian.

In February 1993, when the president went before a joint session of the Congress to talk about his economic package, a quite surprised and uneasy Alan Greenspan found himself sitting between Hillary Clinton and Tipper Gore—involuntarily a poster boy for the new Clinton program. Reich, sitting in a somewhat less favored spot, looked at the president and decided that he seemed to be speaking that night to only one person, Greenspan.[3] Clinton now had a new target for the occasional quick flashes of his anger—his own economic advisers who had turned him into a centrist, cautious politician whose main contribution was going to be limiting the debt. "Goddamnit, I've become Eisenhower," he said.[4] Sometimes, even as he went ahead on this more conservative path, he sounded as if he were arguing with himself. "Where are all the Democrats?" he once said sarcastically. "We're Eisenhower Republicans here and we're fighting the Reagan Republicans. We stand for lower deficits, free trade, and the bond market. Isn't that great?" Then he would go into a tirade that, even if everything worked out and Wall Street reciprocated his favors, "I don't have a goddamn Democratic budget until 1996."[5]

Occasionally he would refer to the people who had pointed him in this direction as "they," as if they were aliens from outside his own government who were forcing him to do things he didn't want to do. His complaints had a touch of self-pity, and he would sometimes protest when he was with more liberal staff members about what had happened. He made it sound as if he were a prisoner of his own administration. There were those who had witnessed similar scenes over issues of foreign policy—an angry, indeed somewhat petulant Clinton railing against the injustice of being president. He was irritated to have to move from campaign rhetoric, which was easy and where you could be for all kinds of good things at the same time, to governance, where you were confronted by a constant series of hard and mean choices. When you campaign, Clinton was learning, there was always a right thing to be for, but when you are president, there was almost never an easy right thing to choose. It was more often than not an imperfect choice of the lesser of two evils.

CHAPTER TWENTY

While Clinton and his senior people were preoccupied with the economics of domestic policy, the crisis in the Balkans stubbornly refused to go away. For what was happening in Bosnia, it was all too clear from the news seeping out of Srebrenica, was a growing humiliation for the West and above all the Clinton administration. In late April 1993, the top Clinton people met again and again over Bosnia, and gradually a consensus began to emerge for lifting the arms embargo and using airpower. On May 1, at a meeting of the principals, the president finally authorized a change in policy, or so it seemed. We would go with lift and strike. The Serbs had to respond to our demands in Bosnia and end their barbarous behavior, or we would help arm their opponents and unleash allied airpower upon them. But the decision had a major catch—we had to have European approval. The secretary of state was assigned to meet with the European leaders and try to get them to agree to the new policy. Additionally, the military component—whether or not the Joint Chiefs would actually go along with it—was still to be declared.

But in truth, the administration's top people, after a prolonged review, had not really made any progress. They had come up with a bastardized proposal that reflected all of their differences; if anything symbolized how ill-prepared and divided the administration was over what would be its first major foreign policy crisis, it was Christopher's trip. To Al Gore, more of a Bosnia hawk than most senior officials, there was a sadness about it all and he had a sense of foreboding. They were sending Christopher on a fool's errand and the Europeans were going to stiff him, Gore was sure. Gore was simply screaming inside, he later said, and he was certain that the secretary felt the same way. Pondering how so dismal a first step could have been taken by bright, talented people who had been working on the subject for so long, Gore would decide that both exhaustion and desperation had led to a policy doomed to failure.

Christopher left for London the night of May 1. The trip turned into an absolute disaster and marked Christopher from the start—a reputation he would work hard to overcome during the next three and a half years—as a weak man personally, who was bearing a weak policy from a weak administration. The policy was poorly thought out and in no way took into account how fierce the European resistance was likely to be. Its key weakness, however, was that the president himself was not entirely convinced of its validity, or that following through on it was worth the price it might extract from his presidency. He was on board, but then again, they might find out that he was not exactly on board.

That was weakness number one. Weakness number two was that the secretary of state, who himself was not a great enthusiast, knew of the president's doubts, his wariness about the potential cost, and therefore felt the leash on him was quite tight. Weakness number three was that the military was in no way for the new policy, nor was the Congress, as a team of deputies from the administration discovered when it talked with congressional leaders on both sides of the aisle. Moreover, the Europeans would probably treat the Christopher visit with disdain. Not only were they going to be opposed to the lift and strike policy because it would put Europeans, not Americans, at risk, but because many European leaders were privately still smoldering over the brashness of the president's use of Bosnia during the 1992 campaign. They resented his almost cavalier trashing of their commitment, no matter how weak and vulnerable it was, especially coming from someone whose country had yet to pay any dues. It had struck them as symbolic of a certain kind of American insolence, the cocksure voice of a young and arrogant politician telling them what they should do and how weak their existing policy was. They already knew all too well that they were wrestling with an issue that had become a horror and that their policy was inadequate.

A Clinton who had talked about ending the crisis by sending American ground troops as well as American warplanes was one thing; a Clinton who criticized what the Europeans were doing on the ground but refused to commit American troops was another. Therefore it was payback time. To the Europeans, American policy on Bosnia, the rhetoric, and now this escalation that would be carried out from thousands and thousands of feet above the ground were characteristic of a country that wanted it both ways. America sought to be internationalist on the cheap and to remain partially isolationist, sure that it had the right to dictate policy for every other country all over the world.

Lift and strike, if it had been undertaken, would have signaled a dramatic change in American policy. Instead the Christopher trip was the high-water mark in the failure to find an acceptable policy. The Bush people, if they had not acted, had at least limited their rhetoric. But the Clinton people had escalated Bosnia as an issue during the campaign, and expectations had risen, particularly in Bosnia. Just before the president took office, American reporters working in the Balkans were constantly being pulled aside by Bosnian Muslims who told them what a great man their new president was.[1] But if Clinton himself was for the new policy, it was in the most tentative way. His doubts still outweighed his certainties. He was for the change in policy, but not for its implications or the cost mandated by that change. He had never made clear to his top people what he really wanted. Thus his own upper bureaucracy was divided, and broad political support for any kind of greater involvement was threadbare. He had already decided that domestic issues were of a far higher priority politically, and he was loath to place his administration and his future domestic policies—all centered around the health of the economy—at risk. So the president might favor the new policy, but he was hardly ready to fight or pay for it.

As for Christopher, his job was not to outline the new policy to the Europeans in terms that they would be forced to deal with, as many of his predecessors had done on other high-priority issues: *I want you to know that the president of the United States has decided to pursue a policy of lift and strike and we would like your support, but we are going to do it in any case.* Rather he would *consult* with them. That struck old hands at the State Department as an odd word. The Europeans were unaccustomed to signature American diplomats consulting in this manner. They were accustomed to someone like George Shultz or James Baker telling them in a nice way that brooked little disagreement what the United States of America intended to do. That was part of Christopher's problem from the start. We were going to consult with people who did not want to be consulted with and would surely oppose any change in the policy.

Barry Schweid, the veteran AP reporter covering State, one of the most senior journalists working the beat, heard that Christopher was going to Europe and that a dramatically new policy was in the works. He immediately called a source of his in the White House. "What's he going to do?" Schweid asked. "He's going to consult with the Europeans on lift and strike," his source said. Consult, Schweid thought, they always say they are going to consult. That was the brush-off they normally gave to reporters when they had something to hide. So he kept calling around, trying to figure out what the new policy really was and why Christopher was going to Europe. Everyone, his best sources who were always straight with him, kept saying it was going to be a consultation, so finally he believed it. But Schweid was sure that Christopher would fail.

The second part of Christopher's problem was the man himself. Among the hawks and doves in the U.S. government on Bosnia, Christopher was somewhere near the center, perhaps slightly on the dovish side. He was, some of the people around him thought, hardly convinced of the validity of the policy he was selling. Years later, when he spoke about the trip with friends, he would describe the president as passive at the time, unwilling to jeopardize other interests. The absence of presidential passion, he would note, affected the entire trip. That was why, it was believed, Christopher presented the policy in a way that could best be described as tentative and in a manner that allowed the Europeans to reject it with a minimum of exertion. His grand tour of Europe started in London. The British were not eager for any change. They had people on the ground and did not want to escalate the dangers under which they served. They opposed lift and strike because they most emphatically did not want more arms pouring into the Balkans, and they were sure that such a policy would escalate the arms race there. Nor did they have any desire to be drawn into a larger military conflict.

Those Americans who were pushing for a more aggressive policy were convinced that British policy had an almost unconscious pro-Serb bias since the British had dealt with them in the past. None of the factions was particularly pleasant to deal with, they were all in the eyes of the British foreign office a rough, uncivilized bunch, but the Serbs appeared to be the strongest force in the region and that was an argument for dealing with them. Or at least not alienating them. Besides, the group that had emerged as their principal opponent in Bosnia were Muslims. They might be Europeanized, they might long ago have dropped many of their Islamic customs, but they were Muslims nonetheless, and there was a certain bias against them.

The Brits were not ready to deal. Far from it. Nor did the State Department have its own people on board. Ray Seitz, the American ambassador in London, was not in any way an admirer of the new administration. The secretary of state, Seitz would later write in his memoirs, with what was extremely faint praise, stood out in the Clinton administration "like an adult in a kindergarten, but Christopher always seemed smaller than the events around him."[2] Seitz was appalled by the change in the policy that his superior was now trying to sell and the irritation it would surely cause his friends in the British government. When the secretary proposed the new policy at a meeting with Prime Minister John Major, Douglas Hurd from the Foreign Office, and Malcolm Rifkind from Defense, Christopher did so, in Seitz's words, "with all the verve of a solicitor going over a conveyance deed." Seitz told how, during a subsequent break, he suggested to Major that he take Christopher aside and point out the impossibility of getting the skeptical British cabinet to accept the new policy, which Major thereupon did. It was a remarkable moment of clientism—an American ambassador telling a foreign prime minister how to shoot down the policy of the ambassador's own country for the benefit of the country to which he was accredited.

Not that the British needed much instruction; they could feel Christopher's lack of enthusiasm. Major was quite emphatic about not changing the policy. His government, he told Christopher, might fall if he backed any escalation in Bosnia. He had no support in his cabinet and none in the Parliament. So London had been tough. But even before the end of the day, as Christopher was on his way to Paris, stories began to leak out of London that the Americans were not going to cut it on this new policy shift, and worse, they had no idea of what was going on in the Balkans. Paris was just as tough. François Mitterrand, who was essentially pro-Serb, was not about to agree to any escalation. "It's immoral to deprive the Bosnian Muslims of arms," he told Christopher, "but we are not going to change." The stories coming out of the European capitals—like reviews of a new play doomed to failure—grew more negative and condescending by the day, saying in effect that this new American team wasn't going to pull it off. The back-channel word already being fed to journalists was no better: the Americans simply did not know what they were doing. It was terrible, one member of Christopher's team noted later. They didn't like our new policy because it might be too strong, but when we delivered it in a somewhat conciliatory manner, then we were too soft for the job.

On the third day of the trip, Christopher was in the Bonn airport when he got a call from Defense Secretary Les Aspin. You might as well forget selling lift and strike, Aspin told him, "the president's gone south on us." The policy, fragile at best, was no longer a policy. No one on the Christopher trip was ever quite sure why Clinton had changed his mind. Perhaps he had never really been on board. Perhaps he had been talking in the interim with the military, specifically Colin Powell. Perhaps he had been reading Robert Kaplan's *Balkan Ghosts,* a book given to him by Powell and which on first reading he apparently thought suggested that it was all hopeless. To Clinton, it seemed to say that the people in the Balkans had been killing each other for centuries and nothing could be done about it.

For whatever reason, Clinton was definitely pulling back. The word spread quickly throughout the top of the bureaucracy that the president had been reading Kaplan's book. His tone had changed and he was now talking about how the people in the Balkans had been doing this forever and would continue to do it. Six years later when Clinton gave a strong speech validating the ferocious high-technology bombing of Kosovo, he decried, in his justification for the American military escalation, those who had argued for standing on the sidelines because these Balkan peoples had been killing each other for centuries. Critics noted that one of the people who had been guilty of that particular rationalization was the president himself when he had tried to justify the failure to push harder on the lift and strike policy in Bosnia.

Christopher returned from his first important trip, as one colleague said, "bullet holes all over him." His own people believed this bad trip had resulted from a poorly thought out policy, taken on by ill-prepared people who did not really support it. They did not even know that, in the final days of the Bush administration, Larry Eagleburger had made a comparable trip, trying to get the Europeans to change the policy. And though, unlike Christopher, he was an old friend of the top European political figures, he had walked right into a stone wall. Bill Montgomery, who had been Eagleburger's top aide, was working in the State Department Operations Center on the day that Christopher's plane was due to return to Washington when he got a call from Beth Jones, Christopher's executive secretary. She said that they were flying back and that Lieu-

tenant General Barry McCaffrey was with them as Colin Powell's representative on the trip. McCaffrey, she said, had been telling them about a similar trip
that Eagleburger had made back in December. "Can you tell us about it?" she
asked. Montgomery was stunned that they knew so little about the immediate
precedent for their trip.

They had all underestimated, Christopher would later note, how strongly
the Europeans were opposed to any change in policy and how hard they would
fight against it. Christopher arrived back on a Friday, and on Saturday he presented his report to the principals. He acknowledged the strength of the European opposition but said that the policy was still doable. To do it they would
have to stay the course, and the president would have to get behind it with
considerable muscle and push the allies very hard. The word *consult* had to be
dropped; the allies would have to be *told*. To do it would require a substantial
use of the president's resources and energies, and much of his attention. The
one thing Christopher remembered saying was *The only way to do it, Mr.
President, is for you to get directly involved.* When Christopher finished, no
one spoke in his behalf, a sign that the phone call he had got in Germany had
been accurate. In some way that he did not understand, the play had changed
while he was overseas, and everyone in the upper level of the bureaucracy
knew that except him. The clearest indication of that was the silence of the
vice president, who might normally have been expected to back him up.
Bosnia, it appeared, was even lower on the list of presidential priorities than
he had imagined when he set out for Europe.

The trip was immensely damaging to the Clinton administration and particularly to Christopher himself. It was supposed to be an exchange of views,
but as Richard Perle, a former assistant secretary of defense, said tartly a year
later before the House Foreign Affairs Committee, "It was an exchange all
right: Warren Christopher went to Europe with an American policy, and he
came back with a European one."[3] Christopher had set himself up as a target
either willingly or unwillingly. He was scarred by it, and that made him, some
members of the Clinton inner circle thought, if not personally more dovish on
Bosnia than he had been before, certainly more cautious about halfhearted
attempts to change the policy. The lesson, the team around Christopher
believed, was that a trip like that should never be taken again. The United
States would not consult. It should decide in advance on its policy and then
explain that policy to its allies.

The Clinton people, apprehensive about foreign policy in general, began to
back off Bosnia immediately in accordance with the president's own lack of
commitment. When a young man in Policy Planning, John Fox, an outspoken
activist, expressed his disappointment about the new administration's failure
to move ahead on Bosnia, his superior, Sam Lewis, remarked, "You must
remember that the foreign policy president now lives in Houston."

Bosnia, Christopher was soon to testify to the Congress, "was the problem from hell," and his trip would cast a shadow over much of his tenure as secretary of state. Later he would talk about how it took more than two years to escape that trip's repercussions and its effect on a host of other issues. Some colleagues thought he never entirely recovered from it. He became the perfect target for blame for critics of the Clinton policies. He seemed out there almost alone taking hits. He never responded to criticism; he was the most stoic of men, who accepted that part of his job was to be a punching bag for the man he served. When criticism was leveled at him, it meant that he was doing his job. His stoicism was perhaps generational, something born of the World War II era. He did not complain, that was not part of his makeup, and showed no self-pity.

Christopher was the most disciplined man any of his aides had ever seen. He got up early every day, ran for several miles, and was at his desk working by 6:30 A.M. If there was a fair amount of criticism of him in the press, and there often was, he used it as a goad to work even harder. When he went home at night, his desk was always clear of paper. At the end of a long, hard day, he might sit in front of a television set in his office, having a single glass of wine. The sign that he was relaxing was when he took his jacket off. He and a few close aides would watch the news, and night after night, there would be a quick, inevitably oversimplified report about him, more often than not, his aides believed, detailing the worst thing that had happened that day. Christopher would watch silently, then say that it had not been their best day, but they would all be back here at the office at 7 A.M.

Having hit a wall with its first rather timid move, the administration now began to back away from Bosnia with a policy called containment, which meant trying to keep things from getting worse without doing very much about it. After all, went the rationale, these people had been killing each other for centuries and we could do little until they decided to stop. That kind of rhetoric had been used in the Bush years and had come from Eagleburger, but the insurgents in the State Department, who had been fighting the old policy and hoping for a change with the Clinton administration, were surprised to find it now coming from the Clinton people.

There was also a new moral ambivalence in Christopher's words that mirrored the political ambivalence of the administration. On May 18, 1993, he went before the House Foreign Affairs Committee and spoke about the acts of genocide committed by Muslims against Serbs. That startled some of his subordinates who had long been wrestling with the problem of the atrocities the Serbs were inflicting on the Muslims. It went against everything that had been said in the campaign, which they had believed was now policy. However, Christopher, knowing that the administration's policy was uniquely vulnerable, had, on the day before he had to face the committee, sent out an urgent request to the department's Human Rights Bureau seeking additional information on Bosnian Muslim atrocities against Serbs. Nothing showed more clearly how the Clinton people were now backing away from their earlier promise than that request. There were, it now seemed, two dogs in that fight and we did not have a favorite.

The summer of 1993 was the start of a bad time for Warren Christopher. The failure to act on Bosnia and the contradiction between American speeches and American actions hung over the department like an immense cloud. The Washington press corps, as norms of entertainment began to dominate old-fashioned journalistic norms, might not be nearly as serious as it once had been. Its attention was focused more than ever on scandal and celebrity, and it was less interested in the rest of the world. But the press corps that covered the State Department was a notable exception. It held to the old norms, and its people were deadly serious about America's relationship with the rest of the world. Its members may have liked Christopher personally and may have felt some sympathy for his dilemma in working with so disengaged a president, but they were tough on him. That summer, as America's failure in Bosnia dominated the larger arena of foreign policy, some senior members of the press corps began to do an imitation of the secretary of state at a press conference, a man searching the room for an Asian or an African face, someone likely to ask about any part of the world except the Balkans.

Thus the Clinton people began their first year in office with the major foreign policy crisis of Bosnia still unresolved, and a major philosophical split dividing them and the military. If they had taken over the White House, they had yet to take over the government—that was a very different thing. They were relatively good when they paid attention, but they were not paying a lot of that to foreign affairs. Preoccupied with deficit reduction and other domestic issues, and giving short shrift to all sorts of dangerous places, they would in time commit a grave foreign policy blunder.

CHAPTER TWENTY-ONE

Without question the most confident and experienced member of Clinton's team, the one holdover from the Bush administration, was General Colin Powell. He knew what the administration wanted to happen in Bosnia. But that policy was, he believed, based on hope, not on reality, and hope was not an acceptable basis for a military commitment. Powell and much of the top-level military based their construct of Yugoslavia on the ferocity and skill with which the partisan guerrillas had fought the Germans during World War II. In situations like this, Powell thought, the head of the JCS had to ponder and estimate the unexpected, not the expected. A lot of bright young people at State and even some in the CIA were saying that the JNA was an overrated army with a high desertion rate and a high level of alcoholism, but Powell remained skeptical. People had said similar things about the Vietcong and the NVA, too. That they had been forced to fight, that their morale was terrible, that kids too young to be of draft age were chained to their machine guns. But it was not true, certainly not when they fought the Americans. Their morale had been quite high, thank you. Perhaps the JNA troops had problems when they fought their own people. But what if they fought what were perceived to be invading Americans on *Yugoslav* territory? That might be very different, with a far stronger appeal to their nationalism. Powell remained dubious.

Clinton, at the head of an administration that was unsure of itself and wanted to avoid any foreign policy commitments, had entered office at the exact moment that Colin Powell was at the apex of his reputation. The Clinton people had won the election, but they were just starting to learn their way. They were members of a political party that had been out of power for twelve years. In contrast, no one inside the government was as experienced, as respected, and as deft in dealing with the Washington power structure as Powell—be it the White House, the Pentagon, the Congress, or the media.

By the fall of 1992, Colin Luther Powell, General of the Army and Chairman of the Joint Chiefs of Staff, had emerged as the most compelling—and trusted—public figure in America. He was many different things to many different people. As a general he was the principal architect of the successful American military intervention in the Gulf War. But like Dwight Eisenhower before him, he did not seem particularly bellicose, and when one critic had spoken of him disdainfully as a reluctant warrior, he had quickly agreed with the characterization. He saw it as a favorable description. He was obviously intelligent; his speeches and his informal television appearances marked him as a man who used language exceptionally well. He had great natural grace and humor; he was a skillful and exceptionally nimble bureaucrat. But Powell was, above all else, a great American success story, a black man who had made it, against considerable odds, to the top in a white man's world, not in some soft, politically correct Ivy League world, but in one of the toughest institutions of all, the U.S. army. Perhaps even more remarkably, he was an ROTC-trained graduate of CCNY in a world of men who had gone to West Point. He had risen to the top by dint of hard work and excellence, and perfect historical timing.

He grew up in the Bronx, the son of Jamaican immigrants, both of whom worked in the garment district; his mother was paid for piecework, and Powell had clear boyhood memories of her every Thursday counting the paper tags that were attached to each garment she sewed, then putting them together in little bundles bound by rubber bands. "That was the way you were paid, a certain amount of money for each tag," he remembered.[1] He was part of a large, extended family of Jamaicans who were either related or knew each other from the old country, and who had become successful in the United States. Education had been central to their experience and success. For a time when he was a boy, he seemed to be slipping behind other members of the family, and below their expectations, someone who was not particularly good at school and had not quite found his niche. He ended up at CCNY instead of NYU in 1954, after a middling high school career, because it was cheaper, and for a while he floundered there as well.

Then he joined the college's ROTC unit, and for the first time he found something he was very good at, the drills and the discipline. He loved it, and the people in the unit liked him and responded to his abilities. He graduated from CCNY in 1958, when the civil rights movement, which would have such an important effect on so many institutions, was still embryonic. There were not that many opportunities for young black college graduates. But the army was changing far more quickly than the country: there were more and more black enlisted men, and much of the professional army cadre was, in the years just after the Korean War, becoming black. Enticed by the many benefits the army offered and the lack of opportunity in civilian life, blacks were staying in and becoming career NCOs, even as whites, with a better shot in the outside world, were leaving, their tours finished. Clearly more black officers were going to be needed.

Powell was obligated upon graduation from CCNY for a three-year tour, and when that tour was up in 1961, just as many white officers, like white NCOs, were getting out, he re-upped. In fact the idea of leaving the army never really entered his mind. What other career was there for a young black man of limited means and connections? he once noted. Work in the garment district like his father and mother? Show oil company executives his CCNY degree in geology and find work drilling for oil in Texas or Oklahoma? If he stayed in the army, he could make $360 a month, or $4,020 a year, which was acceptable middle-class money in those days, especially with the peripheral benefits. The army was, he later wrote, the rarest of professions, one that allowed him to go as far as his talent would take him.[2]

Powell discovered that he was good at being a soldier. He ran into little prejudice on base, even if on occasion he encountered significant prejudice off base, particularly in the South. He liked the camaraderie, the loyalty of men not just to the army but to each other, and that unusual, for modern, affluent America, sense of shared purpose. He liked the fact that what the army wanted of him was always so clear. There were no mixed signals and he usually knew what to expect from the men above him. With a natural gregariousness and charm, blended with great ambition and discipline, he would do well in the army. When the army's own leadership during the war in Vietnam and in the years immediately following betrayed the ethical codes of that institution and severely damaged it, they might as well have been messing with his family—for the army was in a real sense his second family.

For someone who had risen from so humble a beginning to so high a position, Powell had made remarkably few enemies. On occasion he invoked resentment of a traditional kind on the part of those officers who had risen to their positions by dint of command—pure battlefield brilliance—toward those who had risen even a bit higher though they lacked comparable command skills but had served brilliantly as staff men. Or as Norman Schwarzkopf wrote of Powell, when they first started to work together, "His reputation [within the army] was mixed. A lot of people thought of him as half-general, half-politician. In his rise through the ranks, he'd never commanded a division—an important proving ground."[3] Powell was a good guy, talented as hell, but he was a staffy, the combat guys would say on occasion and then note that he had not really been that highly regarded during his two tours of Vietnam. In the first he had served as an adviser, and in his second, he had served with the Americal, a division patched together from other units, one of the worst divisions in army history. Its most ignominious officer was Lieutenant William Calley, who had commanded the troops at My Lai.

Powell enjoyed for a long time—the first fifteen years or so—a good career. But then, just when the promotion lists started to narrow sharply and many talented field officers confronted their weaknesses in other areas and begin either to slip or tread water, his career took off. In an America that was changing rapidly on race, or at least wanted to change, doors that might in the past have remained closed started to open, and his race—which might only recently have worked against him—began to work for him. The army had been a leader in post–World War II America as an equal opportunity employer, constantly well ahead of the national curve, particularly at the entry level. Its leadership realized that it had to match its successes at the bottom of the structure with comparable successes at its upper levels. In 1972, Powell was named a White House fellow and his career began to soar.

As a military man working with civilians, he had no peer. The better he did, the higher he rose, and the higher he rose, the better he did, because the people judging had an ever greater appreciation for the unique quality of his talents. What had been a very good career became a great career. All his special qualities, his intelligence, wit, sensitivity to and awareness of others, and his exceptional discipline and self-confidence, began to set him apart. Powerful civilians in the bureaucracy, men at the cabinet and immediate subcabinet levels, fought for his services, but not because they wanted a token black man sitting in their outer office. They did it because he was very, very good and, they soon began to realize, his talents served to make them look good.

No small part of that came from Powell's discipline. All army men who rise to the top are disciplined, but some seem to be more disciplined than others. That was especially true of the generation of young black officers to which Powell belonged, who entered the officer corps when prejudices were stronger than they would be fifteen years later when he was in midcareer. They were, they knew, *always* being inspected. These young black officers—as Powell's close friend Mike Heningburg once noted—were bonded together by two powerful forces. First, they were black in a white man's world, but a white man's world that seemed to be getting better. Second, they all had had it drummed into them by their parents that if they intended to succeed, they had to be better, much better, than any white person.

Powell was very good, always at his best, because the price for not being good, if you were black, was severe; not only did you not rise quickly, you descended quickly. But what worked for him was more than intelligence and discipline. He had an exceptionally refined sense of anticipation, so important in a bureaucracy, particularly a military one; the ability to sense what was going to happen next, and thereby to help his superior stay ahead of the play. That was valuable at this stage of his career, as he moved into the world of what was called the horse holders, the inner circle of the army's bright young officers who moved up because they were assistants to powerful senior officers. In an earlier time when there was still a horse cavalry, they had held the horses for their superiors as they got ready to mount up.

Powell understood how the army and the upper level of the civilian bureaucracy worked. His job was to protect his superior at all times, know everything that might have an effect on his superior's decision-making, know where potential bureaucratic enemies lay in wait, where the bureaucratic land mines had been planted, and whether anything new had been added to an existing equation in the last twenty-four hours. He also began to exhibit the caution of a man of the bureaucracy. In his book *It's My Party,* a young Republican speechwriter named Peter Robinson wrote that when he had come up with what would be Ronald Reagan's single greatest line—"tear down this wall"— the entire bureaucracy, including the NSC chief Colin Powell, wanted to cut it out. Only Reagan wanted to keep it in.

In time Powell became so talented a figure in the upper level of the bureaucracy that different departments kept trying to pull him into their corner, and he was repeatedly faced with difficult choices between what powerful civilians thought should be his career track, and the very different career track he would have chosen himself. He came to fear that accepting these civilian posts, no matter how flattering the offer and how important the job, was going to cost him his army career. Again and again he was reassured by his army superiors that this would not be true, that in the end the rewards would even out. The civilians who borrowed him and the senior army officers who assured him that he had better take the job being proffered were, in fact, telling the truth.

In a country that loved wonderful stories, particularly those with a Horatio Alger twist, Powell's was one of the best and it tended to please almost all political groups. He was the latest and most admirable personification of the American dream. To many conservatives, resentful of what they saw as government-mandated racial change, he defied the stereotypes of how a black man would behave in a high-level, pressurized, predominantly white world, although their acceptance of him had in some cases taken a bit of time. On the day that Powell's appointment as head of the Joint Chiefs was announced on the front page of the *New York Times,* his friend Vernon Jordan was at the Manhattan heliport when he ran into a leading industrialist, the CEO of a Fortune 500 company. "Vernon, have you seen the paper?" the businessman asked. Jordan said he had not. "Vernon, you know me, and therefore you know better than most people that I'm an equal opportunity man," the man said. *"But chairman of the Joint Chiefs of Staff? Shit!"*

Powell was by the summer of 1992 an imposing and charismatic figure. His hold over the nonideological center of American life was demonstrable. Those in the center of both political parties eyed him eagerly as a future candidate for national office—even for the vice presidency. He was a Republican, a relatively newly registered one to be sure, a Reagan-era Republican, which meant that he had been underwhelmed by the Carter administration's positions on defense, especially its unlikely attempt to rescue the hostages in Iran with a daring heliborne raid that turned out to be a predictable disaster. Powell had emerged politically in the eighties as a centrist, a rather conservative man on national security, and a moderate on larger social policy. He viewed the Republicans he knew as more realistic about national security, and tougher-minded as well. He was conservative, but probably more a Bush centrist than a Reagan conservative. He embodied the best of the country's dreams and possibilities, a Jackie Robinson–like trailblazer working in the military and the national security arena who represented old-fashioned patriotic values and an old-fashioned work ethic. In the early nineties, in the unlikely event he had been able to navigate the tricky shoals standing between any moderate and the Republican presidential nomination, he would probably have been elected to the presidency.

Clinton was aware that Powell, with his exceptional popularity that cut across party lines, might surface as a potential candidate for the presidency four years down the road. Not only was Powell's record on Vietnam in stark contrast to his own, but Powell would deprive Clinton of the support of many liberals, independents, and, of course, blacks, who had until then backed Clinton because he seemed committed to racial equality. Clinton might speak of racial equality, but Powell represented it. If there was a struggle for a benign political center in American public life, something that Clinton had always sought, he knew that Powell would have clearer title to it than he did. In a contest between two American biographies, being a small-town white boy from Hope was not half bad, but it greatly paled beside being the son of black immigrants from the Bronx who went on to lead the nation's military. Powell not only emphasized Clinton's weaknesses, but neutralized his strengths. Clinton, who was always running and scrutinizing the opposition, never took his eye off Powell during his first term.

In a Washington world where most people's social lives had become narrower in recent years because of the rising partisanship, Powell and his wife, Alma, were an exception. They were well connected with the Republican right and the Congress, but they were the rare regulars from the inner Reagan-Bush circle regularly invited to the New Year's Eve party thrown by Ben Bradlee and Sally Quinn of the *Washington Post,* who tended to favor the media elite of the city. It was a reminder of how good Powell was in making a variety of personal connections in a Washington where many people were the products of much narrower professional experiences, were suspicious of anyone with a different experience, and had a hard time finding common ground with each other. Powell, like many military men, might not always like the members of the media, but he got along exceptionally well with them at many levels, the stars as well as the grunts. He never saw the media as some conservatives did, as a liberal enemy incarnate, nor as others who were less sophisticated did, as a monolith. He understood the variables, the vulnerabilities, the dangers, and the uses of the media.

Not by chance was his autobiography called *My American Journey.* The photo on the back showing Powell at about nine was captioned "The life story of a young boy from the Bronx who grew up to live the American dream." It was a sign of his virtually unique position in American life that, at a time when political and military memoirs were usually bombs on the market, his book was a singular success, and his tour of America, run personally by the head of his publishing house, Harry Evans, seemed more like a presidential or at least a prepresidential political campaign than a book tour. His star quality could be evidenced by book sales alone in a publishing world where sales had become more and more a celebrity rather than a literary index. *My American Journey* sold 1,359,000 copies, while *A World Transformed,* a book about the titanic events of the end of the Cold War by George Bush and Brent Scowcroft, sold 49,500.

Like many self-made men, Powell knew his own value. He had been tested again and again in the way few young civilians now coming to power were. He had not only served his country well in Vietnam, he had also gone through the equally difficult post-Vietnam era, when the military was at a low point in its morale and social standing. He had been among the leaders who had brought the army back from those terrible post-Vietnam days. By the time the Clinton people arrived in office, Powell was at the apogee of his power and prestige and was acutely aware of where he stood on the landscape. He had *earned* his authority in things related to national security, even if the president, in terms of constitutional authority, was more powerful. Powell's greatest strength—his résumé—was Clinton's greatest weakness; both of them knew it, and they knew that the Congress and the public at large knew it as well.

Powell knew exactly who he was, what he believed in, and what he represented—the armed forces of the United States of America. He also knew precisely what he wanted to avoid—the careless, poorly thought out, deliberately disingenuous decision-making that had led to the debacle in Vietnam. "In government one of the great undervalued strengths is the power of conviction," noted Les Gelb, a former top-level bureaucrat himself, columnist for the *Times,* and eventually head of the Council on Foreign Relations, "and Colin Powell in many critical meetings was a man of powerful convictions—unshakable ones, born of his own experiences, and it made him a very strong figure inside the government."[4] Powell's feelings about Vietnam and the failure of leadership—both military and civilian—were strong and still emotional, like the anger of a young person toward a willful uncle who has done something both stupid and unethical, squandering the family's wealth, and blackening its name as well. He hated the idea of sending other people's sons off to fight in a war so haphazardly planned, with the military decisions tied to covert domestic political considerations. He despised the class distinctions that had determined who had gone to Vietnam and who had not, which he called an "antidemocratic disgrace." ("I can never forgive a leadership that said in effect: These young men—poorer, less educated, less privileged—are expendable (someone once described them as 'economic cannon-fodder') but the rest are too good to risk. I am angry that so many of the sons of the powerful and well placed and so many professional athletes . . . managed to wangle slots in Reserve and National Guard units."[5]) He hated the lying that many senior officers had participated in, making progress in the war seem greater than it was as a means of selling it politically back home, and thus protecting their own careers.

In waging that war, the top civilians had completely dominated and, in Powell's view and the view of many of his peers, co-opted the Joint Chiefs of Staff. The generals and admirals had been manipulated by the civilians, most notably Lyndon Johnson and Robert McNamara, played off against each other, and in time bought off with parochial packages and goodies. Roles, missions, strategy, and troop levels had never been clearly defined. It was, Powell thought, an earlier commitment based on hope rather than reality. Hope that our military technology would work. Hope that the North Vietnamese would choose not to react if we sent combat troops to the South. Hope that the talented, battle-hardened North Vietnamese infantry, which had fought the French with such skill and bravery, would collapse because it was now fighting Americans and it was no longer a colonial war.

The worst thing about the war—so destructive to the military, so costly to the country, and so grievous to many families—Powell thought, was that the Joint Chiefs had become, willingly or not, coconspirators in so many deceptions. He was an extremely prudent man and a gifted writer who used words carefully. What the Joint Chiefs had done, he said, was a "catastrophe of leadership." They had allowed the president of the United States and his secretary of defense to do something that was truly sinister—to send America to war without forcing its civilian leaders to do it in an honest way. The bill had never been put on the table. "It was *outrageous!*" he said. For Powell and other officers of his generation, the loss of integrity within the army was as shattering as the failure to fight the war effectively. They had seen the corruption reach down into even the lowest levels. "Many of my generation, the career captains, majors, and lieutenant colonels seasoned in that war, vowed that when our turn came to call the shots, we would not acquiesce in halfhearted warfare for half-baked reasons that the American people could not understand or support," he later wrote. "If we could make good on that promise to ourselves, to the civilian leadership, and to the country, then the sacrifices in Vietnam would not have been in vain."[6]

As he faced Bill Clinton and his civilian advisers in the arguments over Bosnian intervention in 1993, Colin Powell was a very cautious and conservative man representing a very cautious and conservative institution. He was unquestionably the single most influential member of Clinton's top national security team, whose other members were new to their jobs and not especially confident of their abilities. Moreover, they all served a new and

untested president who had rather carelessly made a number of commitments during the campaign that he might not be able to fulfill. Eighteen years
after the last Americans had left Saigon, two strong forces were about to
meet in the White House with very different attitudes about the uses of
American power.

CHAPTER TWENTY-TWO

It began almost as a cultural problem. Bill Clinton was ill at ease with the military. Even his salute—as commander in chief—on those occasions when he met with the military was so sloppy that it was a cause for concern among his aides. "The tips of his fingers would furtively touch his slightly bowed head, as if he were being caught at something he wasn't supposed to do," wrote George Stephanopoulos.[1] After a good deal of discussion about who would tell him that he had to change his salute, Tony Lake was finally designated. After all, Lake had spent a lot of time in Vietnam.

The jump from Little Rock to the White House had been harder and more costly than Clinton, so sure of his political gifts, had expected. Clearly the area in which he had the least experience was foreign policy. There the Clinton people intended to deal with a variety of issues in an ad hoc way. The world might be changing, the emerging crises in foreign lands might be driven more by nationalism, tribalism, and the breakdown of an existing order, but no one attempted to adopt a larger conceptual view of how to handle these crises and deal with what foreign policy analyst Les Gelb called "teacup wars." Instead, pragmatic at heart, the Clinton people would handle foreign policy issue by issue, with no guidelines—save the constancy of their awareness of the president's domestic political fortunes. They would do this erratically and episodically throughout his first term.

Part of the reason was the naïveté of a new administration, and part of it was a comparable arrogance. The president was so talented, so politically skillful, he and the others around him believed, that he could come to a meeting at the last minute, well briefed by his staff, and make the right calls on issues of foreign policy. The exasperating thing, thought some of the national security people who dealt with him, was that it was at least partially true. He was so smart, so good at cutting to the essence of any question, that he did, in fact, often respond with exceptional insight, and his involvement greatly aided all discussions. His sense of the politics of every foreign policy issue—both overseas and at home—was usually impeccable. But by the time he entered the discussion, it was often late in the game and the choices had already narrowed.

His foreign policy advisers, in the view of friends and associates who had held similar jobs in previous administrations, were not by any means a strong team. Quite possibly, their greatest weakness was that they were not thought of as prime-time players by the most important person of all, the president they served. Foreign policy was obviously being downgraded—or at least traditional political-military foreign policy. Trade policy, which connected foreign economic policy more directly to domestic policy, was being upgraded, and Mickey Kantor had all the access he wanted to the president. Kantor, a genuine insider, a close personal friend and the key figure on an issue that went to the heart of Clinton's agenda, would soon be seen by some people as another secretary of state, far more influential in policy than Christopher himself, in part because of his greater access.

During much of the Cold War, when America was rich in a world that was poor, trade had always taken a backseat to political concerns. The United States had constantly given up its economic leverage with certain countries to keep them on our side in the great struggle with the Soviets and the Chinese. Nowhere had that been more obvious than in America's relationship with Japan. The Japanese assault upon American industry, exporting freely to us, but keeping their domestic market closed, had taken place largely from 1965 to 1975. American companies operating in Japan had protested bitterly to the ambassadors in Tokyo about the unfairness of that one-way relationship. They pointed out that Japan was no longer a weak and vulnerable economic power rising out of the ashes of World War II. It was well on its way to becoming a major industrial giant. But their complaints had all been ignored because of the primacy of keeping Japan on board as a verbal ally during the Vietnam War. Trade had been unimportant when Cold War politics was the dominant, all-encompassing American concern. But in an infinitely more competitive international economy, the Cold War over, and with American economic hegemony over as well, trade was taking center stage. Now the job of the American ambassador in Tokyo was to squeeze the Japanese to open their markets, not to get them to back us in foreign military ventures.

A sure sign of this change in emphasis rested in access to the president. His top NSC people did not see him much. David Gergen, who had worked in a number of White Houses of different ideological and political bents, thought that under normal circumstances a president spent 60 percent of his time on foreign policy matters. Bush because of his passion for it, and because of the historic events taking place during his administration, had upgraded that to about 75 percent, and perhaps even a bit higher. But Clinton, Gergen believed, because of his uninterest, brought it down in the early years of his administration to 25 percent.

Christopher accepted his minimalist walking papers more readily than some of the others in the Clinton foreign policy team. Tony Lake, his old friends thought, was having an unusually difficult time and appeared edgy because the issues he most cared about were being shortchanged. His access was more limited than what his predecessors had enjoyed. Kissinger, operating out of the White House, had inhaled poor Bill Rogers, the secretary of state under Nixon, a man who was allegedly one of his oldest friends. Brzezinski had charmed Carter from the start and conquered the more proper Cy Vance, who was playing by old-fashioned rules. Scowcroft, more careful and straightforward than Kissinger and Brzezinski, had never challenged James Baker, but he had virtually lived in Bush's office, an obvious alter ego for a trusting president.

Clinton and Lake had no personal ease, which was important, particularly in dealing with someone like Clinton. Lake had always been quite reserved, but over the years he had become much more difficult to talk to, a man who had, it appeared, learned to keep much of what he thought and felt to himself. That was not necessarily an asset. One of the skills necessary for a senior person in the bureaucracy is the ability to create a comfortable ambience where peers and colleagues can talk freely. Scowcroft had been a master of that. But Lake, instead of making people feel more comfortable, tended to make them feel more ill at ease.

Part of the reason was Lake's natural reserve, and part of it was something new, produced by the difficult, unresolved tensions with the president, a belief that if he spoke candidly to others, his words would circulate rapidly around Washington and be used against him. He had become exceptionally secretive, even with his peers, and seemed to be wound very tight. He did not encourage his colleagues to talk, did not return phone calls himself, even to old friends and those who were at a relatively high level in the administration, and in general he made it appear, unless you were one of his own people, that what you thought was of little value. The atmosphere he created was viewed by those outside his immediate circle as quite constipated. He had, one friend thought, an almost pathological fear about leaks, and he was seen so little around Washington that one nickname for him was "the submarine." Rarely had an NSC official been so hard to approach.

The lack of access of James Woolsey, the head of the CIA, became legendary. He simply could not get near the president. Somehow the relationship never worked. Clinton was just not that interested in foreign intelligence, and to the Clinton people, Woolsey, who had been added to the team at the last minute as a necessary concession to the Reagan Democrats, was always a bad fit. Woolsey, they believed, was not really one of them in style and viewpoint, which would turn out to be true. He did not hold the job long and in 1996 endorsed Bob Dole for president. Because the CIA sent over a briefing officer every morning to update the president on what the Agency believed had happened during the last twenty-four hours, Woolsey began to show up with the briefer, hoping to accompany the more junior officer into the meetings with Clinton. Bush, after all, both as vice president and president, had loved the Agency's briefings and had even read the intelligence cables himself.

But Woolsey could not get across the moat. For one thing, Clinton, a speed reader, preferred to read the papers rather than to be briefed. For another, he was indifferent to much of the material. The world had changed, the CIA was less important, and often the stuff in the briefing papers had already been on CNN. At about that time, a psychopath crashed his plane into the White House. Soon, because it was choice Washington gossip that Clinton was cutting off his foreign policy people, particularly the CIA director, the joke spread that the plane had been piloted by Woolsey, who was trying to get in to see the president. At first the DCI was irritated when he heard the story, but then he began to enjoy it—it sounded all too accurate.

Nor was Clinton's relationship with his first secretary of defense, Les Aspin, much better. Aspin, too, was surprised by the distance between himself and the White House. "Wools," Aspin once asked Woolsey, "when you took this job, didn't you think you'd spend a lot of time with the president going over stuff that seemed quite important?" Woolsey said he had. "And have you found that you can't get to him nearly enough on stuff that really matters?" Woolsey said that was also true. "Same with me," Aspin said. He later told friends that he had had two meetings with the president during his entire tour.

If Aspin was frustrated by Clinton, then Clinton was equally frustrated by him. The selection, thought Colin Powell, was probably a mistake from the start. At Powell's first meeting with Clinton, the president-elect had mentioned several of his candidates for the job—Senator Sam Nunn, Congressman Dave McCurdy of Oklahoma, and Congressman Les Aspin—and asked the general for his suggestions. Powell was cautious. It was possible that his endorsement of any candidate—he was, after all, a Bush-Reagan man—might be the kiss of death. Nunn would be good, he replied, but perhaps a bit independent for Clinton and he might be unwilling to give up his senior defense position on the Hill. McCurdy, Powell said, was talented but possibly erratic. Aspin—here Powell had been more openly dubious. Aspin had supported the Gulf War, but Powell and Aspin had fought constantly about a number of issues, and Aspin had often seemed in the past like a man going around with a butcher knife to cut force levels. But they were both big boys and could get past the adversarial roles into which they had been cast institutionally and politically. At a personal level, however, Powell believed it was more complicated. Les was likable, but he was also somewhat erratic. Les is real smart, Clinton ventured. Smart, the general answered, was not necessarily the single most important quality for running the Pentagon. Still, as Powell later noted, he had sensed that Aspin was going to be his new boss.

Aspin had earned his stripes as a congressman, and as a Young Turk on the Hill, he had been one of the leaders in the internal struggle to remove seniority as the only yardstick for chairmanship of a committee. But later he had, as chairman of the House Armed Services Committee, grown careless in tending to his own garden and had just barely beaten off a challenge from dissidents on his committee before he went over to the Defense Department. He had, some thought, begun to lose one of his great strengths, his political skill, the ability to schmooze with all kinds of people who might otherwise disagree with him. Disciplined he was not. Even those who loved Aspin and were charmed by him, and there were many, for he was one of the most likable men in the national security world, thought him chaotic. He was a rumpled hedgehog of a man, overweight, always late to meetings. His shirts were wrinkled and hung out at his waist, and his tie, if not untied, was loosened at the collar, with his collar button open, if it existed at all. These personal habits were not necessarily assets for a man assigned to run a giant institution where the most important inhabitants all wore uniforms that were pressed and starched, ties tied, shirts tucked in, and where meetings always started on time. Even Aspin's close friends held their breath when they learned of the appointment. The question was not one of intelligence, but of discipline and the ability to run a place that was a bureaucratic nightmare.

Moreover, his strengths on the Hill—where he often ran his committee as if it were an ongoing political science seminar and he could choose the issues that interested him and ignore those that did not—might not qualify him to oversee a giant, bone-crushing, man-eating institution like the Pentagon. At the Pentagon, meetings had to run on time, and high officials rarely had the luxury of choosing which issues interested them, ignoring those that did not. Merely exercising control over the complicated maze of warring factions was exhausting. The credentials Aspin brought to the table did not quite fit the job, but Aspin it would be. Powell remained skeptical.

Aspin, regrettably, came to the Pentagon much as he had gone to work at the House. No one knew quite what time he would arrive. Meetings did not start on time and often ran late. All sorts of peripheral people flocked to meetings that were ostensibly for senior officials. His management style could not have been more different from that of the coldly efficient Dick Cheney, a man who, like Aspin, came from the Hill, but whose personality—distant, standoffish—made him right for the job. Whatever else Cheney sought, it was not popularity; and during the Bush administration when congressional issues were raised, he was unimpressed if not openly contemptuous of his former colleagues. Dick Cheney's emotional needs suited him perfectly to handle the brutal job of secretary of defense.

For thirty years Aspin had steeped himself in strategy and weapons systems as if training for the job; few if any in Washington knew more about the intricacies of the military and its weapon systems. But by the time he got to the Pentagon, a new kind of politics dominated the building—a kind of politics he was ill-prepared to deal with. It was about gays in the military, women in the military, and sexual misconduct in the military, subjects of which he wanted no part, and which pulled him away from the things he loved. "Lee," he once told his friend Lee Hamilton, the senior Democrat on the House Foreign Affairs Committee, "you can't believe the amount of time I spend on gays and women in the military. Sometimes it seems like it's all I do." Social-cultural issues had changed the nature of the job for him, Hamilton thought. Instead of playing offense and dealing with the things he knew best, Aspin was working on issues that he knew least, and where he was always going to be on the defensive.

He could not run the Pentagon because he could not run himself. Stories of Aspin's lack of discipline flooded the building from the first day—of his exploding in a rage at a subordinate over some minor infraction, of his eating in a grotesque way—lunch, as one friend said, served too late, potato chips with mayonnaise on them. Powell would tell in his own memoir of a meeting with King Hussein of Jordan in which the king labored mightily to sustain the conversation, while Aspin labored equally mightily to devour the plate of hors d'oeuvres set in front of them, eating thirteen by Powell's count.[2] His health was also a concern to his friends. He had constant heart problems and while in office got a pacemaker. He was a man taunting his own physiological weaknesses in one of the two or three most demanding jobs in America. His tour at the Pentagon was a disaster for the administration, damaging for the country, and absolutely destructive to himself. He was replaced in late 1993, after the catastrophic events in Somalia, and a year and a half later, in May 1995, much mourned by a wide variety of people who had enjoyed his friendship, his intellect, and his service to his country, he died of a stroke.

With less than a year to serve to complete his second two-year tour as chairman of the Joint Chiefs, Colin Powell was both impressed by but more than a little wary of the new president. He was young, smart, and brought with him an innate confidence in his own ability, and he was, on the surface, a good listener. But his foreign policy team was not up to the job. Powell told one close aide that Lake at the NSC, when he was dealing with the other senior people, was like someone driving a team of horses that just weren't there. Meetings at the White House, run by Lake, went on interminably, much like foreign policy seminars. Too many people attended and too many subjects were brought up. One day Powell was shocked to hear one of Lake's subordinates openly contradict him at a meeting. The Professor, Powell sometimes called Lake in private. In his opinion, Lake did not *run* the meetings like Scowcroft and others had run them, and they often lacked focus. Powell thought of the Clinton team, said one of his friends, as being too much like refugees from academe.

More important, Powell did not believe that on those issues where the military power of the United States might be employed, Clinton's people had thought things out carefully. They were almost vague in their attitudes toward the use of force and its consequences, and they were too quick to posture. They, in turn, sensed his disdain for them, as much from his body language as anything else. "You could feel it in the way he looked at us. We were doves, people who had sat out the war while he had fought it, people who had never really paid a price for what we had attained," one senior member of the Clinton administration said. How Powell felt about Clinton and his people could most accurately be gleaned from what he said publicly to George Bush at the latter's final ceremony at the Pentagon. "Mr. President, you have sent us in harm's way when you had to, but never lightly, never hesitantly, never with our hands tied, never without giving us what we needed to do the job."

But that was then and this was now. When he saw old friends from the Bush days, Powell told them they were lucky to be out of it all. The Clinton people, he said, did not seem to understand fully the consequences of their deeds, as if they wanted to try something to see how things turned out, then respond to whatever happened. On one occasion when they had been talking about Bosnia, Aspin said something rather casually to the effect that the United States ought to hit the Serbs hard and see if it worked. "And if it doesn't work?" Powell asked him. "Then we'll try something else," Aspin said. So Powell quoted to Aspin what he believed was a paraphrase of a remark made by General George Patton Jr.: "When you put your hand to the thing, make sure that the thing works."[3]

CHAPTER TWENTY-THREE

The Clinton administration began awkwardly. The president was overloaded, preoccupied with domestic issues. Foreign policy was getting only the most marginal attention; some foreign policy analysts, sensing the short shrift given a number of issues, thought it only a matter of time before the administration stumbled somewhere in the world. The inevitable stumble came in a distant and unbelievably poor country called Somalia, one of those sad, miserable countries whose condition, difficult even in the best of circumstances, was made even worse because it had been caught in the outer periphery of the Cold War. It rested on the Horn of Africa, with the most marginal of economies, a dreadful climate, and wretched, infertile soil. Its people were essentially nomadic, sheep, cattle, and camel herders. But the importance of Somalia had been for a time, for reasons that had absolutely nothing to do with the quality of life for the people there, greatly inflated by the Cold War, as if the outcome of what were always nothing more than their indigenous tribal struggles would in some way help determine a larger, global struggle and show which of the two giant superpowers held the key to the future.

Arms poured in from both superpowers, promises of more aid were made. Warlords were described in the media as either tough, no-nonsense military men (our proxies) or left-leaning radicals (their proxies). In the eyes of the locals, the game of America versus Russia, capitalist versus communist, was largely meaningless. To those in power who got the weapons, it was tribe against tribe and, most important in Somalia, clan against clan. If these strange white men wanted to speak so carelessly of Somalia's critical role in the Cold War conflict, then so be it, as long as they came through with money and guns. They themselves knew what the arms were for—to whack a blood enemy, whose father had been the enemy of your father because his grandfather had been the enemy of your grandfather. The principal social organizations were the clans, which were, in effect, the Somalian form of tribalism. The clans were like giant warring gangs, the forces of any alternative authority were marginal, and the clans or gangs ran the country.

Somalia had had a somewhat checkered history in the Cold War. At one time it had been an American proxy. American weapons poured in. Back in the sixties when the West had chosen not to help, the then Somali rulers, who were anxious to regain territory lost to Kenya and Djibouti, turned to the East. Weapons again poured in, this time from Moscow and Prague. The dominant clan leader at that time was a military man named Mohammed Siad Barre, who staged a coup in October 1969 and quickly took Somalia into the Soviet orbit. But when Siad Barre, feeling a little flush and overconfident because of the massive Soviet aid, initiated a conflict against Ethiopia in 1977, the Soviets withdrew their support. Siad Barre thereupon threw them out of his country.

In time the West returned. The United States, seeking to improve its visibility in a part of the world where it was losing influence, sensitive to the rise of an Islamic regime in Iran, and believing that Somalia was now geographically and geopolitically more important than it had only recently been, began to create a presence there again. In the eighties, American aid poured in, economic as well as military. By 1985, as Bob Oakley and John Hirsch note in their book on Somalia, American economic aid to Somalia was the second-largest amount in sub-Saharan Africa.[1] It was accompanied by hopes for reform, both economic and social, hopes that were essentially unrealistic.

The Americans had at first backed Siad Barre, who, given the power that came with the aid, became ever more authoritarian, and his government more dependent on the clans for its authority. The country was now divided between his clan and related clans against other clans considered less friendly. By 1988 the country was engaged in all-out civil war, in which Siad Barre's growing excesses were a unifying factor among the growing number of dissidents. In the late spring of 1992, even as Bill Clinton was emerging as the leading candidate for the Democratic nomination, Siad Barre, having repeatedly been defeated by forces under the command of General Mohammed Farah Aidid, fled the country.

General Aidid was now the de facto ruler of Somalia. It was not a case of any change in outlook—a nobler vision, or a move toward democracy, or a greater loyalty to the West, or a commitment to the needs of ordinary Somalis—it was, to those who knew the country best, simply one warlord replacing another. The outs were in and the ins were out. Aidid now saw himself as the rightful ruler of the country. He had driven out Siad Barre and stolen it fair and square. Other clan leaders, of course, disputed his claim. It was a division without ideology—warlord against warlord, blood against blood. Even as Siad Barre's forces were in retreat, Aidid continued to battle with other clans, the brunt of the struggle being borne by the citizens of Mogadishu, the capital city, with the internecine warfare, in Oakley and Hirsch's phrase, "virtually destroying the city center, pulverizing the already fragile municipal infrastructure, and inflicting heavy damage."[2] The *Washington Post* reported that nearly one thousand people a week were dying, primarily from random artillery shelling.

By then the great superpowers, no longer engaged in their international rivalry, cared little. There was mass starvation, but relief programs and attempts to help the Somalis ran afoul of the different clans, whose leaders viewed any outside help as a threat to their political control. By the middle of 1992, Somalia had become one of the worst contemporary humanitarian disasters. Hundreds of thousands of refugees were pouring over the border into Kenya, with perhaps as many going to Ethiopia. An estimated one thousand people a day were leaving the country.

It was a classic example of the modern nonstate, a country that was not a country and had, for all intents and purposes, imploded. It could not provide even elemental services to its people, least of all protection from violence; the people allegedly governing the country were the principal source of the cruelty inflicted on their own subjects. The place was hopeless, a horrifying example of the kind of crisis the leaders of the developed world now faced, if they so chose, from the underdeveloped world. The Bush administration was in its last year, and because of the innate cruelty of the Somali leaders, the people who knew anything about the country warned the administration to be cautious. Being drawn in would be exceedingly dangerous, and any commitment should be carefully prescribed. Getting out, they said, was every bit as important as getting in. Any mission should be extremely limited, and any aspirations for political improvement were likely to run into deep-rooted clan resistance.

Yet what was happening in Somalia, despite all the rational warnings about any involvement, was haunting. In time, television cameramen and reporters found their way to Mogadishu, and what might have been shocking photos in the pretelevision age now had far greater force. Instead of still pictures of starving mothers and children, television cameras added a new dimension of horror. Viewers could see the frailest movement of those who were dying; they could see and hear the flies buzzing over the faces of emaciated children. It was powerful stuff and would create something relatively new in American foreign policy: a limited commitment to a country where we had little in the way of traditional ties and where American national security was in no way involved. The policy was driven largely by the power of *images* and the nation's humanitarian instincts. The danger was that the roots of the policy were not deep; it was impelled more by emotion than by the forces that usually created foreign policy, particularly a policy that used the American military. In addition, if you made some kind of humanitarian commitment and it worked according to plan, the cameras, given the extremely limited attention span of the networks' executive producers, would quickly go elsewhere. Among other things, this also meant that the policy was vulnerable to the boredom of the television executives and susceptible to the pull of countervailing emotion and the impact of a different kind of image—the counterimage.

The Bush administration made the first commitment to Somalia. Part of the reason was the pounding it had been taking from the Democrats, particularly candidate Clinton, about places like Bosnia, Haiti, and China as well as Somalia. By the summer of 1992, the televised images of Somalia were, if not worse than the images from Bosnia, certainly more plentiful. The Bosnian refugee camps were extremely difficult to get to, but in Somalia, finding and photographing people who were dying was easy. In July the Bush administration's willingness to do something about Somalia had increased as the outcry over the pictures of starving children grew, and in mid-August it announced that it would fly UN peacekeeping forces to Somalia for humanitarian purposes. This first commitment would escalate into a policy that would have its own organic growth.

In the early fall, the situation in Somalia began to fall apart completely. UN personnel and other relief workers could not get food or medicine to the desperately needy people. The starving population of Mogadishu existed at the mercy of the warlords—and most of the food was going to them. At the same time, the Pentagon began to study its plans for military assistance there. Other options seemed rather limited. The United States, working through the UN, might offer support troops but not ground troops to expedite the food and medical assistance. That would mean a major multinational force that had no American troops at its core. But then in late November, the Pentagon reported at a deputies-level meeting that it would be willing to send as many as two divisions to Somalia. "If you think U.S. forces are needed, we can do the job," Admiral David Jeremiah, Colin Powell's representative on the deputies committee, said.[3] The willingness of the Pentagon to send troops—virtually to *volunteer* them—stunned everyone else at the meeting. It was in sharp contrast to the resistance the Pentagon had always shown about getting involved in Somalia.

But Powell believed that as many as half a million Somali lives could be saved. Americans could protect themselves with a limited but adequate force, perhaps two divisions; and by keeping the mission limited and clearly defined, in time it could be turned over to the UN, thereby enabling the Americans to get out quickly. Looked at that way, he thought the job was manageable. The assumption of others in the NSC and in the Defense Department—especially among the senior uniformed military—was that with the administration under attack on Bosnia and with the images from Somalia growing more haunting, the pressure to do something *somewhere* was forcing the Pentagon's hand. For a variety of reasons Somalia was the better choice, and the mission, though in a more distant country, appeared to be more containable and offer the easiest possibility of extraction.

Sending troops to Somalia, it was widely believed in both the top NSC and Pentagon circles, was Powell's way of doing something humanitarian but, equally important, of *not* sending troops to Bosnia, a place that, as far as he was concerned, was far more dangerous. He did not want to send troops to

Somalia, but he wanted even less to send them to Bosnia. Somalia seemed the easier one, with more control mechanisms. The result was a U.S.-led military mission to Somalia. Brent Scowcroft was worried about an exit strategy and bothered that, while American troops could protect the various groups trying to deliver food, nothing was likely to grow under that costly umbrella. When we left in a few months, the situation on the ground was likely to be the same, with less effective UN troops as the guarantors of safe passage. "We can get in," he had said at one meeting, "but how do we get out?"

The decision was made, however. We would send ground troops for a limited time, a large enough force, over thirty-five thousand men, to be able to protect itself, and once the Americans had established control, they would be replaced by UN troops. It seemed to fit at least part of the Powell doctrine: sufficient force to take on a clearly defined mission with clear rules of engagement and a clear policy for departure. Bush wanted the departure date to be January 19 in order not to burden a new administration with an ongoing troop commitment in so treacherous a place. But that was too early; some of the troops might still be arriving at that time. The agreement was, however, that the troops would be there on a minimal tour.

In the beginning, the chief American political representative there was first-rate. Bob Oakley, who had been ambassador to Somalia from 1982 to 1984, was sent out as Bush's special envoy, and he did exceptionally well in dealing with the different factions, particularly the dangerous Aidid. Oakley had been another of the boys of Saigon, a young political officer who was there with Holbrooke and Lake; Holbrooke, in the Carter years, had made him a deputy assistant secretary at State. Thereafter, he had held a number of exceptionally difficult ambassadorships—Somalia, Zaire, Pakistan—in which he had done well and learned how difficult it was to be guided by good intentions in underdeveloped parts of the world. He was aware of the danger of being grandiose in vision in dealing with the Somalis. He believed that true nation-building was undoable in so godforsaken a place. But because of his earlier time there, he had a good feel for the strengths and weaknesses of the antagonists. "Treat a warlord like a statesman and he will behave like a statesman," he once said. "Treat a warlord like a warlord and he will behave like a warlord." Oakley's political deftness, his understanding that the mission was to be limited, and his sensitivity about how Aidid would see himself in this slightly changed political matrix were considerable assets. He knew just how much to do and how much not to do—and whose toes not to step on. Because of that, in the beginning, the mission was a success, the food was delivered, the very considerable power of the United States was respected, and Aidid and the Americans running the program got along just fine.

In January 1993, the change in administrations had just taken place, and eventually the Americans would have to hand the mission over to the UN.

Here things began to go wrong. The Clinton people were not on top of events. In Washington no one was paying quite enough attention to Somalia. The commitment was not that big and appeared to be going well, and though the equation was about to change, no one in the upper level of the bureaucracy was riding herd on it. Yet there were certainly many warnings about potential dangers in Somalia, particularly the danger of either expanding American policy or in some way letting it free-float. Anyone reading the CIA's estimates would have been extremely cautious about the future. Almost everything the Agency was saying about Somalia was bad. The CIA had, Jim Woolsey believed, some good people who knew the area extremely well. The escalated regional tensions of the seventies and eighties, intertwined as they were with Cold War dictates, had made this a major sphere of conflict, and we had sent some good and knowledgeable people to Somalia. The sum of what they thought was extremely cautionary. In this clan-dominated area, the clans were ruthless and self-absorbed with no larger vision, no concept of civic decency. They were obsessed by only one thing, holding on to power and driving out rival clans. To do that they would destroy everyone and everything in their way.

That view of the country was the same as Oakley's. Any plan that suggested a larger, nobler, or better Somali political order would be seen as a threat to the most delicate balance, a balance arrived at quite violently, and would have no chance of success. No one, looking through the agency cables, would want to get deeply involved in Somalia. No one at the White House, Woolsey soon came to believe, was very much interested in what the CIA had to say about it. Others, old and close and trusted friends of the new administration, were quite pessimistic. Dick Moose, a close associate of some of the people in the Clinton administration, was nervous about Somalia. He was part of a group that included Aspin, Lake, Gelb, and Holbrooke whose roots went back to working together on the Vietnam War. Moose had been with the Senate Foreign Relations Committee in those days. After that they all had served together in the Carter administration, where Moose was assistant secretary for African affairs. That made him extremely knowledgeable about contemporary Somalia. He was now undersecretary of state for management. At the start of the new administration, he had been asked by both Lake and Sandy Berger to write up something for them on Somalia, and he did, stating as bluntly as he could the case for getting out.

Moose had spent endless hours dealing with Somalia in his Carter years, and nothing that had happened in the Bush years—the cruelty the clan leaders inflicted on their own people, if need be—surprised him. He saw only negatives there. The people in Somalia would be different from those in almost any other country we had dealt with, and they would play games with us beyond our wildest imagination, he said. They have survived all these years on an unusually harsh piece of soil, he told Lake and Berger, only by their wits and through the gullibility of others, be it the British, the Russians, and now perhaps us. The idea that we could outwit them on their own turf, where their coming to power was so hard-won and their politics were so brutal, was inconceivable. Moose did not get much of a response to his memo, and he suspected that he was saying something that Tony Lake, his old comrade in arms, did not want to hear.

No one from a senior policy level on the Clinton team even went to Somalia. Later Frank Wisner, who was an undersecretary of defense in the early Clinton years and had been an undersecretary of state in the late Bush years when the original commitment was made, faulted himself for not trusting his instincts and staying on top of the situation. More than anyone else, Les Aspin at Defense was uneasy about everything he knew about Somalia and sensed that the policy was beginning to drift away from the original agreement. He wanted to have a look, and a trip was scheduled in the early days of his tour. He took the requisite shots and had so violent a reaction that the trip had to be canceled. (Some of his friends thought the reaction further damaged his already fragile health.)

The policy was, in fact, changing dramatically, and no one was aware of it. The handover from the American personnel to the UN troops was going badly, well behind schedule. Besides, the limited objectives that were at the core of the policy outlined by Colin Powell were now becoming broader because a critical new player had entered the game, Boutros Boutros-Ghali, the UN secretary general. The agenda of Boutros-Ghali, and therefore the mission he now envisioned (and the higher priority that he, coming from Egypt, gave to the region), was vastly different from that of George Bush, Colin Powell, and Bill Clinton—except that Bush was back in Texas, Powell was on his way out as head of the Joint Chiefs, and Clinton's mind was on other matters.

Boutros-Ghali took a deep interest in Somalia and brought to the table something new, a highly personal loathing for Aidid. The secretary general was an interesting, talented, proud, and prickly man, with no lack of self-confidence. He was often smarter than many of the people he dealt with at UN headquarters—representatives from large, rich, and powerful nations—and his failure to hide the fact that he judged himself intellectually superior to others did not make him many friends in the West. An Egyptian Copt, a Christian in a predominantly Muslim country, he came from an old and prominent family. As a Copt he could rise only so high in the Egyptian government, and he had spent fourteen years as the deputy foreign minister. If he had been denied the right to rise to his proper level by the circumstances of his birth, it had not, even friends of his thought, made him more modest in his appraisal of his abilities.

As the deputy Egyptian foreign minister, Boutros-Ghali had been supportive of Siad Barre, which neither he nor Aidid had forgotten, and which would hang heavily over the unfolding events in Somalia. From the beginning, Boutros-Ghali was interested in not merely handing out food and doing it safely, but in changing the political character of Somalia—which meant trimming, if not ending, Aidid's power. Aidid, who was nothing if not shrewd, was aware of the emergence of a new enemy. Bob Oakley, still on duty in Mogadishu, worked hard to soften Aidid's suspicion of Boutros-Ghali and the UN, but the secretary general's own words and deeds often undercut Oakley.

American troops, sure of their mission, sure of when to fire back, accepted by the locals, post–Gulf War, for the singular military presence they represented, were being replaced somewhat haphazardly by UN troops. The Somalis did not necessarily fear those troops in military terms, but their ruler saw their presence as a political threat. Boutros-Ghali was confident that he knew more about Somalia than almost anyone else he was dealing with, which might have been true, and that his goals were nobler than those of anyone else, which was almost certainly true. He wanted to change the political framework in Somalia to diminish not merely the power of the clans and particularly the power of Aidid, but to end this kind of rogue government once and for all so that future generations would not have to go through the same ordeal in case of a subsequent national tragedy. That was a worthy objective, but whether it could be achieved under the terms of the limited U.S. commitment was quite another question. Some people high in the UN thought that Boutros-Ghali had no idea how much his own background created additional tensions in Somalia; they believed that he should have removed himself on this issue from the beginning.

Somewhat predictably, the question of disarming the clans began to take precedence over everything else. Aidid was alert to the changing nature of the UN mission, and that he was inevitably going to be the target of it. In addition, Oakley, whose role had been so critical in dealing with Aidid and forging a fragile cease-fire, was gone. He had understood that either demonizing Aidid or trying to remove him was pointless. Aidid was not so much the creator of Somalian chaos and violence as he was a reflection of it. If you thought he was the problem, you were mistaken, because who would follow him was likely to be as bad or worse. Oakley had been replaced in early March by Jonathan Howe—an admiral who had been a deputy to Scowcroft and an Al Haig protégé—who was now technically assigned to the UN. The choice had been Tony Lake's. To some in the larger world of security in Washington, the selection of Howe indicated how thin the Clinton administration's bench strength was and how anxious it was, in delicate political-military situations like this, to place a military face on a difficult job. In this case, the military man had worked at a high level in the Bush-Scowcroft NSC and thus could not be accused of being soft. The job was important and demanded great political acumen and, if at all possible, a considerable knowledge of the region.

Howe was a type-A military man, a nuclear-sub guy, who was a good staffer and worked hard at his job. His political skills, however, were considered marginal. "The worst thing about Jon for that job," said one colleague who had worked with him in the Bush years, "was not that he was a military man, but that he was the kind of person who, when the political genes were handed out, simply was absent that day—he had no feel for what would be a very complicated political situation." Sending Howe there, this associate thought, almost guaranteed that some kind of collision would take place between the U.S. and Aidid. It was, he added, "almost a sure thing that Aidid would do something which Howe would take as a personal insult—the leader of a small rabble outfit there crossing and provoking the United States of America—how dare he? When that happened, and it was almost sure to happen, Howe would have to respond. It was not a good choice."

There were two important differences between Howe and Oakley. Oakley had worked for Washington, and Howe worked for the UN; Oakley knew the terrain and its dangers, and Howe did not. In his final days, Oakley had tried to soften Aidid's view of the UN and Boutros-Ghali, but with little success. Clan leaders do not readily change their spots. Their attitude toward their enemies tends to be personal rather than geopolitical. Nor do they think their sworn enemies are capable of changing their spots either. Furthermore, the top UN man in the field, like Oakley skilled at getting along with Aidid, was criticized in New York by Boutros-Ghali for being too close to Aidid and was soon replaced by another UN official, who quickly distanced himself from Aidid. Clearly, the original, narrowly focused American policy and the emerging UN-driven policy were growing apart. In late March 1993 the Security Council passed a resolution calling for "the rehabilitation of the political institutions and economy of Somalia." Madeleine Albright, the administration's ambassador to the UN, spoke vigorously on its behalf. The resolution, she said, represented "an unprecedented enterprise aimed at nothing less than the restoration of an entire country."[4]

That was strong stuff, and Boutros-Ghali wanted whatever force the UN had in the country used to disarm all the Somalis, which given the number of AK-47s they had been supplied by the Russians—one in every house, as one administration official said—was akin to a small handful of FBI men trying to disarm all the right-wing gun lovers in eastern Washington, northern Idaho, and western Montana. Clinton's attention was elsewhere, Christopher's voice was essentially muted, and Lake was not easy to reach. Aspin seemed eager to end the policy and cut back on the commitment, but no one was listening to him. Aspin later complained to his close friend Lee Hamilton that getting instructions from the White House about the policy on Somalia and other issues was hard. "I'll be scheduled for an appearance on one of the Sunday-morning television interview shows, and on Saturday night I'll still be calling around trying to find out what the policy is," he said. But at the UN, Albright was talking about nation-building and the coming of a new and more democratic Somalia, sounding, some people in Washington thought, as if her voice were an echo of Boutros-Ghali's. Her speech, so different from the original mission concept, was a clear sign that Washington was not taking events in Somalia seriously enough, and that no one was really in charge.

There were many telltale signs that things were not going to go as originally planned. George Bush had arrived in Somalia on New Year's Eve for a three-day visit to thank the troops. That visit had gone exceptionally well. But then two days later, Boutros-Ghali had arrived and Aidid had arranged an angry anti-UN demonstration in his honor. So events were now in motion. Aidid began to challenge the UN mission; Howe, in turn, took his resistance as a personal affront. In Aidid's eyes Howe was following the Boutros-Ghali line, favoring disarmament of Aidid's forces. That represented a quantum change in the mission. Though the American commanders in the field felt that their mission was completed and their troops should leave, Howe lobbied Washington to keep them on. The JCS remained unconvinced, and gradually the withdrawal of the original American force began, with some 4,500 assigned to stay on as support troops. Roughly 4,000 Pakistani troops replaced 2,600 marines. But the Pakistani troops did not patrol as much as the Americans and were less sure of their role. When do soldiers of a peacekeeping force return fire on the people they are allegedly protecting? Soon Aidid was slipping his heavy weapons back into town. He was also being told by sources in the UN force friendly to him that the UN command intended to close down his radio station because of the inflammatory anti-UN messages being broadcast. That report proved true.

On June 5, 1993, a day after being told by UN officials that they were going to inspect his weapons depots, Aidid's forces struck at Pakistani patrols throughout Mogadishu. By the end of the day twenty-four Pakistani soldiers were dead and many more wounded. Some of the bodies were badly mutilated—desecrated, really. Only the response of American troops—the Quick Reaction Force—and Italian armored cars kept it from being worse. It was a very bad day for the UN and for Washington, and the cycle of violence now escalated. Aidid would strike at the UN troops, they would respond, and more would die. Each attack triggered another attack, and as the tension grew, Howe would push Sandy Berger and Tony Lake for permission to retaliate. Moreover, in a political corollary to the violence, the demonization of Aidid now fully bloomed. Hunger and poverty and sickness were no longer the enemy: Aidid was.

The skirmishes between the rival forces of the UN and Aidid continued, and in mid-June Howe issued a warrant for his arrest, offering a $25,000 reward for his capture. That too changed the situation. Howe was a UN man, but to the Somalis, and particularly to Aidid himself, he was an American first and foremost. As Aidid was being demonized by the UN (and now the United States), the United States was being demonized in Somalia. The lines had been drawn. Amazingly, there was no high-level national security meeting at which the potential for greater violence inflicted on American troops was fully addressed.

In mid-July American helicopter gunships assaulted Aidid's command headquarters. It was ostensibly a UN mission but approval went all the way up the chain of command to the White House itself. When the American troops pulled back from the site, an angry Somali mob attacked some of the foreign journalists who had arrived to cover the assault, and four of them were killed. It was no longer Aidid against other warlords; it was, in one of the strange twists that these things can take in poor third world countries, the Somalis (under the leadership of Aidid) against all outsiders, including Americans. The very people who had arrived on this most altruistic of missions to end the terrible misery in Somalia had become the targets for the anger that such misery generated. They might as well have been a colonial force.

In Washington, Bob Oakley, a veteran of the same inflated concept of nation-building in Vietnam—and its systematic failures—had a sinking feeling that he was watching a policy without genuine direction. Because of his Vietnam experience and his own common sense, nothing gave him greater concern than the idea of nation-building imposed in the third world at gunpoint. We appeared on the verge of doing that now in Somalia. Nation-building succeeded only when a nation wanted to be built and the forces worked from within—not when well-meaning foreigners, blissfully unaware of their own self-interest, tried to force it upon a distant and alien culture.

Madeleine Albright's comments at the UN and in an op-ed piece in the *New York Times* had particularly disturbed Oakley. The *Times* piece, written in August, had represented a clear mandate for political change: "Failure to take action [against Aidid] would have signaled to other clan leaders that the UN is not serious. . . . The decision we must make is whether to pull up stakes and allow Somalia to fall back into the abyss or to stay the course and help lift the country and its people from the category of a failed state into that of an emerging democracy. For Somalia's sake, and our own, we must persevere."[5] Oakley wondered if she had lost her mind. *Emerging democracy!* He marveled at the words. Nice people, he thought of the Clinton team, well-intentioned, but no one was really in charge. Though his part of the mission had gone well and he was back home in Washington, things were now reaching a crisis point, yet no one from the administration bothered to call him that summer to talk about Somalia.

The top Washington officials were becoming partially aware of the vulnerability of the American troops. In early August, Aidid's forces exploded a remote-control bomb under an American humvee and four Americans were killed. The two people who were minding the store at the Pentagon, Aspin and Powell, were the ones most unhappy with the way the commitment was playing out. The people in charge in Somalia no longer seemed to be in accord with the people who had been responsible for sending the troops in the first place. It was a calamitous equation. To all intents and purposes, Aidid was calling the shots, initiating incidents to which we were responding. Both Powell and Aspin believed that the United States had to get out. Aspin was more and more concerned by the lack of response from the NSC people. He was, he told Powell, pounding on the NSC system, trying to get answers, but the answers were not coming back. That was a huge frustration for Aspin. He was the top civilian at the Pentagon and he was out of the loop. Almost from the start access had been a problem. Tony Lake was a difficult, distant person to reach. In Aspin's view Lake held on to information too closely and did not ventilate the process. "Johnny, can you get anything out of Tony—I'm having a terrible time myself," Aspin asked R. W. (Johnny) Apple, the *Times'* veteran political reporter. Apple thought the question was bizarre, a high-level administration official asking a journalist whether he had greater access to the president's national security adviser than the official himself had. But it was a constant problem for Aspin.

By the summer of 1993, Aspin was desperately trying to get a handle on Somalia, aware that it was slipping out of control and more concerned about the implications of what was happening than anyone else in the government. But he was running into two problems. The first was the lack of energy and interest in the White House on the issue. The second was that all the doubts about his ability to run the Pentagon had been validated. He was not in command there, decisive and in control, knowing exactly what he wanted to do at all times. For that reason he had been a flawed representative of the Pentagon at meetings at the White House. But no one outside the Pentagon was paying enough attention to the looming crisis in Somalia, which now had a dynamic of its own. More troops to protect the forces already there were requested. That had the smell of Vietnam. So both Aspin and Powell were caught between their fear of an escalation and the need, because of their positions in the chain of command, to ensure the safety of American troops and to honor, if at all possible, the requests of their commanders. It was a nightmare.

In late August, both men reluctantly approved a request from Major General Tom Montgomery for a battalion of Rangers and a Delta Force unit, the Pentagon's supersecret commandos. The request had been on the table for some time and they had stiff-armed it before, but now they felt they had to comply. It was exactly what Powell hated: mission expansion, slipping toward an open-ended commitment. Like Oakley, Vietnam had taught Powell to distrust nation-building by well-meaning outsiders. He was torn between two impulses. He did not want to expand the Somalia commitment, but his man on the spot wanted more troops and Powell did not feel he could let him down. Powell told friends we were being nibbled to death in Somalia.

Aspin was equally unhappy with the idea of sending the Rangers and the Delta Force. In late August 1993, just before Dick Holbrooke shipped out for his new job as ambassador to Germany, he had dinner with Aspin in Washington. The dinner was supposed to start at 8 P.M. but Aspin arrived two hours late, looking terrible, drained of energy and absolutely gray in the face. "We've just made a fateful decision," he told his friend. "We're sending the Rangers to Somalia. We're not going to be able to control them, you know. They're like overtrained pit bulls. No one controls them. They're going to push right ahead." The Rangers and the Delta Force became, as Bob Oakley later noted in his book, "a posse with standing authority to go after Aidid and his outlaw band."[6] Aspin was worried and complained to Powell about not being able to get the attention of the other NSC people. In a major speech, Aspin called for a reappraisal of our commitment, suggesting a more narrow, less idealistic policy that reflected a more realistic view of Somalia politics. It was time, he said, to get back to the peace table. That was in direct conflict with what had been coming out of State. But the president and Lake did not seem able to give the administration a clear voice.

Things were reaching a make-or-break point. The UN was going in one direction even as some people in Washington were beginning to hit the brakes, albeit not decisively. Recent assaults on American and UN forces had made the Congress edgier than ever. On September 22, the UN Security Council passed a resolution authorizing a continued policy of what was effectively nation-building. By then the U.S. was moving the other way. Warren Christopher, reflecting a changing attitude in the administration, met with Boutros-Ghali and handed him a memo that explained the American belief that there had to be a new emphasis on finding a political settlement. The search for Aidid had to stop. Somehow—how this was going to be done was never quite made clear—Aidid was supposed to leave Somalia and live under house arrest in a third country, a suggestion that Aidid was certain to reject. Boutros-Ghali was not pleased by what he saw as the American withdrawal from his bold vision for Somalia. He said he intended to bring Aidid to justice. Besides, he said, nothing positive could happen there unless the various forces in Somalia were disarmed. He was in the disarmament business, the Americans were not.

In late September, Powell, facing retirement in a few days, attended what would be his final high-level NSC meeting. All the top people were there, except Clinton: Lake, Aspin, and Christopher, plus Stephanopoulos and Gergen. Most of the meeting was about Bosnia. But toward the end, without having cleared what he was saying with Aspin, which was unusual, Powell spoke about Somalia. He said the United States was being sucked in against its wishes and contrary to the original policy limitations. He said the commander there, General Montgomery, had asked for reinforcements—primarily tanks and armored personnel carriers. Powell remembered that both Stephanopoulos and Gergen looked appalled because the last thing they wanted was to enlarge something that was supposed to be getting smaller. They were, after all, feeling more and more heat from the Hill. When the meeting ended, Powell was worried that Aspin might be irritated because he had spoken on his own without clearing his words. Not at all. Aspin felt even more strongly that the policy had to be curtailed. When they got back to Aspin's office, Powell mentioned Montgomery's request for armor. "It ain't gonna happen," Aspin said. He mentioned the growing pressure from the Hill. It was time to go the other way.

The atmosphere in Mogadishu among the American troops had got uglier and uglier in the summer of 1993. When Bob Oakley eventually returned to Mogadishu, he was appalled by the hatred of the Americans for the Somalis—the view that the only good Somali is a dead Somali. Again it reminded him of Vietnam, where our troops, in their need to survive in such a difficult war, had become even more bitter and spoken of the Vietnamese in the cruelest terms imaginable. Some nation-building, he thought. Three months of escalating combat had completely poisoned the air. Sooner or later there was going to be a tragic confrontation, and on October 3, it took place. It began with a heliborne attempt to capture Aidid and his leadership team at the Olympia Hotel in downtown Mogadishu. A company of Rangers and the elite Delta Force troops took part. So far the Delta Force–Ranger operations had gone well, with no real battles yet, but the elite American troops' disdain for the Somalis was palpable. The Skinnies or the Sammies, these troops called them. Despite the heat in Mogadishu, most of the American troops, heavily laden with gear, did not bother to take two critical items: their water canteens and their night-vision glasses, which would give them a great technological advantage in the event of night fighting. They had made two amazingly arrogant assumptions. First, there would be so little resistance on this hot day that they would never need their water. Second, they believed they would be out so briefly that they would not need their night-vision glasses. Both assumptions turned out to be wrong.[7]

The Americans had the most modern of choppers, Black Hawks, and given the limits of Somali weaponry, they were thought to be virtually indestructible. The Somalis had only leftover Soviet RPGs, primitive, bazooka-like weapons that fired grenades. Against a chopper zipping across the horizon at full speed over an open battlefield, the RPGs might not be effective. But this situation, with a chopper hovering over a hotel as it unloaded troops into a downtown Mogadishu landing zone, was entirely different, and the American chopper pilots knew how vulnerable they were even to the relatively primitive weaponry of Aidid's men. Almost immediately a chopper was shot down by an RPG. The mission changed suddenly from offensive to defensive. Forget about capturing Aidid. Now American troops trapped in an inner city, with their wounded and dead, had to be extricated. American troops, whose greatest asset was their mobility and their capacity to surprise the Somalis, were surrounded. Because of the limits the urban battlefield placed on American technology, with the hovering choppers easy targets in downtown Mogadishu, the battlefield became a horror, one that suddenly favored the Somalis.

Everything continued to go wrong. The Americans on the ground were armed with the latest weapons, and some of the grunts looked like Buck Rogers commandos instead of old-fashioned infantrymen. The technology in the command chopper flying above the battle resembled something out of the Pentagon war room. But the Somalis had their own way of communicating, albeit quite primitive. To alert other Somalis that a battle was taking place, they burned tires where the Americans were now trapped. Thousands of Somalis, all of them, it seemed, armed with AK-47s, poured into the downtown area. They might not have been good soldiers, they might have been poorly trained and inclined to duck down and hold their weapons up to fire away. But some of them were brave, there were a lot of them, and the AK-47 is one of the best infantry weapons of the modern age.

What took place was urban carnage. By the time the battle was over and relief columns were finally able to fight their way through to rescue the trapped units, eighteen Americans had died, at least seventy-four were wounded, and two helicopters had been shot down. Perhaps as many as one thousand Somalis were killed. But it was in all ways an American disaster, and by the end of the day video clips were being broadcast of a dead American soldier being dragged through the streets of Mogadishu to the cheers of local crowds. This was a major league CNN-era disaster. No sight could have been more bitter for ordinary Americans sitting at home to witness: the body of a dead soldier, who had gone so far away on a humanitarian mission, being dragged through the streets, while the people he was there to help cheered his desecration. It was a tragic example of the fickle quality of foreign policy arrived at because of images, in this case, images of starving people, which can quickly be reversed by a counterimage, that of a dead body being dragged through a foreign capital.

Clinton was furious. How could this happen? he ranted. Translated, that meant how could this happen *to me,* and he was deadly serious. He was appalled that the United States was being pushed around by what he called "two-bit pricks."[8] There had been, he decided, a shift in policy without his informed approval. That was the key phrase, *his informed approval,* and in his mind it effectively let him off the hook. Why hadn't anyone told him about the downside of the policy?[9] He believed the people who were supposed to protect him had not protected him. He had been a little careless, more than a little disengaged, in fact, but that did not mean he entirely accepted responsibility for what had happened. His anger needed a target, and gradually it focused on Les Aspin, who had been urging the White House team to clarify the policy and limit the vulnerability of the mission, but whose name, because he had decided to limit the mission just before that tragic day, was *on several pieces of paper* denying the forces in Somalia tanks in September. Some of Clinton's anger was aimed at the UN people who had expanded the mission. Some of his anger was privately aimed at Colin Powell in a personal pique. Talking with reporters in later years, Clinton would often harp on Powell's role in Somalia, that he had signed on to the partial escalation and yet had accepted none of the blame; the president saw this as one of the major injustices of his first term. He felt a lingering irritation with Tony Lake as well, believing that Lake had not adequately protected him on this one. Their relationship, some Clinton insiders thought, was never quite the same.

When it came time for some of the senior military men to respond to questions about Somalia on the Hill, the White House made it clear that it wanted to minimize Lake's role and emphasize that of Jonathan Howe. For much of the concern immediately following the Mogadishu tragedy was over spin: how to make something so disastrous look a little less like a disaster and how to put as much distance as possible between the White House and that disaster. Clinton heard about it while he was traveling in California, and one of the first questions was not what to do about it but how the president should be perceived as responding to it. Should he return to Washington as a means of showing his concern for something so grave, or should he continue on his scheduled trip? Among the people he spoke to were his political consultants and image makers, Stephanopoulos, pollster Stan Greenberg, David Gergen, and Mandy Grunwald. Stephanopoulos and Greenberg thought he should return to Washington immediately; Tony Lake and Gergen thought he should not, fearing that a sudden return would make the crisis seem more important than it was. Clinton continued his trip through California.

Almost immediately both Aspin and Christopher were dispatched to the Hill, but instead of the difficult, somewhat hostile reception they might normally have expected, it was more like a lynching, a vast number of angry congressmen, regardless of party affiliation, screaming at them. To the people on the Hill, what had happened in Somalia smacked of everything that could possibly go wrong. It was a war in a distant country in which we had no vital interest; and it bore the unenviable imprimatur of the United Nations, a humanitarian exercise that had ended with these people—these savages— killing our boys. Neither Christopher nor Aspin arrived with a policy that day. Instead they suggested that members of the Congress help them find a policy. It was as if they had drawn their own blood so that the circling sharks could have a go at them. What was most noticeable about the meeting, some of the veteran congressmen noted, was that Christopher was content to let Aspin do most of the heavy lifting, and to play on his own, if at all possible, a cameo part.

On October 5, Tony Lake called Bob Oakley and asked him to come to the White House for breakfast first thing in the morning. "Why Tony—I've been home for six months," Oakley answered.[10] At the meeting were Lake, Sandy Berger, and Madeleine Albright; they talked for a time in Lake's office and then went into the Oval Office, where they were joined by the president, the vice president, and Les Aspin as well as military representatives. The meeting went on for six hours. In Mogadishu, both Howe and Major General William Garrison, who had actually given the orders for the raid, wanted to continue the search for Aidid. That was no longer a possibility. Aidid had won the round. At this meeting, continuing the old policy, now fully orphaned, was not discussed. It was all about how to get out, or more accurately, how to cut and run without looking like we were cutting and running, to use Lyndon Johnson's old phrase. The answer in the end was that we would reinforce our troops—by God, no one could push us around—and then we would get out as quickly as possible.

Somalia was in all ways a fiasco: a tragedy for the families of the young men killed, a tragedy for an uncertain and up until then somewhat boastful administration, a tragedy for the Somalis, whose cause seemed ever more hopeless. It was also a major tragedy for anyone who believed that America had an increased role to play in humanitarian peacekeeping missions. For the vulnerable of the world in places like Rwanda, Bosnia, and Kosovo, American help, if it came at all, would come later rather than sooner, and it would come smaller rather than larger. It was also a tragedy for U.S.-UN relations, always fragile, but increasingly important if the United States was to become involved in peacekeeping missions in marginal parts of the world. The Congress hated it. Mitch McConnell, an influential Republican senator, was quoted as saying, "Creeping multilateralism died on the streets of Mogadishu."[11] Robert Byrd, one of the Democratic leaders, said afterward of a Senate resolution demanding an early withdrawal from Somalia, "We put an end to the business of the appearance of the UN leading us around by the nose."[12] Whatever else was going to happen in Bosnia, American military aid would be given more grudgingly, and it almost surely would not include ground troops.

It was for the Clinton team not unlike the Bay of Pigs thirty-two years earlier, a devastating blow for a new administration. But the young Jack Kennedy had been a war hero, confident of his own credentials in dealing with the military, and he had a chance relatively soon to recoup his political losses during the Cuban missile crisis. What had happened in Somalia confirmed the worst suspicions about the Clinton administration not merely to its critics, but also to those sitting on the fence. In addition, it also helped confirm Clinton's worst suspicions about foreign policy. It was a tricky, murky business, outside the reach of domestic presidential control, with a greater possibility for negatives than positives, out of which relatively little good would come.

Someone had to pay the piper, and in this case it was Les Aspin, who had been more outspoken about Somalia than anyone else at a high level. He went overboard two months later. The president decided to cast him off, not just because of Somalia, but also because of constant reports that the Pentagon was not being run as it should. Aspin fought back, trying to hold on to his job, and he argued, not without some justification, that Somalia was an unfair test. Clinton wavered. But the private soundings from within the administration and from friends who knew the Pentagon were too loud. Aspin was never going to be the tough, cool administrator needed to run that shop.

Vernon Jordan, who had become Clinton's closest adviser, someone more powerful than ever because he did not actually work for the president and was not in the chain of command, had cautioned Clinton not to change his mind. Aspin, Jordan said, as admirable a person as he might be, was not the right man for the job, and Clinton had to follow through. Jordan used a biblical quote to stiffen the president's spine: "Woe be unto him who puts his hand upon the plow and turns back." A subsequent Senate investigation would fasten on the failure to send the tanks and armored personnel carriers to Somalia, which was laid at Aspin's door. That, rather than the vagueness and drift in the administration's policy, became the hook for the blame.

But Clinton did not escape unscathed. For a president already shaky in his relationship with the military, it was a grave setback. He had been weak before the disaster took place, and now he was weaker still. The domestic implications were frightening. If it had happened in an election year, it could have cost a sitting president reelection. The senior military, already distrustful of the Clinton administration, would become even more distrustful after Somalia. It was a very bad stumble that the administration could ill afford. Colin Powell had retired two days before the events in Mogadishu, but the Powell Doctrine lived on—Somalia was ammo for it. Dick Holbrooke eventually came up with a name for the syndrome that followed the debacle—Vietmalia, combining *Vietnam* and *Somalia*. By that he meant a situation where a great power gets involved in some foreign country where American security is not involved. Because support for the policy is so fragile, and because even the policy makers have considerable doubts about what they are doing, the loss of just a few lives, and the televising of a few funerals, can spell the end of the policy.

The first year ended badly for the Clinton national security team. None of the principals had emerged as a person to be reckoned with. Aspin had been selected to take the fall for the Somalia disaster. But there was another serious stumble to come in the choice of Aspin's successor. Some people wanted Bill

Perry, an Aspin deputy, a man who knew a great deal about high technology and was said to be an excellent administrator. Perry, however, was a relatively low-profile figure in Washington. In contrast, Bobby Ray Inman, a former high-ranking CIA official, was exceptionally well-known, had backing across party lines, and was widely admired in some parts of the media. In recent years he had been working in Austin, Texas, in the world of high technology, trying to create a consortium of American companies to compete with the Japanese, who were less burdened by antimonopoly laws.

The idea of getting someone of a higher profile with great bipartisan connections, who would, at the least, sail through the Senate confirmation hearings, appealed greatly to Clinton. He and his people quickly went after Inman, but it was hard to tell whether Inman really wanted the job. He seemed to think he was doing the country a favor by coming back from the private sector to serve. In one notable public appearance, he had all but implied that rather than the president vetting him, he had vetted the president and found him worthy. Vernon Jordan, briefing Inman for his media moment before he met the press, found him unwilling to resign from the Bohemian Grove, the California establishment enclave that was a rare surviving redoubt of exclusionary male clubbery. Eventually a compromise of sorts was worked out, albeit a rather unsatisfactory one. Inman would resign from the club and be readmitted when he left government service. But Inman, of his own volition, soon withdrew his name from consideration at Defense, perhaps because he felt that the screening process, messy and public as it had become in recent years, was an intrusion into his privacy. As a result Bill Perry was chosen, probably the person who should have been picked in the first place, and who would become by general acclaim the most accomplished member of the Clinton national security team in the first term.

CHAPTER TWENTY-FOUR

The geopolitical consequences of what had happened in Somalia were demonstrated almost immediately in Haiti. It was one of the places where the Clinton administration had been bedeviled from the start, and where, like Bosnia, its rhetoric had been grander than its willingness to act. Few countries in the Western Hemisphere had reached the latter part of twentieth century as poor and as cruelly burdened by the fates as Haiti. It had been governed for years by the Duvaliers, first Papa Doc, François Duvalier, who, upon election to the presidency, had changed the constitution to make himself president for life, thus becoming a role model for countless other dictators; and when his own tyrannical reign was over, by his son Jean Claude, or Baby Doc. The Duvaliers had ruled by fear, the instrument of their will the primitive violence meted out by the Tontons Macoutes, who were government-sponsored terrorists. Not many countries in the world, especially in the Western Hemisphere, presented so dismal a prospect for even the slightest chance of democratic growth. Over the years, talented, educated people either went into exile or were murdered by the Tontons Macoutes. The political act of choice in Haiti was assassination rather than the ballot. Only the poor and the terrified, it was said, had a chance to survive.

During the Cold War, the rule of the Duvaliers had been tolerated by Washington with marginal enthusiasm. They were an embarrassment, but an anticommunist embarrassment, an unlikable ward of the United States. American policy was to look in another direction when the subject came up. In 1971, Papa Doc had died, to be succeeded by his son, Baby Doc, a thin version of what his father had been; and in 1986, he was driven off the island, leaving in a style absolutely befitting a petty dictator whose time had come. Receiving his last political rites from a sponsoring superpower, he departed for the south of France aboard an American aircraft carrier.

In post-Duvalier Haiti, democracy did not exactly flourish. At first there was a military junta, but free elections were held December 1990, and Jean-Bertrand Aristide, a Catholic priest who had been defrocked by the Church because of his radical liberationist theology, was elected president with some 67 percent of the vote. He was not a man widely admired by foreigners for his emotional stability. If those in the West measuring Aristide were somewhat unimpressed and were made uneasy by his volatile and messianic nature, the answer from his supporters was that there was, in fact, no one better. Aristide was popular enough to have served as a rallying point for the Haitian opposition and had survived assassination only because he was a priest. His election was hailed both in Haiti and by the large exile community of Haitians in the United States. It was, after all, a country whose principal export for years had been its most talented, best educated, and most democratically inclined citizens. But after just eight months, Aristide was overthrown by another junta, headed by Lieutenant General Raoul Cedras, whom Aristide had appointed to a high post.

The Bush people tried to keep Haiti on the back burner. At first James Baker said that Cedras would be treated like a pariah, but soon the administration began to soften its criticism. The policy seemed to be that the less we and anyone else knew and said, the better. The one flex of muscle was to ban all commercial trade with Cedras's island. Dick Cheney, as secretary of defense, once asked General Colin Powell what he thought of using military force to restore Aristide to office, and Powell answered that going in would be a piece of cake. "We can take over the place in an afternoon with a company or two of marines," he said. Getting out was the problem. Seething with anger over injustice and poverty, the Haitian people might turn against any identifiable governing authority. The last time the United States had intervened in Haiti was in 1915, and the marines, Powell noted, had stayed for nineteen years. He wanted no invasion.[1] So the Bush administration neither embraced Cedras nor moved him toward democracy. The Cold War might be over, but in the case of Haiti, the old Cold War divisions within the U.S. government remained powerful. The CIA and the Pentagon were generally comfortable with the status quo under Cedras, not so much because they liked him but because they saw no upside to supporting those who claimed the banner of a more democratic country. Therefore, they opposed any policy based on idealism and that might entail American military intervention.

In the summer of 1992, a CIA report portrayed Cedras "as a conscientious military leader who genuinely wished to minimize his role in politics, professionalize the armed services, and develop a separate and competent police force."[2] That was a singularly optimistic bit of reporting. Most independently minded people thought Cedras represented Duvalierism without the Duvaliers, and the junta's principal interest in governing was self-enrichment from the country's limited coffers, while violently suppressing any political opposition. The only American domestic political implication was once again the problem of refugees. By early 1992, the harshness of the Cedras regime, the rash of political murders, and the suppression of any kind of dissent led to a dramatic increase in the number of boat people—Haitians willing to risk their lives in unseaworthy, homemade boats to reach Florida. The Bush administration had returned those Haitians who had succeeded in making the perilous journey.

Then came the 1992 election, and Haiti appeared to be one of those issues where the two parties and the two candidates clearly differed. Clinton, young and idealistic and spotting a great issue with which to nail his opponent, called the Bush policy cruel and unacceptable and promised that he would reverse it. His words implied a clear commitment to a more humanitarian foreign policy. But as he was preparing to take office, the CIA showed him photographic evidence that his election had set off a huge new wave of boat building. Thousands of Haitians were hoping to take advantage of Clinton's new immigration policy and sail to a now more tolerant and open America. The United States could expect as many as two hundred thousand new refugees, the CIA reported.

Clinton immediately backed off his campaign pledge. He was aware of the potential political consequences if too many (nonwhite) refugees arrived in the United States unwanted by local authorities, especially in an important swing state like Florida. As governor of Arkansas, he had tried to do a favor for Jimmy Carter, back in 1979, and had accepted a large number of Cuban refugees at Fort Chaffee to reduce the overload in Florida. Carter, Clinton liked to claim, said it was a short-term deal and the refugees would be moved well before the 1980 election. They were not. The mood both inside the camp among the Cubans and outside among the Arkansans had turned ugly, and Clinton was not pleased. "He [Carter] screwed me," he said years later, convinced that it helped cause his defeat in 1980.[3]

Haiti had no domestic political constituency of any size. The issue was more about race than foreign policy. The Black Congressional Caucus took it seriously and was committed to Aristide's return, but those Americans who cared about political life in Haiti were not likely to vote for the Republicans in any presidential campaign, which, as on so many other issues, diminished the Caucus's leverage. But Clinton *had* spoken those words during the campaign, and they had been unusually clear. So upon entering office, he began to press for changes in Haiti that would expedite Aristide's return. Pressures were exerted—economic ones at first. An international boycott against Haiti was launched, and the shortage of fuel became so acute that the American ambassador's house was lit at night by generators operating on black market gas. Haitian assets in the United States were also frozen, and U.S. navy ships patrolled Haitian waters to stop any would-be refugees from arriving on American shores.

The Clinton administration was badly divided over what to do and how much force to exert against Cedras, divisions that the junta members were quite aware of. Tony Lake, with his special passion for the underdeveloped world, was an activist, more eager to end the junta's rule and reinstate Aristide than most of the others. The Pentagon remained dubious. Driving Cedras out of power would be easy, but none of the senior military men, especially since they lacked confidence that the administration would give them a clear mandate, wanted to undertake a peacekeeping role in a country where the indigenous forces had so violent a history, and where, once they ended the power of the junta, there was so little hope for any true democratic improvement. Among the doubters was Les Aspin. In addition, the CIA was openly opposed to Aristide. Its reporting systematically portrayed him as both unstable and violent, little better than those he would replace. At one point the CIA leaked to conservatives on the Hill its psychological profile of Aristide. It showed that he was unstable, both a megalomaniac and a manic-depressive, and given to the same violent measures as the Cedras regime—among other things necklacing, a quaint Haitian custom of putting a tire around the neck of a political enemy, filling it with gas, and setting it on fire. One of the CIA's principal people in Haiti was Emmanuel (Toto) Constant, the leader of a Haitian right-wing paramilitary group, FRAPH (Front for the Advancement and Progress of Haiti). He was, in fact, on the CIA's payroll and was bitterly anti-Aristide.

The State Department did not appear to have strong views about Haiti. Clinton, those around the White House believed, was a bit more skeptical about Aristide than Lake, but felt that having made a commitment to return him to power, he should follow through. The CIA's reports on Aristide's instability did not bother Clinton greatly. "You know you can make too much of normalcy," he told George Stephanopoulos when he heard about them. "A lot of normal people are assholes." Then Clinton plunged into a long, oddly personal discourse on Abraham Lincoln's profound melancholia.[4]

In early 1993, the United States continued to push for Aristide's return, much of it done through the UN. Eventually an agreement was reached with the junta for a step-by-step transfer of power, and as negotiations proceeded, General Cedras seemed to be softening his resistance, apparently ready to accept Aristide's return, though remaining unwilling to give hard assurances for his safety. In July, an agreement was finally signed to return Aristide to power on October 30. But then in late summer things, as they often did in Haiti, began to unravel amid mounting signs of General Cedras's reluctance to relinquish power. An Aristide supporter was named prime minister as part of the brokered deal, and in return economic sanctions were dropped. But when the Aristide ally, Robert Malval, actually showed up, he was denied any instruments of power. In September an Aristide financial adviser was murdered, and shortly after that, his would-be minister of justice was also assassinated. The two shootings were like warnings; if Aristide returns, they seemed to proclaim, he'll be number three.

Some foreign policy people believed that a major game of chicken was being played, that Cedras was testing the administration. In late September a group of about two hundred American soldiers and twenty-five Canadian engineers were assembled to go to Haiti, where they were supposed to work on nation-building projects under a larger UN agreement and, among other responsibilities, train the police and the Haitian military. Not everyone in Washington wanted them to go. At the Pentagon, Aspin felt strongly that the situation was too volatile to send them. Believing that Cedras was not reliable and might turn on the Americans, Aspin argued for delaying their departure. But others believed the soldiers were the rare bit of muscle in an otherwise weak agreement. Amazingly enough, though the potential for a foreign policy flap of the first order was in the air, the president did not participate in any of the critical discussions.

Off went the troops, the first of some thirteen hundred scheduled to participate in a program that, if it was not nation-building, was certainly nation-cleansing. Though Cedras was giving off every conceivable signal that he did not intend to keep his word, no one had really thought out the consequences. The policy was, as one administration member said, another based on hope and not much more. If the troops ran into trouble when they arrived, there was no backup plan, no real military force that could incrementally be applied. The denouement came on October 11, just a week after the tragic events in Mogadishu. The American soldiers, lightly armed, arrived at Port-au-Prince aboard the USS *Harlan County* but were unable to leave the ship because Cedras had broken his word about providing a docking slip. On the dock was an unusual welcoming party: a mob of more than one hundred jeering Haitians, many of them armed, shouting anti-American slogans and, of course, "Somalia! Somalia!"

It was as if there was a new domino effect. On the front page of the *New York Times,* the lead story was about the incident on the dock at Port-au-Prince with a photo of some of the thugs roughing up the car of Vicki Huddleston, the American chargé d'affaires. Under that was a story headlined "Senators Seek Early Pullout of U.S. Troops from Somalia." What was especially pernicious about the incident was that the thugs on the dock were being choreographed by Cedras's security people, controlled by Emmanuel Constant, still on the CIA payroll. We were, it appeared, helping to fund those who disrupted our foreign policy. For a time, the *Harlan County* hovered just offshore while Washington decided what to do: whether to bring in troops and get our men ashore by force, an act of gunboat diplomacy that would have serious unwanted consequences—a military commitment in Haiti—or to turn tail and depart in a singular humiliation. Any American force sent to escort the soldiers and technicians to their assigned roles might look to the rest of the world like an invasion and, worse, might well end up being one.

It was to be one of the most embarrassing moments in recent American history, and almost surely a low moment for the Clinton administration. The administration was, in fact, badly divided. The hawks were for using military force to land the troops, and the doves, principally Aspin and the Joint Chiefs, at the very least wanted to wait for another day or perhaps try other pressures before we sent in combat troops and possibly got ourselves impaled in a hopeless political environment—or Somalia Two, as it was called.

Certainly no one really wanted a full-scale invasion. Much of the interior debate was about spin and which would look worse—the *Harlan County* waiting out there day by day as they debated further in the White House, or the *Harlan County* turning back. On October 12, the ship pulled away, and on the dock the same Haitian mob danced and jeered. "The theater of the absurd," Lawrence Pezzullo, Washington's chief negotiator in Haiti, called the scene. The political consequences were obvious. "Never again, never again," Sandy Berger, Lake's deputy and Clinton's close friend, a man much more tuned to the president's political needs than Lake, was heard to say.[5] A think piece in the *New York Times* a day later had a devastating headline: "Policing a Global Village: As Peace-Keeping Falters in Somalia, Foes of the U.S. Effort in Haiti Are Emboldened." But no one was ready post-Somalia for any casualties in Haiti.

The return of Aristide would have to wait. Vice President Gore was designated to call Aristide, then in exile in New York, to tell him we intended to keep our promise to restore him to power. It would simply take more time and more planning. Gore expected to find the Haitian leader angry and bitter and was instead chagrined by Aristide's delight at the news. "He's ecstatic," Gore reported to Clinton. The president was not surprised, but was relieved to find that the most important person in the Haitian matrix was not going to be criticizing him. "What would *you* rather do?" Clinton asked Gore. "Go back to Haiti or sip champagne in Harry Belafonte's apartment?"[6] Both in America and the rest of the world, it looked like another major setback at the hands of small-bore third-world tyrants.

Clinton was furious and blamed his NSC staff for putting him in a lose-lose situation. No small part of the problem, he decided once the incident was over, was the lack of positive spin his White House was putting on events, and he suggested to his NSC people that David Gergen, the former Nixon, Reagan, and Bush aide who had recently joined his team, be included in their decision-making. The Reagan people, Clinton yelled at Lake during a particularly violent tirade, were much better at the politics of foreign policy than his team. When Reagan's people lost the marines in Lebanon, Clinton said, they had almost immediately invaded Grenada and that had kept their popularity up.[7] A few minutes after the tirade, Lake sat down in his office with Sandy Berger and George Stephanopoulos and went over the presidential tongue-lashing he had received. "I couldn't," Stephanopoulos wrote later of their meeting, "believe what I was hearing. *Grenada? That's how we should handle things? Like Reagan? The answer to losing 250 marines in a terrorist attack is to stage the invasion of a tiny country? If you really believe that, then why'd we turn the damn ship around?"* They were staggered, not just by the force, but by the nature of Clinton's attack. "He's just so angry," Stephanopoulos later told Lake and Berger, "he doesn't know what he's saying."[8]

Rarely had the United States looked so impotent, its mighty military driven away from a banana republic by a pip-squeak dictator and a hired mob. Robert Kagan's words—that if you are the president of the United States, somehow foreign policy finds you—had rarely been more true. But it was a disaster of the first magnitude, a personal one, and Clinton knew it. Later in his presidency, Clinton was touring Russia when his own and Russian security officers picked up serious reports about a potential assassination attempt against him. Both security forces tried to talk him out of the stop. But he was adamant about making it. "I'm never going to wimp out like I did in Haiti again," he told the people around him.

But in the meantime, even more damage had been done to the Clinton foreign policy team. No wonder then, a few months later, when a small country in the center of Africa imploded into genocidal conflict, the United States stood on the sidelines. Just after the Somalia tragedy and the Haitian debacle, Rwanda went on a barbarous spree of tribal warfare, all of it carefully planned, culminating in violence that, in the words of the writer Philip Gourevitch, represented the most "pure and unambiguous genocide since the end of World War II." At least eight hundred thousand people, most from the Tutsi tribe, were murdered in only one hundred days in what was, Gourevitch added, "the most efficient killing since the atomic bombing of Hiroshima and Nagasaki." The world sat by and watched. In the United States, in the months right after Somalia, a deliberate attempt was made to suppress the issue at the higher level so that the president would not be seen rejecting any option that included sending troops on an errand of mercy. Even the word *genocide* was to be muted in all public discussions. Once again the hope that the United States might stand for a more humanitarian impulse throughout the world was dashed.

Rwanda was, in the eyes of many nonwhite critics of Western geopolitics, the quintessential example not just of the indifference of Americans and Europeans to problems in Africa, but of the double standard used in Washington and other Western capitals to judge the value of African lives compared with Western or Caucasian ones. The West, or at least part of it, they believed, agonized over events in Bosnia, violence inflicted on Europeans by Europeans, but was almost completely unconcerned about violence inflicted on Africans by Africans. Africans were, after all, much more likely to be faceless, without, in Western terms, identities. Europe was historically viewed as the cradle of American society, closer to our shores, more vital to our national security interests. The violence that seeped across borders in Europe always had greater impact on American policy makers than violence that seeped across boundaries in Africa.

No story in early 1994 could have been sadder than that of Rwanda. It had once been known as Rwanda-Urundi, a German colony before World War I that was awarded to Belgium after the war, marginal booty handed off to the winners by the losers. Unlike the neighboring Congo, also Belgian, with its province of Katanga, which was immensely rich in minerals (the uranium for the first atomic bomb had come from Katanga), Rwanda-Urundi had no great mineral wealth. In 1962, independence came and the colony was split into two countries, Rwanda and Burundi. In Rwanda, two distinct tribes were struggling for power, and their antagonisms were historic: the Tutsis, tall, narrower of nose, and thinner of lips, and thus by Western standards of cosmetics, handsome; and the Hutus, shorter, flatter-nosed, and therefore seen as less attractive. Since the Tutsis looked more like a Western ideal, they had been presumed by the Belgians to be more intelligent and became the favored tribe, given key positions in the local hierarchy and a better shot at what limited education was available. The job of the favored tribe, in the way colonial powers operated in that era, was, of course, to help suppress the less favored one.

Since the Tutsis represented 15 percent of the population and the Hutus the other 85, and since colonial regimes were by their very nature brutal and racist, the potential for tribal violence was immense. In the late fifties and early sixties came the early stirrings of a change toward independence throughout Africa. But even before the coming of independence, the Belgians had made a virtually complete switch to favor the Hutus. In 1960, a Belgian colonel named Guy Logiest led a coup in Rwanda, and throughout the country Hutus replaced Tutsis in key positions in government, the police, and the army. When independence came two years later, the country had a Hutu dictatorship; and in the tradition of new African countries, the Hutu leadership did not lack its own instinct for cruelty. It emulated its former colonial masters, lashing out now at the Tutsis, who had long dominated them. Many Tutsis fled the country, others gradually formed into a military political force, the Rwandan Patriotic Front, an army in exile.

In 1990, right after the Berlin Wall fell, the Tutsis invaded Rwanda. The Hutu president, Juvenal Habyarimana, eventually agreed to a peace settlement with them, calling for the sharing of power. To the Hutu extremists around him that peace accord was a sign of weakness; they despised the idea of sharing power with the hated Tutsis, and they worked to destabilize the peace accords. In the uneasy peace, neither side was happy. The Hutu hard-liners were not to be underestimated, and new spasms of violence were launched semicovertly against the Tutsis in what Gourevitch called "the practice massacres of the early nineties."[9]

The rumblings increased, and fearing some kind of explosion by late 1993 the United Nations decided to send in a small peacekeeping mission, UNAMIR (United Nations Assistance Mission in Rwanda), of about twenty-five hundred troops from a number of countries, including Belgium and Ghana. No one thought the mission would be difficult. As in Bosnia, the exact mandate of the UN forces was in some doubt—what they were to do if one tribe attacked the other, and what they could do in their own self-defense. But soon the leaders of UNAMIR learned that dangerous—almost apocalyptic—forces were at work. Major General Romeo Dallaire, the Canadian in charge of the UNAMIR troops, developed a valuable Hutu informant in Habyarimana's inner circle, a member of his security staff. By early January 1994, Dallaire's informant was telling him of very detailed Hutu plans to exterminate all Tutsis. It was nothing less than a blueprint for genocide. Forty secret cells of extremist militia, forty men each, all trained by the Rwanda military, were ready at the signal to kill Tutsis. The militia were known as the Interhamwe, or translated, "those who attack together." The Tutsis were all to be registered by the government and then killed. The informant knew where all the secret arms caches had been hidden away by the Hutus.

Dallaire immediately cabled the details of the plot to his superiors in New York—the informant had been told that his one unit alone should be able to kill one thousand Tutsis in twenty minutes. Dallaire wanted to seize the militia's weapons and head off the massacre. But UN headquarters refused to act. It recalled visions of Mogadishu, where the eighteen Americans and even more Pakistanis had been killed. Or as Iqbal Riza, the chief of staff to the secretary general, said, the feeling in New York was "not Somalia again."[10] Even worse, Dallaire was instructed by New York to tell Habyarimana what he knew, even though the Hutu ruler's inner circle was where the plans had come from. The UN troops on location did not move; therefore it was only a matter of time before the Hutus struck.

In early April 1994, Habyarimana was flying back to Kigali along with the president of Burundi after additional peace talks when his plane was shot down by Hutu extremists. It was the signal for open genocide. Almost everyone in Kigali was stunned by how well organized, albeit primitive, the violence was. As local American cities have radio stations that report the traffic at rush hour, guiding drivers to certain highways, Hutu radio gave out instructions to Hutu murderers about where the Tutsis were hiding. Some of the Tutsi tried to take shelter with the UN forces, but they were badly outnumbered and unsure of their mandate. When a group of ten Belgian soldiers were surrounded, the soldiers were tricked into giving up their weapons. Then the Hutus murdered and mutilated them.

Much of the killing was done with machetes. Often Tutsi feet were chopped off to make them shorter in death than the Hutus who had murdered them. The Hutus believed that if some UN troops were killed, the UN would immediately pull them back. When the UNAMIR leaders cabled to New York that a massacre had begun, New York swept the news under the carpet and announced publicly that this was an internal matter, merely a breakdown in the cease-fire. At one school where some two thousand Tutsis had taken refuge under UN auspices, fearing the coming of the Hutus and knowing that their tribal enemies were doing most of the killing with machetes and knives, they begged the UN officer in command to use their machine guns on them. It was preferable to being hacked to death by the Hutus. What appalled the UN commanders was that it was not a powerful, well-drilled army committing such terrible crimes against innocent, unarmed civilians. It was nothing more than an armed mob. In their opinion, a tiny group of well-trained soldiers could readily have stopped the massacre and rounded up the leaders. As the killings continued, Western nations—France, Belgium, and Italy—sent troops to Rwanda, not to stop the massacre, but to extract their own civilians. In Washington, President Clinton spoke on television to reassure the country that we were doing all we could to protect the 255 Americans there. The genocide succeeded, the UNAMIR noted, because it took place in a moral and political vacuum. Soon the UN decided to withdraw almost all the UNAMIR troops.

Washington wanted no part of Rwanda. The political fallout from Somalia had caused enough damage. As few risks as possible were to be taken, and certainly none in Africa. The State Department's press officers under Clinton, not unlike their predecessors under Bush when dealing with Bosnia, were even reluctant to call it genocide. On April 28, a reporter asked Christine Shelly, a spokesperson for the department, whether the department viewed the violence in Rwanda as genocide. "Well, as I think you know," she said, "the use of the term *genocide* has a very precise legal meaning, although it's not strictly a legal determination. There are other factors in there as well." Reporters covering the department thought it a striking example of bureaucratese, a willingness to talk without saying anything, because anything you said was so morally damaging.

In mid-May as evidence of genocide became more apparent, the UN sent a larger force. The Americans were supposed to help out with matériel. Armored personnel carriers were to be sent to Rwanda to enable the UN troops to get around the country. But their movement through the pipeline was deliberately impeded by debates over the terms of the lease, the color of the APCs, and what kind of stenciling they would have.[11] Week by week the death toll mounted. At one point, estimates placed it at over half a million and growing all the time, but the debate over nomenclature continued in Washington. If it was genocide, then the administration would be culpable for failing to respond. So the new line was that *acts of genocide* had occurred, not genocide itself. On June 10, Ms. Shelly said that the department had every reason to believe that acts of genocide had occurred. A reporter at the briefing asked how many acts of genocide it took to make a genocide. "That's just not a question that I'm in a position to answer," she responded.

"Is it true," another reporter asked, "that you have specific guidance not to use the word *genocide* in isolation but to always preface it with the words *acts of*?" Shelly's answer reflected a government that had lost its way: "I have guidance which, which, to which I—which I try to use as best as I can. I'm not—I have—there are formulations that we are using that we are trying to be consistent in our use of. I don't have an absolute categorical prescription against something, but I have the definitions. I have a phraseology which has been carefully examined and arrived at." George Orwell would have smiled at her confusion.

By mid-July the tribal war was over. Tutsi guerrillas had finally entered the country and defeated the Hutu Interhamwe. Some eight hundred thousand and perhaps as many as one million Tutsis had been murdered. In the words of reporters for *Frontline,* a Boston-based public-television show, the Hutus had killed at a rate three times faster than the Nazis in World War II. Some four years later General Romeo Dallaire, the Canadian commander, went on Canadian television and took full responsibility for the failure of UNAMIR, the failure to protect the Tutsis, and the failure to be able to protect his own troops. Rarely had a commander at such a tragic venue been so unsparing of himself, even though his superiors had not listened to his warnings. Then Dallaire spoke about the larger meaning of the events in Rwanda: "I haven't even started my real mourning of the apathy and the absolute detachment of the international community, and particularly the Western world, from the plight of Rwandans. Because fundamentally, to be very candid and soldierly, who the hell cared about Rwanda? I mean, face it. Essentially how many people remember the genocide in Rwanda? We know the genocide of the Second World War because the whole outfit was involved. But who really is involved in the Rwandan genocide? Who comprehends that more people were killed, injured, and displaced in three and a half months in Rwanda than in the whole of the Yugoslavian campaign in which we poured sixty thousand troops and the whole of the Western world was involved there? . . . Who is grieving for Rwanda and really living it and living with the consequences?"[12]

Almost five years after the massacre, well into his second term, the genocide long over, Bill Clinton flew to Kigali, the country's capital, to offer a partial apologia. He did not actually say he was sorry, and he did not actually apologize, but he did, on behalf of himself and his country, appear to be contrite. He said that he had come to pay his respects to all who had suffered and perished in the genocide. He spoke at the Kigali airport, as part of a larger African tour, met with the families of some of those who were murdered, and gave the president of Rwanda a plaque honoring the dead. In his speech Clinton used the word *genocide* eleven times. He was there a total of three and a

278 / DAVID HALBERSTAM

half hours. He did not leave the airport, and the men piloting *Air Force One* never turned off the plane's engines.[13]

If his administration wanted no part of Rwanda, the Haiti fiasco, coming as it did so soon after Somalia, had been a critical lesson for Clinton. Foreign policy might not help you, but it could certainly hurt you. That danger existed not because people took the new, post-Soviet generation of issues—Bosnia, Somalia, Haiti, Rwanda—that seriously or greatly favored alternative policies toward them. It could hurt you because, unlike most political decisions, what happened after you made them was so visible, a most palpable reminder of something larger and more significant: how the people of your own country measured you and your personal strength as an extension of their strength. Perceived personal strength might be as important, or even more important, than real strength. It had worked well for Ronald Reagan, while the apparent lack of it had significantly damaged Jimmy Carter. Now, however gradually, perceived personal strength became a central factor in the formation of Clinton's foreign policy, a change that started in the middle of the second year of his presidency.

In the summer of 1994, the administration began to search for a policy for Haiti that would restore Aristide, end the rule of the junta, and, if possible, avoid bloodshed. The president's frustrations were obvious. At one point in April, Randall Robinson, a prominent black activist and the leader of TransAfrica Forum, had started a hunger strike to protest American policy in Haiti. When reporters asked Clinton what he thought about Robinson's strike, he amazed them by endorsing it. "He ought to stay out there. We need to change the policy," Clinton said as if he were talking about some other president's foreign policy. That greatly surprised Robinson: "To have the president suggest that a policy should change and I should stay out there on a hunger strike while he abdicates his responsibility is deeply disturbing." Clinton, Robinson added, could change the policy with a stroke of a pen.

Clinton had little to build on. Aristide himself kept sending contradictory signals about whether he wanted to return. Somewhat reluctantly the civilians in the administration began to focus on the use of force, if necessary, to return Aristide and drive the junta out. "Our own Grenada," one administration member called it somewhat skeptically. The politics of it were complicated. There was no immediate political upside; not many people favored a Haitian invasion. The Black Congressional Caucus was for it, but its leverage with Clinton on an issue like this was essentially marginal because it really had nowhere else to go. But now, because of Bosnia, Somalia, Rwanda, and Haiti, there was a sense that foreign policy was slowly affecting the way this administration was perceived; foreign policy was seeping into domestic political perceptions.

So the Pentagon was told to start planning a force for the invasion of

Haiti. It became known as the Bookend policy. One bookend was potentially a bluff: we would go through the motions of an invasion and hope to bluff the junta out, assuming that it would have no desire to meet up with elite American combat units. If the bluff failed, the other bookend was the invasion itself, which would be carried out with considerable force in a quick strike. To make the point, a marine three-star, Jack Sheehan, the man who was putting together the planning of the invasion, was dispatched to meet with Cedras on several occasions. Sheehan was an impressive figure, six feet five, a combat veteran of Vietnam, and bedecked with medals. "I have two sets of uniforms," he told Cedras on one occasion, "my dress uniform and my combat one. You can make the choice which one I'm wearing the next time we meet."

Even if the planning was going ahead, the Pentagon remained cautious, uneasy about Aristide. Walt Slocombe, the undersecretary of defense for planning, was heard at a party to say that he had no intention of risking American lives "to put that psychopath back in power." His colleagues Bill Perry and John Deutch had no doubt about how easy it would be to come in and take over the scene militarily, but they wondered what would happen afterward. The mission lacked clarity as the White House was discussing it. People feared being caught in the middle between feuding Haitian groups. Perry eventually came around on the idea, but slowly, always worried about the postvictory consequences. JCS chairman John Shalikashvili was probably more of an activist. The Clinton presidency, to which he was sympathetic, was obviously in trouble, and success in Haiti could be important in moving away from negative to more positive foreign policy and military images.

On the civilian side, Lake was the most obvious hawk, but Strobe Talbott, now the number two man at State, was a hawk as well. The vice president was also considered an activist. By September, the plan was mostly in place. The orders from the White House were that the invasion was to be kept to a force of under twenty-two thousand men—actually it would end up being closer to twenty-five. The 82nd Airborne would be launched from Fort Bragg. Elements of the 101st Airborne were sitting nearby on a ship ready to join in, and a force of about two thousand marines would hit the shores. To complete the assault, the Tenth Mountain Division would come ashore almost as soon as the airborne troops had landed. Even before the invasion was set in motion, some Special Forces units would go ashore to take out any Haitian armored vehicles.

By early September, invasion plans were fairly complete. Clinton might be getting what he wanted, but he was hardly happy about it. He did not like the current policy, which was, of course, a nonpolicy, he did not like the old policy, which had failed, and he did not like the new policy they had just signed on to because it might end in violence with considerable political repercussions. There were signs of the usual Clinton irritation as he dealt with things he didn't like: "I can't believe they got me into this. . . . How did this happen?

We should have waited until after the elections," he told the people around him.[14]

By mid-September they were ready for the invasion. Then things became complicated. Jimmy Carter, the former president, had valuable contacts in Haiti, including some with members of the junta. He understood that some form of invasion was about to take place and volunteered to lead a negotiating team to try to get the junta to leave peacefully. Clinton was delighted to avoid the outright use of force to remove the junta, but he was also wary of Carter. But he decided that there was no harm in having Carter lead a negotiating team that would permit a peaceful entry of American forces. Carter asked to have his fellow Georgian Sam Nunn for his team. Nunn, still a senator and respected along a broad political spectrum, had openly opposed the use of force in Haiti, which gave him a certain credibility with the junta. He in turn suggested adding Colin Powell to the team. Off they went, aware that a major invasion of military force was already in the works and the clock was ticking. Clinton remained wary of Carter: "Sometimes a wild card, but I took a chance on him in North Korea [in another collision of forces] and that didn't turn out too badly," he told Powell.[15] What bothered Clinton privately was what he considered Carter's considerable ego and his need to validate himself as a self-appointed international peacekeeper and, perhaps most dangerously, what was perceived as his desire to make peace at what might possibly be too great a price. Carter was hardly a White House favorite: the new Democratic president had gone to lengths from the moment he was elected to distance himself from the last Democratic president. Carter, the Clinton people had implied both during the campaign and in the days when they had first come to power, was something of a wimp, and they were going to be different, tougher, more centered. More, any use of him might imply that, if there were not two American presidents, then there were at least two secretaries of State. That of itself might diminish the idea of a Clinton presidency. That this was not a normal mission was obvious from the press release announcing the Carter trip. The original, being finalized in Tony Lake's office, had begun, "With President Clinton's approval, Jimmy Carter . . ."[16] Stephanopoulos took one look and tried to stop it. Clinton had already approved the draft, Lake said. But, Stephanopoulos objected, presidents don't *approve* missions like this, they *order* them. Clinton swung to Stephanopoulos's side.

So it was a politically loaded, somewhat risky idea. In the eyes of the White House, Carter was hard to control, and he tended to freelance and thereby, they feared, play into the hands of the local bad guys. Still, if it was not an ideal option, nothing in Haiti was ideal, and one last effort for peace would be reassuring to other Latin American nations in showing that we had not wanted to practice gunboat diplomacy. So even as the invasion countdown was taking place, Clinton decided to send Carter, Powell, and Nunn.

At this point timing became crucial. The invasion was set for September 19. On September 17, Carter, Nunn, and Powell arrived in Haiti near midday. They had thirty-six hours to convince the Haitian junta to go peacefully. What Clinton wanted more than anything else was to get the deal done: he would prefer the large American force go ashore peacefully, but what he did not want was for it all to go this far and end without a *clear* and *final* resolution—it would seem too much the hallmark of previous stumbles, most specifically the debacle with the *Harlan County*. Whatever else, it must not end up inconclusively, with Cedras able to hedge again—and that was what Clinton began to fear was happening. More, there was a semi-silent player in this pushing him toward the more violent use of force, Aristide himself, who did not want a peaceful takeover, but wanted the American military to come in and wipe out the junta and its leadership for him.

The meetings had a comic-opera, albeit dangerous comic-opera, tone to them, the Haitian leaders talking vaingloriously about their willingness to die for their country, Powell in turn trying to explain what they would face, forces from two aircraft carriers, twenty thousand elite American soldiers, plus tanks and helicopter gunships. No sensible military code, he said, called for the needless sacrifice of lives of either officers or men. Their meetings began to drag on, with the deadline for the invasion, 12:01 A.M. on the nineteenth, getting ever closer.

Even as they were going back and forth on some of the details, the C-130s were leaving Fort Bragg with the 82nd Airborne, the Pentagon press corps had been briefed on the mission, and Tom Johnson, the head of CNN, was calling top people at the Pentagon telling them that CNN knew that planes with the 82nd had already left for Haiti—and it would be easy to figure out the time of the jump. In the Pentagon war room, Lieutenant General Sheehan pleaded with Johnson over the phone not to run anything on the network because it could get kids killed, and Johnson accepted the restraints.

At one point, as his negotiating team was closing in on a deal, Clinton, aware of how little time was left and the danger to them—they could even become hostages—ordered them to get out of the presidential palace and out of the country, but they demanded a little more time. Clinton's order reflected not just the imminent deadline, but a growing irritation with Carter in the White House, which felt Cedras was stalling, and a fear that Carter might be going along with the stall. On the ground, however, it was not just Carter but Nunn and Powell who thought they were close to working out a deal that would allow a peaceful entry of American forces. Just when it seemed that things were at their most chaotic, Brigadier General Philippe Biamby, Cedras's chief of staff, rushed in to tell him, "The Eighty-second Airborne is on its way!" Even then the tensions continued, the Americans buying a little more time from Clinton, the Haitians thundering a little bit more about their pride and manhood before they folded their hands. On board one of the aircraft carriers from which the first troops would debark, aware that time was running out, even as he went down his final checklist for the invasion, was General Hugh Shelton, who commanded all the troops. He and his staff were also watching CNN, where updated details on the negotiations were being fed regularly into the programming. Shelton and his staff would watch the news clips featuring Carter, Powell, and Nunn, then shout at the television set, "Get out of there!"[17] And then, just at the last minute, the macho Haitian mood ended, reality sank in, and a date was fixed for the junta to leave and for Aristide to return. The American troops would arrive peacefully.

But with that, Carter became a problem as far as the Clinton people were concerned. Haiti had been successfully done, force threatened but not used, and Clinton wanted the credit. If it was not exactly a big-time success, it was not a failure, and it was the first foreign policy victory, one badly needed. But Carter did not seem to want to go away; he wanted to stay on and monitor the scene, irritating the White House, which wanted to minimize his role and maximize Clinton's. In time, Carter's phone calls from Haiti, which he had hoped would go through directly to the president or Lake or even Berger, were passed down the line, to be taken by General Sheehan, who had run the military side of it. But all in all, the White House was generally pleased. The president had been partially dewimped, it had been low cost, relatively easy to control. If Haiti would not easily be transformed into a democracy, if Aristide's political world was almost as murky as the one that had preceded it, no one really cared that much. What Haitians did to themselves was always another matter. What mattered in the White House was that we had stood up to dictators, gotten them to leave (albeit on terms rather favorable to them), and reversed the image of the *Harlan County*. That was the lasting image. There were lessons there for the future.

CHAPTER TWENTY-FIVE

Nineteen ninety-four had not been a good year for Clinton and his advisers. The problem of Bosnia remained outside their reach, limiting everything else they did in foreign affairs. One extraordinary media moment had highlighted the administration's frustration as if to remind them that, monopoly superpower or not, our rhetoric was mightier, if not than our sword, then certainly our deeds and will. In the spring of 1994, Christiane Amanpour appeared on a special CNN program and got a rare chance for a correspondent in a war zone to ask the president a question. That network was showcasing its new technological abilities by holding an international town hall meeting featuring Bill Clinton as the principal guest. The occasion was supposed to be ceremonial, and the White House assumed this was a good deed, a favor to CNN, and that Clinton would be asked slow-pitch, softball questions rather than the tough and gritty questions its correspondents normally asked. But when they cut to Amanpour in Sarajevo, she, the correspondent based in what was a living hell, reacted with the obsession that went with the territory. She asked the president why it was taking him so long to come up with a policy on Bosnia. Didn't he think, she added, "that the constant flip-flops of your administration on the issue of Bosnia set a very dangerous precedent?"

Bingo: she had nailed him, live and in color and in front of the entire world. Clinton was not pleased, not expecting this kind of question. He was obviously angry—his face grew hard and his voice icy. "There have been no constant flip-flops, madam," he said. But of course there had been, and well into their second year in office, the Clinton people were still searching for a policy.

With the administration effectively stalemated, the tensions showed on Tony Lake more than anyone else on the NSC team. Christopher was seeking his own measure of distance from the issue, and Sandy Berger, Lake's deputy, was a pragmatist who, more than anything else, reflected Clinton's politics. But these were Lake's issues. He, after all, was the one committed to a new and more active policy in the Balkans, and he had become the most anguished as events remained outside their control. Lake sometimes thought that he and his colleagues in the administration had become what they had all campaigned against two years earlier. But he was caught between his personal beliefs on

Bosnia and his loyalty to the president. From the spring of 1994, well into the spring of 1995, with the Serbs behaving even more aggressively in Bosnia, his frustration steadily mounted.

Issues like this, rather than the strategic Cold War struggle between the world's great powers, were what had driven him for more than two decades. For that reason, Lake's primary interest, even before the collapse of the Soviet Union, separated him from most contemporary national security figures. Despite all the ongoing tensions, he believed our conflict with the Soviets had effectively been settled in a de facto stalemate in the sixties, and it was only a matter of how quickly or slowly the two great powers played out their hands. The important issues of the future, he thought, were more likely to arise in the third world and would concern the implosion of poor countries, the refugee crises thus created, and the ensuing crises of regional destabilization. That made his frustrations over Bosnia all the more painful.

By the fall of 1994, the Serbs had virtually completed carving up Bosnia and had taken nearly 70 percent of the country. Perhaps the worst moment for Lake came in the late fall of 1994, after the off-year election when the Republicans had dealt the Democrats a stunning blow and things were already at a low point in the White House. The Bihac pocket, a small area of Bosnia jutting into the northern part of the Croatian crescent that had already been conquered by Serbs, began to dominate the news from Bosnia. It was extremely vulnerable to the Serbs, its defenders were underarmed, and it was loaded with Muslim refugees from surrounding areas. It was land belonging to Bosnia, but close to Croatia, conquered by the Serbs, and coveted by the Croatians as well. Because of the inventiveness of maps handed down through the ages by everyone involved, it was claimed by all three sides.

The Bihac pocket had become a constant sore point in the war. In October 1994, the Bosnian Fifth Corps, the best unit in the Bosnian army, broke out of the pocket and launched a brief but surprisingly successful campaign against the Serb forces encircling it. Given the limited Bosnian logistical support and the difficulty in sustaining any kind of long-range campaign, the breakout had probably not been a good idea, and the Serbs struck back at the Muslims with a renewed tenacity. By November it appeared likely that Bihac might become the worst humanitarian disaster of the war, a tiny space about four miles by two miles with as many as two hundred thousand Muslims desperately seeking shelter there even as the Serbs pounded it systematically with their artillery.

Bihac again threatened to split the Western alliance because it triggered the elemental divisions that were so basic to allied policy. The Americans wanted to use airpower, but unlike their allies, they still had no troops on the ground. The Serbs kept shelling Bihac despite previous agreements to back off and had used napalm as part of their more recent attacks. Their planes had taken off from a base in Croatia, and American pilots flying NATO warplanes had struck back in retaliation against that airfield. Now the Serbs played their best card. They not only took a number of UNPROFOR troops hostage and encircled other groups of UN soldiers, they threatened to take even more hostages. If the NATO air attacks continued, warned Radovan Karadzic, the Bosnian Serb leader, the UNPROFOR troops would be treated not as peacekeepers but as enemies. It was no idle threat. The UN troops were dispersed in too many small units throughout the country to be able to defend themselves.

Rarely in the entire forty-nine-year postwar history of the Western alliance had relations been so raw nor exchanges between high-level officials so sharp. To the British and the French, the Americans were brilliant kibitzers who were expert on everything that was going wrong, but would not commit their own ground troops. Instead they wanted to be warriors from seventeen thousand or thirty thousand feet, choose your height. One of the most stinging criticisms of American policy in years by a ranking British official had come from Malcolm Rifkind, the British defense minister, who said, "Those who call for action by the world must match words [by] deeds and that doesn't include just a few aircraft."[1] It might become, thought some analysts, the worst division in the Western alliance since the Americans had stopped British, French, and Israeli paratroopers from their sudden assault on the Suez Canal in October 1956.

Lake was caught in a bind. He thought the UNPROFOR troops were a joke, a card we had mistakenly but generously provided Milosevic to use against us and a great impediment to any eventual success there. Little progress could be made unless UNPROFOR was folded up or its troops consolidated into larger units able to defend themselves. But he did not want to shatter the alliance. Moreover, he would be virtually alone in the government if he argued for greater action. Christopher would not be with him, nor would Perry and General John Shalikashvili at the Pentagon. The president, after being deeply embarrassed by the off-year election, was not likely to be in any mood for a greater American commitment in Bosnia. The last thing he wanted was a media crisis if the United States went forward unilaterally and broke with its two most trusted allies.

That placed Lake in an untenable position. He convinced the president to call both François Mitterrand and John Major, but they were immovable. They were not going to jeopardize their troops; they had their own political problems, as Clinton had his. The choice was extremely difficult for Lake. Realpolitik demanded staying with the alliance, but in his heart he wanted to go with an air assault on the Serb forces. He remembered that period well. Thanksgiving, he often said, was his least favorite time of the year because the autumn leaves had already fallen in New England, it was gray and dark, and winter, a season that he did like, had not yet arrived.

Lake thought seriously of resigning that Thanksgiving weekend. He won-

dered if he was becoming the kind of public official he had often privately criticized in the past, a person who believes deeply in something, finds again and
again that he is powerless, and yet stays on in his job, seizing on various rationales to justify not following his conscience. He had pondered resigning
before, aware of the contradiction between the proud words he had written for
the candidate and the administration's subsequent inglorious actions. Now he
assigned an aide to do a study of how long the tour of the average national security adviser had lasted in the past, and the answer came back a year and a half,
which meant that he had already served the requisite time. His close friend and
aide Sandy Vershbow, who had come over from the State Department to be his
top deputy on Balkan policy, was one of the most vocal hawks in the upper
bureaucracy. Vershbow argued with him not to quit. Whoever succeeded him
would not care as much about the Balkans, Vershbow said. The problem was
not going to go away. Stay and fight for another day.

Lake also knew that a resignation now, coupled with his frustrations during
Vietnam, would mark the second time he had served at a reasonably high level
in government and had failed to bring home the policy he advocated on a transcending issue about which he felt passionately. Given the frustrations he had
also felt during the Carter administration about Iran, it would add up to an
unusually bleak career, zero for three on the big ones spanning nearly thirty-
two years. So he decided to stay and wrote a memo for the president saying
that they had to go with the alliance and discontinue the air strikes. "To use
NATO air strikes to prevent the fall of Bihac has only intensified trans-
Atlantic friction. . . . Bihac's fall has exposed the inherent contradictions in
trying to use NATO airpower coercively against the Bosnian Serbs when
our allies have troops on the ground attempting to maintain impartiality in performing a humanitarian mission." Therefore they had to pull back on the idea
of airpower. "The stick of military pressure is no longer viable," he added.[2]

If among the top people in the administration Lake was the most conflicted,
he was also, as one colleague said, the least cynical: "And you must remember that given all the different relentless pressures on the NSC adviser, that is
not necessarily an advantage—it is a job where a very tough exterior shell, a
certain cynicism about human behavior, and the ability to let go of an issue are
almost mandatory. To succeed in that job you have to be able to immunize
yourself against some terrible pressures. I don't think Tony was very good
about letting go of Bosnia—it was probably to his credit as a human being and
to his disadvantage as an NSC adviser."

Lake was a Wilsonian figure in an era that was less and less Wilsonian,
which made him the direct opposite of his onetime superior Henry Kissinger.
The singular strength of Kissinger was not just his skill at dissembling when
necessary, his unusual ability to tell ten different people ten completely different stories about what he was doing on a given issue—and remember

which version of the story he had told to which person. Rather it was an inner emotional toughness, the capacity to immunize himself from the protests on all sides, the right-wingers who felt betrayed by his policies on China, and the liberals and old friends from academe who felt betrayed by his policies in Vietnam. Kissinger was a man of the Old World, of Europe, where morality in foreign policy was generally considered a weakness, and he sometimes seemed to envy the policy makers from authoritarian nations because of the freer hand they could play in negotiations and the lack of competing democratic forces to deal with—not the least, the controlled media in their countries.

Kissinger thought of himself as a realist first and foremost, which meant some curious contradictions existed between his personal odyssey and the policies he sometimes favored. He was the child of refugees who had fled the Holocaust and had benefited greatly from American freedoms and innate political idealism, but he could nonetheless take a cold look at Bosnia and the terrible genocidal crimes committed there and remain immune to them. (Would Henry Kissinger, the power maven, had he been operating in the midthirties at a high level, have pushed for policies that would have allowed Henry Kissinger as a young immigrant boy to come to America? some of his critics sometimes wondered during the Balkan crisis.) Kissinger was the principal non-Wilsonian figure of modern American foreign policy, offending those on both left and right who were driven not only by a sense of the final outcome of events, but by moral and ideological beliefs as well.

Lake was the opposite. He was ambivalent about the use of power; he both liked it and was apprehensive about using it. His view of foreign policy had always had a certain moral rectitude. His grandfather Kirsopp Lake had been a prominent Protestant theologian who taught at Harvard, an almost sure sign that there would be significant Wilsonian traces in the gene pool. Many people who admired Lake and felt they knew him well—such as Nick Katzenbach and others—worried that he was too much a moralist in foreign policy and debated whether he was tough enough for the NSC job. But a part of him also bent over backward periodically to show that, yes, he was plenty tough and pragmatic. During the Clinton years he could and would astonish, if not his critics, then some of his old friends with his ability to be a hard-liner. Yet if he was ambivalent about power and self-deprecatory about his relationship to it—coming aboard and working with the Clinton campaign in 1992 was something to do, he once said, between baseball seasons—he had nonetheless risen, twenty-three years after he had resigned from Kissinger's staff over Cambodia, to become a foreign policy star.

Lake was in his own way a world-class survivor. He might be a shrinking violet in terms of his ambition, but he knew when to shrink and when not to shrink. Whatever doubts he had about power, whatever ambivalence he felt about its uses, a strong part of him still sought it, was comfortable with it, and he gave off the scent to his politically active peers that he wanted to hold and exercise it. He was a skillful infighter during the Clinton years, protecting himself against potential enemies, but he was considered difficult to work with. Critical information did not circulate well in the Lake NSC. His way of operating often frustrated the top people at State, Defense, and Commerce. The senior people at State were furious at the way he had taken over negotiations about Northern Ireland, and their irritation was nothing compared with that of the British, who regarded him as an out-and-out enemy of their policy. He was also the most visible high-level dove from the Vietnam era in the administration, save for the president himself. Vietnam was the prism through which he saw many other issues, and that put him in danger from the political right. Washington had become much more conservative in the dozen years since he had last served in office. Fewer people in high places were able to understand the subtleties of Lake's Vietnam dissent, and his past could now be used to attack him. If he became a target for the right, then it limited his ability and damaged the president he served.

It may have been for that reason that he sometimes tried to distance himself from his past. In the summer of 1995, when some members of the administration were recommending recognition of Hanoi, they found Lake, much to their surprise, to be of little help on an issue they had thought would be close to his heart. Perhaps he was nervous about letting political ghosts into the room. Or perhaps he was reacting to the president's reluctance to reopen an old sore. But as one advocate for recognition said later, dealing with the North Vietnamese was a lot easier than dealing with the White House. That the recognition of Hanoi finally took place was due more to the uncommon generosity of spirit of a number of Vietnam veterans in the Senate—John Kerry, Bob Kerrey, and John McCain, who offered to give the president cover with the Republican Party—than to anything Clinton or Lake did.

Moreover, Lake began to separate himself from some of his oldest friends from previous terms in government who were, like Lake himself, Bosnian activists. He believed that if he spent time with them, he would reveal his frustration with the president and his policy, which would show that he lacked leverage. In a city like Washington, that would mean his blood was in the water, a temptation for all the circling sharks. Old friends began to disappear from his inner circle to be replaced by new people, most of whom worked for him and were about fifteen years younger than he was. When colleagues in the bureaucracy who thought of themselves as trusted confidants, perhaps even peers, called him, often with what they considered important policy suggestions, their calls went unanswered or were returned by junior members of his staff. The first time it happened they might be irritated, thinking it just the sign of someone who was momentarily overloaded; when it happened again and again, it was nothing less than a message.

Lake had always had a Hamlet-like quality, an ambivalence about both power and morality and the intersection of the two. More than the president he served, and far more than some of the others at his level in the Clinton foreign policy team, he personified the contradictions and the doubts about power in the Democratic Party as it had evolved post-Vietnam, the tempered sense of activism and the interest in third world struggles and refugee problems at the expense of larger strategic concerns. These attitudes did not, after all, find much resonance with either the American electorate or the Congress in the nineties. Lake was on many occasions quite ready to exercise power on behalf of the proper cause, but was critical of power nonetheless. The two parts of him, the writer Jason DeParle once shrewdly noted, were like "twin brothers separated at birth."

What made things more difficult was that Lake and Clinton's working relationship remained quite stiff. Lake had no early history with the president and each was unconsciously a bit awkward with the other. Clinton, some observing them thought, began to see Lake as a talented briefer, but not someone he could talk easily to or share his real political feelings with. Lake, with his own considerable reserve, did not seem to know how to get beyond the somewhat stilted connection the two men had forged. Lake wanted to minimize the impact of domestic politics on foreign policy decision-making; but domestic political considerations were rarely far from Clinton's thoughts. The president's greater ease with Sandy Berger, Lake's deputy, was apparent to everyone. Because Berger went back further with the president, they had a personal as well as a professional relationship, and Clinton knew that Berger always understood the essential importance of domestic politics in whatever topic they were discussing.

Lake and Clinton were, in fact, opposite personalities, each something of an alien species to the other. Lake, in contrast to the president, was private and reserved, slow to make new friends, resistant to any kind of intimacy or easy camaraderie, and reluctant to cross social with professional lines. Clinton, always the seducer, was eager to know people a little too quickly and convert them into his admirers, always ready to win over newcomers and thus help his career. Their personal relationship had begun with the most tentative human connection, and both, whether by design or not, succeeded in keeping it that way. Almost everyone else at that level would try to get closer in personal terms to the president. But Lake made a point of keeping his distance. He did not even want to pretend to be the president's pal; he did not want to play hearts with the president on *Air Force One*. If he got too close, he was sure, it would change the nature of his job. He would be reacting more to the personal needs of a friend than to the delicate task of representing complicated choices in a difficult world to its most powerful leader. Lake would become aware of another problem, something that Warren Christopher had warned him about during the transition. "The president," Christopher said with a small smile, "is not a morning person and you get to brief him every morning. Good luck." Clinton was often impatient when Bosnia and other foreign policy issues with no apparent solution pressed in on him. Lake often had to brief him on those issues early in the day when he had not yet emerged from his irritable mood.

Lake seemed to shrink from all the public manifestations into which the NSC job had evolved. Kissinger had helped transform what had once been the almost invisible NSC position into a highly visible one, first making the rounds of Georgetown dinner parties and working the print media gathered there, thereby allowing his star to shine in semiprivate circumstances, then appearing on network-television Sunday talk shows. But Lake largely disdained public appearances. The Sunday talk shows and other comparable forums had become an increasingly important part of the national security adviser's job, but Lake wanted nothing to do with them. He believed that others should speak for the policy. He also held the old-fashioned view that the major decisions on foreign policy should be private, and the more you were seen on television, the more you signaled that you were outside the loop. As a result, he remained almost anonymous. Early in the Clinton administration, a photo of the top NSC officials appeared on the front page of the *New York Times;* Lake was described in the caption as an "unidentified staffer."

Lake had been sensitive to Colin Powell's reservations about the use of airpower in Bosnia. He might, in general, agree with Madeleine Albright about the need for a more aggressive policy, but when she challenged Powell about what use he actually planned for his wonderful army ("I thought I was going to have an aneurysm," Powell later wrote),[3] Lake visibly bristled, and his sympathies had appeared to be more with Powell than with the UN ambassador. Powell had talked to Lake about the danger of airpower: "You're putting a young kid in a fighter bomber which is going about five hundred miles an hour and asking him to take out something which looks to him like a tiny little tube." At one point in early 1994, the air force chief of staff suggested that Lake take a ride in an F-15, and he had done it. They put him through a short training course, sat him in a cockpit, and the pilot explained which lever to pull in case he needed to eject. The technician told him not to worry: "Either way, sir, you're going to end up in a hospital."

Nineteen ninety-four to 1995 was exhausting for Lake. His marriage to Antonia Plehn had long been in jeopardy. They had married right out of college, a perfect couple, one seemingly favored by the gods, who would surely have wanted two such talented, attractive, idealistic, and graceful young people to find each other. Toni Lake, lovely and gentle, had been even more of a doubter than her husband about Vietnam. She had picketed in protest of Nixon's policies while her husband was still working in the White House. They had gradually drawn apart under the pressure of differing sensibilities and ambitions, not the least of which was the requisite workaholism that went with a career like his. After he had accepted the NSC job under Clinton, she stayed in western Massachusetts when he went Washington. Then they decided to give it one last try and she moved to Washington. But the final attempt to work things out had not been a success. Frustrated by events in Bosnia, Lake had become more driven by work than ever.

Many of his old friends, such as Les Gelb, the *New York Times* foreign policy columnist, were pushing hard for a more active policy in Bosnia, and theoretically Lake agreed with them, but he felt himself limited by his role. His friendship with Gelb was old and cherished, and some people felt that Gelb had used his *Times* column to push Lake for the NSC job. They had collaborated on a book a decade earlier that warned about a national security adviser who became too involved in putting forward his own view of policy as Kissinger and Brzezinski had done. Now their friendship was badly damaged, and sharp words had been exchanged over the phone. Once in 1994, Gelb was invited to a dinner at the White House, and Clinton, knowing that Gelb was close to Lake and that this was an unusually stressful time for his national security adviser, suggested that Gelb pay some personal attention to Lake because he badly needed Gelb's friendship. Quoting Seneca, the Roman philosopher, Gelb said that a friend in power was a friend lost.

In the end, the problem was political. Lake was essentially not just an internationalist but a humanitarian one as well. The president he served, however, apart from his campaign rhetoric, was much more cautious. When the crisis in Somalia arose, Clinton had told Stephanopoulos that the American people were essentially isolationist and would back off at the first sight of body bags— unless America's vital interests were engaged. They were, Clinton added, at a gut level on Henry Kissinger's side.[4]

The people who worked for Lake thought the job was taking a considerable toll and they worried about his health. In his first year as national security adviser, he had been testifying before Congress when he collapsed. Aides took him to Bethesda Naval Hospital, where doctors were shocked to find him exhausted and dehydrated. In addition, death threats were made against him from terrorist groups in exile that were taken seriously, and for a time he was moved to Blair House for his safety. The more the administration stumbled, the more defensive Lake became. His dealings with the media were nothing less than a disaster. He gave out little information, and when he did, it was often perceived as being of marginal value. He was querulous—and condescending— with journalists who did not accept a rosy view of the Clinton foreign policy. The dinner parties he did attend with media friends, which were specifically arranged to smooth over tensions and renew old friendships, often deteriorated into confrontational discussions. He, who had once been so friendly with a large number of reporters as a young man in Vietnam, was now astonished by the changes in the media, and the coming of a generation of reporters who went on television and readily gave out their opinions. "When I was young in Saigon and you wanted to know what reporters thought," he said, "you went out to a bar and had a drink. Now all you have to do is turn on a television set and listen to them." Lake was, thought old friends, quite visibly showing the pain and frustration of working as a foreign policy adviser in an administration that was stalemated on a central issue, Bosnia, even as atrocities were still taking place every day.

CHAPTER TWENTY-SIX

In the late spring of 1995, the forces dealing with the crisis in Bosnia were changing. It began in France, where François Mitterrand, who had been a de facto Serb ally, was replaced by Jacques Chirac as president on May 17. Appalled by the humiliation of French forces under the UNPROFOR banner, Chirac was willing to take a harder line against Belgrade. Equally important, though no one would realize it for several months, Croatian forces on what was the Serb western front, somewhat belatedly armed by the outside world, had been in training under former American army officers for more than half a year and could for the first time match the Serbs in firepower.

To Belgrade it indicated that events were coming to a head, and as a result the Bosnian Serbs started to consolidate their gains and cap off their victories with assaults on the three important Bosnian towns that remained outside their control: the so-called safe zones created by the UN at Srebrenica, Zepa, and Gorazde. That move triggered decisions the West had always been reluctant to make. All three towns were small Muslim islands in what had become an ever-expanding Serb ocean. Of the three, the dubious honor of becoming the most famous would fall to Srebrenica. It would become the symbol of all the evil that had transpired for the last three years in Yugoslavia and enter the history books on the list of tragic towns and cities, like Lidice, Katyn, and Nanking in World War II, that were sites of state-ordered genocide.

Srebrenica had undergone a prolonged, bitter siege for almost three years and yet it had not fallen. It stood virtually alone as a place that the Serbs wanted but had not been able to take. It was hardly an important town; most larger maps of Europe did not even show it. It had been predominantly Muslim before the country began to tear apart. The larger community of Srebrenica consisted, according to the 1990 Yugoslav census, of nearly thirty-seven thousand people, three-quarters of them Muslim, one-quarter Serb. The town itself, with a population of about six thousand, was nestled in a steep valley. Any force with decent weaponry could easily defend it against an invader; any force outside with heavy weapons could pummel it unmercifully. It had been by Yugoslav standards a moderately prosperous community with some mining, tourism, and small industry. The name Srebrenica came from the word *srebren,* or silver, in honor of the nearby silver mines.

When the Serbs made their final assault in July 1995, the size of the town itself had nearly quadrupled, to around twenty-three thousand Muslims, many of whom had arrived as desperate survivors from other smaller villages that the Serbs had already cleansed. The unenviable job of protecting the people in this alleged safe zone fell to a Dutch battalion of 429 soldiers, many of them medical and support personnel. With only some light armored vehicles, light antitank weapons, and a few mortars, they were heavily outnumbered and outgunned by the Serb forces surrounding them on all sides. They had little ammunition and not much fuel. If that was not bad enough, like all UN forces they remained unsure of their mandate. Could they fire back in defense of the refugees they were supposed to protect? Or would that mean they had taken sides?

The Bosnian Serbs had already in recent incidents captured UNPROFOR troops and used them as hostages. The UN headquarters, shaken by this and aware that pressures were growing in Washington and some European capitals for countermeasures, did not want the Western allies to take any action, especially the use of NATO airpower, which might trigger the capture of even more hostages. So the stage was set: an aggressive Serb force, which had already captured most of Bosnia and which sensed that the clock might be ticking against it, a nervous and uncertain UN command on location, and a small town swollen with refugees, protected by a tiny combat unit that could not defend the refugees because it could not defend itself. It was the perfect recipe for disaster.

The battle that led to what many would consider the worst war crimes in Europe since World War II began on July 6, 1995, with a Serb mortar attack on an outpost south of Srebrenica manned by the Dutch. From the moment it began, the Dutch defenders were in a virtually hopeless situation. They lacked not only the weaponry with which to defend themselves, but the mandate as well. Their orders were always unclear. By July 9 the Serbs had the first and perhaps the most important of their treasured prizes: thirty Dutch soldiers whom they had encircled and who had surrendered while facing a tank gun pointed right at their small outpost. Without anyone yet realizing it, that sealed the fate of everyone else in Srebrenica.

During the next few days, the Serbs continued to probe and attack, to wait and look for a NATO air response, and then to probe and attack again. Despite the extreme vulnerability of the Dutch troops, requested NATO air strikes failed to take place, certainly not in force and not in any way that would dissuade the Serbs from their assaults. One quick pass at using airpower ended up backfiring. NATO came close to authorizing an air strike, but confusion in the dual chain of command—with both NATO and the UN required to approve air strikes—neutralized Western decision-making. The caution of UN officialdom about a wider war and the weakness of its headquarters command structure were to leave much of the world with an indelible example of incompetence and cowardice.

What followed was a calculated and carefully organized Serb attack and a Dutch-UN response of almost complete uncertainty and confusion. Colonel Ton Karremans, whose great misfortune it was to command the Dutch forces, did not understand until far too late that what had at first appeared to be just another series of probes was, in fact, the ultimate Serb assault. He was never able to get clear instructions from his superiors about what to do: whether to accommodate to the much larger Serb force or try to make a courageous last stand and hope for NATO airpower to save his own force and the Muslims in his care. During the next three days of battle, the Serbs systematically assaulted the tiny little Muslim enclave, while General Ratko Mladic, the commander of the Serbs, promised the UN commander, Lieutenant General Bernard Janvier, that he was not trying to capture Srebrenica.

To the terrified Bosnians caught in this trap, the Serbs were not, as they were politely referred to in the Western press, Bosnian Serbs. They were Chetniks, the feared Serbian monarchist force that had once slaughtered everyone ethnically different in its path—cruel hatreds from the past coupled with the terrifying weapons of the present. Mladic, soon to be named an official war criminal, was the prototypical Serb leader. Those who had known him when he was just an enterprising young army officer and a loyal, ambitious communist never sensed any unusual nationalism in his makeup. As with many people and many things in Yugoslavia, a dark part of his personal history was just under the surface. During the Serb campaigns against the Croats and the Bosnians, however, that darker side emerged, because he had been scarred by his country's cruel fratricidal history. In 1945, Croat fascists, or the Ustashe, as they were known, fighting alongside the Germans had murdered Mladic's father, who was fighting with Tito's partisans. Now it was payback time. A few years earlier during the siege of Sarajevo, when Serb forces were enjoying themselves by lobbing mortar rounds into the city that had been the symbol of Yugoslav pluralism and tolerance, Lieutenant General Lars Eric Wahlgren, the commander of UN forces, had asked Mladic, the man in charge of the shelling, why he continued to assault the city in such a harsh and cruel way. "General, do you remember your father?" Mladic asked. Wahlgren answered that he did. How nice, Mladic remarked bitterly, then said that his father had been murdered when he was only two years old. His own son, he added, would be the first in many generations to know his father: "Because there have been so many attacks on the Serb people, children do not know their fathers."[1]

Mladic's forces had gained several early victories in the war, first in the Krajina against the Croats and then against the Bosnians, usually with minimal opposition from local police and often against people with no arms at all.

They had done it with a singular brutality, which Mladic sanctioned and encouraged. As he won those easy battles, he became increasingly full of himself. He enjoyed giving visiting journalists lectures on the weakness and cowardice of the West. He spoke vaingloriously of attacking—if the West was not careful—cities in Europe. Perhaps Trieste. Perhaps Vienna. A Greater Serb patriot who thinks of himself as Napoleon, decided the French general Philippe Morillon, who clashed with him several times. When Morillon told him that, Mladic was amused by the idea. Morillon reminded him that Napoleon had ended his days alone in exile. Mladic, still pleased by the comparison, remained amused.[2]

Mladic began, in the most dangerous way imaginable, to believe his own myth and the myth of his troops' invincibility. His command of the Serb forces in Bosnia had been personally conferred on him by Milosevic; but as his troops gained their early victories, he became increasingly egocentric and difficult to control. Eventually Milosevic, exhausted by Mladic's self-importance, told Dick Holbrooke that his general was "clinically mad,"[3] an assessment Holbrooke soon came to share. Mladic not only believed that the Western world was foolish and eager enough for noninvolvement to accept what he said at face value, worse, he soon came to believe the truth of his most outrageous statements. He had an answer for everything. Of the terrible photos of Omarska, the town that Roy Gutman had written so passionately about, he said, "Detention camps? Those pictures were faked by the Bush administration to justify the use of American weapons throughout the world."[4] To him the Bosnian Muslims were not fellow members of a once-shared nation, they were the worst kind of foreigners. They were Turks, blood enemies of his nation. His, then, was the holiest of missions: to capture sacred soil for his own people. "The Muslims?" he once said scornfully. "If you make way for one of them, he will come along with five wives, and before you know what is happening, you have a village."[5]

The battle of Srebrenica was fought in a familiar but particularly tragic way. The Serbs continued to take Dutch outposts, one after another, encircling the town and gaining ever better positions from which to rain down their artillery fire. The defenders remained uncertain and confused. The Dutch were still unclear whether they were allowed to defend the Muslims. They believed they could not fight alongside the ragged remains of the Bosnian Muslim forces for fear of losing their status as independent peacekeepers. One last-minute attempt was made to use NATO airpower, but it failed. By the time air strikes were finally about to be carried out, the Serbs had enough Dutch hostages to bluff NATO out of it.

The Dutch began to move as many Muslims as they could to Potocari, a tiny nearby village, where they had set up their own headquarters. That little area, designed to accommodate a few hundred men, was soon overwhelmed by some twenty-three thousand terrified refugees crowding in from Srebrenica. It presented an appalling scene even before the denouement. As one Dutch lieutenant remembered it, "It was absolute chaos. Women were walking around crying, searching for their children, family, or friends. Children were calling for their mothers. . . . [There were] women, men, and children with gunshot and other wounds . . . asking for a doctor. . . . People were fainting. A couple of pregnant women spontaneously went into labor because of the tension. Medics worked overtime with what little material they could use."[6] By July 11 the town of Srebrenica was open to the Serbs.

The crimes of Srebrenica finally pushed the West over the brink. The media seized on them as exhibit A of the brazen willingness of the Serbs to violate every agreement and brutalize their fellow countrymen. Srebrenica became the highly visible symbol of Western indifference. In Washington, the implications of the crisis in Bosnia were escalating rapidly. The politics of the situation were at once amorphous but potentially very real. Bosnia was not an issue in and of itself. Not many Americans were likely to go to the polls in the 1996 presidential election and vote one way or another because of events in Sarajevo or Srebrenica. Rather, its importance was more complicated than that, for it appeared to suggest something larger and far more devastating, an impotence on the part of the Clinton administration not just in this, but in all matters. Events in Bosnia added to the widening suspicion that this administration was facile and articulate and nimble—if anything too nimble—but guilty of believing that words were the equivalent of deeds. The Balkans might become the tip of an iceberg of growing disappointment with an administration that had not yet found its way—nearly two and a half years after coming into office—just as judgment day for the next term was approaching.

The president was frustrated by the situation in Bosnia and irritated with his aides for their failure to provide him a policy. The middle of 1995 was quite possibly the low point in Clinton's presidency. Nothing seemed to be on track. His most important domestic political initiative, the broad, all-inclusive health care plan, had gone down in flames. The benefits that were to come from deficit reduction had not yet kicked in, and many liberal Democrats believed the administration was too conservative. Hillary Clinton, perceived as the chief architect of the health care plan and hailed only months earlier as the prototype of a modern first lady (two chief executives for the price of one, the president often said), was now deftly moved off center stage, her duties—or at least the public perception of them—to be much more traditional for the time being.

Nothing more clearly indicated the deep disappointment in the Clinton presidency than the devastating off-year election, which had given control of the House and the Senate to the Republican Party and heralded the rise of a very conservative right wing in the Congress: the so-called Gingrich revolution, named after Newt Gingrich, the young Georgia Republican and Speaker of the House. Gingrich had become the poster boy for all the new forces coming together in the Republican Party, originating primarily from the South and generated by the political and social changes that had taken place in the twenty-nine years since the Voting Rights Act of 1965 was passed.

That legislation had caused a massive white migration from the Democratic to the Republican Party, and it had produced in Gingrich and the coterie around him a new kind of political radicalism in the rural and suburban South. They represented a complete break with the national Republican Party of the past, particularly those Republicans who had been part of a bipartisan coalition in foreign policy. Their interest in the rest of the world was at best marginal; at least one hundred of Gingrich's new congressmen, Clinton liked to say, did not have passports when they arrived in Washington because they never traveled.[7] Not only were the Republicans in control of the Congress, but their new leadership was less centrist, considerably more partisan and hostile to the administration. Gingrich immediately became the spokesman for this new breed of American conservatives largely backed by religious fundamentalists with a singular cultural agenda of their own; they were out to undo much of the classic, long-standing New Deal doctrines of the past half century. They were the children of the Reagan revolution now coming of age, driven by their own passions and, like many true believers before them, accustomed to talking only with people who agreed with them. They were confident that what they wanted was exactly what the entire country wanted. They were deeply distrustful of the very government that they, like it or not, were now an important part of, but they were apparently unaware that millions of Americans, whatever their ideological tilt, also wanted the country to function well, a mistake that Clinton would eventually use against them with considerable skill.

But the immediate impact of the 1994 election and Gingrich's rise to power was devastating to Clinton. It added to all the failures of the past two years and raised doubts in the entire Clinton team about whether it was up to the job. Warren Christopher, who had become the target for many of Clinton's critics, was in Korea on a state visit when he heard the news that the administration had not only lost both houses of the Congress, but that the new congressional leadership was likely to be ideologically very different from most of its predecessors. He went from Seoul to Indonesia, where he met with Clinton, who was there to talk to APEC (Asian Pacific Economic Cooperation) nations. He found the president, normally the most resilient of public men, to be emotionally down and clearly quite shaken.

Christopher wondered if part of the reason that the Democrats had lost both houses in the election was the lack of clarity and progress in foreign policy. The timing could not have been worse for Christopher. His friends thought he was exhausted physically and, if not actually depressed, certainly badly worn-out by his nearly two years in office and the failure to deal with the number one problem, Bosnia, which blocked progress on so many other issues. He appeared, in the eyes of close aides, to be exhibiting signs of bureaucratic combat fatigue, a man beaten down by his job and a lack of victories. Christopher did not like to show weakness to anyone. When things went badly, he normally just worked harder and became even more stoic, as if willing himself to have an additional layer of emotional protection against those who attacked him. But now for the first time he was not sure whether he was doing the president any good.

One day in late 1994, right after he had returned from Jakarta, Christopher, without discussing it seriously with his aides, went to see the president and, in effect, resigned. (Many within the department believed it the only time he had made a major decision without checking with Tom Donilon, the shrewdest of his political advisers, and Donilon went ballistic when he heard the news.) Perhaps, the secretary thought, it was simply time to go. He liked Washington, but he loved California, and before taking office he had just finished building a handsome new home near the ocean. He had never really lived in it, but he kept a photo of it, panoramic view and all, on his desk as if it was a reminder that easier, less-pressurized days would be ahead.

His resignation stunned Clinton, already under siege himself. His foreign policy team was unraveling. Clinton had already severed himself from Defense Secretary Les Aspin after Somalia, and his national security adviser, Tony Lake, who was wound much too tightly, had become the target of an undercurrent of complaints from his peers and had been thinking of resigning himself. Clinton's CIA director, Jim Woolsey, had not worked out, would leave in early 1995, to the relief of both parties, and would eventually endorse Clinton's opponent in 1996. Now at just the wrong moment, Clinton's secretary of state was getting ready to go home. This potentially quite messy situation was sure to be interpreted by the media as a sign of a larger failure in foreign affairs. Clinton would also have the problem of finding a new secretary of state and getting him (or her) through the Senate, a confirmation process that had not so far been an administration strength, and would surely be more difficult after the off-year election.

Clinton immediately called Vernon Jordan and asked him to come to the White House. "Christopher's resigned," Clinton told his friend. "So what do you want me to do?" Jordan asked. "Call Colin," the president answered. Colin Powell had always fascinated Clinton. He admired him and saw his many strengths but at the same time remained envious of him because he had emerged, so late in life, politically bulletproof. When things had gone wrong in the past, particularly at the time of Somalia, Clinton was wont to pour out his frustration to close aides in tirades about how unfair the media was to him, while it always gave Powell a free ride because he was such a national hero.

Powell, he would add, had as many fingerprints on Somalia as anyone in the White House, but no one called him on it. Well, Clinton would say, by God, just let Colin Powell try running for the presidency and he would find out how many real friends he had in the media and how long they would remain adoring. Hero or not, Powell would quickly discover the other side of the media beast, Clinton liked to say. It would turn on him, too, as it turned on everyone else.

His administration at an absolute low point, his foreign policy team openly scorned, and his secretary of state about to desert what appeared to be a sinking ship, Clinton was returning to an idea he had flirted with in the past: Colin Powell as secretary of state. Having a man in the cabinet with Powell's reputation would give instant credibility to an otherwise not very distinguished and somewhat damaged national security team. It would be immensely popular with the general public, and of course, it would fly through the Senate. No one was likely to speak against Powell. Clinton was always thinking ahead, and Clinton saw Powell as the man who would be hardest to beat in 1996, the one Republican who might have a stronger claim to the political center than he did and would cut across party lines. Therefore, Clinton might gain a talented secretary of state while at the same time neutralizing a dangerous and popular potential presidential challenger in the next election. It would also limit other Republican candidates in that race because the policies they would ostensibly be criticizing were, in part, Powell's. But Powell as secretary of state had a downside as well. It would deed over an incredibly important cabinet portfolio to a man with far better credentials in foreign policy than Clinton himself, and though this was never discussed, a man with much stronger convictions on a number of issues. It would pit a president already vulnerable in foreign and defense policy against a national icon who was not lightly to be disputed in his areas of expertise. That was not an inviting equation; the president might end up as a prisoner of a cabinet officer who towered above him in prestige and authority.

Some of the people around Clinton thought it was about as misguided an idea as possible. They thought he saw Powell as a black icon with whom he would have a connection. For Clinton knew he was skillful with blacks; they had always formed the core of his political base, the group he turned to in moments of need for absolute, rock-solid support. Clinton did not understand, these advisers felt, that Powell was a great deal more than a black man. He was a conservative military-political figure with a national constituency all his own that had no racial borders. "It was all misbegotten," said one of Clinton's top people, "based on a terrible misreading of Powell—that he might, because of Clinton's attitudes on race, come over to our team. But Colin Powell was *never* on our team. He was *always* on the other team. He was a very conservative man on any number of critical issues. His closest friends, the people who he pals around with at the end of the day, were men like Ken Duberstein and Richard Armitage, and they are *very* conservative men, and believe me, neither of them is on our team either. First Reagan and then Bush had made Colin Powell what he was—along with the United States army. To come over to us would have been in his own eyes a profound violation of his loyalty to them, and loyalty was very important to a man like Colin Powell." It was, said the official, a rare example of the president's political instincts, usually so sure, deserting him. An arrogance, born of his skill with dealing with black politicians in the past, misled him into thinking he could handle Powell.

Even so, Vernon Jordan called Powell and asked to come by and meet with him. When the phone had rung, near midnight, Powell was sure he knew who was calling and what the subject was—an offer of secretary of state. "Can you derail it?" he asked Jordan when the latter stopped by his house. "No way," Jordan answered.[8] Jordan himself was sure Powell would not take the job. He was sure Powell would view it as an act of disloyalty to Bush, who had treated him so well and made him chairman of the JCS. Powell was also quite leery of the Clinton team; he did not have very much confidence in its top players, and he feared they might tarnish his own reputation. Besides, he had spent more than three decades in the service; he had just bought an expensive new home in suburban McLean and was enjoying his new options, writing his memoirs, and giving lectures at top-dollar fees. He met with the president and politely turned him down.

Jordan then went on a mission of his own. He drove over to see Warren Christopher and asked just what in the hell he was doing, resigning, and above all doing it without checking with him. Christopher seemed to him to be exhausted, convinced that he had somehow damaged the man he was supposed to serve. So Jordan and a few allies, including Christopher deputies Tom Donilon and Strobe Talbott, orchestrated a campaign to urge Christopher to reconsider, which he did, reenergized by the notion that the president had been willing to accept his resignation and had already turned to Powell. He decided to stay on.

But the episode taking place in late 1994 was a good example of how worn down they all were. Six months later, in the middle of 1995, still pitted against hostile forces from every direction, Clinton appeared to be very much on the defensive. He remained something of an ill-defined figure politically, perhaps more accurately defined by his enemies than by his friends; that is, his enemies seemed surer of what was in his heart, and what was his intent, than his friends. Some more traditional political analysts had begun to study Clinton's moves and failings not in ideological terms as to whether he was of the left or the right of center, but in generational terms. As the first baby boomer president, he was bright and talented but, they believed, spoiled. Like many boomers his expectations outweighed his sense of obligation. His talents—and his charm—were so considerable that they always outweighed his faults. When he disappointed people, they always forgave him, and in time he came to expect that forgiveness. When things went wrong, he was unusually slow, even in private, to accept responsibility himself. The belief that what he represented generationally was critical to his political behavior was shared by some people who worked with him daily. Tony Lake and George Stephanopoulos would often talk about the difficulty they had in dealing with the president, deciding they bookended the boomer generation, Lake just a bit too old and Stephanopoulos a bit too young.

It was against this largely negative political background that the news from Srebrenica was so damaging, a sign of the administration's impotence that could readily translate into a political handicap in 1996. Bosnia had not become an all-consuming issue; it was still peripheral on national television, not yet given a daily network dosage. But a number of the president's top advisers had begun to argue that Bosnia was becoming not just a moral problem but potentially a domestic political one as well. In a way, that group now included, like it or not, Tony Lake, who had from the start pointed out that the failure to come up with a viable policy on Bosnia was a cancer that could destroy the administration's entire foreign policy. Clearly the cancer had begun to spread.

Lake did not connect Bosnia to the coming 1996 election. He did not need to; the consequences were self-evident to the president and everyone around him. In Lake's opinion there had been an equally depressing forerunner of what Bosnia might become. Lake had been Carter's head of Policy Planning in 1979 when the Iranian hostage crisis had taken place, and Lake later came to understand that it had sounded, without anyone realizing it at first, the death knell of the Carter presidency because it had underlined other more vaguely defined weaknesses of his administration. Some close friends of Lake's thought that, among all the others in the upper level of the NSC world, he had been bruised the most by the hostage crisis, perhaps believing that he and the people around him in Policy Planning should have come up with some solution, some formula that would have ended the crisis and saved the president. The rest of them had suffered the difficulty of trying to disengage from the crisis and had seen its catastrophic impact on the president's reelection hopes, but they had eventually accepted the outcome. Every once in a while you are hit by a runaway freight train; that was life. Lake among his peers was considered to have taken the failure quite personally, as if by having been more prescient he might have stopped that train.

As for Clinton, he was beginning to feel pressure from yet another direction. Bob Dole, the Republican Senate majority leader, a likely 1996 presidential candidate and a Bosnian activist, was advocating a resolution that called for a unilateral lifting of the arms embargo. He appeared to have the votes in both the House and the Senate to pass the resolution, and in case the president vetoed it, the votes to override the veto. Some of those votes would stem from genuine repugnance about what was happening in Bosnia—for Dole had become passionate on the subject of the Serb crimes—but others were more likely to be partisan and motivated by the smell of presidential blood.

It was at this point that Jacques Chirac, the new president of France, arrived on the scene. He was a former French army officer who had volunteered for service in Algeria during the bitter colonial war, had been seriously wounded, and thought of that experience as the most important in his life. He was a force not to be underestimated—the nickname for him in France was the Bulldozer. Because of his own service and the bravery shown by his comrades in a difficult and unpopular war, he had a strong Gallic sense of how French soldiers should acquit themselves in uniform. He was furious about the humiliations being inflicted on French troops in Bosnia and their passivity in a moment of crisis. On the first day that Chirac took office, photos were published of French peacekeepers who had been captured and were being used by the Serbs as hostages; some of them had been tied to trees, some chained to Serb artillery pieces. He absolutely exploded at the idea that people in the Balkans, whom the French were trying to help, could do that to his men. "I will not accept this!" he told his aides. "You can kill French soldiers! You can wound them! But you cannot humiliate them! That will end today! France will not accept that! We will change the rules of the game!" Either he was going to beef up the French contingent on the ground and give it new, far more aggressive rules of engagement, or he was going to pull it out. But from now on they would behave with the grandeur and bravery that the French expected of their soldiers—the nobility and courage shown by the last defenders of Dien Bien Phu in French Indochina.

Almost immediately Chirac issued new orders to the French generals in charge in Bosnia—orders that went outside the UN command system. By chance the Serbs, dressed in captured UN uniforms, had just slipped into Sarajevo and captured one of the bridges there. Chirac tongue-lashed the commanding French officers over that incident. His final words before he hung up were "You have twenty-four hours to retake the bridge." They did, though two French soldiers were killed in the recapture. Chirac was a genuine hawk who wanted to do more but was willing, if that was not possible, to do less. He would no longer accept the status quo. He talked with John Major about the creation of a Rapid Reaction Force, an elite French-British unit, far better armed with much heavier weapons, which, with American air support and helicopters, could move quickly and strike the Serbs with genuine force if they violated any more agreements.

Mitterrand, by contrast, had been a man of the old order, who had grown up with a knowledge of the French-Serb alliance in World War I, and of Serbia as a partner and ally during World War II, in an alliance created by mutual distrust of the Germans, and a need for Europe's Slavs—Serbs and Russians—to help counterbalance German expansionism. Of the European leaders, no one had been more sympathetic to the Serb cause. He had always opposed expanding the war: "Don't add war to war," he counseled in a stance which had greatly helped the Serbs.[9] On several occasions when it had appeared that the allies might be moving against the Serbs because of some new outrage, Mitterrand had protected their interests.

Chirac's defining experience had been in Algeria, not World War II. He did not fear Germany in the new Europe, and he felt neither geopolitical dependence upon nor moral kinship with former Slavic allies who were inflicting such terrible crimes on their fellow countrymen. Chirac saw an additional reason to act. What the Serbs were doing was cruel and unspeakable, but it also threatened to destroy something new and noble just being born, the concept of a unified Europe that would reject fratricidal violence and fuse its great energies into positive pursuits. In the new Europe, the senseless shedding of blood in the past could no longer be a justification for the senseless shedding of blood in the present and the future. No one knew this better than the French, who had made their own painful reconciliation with the Germans. Soon after assuming the presidency, Chirac was at a dinner of European leaders when Andreas Papandreou, the Greek prime minister, began to defend the Serbs' actions. The Greeks, for religious reasons, had been steadfast allies of the Serbs in NATO deliberations. Papandreou spoke of the dilemma of the Serbs scattered throughout so large and unwieldy a nation where in some areas they were a minority and were now merely defending their Orthodox faith. Chirac immediately cut him short: "Don't speak to me of any religious war. These people are without any faith, without any sense of law. They are terrorists."[10]

In mid-June 1995, not yet a month in office, Chirac flew to Washington on his way to the G-7 meeting to be held a few days later in Halifax. He met with Clinton and spoke of the need for a tougher line in the Balkans. They could not change the UN mandate, he said, but they could add their own troops to the mandate, use the Rapid Reaction Force (RRF), and in time NATO could end this humiliation. Clinton was largely in agreement and sent him to the Hill to meet with Dole and Gingrich. It had been a helpful visit, a sign to the critics in Congress that the gap between Washington and the Europeans was narrowing.

From there Chirac flew to Halifax for the G-7 meeting, where he surprised everyone by placing Bosnia, though it was not included in the agenda, on the table. His intensity caught everyone unprepared. How could they, he asked the other heads of state, even pretend to talk about conditions in Europe and the world without mentioning Bosnia? He was concerned not just about national security or Balkan atrocities or the future of Europe, but also about the glory that was France. Pure beau geste, said one slightly irritated American. If Chirac surprised the Americans with the immediacy of his call, he surprised his European peers even more. In the past they had been quite uneasy about the Balkans and glad to suppress the subject if at all possible. Chirac instantly became the center of media attention, and photos of him taken in Halifax appeared on many front pages. But perhaps the most interesting thing about his statements was their effect on the president of the United States. Clinton was more than a little jealous of the French president. When Chirac suggested in one of his speeches that "the position of leader of the free world is vacant," it had touched home, and some of the top people in the bureaucracy picked up on it as a way of making the president more proactive on Bosnia. As Clinton had been jealous of Colin Powell's exceptional standing with the American people—unelected and yet revered, with the media having little interest in finding warts—he was now showing signs of being envious of Chirac. In the past two and a half years, he had tried to push the Europeans forward and it had never occurred to him that he might be challenged as the leader of the Western coalition against the Serbs and that another Westerner might become, of all things, *more of a leader* on this issue. Yet it was happening now, led by a man who was not only newer to his job than Clinton but the head of a much smaller and less powerful country.

Chirac's decision to oppose the Serbs changed the rules of the game in Bosnia. "It is easy for the Americans to underestimate how important that decision was in terms of Europe," said one senior foreign policy analyst. "Chirac was choosing a new and as yet uncertain Europe over the traditional past, dark and bloody though that past was." It also gave Clinton a stronger hand if he chose to authorize the use of American ground troops and airpower. Instead of the British and the French being vehemently opposed to an upgraded policy, the president now had an ally who already had troops on the ground and was willing, under the right circumstances, to use more force.

In the view of those European leaders who wanted to escalate the policy in Bosnia, it had always been like a poker game in which the Americans never quite got to the table. They had watched from the sidelines as if the stakes were not high enough for them, and they talked loudly about the need for a bigger game, one worthy of them to play. They had kibitzed and criticized the size of the existing pots, the slowness with which the hands were being played, but so far they had not deigned to sit down, put up any money, and play a hand themselves. The American position, much to the irritation of many Europeans, was mostly posturing; the Americans could safely call for some degree of escalation, sure that the Europeans would block them. Now that was over. "With Mitterrand in power the energy level coming out of France had been, on a scale of ten, about a three," said Peter Tarnoff, the number three man in the State

Department. "With the arrival of Chirac it went to about a nine." With France a much more aggressive player, it put increased pressure on the British to take a more aggressive line.

It also added to Clinton's frustration. To him Bosnia was hardly like Vietnam to Johnson, or even the Iran hostage crisis to Carter. It was more peripheral; it had the capacity to cause damage, but his entire presidency was not riding on it. No American troops were there yet, which meant that he was easier to reach and listened more readily than Johnson ever had. His ego, unlike Johnson's in 1967 as Vietnam began to cast a shadow on his political future, was not yet a factor. But now as the horror of Srebrenica was being revealed, the stakes were going up and his attention was gradually becoming less episodic. It was the simplest of equations: the more open the sore, the less it was about foreign policy and the more it was about presidential effectiveness. Thus it was tied to his political future and he had to pay more attention. He was still quick to blame others, people on his staff who had never been able to give him the policy he wanted. As for the Europeans, he said, they were bumbling around out there, unable to end the thing themselves and yet preventing him from using American airpower. They were whiny, he liked to say, an obstacle to a real policy.

But he was beginning to feel cornered. The French were making their play under Chirac, and that was both an irritant and an asset. The people in the White House talked privately about Chirac and whether he was all bravado. In the Congress, meanwhile, Dole was continuing to put together a veto-proof majority for lifting the arms embargo, which might trigger a politically dangerous chain reaction. If we broke the embargo unilaterally, it would threaten the alliance, with the possibility that the Europeans would decide to pull out. We had already committed armed American helicopters to withdraw UN troops from the most hazardous venues in Bosnia. That would have to be done under the sights of formidable Serb weaponry that, the administration had to assume, was zeroed in on all possible landing zones. We would have to use as many as twenty-five thousand Americans in an exposed and difficult rescue mission. Even worse, as Tony Lake warned, it would take place in the context of a defeat—all that risk, all that danger, with no upside.

The story in Bosnia, then, was in transition from being a foreign one to a domestic one, like Vietnam—though Vietnam had always been a bigger story with so many Americans fighting there. But there were dangers here. The greater the tragedy and the more despicable the atrocities in Bosnia, the more likely the networks and the leading newspapers were to report it, and the more likely it was to come up in press conferences. Clinton was shrewd enough to know that a constituency for action in the Balkans was still relatively small. But it was articulate, morally driven, and an odd amalgam of different people and groups who would in the past have been strange political bedfellows. It existed on both the left and the right, liberal critics of the war in Vietnam like Tony Lewis of the *Times,* and neoconservatives, like Jeane Kirkpatrick, who could normally be depended upon to be critical of each other. It was cerebral and motivated by something relatively rare in politics, a historical if not an actual memory of the Holocaust. That someone like Lewis and others who had been Vietnam doves were now Bosnian hawks irritated Clinton greatly. "What would they have me do?" he asked. "What the fuck would they have me do?"[11]

If these people and groups were not yet large, they were articulate and influential far beyond their numbers, particularly in the print media. They also had a tendency to be slightly ahead of the curve; if they were critical of Clinton in mid-1995, might not their numbers increase by mid-1996? They could not swing an election, but they had the ability to define an issue in what might be a fateful way; moreover, they were the kind of people Clinton badly wanted as well-wishers. They had the capacity to define him and his presidency as he most certainly did not want to be defined—as a man of talent and promise but of little substance or fulfillment. They could wound him severely because many of the things they might say about him on Bosnia were not only true, but might also extend to other aspects of his presidency.

Clinton knew that few Americans had passionate feelings one way or another about the Serbs, Croats, or Muslims, and that the politics of the Balkans were either too remote or too complicated to understand. But a foreign policy crisis that revealed the president of the United States as either passive or politically impotent was quite another thing—potentially devastating. More quickly than anyone else, Clinton was beginning to see that his presidency might be at stake. That realization brought about dramatic change in the White House. The president, like it or not, was becoming immersed in Balkan policy, and he was turning desperately—and often angrily—to the very people he had kept at a distance for the last two and a half years. Tony Lake was now briefing the president every day on foreign policy, and most of the news about Bosnia was bad. It was, Lake later said, as if he walked into each meeting with a giant *B* for Bosnia painted on his forehead. Finally, Clinton's national security adviser had the kind of access that his predecessors had enjoyed.

Still, they did not have a policy. In mid-June, pre-Srebrenica, when Chirac visited the White House, the Clinton team met to go over the outline of what the president should say to this formidable new player about Bosnia. But even with renewed energy, there was clearly no forward movement. The divisions within the American government were as great as ever, and the roadblocks that prevented it from doing anything more active were still sizable. Clinton was infuriated by the images of U.S. helplessness that had been shown on network television, and his aides witnessed some of the worst of his private rages.

They desperately needed to have a policy, the president told his people at one meeting, "or we're just going to be kicking the can down the road again. Right now we've got a situation, we've got no clear mission, no one's in control of events."[12] Then he went on a tirade complaining bitterly about the decision to put troops on the ground, where their hands were tied, and where they themselves presented such easy targets. "The rules of engagement are crazy!" he said. Then Gore spoke about the mounting pressure in Congress led by Dole to lift the arms embargo. Bosnia, the vice president said, echoing what Christopher had said two years earlier, was "the issue from hell."

CHAPTER TWENTY-SEVEN

What took place in the next few months on Bosnia was probably Tony Lake's best moment in government. It began when he was probably at the low point in his government service, completely unable to bring any kind of new direction to Bosnian policy. The worst thing about late 1994 to early 1995, Lake later told his closest associates, was that the critics of the policy were essentially right. What he wanted was often quite close to what they also wanted, but somehow he had always found himself blocked from articulating a better policy.

Bosnia had become an obsession for Lake, his staff members thought, the issue he could not let go of but still could find no daylight on. He would talk with them about how they needed to get the policy right, how he had been up late trying to think of something new. His job had become the hardest one in the government. The national security adviser had the smallest staff, had to deal with the most complicated problems, and was physically closest to the president. On occasion that could be an asset, but on an intractable issue like Bosnia it meant fewer filters between Lake and Clinton, and Lake inevitably ended up taking most of the heat from the president. His job was made considerably harder by Clinton's irritability and his escalating level of personal frustration because Clinton knew he was tied to a big-time policy loser and might become one of its victims.

There was another voice warning Clinton that Bosnia was doing disproportionate damage to his presidency, Richard Morris, a most unusual White House adviser. Morris was a conservative political consultant, a former liberal Democrat who worked primarily with conservative Republicans, and his role in the Clinton White House was semicovert, which he seemed to love. He was, in effect, the purest incarnation of the survive-at-any-cost instinct that had always been part of Clinton's political career. When Clinton sensed that his liberalism and populist beliefs were taking him too far from the political center and getting him into trouble, he would turn to Morris. That Morris, whose relationship with Clinton was complicated, volatile, and finally nothing less than weird, was once again welcome in the White House was a sure sign that the president knew he was in serious jeopardy as he headed toward the 1996 election.

Even close colleagues of the Clintons' always found it difficult to assess how important an influence Morris was on the president. Morris was a shadowy figure who seemed almost pathologically secretive; he liked to use the code name Charley to communicate with the president—the messages he left would say only that Charley had called. He was rarely a part of larger meetings, and because his greatest single talent was probably self-promotion, he tended to inflate his influence and take credit for things in which he was at best a minor player, if a player at all. He was despised by almost all the other Clinton political advisers, seen as a kind of political Darth Vader, a hired gun who wandered into the White House on his way from his primary consultations with conservative Republicans like Jesse Helms and Trent Lott, for whom he continued to consult even after he had reentered Clinton's world. "Having an affair with an intern, that's a stupid, careless mistake but it's not an impeachable offense," one of Clinton's closest advisers said later, "but letting someone like Dick Morris into the West Wing of the White House, *that* is an impeachable offense." Morris was, wrote George Stephanopoulos in what may have been the most impassioned two sentences of his book, "a small sausage of a man encased in a green suit with wide lapels, a wide floral tie, and a wide-collared shirt. His blow-dried pompadour and shiny leather briefcase gave him the look of a B-movie mob lawyer, circa 1975."[1] Others in the Clinton White House disliked Morris because he always seemed to be searching for the lowest common denominator in modern politics. They believed he operated essentially without any moral or ethical restraints. Even more upsetting was what he might tell them about themselves and their role in working for Clinton. Were they, despite all their high-minded hopes and their belief in the value of public service, at their core too much like Morris? Despite the professed idealism that they liked to think drove their participation in politics with Clinton, was it less about issues and helping the vulnerable in society, and more about self-aggrandizement, and therefore their own place at the public trough? When they looked at Dick Morris, those were the questions they posed to themselves. They were not questions they liked to answer.

Morris was an intriguing and bizarre figure, "the dark Buddha whose belly Clinton rubbed in desperate times," Stephanopoulos wrote. For more than a decade Morris had been the adviser Clinton summoned in difficult moments, and only then to represent the hard, dirty underside of the political equation, the side that went contrary to the expressed idealism of the Clintons and their closest advisers. Morris gloried in his semi-outlaw status. In his mind that made him someone from the real world, while the others around the president were the dreamers. "Bill only wants me around when his dark political side is coming out," Morris once said. "He doesn't want anything to do with me when he's in his good-government, Boy Scout mode."[2]

If Clinton was, at his core, the great survivalist, Morris's arrival on the scene signaled more than anything else that Clinton was going into his full-time survive-at-any-cost mode. His entrance into the White House, infuriating as it was to men like Stephanopoulos, Begala, and John Podesta, was a clear sign that Clinton was desperate. He did not need Morris to know that he was in trouble or why. Clinton's own reading of the country and its mood swings was so acute that he could probably learn very little from him. But surrounded by a political staff that was in general younger, more idealistic, and more liberal than he was, he was tired of being pulled one way when his political instincts told him to go another. He wanted Morris as a counterbalance to his other advisors, to reaffirm his own impulse about when to change and tack on a policy. Much to the consternation of some of the White House staff, and Tony Lake in particular, Morris made some tentative moves on foreign policy. Stan Greenberg had not polled on foreign policy because it might imply that the president was making decisions based on polls, and he was replaced by another pollster brought in by Morris, who, in Greenberg's words, "seemed to have no such scruples." Clinton apparently warned Morris against involving himself in foreign policy meetings, and Lake quickly made it clear to the president that Morris was to keep his distance from all foreign policy issues. (Morris later wrote in his memoir of an angry Lake giving him "the evil rodent look he bestowed on me whenever we met in the hallway."[3])

Tony Lake was aware that, as he had predicted from the start, Bosnia had the capacity to hold the administration captive if no one dealt with it. His dilemma was how to jump-start a new Bosnian policy and make sure that the president was truly committed to it. Lake had been getting little help from the top people in the State Department. There was, Lake's aides thought, putting it charitably, a notable absence of energy from State. Christopher and those around him were not eager to take command of an issue from which the secretary obviously wanted to distance himself, and about which the president was also ambivalent. State seemed without answers; our present policy may not be effective, but any new course of action would entail unwanted risks, and Christopher, by nature cautious and getting no clear signal from the president, was nervous about taking risks. If what we were doing did not work, at least it was relatively low cost; anything else we tried might not work either and might become a higher-priced and more visible failure.

Dick Holbrooke, newly returned to Washington from Bonn and just beginning to make his moves as assistant secretary for European and Canadian affairs, might prove to be an important force in seeking a resolution to the Bosnian crisis, but he was not under Lake's jurisdiction—perhaps not under anyone's jurisdiction. Their personal friendship, once so close, had long ago been shattered, and they worked in an atmosphere of barely disguised rivalry and distrust. The Pentagon was still watching events apprehensively. Bill Perry and John Shalikashvili had replaced Les Aspin and Colin Powell, and they might yet prove more accommodating, but for the time being there was no green light for action from the Pentagon. The people there were waiting for the civilians to give a clear signal about what they wanted and how much they were willing to pay.

In this amorphous situation, Lake came up with the beginning of a policy for Bosnia that would help end the White House's drift. He had talked at length with the president earlier in the year about whether they should just let UNPROFOR fold, take the heat, use the requisite American military muscle to pull the various European troops out, and then start anew with a clear field to use American airpower. Clinton was interested, it was a fresh start, but he was worried about the impact on the future of the Western alliance and was not yet ready for that big a jump. To let UNPROFOR collapse on the ground—even if it was done deliberately and a new, stronger policy was in mind—might expose him to additional criticism; it would be seen as a defeat, one that might not lead to a subsequent victory.

Lake had begun by creating a task force to start thinking strategically about this new policy, using two aides who worked extensively on Bosnia, Sandy Vershbow and Nelson Drew, to put it together. Lake was also working for the first time in close alliance with Madeleine Albright, who had always been hawkish, and who like him saw the British, French, and other UN troops on the ground as the single greatest impediment to resolving the conflict. She believed that nothing would expedite policy there better than collapsing UNPROFOR. Lake and Albright's relationship had not been easy in the beginning, but by the spring of 1995, they had come together as allies with a single purpose on this most pressing issue. In late June, Lake's task force was working around the clock. Convinced that the administration's present policy was a product of day-to-day decision-making, reactive rather than creative, Lake was urging the people on his staff to think more strategically. Imagine, he suggested, that they were six months down the road, figure out what they wanted to have taken place by that time, then try to work backward to see how it could be made to happen. What were their goals? Were the UN soldiers an asset or a detriment, and if they were a detriment, how could we overcome that vulnerability?

Soon their objective was clear: a division of Bosnia that would redraw the current boundaries, then with more than 70 percent of the country in Serb hands, to a 51–49 ratio. The map would not be easy to create; it would need a degree of skill as well as logic to keep the divisions relatively secure and as consolidated as possible. The fate of the alleged safe areas in eastern Bosnia—Srebrenica, Zepa, and Gorazde, which were still surrounded by Serb forces—was particularly perplexing. Even as Lake's group began to work on the problem in late June, the Serbs were tightening the noose around these enclaves, above all Srebrenica. The 51–49 map gave the group a goal; the idea of consolidating the UNPROFOR units gave them a substrategy. Lake assigned Sandy Vershbow, who had been his principal staff man on Bosnia, to write up a strategy that offered both carrots and sticks to those who cooperated, for example, the gradual end of economic sanctions as a carrot for the Serbs if they moved toward compliance. The plan was called the Endgame strategy. That was step one. Slowly, almost without anyone else noticing it, Lake was taking over the initiative for a new policy and trying to shape the Washington bureaucracy to his vision. If the raw outline of Endgame was step one, then step two was to bring the president in from the start—to get the hook into him with a certain finality. Clinton wanted to do the right thing on Bosnia, but he wanted to do it with minimal risk to himself, his presidency, and the European alliance. Lake understood those limitations. But for any new policy to work, it had to seem to come from Clinton and have his imprimatur. That was the most important part, to commit a president whose humanitarian instincts had, in the past, put him on one side, but whose political caution had then brought him back to the other. There was a need, once and for all, to get him to commit.

Lake in the next few weeks did something new in his NSC operation: he began to make the bureaucracy work for him. He went to the president and explained what he was working on: a complete and comprehensive new strategy on Bosnia that would work toward a diplomatic settlement. But first more pressure had to be applied on the Serbs on the ground, which could only be exerted by the threat of American military force; that is, airpower, since the use of ground troops was still being ruled out. The Europeans must not be able to block American policy because of the threat posed to their ground troops. Lake intended to move the bureaucracy ahead by at first circumventing it. He was going to go directly to the president, commit him if he could to a course of action without Lake's peers knowing it, and once the president was committed, they would have to follow along. Otherwise, Clinton's top advisers would continue to be as divided as they currently were—without the most important element to end the internal deadlock, presidential leadership. So Lake outlined his plan to the president before he shared it with anyone else in the bureaucracy—that is, Perry, Christopher, or Shalikashvili. In late June Lake met with Clinton to explain how serious a departure this new plan was, and that it might require a significantly greater commitment of American military resources on the eve of an election year. "Mr. President, tell me if you don't want to do this, stop me now because the risks are very clear," Lake told the president, according to Bob Woodward's authoritative notes from their meetings.[4]

The risks were considerable. It would be another major embarrassment if the Endgame strategy failed and caused a rupture with the allies, and it might sink the Clinton administration. The strategy was probably going to necessitate the use of American ground troops in some form to help keep the peace in

Bosnia, and that was not a commitment any president would want to make at the beginning of an election year. Clinton immediately gave his permission to develop the strategy. But Lake wanted to be absolutely sure Clinton understood that if they moved forward, it could easily lead to a wider war with greater American involvement. Yes, he understood that his presidency was on the line, Clinton told Lake. It was an important moment. Lake had begun to make the president his partner in this new strategy, and it would be harder for him to pull back. Lake was to some degree turning the tables on Clinton. After months of presidential complaints about the lack of a new policy, Lake was, in effect, saying, well, I will give you a new policy and it will entail risk, but if I develop it for you, I expect you to be for it.

Now, having loaded the dice with the president, Lake asked for comparable strategic papers from his top colleagues, Perry, Shalikashvili, Christopher, and Albright. Though much of the Endgame strategy was aimed at making the Serbs more amenable to a settlement, one warning was thrown in for the Bosnians. If they did not go along with the new policy, the Americans might pull out completely and leave them even more at the mercy of the Serbs than before. The Europeans, in particular, would like that part—our being tough on the Muslims, too—for up until then the Europeans thought the Americans tilted too much in the Muslims' favor.

There would be carrots and sticks for everyone, economic incentives and military deterrents, the most important of which would be the use of American airpower if need be. Finally the United States would do what it had shirked doing for so long, exert its leadership. Once the policy was agreed upon in Washington and the president was fully committed to it, Lake intended to visit the allies and bring them in. He would say in the most polite way possible that *the president of the United States has decided that we are going to pursue this policy and we would certainly like you to be part of it, but we are going to proceed without your help if necessary.* He would say that we hoped all Balkan parties involved would prefer to negotiate, but we were prepared to use massive American airpower to cajole them into accepting the redrawn map of Bosnia we had in mind. Yes, it would be the same kind of trip that Christopher had made, but with a very different message.

On July 11, Srebrenica fell, and when the Serbs took the town, they did not do it shyly. They swaggered in, fully equipped with their own propaganda units at the ready and their own cameramen to record this historic occasion and great victory. "On to Potocari!" shouted Mladic as he turned toward a Serb television crew, referring to the nearby village where the Dutch battalion was headquartered and where thousands of Muslims had taken refuge.[5] "Finally after the rebellion of the Dahijas," Mladic said, "the time has come to take revenge on the Turks in this region." The reference was to a Serb rebellion against the Turks during the Ottoman Empire, which the Turks had crushed with great brutality in 1804, a mere 191 years earlier. Time clearly stood still in Bosnia. Mladic then said he was presenting this town to the Serbian people as a gift, a new Serbian Srebrenica. To make the gift more perfect, he proposed to rid it of all Muslims.

Because the Serbs gloried in what they were doing, there were many records of that tragic surrender and of Colonel Karremans, defeated, confused, and humiliated by the exuberant Mladic. People knowledgeable about the politics of Europe thought that the Serb leadership had deliberately singled out the Dutch battalion for humiliation because the Dutch had so passionately committed themselves to the concept of a peacekeeping, humanitarian force and the feeling in Amsterdam was particularly hostile to Serb aggression. On Serb television, as in a scripted play, Colonel Karremans was deftly portrayed as an accomplice to the fall of Srebrenica. He appeared to be celebrating the Serb victory—with a glass of champagne perhaps? In reality, it was a glass of water for an exhausted man.

The footage of that surrender was heartbreaking: the sheer swagger of Mladic as conqueror and the humbling of Karremans, a decent man now powerless, sent out on what had appeared to be the most honorable of missions, which had turned into a betrayal of everything he and the people of his proud nation believed in. The terror of the trapped Muslims, when the Srebrenica pocket collapsed and the hated and feared Chetniks arrived, was palpable as they realized that their so-called protectors were now bargaining for their own lives. All the weaknesses, all the failures to act, that had bedeviled the West for the last four years were now being paid for. The Dutch soldiers, impotent, mocked and humiliated by these aggressors, were perfect stand-ins for the Western powers. Now having taken charge of the village, the Serbs started to rid the area of all Muslims. The Serbs might not be good fighters, but they did pogroms very well indeed. They were familiar with the drill, and the entire process had a macabre efficiency.

While the UN forces were still small and numb from the defeat, the Serbs swiftly separated women and children from the men and moved them on buses to other Muslim areas already crowded with refugees. They tried to ease tensions by promising the women that everyone was going to be all right. The men went on buses, too, but they would never be seen again. They were executed and buried in mass graves. Watching the process, the men being separated from the women, a Serb television cameraman asked one of the Dutch doctors, Colonel Gerry Kremer, what was going on. Appalled by the scene, appalled by the question and the source of it, Kremer said, "You know what's going on."[6] Indeed they did. In the next few days, the Serbs under Mladic systematically executed an estimated seven thousand Muslim men.

A handful of men survived and told of the mass executions. Serb soldiers, often fortified with alcohol and armed with Kalashnikovs, an exceptionally murderous weapon (better for use in situations like this, it was said, than machine guns, which were often erratic and jammed), would line up the Muslims and open fire. The Muslims would shout for mercy, one Serb executioner later testified at the War Crimes Tribunal at The Hague: "They begged us, 'Don't shoot us! Our families in Austria will send you money.' One of my comrades yelled at the Muslims, 'Whoever possesses deutschemarks will be spared.' But Branko [the commanding sergeant] said, 'Don't bother, they've [already] taken everything from them in Zvornik.'"[7]

When Srebrenica fell, Clinton and Chirac spoke on the phone. Chirac was enraged. It was, he said, just like the worst of World War II. "We must do something," he said, according to the official notes of their conversation. "Yes, we must act," Clinton agreed.[8] Chirac wanted to use French troops (with American choppers flying them in) to retake the town. The plan was rich in its aura of past French gallantry, full of risk and glory, but did not thrill either the president or the people at the Pentagon. What would happen once Srebrenica was retaken? Clinton asked. Would it really make that great a difference? There was no good answer to that question.

Still, the president was once more enraged; it was as if these small-time Serb leaders were personally taunting him, and on July 14, Clinton blew. Lake might be putting the finishing touches on his Endgame strategy, but it was not quite done and Clinton was furious. Srebrenica was a disaster, the allies remained divided, the demand for action was strengthening in the Congress, and Chirac was taking center stage. Earlier that day in Paris at a Bastille Day celebration and press conference, Chirac had spoken of his eagerness to confront the Serbs, but had noted that regrettably France stood alone in wanting to take action. He talked about the weakness of the West and compared it with the time in 1938 when the West had appeased Hitler as he moved into the Sudetenland. Perhaps in the end, Chirac hinted, France would have to pull out of UNPROFOR. "We can't imagine that the UN force will remain only to observe, and to be, in a way, accomplices in the situation," he said. "If that is the case, it is better to withdraw."[9] It was the ultimate insult to the president, another Western leader speaking of the impotence of Clinton's leadership and accusing the allies of being appeasers.

Clinton's reaction would become known within the White House as the Putting Green Day. Those who had been watching him for the last few weeks had sensed that the presidential temperature was rising and something volcanic was about to happen. He had made more and more exasperated late-night phone calls to aides with the same theme: they *had* to do something, they were stuck and they needed a new plan. So Clinton's explosion, in the early evening, around 7 P.M., was not entirely a surprise. The president, practicing his golf game in the little area known as the Eisenhower Putting Green, was in a rage. Lake was not there, so Clinton inflicted his anger on members of Lake's staff—Berger, Lake's chief deputy, Nancy Soderberg, plus Mike McCurry, the press officer.

They had come to speak to the president about Bosnia and the powerful words coming out of Paris. That McCurry was there with two NSC deputies was a sure sign that they were concerned about questions being asked in the press. They found Clinton in the place where he liked to go late in the afternoon or early evening when he wanted to take a break from the pressures of the office. He would take a bunch of golf balls, scatter them a certain distance from the cup, then practice first chipping and then putting. Clinton kept chipping and putting, and McCurry and the NSC people kept retrieving the balls so he could chip and putt again. Finally, Clinton exploded. He was the president of the United States and he was being checkmated on the most important issue he faced by people who should not be able to checkmate a president.

"This can't continue," he fumed between putts. "I'm getting creamed." They had to have ideas for a new policy, he demanded, then chipped a shot. "This has got to stop. We've got to find some kind of policy and move ahead." Another chip shot. Berger said that Lake was working on the Endgame strategy. That did not seem to ease the presidential pain. He complained about the pressure on him from Chirac. He was being squeezed from all sides. "Why aren't my people doing more for me?" he kept repeating. "Why can't I have a new policy?" Eventually Soderberg, who was scheduled to have dinner with some Nigerian diplomats, excused herself. "Good luck," she quietly mouthed to the less fortunate Berger as she left him behind for the rest of the tirade. Around seven forty-five, after more than three-quarters of an hour of presidential anger, McCurry also left. The last thing he remembered seeing was Berger picking up a club to play, too, and trying to explain to the president various possibilities for action.[10]

The putting green explosion was perfect leverage for Lake. The president wanted a new policy, and that was exactly what Lake was working on. The following Monday, he presented his Endgame strategy to his peers, Christopher, Perry, Shalikashvili, Albright, and Berger. Lake had previously suggested to Clinton that he drop by the meeting. Lake went through his game plan, then, at just the right moment on a prearranged signal, Clinton walked in and expressed his frustration with the status quo. Bosnia was doing immense damage to the United States all over the world, he said. America was being made to look weak. The Serbs had played us skillfully for years. "The only time we make any progress there is when we threaten to use force or use force," he said. The Europeans were no help—all they did was whine, though Chirac's energy was a plus. "We have a war by CNN," Clinton said, meaning that the world was watching. "Our position is unsustainable—it's killing the U.S. position of strength in the world." Then he left the meeting. The last words from Lake were critical: "This is larger than Bosnia. Bosnia . . . is the symbol of U.S. foreign policy."[11] Before the meeting ended, Lake asked the others for their suggestions for a change in policy. These were not as proactive as his Endgame strategy. Essentially both State and the Pentagon still believed in containment, even as it became more and more clear that containment was a formula for humiliation—political *and* military.

But attitudes were changing, and Srebrenica had helped change them. After the town fell, Clinton dispatched both John Shalikashvili and Bill Perry to London to meet with their counterparts to see if they could unsnarl the existing mess and find some mutually acceptable formula that would allow the use of American airpower and end the ability of the Serbs to assault the Bosnians on the ground. In the past, whatever their private feelings, both Perry and Shalikashvili had shared the general reluctance of the Pentagon to embark upon a more proactive policy. Before when Shalikashvili had been sent by the administration to propose upgrading the present policy, he had always known what the response would be: "Shali, until you put your own troops on the ground and share the risks, you can't play." This time it was going to be different.

CHAPTER TWENTY-EIGHT

Nothing characterized the universal—and highly fluid—nature of the modern American social-political experience better than the change-over from Colin Powell to John Shalikashvili in one of the most important and sensitive jobs in public life. It was hard to think of any other great power at any other moment in history that would turn so powerful a position over to men whose backgrounds were, for the highly critical position they held, so countertraditional. Neither man, unlike top-level army officers of the past, was a West Point graduate. But that was just the beginning. If Powell, the son of black Jamaican immigrants and a product of the Bronx and CCNY's ROTC program, was an unusual choice for chairman of the Joint Chiefs of Staff, then John Shali, as he liked to be called, was quite possibly an even more improbable high-ranking American military official with a personal history no less remarkable.

He was a product of the chaos and wreckage of modern Europe, an immigrant who had found sanctuary in America when he arrived in 1952 at the age of sixteen and who learned much of his English from watching John Wayne movies. His father, Dmitri Shalikashvili, was from the Soviet republic of Georgia. His mother, Maria Ruediger, was a Polish national of half-German extraction. His father had fought from 1919 to 1921 with the White Russian army during the Russian civil war. When that was over, he had settled in Poland, married, and trained officers for the Polish cavalry. That was where John Shalikashvili was born in 1936. Dmitri Shalikashvili fought against the Germans early in World War II with the ill-fated Polish cavalry during those heart-breaking days when the most permanent image of the time was of horse cavalry riding valiantly off to counter the mighty German panzer divisions that spearheaded the first great blitzkrieg. He was captured and taken prisoner by the Germans, but his wife, who had influential relatives in Germany, soon helped secure his release. For much of the war, the family had lived in Warsaw. Almost sixty years later, as chairman of the Joint Chiefs, John Shalikashvili had visited Yad Vashem in Jerusalem, and at this memorial to the Holocaust, to the surprise of his hosts, he had broken into tears because of the memories it evoked of the dehumanization of the Jews in the Warsaw ghetto, which he had witnessed as a boy.

After his release from prison, Dmitri Shalikashvili then served with Georgian forces fighting under the German flag, hoping one day for Georgian independence from the Soviets. Known as the Georgian Legion, it was based first along the Normandy coast to repel the Allied invasion. When the Allied forces eventually poured through, he was transferred to another unit, a Georgian battalion under the command of the Waffen SS, fighting in Italy. When John Shalikashvili, during his confirmation hearings in Washington, some fifty years later, learned for the first time of his father's part in this unit, he was stunned and devastated by the news. The rest of the family had been living in Warsaw when the Red Army, having turned the tide of the war at Stalingrad, began to advance to the west. Somehow the Shalikashvilis survived the bombardment of the city and stayed ahead of the Russians. The family found its way to Bavaria, where they had wealthy relatives, and where they were miraculously reunited with Dmitri Shalikashvili, who had survived the Italian campaign, had been captured by the British, and was finally released in 1946. Good novels have been written about odysseys less tortuous than this.

Six years later, through the help of relatives (who kept the days when Dmitri Shalikashvili had served under the SS command a secret) and the Episcopalian Church, the family migrated to the United States, taking root in Peoria, Illinois, where Dmitri Shalikashvili went to work as an accountant in a utility company and Maria as a clerk in a bank. Their son John did well in high school and won a scholarship at Bradley, the local university. There he joined the air force ROTC, hoping to become a pilot, but was hampered because of poor eyesight. Soon after graduation in 1958, he received his draft notice and went into the service. He did well in the army from the start and was soon sent to officer candidate school at Fort Sill. Like Colin Powell before him, he found that he liked the army, and though, unlike Powell, he probably had a broader range of possibilities in civilian life, he was a soldier's son and decided to make the army his career. He went to Vietnam late in 1968 as an adviser to ARVN forces in the area just south of the DMZ.

Shalikashvili was ambitious, hardworking, and, because of his unusual background, in many ways more worldly than his contemporaries. His vision always went beyond America's borders. The army schooled him well; he picked up a master's degree in international affairs from George Washington and attended the requisite number of advanced training courses. What he found, again like Powell, was that he was good at being a soldier. It was a comfortable way of life, unusually welcoming to uncredentialed but talented newcomers who might, in this more iconoclastic era, bring greater respect for authority than the comparably talented children of more traditional and successful American families. He did very well in the post-Vietnam years. He was smart, paid great attention to detail, and estimated the strengths and weaknesses of the people around him with considerable skill. He always turned out to be more intelligent and efficient than those above him thought he was going to be, and with his knowledge of languages—German, Polish, and Russian—he was particularly valuable during his tours in Europe. There he had performed brilliantly as deputy commander of American forces, a three-star slot, during the Gulf War.

Just as that war was about to start, Colin Powell and Norman Schwarzkopf decided to increase the U.S. forces in the Gulf with the addition of some seventy thousand men from the Seventh Corps, which was based in Europe. They also decided on a complete exchange of armored vehicles, from the outdated tanks already in the Gulf to the more modern ones in Germany. It was a monstrous, last-minute logistical assignment, for Christmas was coming up, but Shalikashvili, working closely with German railway officials, managed to move almost all those men and that equipment on the German rail system without impeding normal transportation for local citizens. Using the highways and the barge system in addition to the trains, he got the job done on time. The deadline pressures were enormous because the entire invasion was dependent on everything coming together at just the right moment. What he achieved was nothing less than a military tour de force. His superior in Brussels, General Jack Galvin, who was a four-star, thought that probably no officer in the United States army could have done it as well.

Up until then no one had thought of Shalikashvili as an army superstar. Part of the reason was his last name, which was long and difficult to pronounce. Another part was the way he spoke, with a slight foreign accent; he had learned his English not only from the movies but from antiquated textbooks, which gave his speech an old-fashioned formality. Moreover, when he spoke, his features did not have the easy flex and nuanced movements that signaled various changes of mood that a native son might have had. It made him seem not merely more formal than he was, but also perhaps a bit heavier in style and thought. Though a surprisingly supple man, he made a stolid first impression. So he was reputed to be a good officer, a solid citizen who could get the job done, but not a probable candidate for a top job. In the pressure cooker of the pre–Gulf War logistical preparations, however, his star had finally shone, and no one was more aware of it than Colin Powell. In those days Powell regularly called Jack Galvin in Brussels and would pick up on what Shalikashvili was doing. The admiration in Powell's voice grew all the time, and he would say, "Shali is looking good, isn't he? I mean really looking good," and Galvin would agree.

At the end of the Gulf War, Shalikashvili performed another difficult task. The Kurds, encouraged by the American army's victory, had taken over a number of villages in northern Iraq, but the Iraqi army, no longer opposed by the Americans, had soon gone after them, blasting away at their villages with artillery at point-blank range. Suddenly a major tragedy loomed. The

Kurds had fled into the mountains, perhaps as many as six or seven hundred thousand of them, it was believed, and their condition was desperate. They were without food and water and, in many cases, any shelter. Various relief agencies estimated that they might be dying at the rate of a thousand a day. The Turks barred their entry at the Turkish border—having already absorbed as many Kurdish refugees as they could—so the potential for a humanitarian tragedy grew even larger. The most pressing problem was getting food and water to the refugees, and because he thought it was primarily an airdrop, Galvin assigned an air force two-star named Jim Jameson to run the operation. But soon the mission deepened to become an immensely complicated matter of moving the Kurds out of the mountains into refugee camps where we could protect them and, if need be, hold off the Iraqi army. At that point Galvin switched assignments and put Shalikashvili over Jameson.

Shalikashvili was able to move the Kurds through the mountains to new camps—tent cities—and he created safe zones that he demanded the Iraqi forces respect. Then through deft negotiations with local authorities (and eventually through Saddam Hussein), he enabled the Kurds to return to their villages. The mission, thought Galvin, had been both dangerous and explosive. Finally, fearing that if the new refugee camps were too sturdy, they would become permanent, "like creating another Gaza Strip," in Shalikashvili's own words, he set strict time limits on residency and deliberately made the camps impermanent in order to funnel the Kurds back to their original villages. Some refugee authorities believed that this so-called Operation Provide Comfort saved as many as six hundred thousand lives.

It was a textbook example of the kind of crisis a high-level American officer now had to be prepared to deal with. It also was probably the making of Shalikashvili, the assignment that lifted him above the level of many talented contemporaries and put him on the fastest military track of all. "It was an extraordinary achievement to save that many refugees, and it required exceptional skills and talents," said Mort Abramowitz, then the American ambassador to Turkey, who had served before in Thailand and therefore had an uncommon knowledge of refugee problems and was also an exceptionally tough grader of high-level public servants. "Shali had to protect them from the Iraqis, he had to deal with the Turkish government, which he did with a combination of toughness and flexibility, and then he dealt with the Iraqi military and government with the same combination of qualities. And he did it all, and he moved them back to their villages in three weeks. There was about him something unusual, a sensitivity to refugee problems you did not normally expect to find in military men, a genuinely profound humanitarian streak. He was a superb diplomat as well as an excellent soldier in a very, very difficult moment."

Powell was also impressed. "Shali's looking *very* good these days," he told

Galvin during one of their phone calls as the Kurd refugee crisis came to an end. "I know what you're going to do now," Galvin said. "You're going to tell me that you want him back." That was, in fact, true and Powell brought Shalikashvili to Washington to be his assistant, a powerful and highly visible slot for a three-star. The job as secretary to Powell's staff was a major promotion, not so much in terms of the military ladder, but in terms of exposure to the high-level world of Washington—on the Hill and in the administration, where Powell had excelled in his own career and was so forceful a figure.

Shalikashvili's sensitivity to the plight of refugees was genuine, and it was to be a consistent part of his career. Some of his friends thought it reflected two characteristics that set him apart from most military men at his level. The first was his awareness of what it was like when the world that you had believed was yours had essentially disappeared off the face of the earth and you were nationless, homeless, jobless, dependent completely on the kindness of strangers—and foreigners. The other was an immigrant's special appreciation for America and a belief that this country, not just in the eyes of its own citizens, but in the eyes of much of the world, was the place the least fortunate turned to as the court of last resort. These views were never articulated, but he was to show great sympathy when dealing with refugee problems and an acute awareness of the broad new role that the American military might play in refugee situations. What some officials in refugee work had hoped to find in Henry Kissinger they found instead in John Shalikashvili.

Shalikashvili went back to Europe in 1992, this time as CINC-Europe, and SACEUR, the job from which Galvin had just retired, and a four-star slot. For many Americans a top assignment in Europe was prized because that was where the big boys always went. But for Shalikashvili it had extra importance because it had once been his home. He was far more comfortable there than other Americans and had more genuine curiosity and interest in the region.

When it was time to replace Powell, Shalikashvili was on the chairman's short list. The other leading candidate was Joe Hoar, who was coming off being the CENTO commander. Hoar was the Pentagon's favorite, thought to be stronger, if need be, in standing up for the Pentagon's traditional sense of its territory in any conflict with civilians. When Shalikashvili was interviewed by Clinton, the president posed a number of questions and at the end of their meeting asked him if he wanted to say anything. Yes, Shalikashvili replied. He did not want the job as chairman because he felt he could serve the country better as commander in Europe. He knew the terrain of Europe well, he knew all the top military and political leaders, and he had a feel for both the languages and the cultures.

Shalikashvili would be Clinton's choice. Probably what catapulted him to the head of the class was his handling of the Kurd refugees. His appointment was to mark a critical change in the cast of characters on the American side in terms of Balkan policy. Shalikashvili was not yet more hawkish on Bosnia than Powell, but at least unlike Powell he did not have a doctrine of his own. The differences between the two men were a matter of tone. Shalikashvili was more likely to be *amenable* under certain conditions to the civilians, whereas Powell was more likely to be *arbitrary*. Powell stood so high on the landscape that his shadow had inevitably fallen over and diminished the Clinton people, who had arrived with marginal reputations and confidence and were always aware of his reputation, his achievements, and his confidence.

There was that something else about Shalikashvili, the top people in the Pentagon believed, that the president, always so nuanced personally and politically, would have been quick to pick up on. He would have recognized that Shali's immigrant patriotism, a patriotism perhaps a bit more innocent than that of generals born here, might represent in the ongoing intricate byplay between the White House and the Pentagon, in which so far the military seemed to hold all the cards, a small advantage for the White House. Years later, a number of civilians who had worked in the Bush and Clinton administrations and wanted to escalate the American role in Bosnia would look at the appointment of Shalikashvili as an important step in the slow turning around of the existing policy, a step that had at first not appeared to be a step.

It was daunting for Shalikashvili to replace probably the most respected public figure in America. Shalikashvili was hardly well-known. Henry Kissinger, quick to put down almost any high foreign policy choice by a Democratic administration, told friends "that there were ten others who would have been better choices." Shalikashvili was himself aware of his limitations, that by contrast with Powell he was, to say the least, charismatically challenged. Powell was a tall, striking figure with a great command presence and a formidable capacity to use language. Shalikashvili in the beginning was the exact opposite, the soldier unknown except to his colleagues. He was not a striking figure, although he was greatly admired by the troops who had served under him for his straightness and earthiness. There was always the problem of that name. In all the years he went before the Senate Armed Services Committee, Strom Thurmond, the senior Republican, apparently never once pronounced it correctly.

Shalikashvili knew that in terms of public appeal he was operating out of a deficit position. He was quite awkward at first, and his handlers had to encourage him to make appearances. But people gradually began to recognize the other qualities that Galvin and Powell had seen long ago. He was never going to be the Washington player Powell had been. But he was smart, indeed quietly erudite, he was modest—his ego was never in the way—he was an attentive listener, he used the people around him well, and he was an uncommonly good, thoughtful human being. Tony Lake remembered the time they had visited American troops in Haiti at Christmas in 1994. Shalikashvili was with a group of elite soldiers on December 24 and his words to them were quite simple: "I know you're all tough warriors, and I know that sometimes some of you feel that being here is something of a disappointment and that this is not exactly your kind of mission. But when you wake up tomorrow, I want you to look in the mirror and say to yourselves, 'I think I saved a lot of lives today—I think I've done something of value.' You have a right to feel good about yourselves and I hope you do." Lake thought it a quiet but eloquent performance, reminding these young men and women that elite soldiers can save lives in different ways.

Shalikashvili was not at first proactive on Bosnia, so no tangible change in the policy occurred when he replaced Powell. Yet to the Clinton people, he was a breath of fresh air. In their view, he was more approachable and helpful than his predecessor. He listened and was far more flexible. In contrast to many of the people serving in the White House and the NSC, too young for World War II and even for Vietnam, whose own combat experience was largely limited to an ugly political campaign or two, and whose knowledge of the rest of the world came from vacations, he had lived an uncommon life. The more time the civilians spent with him, the more they found to like. There had been a marvelously revealing moment in September 1994, when the end of the Cold War was celebrated by the retirement of the famed Berlin Brigade, the storied American combat unit that had stood duty in Berlin, a symbol of America's commitment to the defense of Europe and a reminder that if its soldiers had to fight one day, then thousands of other Americans would soon follow. A number of high-ranking American officials had gathered for what was an important ceremony, among them Perry, Christopher, Shalikashvili, and Holbrooke. Waiting for the ceremony to begin, they were comparing notes about when each of them had first visited Berlin. Apparently the earliest visit had been in 1961 just before the hated wall went up. Then Shalikashvili spoke and trumped them all: "It was 1943. During the war. My father brought me here." He was, Holbrooke thought, a fascinating hybrid, a "mixture of the culture and knowledge and sense of the past of Mittel Europe with the strength and the openness and optimism of America."

By the time Shalikashvili became head of the Joint Chiefs in the fall of 1993, Bosnia, the issue that had seemed so manageable in the summer of 1992 when he had returned to Europe as the American commander, had grown completely out of control and NATO was being pulled into a deepening crisis, in danger of failing the first real test it had ever been given. At first Shalikashvili had not been eager to move on Bosnia. Quite the reverse. He was as apprehensive as Powell about deepening America's involvement, and the Pentagon was hardly an eager participant in the search for a new policy. Again like his predecessor, he was disdainful of those who thought all you had to do was unleash American airpower in a lift and strike operation. He knew that a number of people in the administration, the Congress, and Democratic Party circles were enamored of that strategy. But lift and strike, he believed, was foreign policy on the cheap—that is, without the risk of American lives. We would supply the airpower and perhaps some arms for the Bosnian Muslims. But the use of nothing but our high technology, Shalikashvili thought, was a *nutty* idea, one put forward only by civilians who had no knowledge of how complicated it was to coordinate airpower with ground troops.

In truth, he believed it to be one of the most complicated of all military operations, almost impossible to accomplish without people who were well-trained in tactical air support. That had been true in World War II with prop planes, but now with jet fighters and bombers that flew at record speeds, it was even more difficult. The Bosnian Muslims would be ill-trained to play their part, he was sure, and the language problem would be appalling. There would be an inevitable incremental escalation, a small step at first, a demand that we send in American air support liaison men. Just a handful, of course. But if American troops were used as ground observers for the airpower, they would be at risk and make marvelous targets for the Serbs. If they were killed or captured—and the Serbs would not be shy about parading them around Belgrade in front of television cameras—the whole operation might collapse in a day or two, given the lack of popular and congressional support, and the thinness of support in the administration itself. It could easily become a repeat of Somalia. Lift and strike sounded great, he thought, foreign policy at a bargain price—and always painless. So he had dragged his feet.

But the horror of Srebrenica could not be ignored. The Americans were moving toward a new policy, which was being driven in the American bureaucracy for the first time by the president. Under these circumstances Shalikashvili and Perry now climbed on board, both of them accepting the need for a changed policy, moved by the belief that Serb aggression could no longer be tolerated, and that beyond the immediacy of the genocide, the consequences for NATO, for Europe, and for American policy throughout the world had grown in quantum fashion. Srebrenica was about genocide, but it was also about the very fabric of the West. Shalikashvili began to speak of this period, on the occasions when he returned to the Pentagon from meetings at the White House, as a defining moment in the Clinton presidency, and he did it as a means of pushing his colleagues to drive the new policy further. Not everyone at the Pentagon was pleased or completely on board, and there was in certain circles a belief that the civilians had gotten to Shali. These people did not like hearing that they ought to act because it was a defining moment for a president many of them distrusted.

If it had not been for Srebrenica, with the Serbs so brutally and callously overplaying their hand, Shalikashvili thought, they might never have been called on their aggression. But the fall of Srebrenica changed everything. It offended the Western nations and in some odd way made the tragedy personal. That was especially true of the French. The advent of Chirac gave Shalikashvili the beginning of leverage with the allies. Chirac had suggested that they use elite French and British troops in a heliborne assault to retake the town. The Americans were dubious. The risks were great, the upside in case they were successful relatively small. Shalikashvili had run into a badly shaken French colleague immediately after a sharp dressing-down administered by Chirac, and there was no doubt that the French were now more willing to accept the use of force.

It was at this juncture that Shalikashvili made an important point. To ensure that a helicopter assault like this was viable, the Americans would have to conduct a massive bombing raid to take out the Serb air defense system. If that was true, why bother sending in the choppers on a mission that had marginal military value? Why not go directly to the massive air campaign instead, make it the centerpiece of the operation, and take out the Serbs' air defense system, thereby sending them the first of what might be a series of messages? It was a very good question and helped create a bridge over the issues that had divided the allies for so long.

As Shalikashvili pressed this argument, on a trip to London with a small group of colleagues, he found the Europeans still somewhat reluctant, but he also sensed, post-Srebrenica, some cracks in the wall. Then they all went to The Hague to continue the discussion, where he again used the arguments about the future of NATO and the alliance. They could not continue what they were doing, which loomed as a total failure of the alliance on its first real test. If NATO could not deal with this crisis, the Americans asked, if it failed here on European soil, and it was on the brink of failure as they met, what was the purpose of the alliance? Why meet at all? Therefore they had to use airpower, and it could no longer be the little stuff known as pinpricks. It had to be a systematic campaign so that the Serbs would feel some real pain. By the time of the Hague sessions, the Russians were represented, not by a Russian defense minister, but by an ambassador, and they hated Shalikashvili's proposal. But he thought that the French, the British, and the Dutch were coming along; and when he returned from Europe, he began to believe that there was at last a chance to change the policy.

A few days later, Shalikashvili returned to London with Bill Perry and Warren Christopher to a hastily summoned NATO meeting. The turning point, Perry would later call it. There the three men pressured the allies to accept the concept of the use of massive airpower not merely if the Serbs attacked Gorazde or a place like it, but to strike when they seemed ready to mount an assault. They also urged a simplification of the control mechanism used when airpower was to be called in, to take command away if at all possible from Boutros-Ghali and his people, who were regarded as compromised, and get it into the hands of NATO people, primarily its battlefield commanders. Their mission was successful, though it would take some time to work out the exact control system and a number of phone calls from Christopher to Boutros-Ghali to make him give up his key. But for the first time there was an essential agreement on a new and more vigorous air campaign and a simplified, less politicized command structure. A great deal more muscle—so far potential muscle, but muscle nonetheless—had been added to the alliance's threats, and it had been more NATO-ized than UN-ized.

Defense Secretary Bill Perry made a favorable impression on his European colleagues from the start. He was the most admirable of public servants, regarded by his peers much as Brent Scowcroft had been by his. Once back in late 1992 when Tony Lake was working on the foreign policy transition team with Sandy Berger, just before the Clinton people took office, they had discussed qualities that made the ideal public official. They divided potential candidates into four essential categories: talented but high maintenance, talented and low maintenance, not very talented but low maintenance, and not very talented but high maintenance. The rarest person of all, the perfect specimen, was high value, low maintenance. These were talented people with great ego control and a shared sense of common purpose. What they did was not about getting publicity, but about the value of the act itself.

On that scale, Lake, like almost everyone else in the administration, regarded Perry as one of the ablest people to join the Clinton team. Perry had helped stabilize the administration on defense issues and stop the hemorrhaging at the Pentagon. Clinton got him on the third try, after the tragedy of Les Aspin and the debacle of Bobby Inman. Perry was the rarest of public figures who had operated at that level of the Pentagon—a man much respected and fair-minded, with almost no enemies. His confirmation by the Senate was unanimous. He had a low profile outside of the building, but was greatly admired within it. He never had to show that the decisions that were made were his or that he was responsible for any victories, or that he could, if necessary, eat colonels and generals for breakfast. The chiefs not only admired him, they knew how hard it was to fool him. If he was not always on their side, he always played straight with them, which was important.

Perry understood how the Pentagon worked, and he was, unlike most of the other senior Clinton people, up to speed from the start. He had served an earlier tour in the Pentagon under Harold Brown in the Carter administration as undersecretary for research and engineering—the Pentagon's high-tech man. His background was in science—he had a Ph.D. in mathematics from Penn State—and he had spent a lifetime in the world of high technology working with defense-connected industries in California. Much of his time in the eighties before he returned to government had been with Hambrecht and Quist, an investment firm based in San Francisco, which specialized in midwifing the initial public offerings of high-technology firms to potential customers. Unlike most civilians, he knew more about the new high-technology weapons than almost anyone else in the shop. It was a source of great strength in running the Pentagon, but he never exploited it, never flaunted it in front of the uniformed military as others might have. It was simply there and meant that he could not be fooled about weapons systems, an area that tended to befuddle most high-level civilians.

He was older than the president and the bright young people around him, and he did not seem to be in as much of a hurry as everyone else. He was also more given than most of the people in the administration to old-fashioned courtesies—as if to get respect from others you first had to grant them respect. In truth he was perilously close to being of the World War II generation, having enlisted in the army after graduating from high school in 1945. He had served as an enlisted man and went on to Stanford for his undergraduate degree before getting his doctorate in math from Penn State. The favorable impression Perry made on his European colleagues would be instrumental in changing Balkan policy in July 1995. He had time for everyone. He kept in touch with anyone who mattered or who might matter, even if it was just to check in once a week on the phone. If there was a meeting in Europe for the defense ministers, he would have dinner with them one night, the Baltic representatives the next, and the representatives of countries hoping to join NATO the third. He had dealt with many of them in the past, first in the Carter years and then in his first year of the Clinton administration, and he had never tried to muscle them or pull rank. To European officials often weary of being pushed around by brash young Americans who did not even know they were brash, he was a welcome change, a high-level American sensitive to the feelings of people from smaller, less powerful countries.

At one European summit, Clinton, as was his wont, had been twenty minutes late, which to the other heads of state, already familiar with American arrogance, meant he was *very* late. It was insulting to his colleagues because they were supposed to be there on time, but the president of the United States could, if he so chose, arrive late. Helmut Kohl and Jacques Chirac were fuming. It was Bill Perry who sensed the escalating danger of continental distemper and smoothed things over until the president, in his own good time, arrived.

If Perry had hardly been a hawk on Bosnia, at times when the Serbs had acted in an unusually brutal way, he had been quite ready to use American airpower. But in general, his views had coincided with those of the uniformed chiefs. He thought lift and strike an incomplete policy, immensely tempting because it was warfare on the cheap, but full of vulnerabilities. Like Colin Powell, he probably did not worry much about the JNA if it fought in main-force units, but he was worried about what would happen if the Serbs broke it down into smaller units and used them to harass a large American force with a stream of guerrilla assaults. When the uniformed chiefs made arguments like this to him, he was smart enough to take them seriously and not override, manipulate, or try to split them apart, as McNamara had famously done in 1964 and 1965. If the Serbs did that, either in urban or mountainous areas, it could be extremely painful. Hitler, Perry liked to point out, had managed to neutralize Yugoslav guerrilla attacks, but only by unspeakable brutality—savage reprisals against civilians—that would be unacceptable to Americans.

But like the others, Srebrenica had changed Perry, and he referred to it as the galvanizing moment that had crystallized the thinking of the American government and made the Europeans more willing to search for a common policy. It was in London, he believed, that he and Shalikashvili had managed to convince their European allies that the key to success was not the kind of light, pinprick bombing they had done in the past, which the Serbs had clearly scoffed at; it would be massive high-technology bombing. *Carpet bombing* was the phrase, a huge, relentless air campaign. The traditional European objection to the use of that kind of airpower, and the danger to UN troops on the ground, would immediately be addressed. The some twenty thousand UN troops there, scattered in small units, would quickly be consolidated into large units of a thousand men or more and would have sufficient firepower to hold off the Serbs until aircover arrived. Meanwhile, a team of American, British, and French generals would meet with the Bosnian Serb leaders to warn them that if they tried anything from now on, we would pound them as they had never been pounded before; this would be no light dust-off. If they moved against a safe area, they would also be pounded, and if they moved against UN troops, they would be pounded even more.

Finally, Bosnia was on the front burner. Two days after Srebrenica fell, the principals met in the Oval Office. This time it was Gore, long a hawk, but always careful not to embarrass the president and normally quite restrained at meetings like this, who spoke very passionately about Bosnia. If he disagreed with a policy or was bothered by something, Gore dissented with the president in private. Or if they were in the middle of a meeting, Gore would wait for a brief break and speak to the president apart from everyone else.

This time it was different. A long story had appeared in the *Washington Post* over the weekend about a young woman in Srebrenica who had committed suicide by using her belt and a floral shawl to make a noose. The vice president's twenty-one-year-old daughter, Karenna, had seen a photo of the young woman, who was virtually her own age, and asked her father how the administration he belonged to could fail to act in a situation like this. "What am I supposed to tell her?" Gore asked at the Oval Office meeting. "Why is this happening and we're not doing anything? My daughter is surprised the world is allowing this to happen. I am, too.[1] I want you to tell me how to answer her—

my own daughter."[2] The others in the room were surprised by the emotional nature of his words, and by the idea that he might be dissenting from the president. Then it dawned on them that his words were not in dissent; he and the president were together on this issue, which gave it an immediacy it had not had before. Gore then told the meeting he thought that with Srebrenica gone, Zepa would go, too. But they could draw the line at Gorazde, where as many refugees as had jammed into Srebrenica were now cornered. The United States had to end its policy of acquiescence. At the end of the meeting Clinton was talking openly about using American airpower. "The United States," he said, "can not be a punching bag in the world anymore."

CHAPTER TWENTY-NINE

I n the Balkans events on the ground were about to change direction as well because of a new confidence in the Croat military. Despite some reservations at the top in Washington, the United States had authorized the training of the Croat army under the auspices of retired but highly talented American officers and NCOs, all of them operating in the private sector. Eventually a green light was given to the Croats' request for an offensive against the Serb forces still occupying parts of Croatia, despite considerable ambivalence in Washington about their ability to pull it off. They got the go-ahead because Washington was by then desperate.

A good deal of prior work had gone into the decisions that allowed the Croats to arm themselves and undertake the offensive, and one of the men who had advocated it, Peter Galbraith, the American ambassador to Croatia, was hardly a favorite of his boss, Warren Christopher. Galbraith, son of the famed economist John Kenneth Galbraith, had asked for the job because he had already become interested in refugee work and thought that this would be a post where he could make a difference. But he had been appalled by the lack of interest in the area on the part of his superiors. When it came time for him to fly to Zagreb, none of the top people at State wanted to meet with him, and he arrived essentially without instructions. Once settled in Zagreb, Galbraith was more proactive than his government, which was well-known locally, and it made him, as one colleague noted, something of a rock star there, but a pariah back on the seventh floor of the State Department building, where he was regarded as a difficult person representing an unlikable country, and someone who always managed to get too much local press, often, they believed, at the expense of the administration.

Galbraith had long believed that Christopher and the people around him were in deep denial about what was happening in the Balkans, the degree of human destruction and its implications for larger American foreign policy. Galbraith was an activist, and though his government did not particularly welcome or applaud his efforts, some of the things he did in 1993 were to bear fruit two years later, most particularly in limiting tensions between the Croats and the Bosnian Muslims, and creating the foundation for what would eventually become the Bosnian-Croat Federation. His job was hardly easy. The head of state he was working with, Franjo Tudjman, a narrow, brutal, prejudiced man, was almost as unlikable as Milosevic. Tudjman's nationalism was every bit as intense as Milosevic's, but he was not as aggressive in his military pursuit of it because, most Americans believed, he simply lacked the means, not the intent. Still, Galbraith had little doubt about which course to pursue. The Serbs were the aggressors, their deeds were genocidal, and the job of the United States was to use its influence to stop them. Sure from the start that the main threat to the region came from Milosevic, Galbraith was often a step ahead of American policy in trying to get arms to the Bosnians and to limit some of the worst of the bitter internecine and immensely destructive struggles between the Bosnian Muslims and the Croats.

In March of 1994, pushed by the Americans, the Bosnian Muslims and Croats signed a peace treaty in Washington, creating what was called a federation, a two-nation partnership filled with the kind of hatred and distrust rarely matched in such accords. Nonetheless it was, without many people realizing it, an early step in turning the tide against the Serbs. Tudjman, though an architect of the agreement, literally hated what he had wrought because of his dislike of the Bosnian Muslims. He remained unwilling to make the simplest tactical moves that would strengthen a potential ally and weaken a powerful aggressor who had already taken a huge slice of his own territory. Even after the federation was formed, the real result for a long time, like so many things in the Balkans, was an appalling military-political stew. Galbraith liked to tell people that the area he was working in was "like Lebanon placed next to Cyprus."

In the spring of 1994, the desperately underarmed Bosnians went to Tudjman and asked for his permission to let shipments of arms flow through his territory to their own landlocked bases. Tudjman detested the idea, and he answered evasively that he would put the question to the United States. Galbraith had urged Tudjman to give his permission, and now the Croat leader had shrewdly bounced the question back to Washington, suspecting that the United States would turn down the request, as it had once before at the end of the Bush administration when a planeload of arms from Iran had been stopped at the Zagreb airport. Certainly, thought Galbraith, the UN's regional embargo on arms had nothing to do with Tudjman's attitude; the Croats themselves were openly violating the embargo every day.

Galbraith strongly urged Washington to give its approval to arms for Bosnia. What he wanted was a nonresponse response. Washington would not have to say that it was in favor of arms to Bosnia, but it was not to imply that shipments should be blocked. The administration, he suggested, should look the other way on this one. His reasons were simple. It was good for the federation, he believed the Bosnians deserved the arms, and, finally, he felt there was no obligation to enforce the embargo on Bosnia, since everyone else who was involved in the conflict had a source of arms. Back came the word: you have no instructions. Galbraith interpreted that response to mean that Washington had not made a decision.

In fact, Tony Lake had raised the issue with Clinton on *Air Force One* on the way back from Richard Nixon's funeral on April 27, 1994, and Clinton had given his approval. But Galbraith, believing that Washington was hedging again, misunderstood the all-too-discreet answer he had received, and aided by special negotiator Charles Redman, he called the NSC. Jane Watson, the woman on Lake's staff who took his call, told him that he and Redman had carried the day. "Your instructions are to say that you have no instructions," she said, then added, "When Tony passed the instructions on, he said it with a smile and a raised eyebrow." Galbraith and Redman immediately went to see Tudjman. "Mr. President," Galbraith said, "I have no instructions." Then he added, "Please pay attention to what I am not saying." Just to be sure that Tudjman did not misinterpret his meaning, Redman took him aside and emphasized that the United States was not in a position to object to arms going to Bosnia. That would be a significant victory in terms of future events. It meant the Bosnians got some arms (as did, of course, the Croats, who served as unofficial customs officers and took about 50 percent of incoming arms shipments for their own forces) and were not totally at the mercy of the invading Serbs. It also helped save a weak Bosnian alliance with the Croats, who were themselves beginning to strengthen their military position and gradually becoming a competent military force.

If the early skirmishes in the war had not gone well for the Croats and they were forced to fight off what was effectively the JNA with local police, then they had begun in the years that followed to bring themselves up to military parity with the Serbs. They did that first by importing weapons from friendly European countries. The Zagreb airport was a haven for incoming flights bearing arms from all over Europe. An American diplomat who went out to the airport and saw the many new fighter planes that were now part of the Croatian air force asked Gojko Susak, the defense minister, how he got so many of them. "It's easy," he said, smiling. "A fighter plane arrives, we put it in the hangar overnight, and six months later a new airplane is born."

Susak was a member of the greater Croatian diaspora, which was to prove important in the next few years, a Croat who had gone to Canada, prospered as a pizza entrepreneur, and returned to his country at the time of independence. He was not a military man—the Americans sometimes called him the pizza man—but he had strong ideas about the kind of military his country should one day have. It would be built on an American model, and he hoped to maximize the American influence on his military as a first step toward bringing Croatia into NATO. Equally important, to improve the quality of his army, Susak went to an organization in Washington called MPRI, or Military

Professional Resources Incorporated, to do the job. A small, private company uncommonly rich in American military talent, it was headed by two exceptional former four-star generals. One of them was Carl Vuono, a former army chief of staff, the army's highest-ranking officer and its representative on the Joint Chiefs, who was greatly respected within army circles because of his role in modernizing and at the same time downsizing the professional American army post-Vietnam. The other was Butch Saint, a former commander of American forces in Europe. The impetus for their new company was one of the more important changes wrought by Vietnam. Not only was the American army much smaller in general, but the old military advisory groups, or MAGs, could no longer attract quality people to train foreign forces and were being cut back. But the private sector was quite another matter, and Vuono and Saint operated here, filling this vacuum.

Susak gave the Americans a three-part set of objectives. He wanted his army to be like those in the West in order to get into NATO; he wanted to create a professional military under strict civilian control; and as he said, "I want to drive the Serbs out of my country." Vuono and Saint were in a strong position. They knew who all the talented American one-star and two-star generals and colonels were, the kind of men who would be unusually well suited for a complicated challenge like this. They also knew who the top NCOs were. They hired no one but the army's very best. Among those in the first group that arrived in Zagreb was a former senior sergeant major (or highest-ranking enlisted man) who had served in the army in Europe. After finally getting State Department permission, Vuono and Saint sent a team of fourteen people to Croatia in October 1994. There had never been any doubt that their primary assignment was to improve the Croatian military as dramatically and quickly as possible. In only ten months, they helped turn the Croat army into a competent fighting force. Ten months is not a long time to create and train a modern army, but when the competing forces were as poorly trained as they were in this region, and when the needs were so basic, even so brief a period turned out to make a considerable difference. In the land of the blind, as one American officer noted, the one-eyed man is king. At first the Croat army was something of a territorial force—policemen, schoolteachers, blue-collar workers, lower-level bureaucrats—which was not necessarily a disadvantage. It meant that for most of them, particularly the younger men in the lower ranks, there was less to unlearn. In addition, they brought a quality that any good army needs—a broad representation of its country's citizenry.

One thing the Americans set out to do immediately was create an NCO corps, which the Warsaw Pact armies, notoriously more hierarchical, badly lacked. They also worked on basic infantry tactics and how to coordinate medium unit assaults. By the time the Croat offensive against the Serbs began in early August 1995, the first graduates had left the officer training schools the

Americans had set up. The basic infantry skills they had learned there, as well as the psychological lift that came from being trained by so reputable a group of officers, gave the Croats a considerable edge. "We were not there very long—if the Serb-Croat war had been fought in 1999 our fingerprints would have been all over it," said one of the American officers who served there. "But as it was, even in the brief time we were there, we made something of a difference, if only in the confidence we helped instill." Their timing could not have been better. Croatia's bright, young people badly wanted American military advice to modernize their own forces and drive the hated invaders off their land. In addition, the raw material the American tutors found in Croatia was more than worthy: physically tough, exceptionally well-motivated young men, usually of rural rather than urban backgrounds, not yet removed from the hardships of country life. Perfect prototypes for soldiers, they had not lived for several generations in cities or the suburbs, where, many military men believed, human raw material gets more than a little soft.

Most of the lessons taught by their American instructors were of the most basic kind: how to create covering fields of fire, how to use tree lines, how to flank a bunker, and how to minimize casualties. Though not there as advisers, not in the way the Americans had advised at battalion and even company level in Vietnam, nonetheless the instructors were able in a short time to upgrade the Croat army significantly. The instructors also knew that by the summer of 1995 the Croat forces were ready and eager to attack the Serbs in the Krajina. But despite the considerable reputations of Vuono and Saint, and their men working on the ground in Croatia, their belief in the improvement of the Croat military never altered either the Pentagon's or the CIA's view of the forces pitted against each other in Croatia. The top CIA and Pentagon people had been dubious from the start about the entire proposition, mostly because of the old Serbophilia. The leading American military and intelligence people knew all the top JNA people, and by 1994 the Pentagon had, consciously or unconsciously, a vested interest in downgrading the Croats and upgrading the Serbs. Besides, if you downgraded the Croats and hailed the talents of the Serbs, it made it easier to rationalize staying on the sidelines. The Americans were also nervous about the consequences. What if we encouraged the Croats and an even wider war and more killing ensued with little real change on the battlefield? Or worse, what if the Croats attacked and were easily manhandled by the mighty Serbs, who then seized more territory? So even as the Croats prepared for an offensive against the Serbs, the American left hand and the American right hand did not seem to be well coordinated. Both the Defense Department and the CIA kept feeding into the NSC machinery the belief that if the Croats attacked the Serbs, the Croats would readily be defeated.

Earlier—in the middle of November 1994—when the Bosnian and Croatian Serbs were squeezing the Muslims caught in the Bihac pocket, the Croats had queried the Americans about their attitude toward a Croatian offensive. Tudjman summoned Galbraith for talks, but the driving force behind the idea of an offensive, Galbraith thought, came from Susak and the military, rather than Tudjman, who was uneasy about it. If the issue ended up in the UN Security Council, Tudjman asked, would the Americans move to block the possibility of sanctions against the Croats? Galbraith, with some reservations, liked Susak's idea of an offensive. No forward step in any peace negotiations, he was convinced, was going to take place until the Serbs were met by force on the ground and driven back from their earlier conquests. Galbraith also suspected that the Serbs in the Krajina were something of a paper tiger. Washington did not agree with him; it did not think the Croats had the muscle to pull off the offensive, and it did not want a wider war. Galbraith was told to make as strong a case as he could against any offensive.

Tudjman was greatly relieved by Washington's negative response. "See, that's what I told them," he remarked, referring to what he had said to his own military. So the offensive that might have taken place in November was put on hold. In time, the Serb pressure on Bihac eased and the crisis there lessened. But by the summer of 1995, the equation had changed dramatically. The Serbs had badly overplayed their hand. The siege of Srebrenica was taking place, making the status quo untenable. The Serb pressure on Bihac had increased again, and some predicted a human disaster there that might be three times as great as Srebrenica because so many people were crowded in the area. Still, Washington remained apprehensive about a Croat offensive, and the Croats, of course, were all too aware of Washington's doubts. In February 1995, more than two months after the first rejection, Susak had attended a meeting in Munich with Bill Perry and John Shalikashvili. There he made an impassioned plea for a Krajina offensive, but both Perry and Shalikashvili took a dim view of it. They told the Croats it would be nothing less than a disaster. The Americans were saying, in words that could hardly be misunderstood, that the Croats, if they challenged the Serbs, would get their clocks cleaned. Dick Holbrooke had also attended and he noted in his diary that night that it had been a grim meeting.

But then came the destruction of Srebrenica, encouraging the Croats to push forward again. First Susak and then Tudjman summoned Galbraith for talks. They were more secure about the state of their own military now, confident that it was ready to attack. Their troops had fought well in May of 1995 in brief skirmishes in western Slavonia, a section of eastern Croatia, ousting the Serb forces that were occupying it. In addition, far more than the Americans, they had a skeptical view of the Serb military. They believed the Serbs were overextended and the sieges taking place in eastern Bosnia had diverted men and equipment. Again they asked for American protection against sanctions by the Security Council.

Galbraith argued to Washington that we should take the Croat side; the choice, he said, between greater and lesser evil was clear. In the hierarchy of evil, he wrote Washington, the massacre of some forty thousand Muslims in Bihac—which would be a real possibility if the Serbs succeeded—was a much more terrible event than the fall of the Krajina with, inevitably, episodic atrocities there, and with Krajina Serbs driven off their ancestral lands to become refugees. If the Serbs took Bihac, he said, a massacre three or four times greater than the one at Srebrenica had to be expected. With Holbrooke, Bob Frasure, Holbrooke's top deputy, and others also arguing to let the Croats have a shot at it, Washington finally bought the argument, though somewhat ambivalently. Thus, with the Serbs at the high-water mark of their power, Srebrenica and Zepa conquered, and Bihac surrounded, the battlefield picture finally changed. In late July 1995, Tudjman and Bosnian Muslim leader Izetbegovic, nominally rivals with a distrust of each other as old as the centuries, met quietly in Split, pushed to do so by the Americans, and agreed to attack the Serb troops that had encircled the Bihac pocket. The hatred that had caused so many conflicts in the past was still there between the two men, but they had both finally identified a common enemy. If they would not fight exactly together, they would, and this was a breakthrough of considerable importance, fight on a common front and with a shared, common purpose.

Washington still remained ambivalent, wary of a larger war and dubious about both Bosnian and Croat military capacities. In general, the closer officials were to what was happening on the ground, the more they tended to favor a Croat-Bosnian offensive. Both Galbraith and Holbrooke, by then the most important player on the scene, favored unleashing the Croats. In Washington, Lake was an ally, a cool one—he was for a yellow light—as was Madeleine Albright at the United Nations. Christopher was not an enthusiast, nor were the top people at the Pentagon and the CIA, who feared Croat weaknesses and the Serb ability to widen the war. But Washington, living too long with a failed policy, had little in the way of alternatives. When a high-level Croat military official had come up to Bob Frasure during the London conference and unveiled a detailed plan for the invasion of the Krajina, Frasure had looked at the map for some time, smiled, and then said, "Well, do be careful."

Even as the Croats were ready to strike in the west, the Bosnian Serbs, under Mladic, seemed to be invincible in eastern Bosnia. They had completed the siege of Zepa and demanded its surrender. The Western threats to use NATO airpower to protect some surviving safe areas had not included Zepa in the itemized mandate—it was judged too hard to defend. Mladic, vainglorious as ever, quick to pose for the people back home in Serbia, strutted about Zepa as thousands of Muslims surrendered after the city fell. That he had just been indicted as a war criminal seemed not to bother him at all. He boarded one bus filled with Muslim survivors and boasted to them, "Not Allah, not the United Nations, not anything can help you. I am your God."[1]

It was, though no one realized it at the time, least of all Mladic, the high-water mark of Serb battlefield success. For even as Mladic was about to enter Zepa, Croat troops were moving across the Bosnian border to relieve the pressure on Bihac. With that, the tide turned. On August 4, the Croats struck against the Serbs in the Krajina, heading toward Bihac in an offensive called Operation Storm. The Serb forces completely disintegrated and the Croat offensive became a major rout. The Croats advanced and the Serbs fled, not just Croatian Serb soldiers, but thousands of longtime Serb residents of the Krajina. The Croatian advance took place virtually without resistance and with great brutality as Serb villages were systematically torched. Even those who had believed that the Croat forces were vastly improved were stunned by the totality of their success. On August 5, just one day into the offensive, the Krajina Serbs gave up their so-called capitol in Knin without a battle. The Croat troops kept going, and the next day, on August 6, the siege of Bihac was lifted. In only four days the Croats regained all of the territory—some four hundred square miles of land—seized by the Serbs in their 1991 and 1992 assaults.

At virtually the same time, the Bosnian Muslim Fifth Corps, considered the best unit in the Bosnian army, broke out of the Bihac pocket and started driving both south and east. If the Croat-Muslim marriage was imperfect—if it was not, as one American said, the easiest thing to get all their top military men into the same restaurant on the same night and come out unscathed—then, nonetheless, the military link worked. In Washington, the top people at the Pentagon and the CIA were surprised by how well the Croats and Muslim forces were doing, but some of the Americans on the scene, including the former American military officers and NCOs training the Croat army, were not. Dick Holbrooke was irritated with the Pentagon and the CIA because their attitude was too Serb-oriented. They had thought the Serbs would defend the Krajina and would be successful, and that if they got into trouble, Milosevic would send regular JNA troops to help them out. On all these points they had been completely wrong.

Milosevic made no attempt to save the Krajina. He left the Croatian Serbs, some of whom had lived there for centuries, to their fate, which was bitter indeed. Thousands of them were fleeing, mostly into Serb-controlled parts of Bosnia, but Croat and Muslim troops were hard on their trail, leaving their own brutal mark on the villages that they recaptured. Not many people in the other parts of Yugoslavia, where Serb atrocities had become a staple of life, felt much sympathy for the fleeing Krajina Serbs. It was, after all, Milosevic's early aggression, to which many of them had enthusiastically rallied (and from which far too few had dissented), that had broken the accords of the past wherein Serb and Croat had lived in an often uneasy partnership. Relief agencies estimated that more than two hundred thousand Serbs who had lived in Croatia for generations had to flee. The brutality of the Croats toward Serbs in what were once Serb strongholds was one more tragedy of the war. Serb villages were burned and Serbs who stayed behind were killed in the Croats' own form of ethnic cleansing, one more ugly incident in a war where most of the fighting had been waged against civilians.

At almost the same time, his Endgame strategy accepted by his peers and by the president, Tony Lake was preparing to fly to Europe to sell it to the allies. Even as he was getting on the plane, Lake was apprehensive about the response he would get. Sandy Vershbow, who had been working on Bosnia just as long and as hard as Lake and was just as frustrated by it, kept telling him, "Tony, this isn't going to be as hard as you think. It just isn't." When Lake again expressed his doubts, Vershbow dissented: "No, they're going to be more amenable. They're ready for a change. Watch." He was right. The coming of Chirac had placed considerable pressure on the British to favor a more aggressive policy. In addition, the horrendous events in Srebrenica had begun to change British public opinion. When Lake explained to the British what the president wanted and what the Americans were going to do with or without allies, they proved far more amenable than in the past. Later, as the Americans were boarding the plane for their next stop, Lieutenant General Wes Clark, the army officer representing the Pentagon on the team, turned to Lake and said, "The big dog barked today." It had taken two and a half years, but it had finally happened. The Europeans and the Americans were together in a joint strategy to use NATO airpower against the Serbs.

By chance the Croat offensive coincided almost perfectly with Lake's trip. As he sat in his plane with Vershbow and others, they read aloud to each other the earlier intelligence reports from the Pentagon and the CIA with their negative estimates of any Croat assault upon the Serbs. Rarely had pessimistic estimates been so pleasant to read.

Thus for the first time the forces poised to strike not just the Bosnian Serbs, but Milosevic as well, were formidable and, ominously, double-edged. Not only were the Croats and the Bosnians racing across the Krajina, but the West was clearly readying itself for a more aggressive stance against the Serbs, which might include massive air attacks.

CHAPTER THIRTY

The Endgame strategy called for a peace conference to end hostilities in the Balkans, and the role of the principal negotiator would be vital. No one yet knew what form the negotiations would take, where they would be conducted, and who would conduct them. But a special American negotiator would be needed for a job of rare importance and visibility. Technically Lake had the first shot, but he had held back, perhaps because he was overloaded with other work, or perhaps because he sensed that his talents were not especially well suited to the job. That of itself said something about Lake. No one, noted one colleague in the administration, who had ever known Henry Kissinger in his time could imagine him pulling away from such a course in midstream, getting everyone to the peace table and then not putting himself squarely in the spotlight as the principal American negotiator.

Dick Holbrooke, who had been the assistant secretary for European affairs for almost a year, badly wanted the job and had been actively campaigning for it. "I've been preparing for almost thirty years to conduct peace talks like this," he told colleagues. And why not Holbrooke? Who could deal better with Milosevic, Tudjman, and Izetbegovic, none of them, as John Deutch had once said, a candidate for the Thomas Jefferson award. Given the people he was going to have to negotiate with, Holbrooke would be perfect for the job. The only person who might have been better, one friend noted, was Jimmy Hoffa, the former Teamsters leader who had not been seen in years and was believed to be buried under the New York Giants football stadium near Hackensack, New Jersey.

Warren Christopher was another possibility. But he was not familiar with the intricacies of the many different Balkan parties involved, and having conducted the brutal and exhausting Iran hostage negotiations some fifteen years earlier, he had little desire to take on a comparably murderous and exhausting peace conference. Whatever doubts he had had about Holbrooke, Christopher had largely put to rest. Holbrooke had proved to be an admirable deputy, he had made no end runs around Christopher, and the secretary of state knew that the two of them in some unintended way complemented each other. Christopher was always careful and cautious, ever sensitive to what might go wrong, wary of the limelight, the tidiest of men. Holbrooke was the least tidy of men,

342 / DAVID HALBERSTAM

inevitably pulled to the limelight like a moth to a flame and guilty on occasion of shameless self-promotion. "The ego has landed," some of his deputies, who admired him and worked with him on location in the Balkans, would say whenever he arrived in their city during his Balkan shuttle. Yet he was also decisive and audacious, willing to do some things wrong in order to do other things right, willing above all to take risks for policies he believed in.

Moreover, Holbrooke's modus operandi was in sharp contrast to that of diplomats of another era, who valued privacy and secrecy above all else. The coming of Holbrooke—and his closeness to the media—represented one more change wrought by modern communications in the media world it had created. Even in the field of diplomacy, traditionally occupied by gentlemen who kept everything important secret, the torch had been passed to operators who were more rough-hewn and who understood that the diplomat who leaked most artfully and used his press corps as a kind of Greek chorus tended to win out. Holbrooke was hardly Lake's choice for the assignment as peace negotiator. In the previous summer when details of the Endgame strategy were being worked out, Holbrooke had been excluded from the small working team, and cries of anguish were regularly heard from him by almost all his old friends. Lake's doubts about Holbrooke's abilities were obvious. Lake told his peers that Holbrooke would be difficult to control, his ego would be in the way, and he might grandstand. But there was one more critical vote on this one. Bill Perry did not have strong feelings about Holbrooke one way or another, but he did acknowledge that it was the secretary of state's call. As for Clinton, he had come to appreciate Holbrooke and knew that he needed his energy and his ability with the media. So Holbrooke it would be. On August 12, he flew to London, where he met privately with Lake, who gave him the job. "This is what we always dreamed about when we started out in Saigon more than thirty years ago," Lake told him. I'll be with you all the way, he added, "and if it fails, it's my ass more than yours."[1]

That made Holbrooke the bureaucratic comeback kid of 1995. He had started far outside the play in January 1993, taking a post he thought was well beneath him. The Clinton transition period had been the worst of times for him. The Democrats were back in power, and he was fifty-one, at his absolute professional prime, ready to take over one of the top jobs in the new administration. But he had been cut out by the big boys, many of whom were supposed to be old friends, and he was *sure* that some of the people who were getting top jobs were less talented than he was. Even during the transition period, however, he had enjoyed the backing of one critically important sponsor, Strobe Talbott, who had used his influence with Clinton to get Holbrooke the assignment to Germany, and who continued to be his sponsor for an even more important role when he did well in Europe.

The Bonn assignment had caught Holbrooke completely by surprise because he was almost everything but a Europeanist. His doubts about the job were immediate; he feared that he might have fallen too far. Seeking advice, he called Les Gelb, the *Times* foreign affairs columnist who was something of a career consultant in those days to both Lake and Holbrooke. Gelb, a shrewd student of the State Department bureaucracy as well as a knowledgeable expert on Richard C. Holbrooke, was enthusiastic and told him that it was a much better offer than Tokyo, the assignment he had wanted. He had always been typed as an Asian hand, and the Bonn assignment would give him experience in Europe as well, which he would badly need for any additional ascent. Gelb could easily imagine Holbrooke with his talent and energy in action in Germany, the perfect man for an environment where things were no longer static. "It's the best thing that could happen," Gelb said. "It's going to be an exciting time in Germany—it's in flux, and Europe is in flux and you'll be at the center of it, and you'll get a chance to retool yourself in an entirely different region."

Holbrooke's next call was to Frank Wisner, another old friend from the early Vietnam days, and now undersecretary of defense, who took the news without breaking stride and said, "Well, of course you'll take it. It's a very good job and the thing we want from the Germans is . . ." Thereupon Wisner went into an immediate briefing. Then Holbrooke called his mother, who had been born in Germany, had left there before the war at the age of thirteen, and had never been back. She was dismayed by the news. *Germany?* she said, and it was all question mark. Holbrooke's final call, because he was already operational, already making moves, was to Henry Kissinger. He knew Kissinger was the American closest to Chancellor Helmut Kohl, and the call was a way of stroking him. Because they had often been on different sides of the fence, Holbrooke hoped to position Kissinger as much as he could on his side and, above all, did not want Kissinger bad-mouthing him to Kohl.

Holbrooke took the job because a number of his friends thought that Bonn would merely be the first step, that given his abilities and drive, and the weakness in the State Department at the top, he would sooner or later be needed. But he took it as well because he loved government, the byplay and the excitement of the game. Wall Street, though he had made millions there, never excited him as much. He hit the ground running in Germany. It was typical of him that even in a job that was a consolation prize, knowing that some of his peers in Washington were giggling because he had been dispatched to Bonn, he nevertheless seized the day. He quickly retooled himself, and instead of being Asia-centric, he became the very model of a modern Europeanist.

Whatever else could be said about Holbrooke, he was the most intellectually open of men. Even more rare for anyone who operated at his level and whose ego was so large, he knew what he did not know and therefore what he had to learn. He immediately convinced Fritz Stern, an old friend he had met twenty years earlier at Princeton and one of the leading academics in America on German history, to join his embassy for a limited tour as a kind of historian-in-residence and give him a daily two- or three-hour tutorial. Stern had been born in Breslau, had come to America as a boy, and was an academic who knew the contemporary uses of history. He quickly brought Holbrooke up to speed intellectually in his new role. In addition, Holbrooke soon discovered and rehabilitated an ancestor, a grandfather who had fought for the kaiser in World War I. A framed photo of Grandfather, never seen before by any of Holbrooke's old friends in his previous homes, with a suitably Germanic mustache and wearing one of those ludicrous Teutonic helmets, was soon on prominent display.

Holbrooke got on well with Helmut Kohl and was quite influential in convincing Kohl, who had ties by experience and ideology to the Bush administration, to take the new administration seriously. The Clinton people, Holbrooke suggested, were not merely brash, unfinished children, which was the general old-world view; rather, Holbrooke suggested, Clinton would soon emerge as a talented, skillful leader whose exceptional political success so far had not been an accident. Softening Kohl's view of Clinton was no small coup for Holbrooke, and he would help stage-manage Clinton's successful visit to Berlin in 1994. There, Clinton and Kohl, the leaders of the nations that had fought two bitter wars against each other in this century and had then been paired in an uneasy anticommunist alliance, had walked to the Brandenburg Gate together, holding hands, accompanied by their wives. It was such a powerful—and obvious—symbolic moment of the best part of the new world order that Holbrooke always wondered why George Bush had never done it. Unlike Bush, Holbrooke understood, Clinton had an almost perfect anticipatory sense of the right image at the right time.

With Mitterrand's health failing, Kohl had become the most important political figure on the Continent, and Holbrooke dealt ably with him, knowing that with Kohl, as he once said, the principal job for an American ambassador was simply to listen. He understood Kohl's elemental desire to expand NATO so that Germany would no longer be the West's border with Russia as it had been since the end of the war. Kohl wanted Poland to serve that purpose, and therefore as he sought the expansion of NATO, so did Holbrooke within the administration. He sensed a general softness and lack of focus in Clinton's foreign policy, except on trade, where Mickey Kantor was a considerable influence. Holbrooke moved into that vacuum eagerly. Slightly underemployed in Germany, he became something of a force beyond his hierarchical position, what his friend Talbott called "a one-man idea factory on the future of NATO and the security of Europe."

Talbott, who traveled to Moscow regularly, believed that the energy Holbrooke produced was special and would arrange his own trips to stop off in

Bonn to talk with him, thinking him the ablest strategic thinker of the group that was dealing with greater European security. The more time he spent with Holbrooke, the more convinced Talbott became that they needed him back in Washington at a higher level in the department. Some of the stumbles that had marked the first two years of the Clinton administration might have been avoided, Talbott decided, if Holbrooke had come in at a senior level in the beginning. It might have been more chaotic and contentious, but well worth it. Holbrooke, Talbott believed, was well ahead of the administration in his thinking about the Balkans and the dilemma we faced there. Always an activist on the Balkans, Holbrooke thought that we could not deal with any issue of NATO or European security until we dealt with Milosevic because he was such a divisive factor. He exploited and magnified all the existing tensions in the West. It was that simple.

Holbrooke's success in Germany exactly paralleled the failure of the administration's Balkans policy, which he had predicted from day one would be the deciding foreign policy issue of the Clinton presidency. Inevitably, he was called back to Washington to become the assistant secretary for European affairs, returning in the middle of September 1994, not necessarily because Warren Christopher wanted him, but because the department badly needed him. He would be able to fill the conspicuous hole at the top of the department. By then Holbrooke had two sponsors. One was Talbott, who was very much aware of both Holbrooke's strengths and his weaknesses and had once noted of his friend, "Dick is like a great pitcher going into the World Series who is going to strike out more batters than anyone else, but he's also going to hit more guys with beanballs, too—maybe lead the league with hit batsmen." Holbrooke's other sponsor was Tom Donilon, the bright young assistant to Christopher who played a crucial role in his boss's personnel choices and thought the department at the highest level desperately needed Holbrooke's energies and talents, especially since Christopher tended to be only as good as his deputies in any given area. Donilon knew that almost everything critics said about Holbrooke was probably true, but that a great deal of it didn't matter, and much of it was said in jealousy. Donilon understood the one great truth about Dick Holbrooke beyond the peripheral qualities: his career was his life. Succeeding seemed to mean more to Holbrooke than almost anyone else, and failure seemed to mock him far more than most others. Donilon also believed that one criticism of Holbrooke was a great canard, that he operated on his own and never checked in. Never checked in? Donilon told friends—he's *always* checking in. He calls every twenty minutes to let you know what he's just done.

Both Talbott and Donilon were influential with Christopher, and both were Holbrooke fans. Christopher was most assuredly not. He had not been eager to have Holbrooke anywhere near his elbow when he first took over.

Holbrooke's general modus operandi bothered Christopher. Moreover, they had some history together over human rights issues when Holbrooke had struggled with Pat Derian over Marcos and the Philippines. When Talbott and Donilon pressed Holbrooke's case, Christopher would protest. "But Holbrooke is disruptive," he would say. "We could use a little disruption around here," Donilon would reply. Finally Christopher said he would take Holbrooke, but when he made the decision, he turned to Talbott and said, almost pleading, "Now, Strobe, you'll deal with Dick, won't you?"

In a State Department that had become notoriously tentative and unfocused, Holbrooke was an asset from the start. He had a clear idea of what the administration needed, and because he was always aware of the intersection of foreign policy and domestic politics, he knew the danger that events in Bosnia posed to the future of the Clinton presidency. The good thing about the Christopher State Department was the freedom to operate for those who wanted to operate. There were not, in this State Department, tight territorial limitations. If Christopher was not a formidable figure with a clear vision of his own, then he readily deferred to his deputies, and that would be an advantage for Holbrooke. So he came in fully activated, more than two years behind schedule, trying to make up for lost time by taking charge of the Balkans policy.

He was also something of a blowtorch, relentlessly driving the people around him, always demanding excellence and, of course, loyalty. He quickly connected himself to Peter Galbraith, the department's otherwise lonely man in Zagreb, and let him know that Galbraith was back in the loop, but only if he went through Holbrooke. There would be many phone calls to Galbraith, demanding some kind of action, and then at the end a fairly typical Holbrooke reminder: "Just remember, I'm your only friend around here. Everyone else hates your ass. I spend more than half my time defending you. So you better come through for me." Galbraith would try to come back at Holbrooke: "Dick, how come you're my only friend, but all your friends trash you, and I think my friends like me?" So they raged at each other, but Galbraith was aware that Holbrooke was probably right. He was the one man at that level who was on Galbraith's side.

When the handoff from Lake took place in London on August 12, Holbrooke immediately became exactly what he wanted, the point man on Bosnia, and his first job, often working with Peter Galbraith, was to coordinate the Croat-Muslim offensive. Here, Washington and the people in the field differed. Washington wanted greater limits put on the advancing Croats than Holbrooke and his team did. Part of their job was to tell the Croats and the Bosnian Muslims to slow down, instructions that Tudjman and Izetbegovic were hardly eager to hear. Nor did Holbrooke agree. In his mind, every bit of territory regained during the offensive would enormously benefit the eventual peace talks. Simply stated, the more the Croats took, the easier a time Washington's negotiators would have in drawing up a new map. When Holbrooke and his support team met with Tudjman on August 17, one member of the team, responding to Washington's directives, kept pressuring the Croatian president to stop the offensive. Holbrooke felt differently, as did his deputy Bob Frasure, who had already spent a great deal of time negotiating with Milosevic. In the middle of lunch that day, to encourage his boss, Frasure scribbled a note for Holbrooke on his place card and slipped it to him: "Dick: We 'hired' these guys as our junkyard dogs because we were desperate. We need to try to 'control' them. But this is no time to get squeamish about things. This is the first time the Serb wave has been reversed. That is essential for us to get stability so we can get out."[2] That carried the day. The Croat offense would continue.

By mid-September the rout of the Serbs continued. Again Washington was nervous. Tudjman wanted to drive forward, so did the principal Americans he was dealing with, Holbrooke and Galbraith, and so most of all did Izetbegovic. But Washington told both Holbrooke and Galbraith to get the Croats and Bosnian Muslims to stop the offensive. On September 15, Galbraith was ordered to present to Tudjman a démarche, a formal message, telling him to stop. Galbraith, appalled by the message, asked for a revision but was quickly overruled. He had, of course, delivered it, but it went against everything he believed in. Both Holbrooke and Galbraith dissented. Holbrooke believed in Milosevic's essential selfishness; he had written off the Krajina Serbs and was willing to write off, at least partly, the Bosnian Serbs. Holbrooke knew there was no love lost between him and Mladic, and that Mladic was a convenience at best, and quite possibly someone who needed to be brought down a notch.

Holbrooke was by then dealing directly with Milosevic and could see the impact of the changed battlefield in his attitude. Holbrooke believed he had an accurate sense of how far Milosevic was willing to go in response to the Croat-Muslim offensive. Holbrooke was irritated that Washington, which he felt had played this wrong from the start, now wanted to halt the offensive. Tudjman, meeting with Holbrooke and Galbraith in mid-September, shrewdly asked Holbrooke for his personal view on the issue. As carefully as he could, without openly defying his superiors, Holbrooke signaled his support for the offensive. By then the Serb hold on parts of Croatia and western Bosnia had shrunk rather considerably. Milosevic now faced a real political crisis. Thousands and thousands of Bosnian Serbs, just like the Croatian Serbs a few weeks before them, were fleeing their towns and villages, heading back to Serbia, where the city they intended to settle in was Belgrade. Serbia proper had already absorbed more than one hundred thousand Serb refugees, mostly from Croatia, and now with the catastrophic events in Bosnia, the figure that loomed was far greater, perhaps six hundred thousand more, all of them likely to be angry. For Milosevic, that could be a political killer, and he wanted to stop the rout.

He was, for the first time, looking at peace negotiations from a different point of view—the end of someone else's guns.

Holbrooke, aware of Washington's apprehensions but operating under a flexible commission from Christopher, wanted a battlefield that essentially matched the settlement envisioned in Lake's Endgame plan, a 51–49 division of the Bosnian terrain, Croat and Muslim versus the Serbs, and he was prepared to wait just a little while longer. Day by day the Croat-Muslim forces surged ahead, and soon Holbrooke had staff people drawing up maps twice a day showing who controlled how much land. Essentially he was straddling two governments, signaling Tudjman, whose forces were doing most of the fighting, to continue, while trying to hold Washington at bay. In the past the greatest drawback in dealing with the Serbs had been the map they had supplied—with 70 percent of Bosnia in Serb hands. Now that was changing on the battlefield.

If the pressure from the Croat-Bosnian offensive was not enough to convince Milosevic that the tide was turning, late August brought an additional incentive, the first major use of NATO airpower against the Bosnian Serbs, not the pinprick bombings that had failed in the past, but the heavy stuff, delivered with sustained violence and NATO's very considerable technological muscle. That which had distinguished the use of airpower in the Gulf War four years earlier, and which had prompted General Tony McPeak, the air force chief of staff, to tell Colin Powell that airpower alone could make a difference in the Balkans, began to rain down on the Serbs. It had been triggered by a brutal and senseless attack on Sarajevo by Mladic and the Bosnian Serbs on August 28, 1995. Thirty-eight people were killed and another eighty-five wounded in a shelling of the city's marketplace. It was one of the worst incidents of its kind, and coming as it did, when Serb forces were already in flight in the Krajina, it underlined the differences between Milosevic and Mladic. Milosevic was a cold, manipulative figure who could, when it suited him, be a didactic communist, a new-era banker, or a reborn post-Tito nationalist. The only given was his desire to hold power. But Mladic's nationalism was more genuine, approaching, some thought, true madness. Now he had managed to provoke the West just when it wanted to be provoked.

This time the West was ready. "An unexpected last chance to do something we should have done three years earlier," Holbrooke said. The president was on board and the Americans were ready to drive the alliance. On August 30, NATO began the heaviest bombing in its history, using its most modern weapons, including (apparently without clearance from the White House) its Tomahawk cruise missiles. More than sixty aircraft operating from bases in Italy and the carrier *Theodore Roosevelt* participated. One Tomahawk landed with stunning accuracy and took out Mladic's entire communications center. That was an extremely important hit because one of the advantages the Serbs had enjoyed thus far was their vast superiority in communications and the ability, if necessary, to move forces quickly from one venue to another. Now they were, overnight, blind and deaf on the battlefield. The sense of what NATO could do in the future was palpable. Then on September 1, a bombing halt was called. Not all of the Americans were pleased about it, aware that it was always hard to resume bombing after a halt, but it was supposed to give Mladic a chance to negotiate and withdraw. But not much came out of the early talks, and the Americans were eager to resume the bombing, even if all of their allies were not.

What surprised some of the senior American civilians was that the commander of the air attack, Admiral Leighton (Snuffy) Smith, did not want to resume bombing. Smith wore two hats: he was commander of all U.S. forces in southern Europe as well as commander of all American naval forces in Europe. Some of his peers considered him a wonderful ship commander, an old-fashioned, rough, tough figure who regrettably had little feel or interest in the complicated political-military dilemmas of the post–Cold War world. But now, for whatever reason, he did not want to send his young men and women back into combat. He seemed to have no enthusiasm for the Balkan struggle, and he once used the same phrase to Holbrooke that James Baker had uttered a few years earlier: "We don't have a dog in this fight." Clinton would later tell his closest aides that he thought Smith had been insubordinate during this period as well as later when he was in charge of policing the Dayton accords.

Now the dilemma for the civilians was to push Smith to resume the bombing. Lieutenant General Wes Clark, Holbrooke's military liaison, was told to call him and get him to reopen the air war. He reached Smith on a golf course and was reamed out for his trouble. Listening on a cell phone, Holbrooke could hear the roar of Smith's voice and Clark's apologetic yes-sirs and no-sirs. Eventually the issue went to the top and the bombing was resumed, but clearly the fissures between the military and the civilians, which had cast a great shadow over the Balkans from the start, still existed. Moreover, Clark, whom the civilians had begun to think of as helpful, a rare senior military figure who saw the Balkans much as they did, might now be in trouble; a three-star who crossed a four-star was part of an endangered species. Clark was clearly in danger of suffering fatal career wounds, and Holbrooke, Sandy Berger, and Strobe Talbott all immediately lobbied with Shalikashvili on his behalf. But in the complicated, overheated world they lived in, these calls did not go unnoticed, and if they helped protect Clark in the short run, they created even more doubts about him in the Pentagon in the long run.

It was not the first sign that Clark was in some kind of trouble with his own military. During the early days of the Balkan shuttle when he was constantly traveling with Holbrooke, he was given instructions from senior people in the Pentagon that from then on he was to be in as many photo opportunities as possible, as close to Holbrooke as possible. That would show this was not just a civilian operation, but the military was running it as well. In addition, he was no longer to be photographed carrying his briefcase. Generals should not carry their briefcase; that was wimpy. They should look like warriors. Equally troubling were calls from Shalikashvili to Holbrooke to ask whether Clark was working out all right: "Are you okay with Wes?" he would ask. Why? Holbrooke wanted to know. "Well, we're getting a lot of complaints back here," Shalikashvili said. It was an early warning that Clark would be at the center of continued military-civilian tensions, soon to escalate over Kosovo.

But the bombing went on and it was formidable. Nothing had shaken Milosevic quite like the use of the Tomahawk missile. He was aware of the dual nature of his dilemma. Croat forces were advancing across the Krajina, and now NATO's airpower was destroying his troops. He accused the Americans of providing close air support for the Croat troops, which was not true, but the effect was much the same. Finally, one part of the Bosnian campaign was coming to an end. By late September, the Croat-Muslim forces had an open road to Banja Luka, the largest city in Serb-occupied Bosnia. Instead of holding some 70 percent of Bosnian territory, the Serbs in the north were reduced to an ever shrinking island, which with the fall of Banja Luka might disappear completely. Holbrooke was worried about Banja Luka and the refugee catastrophe that awaited the people there if the Croats took it. Three hundred thousand to four hundred thousand Serb refugees were said to be there, all of them having fled the advancing Croat and Bosnian forces. There had already been too much killing, Holbrooke and Galbraith believed, too many helpless people murdered to allow one more city to become infamous, even if the people who were now in danger were the kinfolk of those who had started all this bloody business in the first place.

On September 17, Holbrooke urged Tudjman to hold back on Banja Luka, even as Susak, his defense minister, was meeting with others on Tudjman's team to tell them they were only twenty-four hours from controlling a key mountain outside the city. If they took the mountain, they could have Banja Luka in two more days. Milosevic was clearly eager to talk now. In a note to Christopher on September 20, Holbrooke said, "In only a few weeks, the famous 70 percent division of the country has gone to around 50–50, obviously making our task easier."[3]

On September 17 with Croat-Muslim tanks an estimated seventy-two hours from Banja Luka, Holbrooke told a most unhappy Tudjman to halt his forces short of the city. Izetbegovic was even more unhappy. The rationale Holbrooke used with Izetbegovic had been used against him in the past by Washington: the Serb lines were finally coming together and there was a danger of a counterattack. The offensive that had surprised every Western capital had changed the balance of power on the ground and would set the conditions for the upcoming peace conference. In fact, the Croat-Bosnian offensive made the conference possible. When the peace process began, the Serbs held only 45 percent of Bosnia, and the real negotiating had already been done on the battlefield. The myth of Serb invincibility had been shattered.

CHAPTER THIRTY-ONE

Dick Holbrooke wanted in the worst way to handle the negotiations from the moment it became obvious that some kind of peace process would take place and would be led by the Americans. He was sure he was the right man for the job; he had been preparing for it in one way or another ever since he had virtually forced his way onto the American team that had gone to Paris in 1968 in a failed attempt to end the Vietnam War. What many people did not like about Holbrooke—the excessive energy, the singular sense of purpose, the sheer fearlessness, the willingness to act on and accept responsibility for his views, even the willingness to run over other people if need be—was, his friend Tom Donilon thought, exactly what would be needed in these forthcoming negotiations. Holbrooke wanted the job for the most basic reason: it was the ultimate professional test. You were the man of the hour, all the attention was focused on you. Could you bring it off? All your professional training would be on the line and your country depended on you. Besides, no one was better suited to deal with the particular collection of people from the Balkans who would come to a peace conference. As Bill Clinton later said in a farewell toast to Holbrooke at a dinner in December 2000, "After all, everyone in the Balkans is crazy and everyone has a giant ego. Who else could you send?"

Even before the conference began, Holbrooke had won a major victory over the choice of venue. In Washington, almost no one at the upper level, from either the national security side or the White House political side, wanted the conference held in the United States. The reasoning was obvious. It would be higher profile with more media coverage, and if it failed, which seemed quite possible if not quite likely, it would cause severe damage to a president just about to enter an election year. But Holbrooke, almost alone against the prevailing opinion, had argued vigorously that if you were going to do this, you had to do it right. You had to control it—the logistics, the location, the access to media. The only way to control it, he said, was to conduct the talks on American soil. His friend Talbott strongly disagreed with him but generously helped frame his argument. Given how difficult it was going to be, and how bitter the divisions were between all of the parties, Holbrooke pointed out, if you did not have absolute physical control of the environment, it was likely to turn into a shambles. You might as well take the risk, go for broke, and hold the negotiations here. What he was saying was not what a lot of people in the White House wanted to hear, but in the end his argument, self-evidently true, carried the day. After some debate about the best possible site, the air force volunteered Wright-Patterson Air Force Base in Dayton, Ohio, which was a brilliant suggestion because it would give American negotiators greater control over access—and media—than any other location.

For Holbrooke, it was the role of a lifetime. He loved high visibility, which had been a strength when he was running the Balkan shuttle in the weeks before Dayton, in no small part because he had been so good with the media. He knew just how much to give, and how much not to give, to a hungry press corps. His briefings were a careful blend of genuine information and deft spin, thereby managing to serve both his purpose and the purpose of most reporters. No one since Henry Kissinger and James Baker was as dedicated and skillful in the care and feeding of the media as Dick Holbrooke. Never mind that the central and often most heroic figure in Holbrooke's conversations with journalists tended to be himself—something that angered many of his peers in Washington. Reporters liked him and he was unusually accessible; they might see his flaws, but they thought he was taking this entire process further than anyone else could, and he was good copy. They always got what they needed. His press coverage was good, however, not just because he was a deft briefer, but because he also made things happen. If Holbrooke was pushing on Bosnia, it meant that it would no longer be a grievous, frustrating back-burner issue. It would be a grievous, frustrating front-burner issue.

That was potential consolation for those high-level people who were unenthusiastic about his selection to run the Dayton talks and who were suspicious about the flowering of his ego. If they failed, then, because Holbrooke had been so visible, so close to the media, it was likely to be seen as his failure. The White House would then, it was hoped, be able to separate itself from him. So the plum—was it a plum or a live hand grenade?—fell to Holbrooke. He would be a constant presence in Dayton, someone equal in guile and physical stamina as well as intelligence to the other participants, products though they might be of the Byzantine ways of the Balkans. What the American team was getting, and Donilon and Talbott certainly knew it, was nothing less than a hammer, a person who would pound the Bosnians, the Croats, and the Serbs relentlessly and would be a worthy match for them in toughness and, if necessary, obtuseness and brutality. He would hammer his own countrymen just as hard. His career was in diplomacy, but he was not necessarily a diplomatic man. All the qualities that had once seemed to work against him—the raw edges, the instinct to go where angels fear to tread, the ability to let virtually nothing stand in his way when he wanted something—now worked for him. He had a special strength that most top-level foreign service people lacked—diplomatic niceties meant absolutely nothing to him. Power was what mattered, and because of the changed map in the Balkans he had been handed and the threat of continued NATO bombings, he as a representative of the United States of America held the power.

He would be a match for Milosevic as a user. He could get along with Milosevic if need be, but did not buy into Milosevic's artificial veneer, the earthy bonhomie, a guy you could have a drink and deal with. He saw him as Milosevic had seen countless Western negotiators in the past, someone to be used and manipulated. Holbrooke knew just how much power Milosevic had, and that for all his braggadocio, he was playing with a weaker hand at Dayton than he had held for the last six years. His bluff and that of his proxies had finally been called on the ground by the Croats and NATO. During his Balkan shuttle talks in September, Holbrooke happened to be with Milosevic in Belgrade the day after the Americans had fired their first Tomahawk cruise missile in western Bosnia, with devastating accuracy. Milosevic was clearly shaken by the news of what had happened. So much of his game had been premised on bluster, and now just one Tomahawk missile had wiped out the Serb communications center for the entire region. What kind of weapon allowed a gunner who might be several hundred miles away to fire with pinpoint accuracy as if he could actually see his target when he hit the button? That weapon had not only produced a lethal effect on the ground but a devastating psychological effect as well.

Holbrooke believed that was the moment when Milosevic began to lose some of his bravado. One day in Dayton just after the peace talks began, the Americans took Milosevic and some of the Bosnian Serbs through part of the air base's museum and showed them a Tomahawk missile. It did not seem that big or dangerous, but the Serbs were mightily impressed. "So much damage from something so small," Milosevic said. "It's just so small . . ." Clearly, Milosevic had to worry about that if the conference failed: a continued Croatian-Bosnian assault loosely blended, perhaps, with the awesome airpower of NATO. All for a piece of terrain that did not mean that much to him personally or politically.

Holbrooke intended to waste little time on formalities with these Balkan leaders. He knew when to listen and when to tune out, the rare moments when they were really talking and when it was all propaganda, as if Radio Zagreb or Radio Belgrade or Radio Sarajevo were just spitting out all the hatred and paranoia of the past. He also understood something important about all three groups who would attend the conference: the Serbs, the Croats, and the Bosnian Muslims. They were not only vulnerable to each other because of the blood hatreds, they were vulnerable to themselves. Again and again because of those blood hatreds, they had committed unspeakable acts having grave consequences. It was in the nature of the beast and they did not know how *not* to commit them. Therefore in some bizarre way, they wanted others to stop them from doing the things that by a kind of primitive instinct they felt they had to do.

Holbrooke's job would be not only to limit their claims against each other, but also to create a deterrent force to prevent further Pavlovian acts of violence. He had to be at once a brute, but supple. To understand Milosevic you had to know that though he had helped set the Bosnian Serbs on their murderous mission and they were his instrument, he felt a deep contempt for them, as if they were social inferiors. The fiction that they had nothing to do with him was important to him and his international self-image. From the start, Holbrooke had let Milosevic know that the Americans connected him to the worst deeds of the Bosnian Serbs and the Serb paramilitary.

Yet Milosevic loved his carefully created and nurtured fictions, and he constantly denied any link between the JNA and Arkan and his Tigers, probably the most brutal of the paramilitaries. So in early October 1995, Holbrooke had the CIA prepare a lengthy document on Arkan's activities and exactly how he worked in conjunction with the JNA, or to be blunt, Milosevic. In late October, Holbrooke had broached the subject of Arkan with Milosevic again. "No, no, your information is wrong," the Serb leader said. Holbrooke pointed to the folder the Agency had prepared, carried to the meeting by Jim Pardew, an aide. The evidence is right here, Holbrooke said. Milosevic refused to look at the folder or touch it, and when the meeting broke up, it remained on the conference table. As the Americans were leaving, one of Milosevic's aides told Pardew that he had left his paper on the table. "I didn't forget it," Pardew said. "It belongs to President Milosevic."[1] The implication was obvious—not only was NATO muscle now aimed directly at the Serbs, but the days of easy con jobs were over.

As a very junior member of the Paris peace talks in 1968, Holbrooke had watched a variety of people in Washington undercut Averell Harriman and Cy Vance, the principal U.S. negotiators. Paris had been a bitter learning experience for Holbrooke, and he intended to let no one undercut him at these talks. He would control all information, force the Americans to work as a team, and prevent a split in the alliance by limiting the ability of the different Balkan groups to create mischief by going to their closest European sponsors. He would try to keep the Europeans on board because he needed the threat of more NATO sorties to keep the Serbs in line. It was, given all the divisions on each side, among the Americans, among the Europeans, and among and within the three Yugoslav groups, a large order.

There was no small irony in seeing himself as an airpower hawk, Holbrooke thought. He had always believed the American dependence on airpower in Vietnam as a critical instrument of policy was a serious mistake and it had been of limited value there because of the nontraditional way the enemy, both Vietcong and NVA, operated. But this was a different war with a different enemy, one using relatively traditional, far more stationary battle formations, and thus much more vulnerable to airpower. Equally important, there had been a quantum change in the effectiveness of the instrument itself, the ability to hit targets with great precision and little risk.

There was nothing pretty or just about Balkan history, there was nothing pretty or just about the Balkan wars of the nineties, and there was nothing pretty or just about the Dayton peace conference. The three groups arrived in varying degrees of readiness. The Croats were the most coherent, in effect the real winners in the struggle that had taken place over the previous three years. They were the principal beneficiaries of their recent military assaults, their troops had done most of the fighting, driving the Serbs out of the Krajina and western Bosnia, and they had been on something of a military roll when the cease-fire was declared. In addition, they were as close to being a defined, ethnically unitary nation as it was possible to be in that fractious region. Tudjman was their undisputed leader, with no factions within their delegation. They were on a high after their military victories and likely to become stronger if the fighting continued because they had access to weapons, excellent American training, and might have the advantage of a NATO airshield.

The Serbs arrived much more exposed and divided. Perhaps the most important victory over them had been achieved even before the conference began. For several years Western negotiators had been trying to get Milosevic to exert some control over the Bosnian Serbs, or at least to admit that he had the ability to control them, all to no avail. He had stuck to the fiction of their being an independent force fighting for an independent nation. But after the first major NATO bombing, Milosevic had miraculously shown up at a meeting with Holbrooke with a piece of paper signed by the Orthodox Church patriarch, which in effect gave him control of the Serb delegation that would go to a peace conference. There were to be three representatives from Belgrade and three from Pale, the capital of the Bosnian Serbs. In case of a tie, three to three, the leader of the delegation, Milosevic, would cast the deciding vote. That meant it was his delegation. At one point Holbrooke asked him whether he was sure his friends, the Bosnian Serbs, would go along with it. "They are not my friends. They are not my colleagues," he said. "It is awful to be in the same room with them for so long. They are shit."[2] That meant he was at least partially cutting them loose. Bosnia, unlike Kosovo, upon which he had built his climb to power, was not in his mind sacred Serbian soil.

The Bosnian Muslims were, as they had been from the start, at the greatest disadvantage. Because they were the most pluralistic, they were the most democratic, which meant they were the least unified. The diversity of their delegation made them the most vulnerable to internal divisions among the different ethnic groups. In addition, they had paid the steepest price because of Serb aggression. They had been ill-prepared for the events of 1992–95 and remained ill-prepared now. They arrived in Dayton, their territory partially carved up—to be sure not as badly carved up as it had been two months earlier—with a sense of loss and grievance.

The Bosnian Muslims were indignant about the injuries that had been inflicted on them, but they had significantly less muscle than the Croats. As far back as mid-September, they had been furious when the Americans finally gave the signal to halt the bombing. Not surprisingly, they would prove to be the most difficult group to deal with in Dayton. Relatively weak on the ground militarily, virtually powerless to control the events now unfolding, which affected their country more than any other, they were frustrated, divided, and went home the angriest with the settlement. The other delegates, like the sponsoring Americans, felt that the Bosnian Muslims lacked a sense of reality and, indeed, a sense of gratitude. But the Bosnian Muslims had a deep distrust of those (like the Americans and Europeans) who had had the means to stop the carnage from the start, had done so little for so long, and after finally acting—at so little cost to themselves—had pulled back so quickly. Anything at all that even partially legitimized Serb gains in their eyes rewarded the aggressor. The source of their anger was their dependency; nothing will make the head of a small, defenseless state angrier than dependency upon a large, immensely powerful, but somewhat indifferent superpower. All in all it was not a happy equation.

The conference was chiefly about maps, about trading land for land, and about making as many people as possible equally unhappy. There was a terrible moment late in the talks as things were moving along relatively well, at least for Dayton, when Milosevic, who had not been paying attention to the maps, suddenly realized that instead of a 51–49 split against the Serbs, by mistake it had gone to 54–46. He was furious, sure that he was being tricked—he who had always snookered everyone else. A flurry of pressures got things back to the original goal, as the principals kept trading islands of land to achieve the magical 51–49. Nothing was going to make everyone happy at Dayton.

Late in the negotiations when it appeared the conference might collapse because of Bosnian Muslim resistance, Holbrooke wrote a telling memo for Warren Christopher: "The Bosnians still wish us to believe that they are getting a lousy deal. Yet they know it is not only a good deal, but the best they will ever get. Logically, therefore, they should accept. But the dynamics of their delegation make this a very close call. Izetbegovic spent nine years of his life in jail, and is not a governmental leader so much as a movement leader. He has little understanding of, or interest in, economic development or modernization—the things that peace can bring. He has suffered greatly for his ideals. To him Bosnia is more an abstraction, not several million people who overwhelmingly want peace. Haris [Silajdzic, the prime minister], on the other hand, is more modern and focused heavily on economic reconstruction, something Izetbegovic never mentions."

So it was the victims who were as always the least realistic and had to be squeezed the hardest. The entire three-week conference demanded almost inhuman reserves of energy, toughness, and guile on the part of the lead nego-tiator. One additional strength Holbrooke brought to the talks, a curious one, was a product of his ego, his flair for the dramatic, and his sense that life was in part theater. It was his ability to impress on the others that this was a historic moment and the entire world was watching them. If they did not recognize that and move with it, then history might pass them by. They had to be ready to play their appropriate roles. In the end Holbrooke not only outlasted the various Balkan representatives, he outbullied them, driving them to do what he was sure was good for them even if they did not yet recognize it them-selves. "Why did your man Holbrooke do so well in Dayton?" Jacques Chirac once asked Bill Clinton. "Because he has the same character as Milosevic," Clinton answered. That was both true and untrue, but during that amazing three-week conference, he found the resources to bring home a peace settle-ment from as difficult a group of parties as any negotiator had ever faced.

Holbrooke brought an imperfect peace to a very imperfect part of the world after an unusually cruel war. "Did Dayton," Holbrooke shrewdly asked at the end of his own book on those years, "bring peace to Bosnia or only the absence of war?"[3] There would be two states, a -Croat-Bosnian Federation based in Sarajevo and, surrounding it like a badly designed hat, a Bosnian Serb republic; the contours of both resembled what the battlefield positions had been at the end of the fighting. It was, as Michael Ignatieff wrote, a "de facto ethnic partition." Among the many ironies to that settlement, it was, as some critics believed, only slightly better than the Vance-Owen peace plan that the administration had so arrogantly disdained two and a half years earlier, which, had it gone through, might have saved hundreds of thousands of lives.

The settlement demanded that the Americans station twenty thousand men on the ground as peacekeepers, and that put the president at risk as he was about to enter an election campaign. On the final day of Dayton when it appeared the conference was going to break up without success, a number of Clinton's domestic advisers were greatly relieved, because they feared a set-tlement and worried that if we sent in peacekeepers and events blew up in Bosnia as they had in Somalia, it would hinder the president's reelection. Rarely had Clinton done something of such import with so little ostensible public support. When he committed American troops to peacekeeping in Bosnia, the polls were running roughly 70 percent against the idea. It was, whatever the upside, and the upside was considerable, still a roll of the dice, and it took extraordinary courage on his part to make that decision.

But the peace was incomplete in many ways. The shadows of Vietnam and Somalia still loomed: the possibility of being impaled and losing young Americans in defense of a strategy that had no end. The fear of body bags was always there. The White House, without consultation with the people who had worked out the details of the Dayton plan, decided to put a time limit on the troop commitment—twelve months. It was a sure sign of presidential caution and the apprehensions of his White House political advisers, some of whom had not wanted the Dayton settlement in the first place and had covertly been rooting against it. It was a completely unrealistic deadline that had nothing to do with the problems that any peacekeeping force was likely to encounter on the ground. But it would cover the period of the 1996 election.

It was a waffle of the first order, done strictly for domestic political considerations. If it was designed to send a signal to the Congress and to the American people, it sent an even more powerful one to our European allies, a sign that we were not necessarily committed. It also convinced Slobodan Milosevic that we might have little real staying power. It was exactly the wrong message to send, especially because the Republican Senate leader, Bob Dole, a major Bosnian hawk, was perfectly willing to help Clinton avoid any time limit. Dole was perhaps one of the last figures from the internationalist bipartisan generation of the past, and he had not only been helpful to Clinton on Bosnia, but would not use it as a campaign issue. More typical of the new face of the Republican Party and the Congress was Newt Gingrich, who authorized a resolution supporting the members of the armed forces who might go to the Balkans, but not the policy that sent them there. It was a perfect insight into the schizophrenia of post–Cold War American foreign policy. It passed, 287–141.

CHAPTER THIRTY-TWO

The Clinton people had a settlement in Bosnia, but they still did not have a foreign policy. There was a big difference between the two. They had dealt with Bosnia because it had the potential to go from foreign policy disaster to domestic political problem, and they had shown great skill in negotiating an acceptable settlement in Dayton. The president was taking no small risk in sending more than twenty thousand American soldiers to Bosnia on the eve of a political campaign. Any other policy involved risk as well. But they had pulled it off: Dayton was viewed as a considerable accomplishment, and it greatly steadied Clinton's reputation. It was regarded as his first major foreign policy success. That the talks had been held on American soil added to the resonance of the victory. They had taken that gamble and won.

It would not of itself be a decisive factor in saving Clinton in the 1996 election, but it ended the hemorrhaging caused by all the uncertainty in foreign policy and helped kill off the image of a vacillating Clinton who was not worthy of the larger role of president of the United States. A number of other factors had also come together to work in his behalf. Where he had seemed almost too young in 1992, by 1996 he was fifty. He had aged considerably in his term in office, his hair grayer, his face more lined. He no longer seemed too young— rather he represented the perfect center of the nation's political demographics. Bob Dole, his opponent, surely the last World War II veteran to run for the presidency, seemed by contrast too old, a victim of those same demographics, out of touch in many ways, most notably when he referred to the Dodgers, by then for almost forty years a Los Angeles team, as the Brooklyn Dodgers.

The economy had kicked in and the political risk Clinton had taken early in his first term had been handsomely justified. The Dow had nearly doubled. It had been at around 3,260 on the eve of the election in October 1992 when he ran against Bush; four years later in the middle of the campaign against Dole, it was at 6,029, with most of the rise coming in the last year. Equally important, the Nasdaq, until then a relatively minor economic index, but soon to begin to rival the Dow because of the powerful impact of the new high-technology companies, had also doubled, from 605 to 1,226. Comparably, unemployment was dropping; it had been just under 8 percent in 1992 and was now about 5.5 and falling.

Certainly the signal that the Clinton administration would take on the budget deficit had been a great spur to economic growth, but a number of other economic trends contributed as well, among them the post–Cold War boom as vast parts of Eastern Europe were opened up to a capitalist economy, a benefit that came too late for Bush; the fact that with the Cold War over, the nation could concentrate more and more of its economic—and political—energies on a peacetime economy; and finally the explosion of the new high-tech economy, the beginning of what appeared to be a historic change in the nature of the way people did business. That created (at the upper levels at least) great wealth, record numbers of millionaires and even billionaires. Clinton, surrounded by an unusually able economic team, was president when all these forces came together, leading to an almost unparalleled bull market.

He seemed more comfortable in the presidency. He had mastered the presidential walk; he did not have quite the jauntiness of Reagan, but it was, all things considered, a very good walk. His presidential salute had become smart and crisp. He was finally recognized even by doubters and critics for what he really was, first and foremost an absolutely stunning natural politician, someone who was always on and always working. He had handled perfectly a major assault from Newt Gingrich and his people, letting them overplay their hand when they briefly shut down the government in a battle over the budget. There had been one memorable moment during the shutdown when Clinton met with Gingrich in a private conversation that the Speaker would later relate. "Do you know who I am?" Clinton asked Gingrich. "No," the Speaker answered. "I'm the big rubber clown doll you had as a kid, and every time you hit it, it bounces back up." Clinton paused for a moment. "That's me, the harder you hit me, the faster I come back up." It was a fascinating insight into the way Clinton saw himself and it seemed absolutely accurate. Gingrich had played into his hands. Clinton had once again been lucky in the enemies he had drawn. He knew that the American people might be for some kind of rollback of entitlements as long as they were not *their* entitlements. If they were on occasion displeased by a government that taxed its citizens too promiscuously, they also did not like to see a hard and cruel face on their government.

Clinton understood that among many on the fundamentalist right, there was a veneer of nostalgia for the simpler time of the fifties, when America was a predominantly white society and the old hierarchy still held. But when you pushed through that veneer, it turned out to be thin. A lot of Americans, women, younger people, nonwhites, gays, even middle-class whites, were not nostalgic for an earlier era that they regarded as at least partially repressive. Even those who were nostalgic more often than not wanted their *neighbors* to live as they had in the fifties, creating a society with greater surface civility, while *they themselves* enjoyed the vastly greater freedoms and rewards of the booming economy and the livelier lifestyle of the nineties. Clinton was very much a candidate of the nineties.

He was reelected easily in 1996. He had carved out what he perceived to be a cautious centrism and hewed to that line. Always empathetic—it sometimes seemed to be his ideology—he was, as always, unusually tuned in to the country's voices and its resulting political balances. His constituency by 1996 was not that different from the one that had carried him home the first time. He received a minority of white male votes and did well with nonwhites, women, and gays. He carried the women's vote 54–38. The abortion issue still rested on the shoulders of the Republican Party like a giant albatross in national elections. Foreign policy, naturally, went on the back burner again. There were no easy votes there, but it could on occasion, as it had with Dayton in 1995, polish up the image of a sitting president preparing to run for reelection, just as it could have, if carelessly handled, caused him grave damage.

That meant that Dayton done, the second Clinton administration no longer cared a great deal about the Balkans. But Slobodan Milosevic cared. He had regarded Dayton as something of a victory. If not an all-out winner, he had been a partial power broker there and had departed the scene as Slobodan the Good. It had, ironically, been the Bosnian Muslims, who had suffered for so long before the conference, who were recalcitrant at Dayton, the potential deal breakers, not Milosevic. Now he had his eye on something that had not come up at the peace talks: Kosovo. The Dayton deal done, he thought about the Balkans all the time, while the people in the White House, the reelection over, thought about it as little as possible. There was no eager pursuit of Karadzic or Mladic, the indicted war criminals, no attempt to influence Serbian politics. Some people who had been a part of the Dayton process believed that it was critically important to arrest those two Bosnian Serb leaders. If they remained at large, it would send the wrong signal to Milosevic and throughout Bosnia.

But a serious split quickly reemerged between the military and the civilians, not only about engagement in the Balkans, but also about the Dayton Accords. The civilians believed they would work only if the military enforced them enthusiastically and identified those known troublemakers who were sworn to destroy them. But to some in the military that presented the possibility of placing American troops in too aggressive a role, and becoming too openly involved in local politics, which smacked of a prelude to another Somalia, and they shied away from it. Wasn't going after Mladic and Karadzic the same as going after Aidid? The civilians who had engineered the deal and understood how fragile it was were furious about what they viewed as the essential passivity of the military. Admiral Leighton Smith, the American military commander in the region, appeared to believe that his job was only to keep a military peace and had no interest in arresting anyone who might undermine it. Karadzic apparently glorified in the casual attitude of the American peacekeepers. When Dick Holbrooke, about to return to the private sector, visited Smith for their last meeting in February 1996, he mentioned a *Washington Post* story by John Pomfret about how Karadzic had brazenly driven through four NATO checkpoints in one recent day, two of them manned by Americans. Smith cursed Pomfret, Holbrooke noted, but did not deny the story. His forces, he insisted, would not go after indicted war criminals.

Smith privately infuriated the civilians. Nor did they think that General George Joulwan, the SACEUR, the American military commander of NATO, was pushing Smith or others in his command to make the accords work. The White House was also unhappy with Joulwan, and in the summer of 1997, in what some civilians felt was an upgrade for the Balkan policy, he was replaced by a man who would eventually become a major player in the entire theater, a young four-star named Wes Clark. Clark had been Holbrooke's military counterpart at Dayton, making sure that whatever peace treaty they came up with was enforceable. Some of the civilians who had watched the difficult Dayton negotiations regarded Clark as one of the quiet heroes of Dayton. He had shown considerable courage, they believed, in trying to work out a scenario that would be militarily enforceable, even as he had to know that almost no one in the Pentagon was behind him and many senior people were against any peacekeeping role. He had, they thought, put himself at risk with his own institution. Now returned to Europe as a commander, appalled by the passivity of the troops under his command and the degree to which they were not enforcing the accords, he immediately upgraded their mission.

Clark had a personal loathing for Milosevic by then, having dealt with him for three years. Clark was also aware that many of the senior civilians were very unhappy with the way the military was failing to enforce the Dayton Accords. So he believed he had a mandate to strengthen the agreement, go after Serb war criminals, and cut down the Serb propaganda coming out of their radio center. In September 1997, still quite new on the job, he drew up his plans for a more aggressive military role in support of Dayton's political ends and flew to Washington to show them to Bill Cohen, by then the secretary of defense. Cohen's face fell, Clark remembered, as he outlined some of what he intended to do, a quick warning sign, he sensed. "I'm within your guidelines, aren't I, sir?" Clark asked the secretary. "Just barely," Cohen answered. His reply revealed how deep the rift between civilians and military over the Balkans already was. Other than Clark, the military did not want to make any move that might engage American forces in more than a minimal way.

For the West, it was business as usual, and business was as far from the Balkans as most senior people could get. For Milosevic, it was also business as usual, and business was right there at home, primarily in Kosovo. Kosovo, much more than Bosnia, had always been the most explosive part of Yugoslavia, the raw, unfinished political contradiction handed down by those

364 / DAVID HALBERSTAM

who had drawn up the peace after World War I to those who would eighty years later try to deal with the barely suppressed violence it had created. It was in Kosovo where the past hung most heavily, where the hatreds were most bitter and closer to the surface, and where there was the least pluralism, the least blending of different cultures. Demographically it was primarily settled by the Kosovar Albanians, who were Muslims, though many centuries earlier they had been Christians and had accepted Islam only reluctantly under Ottoman rule. They constituted 90 percent of the population, a percentage constantly going up because their families were larger; it had been closer to 72 percent right after World War II. But in the minds of all Serbs, Kosovo was sacred soil that belonged to them. One additional fact about Kosovo technically limited the leverage of foreign powers to intervene when it became a front-burner crisis. At the time of the breakup of Yugoslavia, it had merely been a *province,* not a republic, and the West had eventually favored independence for the *republics* (Slovenia, Croatia, Bosnia, Macedonia), but not for the provinces. That made it a complicated issue, since it was more clearly part of traditional Yugoslavia, and the question of sovereignty was a greater problem than it had been in Bosnia.

In Kosovo, history had been not only cruel but often whimsical. The only certainty was that today's winners would be tomorrow's losers, and today's oppressors tomorrow's oppressed. That cycle had existed in perpetuity; it knew no beginning and, tragically, no end. Over the years it had produced the cruelest human wounds, the most bitter family histories—every family had lost someone to a sworn ethnic enemy—and, inevitably, the most deeply ingrained ethnic hatreds. The Albanians or the Serbs might temporarily seize power, either on their own or as a part of a new alliance with some great power. But history in Europe had proved fickle over many centuries, and soon there would be another terrible war, followed by another great upheaval. The vanquished would become the victors with the right to torment those who had so recently tormented them. In the ebb and flow of the Balkans and Kosovo, carnage faithfully followed carnage, someone taking vengeance on the person who had only so recently, perhaps a mere century or two before, taken vengeance on him.

In 1908, some eighty-seven years before Milosevic returned to Belgrade from Dayton, the British travel writer Edith Durham had described the hatred between the Serbs and the Kosovar Albanians after a trip to Kosovo: "Blood can be wiped out only with blood." What existed in Kosovo, she wrote, was absolutely primal, men behaving in effect like animals, "an elemental struggle for existence and survival of the strongest carried out in obedience to Nature's law, which says 'There is not place for you both. You must kill—or be killed.' Ineradicably fixed in the breast of an Albanian . . . is the belief that the land has been his rightly for all time. The Serb conquered him, held him for a few passing centuries, was swept out, and shall never return again. He has but done to the Serb as he was done by."[1]

The tensions between the Albanians and the Serbs had been aggravated in recent years with the level of violence steadily mounting. Constitutional changes wrought under Tito in 1974 had given greater autonomy to the Albanians and led to the Albanianization of the region's administrative sector. That, in turn, had enabled the Albanians to squeeze the local Serbs more than in the past. But events outside the province accelerated events inside. Restraints on both the Albanians and the Serbs, never that overwhelming in the best of times, were greatly loosened by the stirrings of nationalism in Eastern Europe and the gradual weakening of Soviet control in much of the rest of what had once been behind the Iron Curtain. As that happened, both sides in the Kosovo dispute were emboldened, the Albanians to seek greater sovereignty, and eventually to unleash new violence on the Serbs, while the Serbs, finally released from Tito's enforced pluralism, felt freer to lash back at the Albanians. The struggle for Kosovo had intensified in the late eighties, helping to catapult Milosevic to power and creating a new ethnic jingoism throughout the country.

To those who knew the Balkans well, Kosovo, not Bosnia, had always been the flash point. Bosnia had seen a constant movement toward some kind of pluralist society until it was torn apart by the deliberate attempts of both Milosevic and Tudjman to destroy that pluralism and escalate ethnic hatreds. That was not true of Kosovo. There the people spoke different languages and had different and completely contradictory histories. Kosovo was like Palestine, sacred land claimed by two bitter combatants. It was not by surprise that the Bush administration had, in its final days, issued the Christmas Warning to Milosevic, saying that the United States would not tolerate any additional aggression against the Albanians in Kosovo.

Kosovo had not been mentioned at Dayton, where the focus was on dealing with *Bosnia*, and neither Milosevic, Tudjman, nor Izetbegovic wanted it on the docket. Dayton had mercifully ended the fighting in Bosnia, but it had left unanswered other questions that still festered there and had escalated the tensions over Kosovo. To complete the deal, Holbrooke and his team badly needed Milosevic's cooperation in bringing his Bosnian Serb underlings along, but they could not have him as a de facto partner and talk about Kosovo. So Kosovo was *never* on the table. Only for one brief moment did Kosovo, in the most peripheral way, come up. Holbrooke and Milosevic were going for a walk around the perimeter of the Wright-Patterson base when they noticed a large group of Albanian-Americans, some of them armed with megaphones, just outside the fence, pleading for the rights of the Kosovars. Holbrooke suggested that they talk to the protesters. No way he was going to do that, Milosevic replied. These people were only there because they were paid for by a foreign power. Besides, he said, Kosovo was an internal problem, not the business of anyone at Dayton except him. Holbrooke disagreed, but that was as far as it went. If Kosovo had come up, there would have been no deal on Bosnia.

In fact, Dayton would make Kosovo more difficult because a political dynamic had been created that would have profound and immediate implications there. For it had undermined the cause of Kosovars like Ibrahim Rugova, who had in the past argued for a nonviolent path to power. Rugova was a classic nonviolent leader. On the wall of his home in Pristina were pictures of Martin Luther King, Gandhi, and the Dalai Lama. Now his critics, younger men and women who had always urged a more violent path to power with the use of arms, could make their case. Look what nonviolence and passive resistance have gotten us: not just more brutal repression by the Serbs, but when the Western powers finally convened a peace conference, we were not invited to the table, nor was our country even mentioned. Only those who had fought and shed blood were treated with respect at Dayton, they could say.

Dayton undermined those who favored a political solution and strengthened those in Kosovo who urged military action, in effect the creation of a guerrilla army. In 1997, two years after Dayton, the KLA, the Kosovo Liberation Army, began to form into a movement. Rarely had any guerrilla group gone so quickly from being a mere idea to becoming a fighting force with important political repercussions. At the time of Dayton, the KLA was virtually nonexistent. Two years later, it had some fifteen thousand to twenty thousand members, arms were flowing in from different nations that wished it well (and wished Milosevic ill), especially from Albania, aided by the Albanian diaspora outside Europe. Moreover, it was the beneficiary of previous events in the Balkans because the media representatives still on hand had something of a post-Bosnia anti-Serb bias, which the KLA would be able to play upon.

By the fall of 1997, the KLA was on the move. It began to strike at the Serbs in classic guerrilla style. Relatively small units, often inadequately trained, but carrying significant weaponry—Kalashnikovs—formed up to hit local Serb officials or policemen who were isolated in small villages and largely defenseless. They struck where the Serbs were most vulnerable, always trying to capture weapons if they could. To those who knew the story of Algeria or Vietnam, it was like instant replay. They also struck at those Kosovars whom they believed had collaborated with or accommodated the Serbs. A militant Kosovo was like a paradox within a paradox, as writer Tim Judah pointed out, for it represented "the ultimate Serbian nightmare: its own Vietnam. That was ironic since Serbian leaders had long promised the West its own Balkan Vietnam should its forces intervene."[2]

The KLA aims were multiple: first to assault the Serbs on the ground, to make them feel vulnerable and reduce their mobility; second, to wrest power away from Rugova by assuming a more aggressive posture; and finally, to escalate tensions and thereby provoke Milosevic and the Serbs to retaliate in a way that would bring the West in as a de facto ally, much as it had finally entered the earlier struggle over Bosnia. The last was the most important. If the KLA struck often and provocatively enough, the Serbs could almost surely be counted on to react ever more violently, and in time a dynamic would be created and the West would once again witness Serb atrocities. Every partner to the conflict, it soon appeared, would play his assigned role. Inevitably the Serbs struck back, and as the violence escalated, the flexibility of everyone involved decreased. The entrance of the KLA meant that it was no longer a two-power dynamic, the West dealing with Milosevic. The KLA was now a third party, hardly able to win a war on its own, but quite able to provoke Milosevic and thus limit or undo any attempt at a compromise that the West might want to offer, perhaps some increased autonomy for the Kosovo Albanians under Serb rule. Even the United States, at first watching from a distance and not paying much attention, would have less control over the situation than it expected.

As the Serbs struck back at the KLA, its leaders got what they wanted, an escalating cycle of violence and, of course, instant martyrs. In mid-October 1997, Adrian Krasniqi, a member of a family of KLA extremists and a supplier of Kalashnikovs to the KLA, became the first KLA soldier to be killed in uniform during a raid on a Serbian police station. Some thirteen thousand people attended his funeral. Incident begot incident. Albanian funerals became political events with as many as fifteen thousand or even twenty thousand people turning out. In late November at the funeral of another KLA activist, a KLA gunman removed his mask and made a political speech. "Serbia is massacring Albanians," he cried. "The KLA is the only force that is fighting for the liberation and the national unity of Kosovo. We shall continue to fight!" The crowd began to chant, "KLA! KLA! KLA!"[3] Despite Rugova's statement that the KLA was a Serbian hoax, it was obviously very real. If the KLA was at first a relative minority without the deep support of the Albanian population, the violence of the Serb reprisals made it increasingly popular. It was a familiar cycle. The Vietminh and Vietcong had done the same thing in Indochina. The Serbs predictably began to ratchet up the pressure, burning villages and murdering those who did not flee into the hills. They kept lists of local villagers, killing anyone who was a potential leader, a businessman, a lawyer, those with an education. The Kosovars, in Milosevic's opinion, were less than human anyway.

The West was slow to act once again. Those who had been activists in round one over Bosnia had a sense of déjà vu as Milosevic danced back and forth, at once denying the violence and his role in it, occasionally suppressing it, and then permitting it again. Washington was hardly on top of things, with a new cast of characters on the scene. A change in the White House staff, begun when Leon Panetta, the president's chief of staff, had departed, had created a game of musical chairs, which in the end left Tony Lake as odd man out. The top contestants to replace Panetta had been Erskine Bowles, from the domestic side, and Sandy Berger, Lake's deputy at the NSC. Bowles at first turned the job down, Berger accepted it, and then a few hours later Bowles changed his mind. With that Berger's future was put on hold and he eventually got the offer of Lake's job at the NSC. That meant finding another job for Lake, who was ticketed to go in any case. It had been an imperfect relationship, neither good nor bad and never very comfortable. Lake had never been entirely forgiven for Somalia. Even before the Panetta-Bowles-Berger switch, Clinton had offered the national security adviser job to Strobe Talbott, probably Clinton's closest friend in the national security complex, and one of his oldest confidants. The offer had been tendered in a very Clintonesque fashion. Much like an expert fly fisherman, he had cast the most desirable of all possible flies right above the largest fish in the stream. Talbott, coming over from magazine journalism, had turned out to be one of the more positive surprises, first in charge of dealing with the Russians, and then as the number two in the department. He had complete control of his ego, never poached on other people's territories, and was committed to the greater good of the administration, even if it meant limiting his own territory. Typically, although he had opposed holding the Bosnian peace conference in this country, Talbott had explained in great detail to his friend Holbrooke how to make the successful case for conducting it here.

Talbott was, however, extremely doubtful about taking the NSC job. He had managed to remain close to Clinton over the first four years, he realized, in no small part because he did not work directly for him. Talbott assumed that if he took the NSC job, the criticism of their friendship would be ugly and personal and would eventually work against both of them. Besides, he thought Berger had earned the job, having put in yeoman work in a difficult period and being by nature well-suited to keeping the hydra-headed NSC complex working. In any case, Talbott was primarily interested in finishing his own work, which was the expansion of NATO, along with trying to allay Russian fears that the East European nations, once Russian satellites, would now be members of an organization that in Russian eyes had for so long been sworn to their destruction. Thus, when the fly offered by the president floated above him, Talbott did not rise to it. But the offer itself had shown that Lake would be leaving.

Lake, meanwhile, was offered a number of ambassadorships and eventually the job as head of the CIA. But his confirmation was not at all assured, and for a time he hung in the wind. Considerable anger and resentment had accumulated against him (and even more against the president he had served—so that striking at Lake was a marvelous way to strike at Clinton). A careless failure to follow through on the paperwork putting his stocks in a blind trust had made him vulnerable on issues of ethics, and he finally went before the Joint Intelligence Committee to testify on the Hill. His appearance there did not go well, and he struck a number of senators as aloof and somewhat hostile. In time he withdrew his name. That meant that Lake, who had pushed harder than anyone else at the top of the administration for some kind of action on Bosnia, now watched from the outside as history repeated itself in Kosovo, frequently calling his old aides in the NSC office to urge them to take a harder line on Milosevic. It also meant that a national security adviser who thought that the impact of domestic politics on foreign policy should be minimized was going to be replaced by Berger, who always reflected, first and foremost, Bill Clinton's political attitudes and agenda.

At State with Warren Christopher retiring, the question of who would succeed him was intriguing and the possible choices reflected different constituencies surfacing in the Democratic Party and in Washington. There were four finalists. The old boy network pushed for either Sam Nunn or George Mitchell. Nunn, politically the most conservative of the candidates, was advanced by Vernon Jordan, a fellow Georgian and very much a traditionalist and Washington insider, while a number of people in the party liked Mitchell, the Maine Democrat who had been a skillful negotiator on Northern Ireland. Mitchell was recommended by Christopher, who was more comfortable with him than he was with anyone else. He was also delighted to be able to favor someone so distinguished with such a fine track record because it meant that he could avoid being for Madeleine Albright without seeming to be against the women's movement.

The candidates from inside the administration were Dick Holbrooke and Albright, who had served at the United Nations. Here the choice was intriguing. Holbrooke had come through for the administration at Dayton, thereby removing foreign policy as a liability in the 1996 campaign. But because he was Holbrooke, he still inspired strong feelings among those who were for him and those who were against him. He would, if chosen, be a formidable secretary of state, but there was the threat that if he got the job, he might take it all too seriously and push the president harder than any other potential candidate. Both Strobe Talbott and Al Gore were for Holbrooke. Gore at one point had even called Holbrooke in Bhutan, where he was vacationing with friends, to tell him to come back to Washington to help make his own case. He was a finalist, but neither Christopher nor Lake supported him. Again and again he was said not to be a team player. He might have dazzled Christopher by his performance in Dayton, but the emotional if not ideological differences between the two men were simply too great, and Christopher remained uneasy about him. With Lake the breach between the two former friends was wider than ever.

The political forces aligned against Holbrooke, if it came down to a choice between him and Albright, were considerable because Albright was backed by a formidable new force within the Democratic Party, an important network of politically active women. Yet the senior Clinton national security people when speaking of her in private rarely showed any enthusiasm. Some of the feelings against her were inevitably sexist, since she was a pioneer in a man's world. However, the general view among her peers was that she was acceptably talented, not exceptional in intellect, and much given, especially with the skills of Jamie Rubin, her press officer, to media grandstanding and self-promotion, which, of course, was also said of Holbrooke. Of the four candidates, she was perceived by those watching the inside game—mostly men, of course—to be the weakest. She had been a hawk from the start on Bosnia and detested Milosevic, but except for one or two occasions, she had not been taken that seriously by her peers.

Nunn was quickly canceled out; he was a good deal more conservative than the president, and the two men were only marginally compatible. Mitchell had something of a problem because the Republicans, led by Trent Lott, told the White House that if he was nominated, it would be payback time for the defeat of John Tower as secretary of defense, a Democratic victory in which Mitchell had played a leading role. Holbrooke's pluses were more obvious as were his deficits: he might well be the most talented, but he was guaranteed to provoke controversy and would be harder to control in office. That Christopher did not back him was damaging. Besides, in the event of some kind of critical mission that demanded an unusually gifted negotiator, he could always be brought in from the outside. His skills were such that the administration might be able to get the best of him without offering him the job he wanted, thus avoiding the Sturm und Drang he might create. For Holbrooke, the decision was devastating. Albright it would be. Clinton had admired her performance before a large and enthusiastic crowd in the Orange Bowl in Miami when she had dusted off Castro—and he knew a rising political star when he saw one. Besides, the temptation to name the first woman secretary of state was irresistible. At Defense, Bill Perry was replaced by Bill Cohen, who had in the past been regarded as something of a Balkan dove.

The new team had not yet begun to tackle the Balkans. The critical missing player, as it had been in round one on Bosnia, was the president. He could not fail to understand the consequences of always being reactive in the Balkans; he knew how relentless—and slippery—Milosevic was and where his primal political instincts would lead him. But Bill Clinton was preoccupied with a far more pressing matter—his very survival as president.

CHAPTER THIRTY-THREE

In early 1998, at exactly the same time that Kosovo was beginning to explode in violence, back in Washington the various groups that had been pursuing the president for several years on whether he had made sexual advances toward a woman named Paula Jones stumbled onto what might have been, in terms of White House promiscuity, a mother lode.

On the morning of January 21, the banner headline in the *Washington Post* was not about Kosovo or Milosevic or the increasing strength of the KLA. Not at all. The headline read: "Clinton Accused of Urging Aide to Lie; Starr Probes Whether President Told Woman to Deny Alleged Affair to Jones' Lawyers." Thus did the nation begin to learn about a young woman named Monica Lewinsky. There was growing evidence that the president had had some kind of sexual relationship with Lewinsky, a twenty-four-year-old former White House intern, who had in one searingly romantic moment seduced him in his own office by flirtatiously lifting her skirt and flashing both her thong underwear and her youthful ass at him. He, a man not famous for his resistance to sexual temptation, apparently took that as an invitation. In that wildly seductive moment, when the culture of *Beverly Hills 90210* met the culture of good old boy Arkansas politics, the entire Clinton administration had been placed in jeopardy. ("I thonged him," Lewinsky later explained to Linda Tripp, her onetime confidante.[1])

When the story broke, Clinton immediately denied the relationship with, as he so gallantly described his paramour, "that woman, Miss Lewinsky." (He used the phrase not so much to distance himself from her, he later confided to his Hollywood producer friend Harry Thomason, but because he had momentarily forgotten her first name.[2]) Not everyone believed his denial, for he had been linked with a long trail of women—Gennifer Flowers, Paula Jones, and now Monica Lewinsky—and some people were ungenerous enough to think that they all had one thing in common: a certain aura of accessibility. (The sexual lure of presidential power, and the notable lack of Clinton's own discipline, meant that his various staff members had always been aware, especially on presidential trips, of the need to keep women away from the president. Someone was usually detailed to say no on his behalf because of fears that it would not be his own instinctive response.) It would take well more than a year of his denials, some of them extremely petulant, and Lewinsky's own testimony to a grand jury before Clinton admitted that she had indeed performed oral sex on him in the White House. What followed was presidential politics not as high art, but as low soap. At times Mike McCurry, the White House press spokesman, found himself trying to explain to a vast horde of journalists (who hungered for more and more of this X-rated sitcom) and to the nation at large—something his parents had almost surely not raised him to do—what the difference was, as the president of the United States of America perceived it, between having sex and having oral sex. Of all the jobs in the federal government at that moment, his might have been the worst. "It's like we're standing under Niagara Falls, looking for a boat to get us out of here," the beleaguered McCurry said at one point.[3]

Ms. Lewinsky, a somewhat insecure young woman who was the product of a broken home in Los Angeles, had constant problems with her weight and seemed to find emotional relief in what was known as American Express therapy, that is, credit card shopping sprees—a true child of the modern American mall. She had been involved with older men before and had virtually stalked one teacher, following him and his family to Oregon. She had obviously been infatuated with Clinton and his power, ready if need be to replace Hillary, who in her mind was cold and unsympathetic. Lewinsky would watch a presidential motorcade with the president and the first lady go by and tell her confidante Linda Tripp that she resented not being the one in the car with him.[4] By December of 1997, she seemed to be too infatuated, and the president tried to break off the relationship, giving her as farewell presents a stuffed animal bought at the Black Dog store on Martha's Vineyard, a pair of goofy sunglasses, a Rockettes blanket, and a box of chocolates. They had parted with what Lewinsky later described as a passionate kiss. But she was unable to keep their special secret entirely to herself. The political carelessness of what Clinton had done was staggering, and yet very Clintonesque, to risk so much for so little at such an important moment in his political career. Though already being pursued by several right-wing posses who were obsessed by his character, or lack thereof, he had still courted danger in his own office, where nothing was ever secret, with an impressionable young woman who would probably, sooner or later, blather. Was there anyone more likely to talk about what had happened between them than an ego-driven, infatuated, somewhat delusional post-teenager from Beverly Hills, not necessarily the citadel of personal restraint and modesty? After all, her greatest moment had been the conquest of the president of the United States, albeit a conquest, she later complained, that had taken place on her knees, saying her real title should have been "Special Assistant to the President for Blow Jobs."[5] She also referred to him as the Big Creep.

Lovelorn because it appeared that the relationship had been more functional than romantic, Lewinsky soon babbled into the hidden microphone of an alleged friend, Linda Tripp, whose purpose was not to offer friendship or to console a young girl in an emotional crisis, but to provide formidable amounts of ammunition for those Americans who wanted to take down William Jefferson Clinton. Later Tripp tried to rationalize her treachery: "I never considered Monica a friend. We never spent time together outside the office, nor discussed my life. I am not a gossip. The idea that I would cultivate this foolish young girl is offensive. I thought she was a pest. But over time I will say that something kicked in, not a sense of pity . . ."[6] The right wing, especially the fundamentalists, had hated Clinton because they always believed he would do something *exactly* like that, and now, by God, he had done it and made them prophets. Details about what Clinton and Lewinsky had done and where they had done it soon began to trickle out and eventually became a flood. Lewinsky, not surprisingly, was terrified by her role in the scandal and the degree to which she had been singled out by history. Yet on occasion, she appeared to be thrilled by her notoriety as well, and when her brief moment of Warholian fame was coming to a close, she seemed to be eager to stay in the spotlight.

Clinton had put at risk his entire second term, all the leverage his comfortable reelection margin had provided him. The nation watched transfixed, millions of ordinary citizens caught between self-dislike for being Peeping Toms and impatience for more lurid details. All sorts of media titans shrugged and spoke of how much they hated covering something like this, then covered it with an energy rarely seen when it came to budget disputes or foreign policy issues. Sam Donaldson, one of the leading personalities on ABC television, went on the air almost immediately and said that if Clinton was not telling the truth, "I think his presidency is numbered in days." That turned out to be absolutely prophetic; his presidency *was* numbered in days, but the number, some three years later when Clinton finally left office, was almost 1,100.

Clinton's wife staunchly defended him on national television against what she called a vast right-wing conspiracy. In one of the lowest moments of his presidency, Clinton also sent the women members of his cabinet out to speak on his behalf, and regrettably they did just that, vouching for a version of the story that was, unfortunately for them, untrue. All of this was the performance not of Clinton the masterful politician who could shrewdly weigh the odds and consequences of every political act and sense what was best for the country, but of Clinton the emotionally truncated man-child, still, some people who knew him thought, more thrilled by the idea of illicit sex than by sex itself. He had never been entirely responsible for his actions and, going back to his Arkansas days, always thought he could get away with whatever he wanted to get away with. And he did get away with it, to a degree. He would be impeached by a partisan vote in the House, but the Senate failed to convict him. Even so, he paid a monstrous price in the coin of his presidency, the coin of what might have been.

All of this meant that the middle of Clinton's second term, instead of being devoted to new initiatives, ones postponed during the first term because of lack of political leverage and pressing economic problems, was devoted to hunkering down to fight off Special Prosecutor Kenneth Starr, a man of uncommon zealotry, and the hard-right Republicans in the Congress, not all of whom had been as faithful to *their* wives as their political righteousness would indicate. (At one point Starr, believing that Ms. Lewinsky had purchased what he believed to be a scatological novel, tried to subpoena the records of her book buying. It was not one of American democracy's finest moments.) Clinton was forced to play defense, not offense, and even when it was all over and he had been impeached but not convicted, he was a badly wounded chief executive, stripped of the prime political capital of any president who intends to bring change, his moral authority. The damage to his presidency was incalculable. The Republicans, as part of their assault on the Democrats in 1998 and 2000, said that Bill Clinton had diminished the office of the presidency. That was probably not true; the presidency rises or falls to the level of the ability and the character of its incumbent. What he had done was something quite different. He had grievously diminished *his own* presidency, which was sinful and foolish enough.

Starting in January 1998 with the first *Washington Post* story, the noose steadily tightened around Clinton's neck. More and more bits of evidence indicated that something had indeed taken place between Clinton and Lewinsky, and that there might, in this age of DNA, be a smoking gun of sorts, in this case a dress stained with presidential semen. Thus it appeared ever more likely that his earlier denials had been lies, and while people might consider him a skilled politician, they did not consider him a paragon of the truth. Now the only real question was whether Lewinsky could hold the line against the special prosecutor's team. As the pressures around the White House grew greater, the bright young men and women who represented the president to the outside world spun the story as best they could. They said that the Lewinsky affair, Monicagate as it was inevitably called, *was not deflecting the president from his appointed duties.* The White House was going on as normal and he was sticking to his job of being president, which was what the American people had elected him to be and wanted him to do. The line was that the president was out there every day selflessly working for all the people, in spite of those vengeful people who would pull him away from his serious responsibilities. That was also the line spun by the Nixon White House when Watergate, a very different kind of scandal, political instead of sexual, had progressed and the young first-lady-to-be Hillary Rodham was working for one of the investigating congressional committees.

Certainly there was not a lot of talk about the scandal in the White House itself, where it was the multiton elephant standing in the corner of the room that was never mentioned. Or as Michael Waldman, a Clinton speechwriter, once noted, "The White House was the one place in the country you could have a two-hour meeting on Bill Clinton and the name Monica Lewinsky wouldn't come up."[7] Despite the public denials, however, the truth about what the president was doing was very different. As soon as the story broke, the White House circled the wagons. All political risks were to be dropped. Coin was to be conserved for this massive winner-take-all political confrontation, and Clinton's vulnerability in other areas instantly went up. A classic example of that came in mid-December 1998 when Secretary of Defense Bill Cohen wanted to bomb Saddam Hussein because he was blocking UN inspectors from certain military sites. Cohen argued first that American credibility overseas depended on such a bombing. If we did not bomb now, Saddam's defiance would only be greater in the future, Cohen said, and other dictators would be encouraged. Then Cohen added the clincher: "If you don't act here, the next argument will be that you're paralyzed." That, as Bob Woodward noted, introduced impeachment (and Lewinsky) into national security decision-making.[8] Such an argument, coming from a long-term Republican politician of notably independent credentials, whose responsibility, along with the Pentagon, was to represent or at least make a read on the Republicans on the Hill, was devastating. Iraq was bombed.[9]

The Clinton presidency was in total jeopardy, and no one knew it better than the president himself. After all, only two people knew for certain that the story was true, Lewinsky, quite terrified by the implications of the events she had set in motion, and the president, who, despite the denials—to his wife, to the country—knew that he was embattled and the clock was ticking against him. The posse was getting closer, and disgrace of monumental proportions possibly awaited him. What Clinton gradually came to face was a Hobson's choice: a short-term personal disgrace of a high order by confessing to egregious misconduct with a young intern, while at the same time trying to hold on to his office and avoid even greater disgrace—impeachment—by claiming that it was personal, not political, misconduct and not grounds for impeachment; or to continue to stonewall his pursuers. Neither choice was particularly attractive. (At one point he even authorized Dick Morris, himself tainted by sexual scandal, to conduct a poll to see if the American people were as yet ready for a public confession. Morris reported back that they were not.) He had played right into the hands of his enemies, and no one knew it better than Clinton.

He was angry and sometimes petulant, and while on occasion he later and somewhat belatedly in public accepted the blame for what he had done, essentially what he really did was blame the fates. "God damn, fuck it," he once said to a friend. "I'm dying [of] a thousand cuts. It's like someone kicked me in the stomach. I've had a knot in my stomach for months." No person, no ordinary citizen, no politician or president, had ever been subjected to anything like this, he complained.[10] To some degree he was right. The sexual behavior of some presidents before him had been comparable and had not been an issue. But this was a different world, and sexual behavior now had a political and media viability it had lacked in the past. Just ask Gary Hart. He had tempted the fates and the fates had bitten him.

Yet even as the Lewinsky scandal played out, both sides escalated the violence in Kosovo. In May of 1998, when Milosevic was beginning to retaliate against the KLA, some people in the administration wanted to use airpower against him. At a meeting in the White House, Bob Gelbhard, who had replaced Holbrooke as the special negotiator, made the case for threatening to use NATO airpower on a list of targets that General Wes Clark had put together, and which they believed would pressure Milosevic to back off in Kosovo. Madeleine Albright had wanted to go ahead and use airpower. Like Clark, she was quite hawkish. But Sandy Berger, who was regarded as a weather vane to Clinton's political mood and needs, and in whose office the meeting was held, quickly and angrily rejected the idea, asking the old Colin Powell question: What happened if airpower did not work? After Berger silenced Gelbhard, no one—not Albright or Strobe Talbott—supported him. Berger had clearly spoken for Clinton. The White House was not yet ready for Kosovo.[11] Too much else was going on at home.

If Albright was the leading hawk in the administration, she backed off for the moment. But in the vacuum that existed in Washington, she was becoming a central player on the Balkans for the first time. She was absolutely certain of her beliefs about what needed to be done in Kosovo. She was convinced the villain was Slobodan Milosevic, and until he was dealt with, nothing good was going to happen. She was also the beneficiary of the dynamic taking place in both Belgrade and Kosovo, where the KLA and Milosevic were tearing at each other in a predictable way, which inevitably made her a prophet because the KLA violence was greeted in much of the world with a degree of sympathy, while the more brutal Serb backlash angered international opinion. As the new secretary of state, Albright would argue for a hard line against the Serbs, saying anything less would only encourage Milosevic. In her opinion negotiations with him were futile and he understood only force. Albright was absolutely sure that Kosovo was a repeat of Bosnia and that the United States would, sooner or later, have to take military action against Belgrade.

No one else in the administration was that certain of events or of what the policy in the Balkans should be; no one else was so ready or so eager to choose that fateful a path. Tony Lake, never entirely tuned to the president, might have been an ally, but he was out of government. Holbrooke might have been on her side, but he, too, was out of government, and his and Albright's personal relationship had always been flawed. They were bitter rivals for the job she had been given, and thus when Holbrooke did come in on special missions—often against her wishes—their combined energy was not as great as it might have been. Moreover, Holbrooke for the moment was not quite as hawkish as Albright; if he was not Milosevic's ally, he had nevertheless worked with him on the Dayton settlement and still believed there might be a solution short of military action. Bill Cohen at Defense was dovish and cautious, an attitude shared by the Joint Chiefs. Sandy Berger was not yet ready for action, and reading him was the purest litmus test as to where the president stood politically on any foreign policy issue. Berger most emphatically reflected the president's desire, if at all possible, to delay any action.

All of this enhanced Albright as a player. In the first Clinton administration she had been very much on the periphery of the decision-making, holding a job that, no matter how extravagant the promises of the president to its would-be occupant, was usually a form of window dressing. Being able to exploit the reputations and distinguished names of former UN ambassadors (Adlai Stevenson, Henry Cabot Lodge, Pat Moynihan, George Bush) was a decided advantage. The post was often given to a well-known figure in the president's party whom the administration wanted to showcase but did not really want to hear from. As a reward for taking such a job, the incumbent ambassadors were often eviscerated by bright young men and women half their age in the NSC office. Albright's tour in Manhattan had not been easy. Representing the United States in the center of the nonwhite political world at a time of waning presidential interest in foreign affairs, and with Jesse Helms chairing the Senate Foreign Relations Committee, was not an enviable task. At the UN, Boutros Boutros-Ghali spoke openly (and snobbishly) about what he considered her shortcomings as a diplomat. In Washington among those who were supposed to be her peers in the administration, the condescension was more muted but no less real.

In part, that reflected the fact that she was an activist at a nonactivist time, and, in part, it meant that the title of ambassador to the UN was often a debit. Some of it, too, was that she was a woman, and power at the top, despite titles, still belonged to the men. It was also true that many of the men occupying the power centers in Washington, in both the executive and congressional branches, did not like her constituents—the poorer and to them noisier nations of Africa and Asia. In Washington, her speech and op-ed pieces on nation-building in Somalia clung to her like a cloak after that disaster. But she seemed to love the UN job, to glory in the celebrity that went with it and the public fascination with her. As a woman in so visible a place, she was something of a star and had access to other stars. She clearly liked that kind of attention and tended to maximize her publicity through the skills of Rubin, her press officer. But that, too, worked against her with her Washington peers, as if she was a little too publicity hungry, which went against the traditional rules of the old boys' club. She was, they said, a bit of a grandstander, though some of the people who said that were known to grandstand themselves.

Of all the high-level people, Albright, along with Holbrooke and Lake, had the fewest doubts about the use of force in Bosnia. She had been especially critical of Colin Powell and the military for their caution. Powell had had reservations about almost all the members of the Clinton team, but she had been a particular irritant, and he often came back from meetings she had attended shaking his head, clearly angered by her. "Madeleine's at it again," he would tell friends. It was all so easy for her, he said. You dropped off a soldier or two here to keep the peace, and a soldier or two there to make the world better, and sooner or later you had a policy. But you would also have American soldiers strung out vulnerably all over the world with little domestic political support.

The ease with which Albright was willing to dispatch troops, some observers thought, was because of all her high-level peers she was the person least affected by Vietnam. It was as if, in foreign policy terms, she had simply skipped a generation. She was literally and figuratively a child of Munich, the Holocaust, and the post–World War II descent of the Iron Curtain, not of the Vietnam experience, and of the American military being impaled in an unpopular, unwinnable war twelve thousand miles away, and the doubts it had created among many of her contemporaries about America's use of its power. The passions of the Vietnam era, though she was just coming of age at that time, graduating from college in 1959, just a few years before Vietnam began to emerge as the dominant concern for the most politically involved people of her generation, always remained distant. Instead, she was very much a product of her personal history. She had arrived in America at the age of eleven, her family barely escaping Czechoslovakia when the Soviets engineered a coup in 1948. Like so many immigrants from Eastern Europe, her family was intensely anticommunist, and she and her parents were unusually grateful for their place in America. As a young woman, Albright was not eager to criticize America or its foreign policy even during one of its most tormented periods; she was not about to disparage the strong, generous hand that had welcomed her and her family. To her, this country even in its darkest moment had been America the hospitable and the just.

Her father, Josef Korbel, who had been a high-level official in the Czech foreign ministry in the years after World War II, had shaped her thinking. The great event forming his postwar political prism was the crude domination of once sovereign Eastern European countries by the local communist governments controlled by Moscow—an invisible occupation supported by a combination of the Red Army and the secret police. Korbel had escaped first the Nazis, then the communists, and had come to America at the age of thirty-nine with a ceiling imposed on his own career. What it might have been had he been born here and what it was for a newly arrived, middle-aged immigrant working in an alien language were very different things. His dreams limited by the upheavals he had witnessed, he would look to Madeleine, the oldest and most intellectually talented of his three children, to fulfill his ambitions.

Friendly government agencies found him a position teaching foreign policy at the University of Denver, and though he might have been moderately liberal on domestic issues, on foreign policy he remained unbendingly anticommunist, a hawk during the Vietnam War, deeply offended by the student protests of that period. He had fled his native land because of the Nazis, knowing that almost all of his and his wife's family had died in concentration camps. He had returned to his home right after the war during that brief time when Czechoslovakia teetered between the West and the East. But even then the vulnerability of his life had made him both smart and nimble, and he understood that the future for Czechoslovakia lay not in its idealism and its democratic aspirations, but in its geography. While serving as the Czech ambassador to Belgrade in 1948, aware that the iron hand of Moscow was about to descend on Prague, he went to the British ambassador and got British visas for himself and his family, receiving them just before the Soviet coup.

Korbel had, it could be said, a hard-earned anticipatory sense of the vagaries of modern European history and the unspeakable price paid in the twentieth century by those who were Jewish. Though both he and his wife were Jews, in May 1941 they had become Roman Catholic, keeping their ethnic origins a secret from their children. The persecution he had already seen in his lifetime was bad enough, and he understood all too well it was soon going to get even worse. He sought no extra burdens, and certainly not in America, once he had arrived as an immigrant in a strange nation that might have its own more covert prejudices. The New World might be more enlightened than the Old, but it was just easier to be Catholic. Or as his wife, Mandula Spiegel Korbel, once told a friend, "To be a Jew is to be constantly threatened by some kind of danger. That is our history."[12] He also dropped the umlaut over the *o* in *Korbel,* thus making the name for those knowledgeable about that kind of thing, and there were a great many of them in Europe, albeit fewer in America, a bit more Germanic. It was one more step in de-Semitizing himself.

What he—a historian and political scientist—did to his own children is a fascinating example of the mind-set and the paranoia of a certain kind of survivor. Korbel sought a fresh start in the New World, not for himself, for he knew the limits of his own career, but for them; he wanted his children as unburdened as possible by the past. But in so doing he denied his own personal history to his children, thereby denying them a crucial part of *their* personal histories. He withheld the true story of the cruel murders of their grandparents, aunts, uncles, and cousins, and he set his daughter up for the terrible embarrassment that would descend upon her at the height of her career. For only after she became secretary of state and a reporter named Michael Dobbs of the *Washington Post* began pursuing what were quite recognizable roadmarks along the path of her own unusual journey did Madeleine Albright find out about her Jewish background. She appeared to be, as someone who knew her said, the last to know, though while she was at the UN, a number of other governments (the Czechs and Israelis, for example) had clearly known the truth of her ethnic roots. It was also clear that several attempts had been made to tell her at least part of the truth of her family's history. Given the number of her relatives who had perished in the death camps, given her mother's maiden name, given what became, as she rose in prominence, little desire to connect to those few who were still alive back in Prague and to learn more about her roots, she apparently understood as an adult exactly how much to know and how much not to know. If the family's harrowing journey had left her father and mother with a need to change what they had been, their daughter was left with a sixth sense that the door to the family attic was never, if at all possible, to be opened.

Josef Korbel was a great survivor; she was a survivor's daughter, raised in a household where circumspection was important. By the time Albright was nominated to be secretary of state, though she had come of age in tumultuous times, there were no statements of hers, except for some ill-fated words on nation-building in Somalia, that could cause her political problems; she had rarely departed from the conventional wisdom on larger issues. That, thought her friends, was not so much conscious as it was instinctive, something she had learned at home. She had gone to a private day school in Denver, then on to Wellesley College, and after graduation she had married Joseph Albright, or more properly, Joseph Medill Patterson Albright, himself just out of Williams College. He was shy and earnest, a descendant of the mighty Medill and Patterson families who had dominated Chicago journalism for generations, and the nephew of Alicia Patterson, the irreverent and iconoclastic woman who had founded *Newsday,* the immensely successful Long Island suburban daily. For their marriage she became an Episcopalian. Two years later, in June 1961, she gave birth to twin daughters.

For a time Joe Albright worked at *Newsday* and was seen as the heir apparent who might one day edit or publish the paper. Thus her career, because of the nature of the era and his connections, was always to be ancillary to his. Even as a young couple, their future seemed already scripted. He would be the worthy, thoughtful publisher of a good, serious newspaper; she would be his wife and partner, perhaps more interested in foreign and domestic policy than other loyal spouses, but a wife and mother nonetheless. Joe Albright had not really wanted to be a newspaperman and had thought about becoming a scientist. It was primarily pressure from his aunt Alicia that had pushed him in that direction. As a journalist he was intelligent, dutiful, hard-working, and steadfast, but not intuitive in the way that makes the profession easier for some reporters. His name may have been more of a burden than an asset. Much was expected from him in a profession where he was never a natural. Later in his career, he gained a considerable level of success as a full-time reporter drawn to serious issues often overlooked by more facile journalists in search of sexier stories.

Almost from the start outside forces affected Albright's original career plan. Alicia Patterson, who had intended to turn *Newsday* over to Joe, died suddenly and unexpectedly of bleeding ulcers in July 1963. She owned 49 percent of the paper, and her far more conservative husband, Harry Guggenheim, owned 51. He was not that impressed by her nephew, his talent, and especially his politics. He did not want Joe anywhere near a position of power and, for a time, brought in Bill Moyers, Lyndon Johnson's former press officer, to be publisher, mistakenly thinking him to be conservative as well. When Moyers inevitably disappointed him, Guggenheim sold the paper to the Chandlers of Los Angeles, apparently believing they were as politically conservative in this generation as they had been in the past. The sale made Joe Albright a wealthy young man, but he was not going to be the top executive of an important paper.

If the ceiling on their ambitions as a couple had been lowered significantly, Madeleine Albright still tried to follow the original script as an earnest, supportive, and conventional wife. Her report to her Wellesley fifth reunion class book in 1964 showed how typical her life was and probably would remain: "In the past five years have moved from Fort Leonard Wood, Missouri, to Chicago to Garden City, Long Island, to Washington, D.C., and back to Long Island. Only unusual accomplishment has been production of twins . . ."[13] Six years after their birth, a third child was born. All were girls. What set the Albrights apart from so many other young couples they knew in the sixties, all of them trying to find their place in what were first the Kennedy, then the Johnson, and finally, and tragically, the Vietnam years, was that they had no money problems. In fact, they had to be careful to spend less than they could for fear of being different and perhaps ostentatious. There was no women's movement at the time, and the idea that Madeleine Albright would one day have a full and rich career—and that it might be more important than her husband's—was unheard of.

But she was her father's daughter. She was a good student, she always worked hard, and even as a housewife, she began to study for a graduate degree in political science. She took classes at the Johns Hopkins School for Advanced International Studies and then at Columbia, where she got a master's and a Ph.D. There she met Zbigniew Brzezinski, who was a rising star in the foreign policy world. Their backgrounds, both exiles from Eastern Europe and children of diplomats, were quite similar (Brzezinski, born in Warsaw, was married to a grandniece of the great Czech democrat Edvard Benes). Brzezinski was, like many Poles, Soviet-phobic. In the late sixties Madeleine Albright was busy being a housewife, working on her Ph.D., but staying essentially apart from that enormous youthful antiwar energy. That made her true to her roots. Her father was a hard-liner, her most important Columbia faculty member was a hard-liner, and her doctoral thesis about contemporary Soviet repression in central Europe could not at that particular moment have been more unfashionable.

In time, with *Newsday* out of the play, Joe Albright became a reporter for the Cox newspaper chain in Washington. He and his wife were not that different from many other ambitious and idealistic young couples in the late sixties and seventies; they were pleasant and industrious, serious but not really glamorous, and obviously a little more privileged than most. Joe Albright's career was to come first; for her initial venture into politics, Madeleine Albright became a board member at the private elementary school their daughters attended. That after all was the most natural role for a serious, quietly ambitious young woman who was a good citizen and wanted to be a part of her community; it allowed her to become involved in something larger than herself while remaining well within her place in the established hierarchy. On that board, she began to make connections with a number of political people in Washington. She was hardworking and intelligent if not brilliant; she was, Brzezinski noted years later, "a very pleasant, amiable, easy-to-get-along-with graduate student," but, as he then added, hardly special.[14]

Like many women tentatively entering the world of politics, Madeleine Albright began by doing the heavy lifting, the so-called donkey work, for a political event or campaign that required a lot of time and effort, offered little glory, and which the men were only too glad to deed over. Ironically, that somewhat limited role kept her from being caught up in the bitter ideological wars of that overheated period, when much of the debate centered not just around Vietnam, but what it said about American foreign policy in general. Years later she had fewer enemies and had made fewer embarrassing statements because in her early political activities she had been given no voice and played so small a role.

Through friends she got to know Ed Muskie, the Maine senator, who was the leading centrist Democrat of the period, though dovish on Vietnam. She proved to be an effective fund-raiser for him, and in 1976 when he faced a difficult reelection campaign, she became his chief fund-raiser. She was hardly a star, but she was beginning to move up the ladder of Democratic politics. She and Joe Albright had a lovely home in Georgetown and enough money to make it the center for other bright young people interested in politics and foreign policy. The Albright wealth was a considerable asset in working the fund-raising circuit; in order to get you had to give as well. Madeleine Albright was slowly but surely becoming both connected and credentialed. In 1976, seventeen years after graduating from Wellesley—nothing came easily for a woman with three young children—she received her Ph.D. from Columbia.

In the brief period when the Democrats came back to power under Carter in 1977 to 1980, a number of the more senior Muskie people went into the administration, creating vacancies in his office and clearing a relatively solid place for Albright on Muskie's staff as chief legislative assistant. That signaled that she was valued, but the idea that in twelve or thirteen years she would be a leading candidate for one of the top jobs in a Democratic administration was still inconceivable. The top candidates of her generation were already in place: Tony Lake at Policy Planning and Dick Holbrooke as an assistant secretary of state, young men who were now moving into positions that would surely guarantee a big ticket the next time the Democrats ruled. Their stars burned brightly; Albright's did not, and she soon left Muskie to work for Brzezinski as a liaison between his NSC office and Congress. Hardworking and steady, she was perceived by some of her peers as the grind who got the job done. She was also, without anyone noticing it, quietly moving ahead of the curve, if not for bright, up-and-coming foreign policy specialists in the Democratic Party, then for *women* in the foreign policy world.

In the early eighties her personal life fell apart. After twenty-three years of marriage, Joe Albright had met a younger woman who was working as a journalist and asked his wife for a divorce. At the time Madeleine Albright was forty-five years old, she and her husband had raised three children, and they had been together as a couple virtually from the moment she had graduated from college. For years she had been a dutiful wife and mother with career coming only after her other responsibilities. She had been raised a Catholic and did not believe in divorce—no one in her family had ever been divorced. Not only had her world been clearly defined, but her *role* in that world had been every bit as well-defined. But now the world she had always counted on was shattered overnight. Some of their mutual friends thought that part of the problem was that his career had hit a plateau and her career had begun to surpass his. The divorce left her quite wealthy; Michael Dobbs, her biographer, estimated that by the time of her appointment as secretary of state in 1997, her net worth was around $10 million. Of the couple, quite visible in the world of Georgetown over the past fifteen years or so, she had been the more extroverted and gregarious; Joe Albright, quieter, more reserved. The divorce also left her with a large number of friends whom she had dealt with loyally and steadfastly, a handsome Georgetown home in which to entertain, and, for a time, a great deal of anger. She was devastated; she had, friends thought, been made to feel old and used and unwanted. Her friends also believed that from that moment on she became career-driven as she had never been before, as if to prove to the now departed Joe Albright who the star in the family really was and what a mistake he had made.

In the eighties and into the early nineties, the Reagan and Bush years and a Democratic wasteland, Albright became increasingly important in insider Democratic politics in Washington, connecting the party's political figures with its foreign policy experts at dinners at her home, which were quite serious and often seemed more like seminars. Now things began to come her way. Because more women were entering the world of international relations, the administrators of the Georgetown School for Foreign Service, a prestigious school not then known for the gender parity of its faculty, offered her a teaching position, a plum job particularly hard won for a woman. It was one more credential to add to her résumé. In the eighties, during two presidential campaigns, she held jobs that were additional credentials—not great ones, given the outcome of the respective elections, but a sign of an ascent still very much in progress. She became foreign policy adviser to Geraldine Ferraro in 1984 during her ill-fated vice-presidential run, and having backed Michael Dukakis early in the 1988 primaries, she served as his chief foreign policy adviser.

That his campaign turned out to be a disaster was not held against Albright. It was widely assumed that Dukakis did not listen to her because, the world of old-line Washington Democrats believed, he did not listen to anyone. She was, however, at least a partial coconspirator in the creation of the catastrophic tank photo. Someone suggested that it might help Dukakis's image if he visited a tank factory (military bases are off-limits to candidates) and thus show he was not a wimp. Albright concurred. Dukakis went to a factory in Sterling Heights, Michigan, got into a tank, and put on a tanker's helmet, thereby violating one of the primary laws of American politics—never wear any hat that might make you look goofy because, as John Kennedy once said, the only thing the voters would remember was a photograph of you in some bizarre hat. Dukakis, helmet on, stuck his head out of the hatch of the tank and grinned while the television cameras rolled away. At first all the Dukakis people were pleased by the coverage. Then they saw the footage. Dukakis did not look combatready: he looked silly. The Republicans were delighted and used the clip for many of their commercials. Albright was partially on the spot. The idea of visiting the factory had been good, she insisted later, but it was Dukakis's fault for putting on the helmet.[15]

The Dukakis campaign had hardly made her a star, but in truth, the Democrats, as they prepared to take office in 1993, had no stars. In many political fields, the constituencies had changed as the country had changed. Only twenty or twenty-five years earlier, for example, the perfect curriculum vitae for a seat on the Supreme Court might have included a WASP background, an education at Harvard or Yale and their respective law schools, and clerking for someone like Earl Warren. But now, especially for Democrats, there were obligations to a much wider variety of interest groups, by ethnicity, gender, and region. The background that had once been an advantage might be a debit; and what had once been a debit might be an advantage. So it was with foreign policy. Joe Albright was a graduate of Groton, an elite New England prep school, which in the old America had helped incubate secretaries of state and would-be secretaries of state (Acheson, Harriman, Bundy, and Bundy) and a national-security kingmaker (Alsop); in the new America, it was the East European ex-wife of a Groton graduate who would earn that title. Credentials were different now. In the years that Albright had struggled upward, more ant than grasshopper, the women's movement had come of age, and gender had become more politicized. The bitter battles over abortion had seen many nominally Republican women switch to the Democratic Party and had made them a powerful force, one that was increasingly well-organized and articulate. Their votes, not the votes of white males, had elected Bill Clinton both times. By 1997 the beginning of an old girls' network was coalescing in Washington. Its leader was Wendy Sherman, who had worked for Maryland senator Barbara Mikulski. The old girls knew what they wanted, and that was a woman as secretary of state, and they had a powerful ally in the White House—Hillary Rodham Clinton. The men, because there were a number of candidates, were divided; the women, because there was only one candidate, were not. Madeleine Albright got the job.

Not unlike Tony Lake, who had been strikingly handsome as a young man and had aged dramatically over the years, Albright's struggle to reach the top showed in the photos of her. It was as if she had never really had a childhood and had always been under considerable subsurface pressure to achieve, to succeed in this country not just for herself but for her father, who had had his career stolen from him by the cruelty of modern history. In addition, the road to power was simply harder for a woman of her generation, despite her achievements. Albright for a long time felt she had not quite gotten her due. Her male peers—such as Tony Lake, Dick Holbrooke, Les Gelb, Win Lord, Frank Wisner, and Dick Moose—were almost automatically named to all kinds of committees and study groups that she was just as automatically left out of. *"The boys,"* she called them in private, and she said it with an edge that implied that they took care of their own, and she was not one of their own and never would be. In her mind (and few women of her generation in the national security world dissented), men automatically said and did exclusionary things without thinking they were sexist. When Colin Powell wrote in his memoir that her more activist attitude about the use of troops in Bosnia had nearly given him an aneurysm, she was infuriated by the phrasing he used to quote his answer to her: "I patiently explained . . ."[16] *Patiently explained* smacked of upper-level sexism in her view, and they exchanged friendly notes about the passage—she signing one of hers, "Forcefully, Madeleine." If you were a woman operating at that level, she once told a friend, you did not seek the battle over gender, but it was there all the time. It sought you.

The years of fighting her way up in male bastions had made Albright both strong and hard, and she emerged during her tour at State as quite territorial, which was not surprising, given the lack of control over territory she had experienced for most of her life. She was immensely sensitive to any criticism, and personal public relations were unusually important to her. It was especially ironic that when she was ambassador to the UN, she had thrived in an almost innocent way not just in the job, but in the star status that went with it. Now the same people who had hindered her career and helped create some of her insecurities made fun of her because she took such pleasure in the perks of her new job. That Henry Kissinger, himself something of a wallflower for much of his life, had blossomed as a sex-symbol star when he attained comparable power and had enjoyed celebrity-hopping and social climbing every bit as much if not more than Albright was not mentioned.

In terms of ideology and beliefs, it was not easy to get a fix on her. Though she had climbed the ladder of the foreign policy establishment slowly and carefully over the years, no one associated her with any particular view or wing of the party. No label seemed to stick to her. But she was passionate about one issue and one man, the Balkans and Milosevic. The reference point she used, again and again when the subject came up, was Munich. He must not be appeased; only force would stop him. At the UN she had been from day one a hard-liner on the Balkans. It was Europe, an area she knew (she also knew the Slavic languages, Russian and Czech); her father, in his last major assignment before the communist coup in Prague, had been ambassador to Belgrade. She had, because of her family history, a powerful antipathy toward military aggression and genocide, and she hated Milosevic as a reincarnation of Hitler and Stalin. From the time she joined the Clinton administration, she had been a hawk on the Balkans, though no one listened to her carefully. Now in 1998, it was her turn to be a signature figure and for her voice to be heard.

Her authority was increasing for two reasons besides the fact that she had a more important position now than she had held in the first Clinton administration. Number one, she was working in something of a vacuum because the administration was preoccupied, most notably with the president's survival in an impeachment trial; and number two, Milosevic systematically played into her hands, the latest Serb atrocities always validating those who wanted to take the hardest line against him.

CHAPTER THIRTY-FOUR

Mid-1998 was not a good time to push ahead too aggressively in the Balkans. As the Lewinsky scandal unfolded and impeachment became a real possibility, both Berger and the president were tiptoeing through a potential minefield. The last thing they wanted was military intervention in Kosovo. A recalcitrant Congress had been resistant to sending even a limited number of American soldiers to Bosnia and had never really liked using them as peacekeepers because, despite the promises, it could become an open-ended commitment. The Congress would certainly not be enthusiastic about bombing threats against Belgrade for fear of what the next military step might be. The Pentagon, as always, resisted military intervention, and the Europeans were once again sounding cautious about any additional use of force. Moreover, the Clinton administration was facing an off-year election in the fall, with every reason to believe the central issue would be the president's personal behavior, and the outcome would help the Republicans. The last thing a besieged presidency needed was to fight politically (and militarily) on another front.

The equation facing Milosevic was familiar and once again quite tempting. The Western powers, which had come together briefly three years earlier on Bosnia, were again divided as he moved on Kosovo. The leadership in the United States was obviously distracted, and eventually, as talks with the West progressed over Kosovo, the Americans appeared to be anxious for some kind of paper accord, willing to go for agreements that gave the appearance of a settlement. Ever aggressive, Milosevic pushed forward, but what was bluff and what was real was hard to tell. To those who had watched him in the past, he was playing an old, familiar game: two steps forward and one step back in order to have his way in Kosovo. Or as Javier Solana, the head of NATO, described it, talking about the limited assault the Serbs were conducting in Kosovo, never pushing so hard that the West would respond—"a village a day keeps NATO away."[1]

But Milosevic himself was at least a partial victim of the dynamic he had created. Kosovo stirred so many emotions in all Serbs and was so basic to his political power that if the bluff did not work and NATO did strike back, he could not easily let go as he had in Bosnia. He might have to fight and let his nation and his people take a pounding for a time—just how long, he would have to figure out—before he conceded anything to the West. Then, instead of betraying the Serb cause, which was sure political death, he would be seen as a descendant of Tsar Lazar, six hundred years before him, who had died rather than surrender, though unlike Lazar, he would surely live to become a hero while his people died and bore the brunt of the suffering.

If Washington was not yet ready to act, people in the administration were taking up their positions. Albright was a hawk. Cohen and the Chiefs were dovish. Clinton and Berger were in the middle, pulled toward choices they did not want to make, hoping to slow down the clock in the Balkans and buy time. To use force in the Balkans, they had to bring in the Europeans as well, and to do that, we had to make more of an attempt to find a settlement with Milosevic. Even if the kind of settlement the Europeans wanted was impossible, we still had to go through the motions of trying to find it in order to prove our good intentions before they would come aboard. But one other important hawk was already aboard, not in Washington, but a major player nonetheless: General Wes Clark. His views by 1998 were close to those of Albright. He believed that Kosovo was a replay of Bosnia, that Milosevic was the primary instigator, that he would negotiate only as a ploy, and that until he was stopped, nothing could be settled. Like Albright he also believed only force would work. When the West negotiated, it used words and thus played into his hands, because words and promises were meaningless to him.

By early 1998, Clark was absolutely sure they were going to have to use force, and the greater the military might they could flash at Milosevic, the more likely they were to get what would be considered a successful settlement. But within the military establishment, Clark's appointment as supreme commander in Europe was controversial, both underlining and aggravating the tensions between the civilians and the military that had existed from the moment the Clinton administration took office. If everyone had eventually come aboard for the policies that had brought the Serbs to Dayton, then the profound differences that divided the Pentagon and the White House over the foreign policy of the United States and the role of the American military in peacekeeping operations were still largely unreconciled. Even Dayton had remained something of a bone in the throat for both sides. The question of how aggressive the military was going to be in pursuing those Serbs who were trying to undermine the Dayton Accords was not easily resolved at first. In the most difficult command of all, Clark would find himself constantly caught between these opposing factions.

The Clinton people had thought of Colin Powell as a hostile and unsympathetic force; they had tried to get along with him at the time, but in retrospect, after he left office, they tended to see him not just as a general who had disagreed with their foreign policy, but as a political opponent, a partially closeted Republican of considerable influence. He, in turn, tended to think of them as neophytes whose rhetoric was greater than their willingness to back it up, the lineal descendants of the architects of the Vietnam War. If the administration had found a sympathetic figure in the military, someone whose beliefs at least *to some degree* paralleled those of the top civilians, it was John Shalikashvili, who had become chairman of the Joint Chiefs after Powell retired in 1993, and whose tour had ended in 1997. Shalikashvili was viewed by the Clinton people as being far more helpful; yet the more helpful he was to the civilians, the greater the suspicions about him remained at the Pentagon.

What was largely unseen, not just by the public at large but by most Washington insiders, was the constant tug-of-war that went on between the administration and the senior military over the top posts. This political game was of great consequence, but no one spoke openly about what was going on, and it was just barely covered by the media. It reflected not merely the divisions in the government, but divisions in the Congress and in the country as well—differences that had a profound effect on the foreign policy of the United States. Among certain circles in the Pentagon, there was a strong belief that the Clinton people had made a practice of shying away from aggressive officers who were classic combat leaders in favor of men who were more amenable. Thus some senior military people admired Shalikashvili but worried that in some way he had allowed himself to become too close to the Clinton people.

In fact, Shalikashvili had worked with great ease with the Clinton people—much of what they wanted was what he wanted. In certain areas—the strengthening and unification of Europe, the expansion of NATO—he as a man of Europe was far more internationalist in his orientation than some of the Clinton people, and was probably a good deal ahead of them in their thinking. But Shalikashvili's beliefs had in general coincided with those of the administration. During his tour as chairman, he had made some progress in trying to bridge the gap between the military and the White House. But that did not mean that resistance to much of what he believed had ended within the very conservative culture of the military, especially his own service, the army. There, he was regarded with some skepticism. To some hard-liners in the Pentagon, Shalikashvili had been chosen by the White House because, as an immigrant and a new citizen, he might be a little too grateful to the civilian officeholders, and a little bit too much in awe of the president of the United States—in effect, an easy mark for the shrewd and manipulative Clinton, as he was viewed in the Pentagon. Not everyone who watched Shalikashvili at work during his four-year term agreed. To them it was not that the White House had gotten Shali, but that Shalikashvili, with stronger beliefs on many issues than the Clinton people, had gotten the White House.

Some thought that Shalikashvili, in tandem with Bill Perry, had a clearer vision of the future of European security than the administration itself, and certainly a stronger view than most people in the State Department. Together

Shalikashvili and Perry had been a more formidable force than State in push-ing for one of the central decisions of the Clinton administration, the expan-sion of NATO into formerly communist countries, including Poland, which bordered on Russia, without appearing to threaten the Russians. Here insiders credited Shalikashvili with considerable influence. He far more than most sen-ior military men (and more than most senior State Department people) believed in a unified Europe. This Europe would include most of the old War-saw Pact nations, where brand-new military ties with the traditional Western democracies might create not just a larger military alliance, but might even enhance democratic forces within each country with the military serving as an important democratic spine. The broader impact of NATO might take the mil-itary, sometimes in the past an antidemocratic force in this part of the world, and make it a pro-democratic force, as these nations struggled through their embryonic experience with democracy. Shalikashvili had also pushed for an additional program, the Partnership for Peace with the Russians, not merely to engage them in joint maneuvers and create healthier relationships, but also to reduce their traditional paranoia about the West (much of it historically well justified). That was especially important if NATO was to be expanded to the Polish-Russian border. Little noted by a national media that did not take things like this seriously, the NATO expansion would stand as one of the more notable achievements of the Clinton administration, one that took place with remarkably little domestic debate.

Shalikashvili had never come up with a Shali Doctrine to replace the Pow-ell Doctrine. But it gradually appeared that he was trying to change—or at least make adjustments to—the core philosophy of the army, particularly in something relatively new, the complicated peacekeeping missions potentially created by the collapse of the old order. What he would later say (quite dis-creetly) was that he had largely agreed with the Powell Doctrine, which was that you did not undertake military missions unless they were completely out-lined, the force levels were agreed upon, and the exit strategy was clear. Indeed he would recall a moment when the Balkans were heating up and Powell as chairman had asked to send a number of American troops to the Macedonian border to make sure that the fighting did not expand there. Shalikashvili had called Powell, slightly surprised by his request, and said, "Colin, *you* want to put some of our troops in Macedonia?" Powell said yes, and it had been done quietly and under UN command, though the troops were never engaged in fighting. What Shalikashvili wanted to change, he said, was the *Weinberger Doctrine,* created by Caspar Weinberger, who was something of a godfather to Powell during his rise in government and had said that military intervention should be used only if the *vital* interests of the United States were at stake. It was the word *vital* that Shalikashvili was taking issue with.

What Shalikashvili had wanted was more flexibility in the use of the army's forces. The military has acronyms for everything, and the acronym here was perfect, OOTW, or Operations Other Than War. He was well aware that now the Cold War was over, military missions were bound to change. In those days Shalikashvili would go around saying that the chairman of the Joint Chiefs did not have the right to put a notice on his door saying, "I'm sorry—we only do the big ones," and signed "John Shalikashvili." He did not, however, by any means represent the majority opinion within the army or the military; his views were still rather unconventional, and the resistance within the culture he was taking on ran deep and strong. He was opposed by men innately uncomfortable with change, uneasy about the direction of policies that took them into uncharted waters, and deeply suspicious of the incumbent politicians, in whom they had little confidence. Shalikashvili had been ahead of most of the chiefs in pushing for American troops to go into Bosnia as part of the Dayton peacekeeping mission, and he had used considerable leverage to bring the force to an adequate level, adjudicating among the CINC, or commander in chief, on the ground, General George Joulwan, and the army chief of staff, back in Washington, General Dennis Reimer. Joulwan wanted around thirty thousand men at first, and Reimer, with a great deal more on his plate and limited enthusiasm for the mission, some friends thought, suggested a reinforced brigade of some five thousand men. What Shalikashvili wanted was about a division, or roughly twenty thousand men, and he told that to Joulwan, though as a sweetener he gave him extra intelligence capabilities so Joulwan could monitor not just the tensions between the various military forces they were separating, but also the reduction of heavy weaponry and some of the civilian mischief that might go on. The army had been something of a hard sell, because it was the branch of service that would have to do the heavy lifting and put the most men on the ground. It was already struggling to keep its budget from being cut and here it was taking on additional responsibilities.

If Shalikashvili was going to change the army, he had not only to change the vision and the training, but also the top personnel. In his search for officers who had a comparable view of what the army's missions might become, Shalikashvili had at a crucial moment reached out and helped get a fourth star for a dazzlingly bright young officer named Wes Clark, even in the face of formidable opposition within the army. Clark had been Shali's J-5, or chief of plans on the joint staff, and he had performed exceptionally well, his analytical abilities of the highest order. Clark was a classic quick study, and his talent for cutting through immensely complicated issues swiftly and thoroughly had long ago set him apart from most of his peers. No one doubted his brightness, the sense that he was the most modern of officers. General Edward (Shy) Meyer, army chief of staff from 1978 to 1983, remembered how smart and alert Clark had been as a division commander at Fort Hood. Clark had been the first officer at that level to talk not just about traditional unit readiness—clean barracks, shined boots, low absenteeism—but to discuss some of the new problems of modern military life—teenage suicide and spousal abuse. Meyer decided that Clark had understood sooner than most that the new professional army, where fewer and fewer soldiers actually lived on base (and where pay scales now had to compete with those of the civilian economy), had to deal with infinitely more complex concerns that reflected the full range of the contemporary domestic social malaise.

Shalikashvili had known Clark since he was a lieutenant colonel, thought him very bright, perhaps a little too brash, but possessing the kind of talent that the army badly needed at that level. In June 1996, Shalikashvili wanted Clark to take the SouthCom job, based in Florida, which would make him a CINC and a four-star. SouthCom, or Southern Command, essentially Latin America and eventually Latin America plus the Caribbean, was viewed by a number of senior military people as the ideal testing ground for an officer ascending to the highest level because he had to deal with all the problems that were endemic to the underdeveloped world—poverty, drugs, and uncommonly fragile civic institutions. It was, as Shy Meyer once said, where you always sent a hot guy because he could learn the most, and where a talented officer who was too rigid in his vision would not be able to handle the wide range of difficulties he would encounter. Shalikashvili agreed and thought SouthCom would be the perfect testing ground for Clark.

Not many people at the upper level of the army favored the idea. Clark had always evoked strong feelings within his own branch of the service among those who felt he represented its best qualities, those who felt he represented some of its lesser qualities, and, on occasion, those who thought he represented both. When it is time to name a CINC, the traditional procedure is for the army, through the chief of staff, to suggest its candidates for the slot, and for the chairman to make the choice, then hand the selection on to the secretary of defense and the White House. But the army did not have Clark on its list. So when Shalikashvili nominated him for the SouthCom post, Dennis Reimer, the chief of staff, was most unhappy and resisted. Shalikashvili reminded Reimer that the chairman still had the right to pick the CINCs, and he asked Reimer, as a personal courtesy, to sign off on the selection. Reimer did so, however reluctantly. The army's attitude was clear: *Well, he's not really the man we want for this one, but if you really want him, you can have him.* That meant the army itself would have been quite content to cut Clark loose and let him retire as a three-star, and that he got a command and a fourth star only because of one man.

A year later the job of SACEUR opened up when George Joulwan left. The Clinton administration had been less than enthusiastic about him, feeling he should have enforced the Dayton Accords more aggressively. The job was crucial, probably the best command in the army ("the prince of Europe—the most powerful man on the Continent," one high-level officer called it). Again the army handed in its list, and again Clark's name was missing. Again Shalikashvili told Reimer that he was going to name Clark for the command and suggested that Reimer sign off on the selection. This time, however, Reimer refused to do it, which meant that the chief of staff of the army was in out-and-out opposition to the chairman on perhaps the most important army personnel selection of his tour. With the Balkans a constant cauldron and with Kosovo as yet to be dealt with, a commander was being sent to Brussels that the army system disliked and distrusted. It was not a good omen for what was to come.

In time, because Clark was by chance both a Rhodes Scholar and from Arkansas, and in the view of many traditional army men, highly political, a belief arose that the Clinton administration was behind him. But contrary to what many people in the military thought, Shalikashvili noted years later, the White House had never pushed for Clark or asked how he was doing or tried to influence his career. Certainly, because he had worked closely with a number of civilians, most notably Holbrooke, before and during Dayton, the civilian activists were supportive of him. Equally certainly, knowing that the SACEUR job was opening up, Clark had, in the way that senior military men often did in situations like this, quietly lobbied for the job, letting some of the top civilians know he wanted it. But as for the president himself, when Clark was nominated for his two CINC posts, Clinton had merely asked Shalikashvili rather casually if Clark was the right person for the job. Nevertheless, the belief that Clark had a Clinton connection persisted—not necessarily an asset in a military culture that deep into the president's second term remained suspicious of him and the people around him.

What the army disliked about Wes Clark, Shalikashvili believed, was an unusual amalgam of the personal and the professional. For all his obvious talents, he was too brash and cocky, too sure that his way was the right way, and therefore not a good listener and difficult to deal with. In addition, people felt that he was so driven and so absorbed in his mission—far too self-absorbed, it seemed to many of his critics—he could be quite hard on the people who worked for him. He lacked the warmth and humanity that truly great commanders need—traditionally highly desirable characteristics in a man who sends younger men and women off to battle. There was more than an element of truth in that belief, Shalikashvili thought. Clark was not the warmest of men; rather he always seemed to bristle with the singularity of military purpose—almost uncompromising if anything ever got in his way. He might be careful and attentive about the condition and the training of his men, and he might send them if needed into battle under optimum conditions, but he did not generate any paternal feelings—*the old man is a hell of a guy.* Nor did he gain one of the those wonderful old-fashioned nicknames that the army traditionally likes to bestow upon its commanders, signifying respect and a kind of reluctant admiration—Cold Steel, Iron Mike, the Gunfighter, Lightning Joe, Buffalo Bill, Coal Bin Willie. He was known as Wes instead of Wesley—that was accommodation enough.

But at Clark's level that was not too critical a debit, Shalikashvili believed, because as CINC Clark would not really mesh that much with the troops, and his subordinates—the division and brigade and battalion commanders—could fill the gap in humanity. More important was the truly superior professional and intellectual ability he would bring to the job; that would be badly needed in Europe with the Balkans still an unfinished crisis and likely to blow. But within the army's structure doubts about Clark ran deep. He was not just too brusque or too cold or too driven. He was in some way alien to the military culture. What those who liked him saw as his confidence, those who did not like him saw as overconfidence. What those who liked him saw as singular purpose, others saw as an overdose of personal ambition. Few senior officers were neutral about him, and a considerable part of the traditional senior army leadership was made uneasy by him. Was he really one of theirs? Was he too political, too likely to grandstand? Did his ambition reach too far?

Clark was named to the most important army command just as the Balkans were about to explode again. Given his personality—he was a classic type A, perhaps even type AA, singularly aggressive and driven, a man who did not believe in downtime—he was not likely to be a passive player. He had gone through his own evolution on the subject of the Balkans. When he had first started out as a player in the Balkans, pre-Dayton, he had shared the military's general apprehension about getting involved there. In 1993, after commanding the First Cavalry Division, he had come to Washington to serve the JCS as a J-5, the officer in charge of strategic plans for political military affairs. His predecessor, Lieutenant General Barry McCaffrey, spoke to him almost immediately about the Balkans, of how difficult a venue they would be, and that it might take several hundred thousand men on the ground to end hostilities there. Clark had essentially accepted that view. Then in 1994 during one of his first trips to the Balkans, Clark had made an appalling blunder. The administration was struggling with the aggressiveness of the Bosnian Serbs when he visited the area. General Michael Rose, the senior British officer in the region, suggested that Clark meet with the Bosnian Serb leaders. Clark was not supposed to do that, but Rose apparently thought it could be done in private—which it was not. Clark unwisely met with General Ratko Mladic, the brutal Bosnian Serb commander, and, even more unwisely, exchanged hats with him. There had been a flash flood of criticism, and for a brief moment his job had hung in the balance.

Holbrooke, still unsure of Clark—he was brash, he was bright, but did he know how to listen?—had rallied to his side and helped save his job. Their relationship had not started auspiciously. They had met earlier in Washington on an intergovernmental committee on NATO expansion that Holbrooke had chaired, and it had gone badly. Clinton had already decided on NATO expansion, but at that meeting Clark, the Pentagon's representative, had challenged Holbrooke—as if the decision had not yet been made. That quickly turned into a firefight. The decision to expand, Holbrooke said, had already been made. "Are you accusing me of insubordination?" Clark then snapped. A real hothead, Holbrooke had decided, but things had gradually been smoothed out.

As J-5, Clark had not been impressed by the various proposals for a settlement that were on the table before him. But gradually he was pulled toward greater activism after spending time with men such as Holbrooke and Chris Hill, and, most of all, by witnessing Milosevic's handiwork close-up. It was events on the morning of August 19, 1995, that made the war intensely personal for Clark. He was part of a convoy going from Mount Igman to Sarajevo when a tragic accident took place. The Mount Igman to Sarajevo road, which Clark and other Americans trying to work on peace proposals had to travel, was known as one of the worst in Europe, winding, unprotected, unreinforced, a nightmare in peacetime and a double nightmare at a time when the Serbs often fired at anything that moved. Holbrooke, who was leading the peace mission, had argued the day before with Milosevic, demanding that he authorize safer passage, but Milosevic had been deliberately unhelpful. The next day two vehicles started out in a convoy to Sarajevo, Holbrooke and Clark in an American humvee, and three of the top deputies on the Bosnian issue, Bob Frasure, Colonel Nelson Drew, and Joe Kruzel, in an armored personnel career. Somehow the APC went over a cliff and tumbled down the mountainside. Clark raced down the mountain to try to help, oblivious to cries from others to watch out for mines, only to find the bodies of his three friends, men much respected and admired by their peers. The American team was devastated, and Clark did not forget the senselessness of those three deaths, nor that Milosevic had lied to them and forced the trip when he could have made it much easier and safer. Clark's feelings about Milosevic were from then on, some friends thought, sealed in blood.

There was no doubt after the accident that the person who influenced Clark the most was no longer Holbrooke, but Milosevic, in Clark's mind a pathological liar always playing for time. At one meeting with the Serb leader just before Dayton in 1995, Holbrooke momentarily left the room and Milosevic started working on Clark, trying to impress him and perhaps hoping that he could get further with his bluster with a military man than a civilian. He boasted that if he was allowed to handle an election in Bosnia, he would be able to do it and bring the Americans the outcome they wanted. After all, he had so much control over events that he could make those Bosnian Serb puppets dance to his orders. If that was true, Clark shrewdly asked Milosevic, then what about Mladic's unspeakable war crimes at Srebrenica?

Why, if Milosevic had all that power, had he allowed Mladic to murder thousands of Muslims there? "Crimes not mine," Milosevic answered. "Crimes those of Mladic. I warn Mladic not do this, but he not listen to me." Clark just sat there and thought to himself, "Yes, you can completely control an election and yet you can't stop your own general from mass murder. I don't think I believe much of what you say anymore."

Clark arrived in Brussels quite hawkish in the middle of 1997, and as tensions between the KLA and the Serbs escalated, he became more of an activist. To him it was a replay of events in Bosnia, and he believed that Milosevic was completely responsible for the increased turmoil. That, of course, put Clark in conflict with the senior military back at the Pentagon on two levels. First, they wanted as little military activism in the Balkans as possible, and second, they were not entirely sure that the Serbs were the sole guilty party. Many senior army officers had considerable skepticism about, and contempt for, the Albanians and the KLA, believing that they might be patriots, but they were also drug dealers and black marketeers. By early 1998, with the administration preoccupied with the Lewinsky affair, Clark become absolutely certain that Milosevic could not be stopped without the use of force.

What made Clark doubly sure was the massacre of the Jashari family. Adem Jashari was a leading KLA fighter and activist, and a previous Serb assault on his home and attempt to arrest or kill him had failed. But on March 5, 1998, the Serbs surrounded the Jashari compound and attacked the family, which was trapped in the basement, with artillery and grenades. Carnage resulted. Besarta Jashari was with her grandmother when someone threw a grenade into the basement. "Grandma was blown into the next room," she later said. "My sister started begging for water. 'Mama! Mama!' she cried."[2] But her mother had already been killed. All told, the Serbs had killed fifty-eight people, including eighteen women and ten children under the age of sixteen.

After that Clark was convinced that the Serb leader felt no compunction about killing Albanians. In fact, Milosevic had once told Clark that the Serbs knew how to handle Albanian nationalists—they had done it once before. When was that? Clark asked. "In Drenica back in 1946, right after the war," Milosevic replied. How did you do it? Clark wondered. "We kill all of them," Milosevic said. "It took several years, but we kill them all."[3] So Clark began to advocate the use of force against the Serbs—at the least the threat of bombing—with both the top civilians and the senior people at the Pentagon. He believed that was the only way Milosevic would negotiate. Otherwise, he was always going to test the limits. The phrase Clark used was that Milosevic was "bumping the high-jump bar," that is, he was like a high jumper trying for a new record, bumping the bar after every jump. Only the use of force by NATO, Clark believed, would stop him.

CHAPTER THIRTY-FIVE

In the spring and summer of 1998, the violence in Kosovo continued to intensify. It was now a three-handed poker game (or four-handed, if the Europeans were included). There were the Serbs, ever more aggressive. There was the KLA, increasingly bold, employing a shrewd strategy that ensured that, even when they lost a battle, they would be seen as martyrs because of the predictable violence of the Serbs and the preconditioned attitudes of the international audience. The KLA was counting on nothing less than Milosevic being Milosevic. As for the Americans, they were tilting toward limiting Serb brutality and hegemony in Kosovo, but not eager to move because of the formidable political hurdles facing the president and a natural reluctance to use force. The last thing Clinton wanted on his plate was any possibility of military intervention in the Balkans. The Europeans, unsure that they wanted to make any new military commitment in the Balkans, were waiting for American leadership. The Europeans were taking cover by talking about having a UN Security Council Resolution before they acted in Kosovo—an impossibility, as they well knew, since the Russians were bound to veto it.

The role of the KLA was to be crucial. When the Americans had tried to deal with Bosnia, their great problem was limiting the Serbs. In Kosovo they would have to stop Serb aggression as well as deal with a clever guerrilla army that delighted in triggering the most violent tendencies of the Serbs. No guerrilla organization had ever coalesced and surfaced as a major force more quickly than the KLA. By the start of 1997, it appeared mostly a figment of Albanian imaginations; by the first few months of 1998, it had, in the writer Tim Judah's phrase, "emerged from the shadows."[1] In early 1998, the UN released figures showing that the KLA was responsible for thirty-one attacks in 1996, fifty-five in all of 1997, and sixty-six in the first two months of 1998, attacks which escalated in seriousness, the level of weaponry, and violence. It was very different from Bosnia. Whereas the Bosnians had not wanted violence and were the victims of it, the Albanians, or at least the KLA, *wanted* it so they would look like victims of Serb reprisals.

Bob Gelbhard, who had taken Holbrooke's former job as America's special envoy to the Balkans, soon managed to alienate both the Albanians and the

Serbs. Some people in the Balkans and Washington pressed for Holbrooke's return to the Balkans and the administration, but for a time Albright resisted. She and Holbrooke might in general want the same outcome in the Balkans, but their personal relationship was abysmal. Finally, with Sandy Berger (pushed by Wes Clark, who thought Holbrooke was badly needed on location) and Strobe Talbott arguing the case, Holbrooke was brought back in. He would eventually make some nine trips to Belgrade to deal with Milosevic. But his hand was weak because of the new triangular game being played on the ground, limited leverage from the White House, and wariness on the part of the Congress. Holbrooke's real marching orders, unspoken but obvious as long as they were in an election year, were to buy time, try to get a settlement, and, if at all possible, make it look better than it was.

If Dayton had been difficult, Kosovo was even more difficult. Holbrooke found Milosevic not only manipulative as in the past, but furious at the way everyone was now aligned against him. He was angry that the Kosovars were doing to him what he had threatened to do to the West—create a Vietnam on his sovereign soil. He complained that he got little sympathy in the West, but in fact sympathy was hardly the word. He had a sense that the West was once again, however slowly, organizing itself to stop him. Holbrooke thought the KLA was every bit as tricky as Milosevic. Shuttling around the disputed territory in the late spring of 1998, he had visited an Albanian village where the KLA had deftly posed one of its guerrillas—armed with a Kalashnikov—next to him in every photo op. Holbrooke knew he had been badly used; he was learning once again that nothing was ever simple in the Balkans. Milosevic was enraged by the photo, thinking Holbrooke was helping to publicize and legitimize a terrorist group.

So Milosevic was now caught in the violent forces he had helped initiate. He had enjoyed some flexibility when it came to Bosnia; he had none in Kosovo. Nor did Western negotiators have that much flexibility to achieve what they wanted, negotiations in which they could pressure Milosevic to grant the Kosovo Albanians greater autonomy. In early 1998, the KLA was doing well, and its troops appeared better prepared for this kind of guerrilla warfare than the Serbs, who had been caught somewhat off guard. But then in July, things began to swing the other way as the Serbs brought more troops and heavier weapons to bear and extracted better intelligence. In July they succeeded in a large-scale ambush of some seven hundred Albanians, a major setback for the KLA. The Serbs now began to lash out with extra harshness, machine-gunning Kosovars, burning crops, and destroying villages. Thousands of Albanians, their departures expedited by Serb police and soldiers, began to flee their villages and move into the hills or neighboring countries. A humanitarian disaster began to loom once again. By August 1998, the UN placed the number of refugees at two hundred thousand. To Western journalists covering the Balkans, it looked all too much like a repeat of Bosnia.

In the fall of 1998, things were at something of a standstill. Wes Clark was aware that he was a greater activist than most of the other people in the military. His briefings both to senior civilians and the military became more and more pessimistic, and at the Pentagon he knew they were regarded as advocacy for war. Perhaps they were. When in late 1998 he spoke with General Dennis Reimer about how badly things were going, he suggested that Reimer ask for additional resources in preparation. "But we don't want to fight there," Reimer answered. Clark agreed, yet suggested that it would be wise to prepare, but felt Reimer was unmoved.[2] Certainly Clark's hatred for Milosevic was so great that he was anxious, some of the people around him thought, to find the right incident that would finalize American policy against him. Clark had studied Milosevic for three years. "I was probably unique among twentieth-century commanders in knowing my adversary so well," he once said.[3] He was sure he even knew when Milosevic was lying and when he had not thought out his lies in advance, for there would be a slight hesitation in his speech as he adjusted his words to his newest line. Clark had also learned to do a skillful imitation of Milosevic trying to con Westerners about his innocence of war crimes in Bosnia.

Clark had spent much of 1998 wanting to increase the pressure on Milosevic. In mid-October, Washington finally agreed—with the consent of the allies—to threaten him with NATO air strikes unless he backed down in Kosovo. B-52 bombers were moved from the United States to England as a way of enforcing the threat. When Holbrooke went to Belgrade in mid-October to deliver a final ultimatum, he took with him Lieutenant General Mike Short, who would be Clark's air commander if there was a NATO air war—the better to impress Milosevic on the gravity of the occasion.

"So you're the man who's going to bomb me," Milosevic said to Short. But Short quickly replied with a line that he and Holbrooke had already rehearsed: "I've got the B-52s in one hand and the U-2 surveillance planes in the other. It's up to you which I'm going to use."

Short was blunt and sure of his purpose, somewhat surprised to find himself in a quasi-diplomatic role, but hardly shy about speaking up. To prevent a NATO bombing, the West was demanding photo reconnaissance flights over Kosovo—without threat from Milosevic's SAM missiles. Short told him to move them out of Kosovo. "General," Milosevic said, "you cannot make me move my SA-6s. They have been in place for many years. A logistical nightmare [to move them]. It would be very difficult for me to move them. I cannot—do not ask me to do that. I will just turn them off and it will be all right."

Short, who had not slept for two days, was on a short fuse. He had been watching the Serb missiles for the last six weeks and knew that Milosevic was moving them to a different site in Kosovo every day. "Mr. President," Short said abruptly, "you're pounding sand up my ass." "What means 'pound sand up my ass'?" Milosevic asked. Short said it meant pulling his chain—another phrase in American military vernacular, which the Serb appeared to understand. Then Short explained that he knew exactly what Milosevic was doing, where he was moving the missiles from, and where he was moving them to. "Now get them out of Kosovo!" Short said. With that, Milosevic seemed to realize that a stage of the game he was playing was over, and they had all advanced to the next stop on the board. It was time to acquiesce, if only momentarily. "You are right," he said. "I will move the missiles."[4]

A day later with rules for some kind of peaceful reconnaissance still stymied, Short turned to his Serb counterpart as the meeting was about to break up unsuccessfully, a failure that would eventually lead to American-NATO air strikes. Short, after all, was the air force man, and he alone in the room knew how formidable his high-technology weaponry was, how much it had advanced in the seven years since Desert Storm. "Why don't you go out now and drive around your city and take one last look at it as it is today, because it will never look that way again," he said. Then he added, "I'm sure that you've spoken to your Iraqi counterparts about what to expect. Well, you can forget what the Iraqis told you. Our air might is far greater and far more lethal and accurate today. Iraq was just the beginning." The bombing, he promised, would be precise, quick, violent, and all-encompassing. "Nothing here will ever be the same, if we do this," he warned.

Holbrooke, dealing from limited leverage from Washington, was delighted by Short's brusque, undiplomatic performance and, watching Milosevic in those October meetings, thought he was truly terrified by the prospect of NATO bombings. Sweat rolled down his face at tense moments. But Holbrooke was aware of the timing of the meetings. Held just before the American election, they were designed to get as good a settlement as possible without using full leverage—the most important missing ingredient being armed ground troops as verifiers. He knew, therefore, that any agreement they reached had a limited shelf life. It might work for a time, but Milosevic *always* looked for wiggle room, and when he did, the ability to stop him might be limited. It would also be limited because it lacked the participation and the goodwill of the KLA, which would almost surely set out to exploit it.

In early November, the American people voted in the off-year election, and though his name was not on any ballot, in many ways the election was about Bill Clinton. He might as well have been running for a third term so much was he, or at least his character, the issue, plain and simple. This election was about his relationship with the American people and he had done, to the surprise of many, extremely well. The Democrats had not lost a few seats, they had gained several. Once again in a corner, Clinton had made a stunning comeback, which underlined his curious and somewhat schizophrenic relationship to the American people. He was not revered as Ronald Reagan was, and it was doubtful that he ever would be. Many Americans who voted for him liked him and thought him quite skilled, but they had learned not to trust him and voted with a certain skepticism. It was as if they had learned, after dealing with him over the years, what he was good at and what he was not good at, which of his promises to believe and which to disregard.

They understood that in political matters as well as in his personal life Clinton was a great flirt and seducer. He was too nimble of mind and feet, and too many conflicting political winds were blowing around for him to be steadfast. Affection, admiration, respect (other than in Hollywood, that great center of artificial emotion, where he was more of a favorite son than Ronald Reagan) might come to him in the future, if and when he was replaced by men who were less interesting and less charming. Then everyone would be able to sit around and talk about how good he had been at empathy, how well he spoke at times of national mourning, and what an exciting cliff-hanger it had been watching him dodge his more righteous and virtuous pursuers on the right. And, of course, how well the economy had done. It was no small thing that the country was in the midst of an almost unprecedented boom. In the meantime, what the American people had with him was, stated bluntly, a deal.

He did not fool them. Nor was he, as he sometimes seemed to believe, smarter than they were. Not at all. It was a relationship of convenience: the American people were every bit as smart about him as he was about them. They seemed to have a sincerity meter with which they could judge him and measure his trustworthy quotient at any given moment. He might be imperfect, but they knew what they were getting, and they suspected the alternatives being offered up were probably a good deal worse. He only fooled them when they wanted to be fooled. Whatever else, however, Clinton offered no meanness of spirit, and it was his particular gift, and that of his wife, to unsettle his many critics and opponents so much that it made *them* seem mean of spirit. It was as if he were always calm and they were always angry. He would gain the center, they would get the fringe. That was no small political skill, to drive your opponents toward mental imbalance and the political extreme. His enemies, particularly those younger conservatives who had come to Congress so full of their own rectitude and so certain of their ideological truths, hated him and his wife with a passion that went well beyond the ideological and became so violently personal that it was almost always self-defeating. Thus in their anger did they play into his hands.

The things that enraged the Republican right and the fundamentalists about Clinton—his apparently loose ways, his infidelity not merely to his wife but to his own words, his co-opting of issues and ideas that had once belonged to them—did not greatly bother the American people. They did not care deeply about the state of his marriage. If they suspected promiscuity, they believed it was none of their business. They would probably prefer to like him a bit more, and certainly to trust him a bit more, but the country was being run well, the economy was surging, and he seemed on domestic matters to be surrounded by talented, able people. He worked hard and was obviously smart. Whoever succeeded him, either from the left or the right, would probably not fit the national mood at the turn of the century as well. Clearly, he was centrist and fair-minded and *modern,* and he wanted to do the right thing for as many people as possible.

Clinton had made the Democrats, at least momentarily, the party of the middle class, not the poor, even if the very wealthy were once again the principal beneficiaries of his administration. In truth, on its own the party was without a center. But issue by issue, image by image, he had carved out a center, and he had done it so shrewdly that he had managed to push the Republican Party much farther to the right than it wanted to be. For many of the young and the people his own age who had voted for him, his political contradictions were not that different from their own. Some of the older people, for whom the cultural and political gap was a little wider, believed that he got the job done and that, in addition, a good deal of the criticism leveled against him was simply unfair, unacceptably harsh and personal. He was doing a good job, that was the deal, and that was why they had elected him.

They knew he was flawed and they accepted his flaws. They might have preferred a more virtuous candidate, but thirty years of living in a media age, where high officials had come under the ever more intense scrutiny of an increasingly sensationalized media, had taught the American people to be somewhat skeptical of those seeking the presidency—or any other high office. For soon Newt Gingrich and some of his more righteous colleagues in the Congress were shown to be leaders whose morality was greater in theory than in practice, men who were casting stones while forgetting that all high-level American politicians now lived in the same glass house.

The American people had become, however involuntarily, a great deal shrewder about political morality in the more than three decades of the marriage of national television and national politics. During that time, for example, the Kennedy family, regarded in the early days of the age of televised politics as the ultimate in romantic politics—all those good-looking, wealthy people who married other good-looking, wealthy people—had been systematically dipped in ex post facto smut. Gradually, the booming celebrity-scandal industry in both print and television had immunized the American people. Ordinary voters might not formulate an equation in which it was presumed that the very nature of the ego required for a life in politics was excessive and that therefore other aspects of political behavior might be excessive as well.

After all, it drove talented men to reject a normal, balanced existence, with loving wives and children and normal working hours and far greater financial rewards, and instead to risk everything by seeking high office and great power, a course that often left family wreckage in its wake. But it seemed obvious that something like that demanded a certain genetic overload (or imbalance) and that very condition might often have a sexual manifestation. There were no longer any great surprises in this area.

So the American people kept their part of the deal. Somehow they sensed that politics, perhaps like Hollywood and sports, was different, that many who were most successful in this profession were not exactly normal people seeking normal jobs and dealing with normal temptations, and that in politics the lust for office and power was often accompanied by other exceptional lusts that went well beyond the norm. No wonder then that, year by year, the American people were less disillusioned when that turned out to be true. They accepted more readily an equation that previous generations might have had more trouble with: that Bill Clinton was at once absolutely brilliant as a politician, both gifted and original, and deeply flawed as a man, both reckless and self-absorbed, and that these seemingly contradictory characteristics were not unrelated. It was in the nature of being a great politician that even when he was paying full attention to you, he was self-absorbed, determined to make you like him, thinking not of you, as it seemed, but only of himself.

What had helped Clinton in the off-year election was a broad public dislike of many of his pursuers. His luck had held once again. Though the Republicans had tried to make him and his morality the central issue of the election, the people of the country apparently had a greater aversion to his various critics than they had for him: the special prosecutor; Linda Tripp, who had wiretapped a young woman who was supposedly her friend; the Republican leadership; and the smut-crazed media, particularly its television pundits, who feasted on the story and talked and talked about it on the air, the people whom the writer Calvin Trillin called "the Sabbath gasbags."

But if Clinton had dodged a potentially lethal bullet, he remained in political terms seriously but not mortally wounded, and his moral authority was greatly diminished. The election news was generally good, but he still faced the terrible threat of an impeachment proceeding.

CHAPTER THIRTY-SIX

With the White House under constant pressure, both domestic and foreign, the key foreign policy player in Washington, the linchpin in a divided government, as one colleague described him, the most important person other than the president himself, was Sandy Berger. He was also the only one of the original principals still operating in the administration in its sixth and soon to be seventh year. Lake was gone, Christopher was gone, Powell and Shalikashvili were both gone, and Cohen was the administration's third secretary of defense, following Aspin and Perry. The president and his advisers paid more attention to Albright as secretary of state than they had when she was at the UN, but even now there was resistance to her pressure for activism. Moreover, something else was missing: she was just not one of the boys. At the start of the Clinton presidency Berger had been Lake's deputy by his own choice, but because of his close personal ties to the president, he had always been a senior player, even before he got the top job.

Berger was the quiet man of the administration, the figure about whom the least was known. He was also both politically and emotionally the closest to the president, with a sure sense of his attitudes, needs, and vulnerabilities at all times. What presidents of the United States require at that level is a combination of undivided loyalty and a very practical kind of intelligence, and Berger offered both. Many of those alleged to be Clinton's close friends, the famed FOB list, were in fact rather casual relationships of mutual self-advantage, some of them long-standing, some of them instant, very few of them deeply rooted and sealed with real trust. Berger's relationship with Clinton was special. In an atmosphere supercharged with ambition and vainglory, it was unusually selfless. Their friendship was mutually solid, had never been tainted, and was distinct from almost any other Clinton working friendship, except perhaps that with Strobe Talbott. But unlike Talbott, Berger had daily access to the president, and anyone who tried to undermine their connection would always lose. Berger's strength was that he did not seek greater power or title, he never let his ego get in the way, and he read Clinton perfectly. Their attitudes on most issues—and the *politics* of these issues—were almost identical.

They had first met during the McGovern campaign in the fall of 1972 at, of all unlikely places, the Alamo. The youthful Berger was writing speeches for

McGovern, driven into politics by the Vietnam War, and Clinton was helping to run the Texas campaign for the South Dakota senator, not the most enviable of assignments. Years later Berger's view of that campaign remained quite enthusiastic. He had realized early on, he said, that its chances of success were limited, but because it had been based on so powerful an idea, ending what was to many in his generation an unacceptable war, and because it had rallied people behind so thoroughly decent a man, it had brought a large number of talented and idealistic young people into the political process for the first time—the next step after their earlier participation in college protests against the war. Berger's first glimpse of the president-to-be was of a quite tall, effusive young man in a white suit—shades of Colonel Sanders—talking incessantly about Arkansas and Southern politics. He was filled with energy, intelligence, and ambition, and in no way depressed about the unlikelihood of his candidate carrying the state to which he had been assigned. Berger remembered one other thing in addition to Clinton's size and energy: he seemed more grounded in his home territory—more rooted, so much a man of Arkansas— than almost anyone else Berger had met at that time. Many of the young would-be political people he knew in Washington, then all in their midtwenties, were ambitious but in some way already partially disconnected from their roots. They had left their hometowns to come to Washington to be part of the larger game working for someone else. Unlike them, Clinton's roots and his political future were entwined. He would run for office at home. He was not looking to exercise power without leaving Washington.

In the eighties their friendship flourished. Berger might be Eastern and Jewish, but he was small-town upstate New York with a boyhood not that different from Clinton's. His father had died when he was eight, and his mother had raised him in difficult economic circumstances. By the eighties Berger had located in Washington, Harvard Law School was behind him, and he was obviously bright and very political so he made an immediate appearance on Clinton's Rolodex, a kindred soul in the nation's capital who was worth staying in touch with. Not long after they had met in Texas, Clinton ran for office and was elected governor of Arkansas. Since he was always looking to connect, and Washington more than Little Rock was a place where you could connect with other bright young men and women, the kingmakers and queenmakers of the future, he visited there frequently, meeting with a small but ever expanding coterie of friends: Carl Wagner, another old friend who also went back to the McGovern campaign when he had run Michigan for the Dakotan; Strobe Talbott, Clinton's old Oxford roommate, a rising star in Washington journalism; Derek Shearer, Talbott's brother-in-law; and of course Berger, who was beginning to make a reputation as a trade lawyer with a Washington firm, but whose primary passion was politics.

Berger was very much taken with Clinton. Though Clinton had no family wealth, he was willing to put himself on the line by running for political office. That meant his views, unlike theirs, could not be abstract: they had to reflect the hard realities of liberalism in the eighties, especially in the South. That impressed Berger greatly. In his view, no other young politician he knew had the rare combination of high intelligence and genuine compassion that Clinton possessed. His range of interests was enormous; there was no book on public policy or history that he had not read, no one he met that he did not try to learn from and, of course, to win over. For Clinton the central issue of American life was race, and the job of any successful American politician, beyond the day-to-day burden of making the state or the country function a little better, was to work toward the immense ongoing task of racial reconciliation. Berger readily agreed with him about the primacy of that task.

It was very much a downtime for Democrats in Washington, and Berger had forged a strong link with Pamela Harriman, who had become a focal point of Democratic Party energy in the capital, having founded a group called Democrats for the Eighties (known privately as PAMPAC). Berger wrote some speeches for her while at the same time introducing her to the bright young aspirants of the party. He not only connected Clinton to her, but also managed to get him on her board, which gave the Arkansas governor reason to come to Washington regularly to meet and be met. Berger wanted to display him as much as he could, sure that every time Clinton met the doyens and doyennes of Washington, he would make a favorable impression. Often he did, using that immense intelligence and charm to convert people who had not intended to be charmed by so young a man from so obscure a place. As early as 1988, Berger thought that Clinton should run for the presidency, especially after Gary Hart self-destructed.

At one point Clinton seemed ready to make the race. An exploratory committee for his candidacy was going to be named and a press conference was scheduled for the announcement in Little Rock. Berger and Mickey Kantor, two of the principal architects of such a run, flew to Arkansas, only to find that Clinton and his wife had been up all night discussing his candidacy and had decided that it was not the right time. There had been enough tension in their marriage—some of the problems that afflicted Hart had also afflicted Clinton—their daughter was still young, and the sum of the negatives was too great. The most lasting image that Berger had of that trip was of walking around the back of the governor's mansion and by chance looking in the window just as Clinton went into the kitchen and told the news to Chelsea, then about eight. She was so thrilled by his declaration of noncandidacy that she jumped into his arms.

Berger was with Clinton in 1988 when he gave his endlessly long speech nominating Michael Dukakis for the presidency. Expectations were high. Everyone connected to Clinton knew how talented and articulate he was, and his coterie was sure that this was his moment and he would hit it out of the park. Perhaps not unlike the young Jack Kennedy, who had seized on his razor-thin defeat for the vice-presidential nomination at the 1956 convention to open his candidacy for 1960, Clinton would open the door for the future with his speech. Instead he went on and on. And on. CBS showed its viewers a red light flashing on the podium, a signal for Clinton to end it. On NBC, Tom Brokaw said, "We have to be here, too," a sign to his audience that he shared its pain. Only when Clinton ad-libbed, "In closing . . . ," was there spontaneous applause.[1] It was, Berger would later say, one of the most painful experiences of his life. The man he had been selling for a decade to others as the brightest young hope of the party had finally gotten his golden moment and had melted down in front of the entire nation, unable to stop, failing to do something that he probably did better than anyone else in the country, read an audience. Berger felt physically ill and had to get away from the convention floor. Just as he was leaving, he ran into the governor and his wife. "That was pretty bad, wasn't it?" Clinton said. Berger agreed that it was.

Two things then happened that impressed Berger. Instead of ducking the media, Clinton immediately went upstairs, in the heat of this calamity, to deal with the national press corps, and a few days later, he called Berger and said, "They want me on *Johnny Carson.* What do you think?" "It's a terrible idea," Berger said, sure that it was some late-night-television producer's dream of the perfect evening: Carson, the great comedian, would take a man who was drowning and hold his head underwater for the final count, upping his own ratings while at the same time presiding over the end of Clinton's national career. But Clinton took that risk. He went on the show, played the saxophone, made fun of himself, and began lancing the boil.

The political twinning of Berger and Clinton, the mix of both idealism and pragmatism, was almost pure. The two men were originally linked by the Vietnam War. Berger, like Clinton, had been a dove. At Cornell, he had taken a course on Southeast Asia taught by the well-known professor George Kahin, one of the war's early critics, and Berger had become convinced that the American involvement in Vietnam was bound to fail. He graduated from Cornell in 1967, just as the protests on the war were obscuring every other issue on the political agenda. Already something of a political junkie, he went to work for Democratic congressman Joe Resnick, who had been elected in a traditionally Republican district in upstate New York—Franklin Roosevelt's own home district, which he himself had never carried. Resnick was young, idealistic, and a self-made millionaire. He had never finished high school and had made his money after World War II producing television antennas. He was one of the more than forty Democrats carried along on Lyndon Johnson's coattails in the 1964 landslide, people elected from what been Republican districts, and Johnson had marked them from the start for special care. He wanted them reelected in 1966 and threw all kinds of favors at them; more than thirty post offices in Resnick's district, Berger remembered, were delivered by the White House.

There is no such thing as a free lunch or a free post office, and of no politician was that more true than Johnson. Resnick was Jewish, and as the Vietnam War escalated, Johnson (incorrectly) decided that Resnick could be helpful with an important Democratic Party constituency with which the president was already having trouble, liberal Jews. He also started sending Resnick to Vietnam, which he would visit some ten times, getting VIP treatment from all the top people there and becoming quite hawkish. That helped endear him to Johnson, as did his dislike of Bobby Kennedy, but it led to a series of heated discussions between Berger and Resnick, even as Resnick decided to run for the Senate in 1968 as the Hubert Humphrey stand-in. It was also the year Berger began to look elsewhere for work before eventually entering Harvard Law School. By 1972, he was out of law school and had landed a job with the McGovern campaign as a speechwriter.

Berger was a dove, but Vietnam had not been the dominating part of his life as it had been for Lake and Holbrooke. Berger would later talk in private about how Clinton and he were different from men like Lake and Holbrooke, for whom Vietnam was an obsessive issue from which so many other things flowed. On reflection Berger felt that the war had had too great an effect on the wing of the party he was part of, the liberal-left McGovern wing. It had happened, he thought, as a natural outgrowth of the anger over Vietnam, but that wing had become too critical of the uniformed military (or at least too distanced from it and not respectful enough), and too critical of American foreign policy engagements elsewhere. The first Democratic politician to try to lead the party back to some semblance of balance in these matters and to figure out a rational and thoughtful defense policy that fit the needs of the changing world, he believed, was Gary Hart, McGovern's old campaign manager, with whom Berger had also become close.

Berger's years in office had solidified his relationship with Clinton. There was a certain modesty to him which helped, though late in his tour, when he had been operating either as the NSC deputy or the NSC adviser for eight years, some friends thought he had become a bit grandiose and began to refer to him privately as Sandy Kissinger. He had an almost perfect sense of pitch for the job, and above all, something critical for any assistant, a sense of how much additional pressure Clinton could absorb at any given time. Berger was not a strategist and made no pretense to be. When asked about that by the *New York Times,* Henry Kissinger, never especially generous with Democratic colleagues, had said somewhat disdainfully, "You can't expect a trade lawyer to be a global strategist."[2] In contrast with Lake, who had been considered a difficult colleague and kept too much to himself,

Berger worked well with the others on the NSC team. He was, not unlike the man he served, exceptionally pragmatic, but he resented it bitterly when critics in the media spoke of him as tilting too much toward an ad hoc policy— as if he and Clinton in the end did not believe in anything larger. The opposite was true, he believed.

Like the president he served, Berger's analytical powers were considerable. He could break issues down to their finer points, he understood the different constituencies affected by each issue overseas, and he was very much aware of the domestic political side of any foreign policy decision. He knew all of Clinton's political priorities. If he was not Clinton's political twin in his outlook toward foreign policy and what the administration might be able to do at any given moment, then no one had ever been able to tell what the perceptible differences between the two of them were. Berger stood at the exact point where the pressures of the outside world and the domestic political pressures on the president intersected. To know what Clinton felt, you only needed to know what Berger felt, and if Berger was not yet ready to take a position on a complicated and pressing issue like Kosovo, it meant that the president wasn't ready either.

On January 15, 1999, shortly after the president's personal vindication in the off-year election, Madeleine Albright stood alone at an NSC principals meeting again pushing for action against Milosevic. She pointed out what was by then common knowledge. The deal that Holbrooke had pulled off in October was falling apart, and she argued strongly for the use of force. But neither the uniformed chiefs nor Bill Cohen wanted to be pulled into the Balkans. Sandy Berger again reflected the White House's doubts. Clinton, still besieged domestically, was hardly eager for a new military adventure. Albright was immensely frustrated by the meeting. "We're just gerbils running on a wheel," she said on her way back to her office.[3]

That was a fateful day. If she could not move the machinery, Albright was sure that sooner or later events would. She did not have long to wait. The last time, in Bosnia, it was Srebrenica that had moved the West to take action. This time, in Kosovo, it was a village called Racak. Events there occurred at almost exactly the same time as the we're-just-gerbils meeting in Washington, though it would be some time before the complete reports reached the principals. What happened at Racak changed everyone, and its political import was obvious: Kosovo, like Bosnia, could no longer be ignored.

Racak was another of those small towns that would come to symbolize something larger than themselves. By the late fall of 1998, the KLA had moved into Racak and used it as a base from which to strike at the Serbs. After a small KLA unit had apparently attacked local Serbs, killing four policemen, a significantly larger, heavily armed Serb unit entered the town. A group of about thirty Albanian men were hiding in a cellar, where the Serbs found them. Young male children were separated from the grown men, and Human Rights Watch, a humanitarian monitoring group, later reported that a conscious decision had clearly been made to execute all the male adults in the town. Twenty-three men were taken from the cellar and marched away. Other men were also apparently taken from different houses in the village.

Soon there were reports of a major massacre at Racak. William Walker, the American who headed the Kosovo Verification Mission, immediately led a convoy to the town. There he found what appeared to be a body lying under a blanket. He lifted the blanket and saw a headless corpse, the beginning of a trail of gore and brutality. Every fifteen or twenty yards Walker and his party discovered another body—all of them riddled with bullets, many of them shot through the head or the eyes. The hill where the first body was found was littered with forty-four other corpses. Walker had served in El Salvador as a diplomat and was no stranger to violence, but this was the worst scene he had ever visited. A few survivors reported that the men had been rounded up, brought to the hill, told to kneel, and then executed.

The massacre at Racak became the critical lever for those in the American government and in allied Western governments to move for military action against the Serbs, a sure sign that the worst of Bosnia would be repeated. Walker, viewed in the State Department as a freelancer whose sympathies were clearly with the Kosovars, did not even check with Washington for instructions. He immediately held an emotional press conference and described what had happened at Racak as a crime against humanity. Albright knew the value of what had happened as well. If there were some people in the administration who thought that Walker had gone too far, she was not one of them. She picked up the phone and called him: "Bill, you're doing a great job. You were right on as far as Racak was concerned."[4]

At NATO headquarters, General Wes Clark felt much the same way. He, too, had been waiting for this. One of his aides remembered hearing him say, when he learned of the Racak massacre, "I have them [the Serbs] where I want them now." Racak finally mobilized the West, greatly lessening the divisions not just between the different countries but within the Clinton administration itself, and made it much harder for the doves to oppose action. Almost certainly there would be a military reckoning.

CHAPTER THIRTY-SEVEN

Once again the Clinton administration found itself pulled by events toward a second unwanted confrontation in the Balkans, with almost none of the larger issues about what America's role there would be, both political and military, as yet resolved. Moreover, the tensions between the administration and the military, most particularly the U.S. army, were not that different from the time almost six years earlier when Clinton had first arrived in office and Colin Powell dominated the play, slowing down the administration's somewhat unfocused vision of a more flexible policy toward peacekeeping missions. The president was obviously somewhat in favor of a wider range of humanitarian missions, but it was hardly policy, and how large a price he would be willing to pay for his beliefs had not been determined. There was no Clinton doctrine, and if the administration had a larger view of what it wanted to do in the world, it had yet to sell it to the Congress or the country.

When the Clinton people spoke about using force in Kosovo, it once again evoked memories of Vietnam to many senior military men. After six years, the debate within the administration between civilians and the military had not really advanced that much, nor was it in truth that much of a debate. Because the issues were so thorny and difficult, both sides generally preferred to talk around what divided them, as if candor would only reveal how divided they really were. Thus the tensions between the senior military and the people in the administration remained substantial. On the surface things seemed to work smoothly. Colin Powell was no longer there to intimidate them. To some degree John Shalikashvili had eased the working relationship, but he had not really brought the two sides closer together. The one person who had helped close the chasm was Bill Perry, who was widely regarded in the Pentagon as one of the superior public servants of the time, a man who was tough but always straight and fair, and who always *listened* to the uniformed officers. He had been replaced in the second Clinton administration by Bill Cohen, a liberal Republican senator from Maine with maverick tendencies, and by 1998 the military jury was still out on him. Though he was likable and intelligent, the general feeling was that he lacked the passion and consuming interest for the job that Perry had shown. He was clearly every bit as bright as Perry, but he seemed neither as knowledgeable nor as *involved* in the running of the Pentagon as Perry had been. Someone who knew them both said that if Bill Perry wrote his autobiography, virtually all of it would be about his years as secretary of defense; if Bill Cohen wrote his autobiography, after a long and successful career in both the House and the Senate, his years at the Pentagon would get one brief chapter.

In the fall of 1997, Shalikashvili was to retire, and the choice for his successor became an immensely important decision, especially with the final chapter on the Balkans still to be written. Given the politics of the administration, the desire to have a more flexible military policy, and Clinton's innate belief that the military was a hostile political constituency (which of course it was), it had not been an easy search. It was never going to be about pure talent, and there was no one sure choice for Shalikashvili's replacement. One of the leading contenders was General Jack Sheehan of the marines. He was a formidable figure, intellectually superior, unusually confident, and just as outspoken, a man not likely to compromise on things he believed important. But he tended to make both civilians and military men nervous with his singular bluntness. He was prone to tell his peers that they were always preparing to fight the last war, not the next one. In strategic terms he agreed with some of the Clinton administration's vision of what America might do in a turbulent and unsettled world to help stabilize it at a relatively low cost. In fact, probably no officer was more critical of the military's failure to adjust and prepare for the new kind of assignments that faced the country—assignments that demanded force restructuring and reevaluation of American military strategy in order to fight smaller, lower intensity wars in the second and third world.[1] Both Clinton and Berger were intrigued by Sheehan's talent and brainpower, but he was by White House standards high-risk. Just a year earlier, at an Aspen Institute conference where many important national security people had gathered, Sheehan had startled his audience by his straightforward talk. Inexpensive military missions, free of casualties, were a pipe dream, he said. If the American military was going to go abroad, then you had better assume that it would cost a great deal of money "and put your sons and daughters in harm's way." Sheehan tended to impress high-level civilians and simultaneously make them quite uneasy. "We really like you and you can have the number two job [vice chairman]," Sandy Berger once told him, "but you won't get the number one job."

Of Sheehan's intelligence, talent, and will there was no doubt. He came in the size the military liked. He was six feet five, a former basketball player at Boston College and a winner of the Silver Star in Vietnam. But the other chiefs were not always fond of him. He had once told an armored commander that his tanks were essentially useless given the technological changes in weaponry and their vulnerability to new, easily fired surface weapons. Shalikashvili had not recommended Sheehan for chairman, fearing resentment among the other chiefs. He was privately considered the brightest of the various candidates, with as good a combat record as anyone else available. In terms of strategy, his vision might parallel that of the Clinton civilians, and that was the rub. If a situation arose where they might have to use force, he would demand a strong commitment—what were the roles and missions, what was the exit strategy, how publicly would the administration back the military, and where was the Congress? Would the military go in and then find, if things got difficult, that it was out there alone? Sheehan, it was judged, would be the hardest of the senior men to control, and in a dispute over strategy, the most likely to resign in protest. That was the nightmare. This formidable, exceptionally impressive marine, who agreed with the Clinton administration's theory of what we should be doing in foreign policy, might go public if it was unwilling to make the necessary commitment. Sheehan would not get the chairman's job.

The man the administration wanted to choose—Bill Cohen's obvious favorite—was an air force general, Joe Ralston. Considered by the Clinton people to be the most subtle of the senior officers, Ralston was comfortable with his colleagues in the military and yet much admired in Washington by many different groups, including the top people in the Clinton NSC and some of the senior people on the Hill. Because of his considerable political skills, he had managed to make both the Clinton civilians and the senior military feel that he was their sympathetic partner. He was intelligent, low-key, knew how the bureaucracy worked, got on with almost everyone, and seemed able to remove obstacles to consensus, rather than create them. Wes Clark, who had his own difficulties with Ralston and the chiefs, later wrote of him, "He was the kind of officer you didn't forget. I remembered thinking at the time [the first time they met] that he certainly knew how to round the edges off an issue."[2] When the Clinton people spoke about Ralston, they invariably said he was helpful. Ralston was tapped by Bill Cohen to replace Shalikashvili, but then Ralston had been forced to move aside because—it was a new age in the military—he acknowledged having committed adultery some ten years earlier at a time when he had been separated from his wife. Given the issues of sexism in the military, that posed a serious problem, particularly at that exact moment. Almost simultaneously, another sex scandal threatened the military. First Lieutenant Kelly Flinn, a graduate of the Air Force Academy, the first woman to fly a B-52 and thus something of a poster girl for the new air force, had had an affair with the husband of an enlisted woman and was threatened with a court-martial, not merely for adultery, but for lying fairly systematically to her superiors about it. That raised the issue of a double standard for a senior officer; and given the cloud that perpetually hovered over the Clinton White House about extramarital sex, it was enough to block Ralston as head of the JCS.

With Ralston out of the picture, the qualities required for the new chairman began to change. He would have to have a squeaky-clean personal life. "Do you have a Ralston problem?" one of the Pentagon's lawyers asked General Hugh Shelton, an army four-star and one of the top candidates for the job. No, he answered. He had known his wife since he was thirteen and she was the only woman he loved. Shelton, the Clinton people thereupon decided, was perfect for the job. He was old-fashioned, not especially verbal but good with the troops, known as a soldier's soldier, apparently crusty, and significantly more laconic, for example, than Wes Clark. Shelton had a worthy combat record and was not likely to break any crockery.

Other military men generally liked Shelton. He was simple, no pomp, no frills, and in no way did they feel threatened by him. Rather they revered what he represented. He was six feet five, his chest was covered with ribbons, and he made a considerable impression on civilians, especially, in the nineties, among the many who had never been in the service. It would be hard to imagine his being as successful in many civilian enterprises as he was in the army—perhaps as a professional football coach, where the physical ambience that a man generates is also important. Moreover, Shelton fit the traditional culture of the military far more readily (and comfortably) than someone like Clark. He knew when to talk and when not to talk, a talent that had proved somewhat elusive for Clark. When Cohen named Shelton chairman, he interestingly enough compared him not to other generals but to two movie stars, Gary Cooper and John Wayne: "tall, straight to the point, not a lot of words."[3]

Shelton had served two tours in Vietnam, the first as a Special Forces A team leader in 1967, and the second as the commander of an infantry company. His record was spotless. He was assistant commander of the elite 101st Airborne during Desert Storm, and later commanded the 82nd Airborne. In 1993 as a commander of the 18th Airborne Corps, he was designated to lead the task force that was to invade Haiti and remove General Raoul Cedras, an invasion that was just about to take place when Cedras, knowing it was all over, stepped down. Shelton had given Cedras and the junta twenty-four hours to get out of the presidential palace. His last message to Cedras was marvelously brief and blunt: "We want you to take everything that belongs to you, and nothing else."[4]

Shelton was, thought his peers, a good man, not brilliant but fair and steady, who represented the virtues, the strengths, the limitations, and the conservatism of the service that had produced him. If some army people were uneasy about Clark's loyalties—were they inside the Pentagon or outside it?—there was no such question about Shelton. He was a man of the institution. He was intelligent, but in civilian-military matters unassertive and obviously often quite uncomfortable in dealing with some of the infinitely complex issues a chairman had to face. His new job was not a natural fit nor one that he would necessarily have sought out. The political responsibilities that went with the job were a constant, yet always seemed alien to Shelton. He had a natural sense of what was good for the army, but many of the other issues he would find troublesome.

Besides, in 1998 as things heated up in Kosovo, the larger question of trust between the Clinton administration—now entering its sixth year—and the senior military remained a problem. There had always been a huge difference of interests and values separating the politicians and the generals, an inevitable suspicion of each side by the other. But now the normal tensions between the two were made considerably more severe by the changing nature of the foreign conflicts potentially being faced, conflicts where the military saw our involvement as being driven by political or moral, rather than national security, concerns. Perhaps even more damaging, the gap between the politicians and the military was greater in this administration and even more difficult to bridge because of the nature of politics in the nineties. The senior military had always been more conservative than the general body politic. For a variety of reasons, not the least of them the issue of gay rights in the military, it was also becoming more identified with the Republican Party than ever before. Gays and people who believed in gay rights tended to identify with the Democratic Party; people who opposed gay rights, such as the senior military, identified with the Republicans, sometimes overtly, sometimes covertly. That meant that in all the struggles between the civilians and the military, the military always knew it had a formidable ally on the Hill with the Republican leadership. Not only did the military know it, but the Clinton administration's senior people knew it as well. The military had stronger philosophical ties with the Republicans and, ironically, greater leverage over the Democrats and a Democratic president, leverage that was a great card as long as it was never really played. It was the threat of it which gave the military power.

The military also had problems with Clinton himself, some of which went back to the way he had handled his draft call. But it went much deeper than that. After all, few of the other senior Republicans (Lott, Gingrich, Quayle, Cheney, George W. Bush) had availed themselves of the chance to go to Vietnam. Phil Gramm, a leading Republican senator who once ran for the presidency, had not gone, but quickly noted that his brother had served. Of that, the columnist Murray Kempton had written memorably, "Thus contentedly and unblushingly does Phil Gramm pronounce his duty done. He is not his brother's keeper, but his brother is conscripted to be his."[5] In the 2000 election the Democrats would nominate a candidate, Gore, who had gone quite voluntarily, and the Republicans would nominate two who had not, but it would not help Gore at all with the military.

Some of the divisions could be traced to the very different nature of politicians and military men. Stated simply, the qualities that made Bill Clinton a superb end-of-the century operator in the fragmented, volatile world of American politics—his skill with words, his immense subtlety, his ability to bridge and tantalize all different kinds of opposing constituencies, his knowledge of what to say to each group at every moment and, above all, whom he might be able to bend just a bit—all of this made the more senior people at the Pentagon singularly distrustful of him. It was cultural. The more naturally gifted a politician was, the more uneasy a high-level officer became, aware that he might be operating out of his league and could have his pocket picked. Politicians used words as ambiguously as possible. Military men often hated ambiguity. What for a politician might be a skill was for a military man quite possibly deception. In the military certain qualities were valued, and you judged your peers in the most elemental way: Would they help carry their wounded off the battlefield under fire? The military people had their doubts that, even in the political sense, Bill Clinton passed that test.

What military men asked about a political leader was whether in a grave military crisis he would be steadfast. (When Wes Clark eventually emerged during Kosovo as an activist, moving closer to the top civilians and away from the senior military, one of his colleagues asked him where his civilian pals were going to be if things went sour. Would they, like the civilians behind the Vietnam debacle, go off to write their books and take their big jobs, the way Mac Bundy and Bob McNamara had done at the Ford Foundation and the World Bank, leaving him to hold the bag?) In the military, someone who was too nimble, too supple with words, too facile, someone who was able to go to different meetings and seem to please opposing constituencies, was not regarded with admiration; he was regarded with distrust. Military men liked their words straight. General David Shoup, who had headed the marines during the Kennedy years, once said that a senior officer's job was not to worry about what the politics of an administration were, but to wait until the president told him to saddle up and go, and then to saddle up and go.[6]

What the military in its codes valued more than anything else was honor; serious military men always knew which of their colleagues had served their time in combat and could be counted on. That was why in private, when they were in uniform among each other, army men often did not display all their ribbons but instead wore the Combat Infantry Badge. It was the army's true badge of honor, and wearing the CIB without other ribbons—even the Silver or Bronze Star—was part of the culture's secret language, the way real army men spoke to each other, deliberately understated. It said in effect that the recipient had been there and done it, and for anyone else who had also been there, that was all you needed to know. And if you hadn't been there, it didn't matter what you thought.

If the military had reservations about the civilians, there were just as many civilian reservations about the military. The most basic frustration—it went back to Madeleine Albright's challenge to Colin Powell about what use he was going to put his fine army to—was that the military always seemed to want too large a force, hundreds of thousands of soldiers to perform any mission—a force level so great that all missions became undoable. Or, as Wes Clark wrote later in his book, the army had gradually become corporatized, "part of the Vietnam hangover." The standard reply (when asked to undertake a mission) was "We'll do it if you direct us, sir, but here are the risks, and we always manage to convey that if you direct us to do this, then you'll be responsible for the losses." To the civilians the military remained too cautious. The second complaint was that though the military men liked to think they were above politics, they were, in fact, very political. They knew how to exploit their leverage with the Republican leadership, and they used a double standard. They were hard on the Democrats who had not gone to Vietnam but paid little attention if it was a friendly Republican politician who had somehow avoided the draft.

Clearly the twain between the military and the Clinton administration had barely met. Clinton had been aware from the start of the doubts about him among the military. Before he could function effectively as president, he knew he would have to overcome at least some of those doubts, and he had worked hard to do that. He had upgraded his personal behavior in dealing with them and had used all of his considerable talents and charm in personal meetings to diminish whatever lingering stereotypes they might have of him. He was not some peacenik left over from the sixties, unwilling to use force when necessary. He could be just as tough and hard-nosed as necessary. He constantly reached out to them, and at times he had tried to end the distrust by offering different leaders of different services more weapons systems than they might have been ready to ask for—an extra aircraft carrier, say, for the navy, are you sure you don't want one? But it had not really taken. They looked for other things. They believed that the White House wanted, as much as it could, to limit the power of the Joint Chiefs, and that given a choice in naming a chief, the Clinton people would always go for the less aggressive officer with the lower visibility on the public landscape.

Many of the top people in the Pentagon had monitored Clinton's behavior from the start. For the military men had their own intelligence systems, unofficial but very good. A military representative was at virtually every important meeting, and he reported back to the Pentagon not merely about the decision that had been made, but about the forces that had driven it, the texture of the meeting, what had been left unsaid, and the subterranean signals the White House was giving out. The military did not like Clinton's decision at the very start of his administration to allow gays to serve openly in the military, but they liked it even less when, facing considerable opposition, he had backed off almost immediately. Nor, when Somalia turned into a disaster, had they been pleased. What had happened there was like a terrible death in the family for the military, but they had been equally disturbed by the interior White House response. First came the preoccupation with spin, about which they were aware, and second, as the White House people prepared to go before the Congress to explain what had happened, they made it clear to the military people who came over to help brief them that the White House wanted to minimize its own culpability in the decision to upgrade the mission and go for nation-building. The Pentagon people believed that decision had been as much Tony Lake's as Jonathan Howe's, but the perception was that the White House wanted to get Lake's fingerprints off it. It was possible that this was wrong, but that was how they saw the administration. To them it showed that what was for them a matter of life and death, of young men dying, could become for the White House all too easily a matter of images.

To many military men the president was charming and talented and seductive. But in their view the primary concern at the White House was not necessarily reality, or at least reality as the military men perceived it. Rather it was the *appearance* of reality—spin. What the people at the White House wanted to do, many military men believed, was to keep certain issues off CNN, or if that was not possible, if they finally exploded out in the world of instant media coverage, to deal with what was going on CNN with an acceptable amount of counterspin—to show they were doing something, even if what they were doing was largely inadequate. Thus, if they could not do anything about the genocide in Rwanda, they would at least use C-130s to drop food, though that was not necessarily the most pressing problem in the region.

By 1998 the senior military men still did not really trust Clinton and the people around him, and he, in turn, still did not trust them. Their purposes were more often than not different, their codes were different, their journeys to the top were different, their Americas were different, and their worlds were different. At the very top it took an unusually skillful man like Shalikashvili or Ralston to satisfy both cultures. Even in the normal byplay between the military and the politicians, both sides tended to speak guardedly, elliptically, and cautiously to each other, editing out or toning down what they really felt, trying to accommodate and find middle ground, and by doing that, ending up not being quite as candid as they should have been. That lack of candor was more exaggerated in the Clinton years, and there was even a certain reluctance, post-Somalia, to put anything about force levels in a combat area down on paper. This was not always obvious to outsiders watching the two cultures trying to blend, or watching Clinton as he tried hard to reach out to the senior military. Nor was it entirely clear to some of the senior civilians themselves.

For the military, especially at the highest levels, was a rare surviving part of America where manners and civility were still important, and by comparison with the rest of the culture, they were almost self-consciously old-fashioned. That, too, was part of the code; all senior civilians were to be treated with respect and courtesy. Thus it was quite possible to mistake the fact that the perfectly groomed three-star whose manners were so exceptional in dealing with you in fact disliked and quite possibly despised much of what you stood for. So if the military and civilians did not exactly talk past each other, they were not straight with each other.

But late in his presidency, Clinton appeared to have an epiphany. It was hopeless to try to turn around the attitudes of much of the upper- and midlevel military; the grievances against him were too deep. The enlisted men, however, were another thing. They were much younger, half his age, they had little or no memory of Vietnam, he was their commander in chief, and when he came to visit them, they were thrilled. The enthusiastic receptions they gave him were especially valuable on the network news shows in trying to erase an old stain. Clinton became in those moments like Harry Truman in 1948. If the owners at countless Midwestern factories did not like him, he would go over their heads and campaign with their workers.

CHAPTER THIRTY-EIGHT

In early 1999 as the possibility of war over Kosovo loomed larger, both the West and Milosevic misunderstood each other. The West thought that it would be just like Bosnia. The threat of bombing, or just a taste of bombing, would do the trick: Milosevic would eventually see the light and bend to our will. Milosevic thought he could divide the West one more time and the alliance would crack if it had to go to war again. He also seemed to believe that his Russian friends would stop any NATO military action, or at the very least grant him access to their newest missiles, which would weaken NATO's strongest card—its use of airpower. Some seven years into the ongoing struggle with the West—a kind of constant brinksmanship—Milosevic had managed to retain the view of many a totalitarian figure before him. He believed that if democracies were slow to act, it was a sign of weakness; if they were affluent, then they were also decadent. In addition, because their politicians and their citizens feared paying the price of war, they could be bullied. He once told the German foreign minister, Joschka Fischer, "I can stand death—lots of it—but you can't."[1] That might or might not be true, but as a NATO bombing campaign became ever more likely, Milosevic finally realized he was now caught in the very same nationalistic forces that he had done so much to create.

In January 1999, when the allies were trying to explain to Milosevic the inevitability of a NATO air campaign against him, Wes Clark once more warned him that the situation was dire. Was it true, he asked the Serb leader, that he had just a few days ago told Dick Holbrooke that it was his neck if he lost Kosovo? "No no, no," Milosevic replied, "I never said that." Well, then, what did you tell Holbrooke? Clark, quite puzzled, asked. "I told him I would lose my *head,* not my *neck,*" Milosevic said in clarification. Head or neck, it was all drawing to a close.

In the wake of the massacre at Racak and in an attempt to end hostilities without the use of force, Madeleine Albright called a conference of both the Serbs and the KLA at Rambouillet, a great French château near Paris. What ensued was not exactly a model of decorum for a peace conference, and it made Dayton, which had its own chaotic quality, look like a paragon of order, symmetry, and purpose. Neither side, the KLA or the Serbs, wanted to be there.

The Serbs thought it was rigged against them, which it probably was, and the Albanians wanted independence instead of some kind of limited autonomy within Serbia, which was what the West wanted. The Serbs sent a B-level delegation; Milosevic did not attend nor did his top people. But even the Albanians had to have their arms twisted to attend, although if they did participate and the Serbs did not, NATO would almost surely go to war on their behalf. Serb stubbornness was nothing new for Western negotiators, but the Albanian intransigence was a major surprise. At one point Albright showed up, apparently believing that a final push by the American secretary of state would get it done. But she found the Albanians not that sophisticated about her position and power. They probably thought, said Dugagjin Gorani, an adviser to the Kosovar delegation, that she was a cleaning woman. "Give us five minutes," one member of the delegation told her, "and go away."[2]

Only pressure from Bob Dole, who was considered a hero by most Kosovars because of his support, eventually convinced them to sign the agreement. "We'll abandon you if you don't sign," he told them. And so reluctantly and belatedly they did sign. Their coming aboard surprised the Serbs, who were sure the Albanians were too arrogant to accept a partial loaf. It was a sign of the lack of clarity within the administration that when Rambouillet essentially collapsed, no one seemed to be sure whether that was a good thing or a bad thing. As some senior administration members noted, Rambouillet at least allowed the administration to show to other NATO nations, still dubious about any military action, that the United States had walked the last mile to bring peace. The conference had failed because of Serb arrogance, and it was therefore now permissible to use force.

It is important to compare two sets of dates to understand the respective domestic and foreign policy pressures that were bringing this struggle to a denouement. Rambouillet began on February 6, 1999, and the Albanians reluctantly signed the agreement on March 18. The siege of Serbia was ready to begin. Back in America, Clinton had been impeached by the House of Representatives on December 19, 1998, and he was acquitted of the charges by the Senate on February 12, 1999. The siege of the White House was over. As Rambouillet fell apart and as the NATO deadline for bombing the Serbs approached in late March 1999, Richard Holbrooke made one last visit to Belgrade to talk with Milosevic. "You understand what will happen when I leave," Holbrooke said, knowing that this was a last fateful moment when the dogs of war could still be leashed. "Yes," Milosevic replied. "You'll bomb us. You're a big, powerful country and you can do anything you want, and there is nothing we can do about it."[3] The bombing, Holbrooke warned, and he had chosen his words carefully in conjunction with senior officers at the Pentagon, "will be swift, it will be severe, and it will be sustained."

Holbrooke thought Milosevic was oddly fatalistic and much less afraid than he was back in October when the Americans had last threatened to bomb. Holbrooke was not sure what had changed him. Perhaps it was the bombing that had taken place during Desert Fox, when the United States had attacked Iraq for seventy hours and then stopped, and Milosevic believed that he could withstand that kind of bombing. Or perhaps he had received from sources within NATO some sense of the limited nature of the NATO bombing orders and believed he could withstand that, too. Or perhaps it was simply a complete mood swing—that happened often enough with him. Whatever the reason, he was much less terrified than he had been a few months earlier, displaying an odd cockiness bordering on indifference.

The Joint Chiefs had accepted the idea of bombing the Serbs without any great enthusiasm. NATO and the White House were aboard, although what level of bombing and which targets remained unanswered questions. It was what the administration wanted, Sandy Berger had given the key signal, and Bill Cohen, filled with doubts, never an enthusiast, went along with it, especially because ground troops were being excluded, which would limit the hostility of opponents in the Congress in the early days of combat. Opposition would still be there, but it would be lurking rather than openly voiced, in most cases. But as the first step in a military action was taken, the Pentagon had its foot on the brake *just as it had on exactly the same issue for exactly the same reason six years earlier.* There was no agreed-upon Plan B. As Powell had often asked, what happens if the bombing does not work?

In the Tank, which was the sanctum where the Chiefs met, the talk had been an unusual blend of both acceptance and doubt. The only enthusiasm for bombing Kosovo was among some senior air force people eager to show what airpower, without ground troops, could do in situations like this. It might help end an important interservice argument that had lingered after Desert Storm. The air force thought that it had not been given proper credit for what it believed was its dominant role in the Desert Storm victory. By the time the ground forces were finally unleashed, the air force people privately believed, the Iraqi forces had been effectively demoralized, if not already defeated. According to that view, the subsequent remarkable four-day ground action had been little more than a tidying-up exercise of a beaten and disheartened Iraqi army.

This was not the first chapter in an old, old argument, nor the last, but Kosovo would allow the air force one more shot at showing what it could do, by unleashing maximum firepower against technologically inferior opponents. Because the casualties were likely to be minimal, it was a seductive path for political leaders facing a dilemma here or anywhere else. Still there were reservations, service by service, especially among the army and the marines, who might be the institutional losers in a mission like this. If those reservations had not been voiced that forcefully in the discussions inside the Tank, being muted because of a sense of which way the play was going, they could be heard as a kind of softer background chorus within the Pentagon in the days and weeks that followed. A policy that placed everything on airpower and therefore went against the most elemental philosophy of the U.S. army, and that had no proviso in case airpower failed, made people unhappy.

So it began, the administration's second act of war over the Balkans in four years. It was to be waged, the civilians and the military men had agreed, if at all possible, entirely through airpower. That was the strength of America and thus the strength of NATO. Or as Sandy Berger sometimes said privately, that was where the West's great advantage lay—an advantage of perhaps one thousand to one in airpower, whereas if it was a struggle with ground troops in terrible terrain, the advantage dropped to seven to one and the terms began to favor Milosevic. Moreover, the Yeltsin government had signaled the allies that while the Russians were unhappy about NATO's use of force against fellow Slavs, they would not come to Belgrade's defense or give the Serbs their newest surface-to-air missiles, which might have made it much more difficult for NATO.

But even so, the White House was in effect tiptoeing into the war, acutely aware of congressional opposition at home and the fragility of the alliance overseas. When the bombing began on March 24, the administration had not made a complete commitment. That night Clinton inserted one critical sentence into his statement, a sentence that would be at the heart of the divisions and the ambivalence of the NATO command in the next three months, reflecting all the unreconciled divisions of the last six years. "I do not intend to put our troops in Kosovo to fight a war," Clinton said. Months later, after it was all over, his top civilian people would privately admit that his statement might have been a considerable mistake. The top military people thought it was, in fact, a catastrophic mistake because it had given the wrong signal to all kinds of people, most notably Slobodan Milosevic.

Ironically, the line may have originated with one of the sterner critics of the administration's Balkan policy, Ivo Daalder, a resident scholar at the Brookings Institute, a former member of the NSC staff and very much an activist on Balkan policy. Daalder, who eventually wrote two thoughtful books on the Bush and Clinton Balkan policies, had become by then one of those talking heads favored on the more erudite television and radio shows, a blossoming star of the more refined media Rolodexes. Because of that, the White House, as it liked to do with such figures, was trying to bring him in on the policy, giving him an early look at it in the hope that if he appeared that night after the announcement was made, his criticism would at least be muted.

On the afternoon of Clinton's speech, Miriam Sapiro, an NSC staff member, called Daalder to outline what the president was going to say and to express her hope that he would support the policy. Of course, Daalder said, he would support greater activism on Kosovo—but what was the president going to say about ground troops? "We're going to say we have no plans to put in ground troops," she answered. "You can't say that because if we have no plans to put in ground troops, we ought to fire the person responsible for drawing up the plans," Daalder said. "So either you don't have plans and you're incompetent, or you're lying, so you can't say that." Then almost unconsciously, for the line was thin between being a man of the NSC and a man of Brookings, he suggested using the word *intention,* saying "something like we have no intention of using ground troops." A little later a sentence to that effect was in the speech, inserted at the last minute by Berger without the knowledge or approval of Albright. That left Daalder wondering if he was responsible, and whether what he had said on the phone to Sapiro was as big a mistake as he had made in quite a while. That night when he went on National Public Radio to critique the speech, he was very hard on the ground-troop exemption.

No matter what the origin of the line, the sentence represented what the Clinton people considered a mandatory political step. They had not even been able to get congressional approval for *peacekeepers* a few months earlier when Holbrooke was trying to lower the level of violence. What they wanted now instead was congressional acquiescence, and the price of acquiescence was that sentence about ground troops. If they had left open the possibility of ground troops, there would have been a congressional uproar. So they had made what appeared to be a commitment not to use ground troops, even though it was not necessarily a promise—it was a hedge, *intend* being the most flexible of words. "We do not want to send ground troops" might have been more accurate.

It was the compromise of all compromises. It would be hard, six years into the Clinton presidency, to think of a sentence more important within the bureaucracy. It summed up with surprising accuracy all the contradictions and the ambivalence of America as a post–Cold War superpower. We were willing to go to war to bring an end to Milosevic's recklessness and some stability to the Balkans. Yes, Kosovo was important, yes, it was worth going to war over, but was it a cause worthy of the lives of our young men and women on the ground? Was there any support for it in the Congress, in the media, in the country? Did we need to rally our people to the cause even as we fought?

Again it was an ad hoc policy, and ruling out ground troops, or seeming to rule them out, was at that moment perhaps the most logical—and easiest—next step to take. But at the Pentagon it rekindled all the old fears and doubts about how steadfast this administration was going to be on this issue. To many military men, it was not a mere throwaway line; rather it seemed to be carved in stone. They had to assume it was their marching orders. What it said to them was *We want this one but how far we are willing to go, we still don't know. Check with us later.* It was a reminder of the ambiguity of the Vietnam decision-making, of civilians who were willing to enter a war zone without any of the hard decisions having been made. As one senior officer said, as far as the military men were concerned, it was accommodating to your political fears even before you put your military strengths into action, especially in a war where the most important lever against a clever authoritarian bluffer was your ability to make him think he was facing the maximum use of power, not the minimum.

That sentence also reflected the White House view that it would be a quickie, a short war; the NATO bombing as it had worked in Bosnia would work just as rapidly this time. White House spokesmen, talking with reporters, made it clear they felt the bombing would last only three or four days; eventually its spokesmen let it be known to reporters that Madeleine Albright had talked that way to them. Indeed she had gone on television that first night with Jim Lehrer and spoken about the war being over quickly. "I don't see this as a long-term operation. I think this is something . . . that is achievable with a relatively short period of time," she told Lehrer. Or as Lieutenant General Mike Short, who would be in charge of the bombing, later said, "I can't tell you how many times the instruction I got was 'Mike, you're only going to be allowed to bomb two, maybe three nights. That's all Washington can stand. That's all some members of the alliance can stand. That's why you've only got ninety targets. This'll be over in three nights.'"[4]

Again, a certain division was at work here. Later, after the war had gone on much, much longer and the early prediction had become something of an embarrassment, some of Albright's people would insist that she had not pulled that figure out of the air; the Defense Department and the CIA must have thrown those estimates at her, they claimed. There were, however, people who thought the war might be more difficult than it might seem on the surface. Within the first few days, Walt Slocombe, the undersecretary of defense for policy, went to the Senate to make the case for the bombing, met with about twenty-five senators, and took a considerable pounding. At one point Robert Bennett of Utah asked him how long he thought the bombing would go on. It will go on until Milosevic stops doing what he's doing, Slocombe answered. Then Bennett said, "I know you can't give us a day for it to end, but if it goes on beyond a certain time, how long would it have to go on before you were surprised?" Three months, Slocombe answered.

CHAPTER THIRTY-NINE

In a war like this, with so much still unresolved and a policy deliberately cloaked in ambiguity for the benefit of the Congress, Clinton's commander in the field, General Wes Clark, would be the man caught in the middle between the conflicting forces: a hesitant White House, a skeptical Congress, a reluctant Pentagon, and of course the other members of NATO, all of them having very different attitudes on how much or how little power to use. His responsibility was to take this limited mandate and maximize it as best he could. A number of allies were hardly enthusiastic at the start and would grow increasingly uneasy day by day if the early use of airpower proved inadequate. If it was not immediately successful, he might have to push for expanded target lists and perhaps eventually for the use of ground troops or at least for the ability to threaten Milosevic with their use.

But because of what Clinton had said about ground troops and the decisions made by the principals about the Kosovo campaign, Clark would be in constant collision with the secretary of defense and the Joint Chiefs, who in time decided he was too hawkish, and as well with his air commander, Mike Short, who soon thought that Clark, most of the civilians in Washington, and almost all of the political leadership in Brussels were going to war halfheartedly and putting his pilots at risk for too little in the way of results. The decision to go with airpower alone might have been something that Clark had signed on to as part of his command. But the ability of the Serbs to endure the early weeks of the bombing campaign, the quite limited nature of the bombing itself, and the narrow target list soon became a major problem. Increasingly frustrated, Clark began to push for a more productive target list and the ability to make ground troops part of his command, if only to increase his leverage over Milosevic.

That would eventually separate him from Cohen and the Chiefs. Their marching orders—in their minds—were quite different. They had never wanted ground troops in the Balkans, and they took the White House's no-ground-troops statement perhaps more literally than the man who had issued it. Nor were they that enthusiastic even about the air campaign, and they were dubious of Clark as well. They did not like his early and constant advocacy of military force long before the fighting started, and they had never wanted him for that job in the first place. Thus were the lines drawn. The tensions between Clark and his colleagues in Washington were never over his talent. His credentials were more than good. They were impeccable. He was, in the army vernacular, a water walker, someone who was so good and whose career was so special that he walked on water. He was the kind of officer whose contemporaries would predict, when he was only a major, that he would surely get several stars, although in Clark's case they were saying it when he was a mere lieutenant. In the fall of 1962 as a plebe, he had begun his career in the army as a wunderkind and had ended it, thirty-seven years later, as a four-star and the American commander of NATO forces in Kosovo, still in a way a wunderkind, as bright and brash as the first day he arrived at West Point, ready to take on the world. Clark was in some ways like the president he served, both of them tapped early on as the brightest boy around, always first in their classes, both of them talented, driven, and unwilling to accept failure in any form.

Clark had been born in Chicago, the son of a Jewish father, Benjamin Kanne, who was a lawyer and minor Democratic Party player, and Veneta Kanne, a Protestant from Arkansas. His blood father died when he was four, and his mother returned to Arkansas and remarried a man named Clark, whose name young Wes took. He was raised as a Baptist, became a convert to Catholicism while in Vietnam, and only learned later in his life that he was half-Jewish. He had excelled as a high school student and several scholarships were available for prestigious colleges, but he wanted West Point. Clark had been first in his class during his plebe year at West Point in 1963, and first in his class when he graduated from the academy in 1966, which marked him as someone to watch. In time he had also been first in his class at the army's most critical trade school, the Command and General Staff School at Fort Leavenworth (where the elite were separated from the not so elite, and where, ironically enough, he had written his master's thesis on Rolling Thunder, the air campaign against the North in Vietnam, deciding that it had signaled weakness rather than strength of resolve), and he had almost always been first on the list for promotion. When in October 1983 the Reagan administration had made a quick strike at Grenada, the first use of force since Vietnam, Clark, then a light colonel, was given one of the two Ranger battalions, a plum assignment, a sign of an up-and-coming officer. Even in the upper level of the army, where everyone was high-powered, ambitious, and almost supernaturally focused, Clark stood out, and it had always been that way. He got his first star when he was only forty-three and commanded the First Cavalry Division at forty-six. He was the most competitive of men. Going back to his early years at West Point, he did not merely want to win; he *had* to win, and he had to win at everything. He had to be first in his class, anything else was unacceptable; he had to win a casual tennis game, which for Clark was not entirely casual. He had to win a regular morning jog with pals—it was friendly, of course, just exercise among friends—but it might as well have been a run at an Olympic event. Even when Clark was an instructor at West Point preparing a few of his cadets for their Rhodes scholarship interviews, they had to do better than candidates prepped by his colleagues. It was not hard to like him, noted one of his friends, just as long as you understood that Wes believed that every minute of every day could be used profitably, and that he had to win, even if he did not understand why he always had to win. The drive that set him apart was an irresistible impulse over which he had little control. To friends it was just Wes being Wes. Winning was a function of character.

He was not by army standards a good old boy, someone who invited intimacy and offered in return comfort and easy camaraderie. Nothing about him was easygoing. As he grew older, he seemed not to age, as if that, too, might be interpreted as a sign of weakness. He refused to gain a single pound, and his manner, the crisp, starched quality of his uniform, the austere, no-nonsense nature of his briefings—was anything ever left out?—seemed to emphasize the intense, unrelenting focus of his entire personality. He was always prepared—no question by a superior would ever catch him unprepared. No one dealing with Clark could ever doubt the totality of his purpose. His vision in terms of his career was singular. He saw brilliantly what was in front of him as if he had some kind of laser scope through which to see things that other mortals might discover only later in their careers. But his peripheral vision, his ability to pick up on what was going on around him and sense the feelings of peers, was considerably more limited. Nor did he necessarily think that was important. He had little sense of the impact his ferocious personality had on those contemporaries who were also bright, but perhaps not quite as bright or as driven or as verbal as he was. He was almost genetically incapable of adjusting to the covert codes of the institution he served, where it was considered a good thing to be intelligent, but to mask your intelligence under a warm, human veneer, to know more about certain things than you let on.

Yet his career was so gilded that in 1981, some sixteen years before he got the NATO command, the *Washington Post Magazine,* which wanted to do a profile of the new exemplary modern army officer, had been steered to Lieutenant Colonel Wes Clark, then only thirty-six. The title was revealing and prophetic: "Battalion Commander: If There's a World War III, Wes Clark May Be Your Man at the Front." He was, the article noted, "among the best the Army has to offer."[1] Later it added, "He approaches the [military] ideal, the perfect modern officer." But even in that article, some of the reservations about him, held by those who had a more traditional view of the army system and were put off by his single-minded sense of purpose, surfaced. One colleague had spoken of him for background: "This battalion [at Fort Carson] did need him, I'll admit that. . . . We all know that before he got here it was the pits. He solved every one of the problems, got it back on its feet. The man is definitely three-star material. He overshadows the battalion. [But] I don't know anyone who feels at ease with him. Nobody wants to give him bad news, so he has a very overrated opinion of morale and is very defensive about anything that might be wrong. Which could be dangerous . . ."[2]

When he left West Point, Clark had gone on to win a Rhodes scholarship, which is not unlike being handed a live hand grenade in the army. It puts you on a fast track, all kinds of powerful people now start looking out for you, but it also means that you may well go against the grain of the culture of the army, which is somewhat suspicious of people who think they are a little too smart and seem to be in too much of a hurry—the hallmark of most Rhodes Scholars. There is a terrific niche within the army for bright young Rhodes Scholars, you can rise reasonably high within a certain prescribed range as a soldier-intellectual (perhaps a brigadier, maybe even a two-star), and you can make yourself valuable over a long period at the Pentagon. Rhodes Scholars were also good advertising that this was a new, more modern, more cerebral army; in addition, it meant that the army had its own bright young men (and women) to deal with the high-powered, bright young civilians in the Defense Department who always wanted to cut its missions and budget, as well as the talented young men and women of the other services who wanted the newest toys for *their* branch. But the army had misgivings about many of them. "Are you a Rhodes?" one bright young officer, who had done brilliantly at the Point and had a glistening curriculum vitae, was asked by his superior on his first day at a new assignment. The officer said apologetically that though he had graduated high in his class, he had just missed the Rhodes. "Good," the commander said. "They all suffer from terminal arrogance before they're thirty." So it was always incumbent on someone who was a Rhodes to show that he was a real army man, a good guy and a straight shooter, one of the boys, as good with the men under him as he was with his superiors, and as much a warrior as he was an intellectual. Within the professional army, some Rhodes Scholars from West Point were eventually accepted by their peers, but they first had to overcome an undertow of distrust—of being perceived as being too favored by the gods.

Wes Clark, however, was not that good at softening the image he presented to others. Moreover, he was a Rhodes Scholar from *Arkansas,* and in the nineties that became something of a problem because it was often assumed that he was close to Clinton, which was not necessarily true. Some of the other officers thought that at times when he had been around Clinton as the J-5 of the Joint Staff during the Haiti operation, Clark had signaled an additional connection. It was almost a light flirt, a hint that the two of them had something apart from everyone else in the room. In reality they were not close, they had not overlapped at Oxford, and they had never been pals during their parallel rise to the top. But they were both small-town boys from the same region who had made good in the big time a long way from home, and there was, if not a friendship, a kind of kinship. Of Clark it could be said, when it was all over, that he was both a beneficiary and a victim of being a Rhodes Scholar from Arkansas. Some in the army pushed him ahead thinking he might help bridge the gap to these alien people in the White House, but even more found their doubts about him growing because they suspected he was working a little too hard trying to bridge that gap.

There was also a kind of all-American innocence to his personality, as if he had believed when he was a boy and still believed as a grown man that the best boy with the best grades who worked hardest would always be justly rewarded. Being with Wes, some friends thought, was like being back in high school and hearing one of the younger players on the football team asking the coach to put him in the game, saying that he could do it, could turn the losing tide around in the final moments. That quality had been true of him from West Point right through to the time he almost did not get his fourth star. "The problem with your General Clark is that he's very bright but he suffers from the gold-star syndrome," a high British officer told one senior American in Brussels during the Kosovo war. What do you mean? the American asked. "Well, don't you remember when you were in the first and second grade and you got a gold star for doing something right? Well, he's been doing that ever since, getting gold stars, and there's a real question as to whether life is about getting a gold star—about what your purpose in doing something is, and in getting ahead. He may be very driven without really knowing why he's so driven."

Those qualities did not necessarily endear Clark to his peers. He had always inspired some resentment, and the higher he went in rank, the more of it there appeared to be. Some of the resentment was driven by jealousy. Go up rapidly in a world like the military, where everyone knows not only your rank but how quickly you got it, and it is hard not to create some jealousy. Many of those most critical of him were men who were unsure of their own abilities and were, in contrast to Clark's rare decisiveness, loath to make a decision. But others who watched him worried whether he was not merely too ambitious, but too self-absorbed.

The criticism of Clark manifested itself in subtle and not so subtle ways. For example, among the many divisions that run through the army, one of the most important, alongside and quite parallel to that of field commander versus staff man, was that of pure warrior versus the military intellectual. Warriors, of course, were greatly favored within the culture, while military intellectuals were generally regarded with suspicion because it was believed that their talents were abstract, that on occasion they tended to play the game of civilian politicians, and that their primary loyalty might not be, consciously or unconsciously, like that of the warriors to their troops. That, many in the army believed, was what had happened in Vietnam. Johnson and McNamara had co-opted too many senior army men, some of them would-be intellectuals, and bent them into accepting the incremental escalation of what was an unwinnable war.

Whatever else, Clark was perceived by many as an army intellectual. But to others who knew him well, he was also, in every sense, the complete warrior. Lieutenant General Dan Christman, later superintendent of West Point and one of Clark's oldest friends in the army—they were a year apart at West Point—admired him greatly. "There is no one I've known in my years in the army who embodies the warrior ethos more completely than Wes—he's excelled as a commander at every level," Christman said. "He's fierce and he's absolutely fearless, and above all he is a *warrior.* He's always ready not merely to go into combat, but to excel. If you were going into battle, you would want him in command—company, battalion, brigade. He would do everything right, he would think out every option, he would be selfless and he would be fearless. *No one would do it better.* But within the army he rarely gets credit for being a warrior."[3]

From the start of his career, Clark was marked for greatness and senior command, but despite all his self-evident talent, some of his superiors always questioned whether he passed one of the army's most critical tests, the ability to show sufficient concern for the men under him, something that distinguishes great commanders. His friends thought that criticism was unfair. No one, they believed, would do a better job preparing his men and bringing them into combat in the best kind of fighting shape, but he would do it coolly and professionally. There would be nothing warm and avuncular about him. His combat credentials were worthy. Clark had graduated from West Point in the middle of the Vietnam War, had commanded a company in the First Infantry Division, and in an early battle had been seriously wounded four times in a single engagement, in the hand, shoulder, leg, and hip. Yet he had continued to command his unit, and for that he had received the Silver Star. The battle and the wounds, some thought, had made him more aggressive than ever; as he rose in rank, he seemed to be on a hair trigger, spoiling for a good fight or a worthy war.

In time Clark had held every command position the army offered and had excelled at each level, but somehow he did not get credit for being a commander. Probably it was a function of his personality. He was never one of the boys. You could, thought one colleague, use Wes as a litmus test on some of his peers: their reaction to him would say as much about them as it did about him. If they were bright and confident, then they overlooked his occasionally irritating qualities. But if they were a little insecure about their own place as they rose to higher ranks where the challenges were more complicated, then Clark, who met those challenges so readily, created resentment. He was, as one colleague noted, the kind of guy who in college took a three-hour exam, was the first to leave the room (by about an hour), and then let you know how easy it was.

There had been only one bad moment when he had slipped and his career was in doubt. When he was at Fort Carson as a battalion commander, the commander there was General Jack Hudachek. He would eventually become well-known within army circles as the one man who had tried to slow down Colin Powell's rapid rise. Powell had had the audacity to try to speak to Hudachek about the slippage of troop morale and had paid a high price indeed. In his memoirs Powell devoted nearly ten pages to Hudachek, none of them especially admiring. Hudachek had not been that enthusiastic about Powell and gave him a mediocre efficiency report that might easily have damaged an otherwise brilliant career. When Clark showed up as one of his battalion commanders, Hudachek did not like him either. Not that Clark had not been warned. Hudachek did not like men from West Point, Clark was told. Nor did Hudachek like young officers who are under the zone, two friends had said about Clark's new commander, using the army term for a bright young officer who keeps getting early promotion and has a golden track record. In Clark's case, the warnings turned out to be all too valid.

When a congressional delegation came to Fort Carson for a visit, Hudachek arranged for some of his best battalion commanders to meet with them. Clark was not selected. He was stunned. Who better exemplified what the modern army wanted to show to the Congress? He was a Rhodes Scholar, a White House Fellow, a combat veteran wounded four times in battle, a Silver Star winner, and almost always first in his class. He had taken a battalion that was in terrible shape and made it one of the best in the division. "I'm afraid the old man [Hudachek] doesn't consider you representative of the battalion commanders," one of the top staff officers told Clark. It was a singular slap in the face; Clark had been judged as somehow different, not one of the boys. His own battalion's excellence—of that there was no doubt—had made no difference. This was some new kind of scoring that he could not fathom, based not on performance, but instead on undefinable qualities of personality. It was a bad omen, but what was to come was worse. When Hudachek prepared Clark's annual efficiency report, which was life-or-death for an officer at that level, where the grading got tougher and the survivors of the system fewer, he was given a comparatively poor grade—block two at a time when it should have been block one to avoid the possible end of a promising career. Hudachek and Clark then spent several hours discussing the report, and finally, it was believed, Hudachek regraded him and put him in the first block.

That same year the brigade command list came out and Clark was not on it. Peers like Hugh Shelton (later four-star and chairman of the JCS) and Dan Christman (eventually a three-star) were on it. For the first time since he had graduated from West Point, Clark was not first in his class, not in the elite group. He was devastated. Then a year later he didn't make the list again and he was even more seriously shaken. He thought of leaving the service, but others told him to stay the course, that even if he was having a hard time at Carson, there would be life after John Hudachek. Clark got past that bad moment, but friends thought it was an early example of the kind of resentment he generated, simply by being who he was. If he was best boy, best boys are not always beloved.

As he rose through the ranks, Clark seemed eager—too eager—to show to the world at large and to powerful civilians in particular that the stereotype of the military man who was slow and inarticulate was completely wrong. So he became almost willfully quick and verbal, and outspoken. One assignment that had showcased not merely his talents, but also some of the qualities that jarred the system, had taken place at the National Training Center at Fort Irwin. At that point he was still a comer but was felt to need more experience—needed, as they say in the army, to be greened. Other officers might have upgraded the program more slowly and with greater tact for the feelings of their peers. Not Clark. He drove it from the day he first arrived. Clark did well at Fort Irwin under a difficult and demanding senior officer, significantly upgrading the entire place, but he made enemies in the process. In the army, given the complicated network of friendships that sometimes went far back, if you were hard on a senior officer, even if he was obviously underperforming, you risked turning all his pals into adversaries. Clark was very result-oriented, one colleague said. He had pushed hard in an environment that was less result-oriented and more driven by cronyism, and he had made some enemies among men who had powerful sponsors. Dennis Reimer, who would be chief of staff of the army when Clark was in Brussels, had come out to visit the NTC and was reportedly unhappy, not with the results, but with the manner in which Clark had operated—too driven, too abrasive, too hard on people.

All of this meant that as the Kosovo war was about to begin, Clark was in a unique and extremely vulnerable position, somewhat isolated from the institution that had produced him, whose top people had not recommended him for the NATO command. His critics had always believed that he might be a little too political. Certainly, he always did exceptionally well with high-level civilians, making an unusually good first impression; those very qualities that kept him from being one of the boys with his peers seemed to help him with civilians. He had in midcareer connected himself to the Nixon people and had for a time been an aide to Al Haig, who had been considered *very* political by fellow army officers. Clark had written speeches for Haig, another indication that Clark, too, might be political. Those doubts arose again when he started operating as a J-5 and was selected to work with Richard Holbrooke, first when he was a special envoy in the Balkans in 1995, and then when Clark served as the military liaison with Holbrooke during Dayton. That, in the last year of dealing with Milosevic, Clark had become as hawkish as some of the civilians did not help him in the Pentagon.

Now Clark was SACEUR, which, given the power of CINCs, made him potentially the single most important military player in the drama now unfolding, more powerful, because of the changed nature of the army's command, than even the chairman of the Joint Chiefs and the army chief of staff. John Shalikashvili, as chairman of the Joint Chiefs, had saved Clark before, and though much of the conflict surrounding Clark was about personality, some was about philosophy as well. He was Shali's kind of guy, but by the time the Kosovo war started, Shalikashvili was gone and the men who had replaced him were not nearly as sympathetic to Clark, nor as eager to adjust the army to more flexible missions that fell outside the guidelines of the Powell Doctrine. It was well-known within the Pentagon by late 1997, first, that Clark was a committed activist, and second, that he was hard to control and tended to operate on his own value system. Clark had had a telltale argument a few months earlier with Joe Ralston, who was vice chairman, over Clark's increasing insistence that they use NATO bombing—or at least the threat of bombing—to rein in Milosevic. In that argument Clark could feel not just Ralston's doubts, but the resistance of the entire Pentagon toward greater activism. Ralston had asked him the old Colin Powell question: What if airpower doesn't work? "It *will* work," Clark had answered. "I know Milosevic, I know how he reacts. It will work." "But what if it doesn't?" Ralston asked. But it will, Clark insisted. "But suppose it doesn't work—do you use ground troops?"[4] That exchange was an early sign of even greater tensions still to come. It reflected the doubts of the other Chiefs, and their belief that Clark was pushing too hard and was too confident; to Clark it showed that the Chiefs were much too cautious, too affected by the Vietnam syndrome.

In the fall of 1998, despite the temporary cease-fire, a cease-fire without teeth, Clark came back to Washington to warn his superiors, both civilian and military, of how serious things were. At the same time he briefed a group of former high-level national security people who were activists on the Balkans and spoke pessimistically about the cease-fire that Holbrooke had negotiated. It was all window dressing, Clark said. It would break down quickly, probably in two or three months, because the verification system was inadequate and therefore Milosevic would exploit it. All we had done was buy ourselves a little time. Milosevic, as he had not honored comparable agreements, would not honor this one, Clark predicted. Two months later, in early January 1999, Clark was back in Washington again to warn the administration that Milosevic was going to violate his word in Kosovo, and we would be faced with hard choices. He met with the same group of Balkan activists and this time was even more pessimistic. There was almost certain to be war, he warned, in a very short time. Because of the course that Milosevic had chosen, it was inevitable. In the fighting, he also warned, Russia would not be pleased with what America and NATO were doing, and there would almost surely be a superpower confrontation. Jim Hooper, the former State Department officer on the Balkans who had put the meeting together, remembered that some people there thought that Clark was much too pessimistic. But a year and a half later when they met again and it turned out that he had been absolutely right in every one of his predictions—what would happen, the timing of it, even the confrontation with the Russians—Hooper told Clark that he had been prophetic.

CHAPTER FORTY

Clark was about to have serious problems not just with the Chiefs, but the new secretary of defense as well, Bill Cohen. When Cohen had interviewed him for the SACEUR job in early 1997, the secretary had spoken quite dovishly about the Balkans. The administration, he said, would never be able to get any kind of military commitment to Kosovo past the Congress. The signal was clear to Clark. Cohen, his boss, did not want the military to be engaged in the Balkans. What Clark now began to hear from Cohen and other senior military was a series of warnings, mostly about becoming too close to the high-ranking civilians. People subtly suggested that some of the civilians who seemed to be his friends and on his side might, in fact, be working in private against him. As the stakes were going up, the game was becoming uglier, and the senior people in the Pentagon, who did not entirely trust Clark, clearly wanted to cut off his access to the civilians.

Nor had things gone well even when, still new to his command, Clark had pushed to toughen the implementation of the Dayton Accords. As early as the summer of 1997 he had also begun to get warnings from Cohen—and in time from Shelton as well—that he ought not to talk to people, to use the Pentagon phrase, on the other side of the river; that is, the civilians at the White House and at State—or to be very specific, Berger, Albright, and eventually Holbrooke. That, Clark decided later, was one more sign of the growing conflict between the senior civilian and military people and of the fear that he was on the wrong side, too close to the civilians and advocating a policy the Pentagon did not want. Even more important, he was, in effect, the swing vote. If it all came to a head over what to do in Kosovo and the CINC lined up with the civilians, that would be a very different equation than if everyone in the military opposed action or gave an unacceptably high figure for what it would take. During one trip to Washington in July 1998, he had carried with him some of the plans for the air campaign. He was scheduled to see General Shelton, but Shelton was unable to see him. The next stop on his schedule was the White House, where he met with Bob Gelbhard, the special negotiator, and Jim Steinberg, a Berger deputy. Shelton, the chairman, he was told, was mightily pissed because the civilians had seen the plans first. The chairman, Clark was told, had said that Clark "had one foot on a banana peel and one foot in the grave."[1] Not long after that, Clark was asked by Cohen and Shelton to submit his itineraries in advance when he came to Washington so they would always know whom he was seeing. That had never happened before. It was, he thought, another warning. He, of course, was not going to play that game. He would continue, despite additional warnings, to keep on checking in with the people on the other side of the river. He did not intend to have so powerful a position and defer to the Pentagon on an issue about which he felt so passionately.

Clark's support system was hardly enviable. His relationship with Denny Reimer, the army chief of staff, was dismal. Reimer was a much more conventional man than General Gordon Sullivan, who had preceded him. The feeling in the army was that Sullivan had been so hard-driving that when he retired, the system needed a break. The lower-key Reimer was ideal for that. He was a decent, honorable man but cautious and conservative as well, leading an institution that was under immense pressure to change, but where the internal culture, especially at the top, resisted change. His relationship with Clark, the army's most important commander, was about as poor as it was possible to get. Reimer had not, after all, placed him on the list for either CINC slot, and on the second, SACEUR, Reimer had deliberately refused to sign on despite Shalikashvili's personal plea.

Those watching Clark and Reimer together at close quarters thought the body language between them was simply dreadful. No one knew what had triggered it, least of all Clark. Had there been an incident long ago when Clark had in some way offended Reimer, had somehow shown that Clark did not think Reimer was quite bright enough? No one was quite sure. But Reimer simply did not like Clark, was decidedly uncomfortable with him, and, in the eyes of some of their peers, clearly threatened by him. To one knowledgeable insider it seemed as if a man of the system could not bear to deal with someone who consciously or unconsciously thought he was better than the system. Their byplay was fascinating: Reimer with his thinly disguised dislike of Clark, and Clark, like an innocent puppy dog, wondering what had caused it. Why, he would sometimes ask friends, does he dislike me? What did I do wrong? It was not the way to start what would eventually become the most delicate command relationship imaginable.

Of all the figures who emerged from the prolonged struggle over the Balkans, no one would reflect the contradictions inherent in his country's policies more clearly than Wes Clark. The fault line in American geopolitical life ran right through him. Nor in the end was anyone else treated as badly by his own institution precisely because of those very same contradictions, America's desire to exercise great power throughout the world, but to do it in a way that caused no (or at least few) American casualties and no larger political problems. It was Clark's fate to run the military side of this unwanted war, fought by an essentially uninterested country, orchestrated by a divided government where the consensus was, at best, extremely flimsy, and where, once the war started, there would be a complex multinational, political command to which he reported. As he went forward with the most limited mandate to achieve what was supposed to be an unlimited victory, he inevitably pressed for more—more bombing targets and, in time, the use of ground troops. But he was carrying out an assignment about which those in charge, both civilian and military, had very different views. In time he would become the combat commander as partial political-military orphan.

His principal adversary was Bill Cohen, who was being pulled in one direction by his own skepticism and the skepticism of the senior military about greater involvement in the Balkans, and in the other by the senior civilians, who wanted to finish an unwanted job. The civilians in the administration might have little enthusiasm for the war, but the alternatives, given the administration's rhetoric, its purpose, and its own role at Dayton, were considered worse. Cohen's position was extremely delicate. He was a Republican moderate from Maine, something of a maverick centrist, the perfect combination for the crusty New England state he represented as it tilted more and more toward the Democratic Party. His positions were never quite predictable. As a young congressman he had first come to national prominence as a House Judiciary Committee member who cast an important vote for Nixon's impeachment.

His maverick side had come all too naturally. He had grown up in Maine, the son of a Jewish father and an Irish mother in a small New England city at a time when mixed marriages of that kind were relatively rare and there was still a good deal of anti-Semitism. Years later, in his memoir, *Roll Call,* Cohen would write poignantly of the divided nature of his childhood. He was torn between wanting to play sports at the YMCA on Saturday and having to attend Hebrew school on the same day. He solved that dilemma by giving two Saturdays to Hebrew school and two to the Y. To carry the name Cohen in playground sports was not easy in those days, he wrote, and when he was pitching in schoolboy baseball and someone yelled, "Send the Jewboy home," he wanted to protest that he was not really Jewish. Tired of being pulled back and forth, he decided not to be bar mitzvahed when he reached thirteen and celebrated by throwing the medal he had received at Hebrew school for scholastic excellence into the Penobscot River, thus declaring himself, for the moment at least, no longer Jewish.[2] (His background was in some ways so similar to that of Wes Clark that Janet Langhart, Cohen's wife, was greatly amused by it; others who worked with both men wondered if the similarities weren't the source of the tensions between two such headstrong, driven men.)

Being different, however, had given Cohen an extra drive, a passion to excel; he had been a very good student and college athlete, and at Bowdoin he thought for a time of becoming a pro basketball player. That was not in the cards; scoring easily against Bates and Middlebury was not the same as playing in the NBA, and he went to law school instead. After graduation, he returned to Maine, entered politics, was elected mayor of Bangor, and eventually arrived in the House in time for the Nixon impeachment proceedings. There, his independence, his good looks, and his intelligence gave him the beginning of a national constituency and helped catapult him in 1978 to a successful Senate run in a state that liked its politicians to be both unpredictable and independent. In the Senate, where Cohen had served three terms, he had emerged as a centrist in a party that was moving away from the center. He earned a reputation for being bright and talented but never entirely engaged. He was interested in military affairs, and he was a quick study and had a good innate feel for the issues. But he was, thought one senior officer who watched him on the Hill, like a bright student who audits the course but never takes the final exam. He would question a military representative carefully and respectfully, sometimes note that the officer's testimony had been unusually illuminating and suggest they have lunch sometime, and then rarely follow up on the invitation.

In the midnineties as he reached what should have been the apex of his political career, Cohen appeared to be somewhat frustrated by the political process and caught in a dilemma that had ensnared many a bright, ambitious young politician before him. There was a ceiling on his possibilities and his head was already touching it. He was a winning, attractive senator whose own party was less than interested in his ideas or his future. He had no chance, given the power of the fundamentalists in the party (and the memories of his vote against Nixon), of a place on the national ticket, and the idea of entering the primaries was quixotic. His sensibilities were slightly different from those of many politicians; he had been a classics major at Bowdoin, knew poetry, could quote it, and liked to write it. He had also written an engaging and thoughtful memoir of his first year in the Senate and had followed it up with several spy novels, and though he wrote reasonably well, his fiction was not distinguished.

Like many of his more moderate peers from both sides of the aisle, Cohen bemoaned the harsher, more partisan, and less collegial tone of contemporary politics, the change it had wrought in the Senate, and the brutality of modern fund-raising. The effect of television on that body, he thought, was powerful, palpable and negative—ever greater posturing and harsher partisanship. In 1996 after three terms, he decided to leave elective politics and not seek a fourth term, which he would probably have won easily. He had become a high-visibility figure in the Washington of the nineties, a politician who had a broad range of friendships. His second wife was a strikingly beautiful woman, the black television personality Janet Langhart, and they were a desirable couple on the Georgetown social circuit, where people with some degree of celebrity were always in demand. Though unlike other senators he was not burdened by fund-raising demands—he was almost unbeatable in Maine and raising money was never a problem—Cohen decided to leave the Senate to start the Cohen Group, a consulting firm in Washington with a primary connection to countries in Asia. Bill Perry, the outgoing secretary of defense, was the first to suggest him to the president as a possible successor, placing Cohen on his own personal short list. Cohen and Clinton talked a few times and Clinton made the offer, which Cohen accepted. He might have been a three-term senator and a prominent and visible one at that, but when Cohen went to the Pentagon no one really knew who he was and what he wanted—what was at the center of him. He was obviously bright, spoke well in the Senate, and made quick, subtle political reads, but he was unpredictable on a number of issues. He had, with some doubts, supported the Gulf War. People were said to know more about what he didn't want—what he rejected—than what he wanted and aspired to.

It was not an easy career switch: he was going from the Congress to the executive branch, and the skills required are very different. Dick Cheney had gone from the executive branch, where his skills—and his emotionally disengaged personality, the lack of a need to be popular—had suited him perfectly, to the legislative branch, which was a much easier exchange, especially for a conservative from Wyoming. In addition to the switch, Cohen was supposed to run an institution deeply suspicious of the administration he served, and he was going from a Republican world to a Democratic one at a time when the level of partisanship in Washington was probably higher than it had ever been. Finally, he was replacing a man who was not merely respected but almost revered within the building. Even as intense a figure as General Barry McCaffrey had spoken of Bill Perry as the very model of a civilian leader in the national security world, "on a par with General George C. Marshall."[3]

At the Pentagon, however, Cohen remained very much a man of the Senate, and when he spoke in White House meetings, he often seemed to be speaking on behalf of the Congress (and the Republican Party), not the administration (and the Democratic Party). The doubts he expressed on many issues were not merely his own doubts, but the doubts of a rather distrustful Congress. In his mind he was warning his new teammates about the opposition they might face on the Hill; but to many in the administration, his words sounded more like those of someone who was in the opposition. Some of the Clinton people wondered if Cohen really was on their team, an issue not helped by his tendency to refer to the Congress as *us* and the Clinton administration as *you.* Finally Sandy Berger took him aside and told him quite gently, "I will regard this administration as a success when you refer to the administration as *we,* and not *you.*" Furthermore, Cohen had been a relatively tough critic of the administration's Bosnia policies in the past, suspicious of greater activism there, and his questioning of John Shalikashvili when he had come before the Senate with the Dayton agreement had been tough, surprising both Shalikashvili and the administration he represented.

In addition, Cohen had to deal with the long-standing resistance within the Pentagon to any policy of activism in the Balkans. Like many of his contemporaries, he had not served in Vietnam, having gotten a graduate school deferment, and that inevitably handed additional leverage to those in the military in any dealings with him. They had been there, and he had not. Moreover, Cohen's instincts in trying to run the Pentagon were more those of a politician than a CEO. He would let the military people understand that he was fair and judicious, as sympathetic as they were going to get from this administration. He made the day-to-day decisions with skill and nuance, but he backed off from the long-range force restructuring decisions that might have torn the Pentagon apart. That bitter struggle would have to wait for someone else. In general, Cohen's political instincts were quite good. But he was obviously very dependent on Ralston, the vice chair, who knew the building and its interior politics better than most and would let Cohen know what decisions he had to make and when to make them.

Growing up in the Vietnam era, Cohen had long been somewhat suspicious of any military intervention. Once during a debate on the Senate floor, he had spoken cautiously of any policy that lightly sends young Americans to die in distant places: "And the hearts that beat so loudly and enthusiastically to do something, to intervene in areas where there is not an immediate threat to our vital interests, when those hearts that had beaten so loudly see the coffins, then they switch, and they say, 'What are we doing there?' "[4] At one high-level meeting as secretary of defense, he had bluntly reminded Clinton, "I voted against your Bosnia policy," not that such a reminder was needed. If Cohen had still been sitting in the Senate, he might well have opposed some of the steps the administration was now taking on Kosovo. The Balkans had always struck him as a notorious geopolitical cemetery, a place, he once said, where people "would rather dig fresh graves than heal old wounds."[5] Mostly he saw pitfalls, things that could go wrong: allies who were dubious about going forward and slow to rally around a policy of activism, difficult terrain that favored the indigenous defender, not the neophyte Western invader. Moreover, a majority in the Congress appeared to share his doubts, and the administration had not yet reached a consensus. It was also extremely cautious about tipping its hand to the Congress about its Balkan policy, and by 1999, some senior people on the Hill, such as John McCain, thought the administration out-and-out disingenuous about what it intended to do.

As secretary of defense Cohen, like most of the senior military, was openly unhappy with most of the military scenarios that were being considered. He did not want NATO to become, as he said, "the air force of the KLA." Eventually, very late in the game, he did come around, and when he did, the rationale was both to stop Milosevic's obscene actions and to save NATO. But he had always questioned the use of the U.S. military on peacekeeping missions. He also believed that the administration should not move ahead without public and congressional support. That was the old congressman and senator in him, and when he voiced his former colleagues' doubts in high-level administration meetings, some thought he was speaking as much for himself as for his former peers.

Those reservations went back to the failure in Somalia and how poorly the administration had been prepared for that disaster. When Les Aspin and Warren Christopher had come to the Congress in the immediate aftermath, Aspin had done most of the talking for the administration, and he had done it very poorly, Cohen remembered. It was one of the worst sessions he had ever been a part of and he was amazed that a former congressman of Aspin's skill and intellect, one of the most senior people from his branch of government, had performed so ineptly. Aspin had asked the attendant members of the Congress— many of them already like hornets whose nest had been attacked—what they thought the administration should do. It was the worst possible phrasing imaginable, Cohen thought. It was one thing to go to the Congress and solicit its input, but quite another to speak the way Aspin had, to imply that the administration had no plan and to ask the Congress what to do. Because of that, the meeting had quickly become ugly, and the Congress remained extremely apprehensive about any future peacekeeping ventures. There was no way to overestimate the damage Somalia had done to the Clinton administration, Cohen believed. When he went to the Hill in the fall of 1998 to ask for seventy-five hundred peacekeepers for Kosovo to support the negotiations that Dick Holbrooke was working on, Cohen was abruptly and coldly turned down by his old colleagues. Part of the reason was that a great many troops were still in Bosnia. They were doing well, with no hemorrhaging, and the American force had already been cut in half. But the original deadline for withdrawal had been extended more than once, and what had happened in Somalia was still in the back of people's minds. Somalia was, Cohen decided, the indelible stain on so many other comparable missions for this administration.

Whatever his own doubts, he was now surrounded by senior military men who were even more dubious of action, especially the use of ground troops. Cohen's views, and the views of most of the senior military, put him in constant and sharp conflict with Madeleine Albright. She spoke on behalf of all the activists in the executive branch who had already been through a long, agonizing first run with Milosevic over Bosnia during Balkans One, and who wanted to jump-start what they thought would be Balkans Two in order to minimize the potential for human suffering they had all witnessed. Cohen, on the other hand, spoke not merely for the military, which did not really want to go ahead, but for the Congress, which the activists essentially intended to bypass, if at all possible. Cohen and Albright's arguments were memorable. She was fierce, sure of her vision, and very much on the attack. He could, in turn, match her readily in argument, if not in passion. Sometimes, when it got heated and the tone almost too personal, he would hold back slightly, but his face would turn quite red.

Watching the intense byplay between those two, Berger thought that one of the differences between Cohen and the activists in the administration like Albright, Clark, and Holbrooke, who was making occasional appearances at the principals' meetings, was that Cohen had not experienced the terrible human wrenching of Balkans One, in which they had stumbled, failed, and agonized over three years before finally patching together a policy that worked. None of the more senior principals ever wanted to go through that again.

CHAPTER FORTY-ONE

The air war in Serbia did not begin well. Part of the problem was the newness of NATO to that kind of assignment. Not only had it never done anything like this before, it had been designed as an essentially *defensive* rather than an offensive instrument. This operation was on-the-job training. NATO also was, as one of the principals said, a lumpy organization, nineteen members now, with all kinds of built-in political constraints. Too few bombers were on hand when the war started, and the targets permitted were not what the two most important commanders, Clark and Mike Short, his top air force man, had hoped for. The complications for Clark's command were obvious from the start. He had wanted to hit the traditional optimum targets to make the Serbs suffer: the power grid, the sources of energy, oil and gas and the refineries, and the communications network. Then he watched the target list shrink under political pressure, some of the targets deleted even as planes were taking off to hit them. Clark was, thought one friend, like a head chef ready to cook what he hoped would be the greatest meal of his life, only to find some twenty other self-appointed chefs, arguing about ingredients and cooking times; instead of making the meal better, each managed to subtract some bit of seasoning, diluting the final product.

There was a significant gap between what the NATO military people had *seemed* to promise Clark before the air war started, and what the NATO political people, more squeamish about bombing Serb political targets, were permitting to be hit. Considerable tensions existed between the more aggressive NATO members, on one hand, and, in this case, what the French and the Italians (the Greeks were always opposed to almost all use of airpower) were willing to go along with. Not surprisingly, frustrations within the command were immense. On the third night of the bombing, Short recalled, he had to cancel a second wave of F-117s because he was already out of targets, particularly ones likely to cause the most pain to Milosevic. As Ivo Daalder and Michael O'Hanlon wrote in their book on Kosovo, *Winning Ugly,* the NATO forces had only 350 planes ready when the bombing began, roughly one-third of the aircraft they finally needed, and one-tenth of the aircraft used in the Gulf War. There was no aircraft carrier in either the Adriatic or the Mediterranean when it began. All in all, it was, noted the authors, "a textbook case of how not to wage war."[1]

It was particularly frustrating for Clark, who hated Milosevic with a passion and had wanted this campaign so badly. Clark was being allowed to use only a small fraction of his full muscle. He was caught in a swirl of political crosscurrents from all sides, a few of them hawkish from his subordinates, but most of them dovish from political types from foreign countries, who might or might not have been his bosses, for no one was ever quite sure. His mandate was so fragile that much of his energy, instead of being spent to demand more force and a better target list, was used to fight off these factions in NATO that wanted to do even less—and were, in fact, calling for a bombing halt, a first step, Clark believed, toward ending the air campaign completely.

Mike Short, who was in the midst of his own private rage against the rules, had little sympathy for Clark. As the air campaign began, Short was furious at the hand he had been dealt, and he blamed Clark and Washington. But since Clark was nearer at hand, most of Short's anger was fixated on his army superior. Long before they had actually initiated the bombing, Short and his most senior colleagues had given Clark a plan for an air campaign not unlike the strategy that John Warden had devised for Desert Storm. It would, in Short's words, put out the lights in Belgrade by targeting the military and civilian communications centers, the petroleum centers, and the transportation network. He intended to make Milosevic and his cronies pay for their adventures in Kosovo. In addition, the ordinary Serbs, whom Short felt should know better and who were getting a free ride on Milosevic's back, would realize, when the lights went out in Belgrade and the bridges came down, that they were also the victims of Milosevic's jingoism and atrocities.

We had this extraordinary instrument of power, and while Iraq and the desert provided easier targets than Serbia and the mountains, Short believed we should use it with a singular intensity. That was especially true because we were putting the young men and women who were flying these missions at constant risk. What American airpower had done in the Gulf War, Short and the other senior airmen believed, was just a beginning. The effectiveness and power of high-precision bombs and the Stealth bombers had increased exponentially in just eight years, and Short was sure that the pressure he could quickly apply to Milosevic would be unbearable and bring him to the table in a short time.

But that plan had never been accepted. Short believed it had never been put forward by Clark to his own superiors, both civilian and military, and they settled on a gradual, incremental plan that Short simply hated. To him it was all too reminiscent of Vietnam, politically acceptable to nervous NATO politicians and the most cautious members of the Clinton team, but diluted at the expense of military excellence. In Short's opinion, it was essentially toothless and squandered and neutered this remarkable new technology. Even worse, he believed it gave an unwanted signal to Milosevic of an America that was faint of heart and thereby encouraged him to try to stick it out. Short's view of what we should have been doing represented the purest distillation of air force ideology, untempered by any sympathy for political complexities. Not all his colleagues, even senior air force officers, agreed with him completely. They understood how he felt, sympathized with his rage, and even knew that if their positions were changed, they might feel much the same way. But they also understood that this mission was something new, that it was a convoluted command, and that the politics of bombing a city in Europe whose citizens had been allies of other European nations were immensely complicated. Short, they felt, was too narrow in his thinking, with little sense of the complexity of Clark's campaign and the terrible political pressures he faced every day. While what Short said was technically right, they felt that he did not understand the interplay of much larger forces taking place around him.

Political niceties and diplomatic sensitivity meant little to Short. He was an old-fashioned commander cut from the rougher, more unsparing human cloth of World War II officers and less sophisticated than most of the modern, high-level military men. He was tough, almost combative. He was who he was, a fighter pilot, he knew his job and he pretended to be—wanted to be—nothing else. He did not believe that he crossed into other people's spheres of influence, and he did not like it when they crossed into his. He saw his duty clearly and wanted no obstructions in doing it. In addition, his sense of the obligations that went with his command were very personal. He took his responsibility for the lives of the people underneath him seriously—especially in a campaign like this, where the risks were, despite our technological advantage, a constant. "My kids," he called the airmen flying the missions, as if they were his, which in one case they were. His own son Christopher was flying a relatively slow and vulnerable A-10 Warthog in the campaign. Sometimes when Short raged against the controls placed on him, especially by French politicians, he would say that if anything happened to his son, his blood would be on Jacques Chirac's hands.

Short had been part of the TAC air mafia that had in the seventies become an important and powerful inner group within the air force. They had wrestled influence away from the SAC people who had once dominated the service, but who, because they had been wedded to nuclear bombers for so long, and nuclear bombs had never been used, had gradually lost their leverage. By the time Short got the Kosovo command, in 1999, he was by air force standards something of a geezer. He had flown his first combat mission thirty-two years earlier, and he was one of the last of that group of air force pilots who had fought in Vietnam in the relatively early going. Nothing over the years had softened his edges; he was famously blunt and ferociously direct. At the time of Kosovo, he was the oldest three-star in the air force. Getting the Kosovo command was within the air force considered something of a last tip of the hat from

General Mike Ryan, the air force chief of staff, to Short. Normally so precious a slot would have been handed off to a bright, ascending young three-star whose brilliance and promise had earned him one last test before receiving his fourth star, rather than someone whose career had leveled out and was essentially awaiting retirement.

Over the years, it was presumed, various attempts to soften Short's rougher edges had failed, which inevitably made him a favorite of the men and the women who served under him, but on occasion jarred some of his superiors. Short was a man without varnish, forthright, confident, someone with absolute faith in his officers and his weapons. His style could not have been more different from Wes Clark's. If Clark was a water walker, a star from the day he had arrived at West Point, Short was the grunt who had made good. Turned down by West Point, he had barely made it to the Air Force Academy, where for a time he had seemed more likely to drown than to walk on water. His great talent was to lead men, which came from being single-minded of purpose, sure of the course he favored, and from facing combat without doubts. That, of course, and transmitting to his subordinates the belief that whatever he asked them to do, he would gladly do himself. But those very qualities made him an edgy deputy in a war as politically delicate as Kosovo.

Short had learned his style at home. His father had been an enlisted man in World War II, had jumped on D day with the 17th Airborne, had fought in the Battle of the Bulge, and had been badly wounded in another war, Korea. At the new Air Force Academy, where he did not do well because he did not have any great feel for the demanding science curriculum, nor for flying itself until they finally flew T-38s. He graduated 443rd in a class of 517, hardly one of the stars of the class of 1965, and he was assigned to fly tankers, not necessarily a slot that went to the academy's more select graduates. By chance, Vietnam was just beginning to escalate, the tanker assignment was canceled, and he arrived in the South in June 1967 assigned to fly in an F-4 as a backseater, or GIB (guy in the back), as the air force people called it. The pilots in the front seat, often underwhelmed by the GIB's contribution, or the lack thereof, had another, less complimentary name for them: "backseat ballast." That assignment was, Short later decided, a turning point in his career. Had he drawn tanker duty, he would surely have done four or five years in the service, gotten out, and ended up flying for a major airline. Instead, he found something he was good at. He liked their mission, providing close air support for embattled American ground units, knowing that even as he was releasing his payload, he might be saving the life and troops of some lieutenant or captain deep in the big muddy. His career had succeeded because he exuded old-fashioned combat abilities in spite of self-evident academic limitations. As he grew more senior, he belied the increasingly sophisticated air force culture.

Short did not have the great natural feel requisite for air-to-air combat, but he liked his role in Vietnam, flying air-to-ground cover, because the result of his work was so palpable: he could see the troops he was protecting. That made going to work easy. By the time he left Vietnam a year later, he had flown 276 missions, but he was aware that he had had, by the standards of the day, a relatively easy war. The army guys were out there humping the boonies, slogging around in terrible terrain under difficult conditions, fighting a tough enemy. Others he knew had it hard, too; some of his air force and navy peers were flying over North Vietnam into heavy missile fire. Of his three roommates when he was based at Cam Ranh Bay, two were killed flying over the North. He was flying primarily in the South—only forty-five missions over the North—where there was little chance of being shot down. At night he slept under clean sheets. Mostly it was thirty minutes over the target and then back to Cam Ranh Bay. He could go to the officers' club, have a drink, and take pride that he might have saved some American lives that day, men who would never know who he was and what he looked like.

Short had found his mission in life: he was a pilot, a good one. He got a Silver Star for a rescue mission in Vietnam, an unusual medal for an air force man, and a Flying Cross. Besides, he began to discover, he was good at command, and his old-fashioned bluntness and candor seemed to work unusually well in the modern age. Being a pilot and a commander fit his personality and his talents. Little of what he brought to the table was wasted. He had no abstract abilities, no philosophical skills. Military theoreticians and intellectuals made him ill at ease, and in private he often spoke disrespectfully of them. In the business he was in, if you were any good, you flew and you led, and if you weren't, then you could teach or write or retire, he liked to say. The only real test in Short's world was how you flew in combat. His abilities did not go unnoticed, and after Vietnam he got a series of good assignments. He was vice commander and then commander of the F-117 Stealth fighter unit back in the mideighties, when it was still black. He did not fly in the Gulf War; the slots had been wrong and he wasn't going to be a wing commander. If a slot had opened up for him, it would have been in photo reconnaissance, something he did not really fancy. Flying into combat and taking pictures was not his style.

Short, his friends thought, would not have an easy time as the air commander for an assignment like Kosovo was going to be. Many of the men around him believed that because his frustrations were so great, he soon came to hate Clark, and it was simply not in Short's nature to understand the more complex equation that faced Clark, nor for Clark to have the human skills to build a bridge to Short. For Short to be Short, he had to push constantly to maximize the target list, nothing less. On occasion, he would talk about how, if he had gotten into West Point as he had originally hoped, he would have been a year ahead of Clark. If he had been a third classman at West Point when Wes

Clark arrived as a plebe, Short liked to say, history might have been a little different. Some of the tensions between the two men were historical, like the tensions between Eisenhower and Patton, or Powell and Schwarzkopf. In addition, Clark was an army man, an infantry soldier at heart, who, in Short's mind, had little sense of what a modern air campaign should look like when properly run. Even before the campaign began, there had been a basic disagreement over their priorities. Clark had asked Short, "Mike, what are you going to do when Milosevic starts killing Muslims in Kosovo?" "Boss," he answered, "I'll attack the leadership in Belgrade." That was the wrong answer, at least for the moment. Neither NATO nor Washington was ready for something that drastic yet. When the bombing campaign began, Clark kept asking Short to go after the Serb Third Army, which was in Kosovo, but Short considered that a waste of airpower. The Third Army, to use the favored air force expression, was not a "center of gravity" for the Serbs in his opinion, and Milosevic did not care what happened to it at all. It was widely dispersed (or would be after the first air attack) and hard to hit. In Short's mind the obvious strategy was to bypass it and cause pain to the Serb leader and his inner circle.

The true center of gravity, Short insisted, was Belgrade, which housed all the instruments critical to Milosevic's hold on power. Short and Clark sometimes argued about what they thought was the right target, the jewel in the crown. "Boss, you and I have known for months that we have different jewelers," Short once told him. "Yes, but my jeweler outranks yours," Clark answered. That debate never really ended, and Short remained—as far as he was concerned—engaged in minimalist missions striking at the Milosevic forces in the field. "Tank plinking," the air force called it, and thought of it as a waste of time, resources, and, potentially, lives. Besides, tank plinking in the Balkans was less rewarding than it had been in the Iraqi desert, because the tanks did not heat up as they did there and did not show up on the thermal targeting systems.

Short was convinced that he and the other airmen had made a better proposal for the air campaign and that Clark, if he did not accept it, should at least have allowed them to go to a higher headquarters with it. Clark later thought that Short had simply not been paying attention. Yes, he himself would have loved to wage an air campaign against Milosevic much like the one we had run in Iraq. But it was not going to happen. The political restraints were infinitely greater in Europe and that changed the entire equation. The European allies were nervous about any attack on Belgrade, and Clark got his first sense of the limitations that would be imposed on him even before the campaign began. In the fall of 1998 when he had talked to the NATO political people about the right to go after prime targets in downtown Belgrade, the word had come back loud and clear: *Absolutely not!*

The case that many nonwhite nations made against American and Western political and military attitudes, that there was always a touch of racism to them, had some justification. Things that were permissible in terms of bombing Iraq—it was after all an Arab nation—were not permissible in Europe. The politics of it were different, and because they were different, the rules of bombing and engagement were different. If the West had used the same ferocious bombing tactics against Belgrade from the very start that it had used against Baghdad, the political opposition in the West would have been greater and might have killed the entire Kosovo campaign. In time, the rules were loosened and critical targets added, but only as failure began to appear ever more likely. The pace of the bombing—how quickly we tightened up the ratchet—was important in the Kosovo war. Some senior air force officials back in Washington talked about the gestation period of the war, the need for it to go on for a time without success, before the civilians, especially the Europeans, were willing to give the military men the targets they asked for.

The divisions, among the Western countries, the military and the politicians, and, finally, one branch of service and another, that hung over the alliance were very real. Clark, in the period when Short was most angry with him in the early weeks of the bombing, had already effectively lost the right to dominate the target list. What Clark really feared once the campaign started were the growing pressures for a bombing pause not just from the Western allies, but from people in the Clinton administration as well. He was convinced that if there was a pause, given the fragility of the mandate he had, the bombing campaign might never resume. That weighed heavily on him, and he had been willing to swap the lack of intensity in the campaign for the right to continue bombing. It was, he later said, only when he reached the Orthodox Easter, some two and a half weeks into the campaign, that he was sure he would not have to deal with a bombing pause. He was also convinced that if he had gone after Belgrade heavily in the first night or two, as he and others had originally wanted to do, the political outcry in Europe might have been so great that the campaign could have ended then and there. He and Short would have been seen as the butchers of Belgrade; they, rather than Milosevic, would have become the principal architects of evil.

None of that satisfied Short. The air campaign, as it was finally manifest, was so weak and soft that for a time he believed some sort of fix was on with Milosevic. In fact, Short told his aides he thought a deal had been made at a level above him. NATO would go through the motions of a bombing campaign to give Milosevic enough political cover to negotiate his way out of Kosovo without bring the wrath of the Serb people down upon him. He would be able to tell the Serbs that he had tried, but NATO had forced his hand with its bombing. Short thought there were too few targets, they were the wrong ones, and the failure to go after what would hurt Milosevic and damage his instruments of power—chop off the head of the snake, in his words—

was now working against us. Short came to hate what he was doing. The campaign as it was proceeding was a long way from the one he had once threatened his Serb counterparts with when he had told them to go out and drive around Belgrade and see it for the last time as it was. The campaign was supposed to show NATO's will and resolution, but in truth, he believed, it was irresolute and signaled weakness and indecisiveness. By the third day, Short had to hold back on using the F-117 Stealth fighters because they lacked adequate targets. Clark kept telling him that more targets were coming, that Hugh Shelton, the chairman of the Joint Chiefs, had an attaché case full of them just waiting for the president—or at least the White House—to approve. That, Short thought, was not reassuring to the young men and women flying in his command, targets in an attaché case half a world away waiting to be checked out by political officials.

At one point during the campaign brief, a young one-star officer in his command spoke up and said, "General Short, I don't want you to take this personally, sir, but it seems to me that what we are doing is randomly bombing military targets with no coherent strategy, sir." To which Short replied, "You wiseass, you're absolutely right!" On two occasions he thought seriously of resigning. Whether he would actually have done it is another matter, but he was so tired, angry, and frustrated that he at least talked about it with his two top aides, Major General Gary Trexler and Brigadier General Randy Gelwix. They, in turn, urged him not to. A new commander would need time to become familiar with so complicated an assignment and gain the respect of most of the NATO military people. No other senior air officer would necessarily deal any better with Clark, they said, and most important of all, Short had not lost any pilots, which meant that for all his frustrations he was handling the assignment well.

A week into the air campaign, the bombing did not seem to be working, or at least working effectively. At fifteen thousand feet, the NATO planes were safe, but so were the Serb forces on the ground. Some evidence suggested that the Serbs were being warned by some friends at NATO headquarters which targets would be hit and when. (That turned out to be true; NATO leaked like a sieve in the early days.) Clark, who had always wanted something that was the opposite of Rolling Thunder, the bombing plan in Vietnam, was now caught in something all too much like it. It took eleven days before Belgrade was hit. Instead of a fierce, full-out attack at the beginning, hammering away at all targets, which the Americans had favored and which had been in their original battle plan, the number of targets, the importance of the targets, and the number of planes had been greatly reduced. The campaign they were carrying out, said General Mike Ryan, the air force chief of staff, reflected a far too optimistic view of what would happen: "Yeah, it's going to be easy, and it's going to be quick."[2]

The larger debate, one that the American and NATO military men were losing in the early weeks of the war, was over target selection. In many cases it was civilians against military, country by country, and certain countries, such as France and Italy, against the United States and Britain. Part of the division between the Americans and some of their European colleagues—particularly the politicians—was due to the differences in attitudes created by vastly different histories. On one side were those who had done the bombing in the past; on the other, those who had been targets of bombing. America during World War II, with the exception of Pearl Harbor, had done the bombing and had not been bombed. In Europe it was a very different story. The devastation of the bombing raids in World War II was a defining experience for the NATO decision-makers. Some of them might have been very young at the time, and some had only heard about it from their parents, but their sensitivity to bombing a European city like Belgrade was far greater than that of the Americans. The Germans had bombed Belgrade early in World War II in one famous and violent night, and some seventeen thousand Yugoslavs had been killed. Those were memories that lasted. The Germans in NATO were notably uneasy about being pulled into any other bombing runs there.

In the early days of the Kosovo war it appeared that each side had grievously underestimated the intentions and the will of the other. If Milosevic had underestimated the propaganda effect of what he was doing in Kosovo on Western public opinion, especially the ethnic clean-and-sweep missions, similarly, the West had underestimated how much more important Kosovo was to his survival than Bosnia, and that he was willing to let his own people suffer and sacrifice before he surrendered. For him to give up Kosovo without some sort of fight was by his political terms suicidal, not unlike asking Bill Clinton to choose domestic policies in 1995 that he knew would surely cost him any chance of carrying California, New York, Pennsylvania, and Illinois in 1996. But Milosevic was aware of and more fixated on the weaknesses of the West rather than its strengths. His fatal mistake was in not understanding how his own actions might finally unite the countries in the alliance against him rather than divide them. He knew the French and the Italians were unhappy about bombing Belgrade, and that the Germans were ambivalent about the air campaign. Perhaps, he hoped, the West would break apart or the Russians would come to his rescue. What he was not aware of was the impact of his own cruel policies in the West among those otherwise bothered by doubts, attitudes reinforced as hundreds of thousands of Albanians were driven out of their homes at the beginning of the war. To the West, he became once again Slobodan the racist, the genocidal warrior.

Slobodan Milosevic was, in fact, far better prepared for war than the West. For months he had been moving a large number of his regular troops, his security forces, and his paramilitary units to the Kosovo border, getting ready for what he was almost certain would come: a NATO bombing campaign but no enemy troops to contest him on the ground. Thus, the moment the bombing started, his forces drove through Kosovo to sweep the Albanians off the land. He had once boasted to Clark that his men could rid Kosovo of all its Albanians in just five days. *"Just five days,"* he had said. *"That's all I need."* What he hoped to provide the allies, as Clark later said, was "a fait accompli to change the demographics of Kosovo." He would de-Albanianize the country. The West would not have to come in to protect the Albanians because there would be no Albanians left.

The prewar population of Kosovo had been estimated at roughly 1.8 million ethnic Albanians. Before the NATO bombing campaign began in late March 1999, some three hundred thousand Albanians had already been forced out of their villages by the earlier Serb assaults, which started in 1998, according to NGO authorities. Now it was far more brutal. What the West saw—captured by still photographers and television cameramen—were the endless lines of Albanian refugees stretching as far as the eye could see, people stripped of their identification papers and driven out of their homes, on their way to some unwanted and unknown destination. A few weeks into the war, it was estimated that three-quarters of the Albanian population had fled their homes, some eight hundred thousand had been driven out of the country, and another five hundred thousand had become refugees within Kosovo, hiding in the hills.

CHAPTER FORTY-TWO

I f Clark was not in the early days of the war getting what he wanted in terms of targets and ground troops, he remained steady and confident because he understood the political equation in which he was now operating. He knew, from the moment the first NATO bombs fell on Serb targets and the war actually began, that unless he *overtly* angered the civilians and the military (perhaps a Somalia-like disaster, where a large number of NATO soldiers were killed in some careless action and it was videotaped and played on national television), he had the whip hand. He was the *commander* now, and Washington, civilian or military, would be loath to lose the war and, if victory or defeat hung in the balance, loath as well to deny the commander what he needed. That meant that a crucial part of his assignment, never openly articulated but always there, especially at this time with this administration, was to keep casualties and aircraft losses to a minimum, something he passed on to Mike Short—as if, Short later said rather angrily, I would have been careless about casualties without those warnings.

So Clark knew, given the dynamic that had been set in motion, the equation had changed with finality and now favored him. Two critical political points were at stake here. First, Washington was not going to lose; if it did not know this yet, it would discover it sooner or later as it became more and more embattled. And second, Washington, if things were going badly, would not want to be portrayed as not having given a commander what he needed to do the job, something that Clark was on occasion not averse to reminding General Hugh Shelton of, thereby making their relationship, hardly ideal, even edgier. Clark's peers in Washington might not have accepted the original rationale for the war—to stop Milosevic and protect the Albanians—but that would change dramatically if things started going badly. The national security and humanitarian rationales would give way to other considerations: the ego and the vanity and the place in history of the Clinton (and Blair) administrations, and the need to show that NATO had not been defeated by some tinhorn dictator. Then Clark would get more of what he wanted: more important targets and perhaps even one day some ground troops. It was in the nature of war that power would pass to him. For Clark was not only a CINC, he was SACEUR, the supreme allied commander in Europe, and that doubly empowered him. CINCs had always been powerful, but with the passage of the Goldwater-Nichols Bill in 1986, that power had been greatly enhanced at the expense of the Joint Chiefs. Goldwater-Nichols had been created to streamline the chain of command and give maximum flexibility to respond to commanders in the field, and it had been expedited by the confusion over the abortive helicopter raid that had been designed to rescue the American prisoners in Teheran in 1980.

But its political impact on the command structure had surprised a good many people within the military. In the past the job as the head of a service— army chief of staff or chief of naval operations—had been the ultimate reward for a successful career. But Goldwater-Nichols changed that. It significantly upgraded the power and leverage of commanders and made the job of service chief more of a support and logistical position. All the real rewards and pleasures—all the fun, if that is the word—went to the CINC, as one military analyst said, "and all the shit jobs went to the service chiefs." Of the chiefs, only the chairman had seen his power enhanced by Goldwater-Nichols, although when the shooting actually started, power tended to pass to the CINC, because he was the man on the spot. Colin Powell had great authority during the Iraqi crisis until the war began, and then power tended to flow to the CINC, Norman Schwarzkopf.

In the beginning, Clark, like others, almost certainly underestimated Milosevic's resistance. Exact records are hard to pin down after Somalia, because a deliberate effort was made not to keep exact records of what was said and promised on the part of every participant. But once the campaign began, Clark drove his command with a singular purpose, intelligence, and skill, handling his immensely complicated and difficult constituencies deftly, knowing full well that he would in time get most of what he wanted, because the great fear in Washington and the European capitals would eventually be defeat. He was soon asking for ground troops, in part because he wanted them (or at least the threat of having them), and in part because in the complicated dynamics that take place between a commander in the field and his superiors and peers in Washington, he knew if they turned him down on that, they would surely have to give in on something else. They would not want NATO to lose the first real war in its history. "What Wes knew, because he was so smart and so far ahead of most of the others on the military side," said one close friend, "is that if they gave him a weak hand at the start, he could always play it into a strong hand. It might be hard, but he *knew* he could do it. He not only knew Milosevic's weaknesses, but he knew Washington's weaknesses as well."

That placed him in an ongoing struggle with Cohen, who, like the Joint Chiefs, was filled with doubts and extremely cautious about the course of action in Serbia. But now the dynamic had shifted. Clark, as the man in the field, had a special kind of power that rivaled or exceeded that of the senior

Pentagon people. Clark and Cohen were supposed to be allies, but they would become antagonists, much more so than the normal, occasionally edgy relationship between a CINC and the secretary of defense. The irony was that Cohen had picked Clark for the job, well aware of the powerful institutional resistance against him within the army. Although he knew some of the army traditionalists thought Clark was too political, Cohen had been impressed by Clark's pure intelligence and his ability to handle the diplomatic side, which would be so important in Brussels. But now under the pressure of a policy that was very much in jeopardy, their relationship was being torn apart. In Cohen's eyes, Clark was putting him in constant conflict with the other senior military, who were opposed to any greater escalation in the Balkans, especially the use of ground troops. That might force Cohen to go against the Pentagon on issues about which he had grave doubts himself. Worse, Clark somehow seemed to be beyond his reach and, in Cohen's mind, always going around him. But Clark's own chain of command as a CINC did not go through the Joint Chiefs; it went directly to the secretary of defense.

Their relationship quickly became a disaster. Even after the bombing started, Clark could never, he later complained, talk to Cohen about substantive things. Whenever he called the secretary to tell him about his problems, Cohen would put him off and try to steer him to the uniformed military. "You better talk to Hugh about that," he would say, clearly not wanting to be caught between an activist CINC and more dovish senior military men. Clark, in turn, decided he was being blocked by a man who was supposed to support him and began to look elsewhere for help. Clark told friends that dealing with Cohen was the worst professional experience he had had since his encounter with Jack Hudachek as a young battalion commander. Cohen felt the same way about Clark. "I rue the day I made him SACEUR," he told aides at one point.

Why it worked out so badly between them, no one was ever sure. Part of it was the terrible issue they faced, a decision to go to war when the military had so many doubts and the top civilians had so little confidence, decision-making therefore deliberately masked in fog. But part of it was personal as well, for some people who knew them well thought that they were very much alike. Both were confident of their own abilities and judgment, both more than a little headstrong, each tending to believe that he was just a bit smarter than everyone else in the institution in which he served. Clark, frustrated by Cohen and the Joint Chiefs, quickly developed moves of his own, which made the people back in Washington even angrier with him. The Chiefs were convinced that he was talking to the people on the other side of the river, telling things to Albright and Berger that they felt he should keep to himself, always lobbying for more, in their opinion loading the dice they all had to play with. Cohen, it was said, would pick up the phone to talk with

Albright or Berger and hear some bit of information that might undermine the Pentagon's position that he was sure could only have come from Clark.

Nor were the top civilians, save Albright, all that enthusiastic about the constant pressure Clark was applying to them to do more. He might be their man, but every nudge from him was a reminder that their policy was in jeopardy, and that their military critics, who had always asked what would happen if airpower alone did not work, might have been right. Some of the senior people in the Pentagon had little sympathy for the SACEUR. To them Clark was being hoisted by his own petard. He had pushed to fight a war that was by army tradition an alien use of American force and had violated every tenet of the Powell Doctrine, which most of them accepted. If Wes Clark was having a hard time now that he was out there on his own, so be it.

What was taking place in the struggle over Kosovo was something new, virtual war from fifteen thousand feet or above. It was an antiseptic war waged by remote control, without casualties, if at all possible, or at least without casualties for the side with the higher level of technology. It was, thought those who were its witnesses and fortunate or unfortunate enough to be near any of the bombing sites, truly surrealistic. The NATO planes flew so high that they were never seen, although on rare occasions there might be a brief glimpse of the bombs themselves falling and then the sound of the explosions. The B-2 bomber pilots flying the missions were based in Missouri, and the question for some of the crews was whether they would get back in time to watch their children's soccer and baseball games. It was war as envisioned by George Orwell or H. G. Wells: invisible planes sent on their missions from scientifically advanced bases elsewhere to pick out unseen targets from high-tech screens and to launch laser-guided or photo-guided weapons of destruction at them. The war, amazingly futuristic in the eyes of men who had fought in other wars, was obviously worthy of a science fiction novel. It seemed to lack only robotic figures at headquarters picking the sites and robotic figures piloting the planes, although in the case of the Tomahawk missiles, propelled by videotape in their electronic brains, the reality was close enough to the futuristic image. Ironically, the new technology of airpower was performing brilliantly—well above expectations—but because the target lists were so limited, the war was going poorly.

This was a new age in war, and one weapon represented just how much warfare had changed in only eight years: the B-2 Stealth bomber. Based at Whiteman Air Force Base in Missouri, its pilots and crews could leave their homes and take off for the fourteen-hour trip to the Balkans, penetrating Serb skies unobserved at night as mere F-117 fighters had been able to do eight years earlier over Iraq. It was an expeditionary force that could sleep in its own beds at night and then go from peace into war over a faraway continent, returning a little more than a day later.

Of the B-2's validity and viability, however, there had always been considerable doubt and controversy. Many wondered whether Stealth technology really worked, including some of the F-117 pilots back in the Gulf War. There had been even greater doubts about the B-2. Some critics claimed it would not fly in the rain. Others said it was an expensive boondoggle. Les Aspin, as an influential congressman, had been dubious and had tried to set a sharp limit on its production.

As they were readied for the Kosovo mission, doubts about the B-2s remained. They had been held out of Desert Fox, the brief air campaign against Iraq in mid-December 1998, for fear of losing one. The same fear still existed on the eve of the Kosovo campaign. Wes Clark also had his doubts, but some persuasive briefings by the younger officers who actually commanded the planes reassured him. Not so at the highest level of the Pentagon. Just before the Kosovo bombing began, Clark told Mike Short, "You know that there are people very high up in your own service who don't want to use the B-2." Short answered that he was sure it was not his chief, Mike Ryan. No, Clark said with just a touch of irony, it was Joe Ralston, the vice chair of the JCS. "Joe's afraid we might lose one," Clark added.[1]

But whatever doubts that still existed about the B-2 were soon dispelled. It became the star piece of equipment of the Kosovo war. It carried the burden in the early weeks of the fighting when the weather was bad and some four thousand sorties by other aircraft had to be canceled. In all, B-2s flew only 3 percent of the missions but hit 33 percent of all the targets. They brought to the war a new dimension of technological excellence, one that seemed to place even greater distance between the warriors and their adversaries.

Even as they took off and headed for the Balkans, immensely sophisticated new devices kept tracking the combat area from satellites and spy planes and fed their information into a system that ended up in the B-2's brain. Two pilots would fly the plane, one of them resting while the other had the controls. They would hit their target, get back to Whiteman, and try to make up some lost sleep while another set of pilots took their turn on the next bombing run.

The bombs they were dropping were, in the complicated terminology of the military, called JDAMs, or Joint Direct Attack Munitions. They were smart bombs, precision-guided and different from missiles because they had no power of their own. JDAMs were two-thousand-pound bombs that could hit their targets with astonishing accuracy and relatively little collateral damage. The radius of accuracy had shrunk dramatically, down now to a few feet, and the striking power had increased just as dramatically in only eight years. The F-117s that had flown over Iraq were called fighters, but they were really small bombers and could carry only two two-thousand-pound bombs. The B-2 bomber, however, could carry sixteen bombs, thus increasing the striking power a minimum of eight times. But because each bomb was so much more accurately guided and the explosive inside so much more powerful—a five-hundred-pound bomb in 1999 was far deadlier than a five-hundred-pound bomb in 1991, more like a two-thousand-pound bomb because of more lethal explosives—the attack capability was probably a factor of far above eight.

The JDAM itself was something of a small but important technological breakthrough, a smart bomb kit that, when attached to a dumb bomb, allowed it to respond to global positioning system (GPS) navigational controls. Bill Perry had helped push through the JDAM program after taking a ride in a B-2 in 1995. Impressed by the plane, he had been appalled to find that adequate munitions were not going to be available, and he had given specific orders to expedite the JDAM program and make it a high priority, a decision that would pay off handsomely in 1999.

The new bombs and missiles were smarter than the old, using the GPS and getting accurate, up-to-the-minute information fed into the B-2's brains even as it was in flight to its targets. In fact, purists now referred to this as an example of *aerospace* power, not airpower, because of the importance of aerospace technology derived from the satellites. Both the B-2 and the much smaller F-117 resembled bats, but the B-2, with a wingspan of 172 feet, resembled a bat on a diet of steroids. Both planes required a special kind of surface that was radar-resistant, and they were designed so that there would be no flat surfaces that might bounce radar beams back to the sender. Thus the enemy radar instruments that liked to play Ping-Pong with hostile aircraft were, in effect, reduced to playing Ping-Pong with themselves, since no one was hitting the ball back. The B-2, like the F-117, also had great control over emissions and carried its weapons inside bomb bays, lest they give off a signal.

The B-2 was designed to look like a small bird on enemy radar rather than a singularly lethal bomber. Or as one air force officer said, it did not come up on radar as a goose that was much too big, but at the most as a sparrow. The degree to which the Stealth technology was effective surprised even its most ardent advocates. One Stealth plane, an F-117 fighter, was shot down early in the war, but the air force later believed that the plane was vulnerable because in the first few days of the fighting some of the pilots did not vary their take-off procedures and flew repetitious routes. The Serbs had placed observers around the Aviano air base, where the F-117s were stationed, knew roughly when they were taking off, and quite likely filled the flight path with anticipatory fire.

One of the B-2's most memorable successes was against the Novi Sad Bridge in downtown Belgrade. Bridges are notoriously tough targets, especially those in urban areas where the flak is heavy. Certain bridges in North Vietnam had been extremely costly, with one the target of the first primitive laser bombs, which used two planes, one to drop the bomb, the other to hold the laser guidance on the target. Even B-2 pilots had considerable doubt that the Novi Sad Bridge could be hit. As it turned out, one B-2 dropping eight JDAMs—six for the center and two for one end—and making just one pass, took the bridge out.

The most notorious bombing mistake of the war was also caused by a B-2, striking Belgrade during the night of May 7–8. The target was a Milosevic logistical center, Target 493, the Federal Procurement and Supply Directorate. But because of a mistake in labeling among the targeteers, the building was, in fact, the Chinese embassy. Four staff members were killed, and an immense diplomatic crisis exploded. It was a reminder that technological brilliance was still at the mercy of human frailty.

The B-2s were used on the first day of bombing and proved to be the most effective new instrument of warfare. They were able to exploit almost all of the new technologies. Not only did they evade Serb radar defenses, but much of the planes' unique value came from their invulnerability to bad weather. They could fly in all kinds of weather and could always find their targets. The laser bombs carried by other planes might be limited by weather, clouds interfering with the laser technology. But the JDAMs, guided by the GPS technology, were always effective. Only one B-2 mission was canceled due to weather, because support aircraft were unable to fly.

In all ways Kosovo presented an entirely new military dilemma. Because we did not want to use ground troops, we depended exclusively on airpower. But though we had the capacity to destroy Milosevic's infrastructure in a matter of days, the nature of the multinational command structure and the fear of punishing the Serbs precipitously resulted in severe restrictions on the use of the awesome new technology. Even so, holding back in its use of power and its target selection, the American NATO military machinery, formidably powerful, was vulnerable to charges of brutality. The war may have started with Milosevic's brutality against the Albanians, but what much of the world was soon watching was a big, rich, technologically advanced nation *bombing* a poor, little country, and doing it in a way that showed its unwillingness to accept casualties itself. Justified as the American and NATO policy might be to those who had authorized it, it was not an attractive picture for the millions of people in other countries who watched it on their television screens.

When Milosevic had attacked the Kosovar Albanians, he had been Goliath; now with NATO airpower being used, the roles had reversed. America, the monopoly superpower, was Goliath, and Milosevic a most unlikely David in a world that never roots for Goliath. Even at home, some traditionally hawkish figures spoke critically of the ethical basis of the war, of NATO and the Americans valuing the lives of their combatants more than they valued the lives of civilians on the ground.

In the early weeks and months of the war when NATO was struggling badly, it did not appear to be Bill Clinton's war. For a time he who was so quick to go on national television in almost any crisis, large or small, to offer a ready and deft touch of presidential empathy now seemed to be the invisible man, keeping a surprisingly low profile. After he made that first statement telling the country we were going to bomb the Serbs, he had vanished. He had authorized the military strike, the country was at war whether it wanted to admit it or not, our bombers were hitting targets in Europe every day, and the country went about its business as usual. It was something stunningly new—war in a time of peace. The president, who by temperament and upbringing did not like the use of force, seemed to shy away from public responsibility for it, loath until much later in the war to make the case for it to the American people.

Instead, the more public figure on the American side, in part by design, in part by accident, became Madeleine Albright. She did not mind; she had advocated the bombing from the start, did not doubt the outcome, if we persevered. Nor was she averse to personal publicity. The cowboy hat and the bomber jacket she favored had always been effective PR ploys, giving the impression that though she was a woman, she could handle herself with the big boys, could if necessary pull a fast draw on the bad guys in the black hats, and therefore was not to be underestimated. In the beginning, it was called Madeleine's War, a title that she did not mind, although she did not like the touch of sexism, the use of her first name. When Vietnam had gone on endlessly, it had been called McNamara's War, and this she thought should be called Albright's War. If the administration wanted her to be point person (at least until it was sure that it was going to work), that was all right with her. What was not all right, some of her allies thought, was the impression that the White House began to give off with the most delicate of leaks that it was annoyed with her because she had promised it would be an easier passage. The war was still going on and some of the scapegoating had already begun.

The other person making the case publicly for the war was Tony Blair, the British prime minister. In contrast to John Major, who had had his foot on the brake during the Bosnia years, Blair had helped NATO move toward a more activist course on Kosovo. Blair was young, articulate, a firm believer that this was the right moral path, and eager to be as visible as possible. He and Clinton had an unusually strong relationship because of their similar backgrounds, politicians who had started out somewhat on the left, had tacked with the changing times, and had moved to the center. Both thrived on their ability to use modern media effectively. If anything, Blair was the first of a generation of international politicians who had learned their craft by studying Clinton and the deft way he handled modern media, choosing which issues he wanted to be associated with, and, of course, which he wanted to avoid.

By early April, restless with the lack of success, Blair went to Brussels to try to find out what was going wrong. He spent several days there, much of the time with Clark, where he soon became Clark's most important convert to the concept of greater force, especially ground troops. Clark was helped in Blair's conversion because most of the senior British military men working with Clark shared his essential viewpoint: if they were going to do it, then they better damn well get it done. When Blair returned to London, he was much more hawkish on the use of ground troops. The White House was not entirely pleased by his conversion and by the appearance of a major figure in the alliance moving slightly ahead of the president. Though delighted to have Blair out front speaking for the war, the White House was not thrilled to have him and his people talking so openly about ground troops, which might cause fissures in the alliance and tended to make the prime minister look more assertive than the president. There was talk in private to reporters that Blair was grandstanding.

It also raised the question of whether Clark was on the team, if in fact there was a team. The White House began to suspect a British-Clark axis, a sense that the Brits, when they wanted something done, worked through Clark, and Clark, when *he* wanted something done, worked through the Brits. Somehow both parties were going through outside channels when it suited them, keeping each other informed of any potential blockages in the American system. Thus began a rather rude awakening, in a White House where none of the senior people had ever hunkered down in a war before, of how the equation of power changed once a war began, and how much more powerful a commander could be than they had suspected. The Bosnia bombing and the quick bombing of Iraq in Desert Storm had been throwaway exercises by comparison. The White House was occasionally quite irritated with Wes Clark, but could not do much about it.

After his visit to Brussels, Blair also recommended to Clinton that they become more aggressive in taking hold of the NATO decision-making machinery; the restraints placed on Clark and Short were unacceptable. That began to have some immediate effect, and the number of political people who could negate targets on the lists was cut back dramatically, although Clark and Short still regarded the French as a problem. Yet in the middle of April, the frustrations continued to mount. The war did not appear to be going well. The target lists were still considered inadequate. NATO, Sandy Berger said much later, was like a new airplane that had never flown before and was having trouble gaining altitude as it took off. In Brussels and Mons, the pressure increased to expand the bombing lists and to follow up with ground troops.

The pressure on Clark was almost unbearable, his aides thought. Everybody in NATO, and everybody in Washington, both civilian and military, knew what he should be doing, and their calls would soon be followed by a call from someone else, often from the same country and of the same or greater rank, telling him *not* to do it. Those around him, even senior officers who disagreed with him on policy or did not always like him personally, thought that Clark was at his very best during this period. He worked endlessly hard, generally treated subordinates well, kept his cool, balanced difficult warring constituencies with considerable grace, and never lost sight of his essential purpose. He was getting little support from his own military, but he did not whine and he remained resolute. To the degree he had allies, they were civilians, not military men. Whatever you thought of Wes Clark—that unusual but occasionally maddening blend of great talent, intelligence, ego, and purpose—this was him at his best. He had the job he had always wanted, and his confidence never flagged.

His calls for expanded target lists were met with growing success. But he had become sure that ground troops would bring Milosevic to heel, if not the actual use of them, then at the very least the threat of them. He did not think Milosevic would take the NATO mission seriously until he began to see ground troops coming. Clark was, after all, an army man, and the army believed that ground troops won wars; airpower, while immensely valuable, had never of its own been the decisive weapon. But that belief put Clark in direct conflict with Cohen and the Joint Chiefs, who were determined to hold the line on ground troops. There was constant sparring over this. Clark would make a move at least partially designed to come closer to the ground troop option, perhaps merely to get some troops in the area, and the Pentagon people would smell it out and try to block him.

At one point, he requested what the army calls a prefloat, a brigade that would be stationed in the area on standby. In this case, it would sit on a ship just off the coast of Greece, waiting for a call, one more obvious dagger aimed at Milosevic, forty-seven hundred elite troops ready to enter battle within twenty-four hours, which would tell him that they were heading toward more, not less, force as the war progressed. Into the Pentagon went the request, back came the rejection. How could they turn you down? one of Clark's aides asked. "They said it was too expensive," he replied. Too expensive? the aide said. How can it be too expensive to have a brigade just sitting there? "They say the whole operation is too expensive and they have major budget problems," Clark answered. That, he and the aides knew, was not true. The truth was the Pentagon did not want ground troops anywhere near him; he was too quick on the draw, too driven, too given to operating on his own, to be trusted with a brigade. Both sides, it was obvious, were onto each other, and they were playing a tough, high-stakes game. At one point, one of Clark's staff members prepared a report for Washington on what would be needed in Kosovo if the allies won, which included among other things a brand-new police system, since the previous one was Serbian and would not be allowed back in the region. The obvious solution was the use of foreign troops to fill the vacuum and police a predictably violent, hate-filled region. That part of the report was ordered deleted in Brussels before it was sent on.

But nothing that happened in the Balkans demonstrated the conflicting tensions as much as the struggle over the AH-64 Apache helicopters, the army's fastest, most modern choppers, especially designed, it was believed, for a situation precisely like this. The Apaches were the army's best and most modern weapon of this kind, designed to elude infantry gunners on the ground, even those armed with simple hand-carried surface-to-air missiles. They had the newest technology available, inventions that would not only keep their engines cool, but cool their exhaust systems as well, thereby protecting them from any heat-seeking missiles. They could also fly at night without showing any lights. Expectations of what the Apaches could achieve in Kosovo were exceptionally high, particularly on the part of those committed to army aviation who wanted to make the army quicker, more mobile, and more flexible in its responses. When the announcement was made that they were being sent to a base in Albania, Kenneth Bacon, the Pentagon's senior press spokesman, suggested that they might change the course of the war and give the United States "the capability to get up close and personal to the Milosevic armored units in Kosovo."

They were to be the military's best weapon for air-to-ground support, particularly against slightly dated enemy armor and its accompanying infantry units. They were faster and more agile, with far greater capacity to scan the battlefield than armored vehicles on the ground, slower and more accurate with their firepower than jet fighters. "Instead," as Dana Priest wrote in the *Washington Post* in a devastating critique of what happened, "the vaunted helicopters came to symbolize everything wrong with the army as it enters into the twenty-first century: its inability to move quickly; its resistance to change; its obsession with casualties; its post–Cold War identity crisis."[2] If the Apaches were a mistake, they were an expensive one. Some $15–$18 billion had been spent not only to make them an exceptional attack instrument, but also to limit their vulnerability to ground fire—the great Achilles' heel of helicopter warfare. Each Apache cost $14.5 million. The end product was considered exceptional: it was fast, could fly just above tree level at high speeds, and even had curved rotor blades to muffle noise. Still they were helicopters, always vulnerable to ground fire if enemy soldiers did not panic. Surprise, stealth, and a limited time in the killing zone were obviously critical to their use.

Ironically, Hugh Shelton, an army man and the chairman of the Joint Chiefs, had been the first to suggest using the Apaches in Kosovo, even before the bombing began. He had rather casually mentioned the idea to Clark, who immediately picked up on it, seeing their potential to fill a critical vacuum in his repertoire. At the very least, he believed, they would significantly upgrade the pressure on Milosevic. But the interior debate over the Apaches was never really about heliborne warfare; it was always about ground troops. What the Pentagon suspected was that Clark wanted the Apaches as a Trojan horse for ground troops. And so, of course, it resisted. A great many neutral observers, as well as a number of Clark's allies, believed the senior military's suspicions were absolutely correct.

In traditional battle plans, drawn up for Pentagon strategists, the Apaches were to be used with a full complement of infantry. But the first condition of the Kosovo commitment was no ground troops, which meant no infantry spotters on the ground for the helicopters. Because he would have no ground troops, Clark wanted to use drones and satellite photos for spotting Serb forces. From the intelligence gleaned that way, the Apaches would then strike at Serb army units. But his superiors in Washington were skeptical. Given the speed of the airships and the richness of the terrain, Dennis Reimer, the army chief of staff, said that it would be like looking for Serb ground troops through a straw. To the Chiefs back in Washington, there was little military upside to the Apaches. To them, the request for their use smacked of the worst kind of incrementalism. What happens if one of the Apaches is shot down? they asked. Won't you have to send in a recovery team *on the ground and in Serb-held territory?* And if the Serbs surround the area with their troops and wait for the recovery team, won't you have to send in an even larger force to protect your own men? To the Chiefs it was a replay of both Vietnam and Somalia. Start with something small and relatively innocent, then something larger and unpredictable is born of it. Were the civilians who had given them what was so far a quite limited mandate ready to open it up for a larger commitment? They doubted it. If they wanted a platform comparable to the Apaches, some senior military men thought, the A-10 Warthog, an air force plane that had been a surprise star of Desert Storm, was perfect and less vulnerable.

In Washington, Clark was virtually without support among the military. Shelton was at the very least ambivalent, and Reimer, the army chief of staff, was against sending them. Back and forth went their discussions, Clark pushing ever harder for the Apaches, Shelton reflecting the Pentagon (and White House) reluctance. "Wes," Clark would quote Shelton as saying, "you should know that I'm having a hard time back here with the Chiefs. The army chief [Reimer] just doesn't want to send them in." But Clark had the perfect answer. Not only were they an ideal weapon for his needs, but, he added, "Surely we're not going to deny a wartime commander in chief the assets we need to win."[3]

For Reimer and others, the Apaches were the first step toward a ground war. Eventually Shelton came up with a compromise solution: send the Apaches to Albania, but don't employ them until more of a consensus favored their use and everyone was more confident about the prospective rate of casualties. If that consensus was reached, Shelton would then make the recommendation to the president. That kicked at least part of the decision back to the White House, which had hardly shown itself eager to get more deeply involved and was still extremely nervous about casualties. The decision to go ahead without really going ahead was made on April 3. Everyone expected that the Apaches would get to Albania within ten days. That prediction, like many others about their usefulness, turned out to be quite optimistic. Now the army slow-walked the Apaches through the pipeline. Its every move seemed greased with molasses. Clearly someone at the very top had sent out a signal saying there was no rush. Deadline after deadline was missed. Excuses piled up. There was always some reason not to proceed. Nor was anyone in the army, one high army officer noted, ever punished for the appalling delay in getting a vital weapon to a hot combat zone.

Of course, no base was ready for the Apaches. Potential sites were studied, and finally the army selected a base near Tirana, close to the Montenegrin border, which offered them a shot at several divisions of Serb troops as well as a major Serb airfield at Podgorica. But the base itself was something of a disaster area, a sea of mud, and the army had to reclaim and rebuild it for the choppers. Enormous amounts of rock fill were brought in. Special landing pads were created, and tanks and armored personnel carriers were ferried over to protect the base. Five thousand ground troops were also sent just in case the Serbs became unusually cocky and attacked the base itself. Five hundred and fifty flights of giant cargo planes were required for the creation of the base and to get all the equipment there at a cost of some $480 million. It was late April before all the helicopters arrived. Clark had requested forty-eight of them; the army sent twenty-four.

Still there was no word on whether the Apaches would be able to fly. Then one crashed during a routine flight because of a mechanical failure, an event that made those already hesitant even more dubious. Back in Washington, Cohen, Shelton, and Ralston still did not want to use them and were telling the White House as much. Given Clinton's own reluctance about taking casualties, as Dana Priest pointed out, that did not make for a difficult sell. There had long been an ongoing debate about projected casualty estimates. Clark and General John Hendrix, the commander of Task Force Hawk, the helicopter unit, were eager to use the Apaches and thought the risks were relatively slight. The senior officers in the Pentagon wanted to know what the casualty estimates might be. At first Clark and Hendrix said that it was hard to give an estimate because this was a new kind of mission. Pressed further, during a telephone linkup with the Pentagon in mid-April, Hendrix said that they would be about five for one hundred sorties, or perhaps even a bit higher. Of the figures being batted around by both sides there remained some question. Hendrix remembered using a figure of five, whereas some of the senior military remembered hearing six to fifteen, the figure given at least once to the White House. At the White House, civilians later said they began to hear figures that were perhaps as high as 50 percent over time. People, it appeared, heard the figure they wanted to hear.

Certainly helicopters were among the most vulnerable of aircraft, and the terrain was mountainous and the foliage thick, which meant it would be difficult and dangerous to fly through, especially when an adversary had countless small hand-held missile launchers. But the American commanders in the field remained eager to go; this was their mission and the first chance to try out a potentially wondrous piece of military equipment. Clark had spent three weeks since the Apaches arrived working with his commanders to make sure they had an acceptable tactical plan, that the choppers could be used with some degree of safety and that they would be a valuable instrument in the fighting. He and his commanders were irritated by the nervousness in Washington.

Like fighter pilots throughout the world, the Apache pilots and their commanders were aggressive, confident, sure they could mold their strategy to the needs of the occasion, anxious to justify all that training. The very nature of their profession demanded risks, and they were all prepared to take them. It was what they had signed up for in the first place and they wanted to get on with it. According to their tactical plan, air force planes would precede them with suppressing fire, and then the Apaches would come in fast, ninety miles an hour, guns blazing, and stay around briefly—five minutes in the battle zone. Overhead jets would provide extra cover.

But the doubts in Washington never went away. To Clark's superiors the risks were constant. One Serb soldier with one hand-held missile launcher might just get lucky and turn what was ostensibly a victory into what would be deemed a defeat, one that CNN and the networks would immediately cover. In addition, it was an obvious place in the ongoing struggle with Clark to draw the line and to gain White House support. The generals back in Washington did not, Clark would later say with considerable bitterness, understand that the Apaches could fly at night and that the hand-held SAM-7s did not have night-sighting. Nor did his superiors understand, Clark said, that the Apaches had infrared jammers that would prevent a SAM-7 from locking on. The army, he would muse later, spent twenty years and all those billions creating a superb instrument and then was afraid to use it.

Eventually, the Apaches returned to their base in Germany. It took thirty trains, twenty ships, and eighty-one C-17 cargo flights to get everyone and everything back to their original bases. The fear of their vulnerability remained so great that despite the immense cost of getting them to Albania, the Apaches of Task Force Hawk engaged in no combat missions, fired no shots, and protected no Kosovar Albanians. When it was all over, Secretary of the Army Louis Caldera noted with a degree of melancholy that we seemed as a nation more willing to take casualties in training than in actual combat.

CHAPTER FORTY-THREE

If he was losing the war on the Apaches, Clark knew that he would win on other fronts. They could not turn him down on everything, and as one colleague said, the Apaches might always have been as much a feint as a real move: "Wes probably sensed that there was a good chance they wouldn't let him use them, but he also knew that if they turned him down on this, they would have to give him something else." But a month into the war the tension points were still considerable, and all of the senior players were becoming edgier and edgier. Nor was international public opinion that good. It tended to focus more and more on what NATO was doing—any bomb that went astray, the hitting of a column of Kosovar refugees—and less and less on what Milosevic had done.

There was still no clear sign of Western will. Of the various senior partners, the British were the most aggressive, the French the least. France was most anxious to set limits on bombing targets, worried not so much about what would happen to Milosevic, but about its long-term relationship with the Serb people if Belgrade was bombed. Some of that tension reflected traditional friendly ties to Belgrade; and part of it reflected instinctive French resistance toward what they considered excessive flexing of American will on the Continent. But certainly part of it also represented something new in the post–Cold War order: an undertow of opposition from former allies—the French, of course, in the lead—to American moves, now that America stood alone as a superpower, a most natural resentment of a rich and powerful nation on the part of those who felt America did not take their wishes seriously enough or consult with them enough.

By that time Clark had become even more passionate about using ground troops. Their enemy, he began to warn, was now the calendar. With nearly a million Kosovars forced to leave their homes, thousands of them living in the hills, they were all facing a humanitarian disaster of enormous proportions when the cruel Balkan winter came. If they were going to help the refugees with a ground operation, they probably had to make the decision by early June in order to get the troops there before the cold weather hit. Clark talked about needing some sixty to ninety days once the order was given. Sooner, he emphasized, was better than later. That meant that time was already pressing in on them. Clark's unofficial deadline for a decision to put the wheels in motion was June 10.

What probably helped save the alliance was that in late April all its members were to meet in Washington for the fiftieth anniversary of NATO, which had been formed in 1949 to limit Soviet aggression in central Europe. In a staggering omission, Clark was originally not going to be invited. His relationship with his Pentagon superiors had deteriorated so much that neither Cohen nor Shelton had wanted him to attend. Some of that, it was believed, also came from the White House, where Clark was considered too aggressive in talking about the need for ground troops. The White House also feared that he was looping around them and linking up with the British, who were also pushing harder and harder for ground troops.

In the end, Clark was invited, indeed, he had to come; it would be a scandal if he did not. He had used Javier Solana, the head of NATO, to press his case, which pleased neither the top military people nor the civilians. His orders, however, were clear. He was to behave with minimum visibility and not to talk about ground troops. He would later recall his arrival for the first meeting, seeing the host American team, headed by Clinton, Albright, and Cohen, and receiving glares from some of its members that told him, in effect, to stay away.

The NATO summit was a turning point. Rather than fragmenting over all the difficult issues that divided it, the alliance came out stronger and more united than ever. Central to what happened was a small dinner meeting that Clinton and Blair and a few of their top aides held the night before the conference began. At that moment, a month into the war, with almost none of the news good, the bombing campaign more than a little anorexic, and Milosevic appearing to have a chance to win his gamble, they were for the first time looking at the possibility of defeat. They had all been so careful about the rules, and about listening to political concerns, that they were not winning the war. In that sense, Mike Short and others who were complaining bitterly about the limits imposed on their air campaign had been right, and the senior politicians were now faced with the consequences of these decisions. The British were by then talking much more openly about the need for ground troops, and Blair himself, having visited Brussels and seized on this issue, was far more out-front and outspoken than the president and irritated with the Americans.

The Americans, for their part, were annoyed with the British for being so public about the use of ground troops, a bridge the Americans were not yet ready to cross politically. At the meeting Blair wanted to push the Americans ahead on the use of ground troops; Clinton wanted to hold the alliance together, fearing their use might tear it apart and wanting to lower the volume on discussing it. That night they reached a compromise. The British would say less about ground troops, and in return the Americans would give permission to go ahead with the planning for their use, an escalation that Belgrade, so wired into NATO through friendships and connections, would know about immediately.

It was only when they faced the prospect of defeat that Clinton and Blair decided they had to win. That was central to the presummit dinner, the sudden awareness that the alternative to winning was unacceptable. What it would do to NATO—effectively signal the end of it—and to their countries (and, it was known but never said, to their own careers and place in history) was also unacceptable, and they vowed in a kind of mutual two-man pact that *they would win. There would be no turning back. They had begun it and they would finish it. If they had to pay a higher price, so be it.* "A metaphorical blood oath," Sandy Berger, one of the handful of witnesses, later called it. There would be no bombing halts. No half-a-loaf negotiations with Milosevic designed to let him off the hook. Instead they would ratchet up the pressure on him. It was, in terms of the war, a fateful decision. A month into the bombing, the most important guide to the conduct of the war, the need to hold the alliance together at all costs for political reasons, was changing. Now the primary goal was to win, and that was a *military* mandate. Clark was given permission to start the early, preliminary paperwork on the use of ground troops.

Clark thought that the differences in attitude on both sides of the Atlantic were the result of a combination of geography and history. The civilians in Washington had never been in a war before, this was not a commitment they had been eager to make, and their attitude had always been one of almost irritation, as if this was some annoying, distant problem that would not go away. For the Europeans, it was more immediate, it was physically closer to them, it was war, and especially among the British, there was a sense of urgency, a belief that the sooner they dealt with what were obvious problems, the better the outcome was going to be for everyone. Whatever else had happened during the NATO summit, Clark thought, the British had managed to convince the Americans of the gravity of the situation and that time was not necessarily on their side.

Because of the summit, the target list was expanded and restrictions on targets in downtown Belgrade were lifted. On May 7, the full force of NATO airpower was used for the first time on targets in the city, with formidable results. Finally, Mike Short told friends, after forty-five days, they were letting him do the things he had wanted to do at the start, and with the change in policy and the willingness to go after targets in downtown Belgrade, the B-2s became even more effective. They did things that no bomber or bombing program had ever done before. It had always been an air force belief that it was virtually impossible to take out and close down an enemy airbase from the air because with so many different possibilities for runways, somehow an auxiliary runway or two could quickly be reopened. But late in the war, a B-2, using all its weaponry, had hit a Serb airbase and had systematically knocked out every runway, closing it down for several days. In addition, the Novi Sad Bridge (the Rock and Roll Bridge from which Belgrade citizens had taunted the United States in the past by using it as a kind of open-air discotheque) had finally been taken out. But even with the new guidelines there were setbacks, and when the Chinese embassy was hit by mistake, strict limits were once again put on targets in downtown Belgrade.

The use of the B-2s showed that the introduction of high technology into warfare was taking place at an ever faster rate. The Gulf War, which less than a decade earlier had been the epitome of a modern high-tech war, now looked oddly old-fashioned. In it, roughly 9 percent of the weaponry had been precision-guided. In Kosovo, that figure went over 60 percent. If one plane could now hit sixteen targets, then the role of the B-2, given the rapid acceleration in technology, was bound to increase in the future. The day was fast approaching when the B-2s would carry perhaps as many as fifty bombs, which would mean that one plane could hit *fifty* targets. John Warden, who had played so pivotal a part in planning the air campaign against Iraq, and who had later decided that it would have taken some six weeks with the airpower available in 1999 to end Hitler's war production and transportation, believed that, with the B-2s, that six-week period would have been shortened even more, now down to three days of bombing. Given the need for the B-2s to go back and forth to Missouri to rearm, this would have translated into six days of war in Kosovo. Later when it was all over and the American targeteers and intelligence people compared notes, they came to believe that they had been more successful even earlier in the war than they had realized. The pain they were inflicting, if not immediately affecting Milosevic and his inner circle back in Belgrade, had been very real for his forces in the field. As the NATO intelligence people came to understand how the Serbs used their forces in the field and moved them around when they were under constant air attack, and as the weather improved dramatically, the air campaign steadily and systematically increased in efficiency, well before it began to register in Belgrade.

Even though the target lists had been expanded, the American targeteers were immensely frustrated by the limitations that remained. In downtown Belgrade, for example, they longed to take out a major communications and telephone switching station, but it was only forty yards from a tenth-century church. The switching station was in the bowels of a building and would be easy enough to hit with two-thousand-pound bombs, but while no part of the church's main structure was apt to be damaged, its beautiful, historic windows might be destroyed. So they let it pass. In addition, they held back on hitting the Yugo factories, even though they knew that Milosevic was using them to repair his mobile radar units and SAMs. But one day, they decided, if the war went on and it came down to something like this, they would be able to take them out, too.

The Serb forces in the field who had once been the hunters had become the hunted, a role they were ill-prepared for. The increased effectiveness of the air campaign was gradual; at no one dramatic moment did it all come together. At first the Serbs had used large formations to attack, as they had been taught by the Russians, but the A-10 Warthogs were brutal, especially on their armored units. "You would think they would have learned from the Iraqis about the Warthogs," one senior air force officer later said, "but I think they were very macho—they thought they were a lot tougher and smarter than the Iraqis, and then they learned it wasn't true." Gradually, however, Serbs broke their forces down into much smaller units and began to park their tanks near houses, so that the NATO pilots, not knowing who lived in the houses, had to be careful.

By early May, Serb reserve units from specific towns that had been called up en masse began to turn against the war, some to mutiny as a group, while others had high desertion rates. Serb police were on a number of occasions forced to turn water hoses on civilians in the towns that the deserters and mutineers had come from. At the same time, the KLA forces were forming into larger units and the Serbs had to deal with them as well as the blistering air campaign. Soon it was an old, many-times-told story in guerrilla warfare: the day belonged to the Serbs, the night to the KLA.

NATO was also becoming more successful in taking out Serb SAMs and radar stations. One of the keys was to find them. The Serbs moved them constantly, but the targeteers began to become expert at looking at a spot where a SAM was and, knowing the limited distance it could be moved, being able to predict where the Serbs would relocate it. By one set of NATO statistics, in the beginning of the fighting the Serbs would move a mobile radar unit roughly every thirty-six hours and a SAM every twelve hours; by mid-May they were moving them every forty-five minutes.

Also by mid-May, for the first time, allied intelligence knew that the air war was having a considerable impact on the Serb political structure. Good sources in Yugoslavia, some of them with connections to the Milosevic regime, began to report the effect of the bombing. Milosevic, they said, was increasingly isolated from some of his closest allies, was becoming more erratic in his personal behavior, and was being seen less and less in public. The population, despite the attempts of Milosevic's propaganda machinery to portray an exuberant, lionhearted Serb people who scoffed at NATO and became more unified with every bomb that fell, was turning surly, its anger focused not only on NATO, but on Milosevic as well. The rate of desertion kept going up especially among conscripts who believed in a Serbian Kosovo but did not want to die for it.

Milosevic's bet that NATO would fragment and be unable to stay the course was illusory. His sources within NATO were reporting that, rather than backing off, NATO was upping the ante, not only bombing the very heart of his political and economic machinery, but moving ahead with preliminary paperwork on ground troops. He was effectively isolated from the rest of the world. The Russians might in theory be supporters of his, critics of NATO, and very unhappy with what it was doing, but because they were immensely dependent upon the West for economic assistance, they were in no position to act. The war so far was not so much showcasing pan-Slavic brotherhood as it was momentary Russian impotence. Milosevic stood alone.

There were other negative signs. The KLA had not been dormant during the bombing. It understood that it now had a wondrous new airshield and renewed its efforts, organizing in larger, if somewhat irregular, units, poorly trained perhaps, but ever more emboldened. By mid-May the weather, which had hampered NATO planes earlier in the bombing runs over Kosovo, had cleared, and NATO was hitting some of Milosevic's armored units, keeping his forces in check, while their indigenous enemies, the KLA, with perhaps as many as ten thousand men under arms, were on the move. Because of that, Milosevic faced an additional dilemma. For the first time he was in danger of being defeated militarily in Kosovo, especially now that the allies were planning on ground forces.

The other issue he had to contend with was his personal control of the country. When he had first come to power, there had been several indigenous protests against his policies and authoritarian moves, but he had always quickly and violently repressed any dissenters and escalated control not merely of the political process but of the media as well. The key to sustaining power, however, as in communist societies past, had been the secret police. But the world around him had changed, and democratic stirrings had not entirely gone away. Now, even with a considerable Serb passion for Kosovo, many of the more democratically oriented Serb citizens, some of whom wanted closer ties to the West and some who did not, were becoming aware that, like it or not, they were at war because of his political excesses, his grandiose flaunting of NATO and his ethnic hatreds. That knowledge, or at least some of it, had always been there. But now it was costing them dearly.

For Yugoslavia or Serbia was, in political terms, something of a halfway house, neither entirely totalitarian nor yet very democratic. In the transition from a Cold War to a post–Cold War society, Milosevic had exploited the existing power vacuum and made a number of critical instruments of democratic life, such as the media, his own, and he had been brutal toward political opponents. But that was not the same thing as gaining popularity; and by May, many Yugoslavs were facing the cumulative effects of Western economic sanctions, isolation from the West, and the knowledge that elsewhere in Europe other once-communist countries were moving toward democracy, while they were still struggling with authoritarian rule. Added to that was the bombing, which was the direct result of Milosevic's ambitions; these were his political moves, but they were the ones who had to pay for them. The Serb people might not like what NATO was doing, but intelligence sources saw signs that they now placed no small part of the blame on Milosevic.

When bombing as a singular instrument of policy had failed before in wartime, it had almost always been against a completely controlled, autocratic society. But Yugoslavia, for all of Milosevic's consolidation of power, was rather different. The country, somewhat in conflict with itself, was a political hybrid, an autocracy with democratic forces momentarily stymied, but still there stirring just under the surface. The bombing underscored the fault line between the two, widening the gap that separated those more drawn to the hatreds of the past and those who hoped for a chance for freedoms, long denied and now delayed. During his rise, Milosevic had used instruments of power and the passions of an unusually cruel nationalism to block equally powerful instincts for democracy. It had worked at first. In the early days of his rule, there was the belief that fierce nationalism and embryonic democratic feelings could be combined. But now that a harsher reality was setting in, a profound separation was taking place between these two forces. Those stirrings for democracy had never gone away, and Milosevic's foreign adventures had taught many Serbs how powerless they really were.

One additional vulnerability that the architects of the bombing played on was that, if Yugoslavia was not exactly like Kenya, an out-and-out kleptocracy, then at the highest levels the Belgrade government was run by a part-capitalist, part-communist mafia, composed of Milosevic, his family, and their closest friends. They were cutting themselves in on all kinds of deals, running state-favored enterprises without any real competition, and gaining immense profits. During the ten years that Milosevic and his family ran the country, a small number of privileged people had eaten handsomely at the public-private trough. There was no greed, some of the Milosevic regime's critics thought, quite like that of former dedicated Marxists when they finally had a chance to bend a partially capitalist system to their wants. The NATO targeteers took great pleasure in singling out those companies that belonged to the Milosevic mafia and destroying their buildings, knowing that this would turn up the pressure on Milosevic. Which it did. Soon reports were emanating from Belgrade about trusted advisers, ministers, and cronies who wanted to leave the country and move their money out as well. Many were trying to get Milosevic to do something to end the war.

For the first time in late May, Washington was somewhat optimistic the bombing was finally working. In Brussels, planning was going ahead for ground forces, as many as 225,000 to 250,000 troops, and the NATO planners were quite open in letting those people suspected of having close Milosevic ties know some of the details—if not exactly the battle plan. The White House was also more confident now. The president gave two good speeches on the war, one at the National Defense University in Washington, then another at the Commonwealth Club in San Francisco. Equally important, on May 18, Clinton pulled back from his original March 24 statement about ground troops. This time he said, "All options are on the table."

Everything was gradually coming to a head. On May 27, the defense ministers of France, Germany, Britain, Italy, and the United States met in Bonn to discuss the use of ground troops. Though Washington was generally moving toward the use of ground troops, Bill Cohen was still something of a holdout. He wanted to continue the air war. The British were quite aggressive and ready to commit fifty thousand of their own men. The French thought it might be too late to get a force there before the winter. The Italians and the Germans were obviously uneasy but did not reject the idea. Right after that meeting, Tony Blair called up thirty thousand British Territorials.

If the White House was slowly moving toward accepting the necessity of ground troops, the JCS remained unconvinced. Clark, coming back to the Pentagon in late May, felt that Reimer was slow-walking him, wanting more time to study his plans. With Joe Ralston, Clark found equal resistance—questions about what would happen if they went ahead with ground troops and hostilities broke out elsewhere, say Korea, and after that the Persian Gulf as well. We were in a shooting war, still needing to win, Clark thought with some irritation, and they are talking to me about a double hypothetical.

At the same time, the Western leaders were also playing the Russian card as boldly as they could. From the start Milosevic had counted on Russian protection. But the new Russia was economically vulnerable, dependent on Western financing and barely able to fend for itself, let alone defend a fellow Slav (whom Boris Yeltsin did not even like). Strobe Talbott, the deputy secretary, had strong Russian connections and had been the contact man with them from the start. Even before the bombing had begun, when Milosevic had looked to Moscow for access to the modern Russian missiles, Talbott had made it abundantly clear to the Russians that we would not tolerate it, that any such lend-lease arrangement would undermine Russia's economic lifeline to the West. From that moment on, a critical part of Milosevic's strategy had failed, and he was isolated in terms of great-power politics, a man without a big brother.

At the time of the NATO anniversary summit, the Western powers had originally hoped to get a senior Russian representative to attend as a symbol that NATO was no longer an anti-Russian instrument but instead part of a larger democratic partnership that could work with the Russians. But the tensions caused by the bombing ended that hope. Yeltsin had originally expected NATO to split apart over the bombing, with the French leading the way, but Jacques Chirac had gone to Moscow and taken a hard line about the war, thus letting Yeltsin know that NATO would probably hold together. During the

NATO summit, Yeltsin had called Clinton and they had had a long, detailed conversation, Yeltsin obviously in considerable political pain because the West was bombing someone he was supposed to help and he had been rendered powerless. That call resulted in Yeltsin's appointing Viktor Chernomyrdin, a former prime minister and a close political ally, as his special envoy to the West on this issue. Chernomyrdin's orders from Yeltsin, he later told others, were "I don't care what you have to do, just end it. It's ruining everything."[1]

Chernomyrdin soon met with Talbott and Vice President Gore, and they came up with a kind of good-cop/bad-cop routine (though Chernomyrdin called it the hammer and the anvil). He would be paired with a neutral figure, who would have to do a good deal of the heavy lifting when they argued with Milosevic, because for a Russian to pound away at a fellow Slav was improper. Madeleine Albright suggested Martti Ahtisaari, the president of Finland. Both the Americans and the Russians quickly agreed he was the ideal choice. For the first time, without anyone realizing it, there was now a serious peace track. Ahtisaari represented a country that was in the European Union but not NATO and was viewed favorably by the Russians as a neutral player. He was also admired by the Americans, as most senior people in the UN were not.

There were more and more signs that Washington had acquired the requisite resolve. The White House had its view of a settlement down to a simple phrase for Kosovo: "Serbs out, NATO in, Albanians back." Sandy Berger, who had been dubious of any kind of air campaign, began to sound more hawkish. On June 2, he met with a number of people from the national security world who were activists on Bosnia and Kosovo, and who had sensed his doubts in the past. "We will win. Period. Full stop. There is no alternative," he told them. "Second, winning means what we said it means. Third, the air campaign is having a serious impact. Fourth, the president has said he has not ruled out any options. So go back to one. We will win."[2] Berger then sat down to write what he thought was a fateful memo for the president, outlining their choices. Even though things were going well, or at least going better, the outcome was still in doubt, and Milosevic's reaction would be unpredictable when he was cornered by NATO with the Russians acting in semiconcert with the alliance. Those who had dealt with him at close range always thought he was the most volatile of personalities, capable of great mood swings. Would he concede relatively quickly or would he force an invasion and watch NATO inflict the full power of its technology on the people of Belgrade before seeking terms? With someone as sociopathic as Milosevic, which was how most senior Western leaders viewed him, there was no telling how he would act in the final, desperate hours of his failed gamble.

Berger's was not the most optimistic of memos. We could invade, he said, but it might not be easy. There was nothing attractive about the ground troop option. We might be sending as many as 250,000 men to Kosovo in the middle of what could be a harsh winter. American tanks would have a hard time going through Kosovo's tunnels. It was, he thought, a hellish choice, sure to be unpopular, especially if the Serbs broke down their units and nibbled at the NATO forces guerrilla-style. Or we could continue the air war, delay the ground war, try to maximize airdrops to the vulnerable Kosovars during the winter, then strike with ground troops in the spring. Or we could arm the KLA and use NATO airpower in conjunction with its forces, although there were long-range dangers in becoming partners with a group like that. At one-thirty in the morning, he finished the memo, laid it out for the president, and went home.

The Talbott-Chernomyrdin-Ahtisaari team made considerable progress almost as soon as it was put in place. Russia signed up along with the G-7, the seven leading industrial democracies, in backing a proposal that called for the removal of Serb troops, police, and paramilitary forces from Kosovo, and their replacement by genuine peacekeeping forces. The first real American-Russian disagreement was, Talbott noted later, over the word *all*. To the Americans and NATO, *all* Serb troops and police and paramilitaries had to go, otherwise it would be far too dangerous for any peacekeeping force, which might be caught in an Albanian-Serb cross fire. The Serbs had responded that they wanted to keep some Serb troops inside Kosovo, the Russians had taken their side, and for a time that slowed things down. The other disagreement with the Russians was whether part of the peacekeeping role would be played by NATO. That was what the West demanded. It did not trust the United Nations, not in this venue, and not after what had happened in Bosnia. That also delayed any agreement.

The Russians, it would turn out, also wanted to play a peacekeeping role with troops of their own in Kosovo. In late May the Russian and American positions seemed frozen, the Americans feeling that the principal resistance came from the Russian military, which had not entirely thawed out in the post–Cold War era. But on the morning of June 3, after a prolonged, thirteen-hour negotiating session, the Russians, apparently under direct orders from Yeltsin, finally agreed that all the Serb forces should leave Kosovo. That was it. In the Russian draft to be taken by Ahtisaari and Chernomyrdin to Belgrade, the phrase "all Serb forces out" was used. The Russian military was furious. There would also be a substantial NATO role in the peacekeeping process.

On June 3, Chernomyrdin and Ahtisaari flew to Belgrade to meet with Milo-sevic. Ahtisaari went through the terms of the agreement with him while Cher-nomyrdin watched. Ahtisaari then warned that if Milosevic did not accept its terms, they would become harsher and the bombing more intensive. NATO would destroy the nation's telephone system and other facets of Belgrade's daily life. As Ahtisaari spoke to him, Milosevic turned to Chernomyrdin for help, received none, and realized that the Russians were now, in effect, on the other side, and the game was over. It was the best deal he could get, Chernomyrdin told him; he had better take it because anything else was going to be worse. Milosevic invited both men to dinner with him. They turned him down. The social game was over, too.[3] The next day he accepted the terms.

Though it had been decided to send in ground troops if necessary, and though Milosevic knew that and it affected his final decision, it was a singular victory for the use of modern airpower, which had just begun to germinate in the Gulf War and had in military terms come to fruition in the Kosovo campaign, however slowly and belatedly. Or as John Keegan, widely regarded as among the most able of military historians, wrote a few days after Milosevic gave up, "There are certain dates in the history of warfare that mark real turning points. November 20, 1917, is one, when at Cambrai the tank showed that the traditional dominance of infantry, cavalry, and artillery on the battlefield had been overthrown. November 11, 1940, is another, when the sinking of the Italian fleet at Taranta demonstrated that the aircraft carrier and its aircraft had abolished the age-old supremacy of the battleship. Now there is a new turning point to fix on the calendar: June 3, 1999, when the capitulation of President Milosevic proved that a war can be won by airpower alone."

One of the early victims of that victory was Wes Clark. Rarely had the commanding general in a victorious cause been treated so harshly. It was all quite deftly done. The other chiefs told the White House that unless they found the right four-star billet for Joe Ralston, he would be forced to retire. The White House was indebted to Ralston, and Bill Cohen was even more so. Ralston had been Cohen's right-hand man, had handled his earlier personal humiliation with grace, had been a valuable team player, and had kept everyone aboard during a tense and edgy time. In the eyes of some, he had been the de facto chairman while serving under Shelton, and there had been talk—never a clear promise—that he might replace him as chairman once Shelton's tour was up in the middle of 1999. The personal problems would be more in the past and the Kelly Flinn case more a part of history, but because of the war, no change was desired and Shelton had gotten a second two-year term.

If they needed a billet, they knew where to look. It would be Wes Clark's. That SACEUR was traditionally an army man's slot no longer seemed to matter. What the other chiefs did not make clear to Berger and Clinton (or at least Berger and Clinton later claimed they did not make clear) was that by signing on to Ralston's new assignment as SACEUR, they were approving a de facto squeezing out of Clark, ending his career, forcing his retirement. Given the nature of the war just over and all the tensions that had been created, it was nothing less than a firing. Clinton signed on, apparently not realizing that he had been snookered. No one on his staff had caught on to the Pentagon move, and it was sold to the White House as a routine assignment, a normal rotation, just one good guy they liked replacing another guy whose tour was up.

Clark had served the usual term, they said, which of course was not true in general. Lauris Norstad had served six and a half years, Al Haig had served five, and in this particular case, Clark, as a triumphant commander who in the most difficult of circumstances had managed to bring them victory, would normally have expected to serve two or three years more. Indeed a critical part of his job would have been to oversee the implementation of the peace he had helped win. Later Clinton was said to have been quite angry about what had happened. So within seven weeks of his victory, Clark had effectively been relieved of his command and replaced by Ralston, who was a much more popular figure on the Pentagon side of the river. It was payback time, and the people at the Pentagon felt there was a lot to pay Clark back for.

So Cohen and the Chiefs had played very hard ball. If anyone was supposed to call Clark and break the news, it was Cohen, who was technically his superior in the chain of command, but the call came from Hugh Shelton, who told Clark he was going to be replaced. The call caught Clark completely by surprise, and because his peers did not trust him and did not want to give him any wiggle room (they feared he might use his Clinton connections to reverse their decision), they had leaked the story to the *Washington Post* that very night. Thus, the next phone call Clark received was from a *Post* reporter asking for confirmation. That meant that even as he was dealing with the stunning news that he would be leaving Brussels, he was being asked by a *Post* reporter what he felt about this unexpected turn of events. Clark immediately got on the phone himself, trying to reach different high officials in the Pentagon to find out what had happened, but they were all quite deliberately unavailable. No, he was told, General Shelton was busy, in a meeting. And Secretary Cohen? Preparing for morning meetings in Japan and couldn't take his call. The more important the figure, the less available he was. The only person he could reach was Ken Bacon, the Pentagon's chief spokesman. There was nothing more Clark could do. It was all over. "I never saw myself as a fifty-five-year-old retired general," he said a few weeks later.[4]

Clark was devastated by the news, a world-class slap in the face, a public rebuke of almost unparalleled proportions. His superiors and peers did not merely dislike him, they hated him and what he had done. Later, Sandy Berger told him that, in effect, the Pentagon had fooled the White House on the changeover, claiming that his tour had been the normal one. But Clark knew he had been had, and he had at his fingertips a list of his predecessors who had stayed on for much longer tours. Because other people had been sacrificed by the White House before, Clark was never entirely sure whether or not to believe Berger's story.

At Clark's retirement ceremonies, the senior military people were notable for their absence. The new army chief of staff, Eric Shinseki, was there, but some of the other Joint Chiefs were missing, most notably Henry Shelton, an army man and the chairman of the JCS, who happened to be on vacation. Some of the members of the Joint Staff, who were in effect Clark's peers, were also missing. That of itself was like a rebuke within a rebuke, as if the Chiefs were rejecting not just the man who had run the war, but the war itself. The civilians did show: Cohen, who presided, Berger, Talbott, Jim Steinberg. Albright was away, but she had let others know she was furious about Clark's treatment.

A year later, as if in atonement, Clinton included Clark on one of the lists for the Presidential Medal of Freedom, but some of Clark's friends remained irate. The Clinton administration, they thought, owed Wes Clark, big time. He had taken on the most difficult of commands, one that the Clinton people had sent him to undertake, and pulled it off, even though he had had to struggle constantly against the undertow of his own people. He had accomplished what he had set out to do against great odds, and if the Clinton people had been tricked by the Pentagon as they later claimed, then the least they owed Clark was to reverse the process they had inadvertently agreed to. But that was not the kind of thing they liked to do, because it would put them in a sharp and unwanted conflict with the uniformed chiefs. Ironically, what happened to Clark created even more doubts about Clinton among many senior military men. They may have had their serious philosophical differences with Clark, but, they felt, Clinton was deeply in debt to him for the way he had run the war. Now when he had been sliced up, Clinton had somehow stood on the sidelines and done nothing. Again it was about codes and loyalty.

More than six years after he had first taken office and begun to struggle with the issue of the Balkans, Clinton had finally and quite reluctantly unleashed American airpower in Kosovo and Serbia. He had won that gamble—at least won it for the time being, because winning in the Balkans was always so problematical. But in the end Milosevic had folded his hand. When he had backed down, Clinton had taken a phone call from Senator Joe Biden of Delaware, the ranking Democratic member of the Senate Foreign Relations Committee. Biden had been almost without equal in urging the administration to act militarily in the Balkans. "Congratulations—you've got your sea legs," he told the president. "Joe, you've been pretty rough on me," the president said. Then he paused and added, as if in apology, something revealing: "Remember I came in as a governor and I didn't have any experience in foreign policy?" It was a nice, friendly call, and it took place in the seventh year of Clinton's presidency.[5]

CHAPTER FORTY-FOUR

This incomplete and in many ways unsatisfactory war was soon followed by an incomplete and difficult peace. Where in Bosnia some traditional forces were working toward pluralism, the forces at play in Kosovo were much more violent and far less likely to find any common ground. The hatreds there between the Serbs and the Kosovar Albanians went deeper—they were almost organic—and were completely mutual. Any peace that followed the fighting would probably not be a genuine peace. Whichever faction was stronger was sure to try to sabotage any peacekeeping effort and exploit its leverage against the momentarily weaker faction. A few months earlier, the villains, by Western consensus, had been the Serbs, trying to de-ethnicize the land by driving the Albanians off it. Now, based on the Serb defeat, and the use of awesome NATO airpower on behalf of the Albanian cause, it was the KLA and related groups that wanted to drive all Serbs out of Kosovo and parts of southern Serbia, which was triggering violent incidents. To the Western forces trying to bring some degree of stability to one of the most unstable pieces of real estate in the world, that meant their recent semi-allies were now potentially their adversaries. In a region where vengeance was a birthright, the great problem was once again deciding who the good guys and who the bad guys were, because they could so readily switch sides. Those who had so recently worn the white hats could wear the black hats, while the black hats could don the white hats.

The past year had greatly strengthened—and emboldened—the KLA and its allied nationalist groups, turning them into a considerable political and military force. Their goal was complete Albanian independence, yet the Western allies that had just fought to protect these same Albanians were pledged to nothing more than some kind of limited autonomy under what would still be overall Serb rule. Thus, the darkest parts of Balkan history—the raw feelings of the Kosovar Albanians and Serbs toward each other—had not been settled. They had been rekindled and were now likely to tear the region apart, with the Western forces that had defeated Milosevic charged with being the new, unsure referee, and largely resentful of being pulled in.

Bill Clinton, who had long minimized the importance of foreign affairs, was the beneficiary of the NATO victory in Kosovo, though there was little political capital to be gained from it. If the intervention had backfired, if the bombing had not worked and ground troops had been needed, there might well have been a political price to pay. It was a valuable lesson for any leader of America-the-superpower in dealing with these so-called teacup wars. If things worked out, if the most optimistic scenario was reasonably accurate, casualties were low (or almost nonexistent), and there was no damaging media coverage, it would nonetheless be of little domestic advantage. But there was always the potential for a downside, the televised capture of American troops, a repeat of Somalia, and a political disaster.

Peace in Kosovo momentarily and only partially accomplished, Clinton in the fall of 1999 was in an oddly ambiguous political position. He had survived impeachment, he had cleared the long-standing shadow of the Balkans from his presidency, the economy was still vibrant, and his standing in the polls was remarkably high, particularly for someone who had been in office for almost two terms. Yet his accomplishments were not necessarily that significant or at least significant in the ways that historians valued them. Much of his energy had gone into limiting the conservative assault upon a broad liberal agenda rather than creating an agenda of his own. After the victory in Kosovo, he had about a year and half remaining to try to define his own vision of the proper legacy of what had been a star-crossed presidency. Clinton was *always* campaigning, and in his last year he was campaigning all out for his place in history, his legacy very much in mind. That was true of most presidents, but for Clinton, a passionate reader and a thoughtful amateur historian himself, it was especially true; he wanted to be sure that historians took the full measure of his presidency—as he measured it himself, of course. There had been signs of this early on. In January 1997, after his reelection, he had sat at dinner next to Doris Kearns Goodwin, who was a member of the Society of American Historians, a group that had just rated the various American presidents, himself included, and had placed him somewhere in the middle. Much of the evening had been devoted to his protests over his mediocre rank and his lobbying for a higher one.

Yet a last-minute upgrade in the legacy business was not an easy accomplishment. His years in office were badly tainted by the Lewinsky affair and the failed impeachment process. Stalemated as he was on the domestic front by fierce, highly personal Republican opposition, it was not likely that he could claim any kind of groundbreaking domestic legislation as a part of his political bequest. Only in the world of foreign affairs could Clinton find some daylight. Thus, in his final year, foreign policy ascended to the top of his political agenda. Though as a candidate he had once criticized Bush for globe-trotting, Clinton had traveled more widely than any other American president, the first to set foot in Botswana, Bulgaria, Kuwait, Slovenia, Denmark, and South Africa. "If it's Monday, this must be Turkey," said a *New York Times* headline in November 1999.

To someone like Marlin Fitzwater, the former Bush press secretary, this was ironic for a man who, Fitzwater noted, had once attacked George Bush in New Hampshire for seeming to care more about Liechtenstein than Littletown and Micronesia than Manchester. Other less partisan critics obviously looked at this development somewhat skeptically, as if Clinton was engaged now in first and foremost a legacy hunt. Another headline in the *New York Times* in January 2000 read, "Clinton's Final Chapter: Singled-Minded Full Steam Run at a Global Agenda." Suddenly Clinton was always on the move, traveling constantly to foreign capitals, where, as analysts pointed out, people cared nothing about the Lewinsky matter and thought the impeachment process (as Clinton himself did) a political travesty. If foreign policy was his only hope to make a mark on history, then that was where he would place his energies.

The change in priorities was dramatic for a man who had a few days before taking office told Lee Hamilton of the House Foreign Affairs Committee that no one in America cared about foreign policy except for a handful of journalists. The old Clinton might have been cautious in midpresidency in moving toward official recognition of Hanoi and had had to be pushed forward by Vietnam veterans serving in the Senate in both parties, but now he was eager to visit the country. He did, and the trip was considered a triumph; old wounds could now be healed just a little faster. There was also in the final months of his second term a good chance that he might visit North Korea, which would have been a first. It would not exactly have been the equal in groundbreaking presidential trips to visiting Moscow or Beijing or even Hanoi, but a first was a first, and in a post–Cold War world with fewer and fewer forbidden cities, you had to take your firsts where you could get them.

Most of Clinton's efforts in his last year went into a highly public, all-out attempt to advance the peace process in the Middle East to a new and final settlement. Clearly this one objective was closer to his heart than anything else on his agenda during the late summer and early fall of 2000. Along with the Israeli prime minister, Ehud Barak, he worked relentlessly toward the next level of a peace accord in a series of nonstop meetings with Palestinian leader Yasir Arafat at Camp David, which ran well into the morning hours. It was obviously the kind of foreign policy role Clinton enjoyed the most. Working to bring peace in the Middle East at Camp David was a more natural part for him to play than sitting around the White House weighing whether to bomb targets in downtown Belgrade. Barak, his partner, seemed equally eager to push forward.

For a brief time, the negotiations appeared to be on the verge of a breakthrough. Arafat was offered a deal that exceeded anything the Israelis had ever before tendered. But because so much of Arafat's position was premised on expected Israeli intransigence, the Palestinian leader seemed totally unprepared by Barak's flexibility. In the end, it was Arafat who blocked the proceedings and the negotiations ended in failure. With the breakup of the Middle East peace process, the last best hope for Clinton to stake his legacy on foreign policy accomplishments collapsed as well.

Clinton liked to tell friends, only partially tongue in cheek, that after the talks failed he received a call from Arafat praising him. "I'm a colossal failure because of you," he answered.[1] Yet what Clinton had done, however reluctantly, in the Balkans was not to be underestimated. The questions facing a president in the post–Cold War years were more difficult to deal with than in the previous, simpler era. This time the enemy was genocide, not Communism. Because there was no direct, immediate threat to the United States during the Balkan crisis, Clinton had received few positive notices for finally using American force in both Bosnia and Kosovo. But quite possibly, with few in the government and even fewer outside realizing it, his administration—and the generation it represented that had come to power after the Cold War—had finally faced a critically important test for the uses of American might, and in answering the question of whether America stood for anything beyond the defense of its own land. Clearly there were no easy answers—or necessarily even right answers—in cases like this, and just as clearly there was little political upside to the intervention. Clinton and his administration had moved slowly at first, perplexed by the equation in front of them and the lack of political support at home. They had frequently stumbled but they had, however awkwardly, and belatedly, met a vital early test of post–Cold War peacekeeping.

Of all the people who had joined the Clinton administration in 1993, Dick Holbrooke ended the eight years, by the consensus of his peers—or at least among those who still intended to serve in a future Democratic administration—as the most successful member of the foreign policy team. Madeleine Albright might be, in terms of celebrity star power, at least momentarily a larger figure because of the nature of her personal story; and because she was the first woman secretary of state, her memoirs would probably sell for a larger sum than those of anyone else who had worked in foreign policy. But it was Holbrooke who had truly impressed his peers, even many who had been dubious of him earlier on.

Probably from the moment he had visited Banja Luka in 1992, Holbrooke had understood not just the evil taking place, but the test it represented for his generation of policy makers and the administration he hoped to join. He had been weaned on one definition of evil in the world, and had been essentially a dove in the earlier construct that was so critical to him as a young man in the beginning of his career in Vietnam. Yet he had adjusted and managed to deal with the very different challenge that the Balkans represented to American policy makers late in his career.

It was not just his successful tour in Germany, the desperately needed energy he had brought to a badly unfocused State Department, and his skillful leadership at the Dayton peace conference. He had finished his tour at the United Nations with a stunning and quite unlikely victory. Through backbreaking work, he had come up with a solution that allowed America to pay its UN dues, long disputed, much of the money targeted for peacekeeping missions. Remarkably the settlement satisfied both the UN leadership *and* the leadership of the Congress, most notably Jesse Helms. Helms had publicly congratulated Holbrooke—a sure sign, in this case, of a tour de force. Old Holbrooke watchers noticed something else about him. He had always wanted, they thought, to be a celebrity. Because of his successes and his high visibility in the past few years, he had finally emerged as something of a star, and the role was becoming to him. He appeared more confident and centered, and those lesser qualities that had bothered people about him in the past had gone sharply into decline. He was finally first in his class.

On the military side, the dominant figure had been Wes Clark. To no small degree, he had broken ranks with the Pentagon because of his belief—effectively taught to him on location by Slobodan Milosevic—that America had to act at certain moments to be the nation it believed it was. Clark had never been popular with his peers; his Balkan activism had made him even less so, and, in the end, he paid dearly for it. But he had handled the most difficult kind of command with skill and intelligence, had lost no troops in actual combat, and had shown future administrations and officers that under certain conditions peacekeeping could be militarily successful at a relatively low cost. He had ended his tour not merely committed to the use of force in such instances, but as a caustic critic of his own branch of service for its conservatism.

At first, the NATO victory did not seem to affect Slobodan Milosevic's hold on power in Belgrade. Yes, his forces had been defeated and his latest military moves had backfired. Yes, he had over more than a decade savaged the Yugoslav economy, and the sanctions levied against Yugoslavia had brought the economy to the edge of ruin while neighboring countries were enjoying unprecedented prosperity. Yes, almost everything he had touched while exploiting the cruelest kind of nationalism had been paid for dearly by his fellow Serbs.

There was one great unanswered question in the months after the Kosovo war came to its unsuccessful (for Serbs) end: In the period right after the collapse of the Berlin Wall, when all their neighbors were enjoying vast improvements in their political and economic status, were there any serious domestic consequences for depriving fellow citizens of their rightful chance for a better, more democratic life? Certainly Milosevic's control over the national media was used to blur any news of the greatly improved lives of those in the surrounding nations, but people in Eastern Europe, accustomed to state-controlled media, had always known when to listen and when not to listen and had traditionally distrusted official sources of information. Still, could Milosevic's ability to manipulate and orchestrate the ugliest aspects of Serb nationalism continue to serve as an acceptable smoke screen for his failure to permit the liberalization of the society that most Serbs hoped for?

Milosevic's hold over the crucial sources of power seemed as complete as ever. His control over the media, especially state television, made any opposition to him on the eve of a presidential election seem frail. The opposition had no real way to make its case, and therefore neither Serbs nor foreigners could gauge how strong it was. If the damage he had inflicted on his own people was palpable, no one was eager to bet against him; he had inhaled all domestic opposition in the past.

Still, elections were elections, and Yugoslavia remained a political hybrid, blending together, in a most unlikely mixture, some elements of nascent democracy with remnants of the old communist apparatus. For Milosevic, the fiction that he was a freely elected president was important when he spoke to the Western world. Vojislav Kostunica, a constitutional lawyer and a Serb nationalist, was chosen to run against him by a group of eighteen opposition parties. At first not many people took Kostunica seriously, but by mid-September, he had clearly become a rallying point for deep-rooted and surprisingly powerful anti-Milosevic feelings, and he was posing a serious challenge to the Serb president. Kostunica was, in the true sense, a more intense nationalist than Milosevic—as one Serb journalist noted, Milosevic's politics were always those of self, with nationalism more a convenience than a genuine passion. With Kostunica, it was a deadly serious business.

On September 24, when the election was held, despite the efforts of the Milosevic camp to jiggle the results, Kostunica obviously won; he had received more than 51 percent of the vote. Milosevic and his people then pressed for a runoff election, deliberately underreporting Kostunica's vote to keep it below 50 percent. But Kostunica would have none of it. He would not participate in a runoff; there was no need to, he said. Suddenly, long-suppressed passions began to come to the surface, and democratic forces rose up to challenge Milosevic. For almost two weeks, he tried to hold the line, and for the first time, the fact that he ran a soft dictatorship, not a harsh one of the old order, and that some form of democratic veneer was important to him, came to the fore. In the past, Milosevic had held power by using inflammatory rhetoric against different ethnic groups and sending his troops against Bosnians, Croats, and Albanians. Now it was *Serbs* who were rallying against him. If he was going to hold on to power, he would have to use his troops against fellow Serbs. Soon the protest spread to the country's miners, angry about both the lack of democracy and the collapse of their earning power in the bankrupt economy. It was a sure sign that the regime was falling apart and Milosevic was no longer able to listen, for when you lose the miners or other critical blue-collar workers in what had for so long been a dictatorship of the proletariat, you are in deep trouble. Milosevic tried to use the army to force the miners back to work, but by then things had gotten away from him. If it came to Serb soldiers firing on Serb miners, he had lost. In the end, the rebellion spread into the army, which refused to fire on fellow citizens.

As the protest increased and became a mass movement, the media, almost as if someone had thrown a giant switch, suddenly gave voice to the pluralism of Serbia's changed politics, and journalists who had so recently been the purest of toadies began to write like free men and women. The isolation from Europe that Milosevic had inflicted on his own people became an issue. "Come home to Europe," Tony Blair told the Serb people, shorthand, as Roger Cohen wrote in the *New York Times,* "for human dignity, democracy, and the rule of law." For Milosevic it was over before it was over: his control of the army and the media was gone, and his secret police could no longer save his regime. By early October, both the regular police and the army were on the side of the demonstrators as hundreds of thousands of Serbs crowded around the Parliament building, a symbol of Milosevic's false democracy, and set it on fire. His thirteen-year regime, based on postcommunist totalitarian rule and dependent on the most violent kind of nationalism, was over. The protest that had destroyed him was, at its core, nonviolent. When the protesters took over the Parliament, they stood on the upper floors and hurled down captured propaganda pamphlets they had liberated, countless posters of Milosevic, and thousands of ballots that were supposed to have been used in the September election, already premarked for him.

The United States stayed in the background as all this took place, glad to see Kostunica come to power, but aware that its imprimatur was, after the Bosnian and Kosovo bombings, not exactly an advantage for anyone succeeding Milosevic. The NATO powers had accomplished their goal, but there were those who wondered what would have happened if they had from the start undertaken a much harsher bombing campaign aimed at downtown Belgrade and Milosevic's instruments of power. Would that also have led to his downfall, or, by its very violence, strengthened Serb resolve and made it harder to drive him from office? In the United States, advocates of a more intense air campaign such as Lieutenant General Mike Short believed that it would have brought the same result much sooner. Others disagreed and believed it might have polarized the Serbs against the West.

The question of Milosevic's legal status became the next dilemma for a country trying to find its way on a new, untried democratic path, and there was also the question of the degree of collective guilt for Serb crimes in Bosnia and Kosovo. Would Milosevic be arrested and turned over to international authorities for trial at The Hague (where he had already been indicted)? Or would he be tried locally for crimes against the Serb people? In late March 2000, local authorities moved to arrest Milosevic. For several days a bizarre scenario played out at his home, which police agents had entered, ready to bring him in. With the police inside his house Milosevic at one point had a pistol and aimed it at his head, threatening to commit suicide. "Do it, Daddy!" shouted his daughter, Maria. "Don't surrender, Daddy!" But finally he did surrender, believing he had worked out a deal whereby he would not be turned over to The Hague. As the police took him off to prison, in the climax of this little melodrama, Maria fired several shots at the departing car.[2]

In the fall of 2000, Al Gore got his chance to run for the presidency and escape the somewhat neutered role of sitting vice president. He had quietly been the leading hawk in the administration, but because the vice president's duty was *never* to be seen in any disagreement with the president, a great deal of what he believed and had wanted to do in the Balkans had been kept completely private. Some insiders in the Clinton administration spoke of the Kosovo campaign as Gore's War, instead of Madeleine's War. Still, he received no bonus points from that, and there was a danger, given the essential indifference of the American populace to foreign policy issues, that if he campaigned too openly and spoke too candidly about his support for the successful use of force there, it might backfire and he would have to defend himself from accusations of being too much of an interventionist.

Gore was an old-fashioned internationalist, a more committed interventionist than the president he had served. But in the spring and summer of 2000, when he needed to clarify the consistency and independence of his views, neither he nor the people immediately around him did a very good job of it. His chief national security operative, Leon Fuerth, himself a Balkan hawk, was by nature so secretive that, when talking to reporters about the vice president's role during Bosnia and Kosovo, he seemed determined to keep Gore's views as much of a mystery as possible. He treated inquiring reporters as if they were representatives of the KGB, thus, however involuntarily, diminishing Gore's role during the Clinton years. Gore was, in fact, experienced and exceptionally well apprenticed, an uncommonly substantive (sometimes *too* substantive) political figure, but curiously clumsy when it came to making the case for himself with the facility requisite in an age of modern communications.

He seemed to be better at governance than campaigning, and during his presidential run he often came across as not merely awkward and stiff, but also prone to saying things that were self-defeating. It was as if his exceptional résumé, obviously better than anyone else's in Washington, was not quite good enough and he had to juice it up just a bit. To those who had studied both Clinton and Gore, the outgoing president was clearly the more skilled politician, his loyalty always calibrated to the needs of the moment, his allegiances, like his thoughts, always inner-directed. Gore, not by any means as gifted a politician, was by contrast the better human being, a man of greater and more consistent beliefs and personal loyalties.

As a presidential candidate, however, he ran an oddly awkward, almost clunky race, a man never entirely in sync with himself, unsure of which Al Gore he really was. Despite his considerable and active involvement in the critical issues of a largely successful and generally popular two-term presidency, he was never able to exploit his superior background or expertise. He had, for example, cast the deciding vote for the economic policies at the start of the Clinton administration, policies, aimed at limiting the deficit, that had helped lead, in time, to unparalleled prosperity. But it was nearly impossible to tell that from listening to him on the campaign trail. He was judged in his three debates with George W. Bush to have done poorly, too aggressive and condescending in the first, then too amenable and almost lobotomized in the second. Rarely had greater knowledge of the issues and a superior curriculum vitae been of less value in a series of presidential debates. Gore, in the end, was generally judged by network pundits to be less likable than George W. Bush, as if they were assessing a college fraternity election, which it often seemed they were.

Despite the economic prosperity the country enjoyed, no small part of Gore's problem was the dilemma of coming to the campaign from the political house of Bill Clinton, and his quite personal (rather than political) need to separate himself from Clinton over the Lewinsky-impeachment scandal. Perhaps a more deft and nimble politician could have done it readily, managing at once to take some credit for the successes of the Clinton years, while avoiding the taint of the administration's lesser aspects. One can easily imagine, if the roles had been reversed and there had been a Gore scandal, that the new candidate, Bill Clinton, finally released from his long years of servitude as vice president, would have embraced the positive in the Gore record while neatly dodging the shadow of the scandal. But Gore was never able to find the proper degree of separation, and his animus toward Clinton appeared very personal for the world of high-level politicians, more like a son who felt betrayed by a parent than a vice president who had learned to be extremely cautious about a talented but careless president.

Foreign policy, an area where Gore held a significant edge in knowledge, experience, and interest over Bush, remained a marginal part of the campaign, and Gore was never able to exploit his vastly greater expertise. To the degree that the Clinton administration was considered a success, it was because of the improvement in the economy; to the degree that it was considered a failure, it was over the scandals that his personal behavior had precipitated. Clinton's foreign policy decisions—most particularly in the Balkans—were barely an issue. The nation's interest still remained inner-directed. To much of the rest of the world, America was immensely powerful, but for a nation that powerful, it was shockingly self-absorbed. George W. Bush, the son of the former president, for whom foreign policy had been his primary political passion, appeared to have little interest in the rest of the world. He had apparently never traveled to Europe, though he had visited Mexico and had stayed with his father when he was the American diplomatic representative to China. George W. Bush's campaign autobiography, as the *New York Times* columnist Maureen Dowd noted, devoted all of one paragraph to his six-week visit to China. The trip, she wrote, "made him applaud free markets and long for Midland [Texas]." In his campaign rhetoric, his foreign policy was limited to the belief that we should spend more money on the military, which he claimed was in bad shape because of Clinton's budget cuts.

In general, when the subject of foreign policy came up, Bush was uneasy and tentative, as if he had walked into the wrong classroom and was being asked to take an exam for a course he had never signed up for. In an obvious difference with Gore in their respective views of the world around them, Bush did say he wanted to pull back from any use of the military in peacekeeping or humanitarian missions. He referred to the Clinton policy in the Balkans as nation-building, which it was not, and Condoleezza Rice, one of his top foreign policy advisers, implied during the campaign that if Bush were elected, he would quickly bring American troops back from the Balkans. That statement enraged people like retired general John Shalikashvili, who had been one of the principal architects of the small American force that was actually helping to keep the peace at a relatively low cost. In all, the debate over the use of the military, such as it was, fit the shrewd assessment of Bruce Herschensohn, the conservative commentator, filmmaker, and political activist who had once run for the Senate in California. The Democrats, he said, always want a small army, but want to send it everywhere, while the Republicans want a very big army and don't want to use it at all.

George W. Bush was considered a more authentic Texan than his father, and the key to his campaign was said to be his likability, as if he were the successor to the much-revered Ronald Reagan rather than to Reagan's more awkward vice president. From the start of the primaries, he had been the candidate of the smart (and big) Republican money, the agreeable young man bearing a famous name who had done so well in Texas that he had been reelected virtually without opposition. The Republicans, believing they were a majority party (they were most certainly a majority *white* American party), and still smarting from two Clinton election victories (they seemed to think that the victories were illegal, that Clinton had somehow stolen the presidency from them), were determined not to stumble on the issue of abortion again.

For that purpose, a great deal of money—some $60 million—had been raised for Bush early in the game, the idea being that he would be able to get by the early ambushes the question of abortion might trigger and thus easily outdistance otherwise minor candidates who might have superior connections to the fundamentalists on the one issue they cared so passionately about. That strategy almost worked, but Senator John McCain, the former POW, ran what was by far the most zestful campaign of all the candidates in both parties, choosing to speak out on what were for many centrist, independent Americans two hot-button issues: the sleaziness of contemporary campaign financing and the power of the fundamentalists in the Republican Party. The McCain campaign eventually forced Bush into a more passionate embrace of the fundamentalists than he wanted during the South Carolina primary. To the degree that any candidate fired the imagination of ordinary centrist Americans in what was generally a grim political year, it was McCain, and his campaign was a reminder that on occasion presidential candidates should have in their curriculum vitae something besides running for office. It was McCain's larger life experience, his ability to survive six years in a North Vietnamese prison camp and come out a richer, more tolerant, more complex human being who appealed to millions of ordinary people. He had created a serious challenge to Bush until he simply ran out of money in midcampaign.

Those who questioned Bush's preparation and readiness for the presidency, his right to lead the world's only superpower, and who were also bothered by what appeared to be glaring deficits in his attention span and curiosity, were reassured by their friends that if he was not exactly a big boy himself, he was surrounded by all the big boys from his father's administration. Just to encourage those people who thought the ticket might be a little short on gravitas, Dick Cheney, good at governance but short on natural charm, and the victim of several heart attacks at a very young age, was made the vice-presidential nominee. Other former top figures from Bush One, such as Colin Powell, often appeared with Bush during the campaign. Even James Baker, in partial exile from the inner Bush circle since the disastrous 1992 campaign, which he had helped manage, was resurrected to be the signature figure in charge of spin during the prolonged struggle over the Florida votes.

The election was extremely close. Gore won the popular vote and might have won the electoral vote as well if the governor of Florida had been a Democrat and not the brother of the Republican candidate. The divisions that had first appeared on the American political landscape starting in the late sixties after the Voting Rights Act of 1965 were still apparent, and the map that the television anchors put up on election night reflected two Americas, a red one and a blue one, which existed uneasily side by side. One America, the smaller, less populated states, with a decided white majority, where what were considered traditional cultural values still dominated, and where the women's movement was not especially powerful, went Republican, often by margins close to 60–40 and sometimes even larger. That particular political-cultural breakdown also placed the senior military on the Republican side of the ledger, for more and more it tended to align itself with the Republicans over issues of values.

In the other America, much stronger in the more populous states, those with larger cities and dramatically different demographics and changed values, the Democrats did well because there were far larger black and Hispanic populations, the women's movement was more powerful, and gays represented a more defined and well-organized political force. In the end some 105 million Americans had voted, 539,897 more for Gore than Bush on the certified results. But on the most important vote of all, that of the Supreme Court of the United States, Bush won a cliff-hanger, 5–4.

Bill Clinton, whose political sense had always been so sure, departed the White House as ingloriously as any president in recent years, save only Richard Nixon. Buoyed in his last months by surprisingly high approval ratings that reached into the midsixties, he had been the omnipresent American figure, flying everywhere and appearing on every television news show to thank people. He clearly enjoyed the final few weeks of his presidency, letting the people of the country know—especially after the grimness of the Bush-Gore campaign—how much they were going to miss him. It was as if he was not merely an outgoing president, but the popular culture's reigning master of ceremonies. Some critics (and friends) might have been left wondering if it was an entirely good thing for a president to exit office so popular. Did that mean he had squirreled away too much of his own political power for too long and not taken enough risks?

Not to worry. Bill Clinton never wore too much success too well for too long, and disaster, as it always did with him, lurked just around the corner. Almost as soon as he left the White House, a firestorm arose over a number of inexplicable pardons he had granted in the last minutes of his presidency, most particularly the one to a fugitive financier named Marc Rich, whose financial and political dealings were one giant mountain of sleaze and corruption. Rich was one of those remarkable refugees who rewards a country that takes him in by seeking to circumvent all its financial laws, and believes as well that his earnings should not go to anything as mundane as paying taxes. Rich had shown not the slightest element of remorse about his thievery, but had devoted himself in his years as a fugitive in Europe to buying access to powerful people through allegedly good works that were the very embodiment of me-first charity. In the Rich case, as in a number of other pardons, Clinton had clearly not checked with the prosecutors, and what he had done was brazen, ugly, and careless, the handiwork of a man who thought he could always get away with whatever he did and would always be forgiven because he was so talented. The pardon to Rich, and a number of other equally improbable and undeserving pardons, stunned even the most loyal of Clinton's inner circle and were devastating to the Democratic Party's leadership.

Oddly enough, another incident was just as revealing about the contradictions within this immensely gifted and equally flawed man. Quietly, in the final hours of his presidency, Clinton worked out a deal with Robert Ray, Ken Starr's successor as independent counsel. Ray would drop the grand jury investigation against Clinton, and as part of the quid pro quo, Clinton agreed to forfeit his Arkansas law license for five years, pay a $25,000 fine to cover legal fees, and not to seek reimbursement for his own attorneys' fees. His had been a long, unpleasant struggle with the independent counsel's office, and though much of it was Clinton's own fault, the righteousness of Starr's pursuit was unbecoming, and one could hardly blame Clinton for seeking on his last day in office what was, in effect, his own pardon. But, in the opinion of some people watching, the deal was distasteful because of Clinton's failure, once it had been agreed upon, to come forward and explain it to the country. Up until then, he who had been everywhere at once, holding impromptu news conferences wherever he went, suddenly disappeared from public view. Instead he sent the White House lawyer and John Podesta, one of his top staff people, to face the country in his place. This, the unwillingness to deal with something so messy, had echoes of the young Clinton who had not merely managed to avoid service in Vietnam, but had played so skillfully with Colonel Holmes, the Arkansas ROTC officer.

Clinton's disastrous farewell allowed George W. Bush a lengthy honeymoon in his early weeks in the White House because so much of the nation's attention was focused—malevolently—on the bizarre final acts of his predecessor. When Bush emerged from the transition period, he was surrounded by those who had been the leading figures in Desert Storm, arguably his father's most dramatic accomplishment. There was Dick Cheney, then secretary of defense, now the vice president, who quickly became the driving force within the White House, and Colin Powell, then chairman of the Joint Chiefs, was now secretary of state. Donald Rumsfeld had been a political opponent of the senior Bush and had often spoken caustically in private of what he considered Bush senior's intellectual limitations. But Rumsfeld was the original sponsor of some of the key Bush people—he had discovered Cheney and had promoted Frank Carlucci, who had, in turn, reached down for Colin Powell. Rumsfeld was named secretary of defense. Condoleezza Rice, the national security adviser, was a Brent Scowcroft protégé. Thus, in terms of foreign policy Bush Two was like something of a reunion of Bush One. Most of the senior people appeared to be cautious about any use of the military for the kind of humanitarian missions that the Clinton people, tentatively and on occasion erratically, had been moving toward. Bush Two was composed of men—and now women—who had dealt well with the final months and weeks of the Cold War, but had not been particularly deft in adapting to the very different circumstances in a changed post–Cold War world.

If anything symbolized that, it was Rumsfeld's passion for a missile shield, something he had been involved with in the past and that loomed as an exceptionally expensive piece of hardware, which might not ever work, and which, if we went after it, would surely siphon immense amounts of money from other very demanding military projects. To many nonpartisan analysts in the world of national security and intelligence, the shield was a kind of high-tech Maginot Line, the wrong idea at the wrong time. America's lead in traditional weaponry was vast and growing greater because of the staggering expense of the technology involved. Thus, rogue states would probably see the gap in aerospace power widen rather than narrow in the years to come. That was one reason not to invest in a missile shield. The other was more basic— a belief among many senior intelligence analysts that the greatest threat to an open society like America came from terrorists, rather than the military power of rogue states, which offered exceptional targets themselves. The real danger to an open society like America was the ability of a terrorist, not connected to any sitting government, to walk into an American city with a crude atomic weapon, delivered, as it were, by hand in a cardboard suitcase.

Early in the new Bush administration, during the inevitable struggle for territory and power, something of a fault line appeared within the national security world, with Rumsfeld and a few people in the White House taking in general a harder line, and Powell at State taking a more moderate one. Of the two factions, the hard-liners appeared to be more influential with this young, neophyte president. On humanitarian issues, the attitude of the new Bush team, said one Washington analyst who had watched them deal with these questions, was more and more like that reflected in the old Jim Baker line, "We don't have a dog in that fight." A dozen years after the end of the Cold War, tensions between the United States and Russia were on the rise, though in no way resembling the continual bipolar crisis that had dominated so much of the second half of the twentieth century. Most Americans did not care very much about Russia as long as it was not a threat, and the ongoing struggle within Russia to keep some form of democracy alive, a great and important story of the new century, did not interest many Americans, especially the executive producers and the anchors of the evening news shows. The role of America in the post–Cold War world, which had not been clearly articulated or defined during the Clinton years, was still murky in January 2001 when the presidential guard changed. Foreign policy was not high on the political agenda, primarily because whatever the forces that might threaten the future of this country were, they were not yet visible.

EPILOGUE

The threat had always been there. And New York was always uniquely vulnerable to it, despite the cinematic protection offered us by Schwarzenegger, Stallone, and Willis, who always got the bad guy in the last sequence of any movie that deigned to deal with terrorism. If anything America dealt with terrorism as a nation in the past by turning to Hollywood; we were, it sometimes seemed, protected more by our fantasy factory than by the reality, perhaps because the reality was so much grimmer. Yet anyone who paid any attention to the way the world was going understood that there were no longer any immunities for Americans and American cities in this world; on the last page of this book which I was in the process of publishing there was a sentence about the missile shield, which has always struck me as a kind of high-tech Maginot Line, saying that the real threat to this country would come not from some rogue state vulnerable to our own power, but from terrorists who could walk into any American city with a crude atomic bomb in a cardboard suitcase. That sentence was born not of any great prophetic sense, but regrettably, of more common sense.

The truth is America—and much of the rest of the West—has had a good deal of time—some twenty, twenty-five years, perhaps more—to understand several things; principal among them, that the great threat to a country like ours was not from some developed nation, which also had a nuclear strike force and against which our immense power was so readily applicable, but from terrorists who did not offer a comparable target, who hated the United States for what it represented in the world (a pervasive, in their eyes, corrupting decadent culture), and for whom its alliances (not just with Israel, but equally important with the allegedly moderate Arab states) were an affront.

It is also, I think, the confrontation between the most modern part of the world and the ultimate antimodernists. We modernists have enraged the antimodernists and they witness us every night by dint of global television. Because we the modernists place a vastly higher priority on education, science, and technology, we have managed, in addition to being infidels, to become *very powerful* infidels, while they are left with being very weak, impoverished believers—enraged, impoverished believers. Ironically, the tensions between the two parts of the world are heightened by one of most modern instruments of communications, television. The poor can now sit in their part of the world and see the vast difference between the quality of their lives and that of the West, and their leaders like Osama bin Laden can sell in that harsh and cruel environment the dubious notion that not only are they poor, and we in the West rich, but they are poor because we are rich. This is a confrontation that I doubt would be taking place if we still lived in a radio era rather than a television era.

That the West, particularly America, was caught napping in the period between the end of the Cold War and September 11 is obvious. America's political and media agenda was uniquely trivial, despite the evidence all around us that the world, post–Cold War, was dangerous in a new and different way, perhaps best described as a more fragmented but no less lethal kind of danger. Was this really the nation, so unconcerned about its relationship with the rest of the world—and all kinds of larger issues—that just two years earlier had submitted itself, in an orgy of self-indulgence, in an impeachment trial of a competent sitting president because he had so stupidly been caught in an assignation with a young intern? The answer is yes. The impeachment trial, post–September 11, seems incomprehensible now, given the real problems that lie before us.

Rarely have the previous agenda and the previous concerns of an earlier period seemed so inconsequential so quickly, that which had seemed important and galvanizing the previous week so trivial, most of it involving stories of petty scandal among celebrities, or would-be celebrities who would not have been very big celebrities without their requisite scandal. The historical demarcation point that we crossed on September 11 is even greater than the one we crossed with the bombing of Pearl Harbor on December 7, 1941: whatever else, in December 1941 there had been all kinds of evidence that the rest of the civilized world, most notably all of our allies, was already deeply involved in a titanic struggle that would surely determine the outcome of civilization as we knew it. The only thing that had not yet been decided was whether we would be a part of it, and whether it would be earlier or later.

The war effort back in 1941, because of the particular nature of the attack on Pearl Harbor, became an immediate extension of America's national will, and of the purest kind imaginable; it is important to remember that an earlier move towards preparedness on the part of President Roosevelt—that is to have a draft—passed by one vote only a few months before. That was the last gasp of the truly isolationist America, which took so much sustenance from the protection allegedly offered by our two great oceans.

The enemy back in 1941 was more easily definable, the definition of the war more traditional, and America's power, industrial and technological, more readily applicable against those two enemies than the unusually elusive enemy we now face operating from among the shadows, often at so great a distance from us, and often, it also turns out, in secret cells and under aliases right among us. Today the more visible the enemy is, the further he is from the magnetic field of our intelligence operations and any potential military strike. It is not that America, as it enters a very different kind of battle, lacks weaponry, it is that the particular kind of weaponry we specialize in lacks targets. This will be a difficult military-intelligence-security challenge: What we do best, they are not vulnerable to. What we do least well, they are vulnerable to. What they do best, we are to a considerable degree vulnerable to.

This then is a brand new era, and the war has come home to us, as it never had before. When I was a young, ambitious journalist some forty years ago, in order to witness the most dramatic conflict of our time I had to volunteer to go some 12,000 miles away to Vietnam to cover a distant war. Now when I am much older, the newest war has come to within five miles of my home.

America then is no longer distant from the conflicts of our time: in that way the attacks on the World Trade Center and the Pentagon ended a unique historical span for us as a great power, one that I would place at nearly a century, or perhaps eighty-four years to be a little more exact, a period in which America has been a major player in the world, but has been given at least a partial immunity from the ravages of modern warfare and weaponry because of the combination of its unique geographical position and the sheer force and magnitude of its almost unparalleled industrial and technological base. It has taken a group of rebels without a country, a ghost nation as it were—that is their particular strength—to become a threat to us.

In that nearly nine-decade period the immense carnage of the modern era was always somewhere else. I am, I think, unusual as an American not just because I have been a foreign correspondent, but because I have always had an obsession with the bloodier landmarks of the modern era, and have always wanted, indeed *needed* to visit them—Verdun, Auschwitz, Dienbienphu, Monte Cassino, Hiroshima, Omaha Beach, the Warsaw Ghetto, and the British cemetery outside Rangoon in Myanmar. The cruelty of the last century has always fascinated me; yet most of my fellow citizens have remained largely indifferent to it, a luxury provided them, of course, by the good fortune of our oceans. Because of our strength and our geography we were for a long time permitted many illusions, some of them existing long after it was obvious that those illusions were in fact just that, and no longer valid.

We became, in no small part because of our geography and our power as that eighty-four-year span continued, somewhat schizophrenic; a curious blend of innate isolationism, a factor of our two great oceans, our size and richness and our self-sufficiency, combined with the quite involuntary role of being the richest, most powerful nation in the world—a democracy, sworn not just to protect our own freedoms, but to shield, in a shrewd estimation of our enlightened self-interest, like-minded democratic regimes. Yet true internationalism has always been a somewhat uneasy role for America, we were not only protected for so long by the oceans, but we were innately large, rich, and self-sufficient (we had our own self-sufficient agriculture, and our own indigenous sources of energy) as a nation. Even on our own continent we seemed invulnerable, as Europeans nations on their continent were not; we have a large neighbor to the north which though different and sovereign, was not really *foreign,* and a neighbor to the south which was historically weak. On our own continent, we were largely unthreatened.

Our isolation, which was physical in one era, clearly ended long ago, but it nonetheless remains a part of our outlook, a formidable undertow to a new reality of this modern age, more psychological than physical now, more a hope than a reality. Our geography therefore has always dominated our psyche, we are by instinct apart from Europe and we *like* being apart from Europe. Our modern history confirms our ambivalence to, and love/hate relationship with, internationalism. In 1914, even as America was beginning to surge forward as a major industrial player, World War I began; we came in three years after the other major powers. With most of Europe already bled white and exhausted, we eventually played a decisive role. Then, still protected by our two oceans, we went back to our old ways and rejected our own president's attempt at internationalism. During World War II, we once again came in later than most of the other players—two years later if you set the clock from the war's beginnings in Europe, longer if you mark Asian events. We became, as Churchill and Roosevelt both understood we would, the arsenal of democracy, our industrial base, unlike the industrial bases of any other major participant, invulnerable from enemy weaponry. We were also the only industrial nation with its own sources of gas and oil.

The war ended with America emerging as a new superpower; we were dramatically more internationalist than when we entered, virtually forced into what were on occasion unwanted connections with the rest of the world by the leaders of the generation that had actually fought the war, had lost their friends and college roommates, and had witnessed the calamity caused by the previous generation's isolationism. It was a generation which also understood the most important new element added to an old equation, that the new weaponry unsheathed at the very end of the war, the atomic bomb and the German V-1 rockets (inventions which were obviously about to be twinned together), made isolationism no longer viable as a possibility. Thus for the first time did we begin to deal with knowledge that some of the immunities or protections that had long been ours no longer existed. That brought us with a certain inevitability into a new kind of internationalism: Europe, shattered by two suicidal wars within twenty-five years, was in ashes; the British, exhausted emotionally, physically, humanly, and financially by the two wars, could no longer sustain their role as the leader of the

West. No bombs had fallen on us: we were rich in a world which was poor, our economy had been brought, kicking and screaming, to the zenith of its power, by the very nature of a war which maximized our production lines.

Thus did we begin an almost unwanted ascent to superpower status. That the ascent has been more unwanted than desired is critically important to understanding how America responds to crises in foreign policy, why it does this more slowly and more awkwardly than other nations, but when finally aroused does it with a certain finality. Our instinct, born of geography, is to be apart. We are a vast country, with all kinds of different ethnic factions and regions and classes; we do not lightly—it is I think, in the long run, a source of both strength and tolerance—respond too quickly for any one single purpose. We have other preoccupations.

It is important to understand one other thing about America, post–World War II, which made it different from most of the rest of the world. Our principal allies, exhausted by those events, were also watching their own colonial eras come to and end. In a world where even the victors were pessimistic and exhausted, America was stronger than ever, more optimistic than ever, and felt better about itself than before the war. In this country, people now spoke readily of an American Century

The period that followed World War II was a new and chilling one. A hot war was followed by a cold one. In Eastern Europe lines were drawn and we, new to our international role, found ourselves in almost immediate conflict with the challenge from a formidable new Soviet empire—worse, a totalitarian one. We were, based on the lessons of World War II and the threat of modern weaponry, involuntarily pulled into a new and once again unwanted (at least in vast sections of the country) internationalism. The lessons of World War II morphed into the new demands of the Cold War. That which had always protected us in the past, and thus defined our essential foreign policy, our geographical isolation, no longer existed; we had been the ocean-protected civilization, and now the oceans had become ponds.

We were, for the first time, becoming internationalist, but almost involuntarily so; it is easy today to forget that even as a terrifying new kind of nuclear threat became evident in those days, one that could easily have undermined many of the then-vulnerable democracies in Europe, there were powerful currents of isolationism at play in America, especially in the Midwest. It is easy to underestimate today the resistance to much of the policy of containment in the forties, of Americans who never again wanted to become involved in Europe and did not want to help strengthen those then quite fragile European allies, and who, in some cases, believed that our old alliances were a source of vulnerability. (In the Midwest the fear that it was the old Eastern Establishment doing the work of the British was powerful. The least Dean Acheson, he of a certain generational anglophilia, with his fancy-the-old-boy manners, his guard's moustache and British tailoring, could do to help an embattled President Truman politically, Averell Harriman once told friends, was to shave off that British guard's moustache.)

Much of the country was still isolationist and resistant to the programs which would form the basis of containment. Resistance to Soviet imperialism could not be sold in too abstract a way, as Senator Arthur Vandenberg of Michigan, a last minute convert in switching from isolationism to internationalism, told Acheson. If Truman wanted his containment policy to go through the Congress, Vandenberg continued, he could have it, "but he will have to go out and scare hell out of the country." That he did, and America became in time both internationalist and anticommunist, though in the end more of the latter than the former. If there was any weakness to the larger American view of the world in the forty-some years from the time that Churchill gave his Iron Curtain speech to the moment when the Berlin Wall collapsed, it was an obsession with communism, a tendency to see complicated parts of the world where the most important issue at stake was nationalism (Vietnam for example) in simplistic terms of communism and anticommunism. This was true right to the end, to the crisis which helped cause the current conflict in the Middle East, when the Americans reached out to those forces in Afghanistan fighting the Russians, and when the Russians finally departed Afghanistan as a defeated enemy, Washington paid no attention to what was left behind, the nature of the vacuum there. The Russians were gone, communism was collapsing—that was enough. From that vacuum came much of today's crisis.

For when the Soviet empire collapsed the bipolar threat that had hung over this country for some forty years also disappeared. The oceans which had become ponds became, in the minds of far too many people here, oceans once again. John Kennedy, writing of the period before England rallied itself to the threat posed by Hitler, once wrote a thesis turned into a small book called *Why England Slept*. If I were looking for a somewhat better subtitle to this current book about America from the collapse of the Berlin Wall in 1989 to September 11, 2001, I might call it, *Why America Napped*. When social historians come to measure us in the future, they may look at the era that just past with unusual distaste, of a time of trivial pursuits and debate in our public sector and singular greed in the private one, and of unacceptable rewards to the heads of our largest corporations. There is a poem that W. H. Auden wrote at the time of the start of World War II. It is called "September 1, 1939." The first five lines go: "I sit in one of the dives/ On Fifty-second Street/ Uncertain and afraid/ As the clever hopes expire/ Of a low dishonest decade."

With luck, and I say this very carefully, with luck, that era of such consummate self-indulgence is passed. What is at stake here, not just in America but in any comparable democratic society, is something both precious and elemental to what we are as a people and a nation, and it is the survival of the open or free society, where in this new era, the very openness of the society makes it unusually vulnerable to its enemies. Those of us who have over the years worked in societies which are not free have, I suspect, treasured more than most this quality about America, not just the freedom to move about, but the freedom to be what you want to be, to be different from those who went before you in your own family, to, if necessary, reinvent yourself and become the person of your own imagination. I believe, as a matter of political faith that freedom, represents not merely an easier more pleasurable life in the simplest sense for the individual, but that all of America's considerable strengths, industrial, scientific, military, and artistic flow from it, that the freer we are, the more we are able to use our fullest talents. In effect, we waste less human potential than any other society that I know of. When other societies suppress some part—or all—of an individual's rights and beliefs, we never know how much of that person's talent they are also suppressing. Simply stated, the freer we are, the stronger we are.

This is a new and infinitely more complicated era for a nation accustomed to exercising its power at a distance, and never being in the immediate firing line. We who are the richest nation in the world—our down cycles are like up cycles for most peoples in the world—face an enemy whose very weaknesses, that is his rootlessness, his alienation from the societies around him, his ability to move around freely at night in the poorest part of the world, has become his strength. What a strange, complicated, and insidious new equation that is for us, an attack against us right here at home. What an irony, that we who have consciously or unconsciously always depended on our scientific and industrial excellence are threatened not by a first world, or even a second world, or even a third world force, but a de facto terrorist or guerrilla group, rootless in terms of nationhood, with, in our view and that of most of the civilized world, a medieval vision of the present and the future, but which has managed to find exceptional financing and to adapt itself surprisingly well to a shrewd if minimalist application of borrowed or stolen modern technology. Even as we reel from this assault, our enemies are trying to buy the most modern weapons of mass destruction, and they have shown an exceptional ability to move money around the world to finance their operations, done in a manner worthy of the most modern multinational corporation. What they have achieved is something quite chilling, and it represents something entirely new, an adversary against whom we have little in the way of an immediate deterrent.

I was seven years old at the time of Pearl Harbor, which I believe to be the previous comparable moment in American life when the world changed so quickly and dramatically for us in just one day. I remember with great clarity hearing the news that Sunday morning, understanding from the hushed voices of my parents that our lives had changed with a certain finality—which they had. My father, who had been a medic in World War I and was now a doctor, went back in the service, and we moved from New York, and our lives were never quite the same.

The America of 1941 was, however involuntarily, very different from the American of 2001, for it was poorer, and expectations were much, much lower, and it was much closer to a certain kind of Calvinist root, and there was a greater sense, I believe, on the part of ordinary citizens of what they *owed* back. This is a much more self-absorbed society, one that demands ever-quicker results: it is accustomed, at its upper, more successful levels, to being rich and secure, and of course, entertained. When things go wrong it is likely to be thought of as someone else's fault, and therefore a mistake that ought to be rectified. And quickly. What is important about this new challenge, especially for a nation like ours at this moment, is that it challenges our attention span.

If there is any vulnerability to the America today it is a kind of national impatience—a need for things to do be done and done quickly. *What! We've bombed the Taliban for four weeks and the war isn't over? How could that be? What! We picked up some traces of anthrax in the mail, and we haven't caught the sender yet and a month has passed?* Part of the reason for that impatience is the result of a nation that is always in overdrive where work is more honored than leisure, part of it is a reflection of the technological inventions of the last fifty years, especially in communications—faxes and the internet—which put more pressure on people for ever-faster answers and ever-faster results. And part of it is the result of a nation where the economic formation is not just a stock-market driven, but driven by a new kind of people's stock market. For in 1941 only a tiny percentage of Americans actually had an investment in the stock market, and most of the heads of big companies were proprietors rather than mangers, and they had a long-term view of business. Now those companies are run by managers, almost everyone has a stake in the stock market, even if it's only through pension plans, and the managers live and die by quarterly reports. Sometimes that works to a company's benefit, and sometimes it creates a hopelessly shortsighted view of the future that is damaging both to the company and the society.

Take our media world, and particularly our television networks for example. Of the many results of the end of the Cold War—the amazing surge in the American economy, six thousand points in six years in the Dow during the Clinton years, the rise of nationalism and tribalism in certain parts of the world—the most surprising, and by far the least predictable, was the almost immediate and quite dramatic trivialization of the American political and media agenda, most especially the decline of the importance in serious news, above all foreign news from our nightly television screens. It was as if the old geopolitical impulse that had preceded World War II and the Cold War, America apart from the rest of the world, had been restored, especially in an era where, because of the quantum breakthroughs in communications, the pull of home screen entertainment became so seductive. Of our many traditional freedoms was added a new one—the right not to be bored in your own home. We became something unique: a de facto monopoly superpower, the richest, most powerful nation in the world, bingeing on self-involvement.

The people who ran the newsrooms in our television networks learned, all too easily, in the eighties that the country was less and less interested in foreign news. It was now considered boring. The world was no longer threatening. Foreign reporters were expensive, and worse, brought low ratings. But celebrity journalism, especially in the period after the end of the Cold War, when the country was bingeing on self-absorption, brought high ratings. People now cared desperately about the lives of celebrities. Would Tom stay married to Nicole? Would O. J. be convicted? Would Monica ever find true love and marry? If it was journalism at its worst then it was economically viable: celebrity journalism was good for the ratings, which was good for the stock, but of course bad for the country. The senior people who ran the network news empires neglected the cardinal rule of a great editor—the need to balance what people *want* to know with what they *need* to know.

We became in the process an entertainment society. We went quite systematically from a serious agenda worthy of a monopoly superpower, to an ever more trivial one of scandal and celebrity; the contradictions of that are self-evident. We have wanted (or needed), in the last decade or so, to exercise our power in certain foreign policy crises, but because of the disconnect between our complex international role and the lack of public support—and a governmental willingness to seek greater support—we have acted with what was a de facto Zero Casualties prohibition on ourselves, especially after the events in Somalia in 1993. Whatever else, that ended on September 11.

Both our politicians and the leading television news personalities, with their parallel sensory perceptions (supported by endless polling of constituents), have understood this change, but the media, I think, has been worse than the politicians. The networks, like the politicians, were all picking up on the same thing, that the American people were tired of serious news, especially foreign news, and they wanted a respite. I would repeat here the importance of one anecdote I tell in these pages: the story of Bill Clinton, a few days before his inauguration, meeting with House Democratic chairman and going around the room asking them their specific problems. When it was the turn of Lee Hamilton, the chairman of the House Foreign Affairs committee, he began to enumerate what was on his plate—problems with China, the difficulties of dealing with Saddam Hussein—before Clinton quickly cut him off. He had been out campaigning for a year, he said, and no one cared about foreign policy except for a handful of journalists. Hamilton, taken somewhat aback, did not note that that might be true, but that foreign policy had a way of defining every one of our recent presidents.

In the months after September 11, there was a sense that America was briefly interested in foreign affairs, driven by these dramatic events that had taken place on domestic soil and that had so seriously shaken the nation. Television news shows that had been featuring fluffy celebrity reporting suddenly became fascinated by events on the Afghanistan-Pakistan border. There was a great deal of talk in certain media circles that Americans had finally woken up to real challenges after a prolonged hibernation. Late hour variety-show hosts competed to have serious public officials like Dick Holbrooke come on and talk seriously about the Middle East (while perhaps telling one self-deprecatory joke or two). Various New York magazine editors vowed that the era of celebrity journalism was over. Not everyone watching all this thought that the dynamic had changed completely, given the economics of the networks, and the need to entertain rather than to inform.

The question of how deep the new interest in foreign policy went was another one. The decline in interest had not been an overnight phenomenon, and it reflected a deeper truth about the country. After all, the senior Bush had clearly been somewhat out of synch with the country when he had shown so much interest in foreign affairs during his one term: the country—and the pollsters—felt that he had become too interested in foreign affairs, a charge that Bill Clinton subtly and not so subtly used against him in 1992. During the Clinton presidency there was a constant ambivalence about how great a priority to pay to foreign policy, especially on the part of a president so nuanced to political winds, who seemed to know how many votes each issue presented him. Certainly late in his presidency, stung by the Lewinsky scandal and looking for some kind of legacy, he had made an all-out effort to bring a settlement to the Israeli-Palestinian dispute.

But the danger of talking about foreign policy in a political campaign remained very much a part of the national fabric. When Al Gore had run for the presidency in 2000 he had been careful to hide his own considerable expertise in foreign affairs—seemingly pretending that he had never been vice president for eight years, played a key role in NSC meetings, had never been a principal activist in the Balkans, and never had exceptionally close and valuable relationships with a number of top Russian officials—it was as if all of these accomplishments might somehow turn into political liabilities. When George W. Bush was elected in 2002 it was clearly as a unilateralist. September 11, at least momentarily changed that.

If the Bush people responded quickly to the military aspect of the September challenge, nonetheless some of the messages they subsequently gave out were mixed, or at the very least a reflection of a divided government. It was as if in this particular region they were willing to be militarily multilateral, but in many other ways, they remained somewhat more unilateral. The Americans were becoming, noted one European foreign minister in February 2002, *minilateral,* as if we only want to be involved with the rest of the world when it served our most immediate purpose.

The administration appeared seriously divided between those who believed that American power was so great that we could wield our influence in the Middle East by military power alone, and others, led by Secretary Powell who appeared to think the world more complex and thought some seemingly easy military moves had consequences that might, in that region, work against the long-range interests of the United States. This debate seemed to center more than anything else on the use of American military force against Iraq—and fears that any additional action against Saddam Hussein might have negative results domestically in Pakistan, in the Palestinian-Israeli conflict, and in how others in the Middle East viewed that conflict.

If anything the very quality of American military high technology sometimes seemed almost too seductive; it inevitably created, however unconsciously, a certain unstated arrogance of might—a belief that you do not really need allies and do not need to consult with others, something our closest allies began to feel was true about us.

Its effect on American policymakers was equally seductive. It tended to have a considerable psychological effect on the architects of policy as well. Because it was extremely effective and something we did very, very well, because the casualties tended to be low, and because no other country could come near matching us in our abilities (and because the other things we had to do in dealing with terrorism were extremely hard and difficult to master), we tended to reinforce what we did well, and neglect things we did not do so well—such as upgrading our ability to come up with traditional forms of intelligence about the other side. The danger here was that the military aspect in a struggle like this remained relatively small. The hard parts, improving domestic security and gaining valuable intelligence on the terrorist operations, were much more difficult to master. Because it clearly was going to be extremely difficult to penetrate the top layer of terrorist cells with human agents, there was a need to use our high technology in gaining intelligence about the enemy leadership and aiding our domestic security people. But here we were well behind the curve—the frustration of the varying intelligence agencies in the months after the terrorist attacks was readily apparent.

How much the country itself had changed, and how genuinely interested it was in foreign affairs—other than a fascination with the events of September 11 and an interest in the military struggles with the Taliban and al Qaeda—was also difficult to determine. In the days and weeks after the terrorist bombings there was a dramatic jump in serious reporting from the Middle East, as well as reporting on the sources of terrorism. But gradually that began to recede. If there was a sign that much of the nation—especially many of the top executives in the media—had not yet changed their real value systems because of September 11, it was the news, in March of 2002, that the executives of Disney wanted to get rid of Ted Koppel and his program *Nightline,* self-evidently the single best program on any network dealing consistently with foreign policy, and replace him with David Letterman because Koppel, in the words of one ABC executive, was no longer relevant. That was staggering—*Nightline* was the jewel in the crown in all of network television, the best and most serious public affairs program on television, and yet the people running the company obviously did not value it.

This then posed a fascinating challenge for the American political system. It was a country pulled in two very different directions, one by the challenge of the new threats, and the other by powerful forces, already at work, for it to keep on as it had been going for years, to stick to business as usual, and because of the pressures in the corporate media world, to continue to present a remarkably trivial agenda.

I had hoped to see a broader kind of change in terms of Washington's attitude towards the rest of the world (and a recognition of the importance of energy in our national security agenda—and thus the beginning of a long-range energy policy that increasingly liberated us from dependence on the Middle East). The overall changes that I had hoped to see in America's attitude toward the rest of the world (and the idea that terrorism is connected to larger issues in foreign policy) had come more slowly than I had hoped. Perhaps that is typically American. Nonetheless, I remain somewhat optimistic about the long-range future.

One of the advantages of being someone older and having some degree of historical knowledge is the faith in the free society that eventually comes with it. The terrible thing about the communists, the poet Allen Ginsberg once told me years ago when I was in Eastern Europe and he had had a difficult little struggle with the Czech and Polish authorities, is that all the clichés about them are true. I would add to that a corollary, that one of the good things about democracies is that many of the clichés about them are true— you just have to stick around long enough to bear witness. But in my lifetime I have seen the resilience of American democracy in action time and again. That encompasses those months after World War II, when we moved so quickly from sleeping isolationist nation, to what we so soon became, an awesome new international power, occasionally vigilant, occasionally not so vigilant, that we are today. When the Cold War was over we spoke too much of who won it, and not of the cool, deliberate, understated leadership of the men who determined our earlier responses, starting with Truman and Acheson and Kennan and others, ironically, much maligned in those early days for being soft even as they rallied the nation for what was then a new and very complicated and somewhat distant challenge. And, post-Sputnik, it reflected our capacity to go all out in space, with the pledge of John Kennedy in 1961 to put a man on the moon, and the ability only eight years later for us to do exactly that.

What I have come to admire over the years, and to believe in, is the degree of muscularity and flex in this society, in the loyalty and energies of free men and women freely summoned, and never to underestimate this country's resolve, once that resolve is focused. More than anything else I have great faith in our pragmatism, our common sense, and our resilience.

What I have also learned is that opponents of the free society—whether it was the Germans (Hitler saying he would wring England's neck like a chicken, and Churchill answering with complete contempt, "*some chicken, some neck*") and the leaders of Imperial Japan in 1941, or the Soviets during the Cold War (Khrushchev saying he would bury us—his son now teaches at my daughter's college in Providence, Rhode Island), and even more recently Slobodan Milosevic, who kept telling America's diplomats that he could out-bluff us because he could accept death and we could not—tend to underestimate our strengths and tend to see our democracy's strengths, the slowness of our responses as weaknesses. The most recent example of that is from Osama bin Laden who was quoted in an interview with the writer Peter Bergen as saying that his battle with America was easier than with the Russians, whose men were more courageous, and above all more patient. Men like that believe, wrongly, I think, that what I consider to be our strength is a certain kind of decadence, because we are slow to act, and we are rarely on a wartime footing.

I have a different view: I think it is easy to underestimate the strengths and resilience of America, that we are, because of our geography, different from other countries, more self-sufficient, more isolated, and therefore slower to act—getting America to change directions and attitudes from one era to another sometimes must seem like trying to change directions in an aircraft carrier while trailing your hand behind it in the water. But our strengths, when summoned and focused, when the body politic is aroused and connects to the top of the political process, are never to be underestimated.

I think this is going to be a difficult period. We are being led by a young man who was elected precisely because he was not interested in the rest of the world. Now, that young man, surrounded by men senior to him, who served his father in another time, is having to learn under what are virtual combat conditions, how to be a wartime president. I retain a certain faith that this country will respond well, but I think it will be a more difficult road than most of my countrymen think, that the military part will be a smaller part of the entire equation, and I believe we are far behind where we should have been in getting our intelligence and security systems up to speed. But in this country we tend to stumble at first, and we are rarely quick in our responses to new challenges—we forget today that the first American troops who fought in North Africa fared poorly, and the British soldiers, much more experienced by then, were contemptuous of their fighting ability in the beginning. We forget as well that we were well behind the Soviets in rocketry when Sputnik orbited in 1957. But somehow, gradually and awkwardly, we turned the full force of our enormous energies to the proper subject, and after muddling through, we got there. As I suspect we will again.

AUTHOR'S NOTE

This book began with a conversation at a party with Les Gelb, the head of the Council of Foreign Relations, in the spring of 1999, when the NATO-American bombing of Kosovo was in full force. At the party I asked him a couple of questions about who within the Clinton administration was driving the bombing campaign, and his answers were so clear, and so different from what I had expected (a critical, forceful, but somewhat covert player, he said, was the vice president, Al Gore) that I thought it might make an interesting magazine piece. Graydon Carter at *Vanity Fair,* immediately and enthusiastically agreed and told me to go ahead. That was very much in character; he has always been a reporter's editor. But after about six weeks of research, I decided it was a book, not a magazine piece. (The same thing had happened to me exactly thirty years earlier when I had begun a magazine article on McGeorge Bundy, which turned into a book about how and why we went to war in Vietnam.) For me this marked the first time I would return to the area of national security reporting since I had finished that book in 1972. The book had done exceptionally well, and I received numerous immediate and handsome offers to do successor books on the same general subject. But since I like to take on questions to which I do not know the answers and to use the four or five years I spend on one of my longer books as a kind of graduate school, I had preferred to go in other directions.

This time, however, I was delighted to return to a venue that I had once known and that had changed so dramatically in recent years. The Cold War was over, and the fear of being called soft on communism, something that had covertly played a large role in the Kennedy and Johnson decision-making, was no longer important. But other things were fascinating to me: for example, the shadow that Vietnam still cast over civilian-military relations, and the question of how truly internationalist this country was, now that the Soviet threat had receded. A number of contemporary issues also intrigued me. The technology of politics was different, the players were different, the political constituencies were quite different, and yet shadows from the past were still there, ghosts that still loitered in the hallways and meeting rooms.

I wanted the book to be a way of looking at America through our decisions in foreign policy; the focal points were places like Bosnia, Kosovo, Haiti,

Rwanda, and Somalia, all of them extremely tough calls, especially for President Clinton, who had so confidently criticized his predecessor's foreign policies during the 1992 campaign. How did Clinton's national security apparatus respond to humanitarian crises and, in some instances, to genocide in distant places where America's national security was not directly involved? How much would they factor in for a president who, despite his campaign speeches, was obsessed first and foremost with domestic politics? How did senior military men, still wary after the civilian architects of Vietnam had given them such a bastardized assignment (and had, in their opinion, helped co-opt a number of their own senior figures), react? And what did the response of, and the divisions within, the foreign policy apparatus tell us about the country itself?

The national security world I was looking at had greatly changed from the one I had encountered so long ago. I first went to Vietnam in 1962, as a correspondent for the *New York Times,* and I was accused of being too young to report or to understand the issues at stake. In those days my contemporaries in the military were mere captains. Now I was older than almost all the players. One chairman of the Joint Chiefs of Staff, Colin Powell, was three years younger than I, and he had retired six years before I began the book. The president of the United States was twelve years younger than I, and the commander of the NATO forces waging war in the Balkans, General Wes Clark, had graduated from West Point eleven years after I graduated from college. At one point I found myself interviewing an army three-star who was seventeen years younger than I was. But significantly, some young foreign service officers whom I had known as a reporter in Saigon in 1963 when they were barely a year out of college, such as Tony Lake and Dick Holbrooke, were now the senior figures of the Democratic Party's national security team.

In writing about America I wanted to capture some of the new forces at work and the important political changes being wrought by a number of nonpolitical factors: the country's remarkable affluence; the advent of the modern media and the rise, post–Cold War, of norms of entertainment at the expense of more serious traditional journalistic standards in much of network television; a change in generational attitudes, post–Cold War, among younger Americans coming of age in a less anxious country in which foreign policy hardly mattered in our national elections; the quantum changes that have evolved in the technology, of war; and, of course, the resulting dramatically changed political structure of the country.

In going back to this world after so long an absence, I was, ironically enough, helped by having spent much of the intervening time writing about subjects that proved quite important in understanding a dramatically altered political landscape. I wrote about the changing technology of communications and what it has done to politics in *The Powers That Be,* and the changing nature of the American economy and its effect on American politics in *The Reckon-*

ing. A third book, *The Fifties,* had taught me the importance of technological developments in effecting social and political change; and in no small part because of that, I was fascinated by the dramatic change in the nature of modern high-technology weaponry and what effect that had on the geopolitics of war.

During Vietnam, high-tech weaponry was in its infancy. In the ensuing three decades that technology advanced exponentially, well beyond the expectations and knowledge of most serious laymen, and, in fact, well beyond the expectations and comprehension of many active senior military men, who still retain great suspicions about the air force's ability to do what it said it could do—win a war with high-tech weaponry alone. Like many correspondents who had covered Vietnam, I had spent much more time with army men in the field than I had with air force officers, and I shared derivatively the doubts reflected by the army men of that era (General Powell would be a good example) of what the air force could accomplish, except in close air support. Like a great many senior army men whose views were fashioned in that earlier era, I now turned out to be quite wrong.

This book was always premised to be about America, not about the Balkans or any other foreign country. I had what was at best a layman's knowledge of the Balkans, and one of the hardest parts of this assignment was getting up to speed on that complicated part of the world where the history is so dark and convoluted.

I should note finally that I did not go looking for the ghosts of Vietnam, but they were often there, and they found me, most notably in the damage done to two institutions critical to general public health and disproportionately affected by that war, the U.S. army and the Democratic Party.

David Halberstam
May 2001

ACKNOWLEDGMENTS

I have listed below various people I interviewed over the years in my research for this book (with the exception of a handful of senior military men who spoke to me with the agreement that I would not use their names). I am especially grateful to my colleagues, journalists, academics, and government officials who helped me to understand the Balkans, either through their books or in interviews, or in some cases both.

A small handful of people refused to talk to me, most notably and puzzlingly Sam Nunn, even though I had dealt amicably with him a few years earlier. Because I like to interview in reverse hierarchical order—lower-level people first, the more senior and powerful people later—I had hoped to see Bill Clinton last. When he left the presidency, he sent me a pleasant handwritten note commenting on an essay I had written about him earlier, and suggesting we get together soon to talk over the issues I had raised. I immediately called his office to set up an appointment. Over six weeks I made many more calls, including one fielded by Betty Currie, but he never responded to any of them.

I am reminded as I complete these notes of my good fortune in being able to do something I love, to write about serious subjects for serious citizens, and to take almost as much time and space as I want to complete my research. It is the rarest of privileges for a working reporter, and my ability to do that this late in a career seems especially precious when so many other journalistic institutions, most notably the television networks, have cut back severely in the seriousness of their coverage of so many critically important issues. People who write books as I do are among the last ma-and-pa enterprises in journalism. But even ma-and-pa proprietors are supported by all kinds of people, in my case by Fred Hills, my editor at Scribner, who loved the idea of the book from the start, and Burton Beals, the line editor, who worked under an unusually pressing deadline; and Carolyn Reidy, Susan Moldow, and Nan Graham, all of Scribner, who always had faith in the book and in me. Others at Scribner to whom I am indebted are Pat Eisemann and Frances Tsay. I am also especially grateful to my lawyer-agents, Marty Garbus and Bob Solomon, both of them always steadfast; Carolyn Parqueth, who is my typist and whose transcribing of my interview notes has always made my life so much easier; Linda Drogin, who is not merely a neighbor and friend but a demon fact-checker; and Doug

Stumpf, my editor at *Vanity Fair,* and Graydon Carter, who have always been supportive. Graydon's support at the beginning of the project was particularly important and very much in character for an editor who treats his writers so generously. Philip Roome, my friend and travel agent, has a rare capacity to take my convoluted schedule and make sense out of it; I remain grateful not merely for his skills but for his friendship as well and the help of his gifted staff. And, of course, to Dr. Leslie H. Gelb, who pointed me in the direction of a changed but fascinating landscape, not for the first time and, I hope, not for the last.

LIST OF INTERVIEWEES

I am indebted to the following people who graciously granted me interviews: Lieutenant General Joseph Abizaid, U.S. Army, Mort Abramowicz, Madeleine Albright, Roger Altman, Christiane Amanpour, R. W. Apple Jr., Ken Bacon, Doug Bennet, Beryl (Mrs. Lloyd) Bentsen, Sandy Berger, Tom Bettag, Senator Joseph Biden, Ray Bonner, Bob Boorstin, James Cannon, Frank Carlucci, Hodding Carter, James Carville, Lieutenant General Dan Christman, U.S. Army, Warren Christopher, General Wesley K. Clark, Bill Cohen, Colonel Joseph Cox, Gregg Craig, Admiral Bill Crowe, Ivo Daalder, Pat Derian, John Deutch, Bob deVecchi, Tom Donilon, Peter Duchin, Fred Dutton, Larry Eagleburger, John Fox, Sol Friedman, Leon Fuerth, Peter Galbraith, General Jack Galvin, U.S. Army, Jeff Garten, Les Gelb, David Gergen, Doris Kearns Goodwin, Michael Gordon, Al Gore, Phillip Gourevitch, Rebecca Grant, Stan Greenberg, Frank Greer, Roy Gutman, Richard Haass, Mort Halperin, Lee Hamilton, Marshall Harris, Chris Hill, James Hoge, Richard Holbrooke, Jim Hooper, Robert Hunter, Richard Johnson, Vernon Jordan, General George Joulwan, U.S. Army, Ret., Tony Judt, General John Jumper, USAF, Ward Just, Donald Kagan, Stanley N. Katz, Nicholas Katzenbach, George Kennan, Bob Kimmitt, Larry L. King, Lieutenant Colonel Tom Klincar, USAF, Ted Koppel, Bill Kristol, Tony Lake, Jim Laurie, Vladimir Lehovich, Joe Lelyveld, Jean-David Levitte, Winston Lord, Senator Richard Lugar, Colonel Douglas Mac-Gregor, David Maraniss, Ed Markey, Mike McCurry, General Merrill (Tony) McPeak, USAF, Ret., Jack McWethy, General Edward (Shy) Meyer, U.S. Army, Ret., Bill Montgomery, Richard Moose, Dee Dee Myers, Colonel Jose Negron, USAF, Robert Oakley, Colonel Robert Owen, USAF, Leon Panetta, Robert Pastor, Bill Perry, Colonel Bob Phillips, U.S. Army, General Colin Powell, U.S. Army, Ret., Dana Priest, Robert Reich, Tom Ricks, David Rohde, Ed Rollins, Tom Rosshirt, General Mike Ryan, USAF, Jack Scanlan, Arthur Schlesinger Jr., Greg Schulte, Barry Schweid, Brent Scowcroft, Louis Sell, Larry Sequith, Daniel Serwer, General John Shalikashvili, U.S. Army,

Ret., General Jack Sheehan, USMC, Ret., Mark Shields, Lieutenant Colonel Chris Shoemaker, Lieutenant General Mike Short, USAF, Ret., Walt Slocombe, Nancy Soderberg, Lieutenant General Ed Soyster, U.S. Army, Ret., Fred Steeper, Jim Steinberg, George Stephanopoulos, Fritz Stern, Bob Straus, Strobe Talbott, Peter Tarnoff, Bob Teeter, General Bernard Trainor, USMC, Ret., Margaret Tutwiler, Richard Ullman, Garrick Utley, Sandy Vershbow, Ed Vulliamy, General Carl Vuono, U.S. Army, Ret., Colonel John Warden, USAF, Ret., Tom Weinberg, Curtis Wilkie, Congressman Charley Wilson, Jules Witcover, Paul Wolfowitz, Bob Woodward, James Woolsey, Jim Wooten, Fareed Zakaria, Warren Zimmermann, Bob Zoellick.

NOTES

CHAPTER ONE

1. Beschloss and Talbott, 434.
2. Ibid., 135.
3. Powell, 532.
4. Beschloss and Talbott, 461.
5. Ibid., 230.

CHAPTER THREE

1. Doder and Branson, 70; interview with Scanlan and Eagleburger.
2. Zimmermann, 59.

CHAPTER FOUR

1. Interview with Eagleburger.
2. Interview with Vulliamy.
3. Interview with Eagleburger.
4. Interview with Scowcroft; Zimmermann, 215.
5. David Owen, 6.

CHAPTER FIVE

1. Reynolds, 29.
2. Schwarzkopf, 318–19.
3. Reynolds, 58.
4. Schwarzkopf, 321.
5. Varying interviews; Reynolds, 128.
6. Gordon and Trainor, 93.

CHAPTER SIX

1. Halberstam, *Children*, 517.
2. Deaver, 130.
3. Atkinson, 94; Powell, 492.
4. Interview with Wooten.

CHAPTER SEVEN

1. Powell, 465.
2. Cramer, 13.
3. Beschloss and Talbott, 26.
4. Tyler, 131.

CHAPTER EIGHT

1. Holbrooke, 26.
2. Gunther, 345.
3. Vulliamy, 5.
4. Rieff, 117.
5. Silber and Little, 29.
6. David Owen, 134.
7. Kaplan, 39.
8. Silber and Little, 29.
9. Kaplan, 40.
10. Doder and Branson, 142.
11. Silber and Little, 37.
12. Doder and Branson, 45, 46.
13. Vulliamy, 52.
14. Zimmermann, 121.
15. Glenny, 35.
16. Judah, 56.
17. Doder, 110.

CHAPTER NINE

1. Interview with Shalikashvili.
2. Interview with Tony Judt.
3. Ibid.
4. Judah, xvii.
5. David Owen, 8.
6. Doder and Branson, 82.
7. Ibid., 91.

CHAPTER TEN

1. David Owen, 9.
2. Doder and Branson, 82.
3. Ibid., 109.
4. Ibid., 95.
5. Ibid., 97.

CHAPTER ELEVEN

1. Interview with Reich.
2. Interview with Shields.

llil

3. Interview with Rollins.
4. Tom Noah, *Slate,* July 27, 2000.
5. Flowers, 125.
6. Interview with Wooten.
7. Goldman et al., 138.

CHAPTER TWELVE

1. Vulliamy, 74–75.
2. Ibid., 83.
3. Holbrooke, 39.
4. Interview with Ullman.

CHAPTER THIRTEEN

1. Rieff, 182.
2. Vulliamy, 101–2.
3. Interview with Johnson; Richard Johnson in Mestrovic, 66.

CHAPTER FOURTEEN

1. Cramer, 87.
2. Noonan, 301.
3. Goldman et al., 407.
4. Ibid., 356.
5. As quoted by John Gregory Dunne, *New Yorker,* "Virtual Patriotism," November 16, 1998.

CHAPTER FIFTEEN

1. Interview with Stephanopoulos.
2. In a talk with the author. We are longtime friends.

CHAPTER SEVENTEEN

1. To the author.
2. Halberstam, "The Decline and Fall of the Eastern Empire," *Vanity Fair,* October 1995.
3. Bonner, 169; interview with Bonner and R. W. Apple Jr.
4. The resident *Times* man was me; we have known each other for thirty-seven years in a sometimes uneven, volatile, but warm friendship.
5. Stephanopoulos, 196–97.
6. Interview with Kagan.

CHAPTER EIGHTEEN

1. David Owen 107.
2. Holbrooke, 50.
3. Ibid., 54.

4. Honig and Both, 84; Silber and Little, 266.
5. Honig and Both, 91.
6. Silber and Little, 270.
7. Powell, 564.
8. David Owen, 289.

CHAPTER NINETEEN

1. Reich, 63.
2. Woodward, *Agenda,* 125.
3. Reich, 72.
4. Interviews with Clinton economic and political aides.
5. Woodward, *Agenda,* 165.

CHAPTER TWENTY

1. Interview with Wooten.
2. Seitz, 328.
3. Interview with Marshall Harris; Marshall Harris in Mestrovic, 242.

CHAPTER TWENTY-ONE

1. Halberstam, *Parade,* September 17, 1995.
2. Ibid.
3. Schwarzkopf, 288.
4. Interview with Gelb.
5. Powell, 148.
6. Ibid., 149.

CHAPTER TWENTY-TWO

1. Stephanopoulos, 132.
2. Powell, 578.
3. Interview with Powell.

CHAPTER TWENTY-THREE

1. Oakley and Hirsch, 7.
2. Ibid., 15.
3. Ibid., 43.
4. Ibid., 111.
5. Dobbs, 355.
6. Oakley and Hirsch, 122.
7. Mark Bowden's *Black Hawk Down* tells in great detail what happened that day and is one of the best pieces of war reporting I have ever read.
8. Stephanopoulos, 214.
9. I am dependent here on background interviews with almost all of the various principals, plus varying memoirs of the period, plus Elizabeth Drew's excellent account in *On the Edge,* the best description of Clinton in that period.

10. Bowden, 309; interviews with Oakley and Lake.
11. Hyland, 59.
12. Ibid.

CHAPTER TWENTY-FOUR

1. Powell, 544.
2. Morris Morley and Chris McGillion, *Political Science Quarterly,* fall 1997.
3. Morris, 5.
4. Stephanopoulos, 219.
5. Ann Devroy and Jeffrey Smith, *Washington Post,* September 25, 1994.
6. Stephanopoulos, 219.
7. Ibid., 217.
8. Ibid., 217–18.
9. Gourevitch, 95.
10. *Frontline,* "The Triumph of Evil," January 16, 1999, transcript.
11. *Frontline,* interview with James Woods, deputy assistant secretary of defense.
12. Gourevitch, 168–69.
13. *Frontline,* "The Triumph of Evil," January 26, 1999.
14. Stephanopoulos, 305.
15. Powell, 598.
16. Stephanopoulos, 313; interviews with him and other White House principals.
17. From an article in the *United States Institute of Peace Press* by Robert Pastor, who was the senior adviser to the Carter trip; interview with Pastor.

CHAPTER TWENTY-FIVE

1. Daalder, 33.
2. Ibid., 34.
3. Powell, 576.
4. Stephanopoulos, 214.

CHAPTER TWENTY-SIX

1. Roger Cohen, 233.
2. Ibid., 234.
3. Doder and Branson, 209.
4. Vulliamy, 107.
5. Ibid., 47.
6. Honig and Both, 28.
7. Jann Wenner, "The *Rolling Stone* Interview with Clinton," January 4, 2001.
8. Powell, 602.
9. Rohde, 25.
10. Ibid., 363.
11. Stephanopoulos, 216.
12. Woodward, *Choice,* 254.

CHAPTER TWENTY-SEVEN

1. Stephanopoulos, 331.
2. Ibid., 333.
3. Morris, 254.
4. Woodward, *Choice,* 258; plus further interviews with principals.
5. Rohde, 167.
6. Honig and Both, xvii.
7. Ibid., 63–64.
8. Woodward, *Choice,* 259–60.
9. Rohde, 301–2.
10. Woodward, *Choice,* 261; plus interviews with Lake, Soderberg, McCurry, Berger, and Vershbow.
11. Woodward, *Choice,* 262; plus interviews with almost all of the principals.

CHAPTER TWENTY-EIGHT

1. Interview with Gore; Woodward, *Choice,* 262.
2. From varying interviews, including with Gore.

CHAPTER TWENTY-NINE

1. Rohde, 330.

CHAPTER THIRTY

1. Interviews with Lake and Holbrooke; Holbrooke, 74.
2. Holbrooke, 73.
3. Ibid., 168.

CHAPTER THIRTY-ONE

1. Holbrooke, 212.
2. Ibid., 106.
3. Ibid., 360.

CHAPTER THIRTY-TWO

1. Judah, xix.
2. Ibid., 156.
3. Ibid., 130–31.

CHAPTER THIRTY-THREE

1. *George,* December 1999.
2. Toobin, 251–52.
3. *Time,* February 2, 1998.
4. *George,* December 2000.
5. *Time,* February 2, 1998.

6. *George,* December 1999.
7. Richard Reeves, *Talk,* September 2000.
8. Woodward, *Shadow,* 493.
9. Ibid., 490–93.
10. Ibid., 495.
11. Daalder and O'Hanlon, 30, 283.
12. Dobbs, 86.
13. Blackman, 141.
14. Dobbs, 197.
15. Ibid., 333.
16. Powell, 576; interview with Albright.

CHAPTER THIRTY-FOUR

1. Daalder and O'Hanlon, 43.
2. *Frontline,* September 22, 2000.
3. Judah, 187; interviews with Clark and Holbrooke.

CHAPTER THIRTY-FIVE

1. Judah, 137.
2. Interview with Clark; Clark, 164–65.
3. *Frontline,* February 22, 2000, Peter Boyer, Michael Kirk, and Rick Young, reporters.
4. Judah, 186; interviews with Short and Holbrooke.

CHAPTER THIRTY-SIX

1. Maraniss, 446.
2. R. W. Apple, *New York Times,* August 25, 1999.
3. Daalder, 70–71; interviews with different principals.
4. *Frontline,* transcript of interview with William Walker, 9.

CHAPTER THIRTY-SEVEN

1. John Barry, *Newsweek,* July 14, 1997.
2. Clark, 82.
3. *Current Biography,* 1998, 529.
4. Elaine Sciolino and Steven Lee Myers, *New York Times,* December 5, 1997.
5. Murray Kempton, *New York Newsday,* February 26, 1995.
6. Halberstam, *Best and Brightest,* 270.

CHAPTER THIRTY-EIGHT

1. Daalder and O'Hanlon, 94.
2. *Frontline,* February 22, 2000.
3. Judah, 227; interviews with Holbrooke and Clark.
4. *Frontline,* February 22, 2000; interview with Short.

CHAPTER THIRTY-NINE

1. Gordon Chaplin, *Washington Post,* May 10, 1981.
2. Ibid.
3. Interview with Christman.
4. Interview with Clark; Clark, 119.

CHAPTER FORTY

1. Interview with Clark and other senior officers; Clark, 126–27.
2. William S. Cohen, 59–62.
3. Dorland, 162–63.
4. Charles Lane, *New Republic,* July 28, 1997.
5. *Frontline,* February 22, 2000.

CHAPTER FORTY-ONE

1. Daalder and O'Hanlon, 19.
2. *Frontline,* February 22, 2000.

CHAPTER FORTY-TWO

1. Interviews with Short and Clark; Grant, *B-2 Goes to War,* 31.
2. Dana Priest, *Washington Post,* December 29, 1999.
3. Interviews with Clark and other generals; Clark, 227.

CHAPTER FORTY-THREE

1. Judah, 274.
2. Ibid., 271.
3. Ibid., 278–79; interview with Talbott; Talbott interview, *Frontline,* February 22, 2000.
4. Laura Silber, *Talk,* April 2000.
5. Interview with Biden.

CHAPTER FORTY-FOUR

1. *Washington Post,* June 28, 2001.
2. Interview with Wooten.

BIBLIOGRAPHY

Ash, Timothy Garton. *History of the Present.* Random House, 1997.

Atkinson, Rick. *Crusade.* Houghton-Mifflin, 1993.

Baker, James A., with Thomas DeFrank. *The Politics of Diplomacy.* Putnam, 1995.

Beschloss, Michael, and Strobe Talbott. *At the Highest Level: The Inside Story of the End of the Cold War.* Little, Brown, 1993.

Blackman, Ann. *Seasons of Her Life: A Biography of Madeleine Korbel Albright.* Scribner, 1998.

Bonner, Ray. *Waltzing the Dictator.* Times Books, 1987.

Boutros-Ghali, Boutros. *Unvanquished.* Random House, 1999.

Bowden, Mark. *Black Hawk Down.* Atlantic Monthly Press, 1999.

Bush, George H. W., and Brent Scowcroft. *A World Transformed.* Knopf, 1998.

Cannon, Lou. *Reagan.* Putnam, 1982.

———. *President Reagan: The Role of a Lifetime.* Simon & Schuster, 1991.

Christopher, Warren. *Chances of a Lifetime.* Scribner, 2001.

Clark, General Wesley K. *Waging Modern War.* Public Affairs Press, 2001.

Cohen, Roger. *Hearts Grown Brutal.* Random House, 1998.

Cohen, Stephen F. *Failed Crusade: America and the Tragedy of Post-Communist Russia.* Norton, 2000.

Cohen, William S. *Roll Call: One Year in the U.S. Senate.* Simon & Schuster, 1981.

Cramer, Richard Ben. *What It Takes.* Random House, 1990.

Crocker, Chester, Ffen Osler Hampson, and Pamela Aall, eds. *Herding Cats.* Specifically the chapter by Robert Pastor, "More and Less Than It Seemed," 507–25. U.S. Institute of Peace Press, 1999.

Daalder, Ivo. *Getting to Dayton: The Making of America's Bosnia Policy.* Brookings, 1999.

Daalder, Ivo, and Michael O'Hanlon. *Winning Ugly: NATO's War to Save Kosovo.* Brookings, 2000.

Deaver, Michael. *Behind the Scene.* Morrow, 1987.

Dobbs, Michael. *Madeleine Albright.* Henry Holt, 1999.

Doder, Dusko. *The Yugoslavs.* Random House, 1978.

Doder, Dusko, and Branson, Louise. *Milosevic: Portrait of a Tyrant.* Free Press, 1999.

Dorland, Gil. *Legacy of Discord.* Brassey's Inc., 2001.

Drew, Elizabeth. *On the Edge: The Clinton Presidency.* Touchstone, 1994.

———. *Showdown: The Struggle Between the Gingrich Congress and the Clinton White House.* Simon & Schuster, 1995.

FitzGerald, Frances. *Way Out There in the Blue: Reagan, Star Wars, and the End of the Cold War.* Simon & Schuster, 2000.

Flowers, Gennifer. *Sleeping with the President.* Anonymous Press, 1998.

Friedman, Thomas. *The Lexus and the Olive Tree.* Farrar, Straus and Giroux, 1999.

Gergen, David. *Eyewitness to Power.* Simon & Schuster, 2000.

Germond, Jack, and Jules Witcover. *Whose Broad Stripes and Bright Stars?* Warner Books, 1989.

Glenny, Mischa. *The Fall of Yugoslavia.* Penguin, 1993.

Goldman, Peter, et al. *Quest for the President 1992.* Texas A&M University Press, 1994.

Gordon, Michael, and General Bernard Trainor. *The Generals' War.* Little, Brown, 1995.

Gourevitch, Philip. *We Wish to Inform You That Tomorrow We Will Be Killed With Our Families.* Farrar, Straus and Giroux, 1998.

Grant, Rebecca. *The Kosovo Campaign: Aerospace Power Made It Work.* The Air Force Association, 1999.

———. *The B-2 Goes to War.* Iris Press, 2001.

Gruff, Peter. *The Kosovo News and Propaganda War.* International Press Institute, 1999.

Gunther, John. *Inside Europe Today.* Harper, 1961.

Gutman, Roy. *A Witness to Genocide.* Element Publishers, 1993.

Haass, Richard. *The Reluctant Sheriff: The United States, After the Cold War.* Council on Foreign Relations Press, 1997.

———. *Intervention: The Use of American Military Force in the Post Cold War World.* Brookings, 1999.

Halberstam, David. *The Best and the Brightest.* Random House, 1972.

———. *The Children.* Random House, 1998.

Holbrooke, Richard. *To End a War.* Random House, 1998.

Honig, Jan Willem, and Norbert Both. *Srebrenica: Record of a War Crime.* Penguin, 1996.

Hyland, William. *Clinton's World: Remaking American Foreign Policy.* Praeger, 1999.

Ignatieff, Michael. *The Warrior's Honor: Ethnic War and the Modern Conscience.* Holt, 1998.

———. *Virtual War: Kosovo and Beyond.* Metropolitan Books, 2000.

Johnson, Haynes. *The Best of Times.* Harcourt, 2001.

Judah, Tim. *Kosovo: War and Peace.* Yale, 2000.

Kaplan, Robert. *Balkan Ghosts: A Journey Through History.* Vintage, 1994.

Kelly, Virginia Clinton, with James Morgan. *Leading with My Heart.* Pocket Star Books, 1994.

Krepinevich, Andrew. *The Army and Vietnam.* Johns Hopkins, 1986.

Lake, Anthony. *Six Nightmares: Real Threats in a Dangerous World and How America Can Meet Them.* Little, Brown, 2000.

Lippman, Thomas. *Madeleine Albright and the New American Diplomacy.* Westview, 2000.

MacGregor, Colonel Douglas. *Breaking the Phalanx: A New Design for Landpower in the Twenty-First Century.* Praeger, 1997.

Malcolm, Noel. *Bosnia: A Short History.* NYU Press, 1994.

Maraniss, David. *First in His Class: The Biography of Bill Clinton.* Simon & Schuster, 1995.

Mazower, Mark. *The Balkans: A Short History.* Random Modern Library, 2000.

McMaster, H. R. *Dereliction of Duty: Lyndon Johnson, Robert McNamara, and the Lies That Led to Vietnam.* HarperCollins, 1997.

Mestrovic, Stjepan, ed. *The Conceit of Innocence.* Texas A&M University Press, 1997.

Morris, Dick. *Behind the Oval Office.* Random House, 1998.

Noonan, Peggy. *What I Saw at the Revolution.* Random House, 1990.

Oakley, Robert, and John Hirsch. *Somalia and Operation Restore Hope.* U.S. Institute of Peace Press, 1995.

O'Shea, Brendan. *Crisis at Bihac.* Sutton, 1998.

Owen, David. *Balkan Odyssey.* Harcourt Brace, 1995.

Owen, Colonel Robert. *Deliberate Force: A Case Study in Effective Air Campaigning.* Air University Press, 2000.

Owens, Admiral Bill, with Ed Offley. *Lifting the Fog of War.* Farrar, Straus and Giroux, 2000.

Perry, William, and Ashton Carter. *Preventive Defense: A New Strategy for America.* Brookings, 1999.

Powell, Colin. *My American Journey.* Random House, 1995.

Reich, Robert. *Locked in the Cabinet.* Knopf, 1997.

Reynolds, Colonel Richard. *Heart of the Storm: The Genesis of the Air Campaign Against Iraq.* Air University Press, 1995.

Rieff, David. *Slaughterhouse: Bosnia and the Failure of the West.* Touchstone, 1996.

Robinson, Peter. *It's My Party.* Warner Books, 2000.

Rohde, David. *Endgame.* Westview, 1997.

Schwarzkopf, Norman. *It Doesn't Take a Hero.* Bantam, 1992.

Seitz, Raymond. *Over Here.* Weidenfeld & Nicolson, 1999.

Shawcross, William. *Deliver Us from Evil.* Simon & Schuster, 2000.

Silber, Laura, and Allan Little. *Yugoslavia: Death of a Nation.* Penguin, 1995.

Stephanopoulos, George. *All Too Human.* Little, Brown, 1999.

Sudetic, Chuck. *Blood and Vengeance.* Norton, 1998.

Thompson, Warren. *Bandits over Baghdad: Personal Stories of Flying the F-117s over Iraq.* Specialty Press, 2000.

Toobin, Jeffrey. *A Vast Conspiracy.* Random House, 1999.

Tyler, Patrick. *A Great Wall: Six Presidents and China.* Public Affairs, 1999.

Udovicki, Jasmina, and James Ridgway. *Burn This House: The Making and Unmaking of Yugoslavia.* Duke University Press, 1997.

Utley, Garrick. *You Should Have Been Here Yesterday.* Public Affairs, 2000.

Vulliamy, Ed. *Seasons in Hell.* St. Martin's, 1994.

Waldman, Michael. *POTUS Speaks.* Simon & Schuster, 2000.

Woodward, Bob. *The Agenda: Inside the Clinton White House.* Simon & Schuster, 1994.

———. *Maestro.* Simon & Schuster, 1994.

———. *The Choice.* Simon & Schuster, 1996.

———. *Shadow: Five Presidents and the Legacy of Watergate.* Simon & Schuster, 1999.

Zimmermann, Warren. *Origins of a Catastrophe.* Times Books, 1996.

INDEX

154–56, 198, 199, 225, 296, 333, 365
budget deficit and, 14, 15, 80, 147, 212–13
Christmas warning of, 155, 365
CIA's relationship with, 243
class attitudes of, 71, 72
Democrats' neutralizing of, 22–23, 58, 190, 250–51
dilatory response to Yugoslav crisis by, 32–46
domestic politics neglected by, 14, 17, 148
in election of 1980, 62–63, 72
in election of 1988, 60, 68, 71, 116, 144, 148, 213
in election of 1992, 9, 11, 14–20, 22–23, 34, 62, 75, 101, 103, 108, 109, 121, 125, 129, 135, 140, 143–44, 148–54, 159, 167, 171, 190, 208, 214, 250–51, 269
and end of Cold War, 9–15, 17, 58, 73, 143, 155–56, 238
final ceremony of, 247
foreign policy as passion of, 14, 57, 58, 61, 62, 70, 147, 158, 193, 229, 242, 482, 483
good manners and civility of, 71–72, 143
Gorbachev's relationship with, 9, 11–14, 32–34
Gulf War and, 9, 12–13, 15–16, 18, 19, 22, 43, 44, 69, 75, 143, 153–54, 208
Haiti policy of, 195, 268–69
health problems of, 148
limitations of, 10–12, 70–72, 143–44, 146
loyalty code of, 11, 12, 60, 72, 149, 150, 301
as media-challenged, 64, 143, 344
memoir of, 65–66, 238
modesty of, 10–11, 143–44
popularity of, 9, 15, 18, 19, 208
post–Cold War issues and, 73–75
principle foreign policy advisors of, 63–68
process emphasized by, 10, 12, 73
public disenchantment with, 14–17, 58, 148, 149
Reagan compared with, 11–12, 58–59, 60, 72–73, 143–46, 151
Scowcroft's relationship with, 43, 58, 65–66, 243

Somalia policy of, 250–52, 254, 257
symbols misused by, 10, 11–12
tax increase and, 14–15, 147, 213
in Texas, 71–72
as vice president, 60, 70, 72–73, 144, 148, 212, 243
Visegrad group and, 155–56
Woolsey in, 192, 193
in World War II, 62, 69, 111, 144–45
Bush, George W., 9, 489–94
in election of 2000, 68, 149, 489–92
as Texan, 60, 72, 490
Vietnam War and, 111, 415
Bush, Prescott, 71
Byrd, Robert, 264

Caldera, Louis, 467
Calley, William, 234
Cambodia, U.S. invasion of, 21, 184–85, 287
Cannon, Jim, 66
capitalism, 24, 74, 215, 361
Milosevic and, 26, 27
Capitol Cities, 163
Carlucci, Frank, 493
Carrington, Lord, 96
Carson, Johnny, 407
Carter, Jimmy (Carter administration), 22, 25, 172, 179, 191, 192–93, 243, 278
Christopher in, 170, 172, 173, 177, 198, 341
Christopher's distancing from, 175
Clinton's relationship with, 175, 269, 280
Cuban refugees and, 269
Democratic split as factor in, 168–69, 170
in election of 1976, 67, 143
Haiti policy and, 280–82
Holbrooke in, 176, 177, 185–86, 252, 383
Iran hostage crisis in, 12, 131, 146, 172, 198–99, 236, 302, 306, 341
Lake in, 20, 185–86, 286, 383
Perry in, 328, 329
Vance's resignation in, 172, 198–99
Carvey, Dana, 10
Carville, James, 222
background of, 116
in election of 1992, 22–23, 101, 109, 116–19, 153, 169
in transition period, 169
Catholic Church, see Roman Catholic Church; Serb Orthodox Catholics

Gore, Al (*cont.*)
  in election of 2000, 415, 488–92
  foreign policy confidence of, 158–59
  Haiti policy and, 272, 279
  as Holbrooke advocate, 369
Gore, Karenna, 330–31
Gore, Tipper, 222
Gourevitch, Philip, 273, 274
Gramm, Phil, 415
Great Britain, 379, 452
  Bosnia policy and, 226–27, 285, 303,
    305, 306, 312, 318, 327, 330, 340
  Churchill Factor and, 17
  Germany feared by, 90
  Kosovo policy and, 461–62, 468,
    469–70, 475
  Lake as viewed by, 288
  as pro-Serb and pro-Belgrade, 88, 89,
    90, 227
  in World War I, 90, 111
  in World War II, 17, 95, 320
Greater Serbia concept, 31, 84, 93, 121,
  126, 356
  see also Serbian nationalism
Greece, 304, 444
Greenberg, Stan, 14, 19, 113, 152, 153,
  263, 311
Greenspan, Alan, 72, 220–23
Greer, Frank, 19
Grenada, U.S. invasion of, 272–73, 427
Grunwald, Mandy, 263
Guggenheim, Harry, 381
gun control, 60–61, 68
Gunther, John, 77
Gutman, Betsy, 98
Gutman, Roy, 96–100
  Bosnia crisis and, 129–34, 166, 296

Habib, Mike, 128–29
Habyarimana, Juvenal, 274, 275
Hague, The, 327
  War Crimes Tribunal in, 316, 488
Haig, Al, 433, 479
Haiti, 267–73
  elections in, 267–68
  international boycott against, 269
  as race issue, 269
  Shalikashvili's visit to, 324–25
  U.S. invasion threat and, 278–82, 414,
    429
  U.S. relations with, 194, 195, 251,
    267–73, 278–82, 324–25, 414, 429
Halifax, G-7 meeting in, 304–5
Halperin, Mark, 114

Hambrecht and Quist, 328–29
Hamilton, Lee, 168, 246, 256, 483
Hapsburg Empire, collapse of, 76, 82
Harden, Blaine, 132, 166
Harlan County, USS, 271–72, 281, 282
Harriman, Averell, 185, 188, 355
Harriman, Pamela, 188, 406
Hart, Gary, 111, 157, 376, 406, 408
health care plan, 218, 297
Hegel, Georg Wilhelm Friedrich, 126
Heinz, Jack, 153
helicopters, AH-64 Apache, 464–68
Helms, Jesse, 26, 62, 310, 377, 485
Hendrix, John, 466
Heningburg, Mike, 235
Herschensohn, Bruce, 490
Hill, Chris, 77, 395
Hirsch, John, 249
Hitler, Adolf, 83, 91, 93, 129, 166, 330
Hoar, Joe, 323
Hoess, Friedrich, 155
Hoffa, Jimmy, 341
Holbrooke, Anthony, 181
Holbrooke, Liddy, 181
Holbrooke, Richard C. (Dick), 175–89,
  260, 325, 337, 341–58, 385
  as activist, 175, 176, 186, 200, 342,
    345
  as ambassador to Germany, 178,
    342–45, 484
  ambition of, 176, 179, 180, 181,
    185–88, 343
  as assistant secretary for European
    Affairs, 345–46
  background of, 180, 181, 187, 344
  Balkans memo of, 199–200
  Bosnia policy and, 177, 179, 199–200,
    311, 346–58, 365–66, 369, 378,
    393, 434
  Bosnia visited by, 124–25, 177, 181,
    199
  in Carter administration, 176, 177,
    185–86, 252, 383
  Christopher compared with, 176, 177,
    341–42
  Christopher's relationship with, 341,
    345–46, 348, 369
  Clark's work with, 350, 363, 393, 395,
    434, 436
  Clinton's relationship with, 179, 188,
    189, 342, 352
  considered for secretary of state
    appointment, 175–78, 369–70, 377
  Croat-Muslim offensive and, 346–47

Clinton's problems with, 204–7, 211, 241, 265, 415–19, 424–25
economic restrictions on use of, 222
gays in, 204–7, 211, 245–46, 415, 417
in Gulf War, 12–13, 15–16, 35, 47–56, 414
Haiti policy and, 268–72, 278–82
lift and strike policy and, 224, 225, 228
new technology and, 12, 16, 35, 44, 47–56, 328–29
sexual misconduct in, 245, 413
Soviet military gap with, 11
women in, 245–46
see also specific services
military advisory groups (MAGs), 335
Milosevic, Maria, 488
Milosevic, Slobodan, 26–28, 30, 42, 91–97, 340, 341, 395–400
Albright's views on, 370, 376, 386, 395
Baker ignored by, 46
Bosnia and, 31, 93, 95–96, 121, 122, 126, 155, 347, 356, 365, 370, 398, 442, 452
Christmas warning and, 155, 365
Clark's views on, 363, 388, 395–96, 399, 434–35, 445, 485
control issues of, 473–74
Eagleburger's relationship with, 26–28, 92
effects of NATO victory on, 485–87
Greater Serbia idea of, 31, 84, 93, 121, 126, 356; *see also* Serbian nationalism
Hitler compared with, 93, 386
Holbrooke's dealings with, 347, 354–59, 365–66, 377, 395, 398, 400, 420, 421–22, 434
Kosovo and, 155, 356, 362–67, 369, 376, 387–88, 396–400, 420–26, 435, 442, 445–46, 449, 450, 452–55, 460, 463, 464, 468–78, 480
Krajina offensive and, 339–40, 347
legal status of, 487–88
media savvy of, 83, 84, 93, 485–86
Mladic compared with, 348
Mladic's self-importance and, 296, 347
in move on Slovenia, 31, 34
opportunism of, 27, 28, 81–82, 83, 127, 129, 387
in peace negotiations, 347–48, 350, 354–59, 362–67, 377
as pro-Saddam, 33

rise of, 80–84, 99
three identities of, 27–28
on Tito, 78
Tudjman compared with, 333
Tudjman's secret meeting with (March 25, 1991), 95–96
weakness of his enemies exploited by, 127
West's dislike of, 91–92
Mitchell, George, 369, 370
Mitterrand, François, 90, 227–28, 285, 293, 303–4, 305, 344
Mladic, Ratko, 203, 295–96, 347
background of, 295
Clark's meeting with, 394
in fall of Srebrenica, 314–15, 396
Milosevic compared with, 348
in peace talks, 349
as war criminal, 295, 338, 362, 396
in Zepa, 338–39
Mogadishu, 249, 250, 251, 255, 257, 261–65
U.S. tragedy in, 261–65, 271, 275
Mondale, Joan, 178
Mondale, Walter (Fritz), 106–7, 178, 191
Monicagate, 371–76, 387, 396, 482, 483, 489
Montenegro, Montenegrans, 44, 126, 466
Montgomery, Bill, 139, 140, 141, 228–29
Montgomery, Sonny, 213
Montgomery, Tom, 259, 261
Moose, Dick, 253–54, 385
Morillon, Philippe, 202–3, 296
Morris, Richard (Dick; Charley), 309–11, 375
Morris, Willie, 102
Moyers, Bill, 61, 381
Moynihan, Pat, 377
MPRI (Military Professional Resources Incorporated), 334–35
MRE (meals ready to eat), 203
MTV, 154
Munich, 337
Murrow, Ed, 160, 161, 164
Muskie, Ed, 170, 172, 199, 382, 383
Muslims, 34, 42
Bosnian, *see* Bosnian Muslims
Kosovar, *see* Kosovo, Kosovars, Albanian Muslims in
Serbs feared by, 94
in World War II, 94–95
My American Journey (Powell), 237–38, 246
Myers, Dee Dee, 192–93

in election of 1992, 108, 117, 119–20,
143, 149
electoral fickleness and, 208–9
empathy, 108
Gulf War and, 153, 154
Lewinsky scandal and, 373
magazine shows for, 160, 162, 164
managerial class and, 161, 163
network, effects of generational
change on, 159–64, 266
political advertising on, 22, 208, 209,
210, 384
Serbian nationalism and, 83
shrewdness about political morality
and, 402–3
Somalia coverage on, 250, 251
star reporters for, 160, 162, 164
vicious cycle for news coverage of,
163–64
Tenth Mountain Division, U.S., 279
Texas:
Bush in, 71–72
politics in, 217, 405, 490
Theodore Roosevelt (carrier), 348
Thomason, Harry, 371
Thornburgh, Dick, 153
Thurmond, Strom, 324
Tigers, Arkan's, 97, 201, 355
Tijanic, Aleksander, 82
Time, 136
Tirana, 466
Tito (Josip Broz), 27, 76, 78–79, 81, 82,
89, 95, 97, 365
Tomahawk cruise missiles, 348–50, 354,
457
Tontons Macoutes, 267
Tower, John, 66, 68, 370
TransAfrica Forum, 278
Treasury, U.S., 63, 67
Bentsen as secretary of, 216, 218–21
Trexler, Gary, 451
tribalism, 74, 241
in Rwanda, 273–77
in Somalia, 248, 249, 250, 253, 255
Trilateral Commission, 72
Trillin, Calvin, 403
Tripp, Linda, 371, 372, 373, 403
Trnopoljie, 123
Tsongas, Paul, 113, 115, 118
Tudjman, Franjo, 37, 122, 333, 341, 356,
365
in arming of Bosnia, 333, 334
Croat-Bosnian offensive and, 338,
347, 348, 350

Galbraith's talks with, 334, 337, 347
Holbrooke's dealings with, 347, 350
Izetbegovic's meeting with, 338
Milosevic's secret meeting with
(March 25, 1991)
neo-Nazi ideology of, 91–92
Turks:
Bosnian Muslims as, 296
Kurds' relationship with, 322
Serbs vs., 84, 91, 314–15
see also Ottoman Empire
Tutsi, 273–77
Tutwiler, Margaret, 132
Tuzla, 203

U-2 surveillance plane, 187, 399
Ukraine, 33
Ullman, Dick, 126
UNAMIR (United Nations Assistance
Mission in Rwanda), 275–77
unemployment, 214, 360
United Nations (UN), 70, 375
Albright as ambassador to, 178, 192,
197, 256, 257, 258, 264, 290, 338,
377–78, 380, 386, 404
Bosnia and, 123, 125–27, 166, 202–3,
204, 275, 285, 293–94, 303, 306,
312–15, 327–28, 330
in Gulf War, 12, 33, 66
Haiti policy and, 270, 271
Holbrooke as ambassador to, 188, 485
Kosovo problem and, 397, 398–99,
476, 477
Pickering at, 191
in Rwanda, 275–77
Security Council of, 204, 256, 260,
337, 397
Somalia policy and, 251, 252, 254–58,
260, 263, 264
Srebrenica and, 202–3, 204, 293–94
U.S. relationship problems with, 147,
264, 476, 485
United States:
affluence in, 101–5
economy of, *see* economy, U.S.
European Community's independence
and, 86, 87
European defense burden shouldered
by, 89–90
foreign policy of, *see* foreign policy,
U.S.
Gulf War victory's effects on, 12–13,
15–16
Haitians in, 268

whites:
    affluence of, 105
    in army, 233, 235
    blue-collar, 105, 209
    middle class, 209
    talk radio and, 209–10
Will, George, 147
Wilson, George, 110
Winfrey, Oprah, 108
Winger, Debra, 111
Winning Ugly (Daalder and O'Hanlon),
    444
Winter Olympics (1984), 122
Wirthlin, Richard, 72
Wisner, Frank, 254, 343, 385
Witcover, Jules, 137–38
Wofford, Harris, 153
Wolfowitz, Paul, 141–42
women:
    Albright supported by, 370
    in Clinton cabinet, 207, 369–70, 373,
        385
    Clinton's support from, 204–5, 362,
        385
    in election of 2000, 491–92
    foreign policy and, 383, 384, 385
    in military, 245–46
    political power of, 204–5, 207, 209,
        385
Wood, Kimba, 207, 211
Woodward, Bob, 313, 375
Woolsey, James, 191–93
    Clinton access as problem for, 243–44
    resignation of, 299
    Somalia policy and, 253
Wooten, Jim, 114–18
World Health Organization, 202
World News Tonight (TV show), 163
World Transformed, A (Bush and Scow-
    croft), 65–66, 238
World War I, 40, 55, 89, 90, 111, 274,
    344, 364, 478
World War II, 17, 37, 45, 62, 75, 94–95,
    118, 182, 295, 478
    air power in, 41, 51, 52, 55, 326, 452
    Allied victories in, 10
    Balkans crisis compared with, 129,
        293, 294, 316, 452
    Bentsen in, 216–17
    Bush in, 62, 69, 111, 144–45
    Gulf War compared with, 13, 16, 52, 55

media and, 160, 161
    patriotism in, 109, 110
    Shalikashvili and, 320–21, 325
    see also specific countries
Wright, Jim, 68

Yad Vashem, 319
Yarborough, Ralph, 217
Yeltsin, Boris, 9, 13, 423, 475–76
Yugoslavia, 76–100
    Baker's trip to (June 1991), 45–46
    breakup of, 17, 24–46, 79, 84, 88–100,
        126, 136, 165, 364
    in Cold War, 76–77, 94
    conflicts and contradictions in, 76–79,
        81
    Eagleburger trip to (Feb. 1979), 25–30,
        92
    economy of, 77, 81, 99, 485, 486–87
    illusion of, 89, 94
    independent communist path of, 77,
        78, 89, 99
    naming of, 76
    suppression of nationalism in, 24, 27,
        76, 78–79
    U.S. post-Cold War attitude toward,
        79–80, 81
    in World War II, 45, 76, 77, 94–95,
        232, 295, 330, 452
    see also Kosovo, Kosovars; *specific
        former Yugoslav republics*
Yugoslav League of Communists, dissolu-
    tion of, 84
Yugoslav National Army (JNA), 31, 37,
    93, 98, 334, 336, 355
    in Bosnia, 122
    dissidents in, 94
    Gulf War and, 33
    overrating of, 34, 232, 337
    Perry's views on, 329–30

Zagreb, 37, 90, 139, 332
    airport in, 333, 334
    TV in, 96
Zaire, 252
Zepa, 293, 312, 331, 338
    surrender of, 338–39
Zimmermann, Warren, 45, 79–81, 140
    Eagleburger's meeting with, 79–80
    Yugoslav opposition groups brought
        together by, 28–29